Remedies in EC Law

Law and Practice in the English and EC Courts

For our families

Remedies in EC law

Law and Practice in the English and EC Courts

Mark Brealey

LLB, LLM, DEA en Droit Communautaire
of Middle Temple, Barrister

Mark Hoskins

BCL, MA(Oxon), Lic Spéc Dr Eur (Brussels),
of Gray's Inn, Barrister

With foreword by Judge David Edward

LONGMAN

© Mark Brealey and Mark Hoskins 1994

ISBN 0 85121 9551

Published by

Longman Law, Tax and Finance
Longman Group Limited
21–27 Lamb's Conduit Street, London WC1N 3NJ

Associated Offices
Australia, Hong Kong, Malaysia, Singapore, USA

A CIP catalogue record for this book is available from the British Library

Printed and bound in Great Britain by Mackays of Chatham PLC, Chatham, Kent

Contents

Part IV: Remedies in EC Courts for Breach of EC law

Part V: Precedents

Foreword

Lawyers, whether practitioners or teachers, are increasingly aware of the relevance of Community law in their daily work.

The question of remedies in Community law is becoming more and more important. The general principle is that the question of how Community rights should be protected is to be determined by the national legal systems of the Member States. This is subject to the conditions, first, that the national rules relating to the protection of Community rights should not be less favourable than those relating to purely domestic rights and, second, that the national rules should not make it impossible in practice to protect Community rights.

However, the Court of Justice has, on occasion, indicated the nature of the remedy which must be available to protect a Community right. Thus, in *Rewe* and *Comet*, the Court recognised a right to restitution where charges had been demanded which were contrary to Community law, thus anticipating the decision of the House of Lords in *Woolwich*. In *Factortame*, the Court held that the English courts could not be prevented by a rule of national law from granting an injunction against the Crown where this was necessary to protect rights under Community law. In *Francovich*, the Court held that failure by a Member State to implement a directive may give rise to a right to damages for individuals who have thereby suffered loss. The recent Opinion of the Advocate General in *Banks* suggests that the Court should now set at rest the doubts remaining after *Garden Cottage Foods*.

So lawyers of all disciplines need to find out in greater detail how Community law interacts with national law, and this book will help them to do it. It covers the existing material in a thorough, but accessible, way and provides clear guidance as to the way in which Community law can be used in the English legal system. In addition, it deals with the direct actions which can be brought before the Court of Justice and Court of First Instance and includes a useful analysis of the Rules of Procedure to be followed before these Courts.

I commend this book to all lawyers who take seriously the duty they owe to their clients to be aware of Community law, and I am sure it will have the success it deserves.

28 October 1993   *David Edward*

Judge of the Court of Justice
of the European Communities

Preface

In 1703 Holt CJ stated in *Ashby v White*:

> If the Plaintiff has a right, he must of necessity have a means to vindicate and maintain it, and a remedy if he is injured in the exercise or enjoyment of it, and indeed it is a vain thing to imagine a right without a remedy; for want of right and want of remedy are reciprocal.

The principle of *ubi jus, ibi remedium* has as much application to EC law in the 1990s as it did to disputed elections in Aylesbury in the 1700s. EC law creates rights for individuals which must be protected. These rights have been described by the European Court of Justice as fundamental and as forming part of our legal heritage. Yet, the extent to which these rights are protected, especially in the national courts, is still unclear. This book attempts to deal with the remedies which are available in the national courts and the EC courts to protect rights afforded to individuals under EC law.

The law is up-to-date to September 1993. Nevertheless the law on remedies in EC law is changing with ever increasing frequency. Chapter 6 on damages in the national courts for breach of EC law will need to be revised in the coming year in the light of Case C–46/93 *Brasseries du Pecheur*, Case C–48/93 *Factortame* and Case C–128/92 *HJ Banks*. All three cases are pending before the Court of Justice and all concern the extent to which national courts are obliged as a matter of EC law to award damages for breach of EC law. This shows how dynamic the subject is. We have been able to incorporate some recent developments, such as the House of Lords' judgment in *R v Secretary for Employment, ex p Equal Opportunities Commission*, in the footnotes. Again, these cases will have to be considered fully in a later edition. In addition, since the completion of the text of the book, the Maastricht Treaty has finally been ratified. The main changes are highlighted in the footnotes to the text.

We would like to express our appreciation to Alison Padfield, William Robinson and Ami Barav for their helpful comments on chapters of the book and to Jeffrey Boloten at Longman. We would also like to thank Judge David Edward for agreeing to write the foreword.

30 March 1994

Mark Brealey
Mark Hoskins
3 Gray's Inn Place
Gray's Inn

Table of Cases

EUROPEAN CASES: ALPHABETICAL LIST

UK CASES

Table of Statutes

Table of Statutory Instruments

Table of Treaties

Table of Regulations

Table of Directives and Decisions

Table of International Conventions

Part I

Application of EC Law in the English Courts

Chapter 1

Sources of EC Law

Sources The main sources of EC law are the treaties which establish the European Communities and the legislation which is passed by the Community institutions to implement those treaties. These sources are supplemented by the case law ('jurisprudence') of the European Court of Justice and the Court of First Instance.

The main legislative sources of EC law may be divided into two categories: primary and secondary legislation.

1. PRIMARY LEGISLATION

The Treaties Primary legislation consists of the treaties which establish the European Communities. There are three main treaties:

(1) The treaty establishing the European Coal and Steel Community ('ECSC' Treaty).[1]

(2) The treaty establishing the European Economic Community ('EEC' Treaty).[2]

(3) The treaty establishing the European Atomic Energy Community ('EAEC' Treaty, also referred to as 'EURATOM').[3]

The EEC Treaty is by far the most important source of primary legislation as it is of more general application than the other two, sectorial, treaties. It sets out:

(*a*) the basic goals or 'Principles of the Community';[4]

(*b*) the 'Foundations of the Community' (namely, the free movement of goods, persons, services and capital, the common market for agriculture and the common transport policy);[5]

(*c*) the 'Policy of the Community' (including competition policy, state aid policy, social policy and environmental policy);[6] and

---

[1] Treaty of Paris, signed on 18 April 1951.
[2] Treaty of Rome, signed on 25 March 1957.
[3] Treaty of Rome, signed on 25 March 1957.
[4] EEC Treaty, articles 1–8c.
[5] EEC Treaty, articles 9–84.
[6] EEC Treaty, articles 85–136a.

3

(*d*) the rules which govern the institutions of the Community.[7]

The EEC Treaty was amended to some extent by the Single European Act[8] and will be subject to further amendment by the European Union Treaty (the Maastricht Treaty).[9]

There are other treaties which constitute sources of primary law, which are less important in everyday practice. These include, notably, the Treaties of Accession by which new Member States joined the Community.[10]

The sources of primary legislation are the legal basis upon which the Community operates. They are, in effect, the constitution of the Community,[11] and as such they take priority over all other sources of law within the Community. The treaties define the limits of the European Communities' competence to act and they provide the legal bases for all secondary legislation. No acts can be adopted which are not justified, directly or indirectly, by the provisions of the treaties. Where there is a conflict between primary and secondary legislation, the primary legislation will prevail.[12]

2. SECONDARY LEGISLATION

Community measures As indicated above, the EEC Treaty sets out the general framework of the European Economic Community. In practice, further detailed legislation is necessary to give effect to the Treaty. The EEC Treaty therefore gives the Community institutions law-making and administrative powers.

There are five basic types of legislative and administrative instruments which the institutions, particularly the Council and the Commission, can adopt. These are regulations, directives, decisions, recommendations and opinions.[13] Each of these instruments is different in character and they are defined in article 189 of the EEC Treaty.[14]

---

[7] EEC Treaty, articles 137–209.
[8] Signed on 17 February 1986, [1987] OJ No L169/1.
[9] Signed at Maastricht on 7 February 1992, OJ No C 191, 29 July 1992, p1. The text of the EEC Treaty, as it will be amended by the Maastricht Treaty, has been published in OJ No C 224, 31 August 1992.
[10] 1972—Denmark, Ireland, United Kingdom; 1979—Greece; 1985—Spain, Portugal.
[11] *Opinion 1/91* [1991] ECR I–6079 para 21 (Opinion concerning the draft Treaty on a European Economic Area).
[12] See, for example, Case 37/70 *Rewe-Zentrale v Hauptzollamt Emmerich* [1971] ECR 23 paras 2–5, Joined Cases 80 and 81/77 *Société Les Commissionnaires Sàrl v Receveur des Douanes* [1978] ECR 927; Case C–21/88 *Du Pont Nemours Italiana SpA v Unità sanitaria locale No 2 di Carrara* [1990] ECR I–889 paras 16–17.
[13] The terminology used for measures under the ECSC Treaty is different: see ECSC Treaty, article 14. In particular, ECSC decisions are equivalent to EEC regulations, while ECSC recommendations are equivalent to EEC directives.
[14] The types of measures listed in article 189 are not exhaustive. See, for example, Case 22/70 *Commission v Council ('ERTA')* [1971] ECR 263 paras 34–42.

(a) Regulations

Definition Article 189 of the EEC Treaty defines regulations as follows:

> A regulation shall have general application. It shall be binding in its entirety and directly applicable in all Member States.

'General application' means that regulations are not addressed to specific Member States or private parties. They are also 'binding in their entirety' which means that their provisions apply in identical terms throughout the Community.

Entry into force A regulation takes effect on the date specified in its text, or, if no such date is specified, on the twentieth day following its publication in the Official Journal of the European Community.[15] A regulation is presumed to be published on the date shown on the issue of the Official Journal in which it appears, unless evidence can be produced that the issue was not in fact available until a later date.[16]

Directly applicable Regulations are 'directly applicable'. This means that as soon as a regulation comes into force, it takes effect automatically in the national legal systems of the Member States. There is no need for the Member States to pass national implementing legislation.[17] The entry into force of a regulation precludes the application of any national legislative measure, even one adopted subsequently, which is incompatible with the provisions of that regulation.[18] Furthermore, Member States are not permitted to modify the scope of application of a regulation by national measures, for example by providing for exemptions which are not contained in the regulation.[19] Once a regulation has entered into force, the Member States have an obligation to repeal all existing national legislation which is incompatible with it. It is not sufficient simply to issue administrative instructions waiving the application of the national law.[20]

---

[15] EEC Treaty, article 191. Where a specific date for entry into force is laid down in the regulation itself, this may be subject to review by the EC Courts, particularly where it would entail retroactive effect: Case 17/67 *Firma Max Neumann v Hauptzollamt Hof/Saale* [1967] ECR 441 at 455–456.

[16] Case 99/78 *Weingut Gustav Decker KG v Hauptzollamt Landau* [1979] ECR 101 paras 2–5; Case 337/88 *Società agricola fattoria alimentare SpA ('SAFA') v Amministrazione delle finanze dello Stato* [1990] ECR 1 paras 8, 12.

[17] Case 34/73 *Variola SpA v Amministrazione Italiana delle Finanze* [1973] ECR 981 para 10; Case 50/76 *Amsterdam Bulb BV v Produktschap voor Siergewassen* [1977] ECR 137 paras 4–6; Case 94/77 *Fratelli Zerbone Snc v Amministrazione delle Finanze dello Stato* [1978] ECR 99 paras 22–24.

[18] Case 84/71 *Marimex SpA v Ministry for Finance of the Italian Republic* [1972] ECR 89 paras 4, 5; Case 34/73 *Variola SpA v Amministrazione Italiana delle Finanze* [1973] ECR 981 paras 14, 15; Case 31/78 *Francesco Bussone v Italian Ministry for Agriculture and Forestry* [1978] ECR 2429 paras 30, 31.

[19] Case 18/72 *Granaria Graaninkoopmaatschappij NV v Produktschap voor Veevoeder* [1972] ECR 1163 paras 14–18.

[20] Case 167/73 *Commission v France* [1974] ECR 359 para 42; Case C–307/89 *Commission v France* [1991] ECR I–2903 paras 12, 13.

Implementation Member States are not permitted to adopt national implementing measures unless this is required, explicitly or implicitly, by the regulation.[21] In particular, Member States are not permitted simply to reproduce the provisions of a regulation in a national law, as this might conceal the Community nature of the rights contained in the regulation.[22]

Member States may adopt national legislative, regulatory, administrative or financial measures where this is expressly required by the regulation[23] or where this is necessary to give effect to the regulation in their national legal system.[24] For example, in Case 31/78 *Francesco Bussone v Italian Ministry for Agriculture and Forestry*[25] a regulation required the Member States to designate official agencies to organise the preparation and distribution of bands and labels with which large packs of eggs had to be provided.

The implementing measures need not be identical in all respects throughout the Community.[26] However, Member States are not permitted to amend the scope of the regulation or add to its provisions, unless this complies with the aim and objectives of the regulation.[27] National implementing measures may reproduce the provisions of a regulation where this is necessary for the sake of coherence and comprehensibility.[28] Where a Member State has adopted implementing measures, the national courts are entitled to review those national measures to ascertain whether they are in accordance with the regulation.[29] In addition, the national measures must respect the general principles of Community law.[30]

---

[21] Case 93/71 *Orsolina Leonisio v Ministry for Agriculture and Forestry of the Italian Republic* [1972] ECR 287 paras 5, 6 and 22; Case 50/76 *Amsterdam Bulb BV v Produktschap voor Siergewassen* [1977] ECR 137 paras 4–8.

[22] Case 39/72 *Commission v Italy* [1973] ECR 101 paras 14–18; Case 34/73 *Variola SpA v Amministrazione Italiana delle Finanze* [1973] ECR 981 paras 9–11; Case 272/83 *Commission v Italy* [1985] ECR 1057 para 26.

[23] See, for example, Case 40/69 *Hauptzollamt Hamburg-Oberelbe v Firma Paul G Bollmann* [1970] ECR 69 paras 2–5; Case 74/69 *Hauptzollamt Bremen-Freihafen v Waren-Import-Gesellschaft Krohn and Co* [1970] ECR 451 paras 2–6; Case 31/78 *Francesco Bussone v Italian Ministry for Agriculture and Forestry* [1978] ECR 2429 paras 30–32; Case 230/78 *SpA Eridania-Zuccherifici nazionali v Minister of Agriculture and Forestry* [1979] ECR 2749 paras 33–35.

[24] Case 94/77 *Fratelli Zerbone Snc v Amministrazione delle Finanze dello Stato* [1978] ECR 99 paras 22–27; Joined Cases 146/81, 192/81, 193/81 *BayWa AG v Bundesanstalt für landwirtschaftliche Marktordnung* [1982] ECR 1503 paras 26–31.

[25] [1978] ECR 2429 paras 26–36.

[26] Case 111/76 *Officier van Justitie v Beert van den Hazel* [1977] ECR 901 para 22.

[27] Case 40/69 *Hauptzollamt Hamburg-Oberelbe v Firma Paul G Bollmann* [1970] ECR 69 paras 2–5; Case 74/69 *Hauptzollamt Bremen-Freihafen v Waren-Import-Gesellschaft Krohn and Co* [1970] ECR 451 paras 2–6; Case 118/76 *Balkan-Import-Export v Hauptzollamt Berlin-Packhof* [1977] ECR 1177 paras 3–6; Case 31/78 *Francesco Bussone v Italian Ministry for Agriculture and Forestry* [1978] ECR 2429 paras 26–36; Case 819/79 *Germany v Commission* [1981] ECR 21 paras 1–11.

[28] Case 272/83 *Commission v Italy* [1985] ECR 1057 paras 21–28.

[29] Case 46/75 *IBC Importazione Bestiame Carni srl v Commission* [1976] ECR 65; Case 230/78 *SpA Eridania-Zuccherifici nazionali v Minister of Agriculture and Forestry* [1979] ECR 2749 para 34.

[30] Case 5/88 *Hubert Wachauf v Germany* [1989] ECR 2609 para 19. General principles are discussed at pp 12–20.

Hierarchy of norms The scope and binding nature of a regulation cannot be affected, during the period of its validity, by the adoption of a subsequent regulation which has the same objectives and which imposes less stringent requirements on Member States, but which does not expressly repeal or amend the original regulation.[31]

(b) Directives

Definition Article 189 of the EEC Treaty provides:

> A directive shall be binding, as to the result to be achieved, upon each Member State to which it is addressed, but shall leave to the national authorities the choice of form and methods.

A directive imposes an obligation on each Member State to which it is addressed to adopt, in that Member State's national legal system, all the measures necessary to ensure that the provisions of the directive are fully effective, in accordance with its objective, while leaving the choice of the forms and methods used to achieve that objective to the Member State itself.[32]

The main difference between a directive and a regulation is that, under the terms of a directive, a Member State has an obligation to pass national implementing legislation to give effect to the directive in its national legal system.[33] Thus, directives are not directly applicable in the same way as regulations. However, in certain circumstances a directive may create legal effects in the national legal systems of Member States before it has been implemented by national legislation. Such rights may arise by virtue of the principles of direct effect[34] or interpretation.[35] In addition, where an individual has suffered loss as a result of a Member State's failure to implement a directive, he may be entitled to recover damages from the State.[36]

Unlike regulations, which are of 'general application', directives may be addressed to particular Member States, although usually they will be addressed to all the Member States.

Implementation A directive will specify a legislative result which must be achieved by each Member State within a given time limit. Generally, each Member State has a discretion as to what national legislative measures are necessary to achieve that result, so that the form and content of national implementing legislation for a directive may differ between Member States.

---

[31] Case C–39/88 *Commission v Ireland* [1990] ECR I–4271 para 9. See also Case C–174/89 *Hoche v Bundesanstalt für landwirtschaftliche Marktordnung* [1990] ECR I–2681 para 23.

[32] For example, see Case C–271/91 *MH Marshall v Southampton and South West Hampshire Area Health Authority*, judgment of 2 August 1993, para 17.

[33] Case 91/79 *Commission v Italy* [1980] ECR 1099 para 6; Case C–287/91 *Commission v Italy* [1992] I–3515 para 7.

[34] See pp 31–39.

[35] See pp 44–50.

[36] Joined Cases C–6/90 and C–9/90 *Francovich and Bonifaci v Italy* [1991] ECR I-5357. See pp 82–85.

However, Member States do not enjoy a complete discretion as to how to implement a directive; they must adopt the most appropriate forms and methods to ensure that a directive is fully effective.[37] In addition, they must respect the general principles of Community law.[38]

A Member State is not obliged to adopt specific implementing legislation which reproduces *verbatim* the provisions of the directive. It may rely on its existing legislative framework, as long as that framework guarantees the full application of the directive in a sufficiently clear and precise manner. This is to ensure that, where the directive is intended to create rights for individuals, the persons concerned can ascertain the full extent of their rights and, where appropriate, rely on them before the national courts.[39] A Member State is not entitled to implement a directive by means of purely administrative practices, as these can be changed by the authorities as they please and are not publicised widely enough.[40] A Member State is free to delegate the task of implementing directives to regional or local authorities. However, the Member State remains responsible for ensuring that directives are correctly implemented.[41]

The fact that a directive has direct effect does not absolve a Member State from its obligation to adopt national implementing legislation.[42]

Implementation period Directives must be notified to those to whom they are addressed and cannot take effect until such notification.[43] Usually, a directive will specify a specific time limit within which it must be implemented.[44] Member States are entitled to maintain potentially conflicting national legislation in force until the implementation period for the directive has expired.[45]

---

[37] Case 48/75 *Jean Noël Royer* [1976] ECR 497 para 75. *Cf* Case 163/82 *Commission v Italy* [1983] ECR 3273 paras 7–10, where the Court of Justice emphasised the Member States' freedom to decide on the most appropriate form and methods for implementation.

[38] Case 230/78 *SpA Eridania v Ministry for Agriculture and Forestry* [1979] ECR 2749 para 31; Joined Cases C–31–44/91 *SpA Alois Lageder and others v Amministrazione delle finanze dello Stato* judgment of 1 April 1993, para 33. See also Case 5/88 *Hubert Wachauf v Germany* [1989] ECR 2609 para 19. General principles discussed at pp 12–20.

[39] Case 29/84 *Commission v Germany* [1985] ECR 1661 paras 22, 23; Case 363/85 *Commission v Italy* [1987] ECR 1733 para 7; Case 131/88 *Commission v Germany* [1991] ECR I–825 para 6; Case C–190/90 *Commission v Netherlands* [1992] I–3265 para 17.

[40] Case 102/79 *Commission v Belgium* [1980] ECR 1473 para 11; Case 145/82 *Commission v Italy* [1983] ECR 711 para 10; Case 168/85 *Commission v Italy* [1986] ECR 2945; Case C–306/89 *Commission v Greece* [1991] ECR I–5863 paras 18–20; Case 235/91 *Commission v Ireland*, [1993] 1 CMLR 325 para 10. *Cf* Case C–339/87 *Commission v Netherlands* [1990] ECR I–851 paras 6–8, where the Court of Justice held that ministerial measures which were published in the Dutch *Official Gazette* and which were capable of creating rights and obligations for individuals could constitute proper implementation of a directive.

[41] Case 96/81 *Commission v Netherlands* [1982] ECR 1791 para 12; Joined Cases 227–230/85 *Commission v Belgium* [1988] ECR 1 para 9; Case C–131/88 *Commission v Germany* [1991] ECR I–825 para 71.

[42] Case 102/79 *Commission v Belgium* [1980] ECR 1473 para 12.

[43] EEC Treaty, article 191.

[44] See p 9 for notification and time limits.

[45] Case 244/78 *Union Laitière Normande v French Dairy Farmers Limited* [1979] ECR 2663 paras 13–15.

(c) Decisions

Definition Article 189 of the EEC Treaty defines decisions as follows:

A decision shall be binding in its entirety upon those to whom it is addressed.

Decisions are not generally applicable and are addressed to specific Member States or private parties. Decisions are used, notably by the Commission, to deal with particular cases. They are issued in many areas of Community competence and it is impossible to give exhaustive examples of their use. They are particularly important in the areas of competition policy[46] and state aids.[47] In Case 249/85 *Albako Margarinefabrik Maria von der Linde GmbH & Co KG v Bundesanstalt für landwirtschaftliche Marktordnung*[48] the Court of Justice held that decisions addressed to a Member State are binding on all the organs of that state, including the courts.

Notification Decisions must be notified to those to whom they are addressed and take effect upon such notification.[49] A decision is duly notified once it has been communicated to the person to whom it is addressed and that person is in a position to take cognisance of it. Actual knowledge is not necessary. Notification will usually take place by a registered letter accompanied by a form headed 'Acknowledgment of Receipt' to be completed by the recipient or delivered by hand against receipt.[50] Regardless of the time of day when the measure in question is notified, time does not begin to run until the end of the day of notification.[51]

(d) Recommendations and opinions

Definition Article 189 of the EEC Treaty states:

Recommendations and opinions shall have no binding force.

Recommendations are generally adopted by the institutions of the Community when they do not have the power under the Treaty to adopt binding measures or when they consider that it is not appropriate to adopt mandatory rules.[52] Although recommendations do not produce binding legal rights which individuals can rely on before national courts, they do have some legal effect. This is clear

---

[46] See Council Regulation No 17/62 of 6 February 1962, First Regulation implementing articles 85 and 86 of the EEC Treaty (as amended), OJ 13, 21 February 1962, p 204 (Special Edition 1959–1962, p 249).

[47] EEC Treaty, article 93.

[48] [1987] ECR 2345 para 17.

[49] EEC Treaty, article 191.

[50] Case 6/72 *Europemballage and Continental Can v Commission* [1973] ECR 215 paras 9, 10; Case 42/85 *Cockerill-Sambre SA v Commission* [1985] ECR 3749 (ECSC) para 10; Case T–12/90 *Bayer AG v Commission* [1991] ECR II–219 paras 17–21.

[51] Case 152/85 *Rudolf Misset v Council* [1987] ECR 223.

[52] Case 322/88 *Salvatore Grimaldi v Fonds des maladies professionnelles* [1989] ECR 4407 para 13.

from Case 322/88 *Salvatore Grimaldi v Fonds des maladies professionnelles*[53] where the Court of Justice held that national courts are bound to take recommendations into consideration in deciding disputes submitted to them, in particular where they are capable of casting light on the interpretation of other provisions of national or Community law.[54]

3. CASE LAW

Court of Justice/Court of First Instance Articles 164–188 of the EEC Treaty establish the basis upon which the Court of Justice functions and the scope of its jurisdiction.[55] Its role is defined in article 164 as follows:

> The Court of Justice shall ensure that in the interpretation and application of this Treaty the law is observed.

The Court of First Instance was created in 1989. Its jurisdiction is more limited than that of the Court of Justice.[56]

Precedent Although the EC Courts are not bound by a strict doctrine of precedent, they will usually follow the principles established in previous judgments.[57] It is normal, therefore, to refer to previous judgments in both written and oral pleadings before the EC Courts, just as it is before the English courts.

Opinions of Advocates-General Reference may also be made to previous Opinions of Advocates-General. The Advocate-General's Opinion is not binding upon any court, but is of strong persuasive value. If it is not followed by the Court of Justice (or Court of First Instance) in its judgment, then it is in some respects like a dissenting judgment in the English courts and may be cited in future cases.[58]

Status of EC Courts' judgments in English law Decisions of the EC Courts are binding on English courts. This is the effect of s 3(1) of the European Communities Act 1972,[59] which provides that:

> (1) For the purposes of all legal proceedings any question as to the meaning or effect of any of the Treaties, or as to the validity, meaning or effect of any Community

---

[53] [1989] ECR 4407 paras 16–19.

[54] See further p 50.

[55] See pp 148–152 and Ch 17.

[56] See pp 252–254.

[57] See the comments of Lord Denning MR in *HP Bulmer Ltd v J Bollinger SA* [1974] 1 Ch 401 at 420C–E; and the comments of Lord Diplock in *Henn and Darby v DPP* [1981] AC 850 at 905B–D.

[58] For examples of English courts referring to Opinions of Advocates-General, see *WH Smith Do-It-All Ltd v Peterborough City Council* [1991] 1 QB 304 at 327B–328B; *Battersea Leisure Limited v Commissioners of Customs and Excise* [1992] 3 CMLR 610 para 34.

[59] As amended by s 2 of the European Communities (Amendment) Act 1986. See *Garden Cottage Foods Ltd v Milk Marketing Board* [1984] AC 130, per Lord Diplock at 141C–D.

instrument, shall be treated as a question of law (and, if not referred to the European Court, be for determination as such in accordance with the principles laid down by and any relevant decision of the European Court or any court attached thereto).

Status of Commission decisions The status of Commission decisions in the English courts is unclear. In *British Leyland Motor Corporation Limited v Wyatt Interpart Company Limited*[60] Graham J considered, *obiter*, that English courts would be bound by decisions of the Commission which had not been overturned by the Community courts. In *Fyffes plc v Chiquita Brands International Inc*[61] Vinelott J stated that 'the Court will attach very great weight to a decision (even a provisional decision) of the Commission'. Further, in *Inntrepeneur Estates Ltd v Mason*[62] M Barnes QC, sitting as a deputy judge of the High Court, stated that an English court should take into account letters written by the Commission which did not have the formal status of comfort letters. Article 189 of the EEC Treaty provides that decisions are binding upon those to whom they are addressed. Therefore, it is arguable that it would undermine 'l'effet utile' of Community law to permit parties who have been the subject of a decision by the Commission to seek to go behind that decision in proceedings before the national courts.[63]

Proving Community law Section 3 of the European Communities Act 1972 contains specific provisions as to proving Community law in the English courts. In particular, it provides that judicial notice must be taken of the Treaties, the Official Journal of the European Communities and decisions of the EC courts.[64] Issues of Community law are to be treated as questions of law.[65] Therefore, in criminal trials, any question of Community law is a question for the judge and not a question for the jury.[66]

In the field of competition law, the Commission has published a 'Notice on co-operation between national courts and the Commission in applying Articles 85 and 86 of the EEC Treaty'.[67] The purpose of this Notice is to encourage the hearing of cases involving Community competition law in the national courts.

---

[60] [1979] 3 CMLR 79 para 14.

[61] [1993] ECC 193 paras 62, 63.

[62] [1993] 2 CMLR 293 paras 31–56. In reaching this conclusion, the judge relied on the 'Notice on co-operation between national courts and the Commission in applying Articles 85 and 86 of the EEC Treaty', issued by the Commission and published at OJ No C 39, 13 February 1993, p6.

[63] *Cf* Case 249/85 *Albako Margarinefabrik Maria von der Linde GmbH & Co KG v Bundesanstalt für landwirtschaftliche Marktordnung* [1987] ECR 2345 para 17, concerning the binding effect of decisions addressed to Member States. See also Opinion of Advocate-General Van Gerven in Case C–128/92 *HJ Banks & Co Ltd v British Coal Corporation* 27 October 1993 at paras 55–61 and Case C–188/92 *TWD Textilwerke Deggendorf GmbH v Germany* (9 March 1994).

[64] Section 3(2) of the European Communities Act 1972, as amended by s 2 of the European Communities (Amendment) Act 1986.

[65] Section 3(1) of the European Communities Act 1972, as amended by s 2 of the European Communities (Amendment) Act 1986.

[66] *R v Goldstein* [1983] 1 WLR 151 at 156A–E.

[67] OJ No C 39, 13 February 1993, p6.

The Notice indicates, *inter alia*, that national courts may, within the limits of their national procedural law, consult the Commission on points of law and obtain information regarding factual data, for example statistics, market studies and economic analyses. Particular difficulties may arise in the English courts in respect of evidence in competition cases as a result of the House of Lords decision in *Rio Tinto Zinc Corporation v Westinghouse Electric Corporation.*[68] The House of Lords held that a party may claim privilege against self-incrimination under s 14(1) of the Civil Evidence Act 1968 in respect of documents which, if produced, might expose it to the imposition of fines by the Commission under the Community competition rules. Furthermore, in *Shearson Lehman Hutton Inc v MacLaine Watson & Co Ltd,*[69] Webster J indicated that he would require a high degree of probability, but less than the standard of proof in criminal matters, to establish an infringement of article 85, as such an infringement could lead to the imposition of fines.

4. GENERAL PRINCIPLES/HUMAN RIGHTS

Introduction The EC courts have recognised certain general principles of law, drawn largely from the national legal systems of the Member States.[70] Community measures and acts of the Member States giving effect to Community obligations must respect these principles. In addition, these principles serve as aids to interpretation of Community law.

(a) Proportionality

Definition In order for a measure to comply with the principle of proportionality:

(1) the means which it employs to achieve its objectives must be capable of doing so and

(2) the means employed must not go beyond what is necessary to achieve those objectives.[71]

When there is a choice between several appropriate measures, recourse must be had to the least onerous. However, where a Community institution is exercising discretionary powers, the EC courts will not strike down a measure simply because they believe that a better approach exists. In such circumstances,

---

[68] [1978] 1 AC 547. See the comments of Advocate-General Edward as to the difficulties of bringing cases based on Community competition law in the national courts in Case T–24/90 *Automec Srl v Commission* and Case T–28/90 *Asia Motor France SA v Commission* [1992] ECR II–2223 at paras 109–116 of the Opinion.

[69] [1989] 3 CMLR 429 paras 283, 284.

[70] See, generally, Jürgen Schwarze, *European Administrative Law* (Sweet & Maxwell, 1992); Schermers, *Judicial Protection in the European Communities*, 5th edn (Kluwer, 1991), 27–94.

[71] Case 66/82 *Fromançais SA v Fonds d'Orientation et de Régularisation des Marchés Agricoles (FORMA)* [1983] ECR 395 para 8; Case 15/83 *Denkavit Nederland BV v Hoofdproduktschap voor Akkerbouwprodukten* [1984] ECR 2171 para 25; Joined Cases 279/84, 280/84, 285/84, 286/84 *Walter Rau Lebensmittelwerke v Commission* [1987] ECR 1069 para 34. Discussed further at pp 116–120.

a measure will be declared invalid only if it is clearly unsuited to the objective which it seeks to pursue.[72]

Community institutions Measures adopted by the Community institutions must comply with the principle of proportionality.[73] In particular, where a penalty is imposed by Community legislation, it must be commensurate with the seriousness of the breach. Thus, a breach of a secondary obligation should not be punished as severely as a breach of an obligation whose observance is of fundamental importance to the proper functioning of the Community system.[74] For example, in Case 122/78 *SA Buitoni v Fonds D'Orientation et de Régularisation des Marchés Agricoles*,[75] Community legislation provided that the grant of import licences for certain goods from outside the Community was conditional on the importer providing security as a guarantee that the goods would, in fact, be imported within the period specified in the licence. The whole of the security was forfeited if the goods were not imported within the specified period or if proof of importation had not been provided within six months after the expiry of the licence. The Court of Justice held that forfeiture of the security for failure to import the goods complied with the principle of proportionality. However, in comparison, it was contrary to the principle of proportionality to impose the same sanction for failure to provide proof within the required period merely to ensure administrative efficiency. In Case 181/84 *The Queen, ex p ED & F Man (Sugar) Ltd v Intervention Board for Agricultural Produce (IBAP)*[76] the Court of Justice summarised this principle in the following way:

> Where Community legislation makes a distinction between a primary obligation, compliance with which is necessary in order to attain the objective sought, and a secondary obligation, essentially of an administrative nature, it cannot, without breaching the principle of proportionality, penalize failure to comply with the secondary obligation as severely as failure to comply with the primary obligation.

Member States Where Member States enact national legislation to give effect to Community law, that legislation must comply with the principle of proportionality. Thus, where national legislation imposes sanctions for breach of a

---

[72] Case 138/78 *Hans-Markus Stölting v Hauptzollamt Hamburg-Jonas* [1979] ECR 713 para 7; Joined Cases 279/84, 280/84, 285/84, 286/84 *Walter Rau Lebensmittelwerke v Commission* [1987] ECR 1069 para 34; Case C–331/88 *R v Minister for Agriculture, Fisheries and Food, ex p FEDESA* [1990] ECR I–4023 paras 12–14.

[73] Case 15/83 *Denkavit Nederland BV v Hoofdproduktschap voor Akkerbouwprodukten* [1984] ECR 2171 paras 24–33. See also Case 5/73 *Balkan-Import-Export GmbH v Hauptzollamt Berlin-Packhof* [1973] ECR 1091 paras 19–23.

[74] Case 240/78 *Atalanta Amsterdam BV v Produktschap voor Vee en Vlees* [1979] ECR 2137 paras 13–16; Case 21/85 *A Maas & Co NV v Bundesanstalt für landwirtschaftliche Marktordnung* [1986] ECR 3537 para 15.

[75] [1979] ECR 677.

[76] [1985] ECR 2889 para 20. Contrast Case 272/81 *Société RU-MI v Fonds d'Orientation et de Régularisation des Marchés Agricoles (FORMA)* [1982] ECR 4167 para 14, where this principle was held to be inapplicable.

Community obligation, the severity of the sanction must not exceed what is appropriate and necessary to attain the objective pursued.[77] Further, where Member States seek to impose restrictions on the free movement of goods in order to protect mandatory requirements, such as consumer protection, any such restrictions must also comply with the principle of proportionality. For example, where a Member State has a choice between various measures in order to attain the same objective, it must choose the means which least restricts the free movement of goods.[78]

(b) Legitimate expectation

Definition The principle of legitimate expectation provides protection for parties who have relied, reasonably and in good faith, on conduct or measures of the Community institutions.[79] The principle has been considered in a wide range of situations and is best illustrated by a number of examples.[80] In Case 120/86 *J Mulder v Minister van Landbouw en Visserij*[81] Mr Mulder, a dairy farmer, had entered into a Community system under which he received payments in return for undertaking not to produce dairy products for a period of five years. After the expiry of the five year period, he applied for a milk quota in order to recommence production. However, because he had not been producing milk in the year prior to his application, his application was rejected. Mr Mulder challenged the validity of the regulation under which he was refused a quota. The Court of Justice held that the regulation upon which the refusal was based was invalid as:

> ... where such a producer, as in the present case, has been encouraged by a Community measure to suspend marketing for a limited period in the general interest and against payment of a premium he may legitimately expect not to be subject, upon the expiry of his undertaking, to restrictions which specifically affect him precisely because he availed himself of the possibilities offered by the Community provisions.

In Case 223/85 *Rijn-Schelde-Verolme (RSV) Maschinefabrieken en Scheepswerven NV v Commission*[82] the Court of Justice annulled a decision of the Commission requiring the Netherlands to recover monies paid to NSV as state aid,

---

[77] Case 203/80 *Criminal proceedings against Guerrino Casati* [1981] ECR 2595 paras 26–29; Case C–210/91 *Commission v Greece* judgment of 16 December 1992 para 20.

[78] Case 261/81 *Walter Rau Lebensmittelwerke v De Smedt PvbA* [1982] ECR 3961 para 12. See pp 116–20 for a discussion of the approach of the English courts to proportionality.

[79] Case T–123/89 *Jean-Louis Chomel v Commission* [1990] ECR II–131 para 25.

[80] For a detailed analysis, see Eleanor Sharpston, 'Legitimate Expectations and Economic Reality' (1990) 15 EL Rev 103.

[81] [1988] ECR 2321 paras 21–28.

[82] [1987] ECR 4617 paras 12–19. *Cf* Case C–301/87 *France v Commission* [1990] ECR I–307 paras 25–28 where delay by the Commission in reaching a decision was justified due to the time required to obtain all necessary information. See also Case 5/82 *Hauptzollamt Krefeld v Maizena GmbH* [1982] ECR 4601 para 22 where the Court of Justice held that the fact that a Member State had followed a certain practice for several years, in breach of Community law, did not give rise to legitimate expectations, even where the Commission had failed to take action to put an end to the breach.

on the ground that the Commission had delayed 26 months before adopting the decision. This delay had established a legitimate expectation on the part of NSV that it would be entitled to retain the monies. In Case 127/80 *Vincent Grogan v Commission*[83] the Court of Justice annulled a Commission decision which reduced the monthly pension payable to the applicant. The Commission decision was adopted pursuant to a Council regulation which adjusted the rates of exchange upon which pensions were calculated. The Court of Justice found that the Council had neglected to rectify exchange rates over a period of about seven years. This had given rise to legitimate expectations amongst pensioners as to the level of pension which they would receive. The Court held that these legitimate expectations were not adequately protected by the new regulation which sought to regularise the position within ten months. The transition period should have been twice as long.

Reasonable reliance In order for reliance to give rise to legitimate expectations, it must be reasonable. Where a particular legal development should have been foreseen by 'prudent and discriminating traders', they cannot challenge its validity on the basis of legitimate expectation.[84] Thus, in areas where the Community institutions enjoy a wide discretionary power and where frequent adjustments to the legislative framework are necessary, such as in relation to the common agricultural policy, the Court of Justice has consistently held that parties cannot have a legitimate expectation that an existing situation will be maintained.[85] Where a party has committed a manifest infringement of a Community measure, he is not entitled to rely on that measure as giving rise to a legitimate expectation.[86]

(c) Legal certainty

Definition The principle of legal certainty requires that every Community measure which produces legal effects must be clear and precise and brought to the attention of the person concerned, so that he can ascertain, with certainty, the time at which the measure begins to produce legal effects.[87] This is particularly important given the short two-month time limit imposed by article 173 of the EEC Treaty for challenging the validity of Community measures.[88] Thus, in Joined Cases T–79/89, T–84/89 and others *BASF AG v Commission*[89] the Court

---

[83] [1982] ECR 869 paras 27–37.
[84] Case 78/77 *Firma Johann Lührs v Hauptzollamt Hamburg-Jonas* [1978] ECR 169 paras 1–10.
[85] Case 230/78 *SpA Eridania-Zuccherifici Nazionali v Minister of Agriculture and Forestry* [1979] ECR 2749 paras 20–22; Case C–350/88 *Société française des Biscuits Delacre v Commission* [1990] ECR I–395 paras 31–38; Joined Cases C–258/90, C–259/90 *Pesquerias De Bermeo SA v Commission* [1992] ECR I–2901 para 34.
[86] Case C–96/89 *Commission v Netherlands* [1991] ECR I–2461 para 30.
[87] Joined Cases T–18/89, T–24/89 *Harissios Tagaras v Court of Justice* [1991] ECR II–53 para 40; Case T–14/91 *Georges Weyrich v Commission* [1991] ECR II–235 para 48.
[88] See pp 198–200.
[89] [1992] II–315 paras 84–100. Cf the Opinion of Advocate-General Van Gerven in Case–137/92P *Commission v BASF AG*, delivered on 29 June 1993, paras 71–82.

of First Instance held that a decision of the Commission was a non-existent act due to the legal uncertainty created by the Commission's failure to follow the proper procedure for its adoption, which made it impossible to identify, with any certainty, the date from which the decision was meant to produce legal effects and the exact content of the decision actually adopted.

The principle of legal certainty must be strictly observed in relation to Community measures which may entail financial consequences.[90] Thus, the Court of Justice has held that:[91]

> rules imposing charges on the taxpayer must be clear and precise so that he may know without ambiguity what are his rights and obligations and may take steps accordingly.

(d) Non-retroactivity

Definition In general, substantive Community measures may not take effect from a date prior to their publication. However, a measure may have retroactive effect where this is necessary to achieve its objective and where the legitimate expectations of those concerned by it are duly respected.[92] In order for a Community measure to be interpreted as having retroactive effect, this consequence must be readily apparent from its 'terms, objective or general scheme'.[93] In addition, the statement of reasons contained in the measure must give particulars which justify the desired retroactive effect.[94] In the context of criminal law, a Community measure cannot validate, *ex post facto*, a national measure which imposed criminal penalties and which, at the relevant time, was contrary to Community law.[95]

Withdrawal of Community measures A Community institution may withdraw an unlawful measure, even retroactively, provided that the withdrawal occurs within a reasonable time and provided that the institution gives proper consideration to the legitimate expectations of those affected by the measure.[96]

---

[90] Case 325/85 *Ireland v Commission* [1987] ECR 5041 para 18; Case 326/85 *Netherlands v Commission* [1987] ECR 5091 para 24; Case C–30/89 *Commission v France* [1990] ECR I–691 para 23.

[91] Case 169/80 *Administration des Douanes v SA Gondrand Frères* [1981] ECR 1931 para 17; Joined Cases 92/87, 93/87 *Commission v France and United Kingdom* [1989] ECR 405 para 22.

[92] Case 98/78 *Firma A Racke v Hauptzollamt Mainz* [1979] ECR 69 para 20; Case 99/78 *Wiengut Gustav Decker KG v Hauptzollamt Landau* [1979] ECR 101 para 8; Case 337/88 *Società agricola fattoria alimentare SpA v Amministrazione delle finanze dello Stato* [1990] ECR 1 paras 13–18.

[93] Joined Cases 212, 217/80 *Amministrazione delle Finanze dello Stato v Srl Meridionale Industria Salumi* [1981] ECR 2735 paras 9, 10.

[94] Case 1/84 R *Ilford SpA v Commission* [1984] ECR 423 para 19.

[95] Case 63/83 R *v Kent Kirk* [1984] ECR 2689 paras 20–23.

[96] Joined Cases 7/56, 3–7/56 *Dineke Algera v Common Assembly* [1957] ECR 39 at 55–56 (ECSC); Joined Cases 42/59, 49/59 *Société Nouvelle des Usines de Pontlieue—Aciéries du Temple (SNUPAT) v High Authority* [1961] ECR 53 at 86–88 (ECSC); Case 14/61 *Koninklijke Nederlandsche Hoogovens en Staalfabrieken NV v High Authority* [1962] ECR 253 (ECSC); Case 111/63 *Lemmerz-Werke GmbH v High Authority* [1965] ECR 677 at 690 (ECSC); Case 14/81 *Alpha Steel Ltd v Commission* [1982] ECR 749 paras 9–12 (ECSC); Case C–248/89 *Cargill BV v Commission* [1991] ECR I–2987 para 20.

However, the retroactive withdrawal of a measure which has conferred individual rights or similar benefits is not permitted[97] unless the measure was based on false or incomplete information provided by the party concerned.[98]

Procedural rules/judgments of EC Courts Changes in procedural rules are generally held to affect all proceedings pending at the time when they enter into force.[99] In addition, judgments of the EC Courts are retrospective, unless the Court itself limits the retroactive effect of its judgment under article 174 of the EEC Treaty[100] or under the doctrine of temporal effects.[101]

(e) Acquired rights

Definition The protection of vested or acquired rights is closely linked to the principles of legal certainty, legitimate expectation and non-retroactivity. In particular, it requires a case to be decided on the basis of the law as it was when the relevant acts or events took place.[102] Further, it may prevent the retroactive withdrawal of an unlawful measure.[103]

(f) Presumption of validity

Definition In the interests of legal certainty, parties are under an obligation to comply with a Community measure, even though it may contain irregularities or contravene general principles of Community law, until it has been annulled or suspended by the EC courts or withdrawn by the institution which adopted it.[104]

(g) Equality

Definition The principle of equality features in specific articles of the EEC Treaty, notably: article 7 (which prohibits discrimination on the grounds of nationality); article 40(3) (which prohibits discrimination between Community

---

[97] Case 159/82 *Angélique Verli-Wallace v Commission* [1983] ECR 2711 paras 8–11.

[98] Joined Cases 42/59, 49/59 *Société Nouvelle des Usines de Pontlieue (SNUPAT) v High Authority* [1961] ECR 53 (ECSC).

[99] Joined Cases 212, 217/80 *Amministrazione delle Finanze dello Stato v Srl Meridionale Industria Salumi* [1981] ECR 2735 para 9; Joined Cases C–121/91, C–122/91 *CT Control (Rotterdam) BV v Commission*, judgment of 6 July 1993 paras 22–28.

[100] Discussed further at pp 200–202.

[101] For example, see Case 43/75 *Defrenne v Sabena* [1976] ECR 455 at 480. Discussed further at pp 133–134.

[102] Case 12/71 *Günther Henck v Hauptzollamt Emmerich* [1971] ECR 743 para 5; Joined Cases 212–217/80 *Amministrazione delle Finanze dello Stato v Srl Meridionale Industria Salumi* [1981] ECR 2735 paras 9, 10; Joined Cases C–121/91, C–122/91 *CT Control (Rotterdam) BV v Commission*, judgment of 6 July 1993 para 22.

[103] Case 15/60 *Gabriel Simon v Court of Justice* [1961] ECR 115 para 3. See pp 16–17.

[104] Joined Cases 7/56, 3–7/57 *Dineke Algera v Common Assembly* [1957] ECR 39 at 60, 61 (ECSC); Case 101/78 *Granaria BV v Hoofdproduktschap voor Akkerbouwprodukten* [1979] ECR 623 paras 4, 5; Joined Cases 46/87, 227/88 *Hoechst AG v Commission* [1989] ECR 2859 paras 62–64. The presumption of validity does not apply to non-existent acts, see further at pp 197–198.

producers or consumers within the context of the Common Agricultural Policy); and article 119 (which provides that men and women should receive equal pay for equal work). However, the Court of Justice has emphasised that these provisions are simply examples of the general principle of equality, which is one of the fundamental principles of Community law.[105] The principle of equality requires that comparable situations must not be treated differently and different situations must not be treated in the same way, unless such treatment is objectively justified.[106] Thus, unequal treatment will not be discriminatory unless it appears to be arbitrary or, in other words, devoid of adequate justification and not based on objective criteria.[107] For example, in Case 230/78 *SpA Eridania-Zuccherifici Nazionali v Minister of Agriculture and Forestry,*[108] the Court of Justice held that differences of treatment of Italian producers in a regulation governing quotas for sugar were justified in the light of the different underlying economic conditions relating to sugar production in Italy when compared with other Member States.[109] The principle of equality prohibits both direct and indirect discrimination.[110]

(h) Procedural rights

Definition The Community institutions must abide by general principles governing the protection of procedural rights, for example the right to be heard[111] and the right of legal privilege.[112] These principles are particularly important in the context of proceedings by the Commission under the competition rules.[113]

(i) Fundamental rights

Definition Fundamental rights form an integral part of the general principles of Community law. Therefore, Community institutions must have regard to fundamental rights in applying and interpreting Community law.[114] In addition,

---

[105] Joined Cases 103/77, 145/77 *Royal Scholten-Honig (Holdings) Limited v Intervention Board for Agricultural Produce* [1978] ECR 2037 paras 25–27; Case 147/79 *René Hochstrass v Court of Justice* [1980] ECR 3005 para 7.

[106] Case 164/80 *Luigi De Pascale v Commission* [1982] ECR 909 para 20; Case 283/83 *Firma A Racke v Hauptzollamt Mainz* [1984] ECR 3791 para 7; Case 106/83 *Sermide SpA v Cassa Conguaglio Zucchero* [1984] ECR 4209 para 28; Case C–217/91 *Spain v Commission*, judgment of 7 July 1993 paras 36–39.

[107] Case 106/81 *Julius Kind KG v EEC* [1982] ECR 2885 para 22.

[108] [1979] ECR 2749 paras 17–19.

[109] See also Joined Cases 117/76, 16/77 *Albert Fuckdeschel & Co v Hauptzollamt Hamburg-St Annen* [1977] ECR 1753 paras 7–10; Case 8/82 *Kommanditgesellschaft in der Firma Hans-Otto Wagner GmbH Agrarhandel v Bundesanstalt für landwirtschaftliche Marktordnung* [1983] ECR 371 paras 18–21.

[110] Case 152/73 *Giovanni Sotgiu v Deutsche Bundespost* [1974] ECR 153 para 11.

[111] Discussed at pp 194–195.

[112] For example, see Case 155/79 *AM & S Europe Ltd v Commission* [1982] ECR 1575.

[113] See Bellamy and Child, *Common Market Law of Competition*, 4th edn (Sweet & Maxwell, 1993), Ch 12; Kerse, *EEC Antitrust Procedure*, 2nd edn (Sweet & Maxwell, 1987), 243–263.

[114] Case 265/87 *Hermann Schräder HS Kraftfutter GmbH & Co KG v Hauptzollamt Gronau* [1989]

Member States must, as far as possible, apply Community rules in accordance with the fundamental rights recognised by Community law.[115] However, the EC Courts do not have power to examine whether national legislation, which falls outside the scope of Community law, is compatible with fundamental rights.[116] The EC Courts have developed these fundamental rights by drawing on two sources, which are: first, the constitutional traditions common to the Member States and, secondly, international treaties for the protection of human rights on which the Member States have collaborated or of which they are signatories.[117] A party cannot invoke a right present in the constitution of a Member State unless that right is recognised generally by the constitutions of all the Member States, so that it can be said to be a fundamental right present in Community law.[118] The fundamental rights recognised by the EC Courts are not absolute. Limits may be placed on fundamental rights in order to facilitate the pursuit of the objectives of the EEC Treaty.[119] However, any restrictions on fundamental rights must not constitute, 'a disproportionate and intolerable interference, impairing the very substance of those rights'.[120]

European Convention on Human Rights The most important source of fundamental rights in the Community legal order is the European Convention on Human Rights.[121] The Community is not itself a signatory to the Convention; however, it has committed itself, politically, to respect fundamental rights.[122]

ECR 2237 paras 13, 14.

[115] Case 5/88 *Hubert Wachauf v Germany* [1989] ECR 2609 paras 17–19.

[116] Joined Cases 60/84, 61/84 *Cinéthèque SA v Fédération nationale des cinémas français* [1985] ECR 2065 paras 25, 26; Case 12/86 *Meryem Demirel v Stadt Schwäbisch Gmünd* [1987] ECR 3719 para 28.

[117] Case 4/73 *J Nold, Kohlen- und Baustoffgroßhandlung v Commission* [1974] ECR 491 paras 12–14 (ECSC); Case C–260/89 *Elliniki Radiophonia Tileorassi AE v Dimotiki Etairia Pliroforissis* [1991] ECR I–2925 paras 41–45. See also Case 29/69 *Erich Stauder v City of Ulm, Sozialamt* [1969] ECR 419 para 7; Case 11/70 *Internationale Handelsgesellschaft mbH v Einfuhr- und Vorratsstelle für Getreide und Futtermittel* [1970] ECR 1125 paras 3, 4.

[118] Case 11/70 *Internationale Handelsgesellschaft mbH v Einfuhr- und Vorratsstelle für Getreide und Futtermittel* [1970] ECR 1125; Case 4/73 *J Nold, Kohlen- und Baustoffgroßhandlung v Commission* [1974] ECR 491 para 14 (ECSC); Case 44/79 *Liselotte Hauer v Land Rheinland-Pfalz* [1979] ECR 3727; Case 63/83 *R v Kent Kirk* [1984] ECR 2689 para 22; Case 374/87 *Orkem v Commission* [1989] ECR 3283 paras 28–30.

[119] See pp 3–4.

[120] Case 265/87 *Hermann Schräder HS Kraftfutter GmbH & Co KG v Hauptzollamt Gronau* [1989] ECR 2237 paras 13–19; Case 5/88 *Hubert Wachauf v Germany* [1989] ECR 2609 paras 17, 18; Case C–62/90 *Commission v Germany* [1992] ECR I–2575 para 23. See also Case 4/73 *J Nold, Kohlen- und Baustoffgroßhandlung v Commission* [1974] ECR 491 para 14 (ECSC); Case 44/79 *Liselotte Hauer v Land Rheinland-Pfalz* [1979] ECR 3727 paras 31–33. Contrast Case C–219/91 *Criminal proceedings against Johannes Ter Voort* [1992] ECR I–5485 para 34, where the Court of Justice held that any measures which are incompatible with rights protected by the European Convention on Human Rights would not be permissible.

[121] Convention for the Protection of Human Rights and Fundamental Freedoms, signed on 4 November 1950.

[122] See the Joint Declaration of the European Parliament, Council and Commission, OJ No C 103/1, 5 April 1977; Preamble to the Single European Act (which refers to the European Convention on Human Rights and the European Social Charter); Declaration of fundamental rights and freedoms by the European Parliament of 12 April 1989; and Treaty on European Union (Maastricht Treaty), article F(2).

Although the European Convention on Human Rights is not directly a part of Community law, the Court of Justice has stated that 'the principles on which that Convention is based must be taken into consideration in Community law'.[123] The Court of Justice has referred expressly to a number of provisions of the European Convention on Human Rights in its case law.[124] For example, in Case 63/83 *R v Kent Kirk*,[125] the Court of Justice held that a regulation could not have retroactive effect as, on the facts of the case, this would have contravened the general principle that penal provisions may not have retroactive effect. This principle is a fundamental right common to the legal systems of all the Member States and enshrined in article 7 of the European Convention on Human Rights and, thus, forms part of the general principles of Community law. In addition, the Court of Justice has recognised the right to enjoy property and the right to pursue an occupation or business,[126] as well as the right to privacy and the protection of medical confidentiality,[127] as fundamental rights.

Other sources The Court of Justice has also referred to the European Social Charter of 18 November 1961 and Convention No 111 of the International Labour Organisation[128] as sources of fundamental rights.[129]

---

[123] Case 222/84 *Johnston v Chief Constable of the Royal Ulster Constabulary* [1986] ECR 1651 para 18; Case C–260/89 *Elliniki Radiophonia Tileorassi AE v Dimotiki Etairia Pliroforissis* [1991] ECR I–2925 para 41.

[124] For example, see Case 130/75 *Vivien Prais v Council* [1976] ECR 1589 paras 8,16 (ECHR, article 9); Case 136/79 *National Panasonic (UK) Ltd v Commission* [1980] ECR 2033 paras 17–20 (ECHR, article 8); Case 44/79 *Liselotte Hauer v Land Rheinland-Pfalz* [1979] ECR 3727 paras 17–19 (First Protocol); Case 222/84 *Johnston v Chief Constable of the Royal Ulster Constabulary* [1986] ECR 1651 para 18 (ECHR, articles 6 and 13); Case 85/87 *Dow Benelux NV v Commission* [1989] ECR 3137 paras 28–30 (ECHR, article 8); Case C–260/89 *Elliniki Radiophonia Tileorassi AE v Dimotiki Etairia Pliroforissis* [1991] ECR I–2925 paras 41–45 (ECHR, article 10); Case C–219/91 *Criminal proceedings against Johannes Ter Voort* [1992] ECR I–5485 paras 33–39 (ECHR, article10); Case C–97/91 *Oleificio Borelli Spa v Commission* judgment of 3 December 1992 para 14 (ECHR, articles 6 and 13).

[125] [1984] ECR 2689 paras 20–23.

[126] Case 265/87 *Hermann Schräder HS Kraftfutter GmbH & Co KG v Hauptzollamt Gronau* [1989] ECR 2237 paras 13–19.

[127] Case C–62/90 *Commission v Germany* [1992] ECR I–2575 para 23.

[128] Case 149/77 *Gabrielle Defrenne v Sabena* [1978] ECR 1365 paras 25–28.

[129] See also Case 374/87 *Orkem v Commission* [1989] ECR 3283 paras 18, 31where the Court of Justice referred to the International Covenant on Civil and Political Rights of 19 December 1966 'United Nations Treaty Series', vol 999, p 171.

Chapter 2

Supremacy of EC Law

1. DOCTRINE OF SUPREMACY

Definition The concept of supremacy[1] deals with the inter-relation of Community law and national law. Where there is a conflict between directly applicable or directly effective Community provisions and a national law, the jurisprudence of the Court of Justice establishes that it is the Community provision which must be applied.

Approach of the Court of Justice The Court of Justice views the EEC Treaty as being a unique source of law, in terms of both international law and national law. In Case 6/64 *Flaminio Costa v ENEL*[2] it stated:

> By contrast with ordinary international treaties, the EEC Treaty has created its own legal system which, on the entry into force of the Treaty, became an integral part of the legal systems of the Member States and which their courts are bound to apply.

Having recognised that the Member States have limited their sovereign rights by virtue of the EEC Treaty, the Court concluded:

> It follows from all these observations that the law stemming from the Treaty, an independent source of law, could not, because of its special and original nature, be overridden by domestic legal provisions, however framed, without being deprived of its character as Community law and without the legal basis of the Community itself being called into question.

The Court clearly viewed the principle of supremacy of Community law as being the necessary corollary of the Community's unique status as a supranational organisation, exercising sovereign powers ceded by the Member States.

Effect in national legal systems The effect of the principle of supremacy on the national legal systems of the Member States was examined in Case 106/77 *Amministrazione delle Finanze dello Stato v Simmenthal SpA*[3] which concerned a preliminary reference made by an Italian court (the *Pretore di Susa*).

---

[1] This is also referred to as the concept of 'primacy' from the French 'la primauté'.
[2] [1964] ECR 585 at 593–594.
[3] [1978] ECR 629.

Under Italian law, only the Italian Constitutional Court could declare that a national law was unconstitutional. The *Pretore*, having found that a subsequent national law conflicted with EC law, asked the European Court of Justice, *inter alia*, whether it was under a duty to disregard the conflicting national law without being obliged to refer the matter to the Constitutional Court. The Court of Justice held that every national court has a duty to apply Community law in its entirety, and to protect the rights conferred on individuals by Community law. National courts are, therefore, under an obligation to disregard any conflicting provision of national law, without waiting for the national law to be set aside by legislative or constitutional means. The judgment of the Court of Justice sets out the following important implications of the principle of supremacy.

(1) The entry into force of a Community measure which is directly applicable or directly effective renders any conflicting provision of national law automatically inapplicable.[4]

(2) The entry into force of a Community measure which is directly applicable or directly effective precludes the valid adoption of new national legislative measures to the extent to which they would be incompatible with the Community measure.[5]

(3) The entry into force of a Community measure which is directly applicable or directly effective imposes an obligation on national courts, of their own motion if necessary, to refuse to apply any national legislative measure, even a subsequent one, which is incompatible.[6]

(4) Any provision of a national legal system and any legislative, administrative or judicial practice which might impair the effectiveness of Community law by withholding, from the national court having jurisdiction to apply such law, the power to do everything necessary at the moment of its application to set aside national legislative provisions, which might prevent Community rules from having full force and effect, are incompatible with Community law.[7]

Criminal proceedings Community law has supremacy over national criminal legislation.[8] Thus, where a conviction is obtained on the basis of a national legislative measure, which is contrary to Community law, that conviction is also incompatible with Community law.[9]

---

[4] Ibid para 17.

[5] Ibid para 17. See also Case 43/71 *Politi SAS v Ministry for Finance of the Italian Republic* [1971] ECR 1039 para 9.

[6] Case 106/77 *Amministrazione delle Finanze dello Stato v Simmenthal SpA* [1978] ECR 629 para 21. See also Case 6/64 *Flaminio Costa v ENEL* [1964] ECR 585 at 593-594; Case 34/67 *Firma Gebrüder Lück v Hauptzollamt Köln-Rheinau* [1968] ECR 245 at 251; Case 84/71 *Marimex SpA v Ministry for Finance of the Italian Republic* [1972] ECR 89 para 5; Case C–184/89 *Helga Nimz v Freie und Hansestadt Hamburg* [1991] ECR I–297 paras 16–21, Joined Cases C–87–89/90 *A Verholen v Sociale Verzekeringsbank* [1991] ECR I–3757 paras 11–16.

[7] Case 106/77 *Amministrazione delle Finanze dello Stato v Simmenthal SpA* [1978] ECR 629 para 22. See also Case C–213/89 *R v Secretary of State for Transport, ex p Factortame Ltd* [1990] ECR I–2433.

[8] Case 82/71 *Pubblico Ministero Italiano v SAIL* [1972] ECR 119 para 5.

[9] Case 88/77 *Minister for Fisheries v CA Schonenberg* [1978] ECR 473 para 16; Case 269/80 *R v Robert Tymen* [1981] ECR 3079 paras 15–17.

Validity of Community law cannot be challenged by reference to national law A further aspect of the principle of supremacy is that the validity of a Community legislative measure cannot be challenged by reference to national legal or constitutional principles. This is established by the judgment of the Court of Justice in Case 11/70 *Internationale Handelsgesellschaft GmbH v Einfuhr-und Vorratsstelle für Getreide und Futtermittel*.[10] This case involved a preliminary reference from a German court which considered that a Community regulation was contrary to the German Basic Law. The Court of Justice held that the validity of the regulation must be decided in the light of Community law, not national law.

2. APPLICATION IN ENGLISH COURTS

Effect on English courts The practical effect of the case law of the Court of Justice, concerning the principle of supremacy, is that, if an English court is confronted with a conflict between a national law (whether case law or statute law) and a directly applicable or directly effective Community measure, the judge is obliged to apply the Community measure in preference to the national law. This is the case regardless of whether the English law was passed before or after the Community measure. Furthermore, the judge is not entitled to wait for the conflicting English provision to be set aside by legislative or administrative intervention.

European Communities Act 1972 Section 2(1) of the European Communities Act 1972 provides that:

All such rights, powers, liabilities, obligations and restrictions from time to time created or arising by or under the Treaties, and all such remedies and procedures from time to time provided for by or under the Treaties, as in accordance with the Treaties are without further enactment to be given legal effect or used in the United Kingdom shall be recognised and available in law, and be enforced, allowed and followed accordingly; and the expression 'enforceable Community right' and similar expressions shall be read as referring to one to which this subsection applies.

Section 2(4) of the European Communities Act 1972 provides:

... any such provision ... as might be made by Act of Parliament, and any enactment passed or to be passed ... shall be construed and have effect subject to the foregoing provisions of this section; ....

Approach of English courts The English courts have recognised and given effect to the principle of supremacy in the national legal system.[11] In *Stoke-on-Trent City Council v B&Q plc*,[12] Hoffmann J stated that 'The EEC Treaty is the

---

[10] [1970] ECR 1125 paras 3, 4. See also Joined Cases 97–99/87 *Dow Chemical Ibérica v Commission* [1989] ECR 3181 paras 37–39.

[11] See the judgments of Lord Denning MR in *Application des Gaz SA v Falks Veritas Ltd* [1974] 1 Ch 381 and *HP Bulmer Ltd v J Bollinger SA* [1974] 1 Ch 401, for an early recognition of the principle of supremacy in English law.

[12] [1991] Ch 48 at 56D.

supreme law of this country, taking precedence over Acts of Parliament'. However, rather than analysing the principle of supremacy as stemming from the unique character of the Community legal order, the English courts have tended, instead, to base their reasoning on s 2 of the European Communities Act 1972.[13]

An example of the approach of the English courts is illustrated by the decision in *Macarthys Ltd v Smith*,[14] which concerned the interpretation of the Equal Pay Act 1970 and its relationship with article 119 of the EEC Treaty, which establishes the principle that men and women should receive equal pay for equal work. Lord Denning MR held that:

> In construing our statute, we are entitled to look to the Treaty as an aid to its construction: and even more, not only as an aid but as an overriding force. If on close investigation it should appear that our legislation is deficient—or is inconsistent with Community law—by some oversight of our draftsmen—then it is our bounden duty to give priority to Community law. Such is the result of section 2(1) and (4) of the European Communities Act 1972.

The House of Lords considered the effect of the principle of supremacy in *R v Secretary of State for Transport ex p Factortame Ltd (No 2)*.[15] In that case, owners of Spanish fishing boats sought an interim injunction suspending the application of Part II of the Merchant Shipping Act 1988 pending final judgment in their application for judicial review, on the basis that the Act was contrary to EEC law. The House of Lords, when the case first came before it, held, *inter alia*, that the English courts could not grant such an injunction because of the rule in English law that an injunction cannot be granted against the Crown.[16] A preliminary reference on this issue was made to the Court of Justice, which held that, where an application was made for interim relief in a case concerning Community law, and a national court considered that the only obstacle which precluded such relief was a rule of national law, that court must set the rule aside.[17] When the House of Lords reconsidered the matter in light of the Court of Justice's ruling, it decided to grant the injunction sought. Lord Bridge made the following observations concerning the principle of supremacy:[18]

> Under the terms of the Act of 1972 it has always been clear that it was the duty of a United Kingdom court, when delivering final judgment, to override any rule of na-

---

[13] An exception is the decision of Oliver LJ in *Bourgoin SA v Ministry of Agriculture, Fisheries and Food* [1986] QB 716 at 774D–775A, where he relied directly on Case 106/77 *Amministrazione delle Finanze dello Stato v Simmenthal SpA* [1978] ECR 629 as providing authority for the supremacy of Community law. See pp 21–22.

[14] [1979] ICR 785 at 788C–789F. See also the further judgment as to costs reported at [1981] 1 QB 180 at 200E–G, where Lord Denning MR reiterated the effect of the principle of supremacy in English law. See also *Shields v E Coomes (Holdings) Ltd* [1978] 1 WLR 1408, per Lord Denning MR at 1414B–1416B; *Aero Zipp Fasteners v YKK Fasteners (UK) Ltd* [1974] RPC 624 at 625; *WH Smith Do-It-All Ltd v Peterborough City Council* [1990] 3 WLR 1131 at 1139E–F.

[15] [1991] 1 AC 603.

[16] *R v Secretary of State for Transport ex p Factortame Ltd* [1990] 2 AC 85.

[17] Case C–213/89 *R v Secretary of State for Transport ex p Factortame Ltd* [1990] ECR I–2433, [1991] 1 AC 603 at 640.

[18] [1991] 1 AC 603 at 659A–C.

tional law found to be in conflict with any directly enforceable rule of Community law. Similarly, when decisions of the European Court of Justice have exposed areas of United Kingdom statute law which failed to implement Council directives, Parliament has always loyally accepted the obligation to make appropriate and prompt amendments. Thus there is nothing in any way novel in according supremacy to rules of Community law in those areas to which they apply and to insist that, in the protection of rights under Community law, national courts must not be inhibited by rules of national law from granting interm relief in appropriate cases is no more than a logical recognition of that supremacy.

The decision of the House of Lords in *Factortame* is particularly important as it recognises the full extent of the principle of supremacy. The law that an injunction could not be obtained against the Crown was, in effect, a constitutional rule, based on the principle that the courts are merely an extension of the Sovereign's right to rule. In granting an interim injunction, the House of Lords recognised the supremacy of EEC law over national constitutional principles.

Potential limitation A practical difference between the general approach of the English courts to the principle of supremacy and the approach of the Court of Justice might arise if the United Kingdom Parliament deliberately chose to pass an Act with the intention of repudiating its Community obligations. In *Macarthys Ltd v Smith*[19] Lord Denning MR observed that in such a case the English courts would probably be under a duty to follow the United Kingdom statute rather than the EEC Treaty. However, unless there is an intentional and express repudiation of the EEC Treaty, the English courts are under a duty to give priority to the Treaty.

---

[19] [1979] ICR 785 at 789E–F, per Lord Denning MR. See also the judgment of Lawton LJ at 796 C–D and *Blackburn v Attorney General* [1971] 1 WLR 1037 at 1040–1041, per Lord Denning MR.

Chapter 3

Direct Effect

1. INTRODUCTION

Definition The principle of direct effect means that private parties are entitled to rely on rights derived from a Community measure in the national courts even if that measure has not been implemented by national legislation.[1]

English law Section 2(1) of the European Communities Act 1972 provides that:

> All such rights, powers, liabilities, obligations and restrictions from time to time created or arising by or under the Treaties, and all such remedies and procedures from time to time provided for by or under the Treaties, as in accordance with the Treaties are without further enactment to be given legal effect or used in the United Kingdom shall be recognised and available in law, and be enforced, allowed and followed accordingly; and the expression 'enforceable Community right' and similar expressions shall be read as referring to one to which this subsection applies.

Directly effective Community provisions fall within this section and, therefore, are recognised and enforced by English courts without the need for enactment in national legislation.[2]

Relationship between direct effect and direct applicability Article 189 of the EEC Treaty states that regulations are 'directly applicable'. This means that they automatically take effect in the national legal systems of all the Member States without the need for national implementing legislation. However, not all regulations are directly effective in the sense of creating rights for private parties, either against the State or as between themselves.[3]

---

[1] Case 26/62 *Van Gend en Loos v Nederlandse administratie der belastingen (Netherlands Inland Revenue Administration)* [1963] ECR 1. For early recognition of the principle of direct effect in English law, see *Shields v E Coomes (Holdings) Ltd* [1978] 1 WLR 1408 at 1414B–1416B, per Lord Denning MR.

[2] For example, see *Garden Cottage Foods Ltd v Milk Marketing Board* [1984] 1 AC 130 at 141C–D per Lord Diplock; *MH Marshall v Southampton and South-West Hampshire Area Health Authority* [1990] 3 CMLR 425, [1991] ICR 136, per Staughton LJ.

[3] The relationship between direct applicability and direct effect is discussed further at pp 30–31.

Relationship between direct effect and supremacy[4] The principle of supremacy obliges national courts to give precedence to directly effective Community provisions over conflicting national law, whether that law was passed prior or subsequently to the Community provision.[5] In addition, the Member States are under an obligation not to pass any new laws which conflict with directly effective Community provisions and to repeal pre-existing national laws which conflict.[6]

Creation of the principle of direct effect The principle of direct effect is not expressly established by any provisions in the EEC Treaty. It was created by the Court of Justice in Case 26/62 *Van Gend en Loos v Nederlandse administratie der belastingen (Netherlands Inland Revenue Administration).*[7] In that case, a Dutch company (Van Gend en Loos) imported goods into the Netherlands from West Germany. The Dutch revenue authorities levied an import duty of 8 per cent on the goods. Van Gend en Loos challenged their liability to pay this duty before the Dutch courts, relying on article 12 of the EEC Treaty, which requires Member States to refrain from introducing new customs duties on intra-Community trade or increasing existing duties. Van Gend en Loos argued that the Dutch Government was in breach of article 12 as it had raised the import duty on this classification of goods from 3 per cent to 8 per cent. The Dutch court made a preliminary reference to the Court of Justice and one of the questions which it asked was whether article 12 creates rights for individuals which the national courts are obliged to protect. The Court of Justice held that article 12, which is clear and unconditional in its terms, does have direct effect.[8] The Court justified this finding on the basis that:

> ... the Community constitutes a new legal order of international law for the benefit of which the states have limited their sovereign rights, albeit within limited fields, and the subjects of which comprise not only Member States but also their nationals. Independently of the legislation of Member States, Community law therefore not only imposes obligations on individuals but is also intended to confer upon them rights which become part of their legal heritage. These rights arise not only where they are expressly granted by the Treaty, but also by reason of obligations which the Treaty imposes in a clearly defined way upon individuals as well as upon the Member States and upon the institutions of the Community.

In addition, the Court of Justice rejected the argument that breaches of Community law by Member States could be adequately sanctioned by proceedings under articles 169 and 170 of the EEC Treaty. Proceedings under these articles can only be brought by the Commission or the Member States and, therefore, cannot provide individuals with a means of obtaining direct legal protection of their rights. The Court recognised that the binding effect of Community measures would be more likely to be enforced if individuals could rely directly on those rights in the national courts.

---

[4] See Ch 2 in relation to the principle of supremacy.
[5] Case 148/78 *Pubblico Ministero v Tullio Ratti* [1979] ECR 1629 para 23.
[6] For example, see Case 167/73 *Commission v French Republic* [1974] ECR 359 paras 34–48.
[7] [1963] ECR 1.
[8] Ibid at 11–13.

The importance of this judgment cannot be underestimated. Instead of being simply an international treaty which imposes obligations on the signatory states alone, the EEC Treaty has become a new and independent source of law which is integrated into the national legal systems of all the Member States, thus creating rights for individuals in the same way as national legislation. Furthermore, national courts have become, in essence, Community courts at a national level, as they are obliged to provide effective protection for directly effective Community law rights. In later judgments, the Court of Justice refined the test to be applied in deciding whether any given provision has direct effect or not and also extended the scope of the principle to include decisions and directives.[9]

2. TEST TO ESTABLISH DIRECT EFFECT

Test for direct effect The test to establish direct effect has been applied many times and has been put in many different ways. Put very simply, in order to have direct effect, the Community provision in question must be clear, precise and unconditional and must be capable of creating rights for individuals.[10] This test is not merely a mechanical formula to be applied to a given provision in order to produce the 'correct' answer. In many cases, the application of the test will involve a degree of subjectivity on the part of the court which is considering the issue.

Meaning of 'clear' In order to be 'clear', a Community provision should be precise enough to give rise to legal rights.[11] This was the approach adopted by Advocate-General Warner in Case 131/79 *R v Secretary of State for Home Affairs ex p Mario Santillo*.[12] He rejected the submission of the United Kingdom Government that 'clear' in this context meant 'unambiguous' on the basis that:

> Ambiguity in legislative provisions is one of the things that courts exist to resolve. It is not the same as lack of precision. We are only too familiar in this Court with ambiguities in regulations. No-one has ever suggested however, and quite rightly, that an ambiguity in a regulation meant that it could not have direct effect. The same is true of directives, as the Court held in the *Van Duyn* case.

Meaning of 'unconditional' A provision will be 'unconditional' where there is no need for further action by the Community institutions or Member States in order to define its content.[13] For example, in Case 203/80 *Criminal Proceedings against Guerruno Casati*[14] the Court of Justice held that article 67 of the EEC

---

[9] Case 57/65 *Alfons Lütticke GmbH v Hauptzollamt Saarlouis* [1966] ECR 205 is another important example of an early Court judgment finding that an EEC Treaty article has direct effect (article 95).

[10] For example, see Case 9/70 *Franz Grad v Finanzamt Traunstein* [1970] ECR 825 para 9; Case 8/81 *Becker v Finanzamt Münster-Innenstadt* [1982] ECR 53 para 25.

[11] Discussed further in the context of directives at pp 32–35.

[12] [1980] ECR 1585 at 1611.

[13] Discussed further in the context of directives at pp 32–35.

[14] [1981] ECR 2595, paras 8–13.

Treaty, which provides for the free movement of capital, does not have direct effect. The Court reached this conclusion on the basis that the obligation to liberalise capital movements in article 67 is not absolute, but is limited, to the extent that liberalisation 'is necessary to ensure the proper functioning of the Common Market.' This limitation recognised the fact that capital movements are closely connected with the economic and monetary policies of the Member States and, therefore, to avoid creating imbalances, liberalisation was subject to the assessment of the Council on what was necessary and appropriate, at any given time, in light of the degree of integration achieved between the Member States. The fact that the need for liberalisation was subject to the continuing assessment of the Council prevented article 67 having direct effect.

Capable of producing rights for individuals The provision in question must be 'capable' of creating individual rights in the national courts. For example, in Case 6/64 *Flaminio Costa v ENEL*,[15] the Court of Justice held that article 102 of the EEC Treaty imposes obligations on the Member States alone and is not capable of creating rights for individuals. Article 102 imposes an obligation on Member States to consult with the Commission where they fear that a proposed national measure might distort competition within the Common Market.

Vertical and horizontal direct effect There is an important distinction to be made between 'vertical' and 'horizontal' direct effect. A Community measure with vertical direct effect creates rights and obligations between individuals and the State. A Community measure with horizontal direct effect can be relied on by a private party against other private parties. The distinction is particularly important in relation to directives, as the Court of Justice has held that these are capable of having only vertical direct effect.[16]

3. DIRECT EFFECT OF TREATY ARTICLES

Treaty articles Many Treaty articles have been recognised as having direct effect. In 1983, the Commission produced a list of the Treaty provisions which the Court of Justice has established as having direct effect, as well as those provisions which have been held not to have direct effect.[17]

Vertical and horizontal direct effect Directly effective treaty articles may have both vertical and horizontal direct effect. An example of horizontal direct effect is provided by the competition rules of the EEC Treaty, articles 85 and 86, which can be invoked by economic undertakings against each other in the national courts.[18]

---

[15] [1964] ECR 585 at 595. See also Case 380/87 *Encihem Base v Comune di Cinisello Basamo* [1989] ECR 2491 paras 3, 6–9. Discussed further in the context of directives at p 34.

[16] Discussed at pp 35–7.

[17] OJ No C 177, 4 July 1983, p 13. Reproduced in Appendix A, pp 295–296.

[18] For example, see *Garden Cottage Foods v Milk Marketing Board* [1984] AC 130.

In Case 36/74 *BNO Walrave and LJN Koch v Association Union Cycliste Internationale*[19] the Court of Justice held that article 7 (general prohibition of discrimination), article 48 (free movement of workers) and article 59 (freedom to provide services), all have horizontal direct effect and can be invoked in the national courts by private parties against other private parties, in this case, an international sporting federation. In Case 43/75 *Gabrielle Defrenne v Sabena*,[20] the Court of Justice held, similarly, that article 119, which establishes the principle of equal pay for men and women, has horizontal direct effect.

4. DIRECT EFFECT OF REGULATIONS

Regulations Article 189 of the EEC Treaty expressly provides that regulations are 'directly applicable' in all Member States.[21] The Court of Justice has often used the terms 'directly applicable' and 'directly effective' interchangeably, but has never expressly considered whether there is, in fact, a difference between the two concepts.[22] Logically, it must be the case that while all regulations are directly applicable, in the sense that they automatically become integrated into the national legal systems of the Member States without requiring national implementing legislation, they do not necessarily create rights which individuals can rely on in the national courts.[23] Support for this is found in Case 87/82 *Rogers v Darthenay*,[24] where a regulation provided that, 'No device shall be used by means of which the mesh in any part of a fishing net is obstructed or otherwise effectively diminished. This provision does not exclude the use of the devices referred to in the detailed implementing rules to be adopted in accordance with the procedure laid down in Article 20'. The Court of Justice did not assume that because a regulation is directly applicable it must necessarily have direct effect. Rather the Court applied the normal test for direct effect in holding that this was an 'independent and perfectly clear provision' which could, therefore, be relied on in the national proceedings. Indeed, if a regulation is not clear, precise and unconditional and is not capable of creating individual rights, it is not clear how a national court could protect such a 'right'.[25] For example, further national or

---

[19] [1974] ECR 1405.

[20] [1976] ECR 455 para 39.

[21] See p 5.

[22] In Case 34/73 *Variola SpA v Amministrazione Italiana delle Finanze* [1973] ECR 981 and Case 83/78 *Pigs Marketing Board v Redmond* [1978] ECR 2347 paras 66, 67, the Court of Justice seemed to suggest that a directly applicable regulation would automatically be directly effective.

[23] See Case 31/74 *Filippo Galli* [1975] ECR 47, Opinion of Advocate-General Warner at 70; Case 74/76 *Ianelli & Volpi SpA v Ditta Paolo Meroni* [1977] ECR 557, Opinion of Advocate-General Warner at 583; and Case 131/79 *R v Secretary of State for Home Affairs, ex p Mario Santillo* [1980] ECR 1585, Opinion of Advocate-General Warner at 1608–1609. See also the legal submissions referred to in the judgment of Lloyd LJ in *An Bord Bainne Co-operative Ltd v Milk Marketing Board* [1988] 1 CMLR 605 paras 12–17.

[24] [1983] ECR 1579 para 11.

[25] See Case 43/71 *Politi SAS v Italy* [1971] ECR 1039 paras 8, 9; Case 84/71 *Marimex SpA v Italy* [1972] ECR 89 paras 4, 5; Case 93/71 *Leonisio v Italy* [1972] ECR 287; Case 65/75 *Riccardo Tasca* [1976] ECR 291 paras 15, 16; and Case 148/78 *Pubblico Ministero v Tullio Ratti* [1979] ECR 1629 para 19. All of these cases appear to suggest that a regulation can have direct effect

Community legislation may be necessary to define individual rights under a regulation. Alternatively, the content of a regulation may not be suitable for creating individual rights. It may impose obligations on the Member States, as between themselves, which are irrelevant when considered in terms of individual rights (for example, obligations concerning economic or monetary policy).

5. DIRECT EFFECT OF DECISIONS

Decisions Decisions are capable of having direct effect. This was established in Case 9/70 *Franz Grad v Finanzamt Traunstein*,[26] where the Court of Justice was concerned with the combined effect of provisions contained in a decision and a directive. The Court emphasised that under article 189 of the EEC Treaty a decision is binding in its entirety upon those to whom it is addressed. Thus, where the Community authorities have imposed an obligation on a Member State to act in a certain way by means of a decision, the effectiveness (*l' effet utile*) of such a measure would be weakened if private parties could not invoke it in the national courts and the national courts could not take it into consideration as part of Community law. The fact that a decision permits a Member State to exercise certain derogations from clear and precise provisions does not prevent those provisions from having direct effect.[27] Where a decision sets down a time limit for compliance with its provisions, it cannot have direct effect until that time limit has expired.[28]

6. DIRECT EFFECT OF DIRECTIVES

(a) Recognition of direct effect of directives

Directives Case 41/74 *Yvonne van Duyn v Home Office*[29] concerned a woman of Dutch nationality who was refused leave to enter the United Kingdom to take up employment as a secretary with the Church of Scientology. Leave to enter was refused as the Government considered that the activities of the Church were socially harmful. On a preliminary reference from the High Court, the Court of Justice held that article 3(1) of Council Directive 64/221,[30] which provides that

---

only if it is 'capable of creating individual rights'.

[26] [1970] ECR 825 paras 3–5.

[27] Case C–156/91 *Hansa Fleisch Ernst Mundt GmbH & Co KG v Landrat des Kreises Schleswig-Flensburg* judgment of 10 November 1992 paras 11–17.

[28] Ibid paras 18–20.

[29] [1974] ECR 1337 paras 9–15. See also Case 33/70 *SpA SACE v Ministry for Finance of the Italian Republic* [1970] ECR 1213 para 15, where it was held that a directive addressed to the Italian Government, which was intended to implement directly effective treaty articles, had direct effect itself.

[30] Council Directive 64/221 of 25 February 1964 on the co-ordination of special measures concerning the movement and residence of foreign nationals, which are justified on grounds of public policy, public security or public health, OJ Special Edition, 1963–1964 at 117.

measures taken to restrict entry to a Member State on grounds of public policy or public security should be based exclusively on the personal conduct of the individual concerned, has direct effect. The Court of Justice held that it would be incompatible with the binding effect attributed to directives by article 189 of the EEC Treaty to exclude, in principle, the possibility that they could be relied on by private parties before the national courts. The Court repeated that, where the Community authorities have imposed on Member States, by means of a directive, the obligation to pursue a particular course of conduct, the effectiveness (*l'effet utile*) of such an act would be weakened if individuals were prevented from relying on it before their national courts and if the courts themselves were prevented from taking it into consideration as an element of Community law. By allowing private parties to rely on directives in the national courts, the proper application of binding Community law would be more likely to be achieved throughout the Community.[31]

(b) Test for direct effect of directives

Test In order for a directive to have direct effect, a three-fold test must be satisfied:

(1) the relevant obligation(s) must be clear, precise and unconditional;[32]

(2) the nature of the directive must be capable of creating rights for individuals;[33] and

(3) the implementation date for the directive must have expired.[34]

Clear, precise and unconditional The status of directives is somewhat special because, theoretically, a Member State always has a degree of discretion as to the choice of form and methods by which to implement a directive into national law. However, this discretion as to form and method of implementation does not prevent a directive from having direct effect, so long as the *result* required to be achieved is sufficiently clear and precise.

Discretion as to implementation Where the result to be achieved by national implementing legislation is clear, the fact that a Member State has a discretion as to how to achieve that result does not prevent a directive having direct effect.[35] For example, in Case 71/85 *Netherlands v Federatie Nederlandse Vakbeweging*,[36] the Court of Justice considered article 4(1) of Council Directive

---

[31] See also Case 190/87 *Oberkreisdirektor des Kreises Borken v Handelsonderneming Moormann BV* [1988] ECR 4689 paras 21–24 where the Court of Justice stated that the direct effect of directives is based on the combined effect of articles 189 and 5 of the EEC Treaty.

[32] Case 8/81 *Becker v Finanzamt Münster-Innenstadt* [1982] ECR 53 paras 17–25; Joined Cases C–6/90, C–9/90 *Francovich and Bonifaci v Italy* [1991] ECR I–5357 para 11.

[33] Case 8/81 *Becker v Finanzamt Münster-Innenstadt* [1982] ECR 53 para 25; Case 380/87 *Enichem Base v Comune di Cinisello Balsamo* [1989] ECR 2491 paras 3, 6–8.

[34] Case 148/78 *Pubblico Ministero v Tullio Ratti* [1979] ECR 1629 paras 24, 39–46.

[35] Case 8/81 *Becker v Finanzamt Münster-Innenstadt* [1982] ECR 53 paras 28–30; Case 286/85 *McDermott and Cotter v Minister for Social Welfare and Attorney-General* [1987] ECR 1453 para 15; Case C–271/91 *MH Marshall v Southampton and South-West Hampshire Area Health Authority* judgment of 2 August 1993 paras 33–38.

[36] [1986] ECR 3855 paras 12–23.

79/7[37] which precludes all discrimination on grounds of sex with regard to social security. Article 5 of the Directive obliges Member States to take, 'the measures necessary to ensure that any laws, regulations and administrative provisions contrary to the principle of equal treatment are abolished'. The Court held that the result to be achieved by virtue of article 4(1) was sufficiently precise to have direct effect and the fact that the Member States had a discretion as to the measures to be adopted under article 5 did not prevent article 4(1) from having direct effect.

In contrast, in Joined Cases C–6/90 and C–9/90 *Francovich and Bonifaci v Italy*[38] the Court of Justice held that Council Directive 80/987 on the protection of employees in the event of their employers' insolvency[39] did not have direct effect. The Directive required the Member States to set up a guarantee system to meet employees' outstanding claims against insolvent employers. The Court found that the provisions of the Directive defining those entitled to the guarantee and the content of the guarantee were clear, precise and unconditional. However, the Directive could not have direct effect as it gave the Member States a wide discretion as to the organisation, operation and financing of the institutions who were to be responsible for providing the guarantee.

Choice as to result to be achieved Where a directive provides a choice as to the result to be achieved, an individual may enforce the directive against the Member State on the basis of the option which places the least onerous burden on the State. For example, in Joined Cases C–6/90 and C–9/90 *Francovich and Bonifaci v Italy*[40], Council Directive 80/987 permitted Member States to choose between three methods of calculation as to the period to which the guarantee of payment was to relate. Thus, Member States could provide that employees should be entitled to back-pay: (1) up to the date of the onset of their employer's insolvency; (2) up to the date that a notice of dismissal was issued on account of the insolvency; or (3) up to the date of the onset of insolvency alternatively of the discontinuance of the employment relationship. This particular provision was clear and unconditional as it was possible to determine the minimum guarantee provided for by the Directive by taking the date which entailed the least liability for the guarantee institution — namely, the onset of the employer's insolvency. This choice was the least onerous as it would provide for the shortest duration of the guarantee period.

Result is clear, but Member State is permitted certain derogations Where a directive requires a clear result to be achieved, it is not prevented from having direct effect by virtue of the fact that the Member State could have exercised

---

[37] Council Directive 79/7 of 19 December 1978 on the progressive implementation of the principle of equal treatment for men and women in matters of social security, OJ No L 6, 10 January 1979, p 24.

[38] [1991] ECR I–5357 paras 10–27.

[39] Council Directive 80/987 of 20 October 1980 on the approximation of the laws of the Member States relating to the protection of employees in the event of the insolvency of their employer, OJ No L 283, 28 October 1980, p 23.

[40] [1991] ECR I–5357 paras 15–20.

certain derogations if it had implemented the directive.[41] For example, by way of analogy, in Case 41/74 *Yvonne van Duyn v Home Office*,[42] one of the questions referred to the Court of Justice was whether article 48 of the EEC Treaty had direct effect. Article 48(1) imposes an obligation on Member States to ensure the free movement of workers within the Community. However, this obligation is not absolute as article 48(3) permits Member States to impose restrictions on that freedom on the grounds of public policy, public security or public health. The Court of Justice held that article 48 imposes a precise obligation on the Member States to ensure the free movement of workers which does not require the adoption of any further measure on the part either of the Community institutions or of the Member States and which leaves them, in relation to its implementation, no discretionary power. Although article 48(3) permits a Member State to impose limitations on that freedom, this did not prevent the basic right established in article 48(1) from having direct effect.

Severance of directly effective obligations Particular obligations which are capable of having direct effect, but which are contained in a directive which, as a whole, is not capable of having direct effect, may be 'severed' from the general provisions. Thus, in Case 8/81 *Becker v Finanzamt Münster-Innenstadt*,[43] the Court of Justice held that, whilst certain provisions of the Sixth VAT Directive could not have direct effect, other provisions which were capable of having direct effect standing on their own and which could be severed from the general body of provisions and applied separately, could be relied on by private parties in the national courts. It follows from this approach that the relevant question is not necessarily whether a directive as a whole has direct effect, although this may indeed be the case, but whether particular provisions sought to be relied on within the directive can stand on their own and have direct effect.

Capable of creating rights for individuals A directive cannot have direct effect if, by its nature, it does not give rise to rights for individuals. For example, in Case 380/87 *Enichem Base v Comune di Cinisello Balsamo*[44] manufacturers of plastic bags sought to rely on Council Directive 75/442[45] in the national courts in order to challenge the validity of an Italian ban on the sale of plastic bags. However, the Court of Justice held that the directive did not create rights for individuals as its purpose was to harmonise Member States' legislation in order to avoid barriers to intra-Community trade and to further environmental objectives at a Community level.

Direct effect cannot arise until the implementation date has expired As directives must be implemented by Member States into their national law, a directive usually will set out a final date by which the directive must be imple-

---

[41] Case 71/85 *Netherlands v Federatie Nederlandse Vakbeweging* [1986] ECR 3855 paras 12–23, in particular para 19; Joined Cases C–19/90 and C–20/90 *Marina Karella v Minister of Industry, Energy and Technology* [1991] ECR I-2691 paras 17–23.
[42] [1974] ECR 1337 paras 4–8.
[43] [1982] ECR 53 paras 29–30.
[44] [1989] ECR 2491 paras 6–11.
[45] Council Directive 75/442 on waste, OJ No L 194, 25 July 1975, p 39.

mented, 'the implementation date'. After the implementation date has passed, if the Member State has not adopted the necessary implementing legislation, a private party can rely on the direct effect of the directive in an action against the Member State and the directive will prevail over national law inconsistent with the directive. However, a directive cannot have direct effect until the implementation period specified has expired.[46] Until that date a Member State is free to rely on existing national law, even if it conflicts with the provisions required to be implemented by the directive.[47]

Position once a directive has been implemented Once a directive has been properly implemented by national legislation, a private party must rely on the national legislation rather than on the direct effect of the directive.[48] However, a private party may continue to rely on the direct effect of a directive where the legislation introduced by a Member State does not properly implement the directive.[49]

National limitation periods In Case C–208/90 *Theresa Emmott v Minister for Social Welfare*,[50] the Court of Justice held that, in proceedings based on a directly effective directive, the limitation period in respect of actions against the State provided for by national law cannot begin to run until the directive has been properly implemented.[51]

(c) Vertical direct effect only

No horizontal direct effect In Case 152/84 *MH Marshall v Southampton and South-West Hampshire Area Health Authority*,[52] the Court of Justice held that directives can only have vertical direct effect. This means that, in proceedings in the national courts, a private party can rely on a directly effective directive against a Member State which has failed to implement that directive, but cannot

---

[46] Case 148/78 *Pubblico Ministero v Tullio Ratti* [1979] ECR 1629 paras 24, 39–46. See also the Opinion of Advocate-General Jacobs in Case C–156/91 *Hansa Fleisch Ernst Mundt v Landrat des Kreises Schleswig-Flensburg* judgment of 10 November 1992 paras 17–22 of the Opinion, where he rejected an argument that a directive could have direct effect against a Member State even before the deadline for implementation has passed where the State has attempted to implement the directive before the end of the prescribed period, but has done so incorrectly.

[47] Case 244/78 *Union Laitière Normande v French Dairy Farmers Limited* [1979] ECR 2663 paras 13–15.

[48] Case 102/79 *Commission v Belgium* [1980] ECR 1473; Case 270/81 *Felicitas Rickmers-Linie KG & Co v Finanzamt für Verkehrsteuern, Hamburg* [1982] ECR 2771 para 24; Case 222/84 *Johnston v Chief Constable of the Royal Ulster Constabulary* [1986] ECR 1651 para 51.

[49] Case 51/76 *Verbond van Nederlandse Ondernemingen v Inspecteur der Invoerrechten en Accijnzen* [1977] ECR 113 paras 23, 24; Case 38/77 *Enka BV v Inspecteur der Invoerrechten en Accijnzen* [1977] ECR 2203; Case 102/79 *Commission v Belgium* [1980] ECR 1473 para 12; Case C–208/90 *Theresa Emmott v Minister for Social Welfare* [1991] ECR I–4269 para 20.

[50] [1991] ECR I–4269 paras 21–23.

[51] This principle was applied by the Employment Appeal Tribunal in *Cannon v Barnsley Metropolitan Borough Council* [1992] ICR 698 at 705C–D, [1992] 2 CMLR 795 para 11.

[52] [1986] ECR 723 paras 48, 49; Case C–221/88 *ECSC v Acciaierie e Ferriere Busseni (in liquidation)* [1990] ECR I–495 paras 22, 23 (ECSC).

rely on the directive against another private party. One result of the Court of Justice's case law in this area is that while employees of State bodies can rely on directly effective rights in the national courts against their employers, private employees cannot do so. The United Kingdom Government has argued that this constitutes an arbitrary and unfair distinction.[53]

Estoppel The Court of Justice has consistently stated that the basis for the vertical direct effect of directives is that a Member State, which has not adopted the implementing measures required by a directive within the prescribed period, may not plead, as against individuals, its own failure to perform the obligations which the directive entails.[54] Therefore, the justification for vertical direct effect can be seen as a form of 'estoppel' operating against a Member State, which precludes the principle of horizontal direct effect.[55]

Sword or shield The use of the term 'estoppel' is inappropriate to a certain extent as, in contrast to the common law notion of estoppel, a private party can rely on directly effective rights as a 'sword or a shield' in an action involving a Member State. In other words, a private party can rely on directly effective rights to found an action against a Member State and can also rely on such rights as a defence to an action brought by a Member State.[56]

Member States cannot rely on directly effective directives against individuals This is the logical result of the analysis of the direct effect of directives set out in *Marshall*, where the Court of Justice held that:[57]

> a directive may not of itself impose obligations on an individual and ... a provision of a directive may not be relied upon as such against such a person.

On the basis of this passage, the Court of Justice concluded in Case 14/86 *Pretore di Salò v Persons Unknown*,[58] that a directive which has not been imple-

---

[53] Case 152/84 *MH Marshall v Southampton and South-West Hampshire Area Health Authority* [1986] ECR 723 para 51. Certain Advocates-General have argued in favour of horizontal direct effect for directives. See Case C–271/91 *(Marshall (No 2))* para 12 of the Opinion of Advocate-General Van Gerven [1993] 3 CMLR 293 and Case C–316/93 *Nicole Vaneetveld v SA Le Foyer*, Opinion of Advocate-General Jacobs, delivered 27 January 1994, paras 16–36.

[54] For example, see Case 148/78 *Pubblico Ministero v Tullio Ratti* [1979] ECR 1629 para 22; Case 8/81 *Becker v Finanzamt Münster-Innenstadt* [1982] ECR 53 para 24; Case 152/84 *MH Marshall v Southampton and South-West Hampshire Area Health Authority* [1986] ECR 723 para 47.

[55] See, generally, *Wyatt* [1983] 8 ELR 155; *Easson* [1981] YBEL 1; *Green* [1984] 9 ELR 295. In Case 80/86 *Kolpinghuis Nijmegen BV* [1987] ECR 3969, Advocate-General Mischo explicitly referred, in para 7 of his Opinion, to the concept of estoppel in this context. Compare Case C–188/89 *A Foster v British Gas plc* [1990] ECR I–3313, where Advocate-General van Gerven identified the basis of the judgment in Case 152/84 *Marshall* [1986] ECR 723 as deriving from the principle *nemo auditur propriam turpitudinem allegans* or 'the State cannot plead its own wrong' (para 5 of the Advocate-General's Opinion).

[56] See the Opinion of Advocate-General Sir Gordon Slynn in Case 152/84 *Marshall* [1986] ECR 723 at 734. *Marshall* itself is an example of an individual relying on the principle of direct effect as a 'sword'. See also Case 188/89 *A Foster v British Gas plc* [1990] ECR I–3313. Case 148/78 *Pubblico Ministero v Tullio Ratti* [1979] ECR 1629 is an example of direct effect being used as a 'shield'.

[57] Case 152/84 *Marshall* [1986] ECR 723 para 48.

[58] [1987] ECR 2545 paras 19, 20. See also Joined Cases 372-374/85 *Ministère Public v Oscar Traen* [1987] ECR 2141 paras 23–26; Case 80/86 *Kolpinghuis Nijmegen BV* [1987] ECR 3969 paras 6–10.

mented by national legislation cannot impose obligations on individuals, either in regard to other individuals or, *a fortiori*, in relation to the State itself.[59] Thus, for example, a Member State cannot rely on a directly effective directive which has not been implemented in order to establish or aggravate the criminal liability of private parties who are alleged to have breached the directive.[60]

(d) Definition of 'the State'

Test If directly effective directives can only be invoked against 'the State', then, clearly, the definition of what constitutes the State is very important. The Court of Justice's approach is very broad. In Case 188/89 *A Foster v British Gas plc*,[61] the Court of Justice established the general principle that an individual can rely on a directly effective directive in proceedings in the national courts against an organisation or body, whatever its legal form, which is:

(1) subject to the authority or control of the State; or

(2) which has special powers beyond those which result from the normal rules applicable to relations between individuals.[62]

The Court of Justice appeared to set down the test in disjunctive terms: a body will be equivalent to the State if, *either* it is subject to the authority or control of the State *or* it has special powers. It is for the national courts to decide whether a particular body falls within this definition of a State body.[63]

Capacity in which body acts is irrelevant The Court of Justice has consistently held that where a body falls within the above definition of a State body, then, in an action before the national courts, an individual can rely on a directly effective directive against that body or organisation, regardless of the capacity in which the latter is acting, whether acting in the realm of public law, as a public authority, or in the realm of private law, for example, as an employer.[64] Thus, the Court has indicated that an individual may rely on a directly effective directive against: national tax authorities;[65] public authorities providing public health services;[66] constitutionally independent authorities responsible for the maintenance of public order and safety;[67] and local or regional authorities.[68]

---

[59] See *Organon Laboratories Ltd v Department of Health and Social Security* [1990] 2 CMLR 49 paras 51–52, per Mustill LJ, for a recognition of this principle by the English courts.

[60] Case 14/86 *Pretore di Salò v Persons Unknown* [1987] ECR 2545 paras 19, 20.

[61] [1990] ECR I–3313 paras 16–22.

[62] Ibid para 18.

[63] Case 152/84 *MH Marshall v Southampton and South-West Hampshire Area Health Authority* [1986] ECR 723 paras 49–50; Case 188/89 *A Foster v British Gas plc* [1990] ECR I–3313 paras 13–15.

[64] Case 152/84 *MH Marshall v Southampton and South-West Hampshire Area Health Authority* (above) para 49; Case 222/84 *Johnston v Chief Constable of the Royal Ulster Constabulary* [1986] ECR 1651 para 56; Case 188/89 *A Foster v British Gas plc* [1990] (above) para 17.

[65] Case 8/81 *Becker v Finanzamt Münster-Innenstadt* [1982] ECR 53.

[66] Case 152/84 *MH Marshall v Southampton and South-West Hampshire Area Health Authority* [1986] ECR 723 para 50.

[67] Case 222/84 *Johnston v Chief Constable of the Royal Ulster Constabulary* [1986] ECR 1651 para 56.

[68] Case 103/88 *Fratelli Costanzo v Comune di Milano* [1989] ECR 1839 para 31.

Approach of the English courts When the House of Lords considered the *Foster* case in light of the Court of Justice's ruling,[69] Lord Templeman held that the test to be applied was whether the British Gas Corporation (BGC), 'pursuant to a measure adopted by the state, provided a public service under the control of the state *and* exercised special powers' (emphasis added).[70] He went on to examine the statutory provisions (particularly the Gas Act 1972) which established the BGC as a body corporate and found that the 1972 Act created a body (the BGC) which provided a public service (the supply of gas) to citizens of the State generally. This was done under the control of the State, which could dictate the BGC's policies and retain its surplus revenue. Furthermore, the BGC was equipped with a special monopoly power which was created, and could only have been created, by the legislature. Lord Templeman concluded, therefore, that the BGC was a body against which the relevant provisions of the Directive could be enforced.[71]

The speech of Lord Templeman could be understood as setting down a conjunctive test for what constitutes a State body. The body must be subject to the authority or control of the State *and* it must exercise special powers. In contrast, the test set down by the Court of Justice is disjunctive as it held that a State body is one which is subject to State control or authority *or* which has special powers. The different formulation by Lord Templeman did not affect the result in *Foster* as, even applying a conjunctive test, the BGC was held to be a State body.

Applying the test in a conjunctive, rather than disjunctive, manner may affect the result of a case. In *Rolls-Royce plc v Doughty*,[72] an ex-employee of Rolls-Royce wished to rely on a directly effective provision of a directive in an action against the company in the national courts. Rolls-Royce was a public limited company in which all the shares were held by nominees on behalf of the Crown. Furthermore, Rolls-Royce had a particularly close trading relationship with the State in respect of its military production. Mustill LJ gave the judgment of the Court of Appeal and held that Rolls-Royce did not fall within the test enunciated in *Foster*, as it did not have 'special powers' of the type enjoyed by the British Gas Corporation, nor did it provide public 'services' by virtue of its importance to the defence of the realm. In fact, it was 'a commercial undertaking which as part of its business traded with the state on terms which were negotiated at arm's length'. It is debatable whether the Court of Appeal properly applied the test laid down by the Court of Justice in *Foster* as, rather than applying the disjunctive general test, the Court of Appeal rejected the ex-employee's argument that it was sufficient to show that the entity in question fell under the control of the State in order to come within the test established in *Foster*.[73] The Court of Appeal also indicated that the test in *Foster* (as interpreted by the Court of Appeal itself) is not conclusive. However, it held that if a body satisfies all the factors of the *Foster* test, it is only in exceptional circum

---

[69] *A Foster v British Gas plc* [1991] 2 AC 306.
[70] Ibid p 314G–314H.
[71] Ibid p 315H–316A.
[72] [1992] ICR 538.
[73] Ibid at 550F–G and 551F–G.

stances that the body will not be identified with the State. Conversely, the absence of a factor will not necessarily preclude a body from being identified with the State.[74] As indicated above, the general test set down by the Court of Justice in *Foster* implies that it is sufficient for an entity to be subject to the authority or control of the State for it to be subject to directly effective rights under a directive.[75]

7. RECOMMENDATIONS AND OPINIONS

No direct effect Recommendations and opinions do not have direct effect. This follows from the wording of article 189 of the EEC Treaty which states that:

> Recommendations and opinions shall have no binding force.

Therefore, they cannot impose obligations on, or create rights for the benefit of, individuals.

Legal effects This does not mean that recommendations can never produce any legal effects in the national legal systems of Member States. National courts are under an obligation to take recommendations into account in interpreting national legislation.[76]

8. DIRECT EFFECT OF INTERNATIONAL AGREEMENTS

International agreements A provision of an international agreement made by the Community with third countries will have direct effect when, having regard to the wording, purpose and nature of the agreement itself, the provision is sufficiently clear, precise and unconditional.[77] For example, in Case 104/81 *Hauptzollamt Mainz v Kupferberg*,[78] the Court of Justice held that a provision of the free-trade agreement between the Community and Portugal (which was not at that time a member of the Community) had direct effect within the Community. The Court emphasised that, according to article 228(2) of the EEC Treaty,

---

[74] Ibid at 552B–C.

[75] See also *R v London Boroughs Transport Committee, ex p Freight Transport Association Ltd* [1990] 3 CMLR 495 where Neill LJ (at paras 30, 31) relied directly on the test enunciated by the Court of Justice in *Foster* in holding that the London Boroughs Transport Committee was an emanation of the State. See also per Sir Roger Ormrod at para 57. This issue was not discussed by the House of Lords on appeal.

[76] Case 322/88 *Grimaldi v Fonds des Maladies* [1989] ECR 4421. Discussed further at p 50.

[77] Case 12/86 *Demirel v Stadt Schwäbisch Gmünd* [1987] ECR 3719 para 14 (Association Agreement between the EEC and Turkey); Case C–18/90 *Office national de l'emploi v Bahia Kziber* [1991] ECR I–199 para 15 (Co-operation Agreement between the EEC and Morocco). See also Case 87/75 *Bresciani v Amministrazione Italiana delle Finanze* [1976] ECR 129 paras 16–26 (Yaoundé Convention); Case 17/81 *Pabst & Richarz KG v Hauptzollamt Oldenburg* [1982] ECR 1331 paras 25–27 (Association Agreement between the EEC and Greece). In *R v Secretary of State for the Home Department, ex p Narin* [1990] 1 CMLR 682 the Queen's Bench Division considered whether the EEC-Turkey Association Agreement had direct effect.

[78] [1982] ECR 3641 paras 9–27.

agreements concluded by the Community with non-member states or international organisations under powers conferred by the EEC Treaty are binding on the Community institutions and the Member States. By recognising the direct effect of such agreements, the Court could ensure that the ensuing obligations were uniformly applied by all the Member States. Similarly, in Case C–192/89 *SZ Sevince v Staatssecretaris van Justitie*,[79] the Court of Justice held that decisions adopted by the Council of Association, established under the Association Agreement between the EEC and Turkey, had direct effect.

GATT In Joined Cases 21–24/72 *International Fruit Company NV v Produktschap voor Groenten en Fruit*[80] the Court of Justice held that, insofar as the Community has assumed the powers previously exercised by the Member States in relation to the General Agreement of Tariffs and Trade, the provisions of the Agreement bind the Community. However, those provisions do not have direct effect (that is, they do not create rights for private parties) due to the 'great flexibility' of their nature.[81]

Interpretation of directly effective provisions of international agreements The fact that an international agreement contains directly effective provisions similar in content to articles of the EEC Treaty does not mean that those provisions will be interpreted by the Court of Justice in an identical manner to the analogous EEC Treaty articles. The provisions of an international agreement must be interpreted in the context of the agreement itself and with reference to its own specific terms and objectives.[82]

---

[79] [1990] ECR I–3461 paras 13–26. See also Case C–188/91 *Deutsche Shell AG v Hauptzollamt Hamburg-Harburg* judgment of 21 January 1993 paras 13–19.

[80] [1972] ECR 1219. See also Case 266/81 *SIOT v Ministero delle Finanze* [1983] ECR 731 paras 26–31; Joined Cases 267–269/81 *Amministrazione delle Finanze dello Stato v Società Petrolifera Italiana SpA and SpA Michelin Italiana* [1983] ECR 801 paras 21–26.

[81] See also Case 9/73 *Schlüter v Hauptzollamt Lörrach* [1973] ECR 1135 paras 24–34 in which it was held that, although certain provisions of GATT do not have direct effect, a specific provision agreed in the context of GATT, which was, in itself, sufficiently clear, precise and unconditional and which had been incorporated into a Community regulation, did have direct effect. See also Case 70/87 *Fédération de l'industrie de l'huilerie de la CEE (Fedoil) v Commission* [1989] ECR 1781 paras 18–22 where the Court of Justice interpreted and applied GATT rules in the context of an action under article 173 of the EEC Treaty.

[82] Case 270/80 *Polydor v Harlequin Record Shops* [1982] ECR 329; Case 104/81 *Hauptzollamt Mainz v Kupferberg* [1982] ECR 3641 paras 28–31.

Chapter 4

Interpretation

1. INTERPRETATION OF COMMUNITY LAW

English courts Section 3(1) of the European Communities Act 1972[1] obliges the English courts to follow the same principles of interpretation as the EC Courts in relation to Community law provisions.[2]

Uniform interpretation Terms used in Community law must be interpreted and implemented uniformly throughout the Community, except when an express or implied reference is made to national law.[3]

Language versions The official language versions of a Community measure are all equally authentic.[4] Where there is doubt as to the meaning of a provision of Community law, reference should be made to the wording of the provision as it appears in the other official language versions.[5] The different language versions of a Community provision must be given a uniform interpretation. Therefore, in the case of divergence between the different versions, the provision in question should be interpreted by reference to the purpose and general scheme of the rules of which it forms a part.[6]

---

[1] Reproduced at pp 10–11.
[2] See *HP Bulmer Ltd v J Bollinger SA* [1974] 1 Ch 401 at 419C–G, 425C–426E, per Lord Denning.
[3] Case 49/71 *Hagen OHG v Einfuhr- und Vorratsstelle für Getreide und Futtermittel* [1972] ECR 23 para 6 and Case 327/82 *Ekro BV Vee en Vleeshandel v Produktschap voor Vee en Vlees* [1984] ECR 107 para 11. See also Case 29/69 *Erich Stauder v City of Ulm, Sozialamt* [1969] ECR 419 paras 3, 4.
[4] Case 283/81 *Srl CILFIT v Ministry of Health* [1982] ECR 3415 para 18.
[5] Case 19/67 *Bestuur der Sociale Verzekeringsbank v JH van der Vecht* [1967] ECR 345 at 354; Case 9/79 *Marianne Wörsdorfer, née Koschniske v Raad van Arbeid* [1979] ECR 2717 paras 5–9. See *National Smokeless Fuels Limited v Commissioners of Inland Revenue* [1986] 3 CMLR 227 para 25 for English authority concerning the use of different language versions of Community provisions.
[6] Case 6/74 *Johannes Coenrad Moulijn v Commission* [1974] ECR 1287 paras 10, 11; Case 80/76 *North Kerry Milk Products Ltd v Minister for Agriculture and Fisheries* [1977] ECR 425 para 11; Case 30/77 *R v Pierre Bouchereau* [1977] ECR 1999 paras 13, 14; Case 803/79 *Criminal proceedings against Gérard Roudolff* [1980] ECR 2015 para 7.

Purposive or teleological approach In interpreting provisions of Community law, it is necessary to adopt a 'teleological' or 'purposive' approach to legislative interpretation. This means that as well as considering the wording of a provision, the context in which that wording appears and the purpose of the specific legislative framework of which it forms a part should also be considered.[7]

In Case 67/79 *Waldemar Fellinger v Bundesanstalt für Arbeit, Nuremberg*[8] Advocate-General Mayras stated:

> ... this Court may not substitute its discretion for that of the legislature; when the meaning of the legislation is clear it has to be applied with that meaning, even if the solution prescribed may be thought to be unsatisfactory. That is not to say, however, that the literal construction of a provision must always be accepted. If such a construction were to lead to a nonsensical result in regard to a situation which the Court believed the provision was intended to cover, certain doubts might properly be entertained in regard to it. In other words, the clear meaning and the literal meaning are not synonymous.
>
> There have been many cases in which the Court has rejected a literal interpretation in favour of another which it found more compatible with the objective and the whole scheme of the legislation in question.

This approach applies equally to the Brussels Convention on Jurisdiction and the Enforcement of Judgments in Civil and Commercial Matters and related conventions and to the Rome Convention on the Law applicable to Contractual Obligations.[9] The House of Lords has recognised that English courts must adopt a purposive approach when interpreting Community law.[10]

Consistent with the Treaty When the wording of secondary legislation is open to more than one interpretation, preference should be given to the interpretation which renders it consistent with the EEC Treaty and the general principles of Community law.[11]

Laws of third countries A Community provision must be interpreted solely in the context of Community law, unless it expressly refers to the laws or customs of a third country.[12]

---

[7] Case 50/76 *Amsterdam Bulb BV v Produktschap voor Siergewassen* [1977] ECR 137 paras 9 and 28; Case 292/82 *Firma E Merck v Hauptzollamt Hamburg-Jonas* [1983] ECR 3781 para 12; Case C–136/91 *Findling Wälzlager Handelsgesellschaft mbH v Hauptzollamt Karlsruhe*, judgment of 1 April 1993, para 11.

[8] [1980] ECR 535 at 550.

[9] Case 133/81 *Roger Ivenel v Helmut Schwab* [1982] ECR 1891 paras 10–20; Case 201/82 *Gerling Konzern Speziale Kreditversicherungs-AG v Amministrazione dello Stato* [1983] ECR 2503 para 11. See also *Re Harrods (Buenos Aires) Ltd* [1992] Ch 72, per Bingham LJ at 98G–99C.

[10] *Pickstone v Freemans plc* [1989] 1 AC 66; *Litster v Forth Dry Dock & Engineering Co Ltd* [1990] 1 AC 546 at 558E, 559E; *A Foster v British Gas plc* [1991] 2 AC 306 at 315C–316A. See also *Thomas v Chief Adjudication Officer* [1991] 2 QB 164, per Slade LJ at 179–182.

[11] Case 218/82 *Commission v Council* [1983] ECR 4063 para 15; Joined Cases 201/85, 202/85 *Marthe Klensch v Secrétaire d'Etat à l'Agriculture et à la Viticulture* [1986] ECR 3477 para 21; Case 220/83 *Commission v France* [1986] ECR 3663 para 15; Case C–314/89 *Siegfried Rauh v Hauptzollamt Nürnberg-Fürth* [1991] I-1647 para 17; Joined Cases C–90/90 and C–91/90 *Jean Neu v Secrétaire d'Etat à l'Agriculture et à la Viticulture* [1991] ECR I–3617 para 12.

[12] Case 12/73 *Claus W Muras v Hauptzollamt Hamburg-Jonas* [1973] ECR 963 paras 5–8 which concerned the interpretation of a regulation governing export refunds in respect of exports by Community producers to third countries.

Preambles/preparatory measures Courts may refer to the preamble to a Community measure which will usually state the objectives of that measure,[13] as an aid to its interpretation.[14] Where there is a discrepancy between the preamble and the text of the measure, the latter will prevail.[15] Courts are also entitled to refer to working documents (*travaux préparatoires*) as an aid to interpretation.[16] In certain cases the Court of Justice has been prepared to rely on declarations of the Commission and/or Council.[17] In *R v London Boroughs Transport Committee v Freight Transport Association Ltd*[18] the House of Lords referred to a Commission Green Paper as an aid to interpretation.

Preliminary references The fact that the Court of Justice is generally in a better position than a national court to give a purposive interpretation of a Community provision in the light of all its different language versions is an important factor for an English court to consider in deciding whether to make a preliminary reference to the Court of Justice under article 177 of the EEC Treaty.[19]

Derogations Derogations from the fundamental principles of Community law must be narrowly construed.[20]

General principles/fundamental rights The Community courts draw on general principles, such as proportionality, legitimate expectation, legal certainty and fundamental human rights, as aids to interpretation.[21]

---

[13] See Case C–346/88 *Schweizerische Lactina Panchaud AG v Germany* [1989] ECR 4579 para 10.

[14] For example: Case 63/75 *Fonderies Roubaix-Wattrelos Sa v Société Nouvelle des Fonderies Roux* [1976] ECR 111 paras 17–19; Case 50/76 *Amsterdam Bulb BV v Produktschap voor Siergewassen* [1977] ECR 137 paras 9–11; Joined Cases C–71/91, C–178/91 *Ponente Carni SpA and Cispanda Costruzioni SpA v Amministrazione delle Finanze dello Stato* judgment of 20 April 1993 paras 19, 20. For English authorities concerning the use of a preamble in interpreting a Community provision, see *R v Robert Tymen* [1980] 3 CMLR 101 paras 28, 29; *National Smokeless Fuels Limited v Commissioners of Inland Revenue* [1986] 3 CMLR 227 para 24.

[15] Joined Cases 154/83, 155/83 *Joseph Hoche v Bundesanstalt für Landwirtschaftliche Marktordnung* [1985] ECR 1215 para 13.

[16] Case 15/60 *Gabriel Simon v Court of Justice* [1961] ECR 115 at 124, 125; Case 18/76 *Germany v Commission* [1979] ECR 343 para 5; Case 130/87 *François Retter v Caisse de pension des employés privés* [1989] ECR 865 para 16.

[17] Case 29/69 *Erich Stauder v City of Ulm, Sozialamt* [1969] ECR 419 para 5; Case C–310/90 *Nationale Raad van de Orde van Architecten v Ulrich Egle* [1992] ECR I–177 para 12. However, the Court of Justice held that no reliance could be placed on such a declaration in Case 429/85 *Commission v Italy* [1988] ECR 843 paras 8, 9 and Case C–292/89 *R v Immigration Appeal Tribunal ex p Antonissen* [1991] ECR I–745 paras 17, 18.

[18] [1991] 1 WLR 828 at 839A–841B.

[19] *Customs and Excise v ApS Samex* [1983] 1 All ER 1042 at 1055G–1056B. See also Case 283/81 *Srl CILFIT v Ministry of Health* [1982] ECR 3415 paras 16–21. Discussed further at p 139.

[20] For example: Case 46/76 *WJG Bauhuis v Netherlands* [1977] ECR 5 para 12 (free movement of goods, article 36, EEC Treaty); Case 41/74 *Yvonne van Duyn v Home Office* [1974] ECR 1337 (free movement of workers, article 48(3), EEC Treaty); Case 262/84 *Beets-Proper v F Van Lanschot Bankiers NV* [1986] ECR 773 para 38 (equal treatment legislation); Case 2/74 *Jean Reyners v Belgium* [1974] ECR 631 para 43 (freedom of establishment, EEC Treaty, article 55).

[21] Discussed at pp 12–20.

2. INTERPRETATION OF NATIONAL LAW

Rules of interpretation The normal approach to statutory interpretation under English law is that the intention of Parliament must be ascertained from the words used in the legislation and those words are to be construed according to their plain and ordinary meaning. However, as a result of the case law of the Court of Justice, special rules of construction apply in relation to national legislation which falls within an area of Community competence. In particular, the national courts are under an obligation to interpret national law in conformity with Community law whenever possible. This obligation applies to all national legislation, whether it was specifically adopted to implement a directive or not, and whether it was adopted before or after the implementation date of a directive. However, national courts are not obliged to distort the meaning of national legislation.

Relationship with direct effect The obligation to interpret national law in conformity with Community law is of particular importance where a directive does not have direct effect or in cases between private parties. Directives do not have horizontal direct effect; a private party cannot rely on an unimplemented directive against another private party in the national courts.[22] However, where the national legislation is capable of being interpreted in accordance with a directive, the practical result of the obligation of interpretation is that a private party may be able to rely indirectly on the directive as against another private party (so-called 'indirect effect').

Obligation of interpretation The obligation of interpretation was recognised by the Court of Justice in Case 14/83 *Sabine von Colson and Elisabeth Kamann v Land Nordrhein-Westfalen*.[23] The Court held that:

> ... the Member States' obligation arising from a directive to achieve the result envisaged by the directive and their duty under Article 5 of the Treaty[24] to take all appropriate measures, whether general or particular, to ensure the fulfilment of that obligation, is binding on all the authorities of Member States including, for matters within their jurisdiction, the courts. It follows that, in applying the national law and in particular the provisions of national law specifically introduced in order to implement [a directive], national courts are required to interpret their national law in the light of the wording and the purpose of the directive in order to achieve the result referred to in the third paragraph of Article 189.

National legislation pre-dates Community provisions Following the decision in *von Colson*, the obligation of interpretation was applied in subsequent cases in respect of national legislation which had been specifically passed to im-

---

[22] See pp 35–37.
[23] [1984] ECR 1891 para 26.
[24] Article 5 of the EEC Treaty provides, *inter alia*,

Member States shall take all appropriate measures, whether general or particular, to ensure fulfilment of the obligations arising out of this Treaty or resulting from action taken by the institutions of the Community.

plement a directive.[25] However, it was only Case C–106/89 *Marleasing SA v La Comercial Internacional de Alimentación SA*[26] that the Court of Justice clarified the general scope of the obligation to interpret *all* national legislation in conformity with a directive where possible and not just national legislation which had been passed specifically to implement a directive or legislation passed after the implementation date of the directive had expired. In this case, Marleasing SA brought an action in the Spanish courts seeking, *inter alia*, the annulment of the contract of association of La Comercial on the basis that its establishment was a sham transaction designed to defraud the creditors of one of the founders of La Comercial. Marleasing relied on certain articles of the Spanish Civil Code which provided that contracts without 'cause', or of which the 'cause' was unlawful, had no legal effect. However, article 11 of Directive 68/151,[27] which post-dates the Spanish Civil Code, contains an exhaustive list of the grounds upon which the nullity of a company may be ordered. These grounds do not include lack of 'cause'. At the time of the case, the Spanish Government had not yet implemented Directive 68/151. The Court of Justice held that:[28]

> in applying national law, whether the provisions in question were adopted before or after the directive, the national court called upon to interpret it is required to do so, as far as possible, in the light of the wording and the purpose of the directive in order to achieve the result pursued by the latter. . . .

In *Webb v Emo Air Cargo (UK) Ltd*,[29] Lord Keith recognised that the decision in *Marleasing* imposes an obligation on the English courts to interpret national law in accordance with Community law as far as possible, regardless of whether the national legislation was adopted before or after the Community legislation.[30]

---

[25] Case 79/83 *Dorit Harz v Deutsche Tradax GmbH* [1984] ECR 1921 para 26; Case 222/84 *Johnston v Chief Constable of the Royal Ulster Constabulary* [1986] ECR 1651 para 53; Case 80/86 *Criminal proceedings against Kolpinghuis Nijmegen BV* [1987] ECR 3969 para 12; *Apple and Pear Development Council v Commissioners of Customs and Excise* [1987] 2 CMLR 634 at 654, per Lord Brightman at para 27; Case 125/88 *Criminal Proceedings against HFM Nijman* [1989] ECR 3533 para 6; *J Rothschild Holdings plc v Commissioners of Inland Revenue* [1989] 2 CMLR 621 paras 53, 54.

[26] [1990] ECR I–4135.

[27] Council Directive 68/151 on co-ordination of safeguards which, for the protection of the interests of Member States and others, are required by Member States of companies within article 58 of the EEC Treaty, with a view to making such safeguards equivalent throughout the Community, OJ No L 65, 13 March 1968, p 8, Special Edition 1968(I) at p 41.

[28] Case C–106/89 *Marleasing SA v La Comercial Internacional de Alimentación SA* [1990] ECR I–4135 para 8.

[29] [1993] 1 WLR 49, per Lord Keith at 59G.

[30] To the extent that the judgments in *Duke v GEC Reliance Ltd* [1981] 1 AC 618 and *Finnegan v Clowney Youth Training Programme Ltd* [1990] 2 AC 407 suggest otherwise they should be treated as incorrect following the decision of the Court of Justice in *Marleasing SA v La Comercial Internacional de Alimentación SA* (above) and the House of Lords decision in *Webb v Emo Air Cargo (UK) Ltd*.

National legislation must be open to interpretation Following the decision in *Marleasing*, there has been considerable academic debate[31] as to whether the Court of Justice in effect had introduced the principle of horizontal direct effect for directives by means of the obligation of interpretation. This argument rests on an analysis of the judgment which states that the national courts are under an absolute duty to interpret national law in conformity with a directive, even where, on its face, the national law conflicts with the directive. This 'absolutist' view of *Marleasing* is not borne out by a careful analysis of the decision. The Court of Justice specifically emphasised[32] that directives cannot have horizontal direct effect, as established in Case 152/84 *MH Marshall v Southampton and South-West Hampshire Area Health Authority*.[33] Furthermore, the Court of Justice held that the obligation to interpret national law in light of a Community directive only applies 'as far as possible'.[34]

Admittedly, the decision of the Court of Justice in *Marleasing* lacks depth of argument. However, the Opinion of Advocate-General Van Gerven is more fully argued and dispels the view that *Marleasing* imposes an absolute obligation of interpretation on national courts. The Advocate-General describes the obligation of interpretation in the following terms:

> The obligation to interpret a provision of national law in conformity with a directive arises whenever the provision in question is to any extent open to interpretation. In those circumstances the national court must, having regard to the usual methods of interpretation in its legal system, give precedence to the method which enables it to construe the national provision concerned in a manner consistent with the directive.[35]

On the particular facts of the case, Advocate-General Van Gerven considered that the Spanish law was open to interpretation in order to conform with the directive.[36] This view is borne out by the decision in *von Colson* itself, where the Court of Justice stated that the obligation on a national court to interpret national law in conformity with Community law applies only, 'insofar as it is given discretion to do so under national law'.[37]

Thus, it appears that, according to the case law of the Court of Justice, national courts are obliged to interpret national legislation in conformity with a directive only where the legislation is open to such an interpretation. They are not obliged to interpret the national legislation *contra legem*, in a way which is clearly contradictory to the words used.[38] The judgment of the Court of Justice

---

[31] For example, see Mead 'The Obligation to Apply European Law: Is *Duke* Dead?' (1991) 16 EL Rev 490; de Búrca 'Giving Effect to European Community Directives' (1992) 55 MLR 215; Greenwood 'Effect of EEC Directives in National Law' (1992) CLJ 3; Maltby '*Marleasing*: What is All the Fuss About?' (1993) 109 LQR 301.

[32] *Marleasing SA v La Comercial Internacional de Alimentación SA* [1990] ECR I–4135 para 6.

[33] [1986] ECR 723. See p 35

[34] *Marleasing* (above) para 8.

[35] *Marleasing* (above) para 8 of the Opinion.

[36] *Marleasing* (above) para 20 of the Opinion.

[37] [1984] ECR 1891 para 28.

[38] See also the Opinion of Advocate-General Van Gerven of 26 January 1993 in Case C–271/91 *MH Marshall v Southampton and South-West Hampshire Area Health Authority* at para 10 ('*Marshall No 2*') [1993] 3 CMLR 293 (ECJ).

in *Marleasing* appears to be consistent with the view of the English courts that they are not obliged to 'distort' the meaning of national legislation. In *Duke v GEC Reliance Ltd*,[39] a case which pre-dated *Marleasing*, the House of Lords was required to consider whether the United Kingdom Equal Pay Act 1970 and Sex Discrimination Act 1975 should be interpreted in a manner which gave effect to the EEC Equal Treatment Directive[40] which was adopted in 1976. Lord Templeman held:[41]

> Of course a British court will always be willing and anxious to conclude that United Kingdom law is consistent with Community law. Where an Act is passed for the purpose of giving effect to an obligation imposed by a directive or other instrument a British court will seldom encounter difficulty in concluding that the language of the Act is effective for the intended purpose. But the construction of a British Act of Parliament is a matter of judgment to be determined by British courts and to be derived from the language of the legislation considered in the light of the circumstances prevailing at the date of enactment.

Lord Templeman concluded that the British courts were not entitled to distort the meaning of a British statute in order to give effect to Community legislation and held that, in the particular case, the relevant words of the British statute were not 'reasonably capable' of bearing a meaning which conformed with Community law.[42]

Lord Keith considered this issue in *Webb v Emo Air Cargo (UK) Ltd*[43] where he held that:[44]

> ... it is for a United Kingdom court to construe domestic legislation in any field covered by a Community Directive so as to accord with the interpretation of the Directive as laid down by the European Court of Justice, if that can be done without distorting the meaning of the domestic legislation: *Duke v GEC Reliance Systems Ltd* [1988] AC 618, 639–640, per Lord Templeman.

Lord Keith analysed the *Marleasing* decision as imposing an obligation in these terms:[45]

> ... a national court must construe a domestic law to accord with the terms of a Directive in the same field only if it is possible to do so. That means that the domestic law must be open to an interpretation consistent with the Directive whether or not it is also open to an interpretation inconsistent with it.

Where the national law will not support a construction which conforms with EEC law, it is for Parliament to make the necessary amendments to the national

---

[39] [1988] 1 AC 618. Applied in *Organon Laboratories Ltd v Department of Health and Social Security* [1990] 2 CMLR 49 at paras 48–50, per Mustill LJ. See also *Garland v British Rail Engineering Ltd* [1983] 2 AC 751.

[40] Council Directive 76/207 on the implementation of the principle of equal treatment for men and women as regards access to employment, vocational training and promotion, and working conditions, OJ No L 39, 14 February 1976, p 40.

[41] *Duke v GEC Reliance Ltd* [1988] 1 AC 618 at 638F–G.

[42] Ibid at 639H–639A.

[43] [1993] 1 WLR 49.

[44] Ibid at 59F.

[45] Ibid at 60F.

law in order to prevent the United Kingdom from being in breach of its Treaty obligations. Where Community law is unclear, a reference to the Court of Justice will usually be appropriate.[46]

Purposive approach — implying words into national legislation Shortly after the decision in *Duke v GEC Reliance Ltd*, the House of Lords was required to consider the question of interpretation of United Kingdom legislation in the context of Community law in *Pickstone v Freemans*,[47] and *Litster v Forth Dry Dock and Engineering Co Ltd (In Receivership)*.[48] The speeches in those cases recognised that the English courts are under an obligation to adopt a purposive approach to the interpretation of United Kingdom primary and subordinate legislation enacted to give effect to the United Kingdom's obligations under the EEC Treaty. Thus, where legislation can be reasonably construed so as to conform with the United Kingdom's Community obligations, the English courts must do so, even if this involves a departure from the strict and literal application of the words used in the legislation.[49] Indeed, in both the above cases[50] the House of Lords held that, as a matter of language, the United Kingdom legislation at issue was 'unequivocal' and 'unambiguous' on its face. However, adopting a purposive approach, the House in both cases implied words into the legislation in order to comply with the United Kingdom's Treaty obligations.

Implementation period of directive has not expired A directive cannot have direct effect before the expiry of the time limit laid down for its implementation.[51] It can be argued, by analogy, that no obligation to interpret national legislation in conformity with a directive should arise until the implementation period of the directive has expired. However, in Case C–156/91 *Hansa Fleisch Ernst Mundt v Landrat des Kreises Schleswig-Flensburg*,[52] Advocate-General Jacobs argued that the obligation of interpretation should arise prior to the expiry of the implementation date of a directive where a Member State has chosen to introduce national implementing legislation at an earlier date. In all other cases he considered that the obligation of interpretation could not arise until the implementation date for the directive had expired.

The judgment in Case 80/86 *Kolpinghuis Nijmegen*[53] has been relied on as authority for the principle that the obligation of interpretation applies even before the expiry of the implementation date.[54] However, on close analysis, it

---

[46] As in *Webb v Emo Air Cargo Ltd* [1993] 1 WLR 49.
[47] [1989] 1 AC 66.
[48] [1990] 1 AC 546.
[49] *Pickstone v Freemans* (above) at 112C–D, per Lord Keith, at 125F–H and 127H–128A, per Lord Oliver; *Litster v Forth Dry Dock and Engineering Co Ltd (In Receivership)* (above) at 558E, 559E–F per Lord Templeman.
[50] *Pickstone v Freemans* (above) at 125F–H, 126A–D, 126H–127C and 127H–128D, per Lord Oliver; *Litster v Forth Dry Dock and Engineering Co Ltd (In Receivership)* (above) at 554G–H, per Lord Keith and at 576D–577D, per Lord Oliver.
[51] Case 148/78 *Pubblico Ministero v Tullio Ratti* [1979] ECR 1629 paras 24, 39–46. See pp 34–35.
[52] Opinion of Advocate-General Jacobs, judgment of 10 November 1992 paras 23–27.
[53] [1987] ECR 3969.
[54] See the Opinion of Advocate-General Van Gerven in Case C–106/89 *Marleasing SA v La Comercial Internacional de Alimentación SA* [1990] ECR I–4135 at fn 16; and Schermers, *Judicial Protection in the European Communities*, 5th edn (Kluwer 1991), para 255.

appears that the judgment does not provide support for this argument. In this case, the Court of Justice answered the third question of a preliminary reference from the *Arrondissementsrechtbank*, Arnhem, by re-affirming that national courts are required to interpret their national law in light of a relevant directive. However, the Court then stated that this general obligation of interpretation is limited, in that a directive which has not been implemented by national law cannot determine or aggravate the criminal liability of persons who act in contravention of the directive. The fourth question asked by the Dutch court was, *inter alia*, whether it made a difference to the answer to the third question if the implementation date for the relevant directive had not yet expired. The Court of Justice replied as follows:[55]

> As regards the third question concerning the limits which Community law might impose on the obligation or power of the national court to interpret the rules of its national law in the light of the directive, it makes no difference whether or not the period prescribed for implementation has expired.

It appears from this passage that the Court was emphasising that the fact that the implementation date for a directive has not yet expired does not affect the principle that a directive which has not been implemented by a national law cannot create or aggravate criminal liability. The Court did not address the question of whether the general obligation of interpretation is affected by the fact that the implementation date for a directive has expired or not.[56]

Obligation of interpretation applies to directives even if they are not 'unconditional and sufficiently precise' This is a further difference between the obligation of interpretation and the doctrine of direct effect, as was recognised by Advocate-General Darmon in Case 177/88 *Elisabeth Johanna Pacifica Dekker v Stichting Vormingscentrum voor Jonge Volwassenen (VJV-Centrum) Plus*:[57]

> It should be noted that my approach leads — as indeed previous judgments of the Court have done — to a distinction which has not often been stressed, between the possibility of relying on a directive, in cases where there are no national rules giving effect to its aims, so as to have its provisions applied directly (doctrine of 'direct effect') and reliance on a directive for the sole purpose of the interpretation of national law, including an interpretation of national provisions intended to implement the Community instrument (the doctrine of *interprétation conforme*). Whereas the former is confined to those provisions in directives which are sufficiently precise and unconditional, and cannot, according to the case-law, govern relations between individuals, the latter is very broad in scope, regardless of whether or not the directive has direct effect and regardless of the parties involved.

---

[55] Case 80/86 *Kolpinghuis Nijmegen BV* [1987] ECR 3969, paras 15, 16.
[56] This analysis of Case 80/86 *Kolpinghuis Nijmegen BV* [1987] ECR 3969 is supported by the Opinion of Advocate-General Jacobs in Case C–156/91 *Hansa Fleisch Ernst Mundt v Landrat des Kreises Schleswig-Flensburg*, judgment of 10 November 1992, para 26 of the Opinion.
[57] [1990] ECR I–3941 para 15 of the Opinion. See also Opinion of Advocate-General Van Gerven in Case C–106/89 *Marleasing SA v La Comercial Internacional de Alimentación SA* [1990] ECR I–4135 at fn 11.

Obligation of interpretation and criminal liability In Case 80/86 *Kolpinghuis Nijmegen BV*,[58] the Court of Justice held that the obligation of interpretation is limited by the general principles of Community law and, in particular, the general principles of legal certainty and non-retroactivity. Thus, a directive which has not been implemented by national law cannot determine or aggravate the criminal liability of persons who act in contravention of the directive.

Recommendations Although article 189 of the EEC Treaty states that 'Recommendations and opinions shall have no binding force', so that they cannot have direct effect, they do have some legal effect in the national legal systems. In Case 322/88 *Salvatore Grimaldi v Fonds des maladies professionnelles*[59] the Court of Justice held that national courts are bound to take recommendations into consideration in deciding disputes submitted to them, in particular where they cast light on the interpretation of national measures adopted in order to implement them or where they are designed to supplement binding Community provisions.

---

[58] [1987] ECR 3969 paras 11–14. Compare the position in relation to the direct effect of directives, pp 36–37.
[59] [1989] ECR 4407 paras 16–19.

Part II

Remedies in English Courts for Breach of EC law

Chapter 5

Effective Protection of EC Law Rights

1. PRINCIPLE OF EFFECTIVE PROTECTION

Duty on national courts Pursuant to article 5 of the EEC Treaty, it is the duty of national courts to ensure the legal protection of rights which individuals derive from Community law.[1] In defining this duty of 'sincere co-operation' between national courts and the Community, the Court of Justice stated in Case 13/68 *SPA Salgoil v Italian Ministry for Foreign Trade*[2] that national courts are required to protect the interests of persons who may be affected by any possible infringement of the Treaty, 'by ensuring for them direct and immediate protection . . .'. Referring to this judgment, the Court of Justice stated in Case 179/84 *Bozzetti v Invernizzi SpA and Ministerio del Tesoro*[3] that rights conferred on individuals by Community law, 'must be effectively protected in each case'. An effective remedy is one which ensures the effectiveness of Community law rights. Thus, national courts cannot be inhibited by any provision, precedent, practice or presumption which might impair the effectiveness of such rights. As the Court of Justice stated in Case 106/77 *Amministrazione delle Finanze dello Stato v Simmenthal SpA*:[4]

> any provision of a national legal system and any legislative, administrative or judicial practice which might impair the effectiveness of Community law by withholding from the national court having jurisdiction to apply such law the power to do everything necessary at the moment of its application to set aside national legislative provisions which might prevent Community rules from having full force and effect are incompatible with those requirements which are the very essence of Community law.

All available remedies Regard should be had to all available national remedies and the conditions under which they can be granted, in order to determine

---

[1] Case C–213/89 *R v Secretary of State for Transport ex p Factortame (No 2)* [1990] ECR I–2433; [1991] 1 AC 603 para 19; Case C–2/88 *JJ Zwartveld v European Parliament* [1990] ECR I-3365 para 18 and Case 33/76 *Rewe-Zentralfinanz eG v Landwirtschaftskammer für Saarland* [1976] ECR 1989 para 5.

[2] [1968] ECR 453 at 463.

[3] [1985] ECR 2301 at 2317, 2318.

[4] [1978] ECR 629 paras 21, 22.

whether Community law is being effectively protected. The principle of effective protection is, therefore, an elastic and, indeed, a subjective concept. For example, in *Bourgoin SA v Ministry of Agriculture, Fisheries and Food*[5] Parker
LJ, with whom Norse LJ agreed, considered that the remedy of judicial review
for an innocent, yet unlawful, breach of article 30 of the EEC Treaty by the Ministry provided adequate protection to the individuals affected.[6] In contrast, Oliver LJ considered that judicial review in itself was not an effective remedy for
such a breach. A denial of a remedy in damages for past loss caused by the act
complained of would, he considered, infringe the principle of effective protection.[7]

Nature of the right infringed   In applying the principle of effective protection,
national courts must have regard to the objective and the purpose of the EC provision which gives rise to the right alleged to have been infringed. In *Marshall v
Southampton and South-West Hampshire Health Authority Teaching (No 2)*[8]
Miss Marshall successfully claimed that she had been forced to retire because of
a discriminatory policy which was contrary to Council Directive 76/207[9] on
equal treatment for men and women. The industrial tribunal assessed Miss Marshall's financial loss at £18,405. At the relevant time, however, the statutory
limit on the compensation which could be awarded was £6,250. The Court of
Justice applied the principle of effective protection (enshrined in article 6 of the
Directive) in the light of the objective of the Directive, which is to arrive at real
equality of opportunity. This meant that there should be full compensation for
the damage sustained as a result of the discrimination. Consequently, the industrial tribunal was required to set aside the statutory limit on the amount of compensation which could be awarded to Miss Marshall.

2. RIGHT TO JUDICIAL CONTROL

Access to the courts   The existence of a judicial remedy is essential if an individual is to be able to seek effective protection of his Community law rights. In
short, there must be a right to judicial control. This requirement was laid down
by the Court of Justice in Case 222/84 *Johnston v Chief Constable of the Royal
Ulster Constabulary*.[10] In this case, Mrs Johnston had been in the full-time reserve of the Royal Ulster Constabulary and, as a result of the decision not to arm

---

[5] [1986] 1 QB 716. Discussed at pp 78–81.
[6] Ibid at 785D–E.
[7] Ibid at 769E–771G.
[8] [1990] ICR 6 (EAT), [1991] ICR 136 (CA), Case C–271/91 [1993] 3 CMLR 293 (ECJ). See also
     Case 14/83 *Sabine Von Colson & Elisabeth Kamann and Land Nordrhein-Westfalen* [1984] ECR
     1891 para 18.
[9] Council Directive 76/207 of 9 February 1976, OJ No L 39, 14 February 1976, p 40, on the
     implementation of the principle of equal treatment for men and women as regards access to
     employment, vocational training and promotion and working conditions.
[10] [1986] ECR 1651 paras 13–21: applied generally in Case 222/86 *UNECTEF v Heylens* [1987]
     ECR 4097; Case C–340/89 *Vlassopoulou* [1991] ECR I–2357 para 22; Case C–97/91 *Oleificio
     Borelli*, judgment of 3 December 1992: and Case C–19/92 *Dieter Kraus v Land Baden-
     Würtemberg*, judgment of 31 March 1993, para 40.

women police officers, did not have her contract of employment renewed. On her application, under the Sex Discrimination (Northern Ireland) Order 1976, to the industrial tribunal, the Secretary of State signed a certificate under article 53(2) of the Order, which was conclusive evidence that the applicant had been refused full-time employment on the grounds of national security, public safety and public order. The Court of Justice held that this denial of access to the courts was a clear and unconditional breach of article 6 of Directive 76/207 on equal treatment for men and women,[11] which enables all persons who consider themselves wronged by discrimination 'to pursue their claims by judicial process'. The Court of Justice held that this requirement reflected a general principle of Community law which underlies the constitutional traditions common to the Member States and which has been enshrined in articles 6 and 13 of the European Convention on Human Rights.

Similarly, in Case 178/84 *Commission v Germany* ('the beer case')[12] the Court of Justice stated that article 30 of the EEC Treaty did not prevent Member States from subjecting the use of certain food additives to prior authorisation. However, the principle of proportionality underlying article 36 of the EEC Treaty dictates that importers must have access to a system of authorisation and that they should be able to challenge any refusal to grant authorisation before the national courts .

Duty to give reasons In Case 222/86 *UNECTEF v Heylens*[13] the Court of Justice held that national authorities must give reasons for decisions which impinge upon directly effective rights, so as to enable individuals properly to exercise their right to judicial control. In this case, Mr Heylens, a Belgian national, was employed as a football trainer for a French football club. Under French law, a person either had to possess a French diploma or a recognised foreign diploma in order to practise as a football trainer. The French Minister for Sport refused to recognise Mr Heylens' Belgian diploma. There was no requirement under French law for the Minister to provide reasons for the refusal and no provision was made for any specific legal remedy against the decision. The Court held that the inability to appeal against the decision and the failure to give reasons infringed the right to judicial control. The Court stated:[14]

> Effective judicial review, which must be able to cover the legality of the reasons for the contested decision, presupposes in general that the court to which the matter is referred may require the competent authority to notify its reasons. But where, as in this case, it is more particularly a question of securing the effective protection of a fundamental right conferred by the Treaty on Community workers, the latter must also be able to defend that right under the best possible conditions and have the possibility of deciding, with a full knowledge of the relevant facts, whether there is any point in

---

[11] Council Directive 76/207 of 9 February 1976, OJ No L 39, 14 February 1976, p 40, on the implementation of the principle of equal treatment for men and women as regards access to employment, vocational training and promotion and working conditions.

[12] [1987] ECR 1227 paras 44–46.

[13] [1987] ECR 4097.

[14] Ibid para 15.

their applying to the courts. Consequently, in such circumstances the competent national authority is under a duty to inform them of the reasons on which its refusal is based, either in the decision itself or in a subsequent communication made at their request.

Preparatory measures The right to judicial control and the duty to state reasons only concern final decisions and do not extend to Opinions and other measures occurring in preparatory or investigative stages leading to a final decision.[15]

Directives Directives sometimes specifically require that there should be access to the courts or that there should be a duty to state reasons on the part of national authorities. For example, Directive 79/279 on official stock exchange listing[16] requires Member States to ensure that decisions of the stock exchange refusing or discontinuing the listing of a company's shares are subject to review by the courts. Article 6 of Directive 76/207 on equal treatment for men and women, enables all persons who consider themselves wronged by discrimination 'to pursue their claims by judicial process'.[17] Similarly, Directive 89/665,[18] on public procurement remedies, provides that decisions concerning public procurement should be reviewed effectively and as rapidly as possible and that courts or separate review bodies should have the power to grant interim relief, quash any unlawful decision and award damages. Article 2(8) of the Directive provides that where the bodies responsible for review procedures are not judicial in character, written reasons for their decisions should always be given and their decision should be subject to review by a court or tribunal within the meaning of article 177 of the EEC Treaty.

3. AVAILABILITY OF PARTICULAR REMEDIES

Jurisdiction to grant certain remedies Since it is the task of national courts to protect Community law rights in the national legal order, it is primarily the task of those courts to consider whether the available remedies afford effective protection. On occasions, however, the Court of Justice has ruled that individuals must have the right to seek, albeit not necessarily to obtain, a particular remedy, in order effectively to protect rights derived from Community law. The Court has held that individuals have a right to restitution of charges levied by Member

---

[15] *UNECTEF v Heylans* [1987] ECR 4097 para 16.

[16] Council Directive 79/279 of 5 March 1979, OJ No L 66, 16 March 1979, p 21, co-ordinating the admission of securities to official stock exchange listing. Access to the courts does not extend to shareholders in a company. See the Court of Appeal in *R v International Stock Exchange of the United Kingdom and the Republic of Ireland Limited ex p Else (1982) Limited* [1993] QB 534.

[17] Council Directive 76/207 of 19 February 1976, OJ No L 39, 14 February 1976, p 40, on the implementation of the principle of equal treatment for men and women as regards access to employment, vocational training and promotion and working conditions.

[18] Council Directive 89/665 of 21 December 1989, OJ No L 395, 30 December 1989, p 33, on the co-ordination of the laws, regulations and administrative provisions relating to the application of review procedures to the award of public supply and works contracts. See also Council Directive 92/13 of 25 February 1992, OJ No L 76, 23 March 1992, p 14, co-ordinating the laws, regulations and administrative provisions relating to the application of community rules on the procurement procedures of entities operating in the water, energy, transport and telecommunications sectors.

States contrary to Community law,[19] a right to damages from the State for loss suffered due to the State's non-implementation of directives,[20] a right to obtain full compensation without limitation,[21] a right to interest on compensation[22] and a right to an interlocutory injunction to disapply an Act of Parliament in order to protect putative Community law rights.[23]

Procedural, substantive and evidential conditions In the absence of any Community legislation or ruling by the Court of Justice laying down the procedural, substantive or evidential rules relating to a particular remedy, it is for the national courts to apply their own rules. The Court of Justice has held that limitation periods,[24] rates of interest,[25] the availability of a defence of set-off[26] or unjust enrichment[27] and the severance of clauses in contracts which infringe the EC competition rules[28] are all matters for the national courts. However, these rules cannot be less favourable than those relating to similar national claims and they cannot make it virtually impossible or excessively difficult to obtain the particular remedy.[29]

Discriminatory conditions Any national condition concerning admissibility, substance or procedure is unlawful, insofar as it discriminates against other EC nationals or against any person bringing a claim under EC law.[30] Thus, in Case

---

[19] Case 33/76 *Rewe-Zentralfinanz eG v Landwirtschaftskammer für Saarland* [1976] ECR 1989; Case 199/82 *Amministrazione delle Finanze v San Giorgio* [1983] ECR 3595. See Ch 8 on Restitution.

[20] Joined Cases C–6/90, C–9/90 *Francovich and Bonifaci v Italy* [1991] ECR I–5357. See Ch 6 on Damages.

[21] Case C–271/91 *Marshall v Southampton and South-West Hampshire Health Authority (Teaching) (No 2)* [1993] 3 CMLR 293. See also the Opinion of Advocate-General Van Gerven in Case C–128/92 *HJ Banks & Co Ltd v British Coal Corporation*, delivered on 27 October 1993.

[22] Case C–271/91 *Marshall v Southampton and South-West Hampshire Health Authority (Teaching) (No 2)* [1993] 3 CMLR 293.

[23] Case C–221/89 *R v Secretary of State for Transport ex p Factortame Limited (No 2)* [1991] ECR I–3905, [1991] 1 AC 603. See Ch 7 on Injunctions.

[24] Case 33/76 *Rewe-Zentralfinanz eG v Landwirtschaftskammer für Saarland* [1976] ECR 1989; Case 45/76 *Comet BV v Produktschap voor Siergewassen* [1976] ECR 2043 (reasonable time limits). See also Case C–208/90 *Theresa Emmott v Minister for Social Welfare* [1991] ECR I–4269 (time limit concerning implementation of directives).

[25] Case 130/79 *Express Dairy Foods v Intervention Board for Agricultural Produce* [1980] ECR 1887; but note Case C–271/91 *Marshall v Southampton and South-West Hampshire Health Authority (Teaching) (No 2)* [1993] 3 CMLR 293. See also the Opinion of Advocate-General Van Gerven in Case C–128/92 *HJ Banks & Co Ltd v British Coal Corporation*, delivered on 27 October 1993.

[26] Case 177/78 *Pigs & Bacon Commission v McCarren* [1979] ECR 2161.

[27] Case 68/79 *Hans Just v Danish Ministry for Fiscal Affairs* [1980] ECR 501.

[28] Case 56/65 *Société La Technique Minière v Ulm* [1966] ECR 235; applied in *Chemidus Wavin Ltd* [1978] 3 CMLR 514; *Inntrepreneur v Mason* [1993] 2 CMLR 293; *Inntrepreneur v Boyes*, not yet reported (CA).

[29] For example, see Case 33/76 *Rewe-Zentralfinanz eG v Landwirstchaftskammer für Saarland* [1976] ECR 1989 para 5; Case 45/76 *Comet v Produktschap* [1976] ECR 2043 paras 12–19; Case 61/79 *Amministrazione delle Finanze v Denkavit* [1980] ECR 1205 para 25; Case 826/79 *Amministrazione delle Finanze v Sas MIRECO* [1980] ECR 2559 para 13; Case 199/82 *Amministrazione delle Finanze v San Giorgio* [1983] ECR 3595; Joined Cases C–6/90, C–9/90 *Francovich and Bonifaci v Italy* [1991] ECR I–5357, [1993] 2 CMLR 66 para 42.

[30] Case 158/80 *Rewe v Hauptzollomt Kiel* [1981] ECR 1805 para 44; Case 199/82 *Amministrazione delle Finanze v San Giorgio* [1983] ECR 3593 para 12; Joined Cases C–6/90, C–9/90 *Francovich and Bonifaci v Italy* [1991] ECR I–5357 para 43.

C–20/90 *Anthony Hubbard v Peter Hamburger*[31] Mr Hubbard, an English solicitor acting in his capacity as executor of a will in England, applied to the German courts for the transfer to his name of assets located in Germany which were part of the estate. Under German law he was obliged, as a foreign national, to provide security for costs. The Court of Justice held that this requirement was discriminatory and contrary to articles 59 and 60 of the EEC Treaty on the basis that German nationals were not required to provide such security in a similar situation.

The question has arisen whether English procedural rules on security for costs are also discriminatory. RSC Ord 23, r1(1)(a) provides that where the plaintiff is ordinarily resident out of the jurisdiction, the court may, having regard to all the circumstances of the case, order the plaintiff to give such security for the defendant's cost of the action as it thinks just. In *Berkeley Administration Inc v McClelland*[32] the Court of Appeal held that Ord 23 and, in particular, the residence requirement, did not result in any unlawful discrimination. The majority of the Court of Appeal (Parker and Russell LJJ) held that there was no discrimination on the grounds of nationality. Residence abroad was not, in itself, a ground for making an order under the rule, it was merely a pre-condition to the existence of the jurisdiction. Moreover, the rule applied wherever the plaintiff was resident abroad, whether in a Member State or a non-Member State, and it applied no matter what the nationality of the plaintiff was. Perhaps the better view is contained in the judgment of Staughton LJ who considered that the residence requirement was tantamount to discrimination on the grounds of nationality but was objectively justified.

Impossibility in practice Any national condition concerning admissibility, substance or procedure is unlawful, insofar as it makes it impossible in practice or excessively difficult to exercise rights which derive from Community law. In Case 199/82 *Amministrazione delle Finanz dello Sta VSpA San Giorgio*[33] an Italian trader had paid charges to the Italian authorities, which had been levied in breach of Community law. Italian law recognised the right to restitution where charges had been levied contrary to national law and Community law. However, the law presumed that the person who had paid the charges would pass them on to the consumer. To recover the charges from the Italian authorities the trader had to prove, by documentary evidence, that they had not been passed on. The Court of Justice considered that the requirement to prove a negative by documentary evidence, although not discriminatory, made it impossible, in practice, to exercise the right to restitution guaranteed by Community law. As a result, the Court held that the requirement was unlawful.

Similar principles apply where national laws are passed to limit the right to reimbursement of charges which have been declared contrary to Community law. In Case 309/85 *Barra v Belgium*[34] Mr Barra sought reimbursement of en-

---

[31] Judgment of 19 July 1993. See (1993) *The Times*, 16 July.

[32] [1990] 2 WLR 1021. See also *Porzeleck KG and Porzeleck UK Limited* [1987] 1 WLR 420.

[33] [1983] ECR 3595; applied in Case 331/85 *Bianco v Directeur Général des Douanes* [1988] ECR 1099. Compare case 68/79 *Hans Just v Danish Ministry for Fiscal Affairs* [1980] ECR 501.

[34] [1988] ECR 355. See also Case 240/87 *Deville v Administration des Impôts* [1988] ECR 3513.

rolment fees which he had paid before 13 February 1985, the date on which the Court of Justice gave judgment in Case 293/83 *Gravier v City of Liège*[35] in which case the Court had held that the enrolment fee was unlawful. Approximately four months after the date of the Court's judgment, the Belgian state passed a law which provided that there would be no reimbursement except to those students who had brought court proceedings before the date of the *Gravier* judgment. This excluded Mr Barra, who had brought his action in March 1985. The Court of Justice ruled that such a law made it impossible to exercise the right to reimbursement of the fee which was guaranteed by Community law and should, therefore, be disapplied.[36]

Public policy limitations The principle of effective protection does not mean that a remedy must be granted in every case where an individual's directly effective rights have been infringed. Considerations of public policy may limit the entitlement to the remedy in a particular case, but may not exclude jurisdiction to grant that remedy in all cases. In Case 33/76 *Rewe-Zentralfinanz eG v Landwirtschaftskammer für Saarland*[37] the Court of Justice ruled that reasonable limitation periods could bar a claim to restitution for monies levied by the State in breach of Community law. The Court stated that:

> The laying down of such time-limits with regard to actions of a fiscal nature is an application of the fundamental principle of legal certainty protecting both the tax payer and the administration concerned.

On this basis, therefore, strict (but not impossible) conditions may legitimately be imposed in the public interest where, for example, an individual seeks an interim injunction to disapply an Act of Parliament which is allegedly contrary to Community law.[38] Similarly, public policy considerations may limit an individual's ability to receive damages from the State for loss suffered due to a breach of Community law for which the State is responsible.[39]

4. OBLIGATION TO CREATE A REMEDY

No obligation to create remedies The duty of national courts to ensure the legal protection which individuals derive from Community law is unlikely to involve the invention of new remedies. On this basis, French courts could not be obliged to recognise the concept of equitable remedies known in English law in order to protect Community law rights. The Court of Justice has stated, *obiter*, that:[40]

---

[35] [1985] ECR 593.

[36] Only the EC Courts have power to impose temporal limitations on the effect of their judgments. National courts may not do so. See pp 133–134 and 201–202.

[37] [1976] ECR 1989. See also Case 45/76 *Comet BV v Produktschap* [1976] ECR 2043 para 5.

[38] Case C–213/89 *R v Secretary of State for Transport ex p Factortame (No 2)* [1990] ECR I-2433; [1990] 2 AC 85; [1991] 1 AC 603. See Ch 7 on Injunctions.

[39] See the rationale for the decision by the majority in *Bourgoin v Ministry of Agriculture Fisheries and Food* [1986] 1 QB 716. See Ch 6 on Damages.

[40] Case 158/80 *Rewe v Hauptzollomt Kiel* [1981] ECR 1805 para 44.

... although the treaty has made it possible in a number of instances for private persons to bring a direct action, where appropriate, before the Court of Justice, it was not intended to create new remedies in the national courts to ensure the observance of Community law other than those already laid down by national law.

Obligation to create jurisdiction It is unclear whether national courts must establish or create jurisdiction to exercise existing remedies where no such jurisdiction existed before, in order, effectively, to protect Community law rights. In *Marshall v Southampton and South-West Hampshire Health Authority (Teaching) (No 2)*[41] the Employment Appeal Tribunal, in assessing compensation in accordance with ss 65 and 66 of the Sex Discrimination Act 1975, awarded Miss Marshall compensation for loss of earnings, but held that an industrial tribunal was not a court of record and had no inherent power to award interest on any monetary award. On appeal, Dillon LJ, in relation to the lack of jurisdiction to award interest, stated:[42]

> It is one thing, however, to write out of a national statute, by a form of estoppel ..., a limitation in the statute on the power conferred by the statute on the national court to award compensation. It is not necessarily the same thing to write into the statute a power that is not there so as to enable the national court to make an award which the terms of the national statute give it no discretion to make.

The reply given by the Court of Justice was that a victim of sex discrimination was entitled to full compensation including a right to interest. As a result, the Member States are under an obligation to ensure that interest in respect of such claims is available in their national legal systems. The Court of Justice expressly did not deal with the issue of whether Community law provided the Industrial Tribunal with jurisdiction to grant interest even if it had not yet been granted such jurisdiction under the relevant national statute.

In *R v Secretary of State for Transport ex p Factortame Limited (No 2)*[43] the House of Lords considered that, as a matter of English law, it could not grant an interim injunction in judicial review proceedings which sought to disapply an Act of Parliament in order to protect putative Community law rights because:

(1) Supreme Court Act 1981, s 31 did not give the courts the power; and

(2) an Act of Parliament was presumed valid until declared invalid.

However, on a reference under article 177 of the EEC Treaty, the Court of Justice ruled that the House of Lords should disapply these rules in so far as they precluded it from granting such interim relief.[44] Lord Bridge said of the ruling:

---

[41] [1990] ICR 6 (EAT), [1991] ICR 136 (CA), Case C–271/91, judgment of 2 August 1993 (ECJ). See also Case 14/83 *Von Colson & Kamann v Land Nordrhein-Westfalen* [1984] ECR 1891. Compare the approach of Lord Templeman in *Duke v Reliance Systems Limited* [1988] 1 AC 618 at 641.

[42] *Marshall v Southampton and South West Hampshire Health Authority (Teaching) No 2* [1991] ICR 136 at 143E. Dillon LJ was, however, prepared to give the tribunal the power. The Court of Appeal held by majority that, whether or not the Industrial Tribunal had power to award interest, the statutory limit on the amount of compensation that could be awarded provided a complete defence to her claim for full compensation. This limitation was ruled unlawful by the Court of Justice.

[43] [1990] 1 AC 603.

[44] Case C–213/89 *R v Secretary of State for Transport ex p Factortame Ltd (No 2)* [1990] ECR I–2433, [1991] 1 AC 603.

My Lords, when this appeal first came before the House last year ... your Lordships held that, as a matter of English law, the courts had no jurisdiction to grant interim relief in terms which would involve either overturning an English statute in advance of any decision by the European Court of Justice that the statute infringed Community law or granting an injunction against the Crown. It then became necessary to seek a preliminary ruling from the European Court of Justice as to whether Community law itself invested us with such jurisdiction ...

In June of this year we received the judgment of the European Court of Justice ... affirming that we had jurisdiction, in the circumstances postulated, to grant interim relief for the protection of directly enforceable rights under Community law and that no limitation on our jurisdiction imposed by any rule of national law could stand as the sole obstacle to preclude the grant of such relief.[45]

It would appear that the House of Lords considered that Community law vested the Courts with the jurisdiction to grant an injunction where none existed before; on a closer analysis, however, the Court of Justice did not actually intend that its ruling should be so interpreted. Its ruling is based on the point that English Courts had jurisdiction, but were prevented from exercising it 'by the old common law rule that an interim injunction may not be granted against the Crown, that is to say against the Government, in conjunction with the presumption that an Act of Parliament is in conformity with Community law until such time as a decision on its compatibility with that law has been given'.

Creation of new procedural rules Courts will have to create new procedural rules to deal with claims arising under Community law if none already exist. In *Cannon v Barnsley Metropolitan Borough Council*,[46] which concerned a claim of sex discrimination contrary to Council Directive 76/207,[47] Knox J, in the Employment Appeal Tribunal, remarked that there was no relevant provision in national law setting out a particular time period in which to bring a claim under Community law. He held that, in principle, English law was perfectly capable of creating such a time limit, if necessary by analogy to statutory or common law time limits. Similarly, in *Livingston v Hepworth Refectories plc*,[48] the plaintiff had retired and, at the same time, had signed an agreement whereby, in exchange for payment to him of £20,400, he had waived all claims against his employer. Thereafter, he claimed that his pension fund had been operated contrary to Community law. The Industrial Tribunal dismissed the action for want of jurisdiction on the basis that the agreement waived all claims. Wood J, in the Employment Appeal Tribunal, held that the absence of specific procedural rules to deal with Community law claims relating to the plaintiff's pension should be filled by applying the procedures contained in the Sex Discrimination Act 1975. This Act included a code to protect employees against bad bargains. Consequently, the agreement was no bar to the action under Community law.

---

[45] [1991] 1 AC 603 at 658A–E.
[46] [1992] ICR 698.
[47] Council Directive 76/207 of 9 February 1976, OJ 1976 L 39, 14 February 1976, p 40, on the implementation of the principle of equal treatment for men and women as regards access to employment, vocational training and promotion and working conditions.
[48] [1992] 3 CMLR 601.

Chapter 6

Damages

1. ACTIONS AGAINST PRIVATE PARTIES

Need for an actionable wrong Before damages can be recovered, an actionable wrong must have been committed. As Lord Wright stated in *Bourhill v Young*,[1] a case which concerned the tort of negligence:

> Damage due to the legitimate exercise of a right is not actionable, even if the actor contemplates the damage. It is *damnum absque injuria*. The damage must be attributable to the breach by the defendant of some duty owing to the plaintiff.

On the same basis, not all breaches of Community law can give rise to an action for damages against private parties, since not all provisions of Community law impose duties or obligations on individuals. For example, a directive does not have horizontal direct effect and cannot, by itself, impose obligations on individuals. Consequently, a breach of a directive is not a wrong actionable at the suit of another.[2]

Available remedies The basic forms of private law remedies available in English law are damages, restitution, injunctive relief and declaratory relief. Although it is for the national legal systems to decide on the form of protection available in respect of directly effective Community law rights, the protection granted cannot make it impossible, in practice, to exercise those rights.[3] Injunctive or declaratory remedies can only provide future protection for Community law rights; they do not have any retrospective effect. Past loss or damage caused by a breach of Community law can only be effectively protected by the award of damages or restitution. It follows, therefore, that as a matter of Community law, where damages constitute the only effective remedy in a particular case, there is an obligation on the courts to ensure that such a remedy is available to the parties affected.[4]

---

[1] [1943] AC 92 at 106.

[2] See further at pp 35–37 for a discussion on the lack of horizontal direct effect of directives.

[3] Case 33/76 *Rewe-Zentralfinanz eG v Landwirtschaftskammer für Saarland* [1976] ECR 1989; Case 45/76 *Comet BV v Produktschap voor Siergewassen* [1976] ECR 2043. See pp 56–59.

[4] See the opinion of Advocate-General Mischo in Joined cases C–6/90 and C–9/90 *Francovich and Bonifaci v Italy* [1991] ECR I–5357. Similar reasoning was adopted by Lord Diplock in *Garden Cottage Foods Ltd v Milk Marketing Board* [1984] 1 AC 130 at 144A–145G. See also

Interest Where there is a right to damages as a result of a breach of Community law, the plaintiff is entitled to recover interest on any damages awarded to reflect the effluxion of time prior to judgment being obtained. The rate of interest remains within the discretion of the national court, provided that it reflects the plaintiff's right to obtain effective compensation.[5]

Causes of action The English courts have accepted that an actionable wrong is committed where an individual breaches a duty imposed on him by a directly effective provision of Community law. However, uncertainty remains as to how to categorise the nature of the breach and how to determine the relevant cause of action. A private action for damages for a breach of a directly effective provision of Community law could, potentially, be brought on the grounds of the following tortious causes of action:

    (a) breach of statutory duty;

    (b) economic torts; or

    (c) innominate torts.

Given the under-developed state of this area, it is advisable to plead alternative causes of action where possible (see Precedent A).

(a) Breach of statutory duty

(i) Breach of Community law categorised as breach of statutory duty

Garden Cottage Foods In *Garden Cottage Foods Ltd v Milk Marketing Board*[6] a majority of the House of Lords gave a very strong indication that damages are available to compensate loss suffered due to a breach of article 86 of the EEC Treaty. In this case, the Milk Marketing Board allegedly held a dominant position in the supply of bulk butter in England and Wales. When it refused to supply Garden Cottage Foods Ltd, the company brought an action in the English courts for, *inter alia*, an injunction, restraining the Milk Marketing Board from withholding supplies of butter. This refusal, it was argued, constituted an abuse of a dominant position contrary to article 86. Parker J, at first instance, refused to grant the injunction on the basis that damages would be an adequate remedy. When the case reached the House of Lords their Lordships had to consider the issue of whether damages could be awarded for a breach of article 86.

    Lord Diplock, with whom three other members of the House of Lords agreed, categorised a breach of article 86 as a breach of a statutory duty. He stated:[7]

Bourgoin SA v Ministry of Agriculture, Fisheries and Food [1986] 1 QB 716 at 770C–773E, per Oliver LJ (dissenting). See pp 53–54.

[5] Case C–271/91 *MH Marshall v Southampton and South-West Hampshire Area Health Authority* [1993] 3 CMLR 293. See also the Opinion of Advocate-General Van Gerven in Case C–128/92 *HJ Banks & Co Ltd v British Coal Corporation*, delivered on 27 October 1993; Case 130/79 *Express Dairy Foods Ltd v Intervention Board For Agricultural Produce* [1980] ECR 1887.

[6] [1984] 1 AC 130. See also the Opinion of Advocate-General Van Gerven in Case C–128/92 *HJ Banks & Co Ltd v British Coal Corporation*, delivered on 27 October 1993, where he stated that damages should in principle be awarded as a result of a breach of the competition rules set out in the ECSC Treaty.

[7] Above at 141 C–E.

This article of the Treaty of Rome (the E.E.C. Treaty) was held by the European Court of Justice in *Belgische Radio en Televisie v SV SABAM* (case 127/73) [1974] ECR 51, 62 to produce direct effects in relations between individuals and to create direct rights in respect of the individuals concerned which the national courts must protect. This decision of the European Court of Justice as to the effect of article 86 is one which section 3(1) of the European Communities Act 1972 requires your Lordships to follow. The rights which the article confers upon citizens in the United Kingdom accordingly fall within section 2(1) of the Act. They are without further enactment to be given legal effect in the United Kingdom and enforced accordingly.

A breach of the duty imposed by article 86 not to abuse a dominant position in the common market or in a substantial part of it, can thus be categorised in English law as a breach of statutory duty that is imposed not only for the purpose of promoting the general economic prosperity of the common market but also for the benefit of private individuals to whom loss or damage is caused by a breach of that duty.

It was, in his Lordship's view, unnecessary to invent new causes of action to deal with breaches of articles of the EEC Treaty. Furthermore, he could not see any other categorisation which could give rise to a civil cause of action in English private law on the part of a private individual who sustained loss or damage by reason of a breach of a directly effective provision of the EEC Treaty. Although his Lordship conceded that his categorisation was not beyond argument, he considered that if a breach of article 86 gives rise to a civil cause of action at all, it must be a cause of action for which damages are available. He stated:[8]

I, for my own part, find it difficult to see how it can ultimately be successfully argued ... that a contravention of article 86 which causes damage to an individual citizen does not give rise to a cause of action in English law of the nature of a cause of action for breach of statutory duty; but since it cannot be regarded as unarguable that is not a matter for final decision by your Lordships at the interlocutory stage that the instant case has reached. What, with great respect to those who think otherwise, I *do* regard as quite unarguable is the proposition ... that if such a contravention of article 86 gives rise to any cause of action at all, it gives rise to a cause of action for which there is no remedy in damages to compensate for loss already caused by that contravention but only a remedy by way of injunction to prevent future loss being caused.

Lord Wilberforce dissented. He considered that the question of whether damages were available for breach of article 86 was open to argument and he was not prepared to decide what he considered to be a difficult question of law during interlocutory proceedings. His Lordship stated:[9]

So far as the Community is concerned, article 86 is enforced under Regulation No 17 by orders to desist (article 3), and if necessary by fines (article 15), and the Court of Justice has similar powers on review. Fines are not payable to persons injured by the prohibited conduct, and there is no way under community law by which such persons can get damages. So the question is, whether the situation is changed, and the remedy extended, by the incorporation of article 86 into our law by section 2 of the European Communities Act 1972. To say that thereby what is prohibited action becomes a tort or a 'breach of statutory duty' is in my opinion, a conclusionary statement concealing a vital and unexpressed step. All that section 2 says (relevantly) is that rights arising

---

[8] Above at 144 B–D.
[9] Above at 151G–152D.

under the Treaty are to be available in law in the United Kingdom, but this does not suggest any transformation or enlargement in their character.

Subsequent cases Subsequent cases have adopted the approach of the majority of the House of Lords in *Garden Cottage Foods*. Thus, in *An Bord Bainne Co-operative v Milk Marketing Board*[10] Neil J stated that although the House of Lords in *Garden Cottage Foods* did not decide definitively that a breach of article 86 gives rise to a cause of action in English law:

> the speeches provide compelling support for the proposition that contraventions of EEC regulations which have 'direct effects' create direct rights in private law which the national courts must protect.

Similarly, in *Bourgoin SA v Ministry of Agriculture, Fisheries and Food*,[11] a case concerning article 30 of the EEC Treaty, Parker LJ considered that *Garden Cottage Foods* was 'clear authority that a private law action for breach of article 86 against an undertaking sounds in damages'. In *Plessey Co plc v General Electric Co plc and Siemens*[12] Morritt J stated:

> ... a breach of Article 85 is, in English law, the equivalent to the breach of a statutory duty imposed for the benefit of private individuals to whom loss or damage is caused by a breach of that duty. As *Garden Cottage Foods* makes plain, the rights so created in favour of individuals are ones which the national courts must protect by the normal remedies of damages or injunctions.

Breach of a directly effective provision of Community law which constitutes a breach of statutory duty has been described as a 'Eurotort'.[13]

(ii) Analysis of the tort
Definition Despite the speech of Lord Diplock in *Garden Cottage Foods*, the principles upon which a breach of a directly effective right becomes a breach of a statutory duty remain unclear. For example, in *Bourgoin SA v Ministry of Agriculture, Fisheries and Food*[14] the Court of Appeal held that a breach of article 30 of the EEC Treaty by the Ministry of Agriculture, Fisheries and Food was not a breach of a statutory duty, despite the fact that article 30 has direct effect. Consequently, whether breach of statutory duty is the appropriate cause of action for a breach of directly effective provisions of Community law is open to debate. In order to establish a cause of action based on breach of statutory duty, a plaintiff must show that:[15]

    (1) the loss suffered is within the scope of the statute;
    (2) the statute gives rise to a civil cause of action;

---

[10] [1984] 1 CMLR 519 at 528.
[11] [1986] 1 QB 716 at 787D. Nourse LJ, at 790D–E, stated that he was in 'entire agreement' with this view.
[12] [1990] ECC 384 at 393, 394. See also: *Cutsforth v Mansfield Inns Ltd* [1986] 1 WLR 558 at 563G, per Sir Neil Lawson; *Argyll Group v The Distillers Co* [1986] 1 CMLR 764 at 767 and 769, per Lord Jauncey; *Merson v Rover Group* judgment of 22 May 1992, unreported.
[13] Henry J in *Barretts & Baird (Wholesale) v IPCS* [1987] IRLR 3 at 5.
[14] [1986] 1 QB 716, discussed at pp 78–81.
[15] See, generally, *Clerk and Lindsell on Torts*, 16th edn (Sweet & Maxwell, 1989) Ch 14.

(3) there has been a breach of statutory duty; and

(4) the breach has caused the loss complained of.

(1) Loss suffered is within the scope of the statute

Imposition of a duty Whether the loss suffered is within the scope of the statute depends upon whether the statute imposes a duty for the benefit of the particular individual harmed. At common law, where a duty is imposed for the benefit of individuals, a correlative right arises in those persons who may be injured by its contravention.[16] The statutory duty need not be owed to a particular class of persons, but can be owed to persons generally. Thus, in *Monk v Warbey*[17] the Court of Appeal held that a statutory duty imposed by the Road Traffic Acts, to insure vehicles, was for the benefit of all road users.

Concept of direct effect The concept of direct effect appears neatly to satisfy this first condition to establish a cause of action. A directly effective provision of Community law imposes, upon one person, a clear and unconditional obligation, which in turn creates rights in others to whom that duty is owed. As the Court of Justice has stated, a directly effective provision of Community law is:[18]

> a direct source of rights and duties for all those affected thereby, whether Member States or individuals, who are parties to legal relationships under Community law.

These rights are fundamental rights since Community law:[19]

> not only imposes obligations on individuals but is also intended to confer upon them rights which become part of their legal heritage.

Since s 2(1) of the European Communities Act 1972 provides the statutory basis for the recognition of directly effective rights and duties in the English legal system, any breach of a directly effective Community provision by a private party can be said to constitute a breach of the statutory duty imposed by the European Communities Act 1972. Therefore, Lord Diplock's analysis in this respect appears to be sound.

(2) Statute gives rise to a civil cause of action

Duty to protect Since national courts are bound to protect directly effective rights which are conferred on individuals, any breach of a directly effective provision of Community law must, *a fortiori*, give rise to a civil cause of action.

Other means of protection In English law, a civil cause of action may be denied where the right conferred by the statute is protected in some other way, for example, by a criminal sanction.[20] It is clear that Community law rights may

---

[16] *Butler v Fife Coal Co Ltd* [1912] AC 149 at 165, per Lord Kinnear.

[17] [1935] 1 KB 75. See also Atkin LJ in *Phillips v Britannia Hygienic Laundry Co* [1923] 2 KB 832 at 841.

[18] Case 106/77 *Administrazione Delle Finanze dello Stato v Simmenthal SpA* [1978] ECR 629 para 15.

[19] Case 26/62 *Van Gend en Loos v Nederlandse administratie der belastinge (Netherlands Inland Revenue Administration)* [1963] ECR 1 at 12.

[20] *Lonrho Ltd v Shell Petroleum Co Ltd (No 2)* [1982] AC 173: *Monk v Warbey* [1935] 1 KB 75.

be protected by other means. The Commission or Member States, respectively, may bring proceedings before the Court of Justice under article 169 or 170 of the EEC Treaty for a declaration that a Member State is in breach of its Treaty obligations. In relation to competition law, the Commission may act pursuant to Regulation 17, ordering the termination of a restrictive practice or imposing fines for breach of the competition rules.[21] However, these other means of protecting directly effective rights cannot prevent individuals from invoking their rights before the national courts. As the Court of Justice stated in Case 26/62 *Van Gend En Loos v Nederlandse administratie der belastungen (Netherlands Inland Revenue Administration)*:[22]

> ...the argument based on Article 169 and 170 of the Treaty put forward by the three Governments which have submitted observations to the Court in their statements of case is misconceived. The fact that these Articles of the Treaty enable the Commission and the Member States to bring before the Court a State which has not fulfilled its obligations does not mean that individuals cannot plead these obligations, should the occasion arise, before a national court, any more than the fact that the Treaty places at the disposal of the Commission ways of ensuring that obligations imposed upon those subject to the Treaty are observed, precludes the possibility, in actions between individuals before a national court, of pleading infringements of these obligations.
>
> A restriction of the guarantees against an infringement of Article 12 by Member States to the procedures under Article 169 and 170 would remove all direct legal protection of the individual rights of their nationals. There is the risk that recourse to the procedure under these Articles would be ineffective if it were to occur after the implementation of a national decision taken contrary to the provisions of the Treaty.

(3) Breach of the statutory duty

Strict liability Liability for breach of statutory duty is usually strict or absolute. However, the courts have occasionally rejected a plaintiff's claim on the basis that the defendant took all reasonable steps to comply with the duty or on the basis that the breach was unavoidable. Whether liability depends on fault or not is determined by the true construction of the statute.[23] By contrast, since directly effective provisions of Community law, by definition, impose clear and unconditional duties, liability for breach of statutory duty in respect of Community law is likely to be strict or absolute. A breach of Community law is examined objectively and requires no examination of reasonableness.[24] For

---

[21] Council Regulation No 17/62 of 6 February 1962, First Regulation implementing articles 85 and 86 of the EEC Treaty (as amended), OJ No 13, 21 February 1962, p 204 (Special Edition 1959–1962, p 87).

[22] [1963] ECR 1 at 13. See also Case 28/67 *Firma Molkerei-Zentrale Westfalen/Lippe GmbH v Hauptzollamt Paderborn* [1968] ECR 143. In respect of competition matters see Case 127/73 *BRT v SABAM* [1974] ECR 51 at 63; and Lord Diplock in *Garden Cottage Foods Ltd v Milk Marketing Board* [1984] 1 AC 130 at 146H.

[23] See *Clerk and Lindsell on Torts*, 16th edn (Sweet & Maxwell, 1989) para 14–14.

[24] See p 164 for a discussion of the objective nature of Member States' failure to fulfil EEC Treaty obligations in the context of article 169.

example, there is no scope for an English court to hold that, on the true construction of article 86, an undertaking is not in breach because it has acted reasonably.

(4) Breach has caused the loss

Causation The plaintiff must show that, on a balance of probabilities, the breach of duty caused, or materially contributed to, his loss.[25] This is a simple, factual, 'but for' test of causation: would the damage have occurred but for the breach? Unlike in the tort of negligence, it is not necessary to prove that the damage was a reasonably foreseeable result of the breach. Furthermore, damages for economic loss may be recovered in an action for a breach of statutory duty.

Co-extensive duties on defendant and plaintiff The situation may arise where both the plaintiff and the defendant are under a statutory duty not to breach a directly effective provision of Community law. For example, an agreement between a supplier and a distributor may contain an export ban prohibiting the distributor from selling outside the contract territory. If the export ban is subsequently invalidated as being contrary to article 85 of the EEC Treaty, which prohibits agreements which distort competition in the Common Market and which affect trade between Member States, can the distributor sue the supplier in damages for lost sales? It could be argued that, since both parties to the contract are under a duty not to breach article 85, the distributor might be unable to recover. As Lord Diplock stated in *Boyle v Kodak*,[26] 'To say "you are liable to me for my own wrongdoing" is neither good morals nor good law'. However, in order to determine whether this defence is available to the defendant in this situation, the courts seek to ascertain who is primarily at fault. If it is decided that the breach was entirely the fault of the plaintiff, the plaintiff cannot recover; but, where the plaintiff is not entirely to blame, the courts may apportion liability and award the plaintiff damages, albeit subject to a reduction.[27] As a result, it is arguable that, in the above example, the distributor may recover some of his loss, which was caused by the export ban, especially where the distributor is in a weaker bargaining position or has signed on the supplier's standard terms and conditions.

Moreover, it is unlikely that in the above example the defendant supplier could successfully rely on the defence of *ex turpi causa non oritur actio*. Although the plaintiff distributor may need to prove the unlawfulness of the export ban to found a claim, arguably there is no affront to the public conscience that the weaker or innocent party, not being *in pari delicto*, should be allowed to recover his loss.[28] Obviously, different considerations may apply where one

---

[25] See *Bonnington Castings Ltd v Wardlaw* [1956] 1 AC 613. See also *Clerk and Lindsell on Torts*, 16th edn (Sweet & Maxwell, 1989) para 14–16.

[26] [1969] 1 WLR 661 at 673. See also *Ginty v Belmont Building Supplies Ltd* [1959] 1 All ER 414; *Ross v Associated Portland Cement Manufacturers* [1964] 1 WLR 768.

[27] In *Boyle v Kodak* the plaintiff was awarded one half of the sum assessed as damages, to take account of his breach of statutory duty.

[28] This being the appropriate test. See generally *Shelley v Paddock* [1980] 1 QB 348; *Thackwell v*

member of a price fixing cartel sues the other members for loss suffered as a result of its operation.

(iii) Limitations on policy grounds?

The problem The wide class of individuals to whom a statutory duty may be owed, the absolute nature of breach and the 'but for' test of causation potentially expose a defendant to an indeterminate amount of damages payable to an indeterminate number of plaintiffs. The exposure to such liability for what may be an unintentional breach of a directly effective provision of Community law raises doubts as to the suitability of breach of statutory duty as the relevant cause of action against a private party. The courts may, therefore, need to refine the conditions for liability.

Reasonableness One possible limitation would be to recognise that not every breach of directly effective Community law necessarily gives rise to a right to damages. It remains to be seen whether the EC courts would accept a defence of reasonableness, on policy grounds, in order to avoid strict liability in cases where an unintentional breach of Community law might incur massive liability for the defendant; for example, private water companies supplying water contrary to EC health standards.[29]

Remoteness Another possible limitation would be to relax the 'but for' test for causation, the danger of which is particularly relevant in the competition field. For example, if a dominant manufacturer sets a price for its products which is held to be excessive and abusive, who can sue the company for breach of article 86—wholesalers, retailers, the ultimate consumer? In order to avoid such a situation, the courts may have to adopt a stricter approach to causation and award damages only to those who have suffered as a direct consequence of the unlawful conduct. The requirement of a close causal link would prevent recovery for damage which is too remote. This is the approach of the Court of Justice in actions for damages against Community institutions under article 215 of the EEC Treaty.[30] It is also the approach adopted by Advocate-General Van Gerven in *HJ Banks & Co Ltd v British Coal Corporation* in relation to damages for breach of the competition rules under the ECSC Treaty.[31]

Barclays Bank [1986] 1 All ER 676; *Saunders v Edwards* [1987] 1 WLR 1116; *Euro-Diam Ltd v Bathurst* [1990] 1 QB 1; *Howard v Shirlstar Container Transport Ltd* [1990] 1 WLR 1292; *Tinsley v Milligan* [1993] 3 WLR 126.

[29] By analogy with *Read v Croydon Corporation* [1938] 4 All ER 631 at 651 (where a statutory duty to supply pure water was construed as a duty to take all reasonable care). See also *Atkinson v Newcastle and Gateshead Waterworks Co* (1877) LR 2 Ex D 441.

[30] See pp 235–237.

[31] Opinion of Advocate-General Van Gerven in Case C–128/92 *HJ Banks & Co Ltd v British Coal Corporation*, delivered on 27 October 1993.

(b) Economic torts

(i) Unlawful interference with trade or business

Nature of the tort The tort of unlawful interference with trade or business is a relatively recent judicial development.[32] Although the precise limits of the tort have still to be defined, it appears that in order to establish a right to damages for unlawful interference, it is necessary to show:

(1) that there was an unlawful act;

(2) which foreseeably caused injury to the interests of another or which was done with the intention of harming another.

Unlawful act In *Lonrho plc v Fayed*[33] Dillon LJ indicated that the mere fact that an act is in breach of a statutory prohibition does not render it 'unlawful' for the purposes of the tort of unlawful interference. The complainant must show that on its true construction the statute which imposes the prohibition gives rise to a civil remedy. Since directly effective Community provisions create rights for individuals which the English courts are bound to protect, breach of a directly effective provision should be considered 'unlawful' for the purposes of this tort. The considerations underlying 'an unlawful act' are similar to the first two conditions necessary to satisfy a breach of statutory duty.[34] Indeed, in *Barretts & Baird (Wholesale) v IPCS*[35] Henry J considered that a breach of statutory duty was, itself, unlawful.

Intention/Foreseeability It is not necessary to prove that the predominant purpose of the tortfeasor was to injure the victim. In *Lonrho plc v Fayed*[36] Dillon LJ held that 'It has to be proved by a plaintiff who seeks to rely on this tort ... that the unlawful act was in some sense directed against the plaintiff or intended to harm the plaintiff'. Woolf LJ stated that 'If a defendant has deliberately embarked upon a course of conduct, the probable consequences of which to the plaintiff he appreciated, I do not see why the plaintiff should not be compensated'. It is the requirement that there be some degree of intention or foreseeability which distinguishes this tort from the tort of breach of statutory duty. From a plaintiff's point of view, breach of statutory duty is easier to establish. In suitable cases, a defendant may be advised to argue that the tort of unlawful interference with trade is the more appropriate cause of action for breach of a directly effective provision, especially given the potentially wide ambit of breach of statutory duty.[37]

---

[32] See *JT Stratford & Son Ltd v Lindley* [1965] AC 269, per Lord Reid at 324, per Viscount Radcliffe at 328; *Merkur Island Shipping Corp v Laughton* [1983] 2 AC 570, per Lord Diplock at 609, 610; *Lonrho plc v Fayed* [1990] 2 QB 479 (the House of Lords affirmed the decision on other grounds). See also *Clerk and Lindsell on Torts*, 16th edn (Sweet & Maxwell, 1989) paras 15–19, 15–20.

[33] [1990] 2 QB 479 at 488E–G.

[34] Namely, (1) the loss suffered is within the scope of the statute; and (2) the statute gives rise to a civil cause of action. See pp 65–67.

[35] [1987] IRLR 3 at 6.

[36] *Lonrho plc v Fayed* [1990] 2 QB 479 at 489E, 494D.

[37] See pp 67–69.

Examples The tort of unlawful interference could form the basis of a cause of action where a company in a dominant position is engaged in a campaign of predatory pricing, with the specific intention of driving a competitor out of the market or of dissuading a potential competitor from entering that market. The tort could also arise where a supplier gave instructions to his distributors not to supply a particular company which wished to undertake parallel imports of the goods concerned.

(ii) Conspiracy

Nature of the tort Liability for civil conspiracy may take two forms:[38]

(1) where two or more parties combine, with the predominant intention of causing injury to another, even though the means used are lawful; or

(2) where two or more parties intentionally injure another by use of unlawful means, even if their primary purpose is to further or protect their own interests.[39]

Example The tort of conspiracy may be applicable to the operation of a cartel. A claim based on the second type of civil conspiracy might be appropriate where there has been a breach of article 85, for example, where a group of companies enter into a price-fixing agreement in an attempt to gain an advantage over other competitors. Although the primary purpose of the participants in the cartel may be to retain market share and protect their own interests, their conduct may be tortious if there is also an intent to injure a competitor. Consequently, any competitor which suffers loss as a result of the cartel may seek to rely on the tort of conspiracy. Breach of statutory duty should be pleaded in the alternative, as the necessary conditions are easier to satisfy.

(c) Innominate torts

Rejection of the concept In *Application des Gaz SA v Falks Veritas Ltd*[40] Lord Denning MR stated, *obiter*, that as articles 85 and 86 of the EEC Treaty have direct effect, they are part of English law and create new torts or wrongs called 'undue restriction of competition within the common market' and 'abuse of dominant position within the common market'. However, this approach of creating new torts to compensate for breaches of Community law was firmly rejected by Lord Diplock in *Garden Cottage Foods Ltd v Milk Marketing Board*[41] who stated that there was no reason to invent a wholly novel cause of action in order to deal with breaches of articles of the EEC Treaty which have the same

---

[38] *Lonrho Plc v Fayed* [1991] 3 WLR 188 contains a thorough analysis of the relevant case law. See also *Clerk and Lindsell on Torts*, 16th edn (Sweet & Maxwell, 1989) paras 15-21–15-26.

[39] The same arguments applicable to 'unlawful means' in the context of the tort of unlawful interference should also apply to the tort of conspiracy. See p 70.

[40] [1974] 1 Ch 381 at 395H–396C. See also the judgment of Lord Denning MR in *Garden Cottage Foods Ltd v Milk Marketing Board* [1982] 3 WLR 514 at 516B–G.

[41] [1984] 1 AC 130 at 144F–G. See also the doubts expressed by Roskill LJ in *Valor International Limited v Application des Gaz SA* [1978] 3 CMLR 87 at 99, 100.

effect in the United Kingdom as statutes. Furthermore, in *Bourgoin SA v Ministry of Agriculture, Fisheries and Food*[42] Mann J, at first instance, described the formulation of a claim based on an innominate tort as 'obsolete'. Although the above authorities appear to indicate that a claim pleaded on the basis of an 'innominate tort' would have little chance of success, this basis of liability cannot be discounted since it has not yet been definitively decided what the correct cause of action is for a breach of a directly effective provision of Community law.

2. ACTIONS AGAINST THE STATE

(a) General principles of liability

Principle of State liability National courts must have jurisdiction to award damages against the State if the State causes harm to individuals in breach of Community law. The principle of State liability was established by the Court of Justice in Joined Cases C–6/90, C–9/90 *Francovich and Bonifaci v Italy*[43] where it was held that:

> it is a principle of Community law that the Member States are obliged to make good loss and damage caused to individuals by breaches of Community law for which they can be held responsible.

Basis of liability The principle of State liability is based on two premises. First, it is inherent in the EEC Treaty, and particularly article 5, that Member States take all appropriate measures to ensure fulfilment of their EEC Treaty obligations, which includes nullifying any unlawful consequences due to their breach of Community law.[44] Secondly, State liability is based on the principle of effective protection of Community law rights. As the Court stated in *Francovich*:[45]

> ... it has been consistently held that the national courts whose task it is to apply the provisions of Community law in areas within their jurisdiction must ensure that those rules take full effect and must protect the rights which they confer on individuals ...
>
> The full effectiveness of Community rules would be impaired and the protection of the rights which they grant would be weakened if individuals were unable to obtain redress when their rights are infringed by a breach of Community law for which a Member State can be held responsible.

Limitation on policy grounds? The scope of the principle of State liability is, potentially, very far-reaching. Breaches of Community law by Member States are ascertained objectively; there is no element of fault involved in determining

---

[42] [1986] 1 QB 716 at 734B–F, following a concession by counsel. See the comments of Oliver LJ in [1986] 1 QB 716 at 775C–G.

[43] [1991] ECR I–5357 paras 31–37. See also Case 60/75 *Russo v AIMA* [1976] ECR 45 para 9 and Case 6/60 *Humblet v Belgium* [1960] ECR 559 for State liability under the ECSC Treaty.

[44] Joined Cases C–6/90, C–9/90 *Francovich and Bonifaci v Italy* [1991] ECR I–5357 para 36.

[45] Ibid paras 32, 33. For the principle of effective protection see Ch 5.

a breach.[46] If State liability in damages is based purely on breach, Member States may be faced with liability 'in an indeterminate amount for an indeterminate time to an indeterminate class'[47] in respect of legislative, quasi-legislative, or administrative acts. In order to avoid this situation, the principle of State liability may need to be limited on policy grounds by introducing some element of culpability. It is thought that this would be consistent with the principle of effective protection.[48]

Advocate-General Mischo in *Francovich* considered that State liability should be subject to the same conditions as the grant of damages by the Court of Justice, under Article 215 of the EEC Treaty for breach of Community law by a Community institution. On this basis, a Member State would not be liable for the adoption of a legislative measure unless a sufficiently serious breach of a superior rule of law for the protection of the individual could be shown; mere unlawfulness of the measure would not suffice. The rationale for the stricter test is based on policy considerations. State authorities should not be unduly hindered in making decisions by the spectre of indeterminate liability and individuals must accept that their economic interests may be affected by State measures adopted in the public interest. This risk is not so great in purely administrative measures and, consequently, the Court of Justice does not require the stricter test to be satisfied when a plaintiff is seeking damages for an administrative measure adopted by the Community.[49]

If this approach were adopted by the English courts, it should be noted that not every provision of Community law would constitute a superior rule of law for the protection of the individual. Arguably, discrimination on the ground of nationality contrary to article 7 of the EEC Treaty would be such a rule, whereas a breach of a directive harmonising labelling laws would not be. Indeed, the Court of Appeal has already drawn on article 215 principles in holding that not every breach of Community law gives rise to a cause of action in damages. In *Bourgoin v Ministry of Agriculture, Fisheries and Food*[50] the majority of the Court of Appeal held that an abusive breach of article 30 of the EEC Treaty had to be proved before the Ministry could be held liable in damages. The policy consideration of not unduly hindering Member States in taking legislative action was illustrated by Parker LJ in the following example. A Member State may be advised by experts that a particular drug has harmful side effects which makes it necessary to impose an import ban on health grounds. The Court of

---

[46] Case 415/85 *Commission v Ireland* [1988] ECR 3097 para 9; Case 416/85 *Commission v United Kingdom* [1988] ECR 3127 para 9; Case C–209/89 *Commission v Italy* [1991] ECR I–1591 para 6. See pp 164–166.

[47] *Ultramares Corporation v Touche* [1931] 174 NE 441 at 444, per Cardozo J.

[48] See p 59.

[49] Joined Cases C–6/90, C–9/90 *Francovich and Bonifaci v Italy* [1991] ECR I–5357 para 71 of the Opinion. This policy argument has been accepted by the Court of Justice in the context of tortious liability of Community institutions under article 215 of the EEC Treaty. See Joined Cases 83/76, 94/76, 4/77, 15/77, 40/77 *Bayerische HNL Vermehrungsbetriebe GmbH & Co KG v Council and Commission* [1978] ECR 1209; Case 143/77 *Koninklijke Scholten Honig NV v Council and Commission* [1979] ECR 3583. Discussed further in Ch 15.

[50] [1986] 1 QB 716. See p 78.

Justice, after hearing a mass of conflicting evidence, rules that the ban cannot be so justified and that it is contrary to article 30 of the EEC Treaty. In such a case, the mere breach of article 30 would render the Member State liable for substantial damages which, in his Lordship's view, was an untenable proposition.

Conditions of liability In contrast to Advocate-General Mischo, the Court of Justice in *Francovich* declined to lay down general conditions of State liability, merely indicating that the right to compensation depends 'on the nature of the breach of Community law giving rise to the harm'.[51] In the absence of any Community legislation or ruling by the Court of Justice laying down the conditions for State liability, the national courts must apply their own conditions of liability, provided that they are not less favourable than those relating to similar claims under national law (ie not involving Community law) and do not make it virtually impossible or excessively difficult to obtain compensation.[52] Thus, subject to these requirements of Community law, it is for national courts to determine the cause of action appropriate for the claim in damages and to rule on issues such as the foreseeability, remoteness and quantum of damage.[53] The emphasis by the Court of Justice on 'the nature of the breach' leaves it open to national courts to adopt Advocate-General Mischo's approach or impose some other limitation to reflect the State's culpability. It also means that the conditions of liability may differ according to whether the State has adopted an act contrary to Community law, whether it has failed to abolish an act which is contrary to Community law, whether it has failed to implement a directive or whether it has incorrectly implemented a directive. Moreover, different causes of action may apply, depending on the nature of the breach.

State acting *qua* state Different considerations will apply depending on whether the State is acting in a public or private capacity. For example, if the Government fails to implement a directive on sex discrimination, the claims by its own employees for damages for sex discrimination based on the direct effect of the directive will probably be different in nature to any damages claims brought against it by other employees of private parties in respect of the failure to implement the directive.[54]

Interest Where an individual obtains damages against the State for breach of Community law, the individual is entitled to recover interest on any damages awarded to reflect the effluxion of time prior to judgment being obtained. The rate of interest remains within the discretion of the national court, provided that it reflects the individual's right to obtain effective compensation.[55]

---

[51] Joined cases C–6/90, C–9/90 *Francovich and Bonifaci v Italy* [1991] ECR I–5357 para 38.

[52] Ibid paras 42, 43. See pp 56–59.

[53] Opinion of Advocate-General Van Gerven in Case C–271/91 *MH Marshall v Southampton and South-West Hampshire Area Health Authority (No 2)* [1993] 3 CMLR 293. See also the Opinion of Advocate-General Van Gerven in Case C–128/92 *HJ Banks & Co Ltd v British Coal Corporation*, delivered on 27 October 1993.

[54] Indeed, the public employees may have a dual line of attack: one based on the direct effect of the directive and the other based on failure to implement the directive.

[55] Case C–271/91 *MH Marshall v Southampton and South-West Hampshire Area Health Authority*

(b) Potential causes of action in English law

Causes of action English case law in relation to State liability in damages is
under-developed. In *Bourgoin SA v Ministry of Agriculture, Fisheries and
Food*[56] the Court of Appeal held that the relevant cause of action for a breach of
Community law by the Ministry was misfeasance in public office. This case
concerned the allegedly abusive revocation of a system of licences by the Minister, who was acting pursuant to a statutory power. The tort of misfeasance in
public office, therefore, appeared a legitimate cause of action to deal with this
kind of malpractice. The case of *Bourgoin* was decided before *Francovich* and
before it was realised that the United Kingdom could be liable in damages for
failing to comply with Community law. There is now doubt whether *Bourgoin*
remains good law and whether misfeasance in public office is apt to cover all
types of breach of Community law for which the United Kingdom may be liable
in damages.[57] Consequently, when considering whether to bring an action
against the State in the English courts all of the following causes of action
should be considered (see Precedent B):

    (1) misfeasance in public office;
    (2) breach of statutory duty;
    (3) innominate tort; and
    (4) negligence.

(i) Misfeasance in public office

Definition In order to found a cause of action upon the tort of misfeasance in
public office, it is necessary to prove either malice or actual knowledge of the
ultra vires or unlawful act.[58] Malice and knowledge are alternatives. As Mann J
stated in *Bourgoin*:[59]

> There is no sensible distinction between the case where an officer performs an act
> which he has no power to perform with the object of injuring A (which the defendant
> accepts is actionable at the instance of A) and the case where an officer performs an
> act which he knows he has no power to perform with the object of conferring a bene-
> fit on B but which has the foreseeable and actual consequence of injury to A (which
> the defendant denies is actionable at the instance of A).

The Court of Appeal unanimously agreed with this proposition. Oliver LJ
stated:[60]

    [1993] 3 CMLR 293. Also Case 130/79 *Express Dairy Foods Ltd v Intervention Board For Agri-
cultural Produce* [1980] ECR 1887.
[56] [1986] 1 QB 716.
[57] See pp 78–81.
[58] It appears that actual knowledge must be proved; *Everett v Griffiths* [1921] AC 631 at 695, per
Lord Moulton.
[59] *Bourgoin SA v Ministry of Agriculture, Fisheries and Food* [1986] 1 QB 716 at 740E–F. See *R v
Secretary of State for the Environment ex p Hackney London Borough Council* [1983] 1 WLR
524 at 539, per May LJ; *Dunlop v Woolahra Municipal Council* [1982] AC 158 at 172E, per Lord
Diplock; *Calveley v Chief Constable of the Merseyside Police* [1989] AC 1228 at 1240C–D, per
Lord Bridge. See also Wade, *Administrative Law*, 6th edn (Oxford University Press, 1988),
pp 777–783.
[60] *Bourgoin SA v Ministry of Agriculture, Fisheries and Food* [1986] 1 QB 716 at 777H.

If an act is done deliberately and with knowledge of its consequences, I do not think that the actor can sensibly say that he did not 'intend' the consequences or that the act was not 'aimed' at the persons who, it is known, will suffer them.

Public office In general, a person will be said to hold a public office where he discharges a duty for the benefit of the public and does not act for private profit.[61] There is, however, no precise definition of public office and it is questionable whether the English courts would hold that nationalised and privatised companies could be liable for misfeasance in public office, albeit that they may constitute an 'emanation of the State' as defined by the Court of Justice.[62]

Legislative and administrative acts: A claim for misfeasance in public office is available regardless of whether the abusive act complained of is legislative, quasi-legislative or purely administrative in nature.[63]

Damages Misfeasance in public office is a tort which sounds in damages. It may also be appropriate to include a claim for exemplary damages. In *Rookes v Barnard*,[64] Lord Devlin indicated that exemplary damages could be awarded in respect of 'oppressive, arbitrary or unconstitutional action by the servants of the government'. However, it is only abuse of governmental or executive power which gives rise to exemplary damages, not an abuse by a nationalised body, albeit that it might constitute an emanation of the state as defined by the Court of Justice.[65]

Vicarious liability The State can be vicariously liable for the tort of misfeasance in public office committed by a public officer. Thus, in *Racz v Home Office*[66] the House of Lords held that the Home Office could be vicariously liable for unauthorized acts of prison officers that amounted to misfeasance in public office. Similarly, it has been held that Government departments may be sued in the tort of misfeasance in public office where the minister has knowingly introduced protectionist legislation in breach of Community law.[67]

(ii) Breach of statutory duty
Definition In order to establish a cause of action based on breach of statutory duty, a plaintiff must show that:
(1) the loss suffered is within the scope of the statute;

---

[61] *Halsbury's Laws of England*, 4th edn (Butterworths, 1989), Vol 1(1), paras 6–9.
[62] Case 188/89 *A Foster v British Gas Corporation* [1990] ECR I–3313. See further at pp 37–39.
[63] *An Bord Bainne Co-operative Limited v Milk Marketing Board* [1988] 1 CMLR 605 paras 18–36. Compare the position under article 215 of the EEC Treaty, where the Court of Justice has drawn a distinction between legislative and administrative measures. Discussed further at p 231.
[64] [1964] AC 1129 at 1226, per Lord Devlin.
[65] *AB v South West Water Services Ltd* [1993] 2 WLR 507. For discussion of the definition of what constitutes an emanation of the State see pp 37–39.
[66] [1994] 2 WLR 23.
[67] For example *Bourgoin v Ministry of Agriculture, Fisheries and Food* [1986] 1 QB 716. As to the relationship between Ministers and the Crown see, generally, *M v Home Office* [1993] 3 WLR 433 where the House of Lords held that it was appropriate to make a finding of contempt against a government department or minister of the Crown acting in his official capacity, where an individual minister had committed acts which amounted to a contempt.

(2) the statute gives rise to a civil cause of action;

(3) there has been a breach of statutory duty; and

(4) the breach has caused the loss complained of.

Direct effect A breach of a directly effective provision of Community law by the State can be categorised as a breach of s 2(1) of the European Communities Act 1972 and, thus, a breach of statutory duty giving rise to a civil cause of action.[68] Breach of statutory duty was accepted by the House of Lords in *Garden Cottage Foods Ltd v Milk Marketing Board*[69] as the correct cause of action in cases concerning private law rights (*in casu* article 86 of the EEC Treaty), but was rejected by the Court of Appeal in *Bourgoin* as the correct cause of action in cases concerning public law rights (*in casu* article 30 of the EEC Treaty). Nevertheless, following the judgment of the Court of Justice in *Francovich and Bonifaci v Italy*[70], this tort cannot be discounted and should be pleaded in all actions for damages against the State.

Breach of statutory duty by the Crown Section 2(2) of the Crown Proceedings Act 1947 provides that the Crown is liable for breach of statutory duty where the duty is binding also upon persons other than the Crown and its officers. Attempts by the Crown to exclude liability for breaches of Community law by reference to this section have not succeeded. In *Bourgoin SA v Ministry of Agriculture, Fisheries and Food*[71] the Crown relied on s 2(2), arguing that it could not be liable for breach of statutory duty in infringing article 30 of the EEC Treaty because this article only imposes a duty on Member States. This argument was rejected. Oliver LJ noted that, as well as imposing obligations on the State to ensure the free movement of goods, this article also imposes obligations on private parties in respect of the exercise of intellectual property rights. In any event, even if article 30 had bound only the Crown, Oliver LJ indicated that s 2(2) would have been overridden by the principle of supremacy of Community law.

(iii) Innominate torts

Special duty If existing causes of action known to English law are considered inappropriate, it will be necessary to invent a new cause of action to deal with the special duty imposed by Community law on the State to comply with Community law and not to infringe individuals' directly effective rights. The innominate tort has not found favour with the courts. At first instance in *Bourgoin SA v Ministry of Agriculture, Fisheries and Food*,[72] following a concession by counsel for the plaintiff, Mann J described the formulation of a claim based on an

---

[68] For a discussion of breach of statutory duty see pp 63–69.

[69] [1984] AC 130.

[70] [1991] ECR I–5357.

[71] [1985] 3 WLR 1027 at 1073G–1075B, per Oliver LJ. In *An Bord Bainne Co-operative Ltd v Milk Marketing Board* [1988] 1 CMLR 605, the argument was advanced but not fully developed.

[72] [1986] 1 QB 716 at 734B–F. See also the comments of Oliver LJ at 775C–G. See also pp 71–72 in respect of private law actions.

innominate tort as 'obsolete'. However, due to the uncertain state of the law determining the relevant causes of action with regard to State liability, this tort cannot be ignored. Indeed, pleadings in national proceedings often allege a breach of 'a special duty' not to infringe Community law as a catch-all cause of action.

(iv) Negligence

A further cause of action against the State, which appears to have been largely ignored, is the negligent exercise of statutory power.[73] This tort is flexible enough to impose liability for the negligent, but *bona fide*, exercise of discretionary power. However, it is doubtful whether the courts will recognise a duty of care not to breach Community law in the light of the restrictions placed on the development of the tort of negligence. Novel categories of negligence are now developed incrementally and by analogy with established categories.[74] Moreover, the courts have been reluctant to impose a duty of care on public authorities not to breach their statutory powers on the basis that the developed law of misfeasance in public office would be rendered 'otiose'.[75]

(c) Adoption of acts contrary to Community law

(i) Breach of Community law categorised as misfeasance in public office
Bourgoin In *Bourgoin SA v Ministry of Agriculture, Fisheries and Food*[76] the Ministry of Agriculture, Fisheries and Food (MAFF) introduced a system of licences for the import of turkeys into the United Kingdom. This restricted the import from countries where Newcastle disease, to which turkeys are prone, was controlled by vaccination rather than slaughter. The effect of the system was to prevent the import of turkeys from France, with the result that the plaintiffs, who were French turkey producers, were no longer able to trade in the United Kingdom. In subsequent proceedings brought by the Commission under article 169 of the EEC Treaty, the Court of Justice held that the system constituted a restriction on inter-state trade, contrary to article 30. The ban could not be justified on animal health grounds under article 36. The Court found, as a fact, that the ban was not part of a seriously considered health policy, but was in reality a disguised restriction on trade designed to protect British poultry producers from French competition.[77]

After the Court of Justice's judgment, MAFF revoked the system, thus allowing the import of French turkeys to resume. The plaintiffs, thereupon, sued MAFF for £19 million in lost sales. The plaintiffs claimed damages for: (1) breach of statutory duty; (2) commission of an innominate tort and (3) mis-

---

[73] See, generally, *Halsbury's Laws of England* 4th edn (Butterworths, 1989), Vol 1(1) para 204; and Salmond and Heuston, *The Law of Torts*, 20th edn (Sweet & Maxwell, 1992), 242–244.

[74] See *Caparo Industries plc v Dickman* [1990] 2 AC 605 and *Murphy v Brentwood District Council* [1991] 1 AC 398.

[75] Hirst J in *Irish Aerospace v Eurocontrol* [1992] 1 Lloyds Rep 383 at 401.

[76] [1986] 1 QB 716.

[77] Case 40/82 *Commission v United Kingdom* [1982] ECR 2793.

feasance in public office. Mann J, at first instance, held that (1) and (3) disclosed a cause of action, but (2) did not. The Court of Appeal agreed with Mann J that (2) disclosed no cause of action and that (3) did. However, a majority (Parker LJ and Norse LJ, Oliver LJ dissenting) held that (1) disclosed no reasonable cause of action.

Mere breach does not constitute a breach of statutory duty or an innominate tort The majority in *Bourgoin* considered that a mere breach of article 30 could not constitute a tort.[78] Although the House of Lords in *Garden Cottage Foods* had indicated that a breach of article 86 constituted a breach of statutory duty, this case was distinguished on the ground that it did not involve the liability of a Member State and was not, therefore, concerned with public law. Parker LJ held that the right conferred on individuals by article 30 lay in the public law field, not the private law field and, consequently, only the remedy of judicial review was available for a mere breach of article 30 by a Member State. This view was justified on the ground that the Community itself could not be liable in damages for a mere breach of the EEC Treaty; instead it is necessary to prove that the institution has committed a 'sufficiently serious breach of a superior rule of law for the protection of the individual'.[79] By analogy with this approach, the majority held that the Minister could only be liable in damages if an abusive breach and not merely an innocent breach of the EEC Treaty was proved. The only cause of action available to the plaintiffs was, therefore, misfeasance in public office.

Oliver LJ, dissenting, concluded that the right afforded to individuals by article 30 was a private law right rather than a public law right. The Court of Justice had held that individuals have a right to restitution of monies demanded by a public authority in breach of article 30 and he could see no difference between a claim for damages and a claim for restitution for a breach of Article 30. The fact that article 30, unlike article 86, was addressed to Member States, did not alter the private nature of the right. It remained a right personal to each individual and one which the United Kingdom had a duty to protect. Oliver LJ, therefore, agreed with Mann J at first instance and, applying *Garden Cottage Foods,* held that a mere breach of article 30 amounted to a breach of statutory duty (the duty being one imposed by article 30 and s 2(1) of the European Communities Act 1972), which in private law gave an individual the right to claim damages.

Nature of the right If the approach of the majority in *Bourgoin* is followed, it is necessary to examine whether the individual right breached by the State lies in public law or in private law. If the right lies in the public domain and the breach is *bona fide*, the appropriate remedy is judicial review by anyone with sufficient interest and a declaration of the invalidity of the act. If the public law

---

[78] The argument on innominate tort was not pressed strongly either before Mann J (at 734B–F) or before the Court of Appeal (at 775C–G).

[79] Joined Cases 83/76, 94/76 *HNL v Council* [1978] ECR 1209 and Case 101/78 *Granaria BV v Hoofproduktschap* [1979] ECR 623. See pp 231–241.

right is breached in an abusive manner the appropriate cause of action is misfeasance in public office, for which damages may be awarded. If the right is a private law right, it is likely that a *bona fide* breach will give a cause of action for breach of statutory duty. The examination of the nature of the right may prove to be a difficult exercise, however, and not all Community provisions which are addressed to Member States necessarily afford rights in public law. For example, Directive 76/207,[80] which provides that Member States should ensure that men and women are treated equally, affords a private right to individuals not to be subject to sex discrimination; thus, a *bona fide* breach of that directive by a public body as regards its employees is a tort and exposes the body to a claim for damages.[81] Arguably, the distinction between private law rights and public law rights, which is notoriously difficult to make, is not apt to cover directly effective rights under Community law, since they are, by their nature, rights personal to each individual.

Is *Bourgoin* still good law after *Francovich*? In Joined Cases C–6/90, C–9/90 *Francovich and Bonifaci v Italy*[82] the Court of Justice held that it was a general principle of Community law that Member States pay compensation for harm caused to individuals by breaches of Community law for which they can be held responsible. Although it has been doubted whether *Bourgoin* can be considered good law after *Francovich*[83], the rejection by the Court of Appeal of liability for damages for a mere breach of Community law is probably consistent with *Francovich*. What national courts cannot do in the light of *Francovich* is to deny any right to damages against the State and, in this respect, it should not be forgotten that the Court of Appeal in *Bourgoin* accepted the principle of State liability in the guise of misfeasance in public office. The Court of Justice has expressly affirmed the power of national courts to lay down the conditions of State liability, provided that they do not make it excessively difficult to obtain damages against the State. A more difficult question is whether the conditions necessary to prove misfeasance in public office make it impossible in practice to obtain compensation from the State.

Does misfeasance provide effective protection? The extent to which misfeasance in public office provides effective protection for Community law rights must await further judicial consideration. Nevertheless, the conditions necessary to prove misfeasance give cause for concern that the tort might not provide effective protection. First, the requirement of malice and actual knowledge are essentially mental elements, which may be impossible to prove in the

---

[80] Council Directive 76/207 of February 1976, OJ No L 39, 14 February 1976, p 40, on the implementation of the principle of equal treatment for men and women as regards access to employment, vocational training and promotion and working conditions.

[81] For example damages for sex discrimination provided for by ss 65 and 66 of the Sex Discrimination Act 1975 and, generally, *Marshall v Southampton and South-West Hampshire Health Authority No 2* [1990] ICR 6 at 16C (EAT), [1991] ICR 136(CA). Case C–271/91, judgment of 2 August 1993.

[82] [1991] ECR I–5357.

[83] See *Kirklees Metropolitan Borough Council v Wickes Building Supplies Ltd* [1993] AC 227 at 281C–282C, per Lord Goff.

case of the adoption of acts for which no individual natural person is responsible. Secondly, if malice or actual knowledge are the only grounds to found liability, the tort is far narrower in scope than the conditions for tortious liability of the Community under article 215 of the EEC Treaty which so attracted the majority in *Bourgoin* and Advocate-General Mischo in *Francovich*. In its present state, the tort does not provide for liability where an official has acted in good faith but has committed a manifest breach of a superior rule of law for the protection of the individual. In short, the fact that the tort does not impose liability for an innocent but serious breach of Community law may make it impossible, in practice, to obtain compensation from the State.

(ii) Other causes of action

Breach of statutory duty or innominate tort If misfeasance in public office is not considered to provide an effective or appropriate remedy in the event that the State adopts an act contrary to Community law, another cause of action will need to be pleaded. For example, it is not yet decided whether misfeasance in public office is the correct cause of action for loss suffered due to the passing of an Act of Parliament. Consequently, the commission of an innominate tort or the breach of statutory duty remain possible causes of action, despite their apparent rejection by the Court of Appeal in *Bourgoin* (see Precedent B).

(d) Failure to abolish acts contrary to Community law

Liability in damages The principle of State liability laid down in *Francovich* must also apply to a failure by the State to abolish acts contrary to Community law. Indeed, in *Kirklees Metropolitan Borough Council v Wickes Building Supplies Ltd*,[84] where the House of Lords held that the plaintiff council was entitled to an injunction to enforce the ban on Sunday trading contained in s 47 of the Shops Act 1950 without giving a cross undertaking as to damages, Lord Goff proceeded on the basis that if s 47 were held invalid as being in conflict with article 30 of the EEC treaty 'the United Kingdom may be obliged to make good damage caused to individuals by the breach of article 30 for which it is responsible'.

Conditions of liability Any failure to repeal a national measure which is contrary to Community law will constitute a breach by a Member State.[85] This creates particular problems due to the fast-evolving nature of Community law. A national measure which has been in existence for many years may suddenly become contrary to Community law due to a decision of the Court of Justice or the enactment of Community legislation. It is a near impossible task for a Member State to ensure that, at any given time, no national measures exist which are contrary to Community law. The courts may, therefore, be particularly inclined to impose limitations on the principle of State liability in respect of such breaches.

---

[84] [1993] AC 227 at 281C–282C.
[85] For example, see Case 167/73 *Commission v France* [1974] ECR 359 para 41.

Causes of action Since the tort of misfeasance in public office may not constitute the correct cause of action, especially in the case of a failure by the legislature, a breach of statutory duty or commission of an innominate tort should also be pleaded.

(e) Failure to implement directives

Liability in damages for failure to implement a directive In Joined Cases C–6/90, C–9/90 *Francovich and Bonifaci v Italy*[86] the Court of Justice held that Member States which fail to implement directives within the implementation period are, in principle, liable to compensate individuals who have thereby suffered loss. The possibility of obtaining compensation from a Member State is particularly important in the event of non-implementation of directives, because the full effectiveness of the Community rules are subject to implementation by the State. A directive may not have direct effect and thus cannot be relied on by an individual in the national courts. In the absence of implementing measures, therefore, individuals cannot vindicate the rights intended to be conferred upon them.

Francovich Directive 80/987 provides that Member States must establish institutions to guarantee payment of employees' outstanding claims in the event of their employer's insolvency.[87] Member States were required to implement the directive by 23 October 1983. In proceedings brought by the Commission under article 169 of the EEC Treaty, the Court of Justice held that the Italian Republic had failed to comply with that obligation.[88] Mr Francovich was employed by CDN Elettronica and only received periodic payments of his salary. He instituted proceedings before the Italian courts, which ordered CDN to pay 6,000,000 lira. When Mr Francovich was unable to satisfy his claim against the company because of its insolvency, he brought proceedings against the Italian Republic, claiming either the guaranteed payment envisaged by Directive 80/987 or damages. Two questions arose. First, whether Mr Francovich could rely on the Directive against the State in order to claim the guaranteed sum. Secondly, whether Mr Francovich could sue the State in damages for the loss which he had suffered by virtue of the non-implementation of the directive. The Court of Justice held that the directive, as a whole, was not sufficiently precise and unconditional for Mr Francovich to rely on it against the State in order to claim payment. Thus, there was no directly effective right to payment which could be relied on in the national courts. There was, however, a right to compensation founded directly on Community law.

Conditions of liability for damages The court, in *Francovich*, held that where a Member State fails to fulfil its obligations under article 189(3) of the EEC

---

[86] [1991] ECR I–5357.

[87] Council Directive 80/987 of 20 October 1980 on the approximation of the laws of the Member States relating to the protection of employees in the event of the insolvency of their employer, OJ No L 283, 28 October 1980, p 23.

[88] Case 22/87 *Commission v Italy* [1989] ECR 143.

Treaty, to take all measures necessary to achieve the result prescribed by a directive, there should be a right to compensation where three conditions are satisfied:

(1) the result of the directive should entail the grant of rights to individuals; and

(2) it should be possible to identify the content of those rights on the basis of the provisions of the directive; and

(3) there should be a causal link between the breach of the State's obligation and the harm suffered by the injured parties.

In Mr Francovich's case, the infringement of Community law by the Italian Government as a result of the non-implementation of Directive 80/987 within the implementation period had already been established by the Court of Justice in the article 169 proceedings. The result laid down by that directive included the grant to employees of a right to a guaranteed payment of outstanding claims relating to their remuneration. The scope of that right could be identified on the basis of the provisions of the directive. All conditions were, therefore, satisfied. In those circumstances, the Court held that employees, such as Mr Francovich, had a right to obtain compensation for damage which they might have suffered by the non-implementation of the directive.

The three conditions of liability are sufficient to give rise to a right on the part of individuals to compensation. National courts cannot impose additional conditions. For example, it is unlikely that national courts can require proof of actual knowledge or malice, which are essential ingredients in the tort of misfeasance in public office. Nevertheless, in applying the three conditions it is for the national courts to apply their own substantive and procedural rules, provided that they are no less favourable than those relating to similar claims under national law and they do not make it impossible in practice, or excessively difficult, to obtain compensation. Consequently, it is for the English courts to apply their own rules on causation and, in this respect, it would be permissible to require a direct link between the loss suffered and the failure to implement.

Cause of action It is far from clear what the relevant cause of action is for failure to implement a directive. Since conditions of liability cannot be imposed in addition to the three conditions set out by the Court of Justice, the tort of misfeasance in public office does not appear particularly appropriate, since it requires proof of either malice or knowledge on the part of the Defendant. In reality, failure to implement a directive is unlikely to be attributable to a conscious decision by any one public officer, but rather a collective failure of the machinery of government. Therefore, it appears that, in most circumstances, breach of statutory duty or commission of an innominate tort will provide the most appropriate cause of action.

The grant of rights to individuals The first condition of liability laid down by the Court of Justice was that the result prescribed by the directive should 'entail the grant of rights to individuals'. What is immediately striking about this condition is that the directive need not have direct effect. In *Francovich*, the Italian State was required to make good damage to individuals arising from the non-implementation of Directive 80/987, despite the fact that the directive did not have direct effect. The directive, itself, created no rights for individuals which national courts had to protect; instead the emphasis was on the right intended by the directive to be created by national implementing legislation (ie the right of employees to a guaranteed payment).

This first condition will not always be satisfied, since many directives do not involve the creation of rights for individuals, albeit that they impose obligations on Member States. For example, in Case 380/87 *Enichem Base v Comune di Cinisello Balsamo*[89] the Court of Justice rejected a claim by plastic bag manufacturers that an Italian ban on the sale of plastic bags was contrary to Directive 75/442 on waste.[90] That directive aimed to harmonise national laws relating to waste and to avoid barriers to inter state trade. On its true interpretation the directive did not give individuals the right to sell plastic bags. On the basis that the directive did not intend to create rights for individuals, any failure to implement the directive (had it occurred) would not have given rise to State liability in damages.

Causation The judgment in *Francovich* will be particularly significant to an individual who is precluded from relying on a directly effective provision of a directive against another individual, by virtue of the fact that directives do not have horizontal direct effect. The case of *Duke v GEC Reliance Ltd*[91] provides an example. In this case, Mrs Duke was made to retire at the age of 60, whereas had she been male she would have retired at 65. The Equal Treatment Directive 76/207[92] provided that there should be no discrimination on grounds of sex relating to dismissal. The time for implementation of the directive expired on 12 August 1978. The United Kingdom Government considered that s 6(4) of the Sex Discrimination Act 1975, which permitted discrimination relating to retirement, complied with the directive. In Case 152/84 *MH Marshall v Southampton and South-West Hampshire Area Health Authority*[93] the Court of Justice decided that 'dismissal' was wide enough to cover retirement. The United Kingdom subsequently enacted the Sex Discrimination Act 1986, which amended s 6(4) of the Sex Discrimination Act 1975 so as to render unlawful discriminatory retirement ages as between men and women. The 1986 Act was not retrospective and did not therefore avail Mrs Duke. She could not rely on Directive 76/207 against her employer, GEC Reliance, because of the horizontal nature of the litigation. On facts such as these, the question arises whether Mrs Duke could have sued the United Kingdom in damages for the loss suffered due to the non-implementation of the directive. The answer depends upon whether there is a sufficient causal link between non-implementation and the loss suffered. In other words, is this a breach of Community law for which the State 'can be held

---

[89] [1989] ECR 2491.
[90] OJ 1975 No L 194/39.
[91] [1988] 1 AC 618.
[92] OJ No L 39, 9 February 1976, p 40.
[93] [1986] ECR 723.

responsible'.[94] According to Advocate-General Mischo in *Francovich*, the State would be liable in such a situation. He stated:[95]

> One might nevertheless ask whether, within the category of directives which do not give rise to direct effect, a distinction should be made between those whose purpose it is to impose obligations on the State and those whose purpose is to impose obligations on private undertakings, there being no liability on the part of the State in the latter case. After all, in that case the state is responsible only for the failure to implement the directive and not for the circumstances which are the direct cause of the harm suffered by the citizen, such as the non-payment of wages, the insufficient remuneration of a woman, or the defective nature of a product.
>
> Conversely, where the directive imposes obligations on the State itself (or on an organization which must necessarily be identified with the State), its offence is twofold: failure to implement the directive and failure to comply with the obligations which the directive imposes.
>
> I do not, however, think it is possible to make such a distinction, for the whole of the reasoning set out above is based on the principle that any failure to implement a directive *ipso facto* constitutes an infringement of Articles 5 and 189 EEC, that is to say an unlawful act which must be made good by the State where it has caused harm to an individual.

(f) Incorrect implementation of a directive

Liability in damages for incorrect implementation The statement by the Court of Justice in *Francovich*, that there is a right to compensation when the State fails 'to take all the measures necessary to achieve the result prescribed by a directive' is wide enough to cover incorrect implementation of a directive, as well as a total failure to implement. Advocate-General Mischo in *Francovich* expressly stated that 'an incorrect implementation constitutes an unlawful act which can give rise to liability on the part of the state if all other conditions are met'.[96] Similarly, in Case C–271/91 *Marshall v Southampton and South-West Hampshire Area Health Authority (No 2)*[97] Advocate-General Van Gerven stated:

> ... following the Court's judgment in *Francovich* the Member States may be ordered in certain circumstances to pay compensation on account of their failure correctly to implement directives.

Conditions of liability for damages In *Francovich* the Court of Justice made no distinction between the conditions of liability for failing to implement, and incorrectly implementing, a directive. However, the Court was faced in that case with a total failure to transpose Directive 80/987 into Italian law, so that the conditions for liability for incorrect implementation remain susceptible to analysis. Indeed, it is arguable that the conditions should not be the same, on the basis that there is not the same degree of culpability. In the case of non-

---

[94] Joined Cases C–6/90, C–9/90 *Francovich and Bonifaci v Italy* [1991] ECR I–5357 para 37.

[95] Ibid, paras 67, 68 of the Opinion. Note also the comments of Kennedy LJ in *R v Employment Secretary ex p Equal Opportunities Commission* [1993] 1 WLR 872 at 896D–E.

[96] [1991] ECR I–5357, para 76 of the Opinion.

[97] [1993] 3 CMLR 293, para 12 of the Opinion.

implementation, the breach of Community law is obvious and inexcusable. In the case of incorrect implementation, the breach may have been made innocently and bona fide. It remains to be seen, therefore, whether the Court of Justice (or indeed national courts) will impose extra conditions of liability to reflect this difference in culpability.

Causes of action As with the failure to implement Community legislation, the tort of misfeasance in public office will only apply in very limited circumstances due to the need to prove malice or knowledge. Breach of statutory duty or commission of an innominate tort are of much wider application and would, therefore, appear to be more appropriate causes of action.

(g) Procedure in actions involving the State

Appropriate procedure Where a claim for damages raises public law issues, the plaintiff must consider whether to proceed by way of judicial review pursuant to RSC Ord 53 or by way of writ. Choosing the wrong procedure may lead to the claim being struck out as an abuse of the process of the Court.[98]

Private law actions involving the Crown Special rules governing private law proceedings by and against the Crown are set out in the Crown Proceedings Act 1947 and RSC Ord 77.[99] Section 17 of the Crown Proceedings Act 1947 establishes the appropriate parties in actions involving the Crown. Civil proceedings against the Crown should be brought against the appropriate authorised Government department.[100] Where no Government department appears to be appropriate, or where there is doubt as to the appropriate department, the action should be brought against the Attorney General.[101]

---

[98] This is discussed at pp 110–112.

[99] These rules deal, in particular, with service of proceedings, discovery, summary judgment, default judgment and execution of orders.

[100] Section 17(1) of the Crown Proceedings Act 1947 requires the Minister for the Civil Service to publish a list of the 'authorised' departments for the purposes of the Act.

[101] Section 17(3) of the Crown Proceedings Act 1947.

Chapter 7

Injunctions

1. ACTIONS AGAINST PRIVATE PARTIES

(a) Jurisdiction to grant injunctions

Availability of injunctions A private person can obtain a final or interim injunction to restrain another private person from infringing his directly effective Community law rights. In the context of preventing a breach of article 85 of the EEC Treaty Peter Gibson J, in *Holleran v Daniel Thwaites*[1] stated that:

> the Court has power to prevent a person from abusing his rights, whether conferred on him by statute or contract, in order to create a breach of Community law.

Similarly, in *Garden Cottage Ltd v Milk Marketing Board*[2] the House of Lords was unanimous in stating that the English courts have jurisdiction to grant an injunction to prevent an undertaking abusing its dominant position contrary to article 86 of the EEC Treaty. Lord Wilberforce stated:[3]

> It can I think be accepted that a private person can sue in this country to prevent an infraction of article 86. This follows from the fact, which is indisputable, that this article is directly applicable in member states ... Since article 86 says that abuses of a dominant position are prohibited, and since prohibited conduct in England is sanctioned by an injunction, it would seem to follow that an action lies, at the instance of a private person, for an injunction to restrain the prohibited conduct.

(b) Principles applicable to interim injunctions

***American Cyanamid* principles** The jurisdiction of the English courts to grant interim injunctions is contained in s 37 of the Supreme Court Act 1981 under which the court has power to grant an injunction where it appears to be just and convenient to do so. Guidelines for the exercise of the court's discretion were laid down by the House of Lords in *American Cyanamid Co v Ethicon Ltd*[4]

---

[1] [1989] 2 CMLR 917 para 51. See also *Cutsforth v Mansfield Inns Ltd* [1986] 1 WLR 558.
[2] [1984] 1 AC 130. The majority (Lord Wilberforce dissenting) considered that the relevant cause of action was a breach of statutory duty (see pp 63–65).
[3] Ibid at 151E–F.
[4] [1975] AC 396.

in the speech of Lord Diplock. Pursuant to these guidelines the grant of an interim injunction is usually examined under three headings:

(1) serious question to be tried;
(2) adequacy of damages to either party; and
(3) the balance of convenience.

Serious question to be tried No serious question arises where the court is satisfied that the claim is frivolous or vexatious or where the material before the court discloses that the plaintiff has no real prospect of succeeding in his claim for a permanent injunction. However, it is not necessary for the plaintiff, to show a *prima facie* case for substantive relief. It is not part of the court's function at this threshold stage to try to resolve conflicts of evidence on affidavit or to decide difficult questions of law which call for detailed consideration. If the plaintiff can show that there is a serious question to be tried the court can address itself to the next question, ie whether it is just and convenient to grant an injunction.[5]

Adequacy of damages If damages to the plaintiff would be an adequate remedy an interim injunction will not normally be granted. However, where the defendant's undertaking to pay damages would not adequately compensate the plaintiff, the court will consider whether, if an injunction were granted against the defendant, the plaintiff's cross-undertaking to pay damages would adequately compensate the defendant if the defendant were successful at trial. If the court considers that such a cross-undertaking would provide an adequate remedy, the plaintiff will usually be granted an interim injunction.

These principles were applied by the House of Lords in a Community law context in *Garden Cottage Foods Ltd v Milk Marketing Board.*[6] In this case the Milk Marketing Board (MMB), which was the major producer of bulk butter in England, rationalised its sales policy by selling directly to only four distributors. As a result, supplies of butter to the plaintiff ceased. The plaintiff's business consisted of buying butter from the MMB and reselling it to other traders. The plaintiff applied for an injunction to restrain the MMB from withholding direct supplies to it, arguing that the MMB's refusal to sell constituted an abuse of a dominant position contrary to article 86 of the EEC Treaty. Parker J declined to grant the injunction, on the ground that damages would constitute an adequate remedy. The majority of the House of Lords agreed. The purchase of butter from one of the four distributors, instead of directly from the MMB, would merely reduce the plaintiff's margin. This loss could be quantified; indeed, Lord Diplock considered that there could hardly be a clearer case of damages being an adequate remedy.

Balance of convenience If there is doubt as to the adequacy of damages to both parties, the court will consider 'the balance of convenience' which entails

---

[5] Ibid at 407, 408, per Lord Diplock.
[6] [1984] 1 AC 130. See also *Cutsforth v Mansfield Inns Ltd* [1986] 1 WLR 558 at 567E–H (damages were not an adequate remedy to the plaintiffs); *Holleran v Daniel Thwaites* [1989] 2 CMLR 917 para 51; *Argyll Group plc v The Distillers Company plc* [1986] 1 CMLR 764.

balancing the risk of injustice to either party of granting or refusing an injunction. As Lord Bridge stated in *R v Secretary of State for Transport ex parte Factortame Ltd*:[7]

> A decision to grant or withhold interim relief in the protection of disputed rights at a time when the merits of the dispute cannot be finally resolved must always involve an element of risk. If, in the end, the claimant succeeds in a case where interim relief has been refused, he will have suffered an injustice. If, in the end, he fails in a case where interim relief has been granted, injustice will have been done to the other party. The objective which underlies the principles by which the discretion is to be guided must always be to ensure that the court shall choose the course which, in all the circumstances, appears to offer the best prospect that eventual injustice will be avoided or minimised.

For the purpose of deciding where the balance of convenience lies, the court will consider all the circumstances of the case. Where factors appear to be evenly balanced the court is likely to seek to preserve the status quo. The court will look at the state of affairs existing during the period immediately preceding the writ, not at the period prior to the defendant's conduct which is complained of. However, the duration of the period prior to the writ must be more than minimal; otherwise the state of affairs prior to the commencement of the conduct complained of will be the status quo.[8] Another factor in deciding where the balance of convenience lies is whether one person will suffer irreparable damage to a greater extent than the other. If the extent of irreparable damage to each party would not differ widely, the courts may take into account the strength of each party's case in tipping the balance. An examination of the merits of the case is, however, an exceptional course.

Special cases The courts will not apply the *American Cyanamid* principles where the grant or refusal of the interlocutory injunction will have the practical effect of putting an end to the action by giving one party summary judgment.[9] This was the approach adopted by Morritt J in *Plessey Co plc v General Electric Co plc*.[10] In this case the plaintiff target company sought an interlocutory injunction, to prevent the defendant company from making a takeover bid, on the basis that the takeover would be contrary to article 85 of the EEC Treaty. Morritt J refused to grant an interim injunction preventing the defendant from making any offer for the shares, because to have done so would have prevented the defendant from complying with the Takeover Panel's rules and timetables. This would have prevented the defendant from making any bid at all. It was only by refusing the injunction that final judgment in favour of the plaintiff was avoided.

---

[7] [1991] 1 AC 603 at 659D–F. See also May LJ in *Cayne v Global Natural Resources plc* [1984] 1 All ER 225 at 237H; *Francome v Mirror Group Newspapers Ltd* [1984] 1 WLR 892.

[8] *American Cyanamid v Ethicon* [1975] AC 396 at 408G, per Lord Diplock. See also *Garden Cottage Foods v Milk Marketing Board* [1985] 1 AC 130 at 140C, per Lord Diplock.

[9] *NWL Ltd v Woods* [1979] 1 WLR 1294 at 1306; *Cayne v Global Natural Resources plc* [1984] 1 All ER 225.

[10] [1990] ECC 384.

Further, the *American Cyanamid* principles are not applied in the case of interlocutory mandatory injunctions. A mandatory injunction (eg an order that a patent licence be granted) can be more drastic than a prohibitory one. Normally, therefore, the case must be strong and clear before an interlocutory mandatory injunction will be granted. However, where the practical reality of the situation is such that it is necessary for some form of mandatory order to be made in the interim, the court may make the order whether or not the high standard of probability of success at trial is made out.[11]

2. ACTIONS INVOLVING THE STATE

(a) English rules on jurisdiction to grant interim relief

Stay of proceedings Applicants seeking interim relief in judicial review proceedings may seek a stay of proceedings under RSC Ord 53, r 3(10)(a). An application for a 'stay of proceedings' embraces not only judicial proceedings, but also decisions of ministers and the decision-making process (if it has not been completed).[12] Although a stay and an interim injunction may, on occasions, lead to the same result, it is clear that a stay is of more limited application. A stay is not coercive in the sense that it cannot direct a Minister to act in a particular way. Moreover, it is doubtful whether the power granted under RSC, Ord 53, r 3(10)(a) could be used to suspend the operation of an Act of Parliament as an Act is not a 'proceeding'.

Interim injunctions RSC Ord 53, r 3(10)(b), which is given statutory force by s 31 of the Supreme Court Act 1981, provides that applicants may seek an interlocutory injunction in judicial review proceedings. In *M v Home Office*[13] the House of Lords interpreted these provisions as giving the English courts jurisdiction to grant interim injunctions against the Crown. Lord Woolf, giving the leading speech, considered that the unqualified language of s 31 gave the courts jurisdiction to make coercive orders, such as injunctions, against Ministers of the Crown acting in their official capacity. Therefore, under RSC Ord 53, r 3(10)(b), the court can grant injunctions against Ministers where it is just and convenient to do so. The House of Lords effectively overruled its previous decision to the contrary in *R v Secretary of State for Transport ex p Factortame Ltd (No 2)*[14] where Lord Bridge, giving a narrow and technical interpretation to s 31 and RSC Ord 53, r 3 (10)(b), had concluded that no such power existed.

---

[11] *Leisure Data v Bell* [1988] FSR 367. See also *Redland Bricks v Morris* [1970] AC 652, per Lord Upjohn; *Films Rover International Ltd v Cannon Films Sales Ltd* [1987] 1 WLR 671.
[12] *R v Secretary of State For Education and Science ex p Avon County Council* [1991] 1 QB 558. See also Lord Woolf in *M v Home Office* [1993] 3 WLR 433 at 463D–F.
[13] [1993] 3 WLR 433.
[14] [1990] 2 AC 85.

(b) Interim injunctions disapplying national law alleged to be incompatible with EC law

(i) Jurisdiction

Jurisdiction to grant injunctions against the Crown The principles of supremacy of Community law and effective protection of Community law rights require national courts to disapply any national provision which is found to be incompatible with a directly effective provision of Community law. However, the English courts initially proved reluctant to grant an interim injunction against the Crown requiring it to disapply national law to protect putative Community law rights (ie rights which are only alleged, not established). In *R v Secretary of State for Transport ex p Factortame Limited (No 2)*[15] the House of Lords considered that, as a matter of English law, there were two barriers to the grant of an interim injunction in judicial review proceedings to disapply an Act of Parliament or subordinate legislation which allegedly infringed Community law rights. These were:

(1) s 31 of the Supreme Court Act 1981 did not give the courts the power;[16] and

(2) the presumption that an Act of Parliament is valid until proved invalid prevented the grant of such an injunction.

However, on a reference by the House of Lords under article 177 of the EEC Treaty, as to whether these barriers were compatible with Community law, the Court of Justice held that the same principles of supremacy and effectiveness dictate that national courts must at least have jurisdiction to grant interim relief to disapply a national law to protect putative rights in Community law.[17]

Factortame **litigation** This case concerned the common market fishing policy under which the Community fixes quotas for the amount of fish which each national fishing fleet may catch. A practice known as 'quota hopping' arose whereby, according to the United Kingdom, its fishing quotas were plundered by vessels flying a British flag but lacking any genuine link with the United Kingdom. In December 1985 the Government made it a condition for the grant of a fishing licence that 75 per cent of the crew should be resident in the United Kingdom. The Government also introduced a new register for fishing vessels under the Merchant Shipping Act 1988 and subordinate regulations. To be registered, owners and operators of the vessels had to be British nationals (or, in the case of companies, at least 75 per cent of the shares had to be owned by British nationals) and the owners and operators (and shareholders and directors)

---

[15] Ibid.

[16] Overruling *R v Licensing Authority established under Medicines Act 1968 ex p Smith Kline and French Laboratories (No 2)* [1990] QB 574; and *R v Secretary of State for the Home Department ex p Herbage* [1987] QB 872. However, the House of Lords has departed from this narrow interpretation in *M v Home Office* [1993] 3 WLR 433.

[17] *R v Secretary of State for Transport ex p Factortame Ltd (No 2)* [1990] ECR I–2433; [1991] 1 AC 603.

had to be resident in the United Kingdom. The applicants (companies incorporated under United Kingdom law and their directors and shareholders, most of whom were Spanish nationals) owned, between them, 95 sea-fishing vessels. They did not meet the new nationality and residence conditions laid down by the 1988 Act. On an application for judicial review of the 1988 Act, the applicants argued that the conditions were contrary to article 7 of the EEC Treaty (discrimination on the grounds of nationality), article 52 (principle of freedom of establishment) and article 221 (non-discrimination as regards participation in the capital of companies or firms).

The divisional court of the Queen's Bench Division (Neill LJ and Hodgson J) requested a preliminary ruling from the Court of Justice in accordance with article 177 of the EEC Treaty, as to the compatibility of the 1988 Act with Community law.[18] Although the applicants had been seeking a final and not an interlocutory order, the reference to the Court of Justice raised the issue of interim relief in respect of the period prior to the Court giving its ruling. On the applicants' motion, the Divisional Court granted interim relief, ordering that:[19]

> the operation of Part II of the Merchant Shipping Act 1988 and the Merchant Shipping (Registration of Shipping Vessels) Regulations 1988 be disapplied, and the Secretary of State be restrained from enforcing the same . . . .

The Court of Appeal (Lord Donaldson MR, Bingham and Mann LJJ) allowed the Secretary of State's appeal on the issue of interim relief and held that there was no jurisdiction in the court to disapply an Act of Parliament unless and until incompatibility with Community law had been established. Lord Donaldson MR stated:[20]

> Looking at British national law without reference to the European Communities Act 1972, it is fundamental to our (unwritten) constitution that it is for Parliament to legislate and for the judiciary to interpret and apply the fruits of Parliament's labours. Any attempt to interfere with primary legislation would be wholly unconstitutional. That apart, there is a well settled principle of British national law that the validity of subordinate legislation and the legality of acts done pursuant to the law declared by it are presumed unless and until its validity has been challenged in the courts *and* the courts have fully determined its invalidity (see *Hoffman La Roche v Secretary of State for Trade* [1975] AC 295 at 365, per Lord Diplock). The position in relation to primary legislation must be the same.

The House of Lords affirmed the decision of the Court of Appeal with regard to the lack of jurisdiction. Lord Bridge said of the order for interim relief:[21]

---

[18] *R v Secretary of State for Transport ex p Factortame Ltd* [1989] 2 CMLR 353 at 357. In reply to the reference made by the divisional court as to the substantive issue, the Court of Justice subsequently held in Case C–221/89 *R v Secretary of State for Transport ex p Factortame Ltd and others* [1991] ECR I–3905 that the nationality and residence requirements imposed by the United Kingdom legislation were contrary to EC law. The Commission also took parallel proceedings against the United Kingdom under article 169 of the EEC Treaty. In the course of these proceedings the Court of Justice made an order pursuant to article 186 of the EEC Treaty requiring the United Kingdom to suspend the application of the nationality requirements in Case 246/89R *Commission v United Kingdom* [1989] ECR 3125.

[19] [1989] 2 CMLR 353 at 400 para 26.

[20] *R v Secretary of State for Transport ex p Factortame Ltd* [1989] 2 CMLR 353 at 392 para 19.

[21] *R v Secretary of State for Transport ex p Factortame Ltd* [1990] 2 AC 85 at 142, 143.

Any such order, unlike any form of order for interim relief known to the law, would irreversibly determine in the applicant's favour for a period of some two years rights which are necessarily uncertain until the preliminary ruling of the ECJ has been given. If the applicants fail to establish the rights they claim before the ECJ, the effect of the interim relief granted would be to have conferred upon them rights directly contrary to Parliament's sovereign will and correspondingly to have deprived British fishing vessels, as defined by Parliament, of the enjoyment of a substantial proportion of the United Kingdom quota of stocks of fish protected by the common fisheries policy. I am clearly of the opinion that, as a matter of English law, the court has no power to make an order which has these consequences.

However, the House of Lords made a further preliminary reference to the Court of Justice enquiring whether Community law empowered or obliged an English court, irrespective of the position under national law, to provide effective interim protection of the putative rights under Community law claimed by the applicants. The Court of Justice, following the opinion of Advocate-General Tesauro, ruled that the national courts must disapply any rule or presumption which prevents the court from at least having jurisdiction to protect putative, as well as established, rights under Community law. Referring to its earlier judgment in Case 106/77 *Amministrazione delle Finanze dello Stato v Simmenthal SpA*,[22] the Court of Justice stated that a national court must have the power to set aside national law which prevents Community rules from having full force and effect. The Court deduced from this that the full effectiveness of Community law would be impaired if national courts could not act to protect rights alleged to exist under Community law. The Court stated:[23]

> ... the full effectiveness of Community law would be just as much impaired if a rule of national law could prevent a court seised of a dispute governed by Community law from granting interim relief in order to ensure the full effectiveness of the judgment to be given on the existence of the rights claimed under Community law. It follows that a court which in those circumstances would grant interim relief, if it were not for a rule of national law, is obliged to set aside that rule.

Applying the ruling of the Court of Justice, the House of Lords granted the interim injunction sought on the basis that the applicants had strong grounds for challenging the validity of the provisions in the Merchant Shipping Act 1988 relating to residence and domicile.[24] In the *Agegate* case[25] the Court of Justice had rejected, as invalid, a condition of a fishing licence that 75 per cent of the vessel's crew be resident in the UK. Consequently, if such a residence qualification was rejected in respect of the crew it was difficult to see how a similar condition could be upheld in respect of owners and operators. Moreover, the House of Lords was also persuaded that serious and irreparable damage would be suffered by the applicants if an interim injunction were not granted.

---

[22] [1978] ECR 629.
[23] Case C–213/89 *R v Secretary of State for Transport ex p Factortame Ltd* [1990] ECR I–2433 para 21.
[24] *R v Secretary of State for Transport ex p Factortame Ltd (No 2)* [1991] 1 AC 603. See pp 94–99 for conditions imposed on grant of interim relief in such cases.
[25] Case 3/87 *R v Ministry of Agriculture, Fisheries and Food ex p Agegate Ltd* [1989] ECR 4459; See also Case C–216/87 *R v MAFF ex p Jaderow Ltd* [1989] ECR 4509.

Circumstances where an application for interlocutory relief may be made National courts may be faced with interlocutory applications to disapply national law in the following situations:

(1) where a public authority or the State seeks an interim injunction to prevent a breach of United Kingdom law and the private party argues that no such injunction should be granted as the relevant national law is invalid under Community law;[26]

(2) where a private party seeks an interim injunction to prevent the Crown enforcing a United Kingdom law which is alleged to be invalid under Community law.[27]

Moreover, as a result of the judgment of the House of Lords in *M v Home Office*,[28] English courts have jurisdiction to grant interim relief not only to protect putative, directly effective rights, but also to prevent a breach of non-directly effective provisions of Community law. For example, a directive may direct Member States to impose certain obligations on individuals. The United Kingdom may implement the directive but may impose stricter obligations than is required by the directive. Although the provisions of the directive may not be sufficiently clear and unconditional to be directly effective, arguably the individuals can seek an interim injunction against the Crown to disapply the implementing measure.

(ii) Conditions for the grant of interim relief

National law is applicable In its reference to the Court of Justice in *Factortame* the House of Lords asked, *inter alia*, what the criteria would be in determining whether to disapply national law on an interim basis in order to protect putative Community law rights. The Court of Justice did not answer this question. At present, therefore, in the absence of any Community law determining the conditions for the grant of interim relief where national law is allegedly inconsistent with Community law, it is for the English courts to apply their own national rules based on the guidelines laid down by Lord Diplock in *American Cyanamid*[29] and modified as necessary. Thus, in applying the ruling of the Court of Justice in *Factortame*,[30] the House of Lords exercised its new-found jurisdiction and granted an interim injunction restraining the Secretary of State from withholding or withdrawing registration of the applicant's vessels in the register maintained under the Merchant Shipping Act 1988. In so doing, the majority of the House of Lords applied the guidelines laid down by Lord Diplock in *American Cyanamid*, albeit with some modification to take account of the public interest in ensuring that the law was enforced. The grant of an interim injunction to restrain a breach by the State of putative rights in Community law will be examined under three headings:

---

[26] For example, *Kirklees Metropolitan Borough Council v Wickes Building Supplies* [1993] AC 227, one of the 'Sunday trading' cases.

[27] For example, the *Factortame* cases. See pp 91–93.

[28] [1993] 3 WLR 433.

[29] This was the view adopted by Advocate-General Tesauro in *Factortame* [1990] ECR I–2433.

[30] *R v Secretary of State for Transport ex p Factortame Ltd (No 2)* [1991] 1 AC 603.

(1) a serious question to be tried;
(2) adequacy of damages to either party; and
(3) the balance of convenience.[31]

Serious question to be tried The majority of the House of Lords in *Factortame*[32] considered that, at the threshold stage, it is sufficient for the applicant to show that the claim is not vexatious or frivolous, but that there is a serious question to be tried. Once this threshold stage has been passed, the court can address itself to the question of whether it is just or convenient to grant the injunction. Lord Jauncey disagreed with this approach. He considered that the presumption of validity of national legislation made the *American Cyanamid* test, of a serious question to be tried, inappropriate.[33] Rather, he believed that a person seeking to challenge the validity of national legislation should show at least a strong *prima facie* case of incompatibility with Community law in order to cross the threshold. In practical terms, the two approaches are not very different. It is only in exceptional cases that an injunction will be granted where the applicant cannot show that he is likely to succeed. The difference between the two approaches is mainly at which stage the applicant must discharge this burden. In the opinion of Lord Jauncey, failure to show a strong *prima facie* case will mean that the application for an injunction will not pass the threshold test. However, in the opinion of the majority of the House of Lords, failure to show a strong *prima facie* case would, in most cases, lead to the balance of convenience being weighed in favour of the Crown.

Adequacy of damages Lord Goff in *Factortame* considered that, in cases involving law enforcement and the public interest, the problem as to whether an injunction should be granted would not usually be solved at the damages stage, for two reasons. Firstly, where the Crown or a public authority is seeking to enforce the law it is unusual to impose upon the Crown or the public authority the usual undertaking or cross-undertaking in damages.[34] Secondly, due to the restrictive approach adopted by the Court of Appeal in *Bourgoin SA v Ministry of Agriculture Fisheries and Food*,[35] in relation to awarding damages against the State, damages would rarely be an adequate remedy.

The question of whether an individual would be compensated in damages must be reconsidered in the light of the judgment by the Court of Justice in Joined Cases C–6/90, C–/90 *Francovich and Bonifaci v Italy*, which introduces a general principle of State liability in damages for breach of Community law.[36]

---

[31] Ibid, per Lord Goff giving the leading speech. See also *R v Secretary of State For The National Heritage ex p Continental Television BV (Red Hot Dutch)* [1993] 2 CMLR 333, [1993] 3 CMLR 387 (CA); *R v HM Treasury ex p British Telecommunications Plc* (1993), unreported.

[32] *R v Secretary of State for Transport ex p Factortame Ltd (No 2)* [1991] 1 AC 603.

[33] Ibid at 679B.

[34] *F Hoffmann-La Roche & Co AG v Secretary of State for Trade and Industry* [1975] AC 295 (insofar as it applies to the Crown); and *Kirklees MBC v Wickes Building Supplies* [1993] AC 227 (insofar as the principle applies to public authorities).

[35] [1985] ECR 1027. There would be no remedy in damages available to the applicants for any loss suffered by them on the basis that the government would not be liable in damages for an innocent breach of Community law. See pp 78–79.

[36] Joined Cases C–6/90, C–9/90 *Francovich and Bonifaci v Italy* [1991] ECR I–5357. Discussed at pp 72–74 and 82–86. See also p 80.

However, the precise grounds on which such liability will arise are not clear. The cases where damages are awarded to an individual who has suffered loss as a result of a breach of Community law by the State are likely to be exceptional. Even if damages are available as a remedy, they may prove to be an inadequate remedy.

Cross-undertaking in damages Public authorities[37] and the Crown[38] will not, in general, be required to give an undertaking or cross-undertaking in damages. Where the Crown or a public authority seeks to enforce what is *prima facie* the law of the land, the individual seeking to disapply that law in interlocutory proceedings must show very good reason why the Crown or the public authority should give an undertaking to pay damages in the event of the individual succeeding at trial. In doing so, regard must be had to all the circumstances of the case, For example, in *Kirklees Metropolitan Borough Council v Wickes Building Supplies*[39] the plaintiff council applied for an interlocutory injunction to restrain the defendant from trading on Sunday contrary to the Shops Act 1950. The defendant argued that the Shops Act 1950 conflicted with article 30 of the EEC Treaty. The question arose as to whether the plaintiff council should give a cross-undertaking in damages as a condition of being granted interlocutory relief. The House of Lords held that Mervyn Davies J, at first instance, was fully entitled to hold, on ordinary principles of English law, that no cross-undertaking should be given. Relevant factors were:

(1) the defendant company would, unless restrained, continue to act in contravention of the Act;

(2) an injunction was the only practical means of enforcing the law, as fines were not a sufficient deterrent due to the maximum amounts which could be imposed under the relevant legislation;

(3) the effect of requiring an undertaking in damages from the council would be to cause the collapse of the law enforcement process in this area of law;

(4) it was arguable that small retailers might suffer if large retailers were able to continue to trade;

(5) the plaintiff council's prospect of success in the action could not be described as 'slight';

(6) the council was seeking to enforce the law of the United Kingdom; if the law were subsequently held to be invalid, the proper party to pay damages would be the State, not the public authority. There could not be guilt by association.

Balance of convenience In determining where the balance of convenience or the risk of causing an injustice lies, the courts must have regard to the wider con-

---

[37] *Kirklees Metropolitan Borough Council v Wickes Building Supplies* [1993] AC 227.
[38] *F Hoffmann La Roche & Co AG v Secretary of State for Trade and Industry* [1975] AC 295.
[39] [1993] AC 227.

siderations of the public interest, particularly in cases involving the application of the criminal law.[40] In this context, Lord Goff stated in *Factortame No 2*:[41]

> ... particular stress should be placed upon the importance of upholding the law of the land, in the public interest, bearing in mind the need for stability in our society, and the duty placed upon certain authorities to enforce the law in the public interest. This is of itself an important factor to be weighed in the balance when assessing the balance of convenience. So if a public authority seeks to enforce what is on its face the law of the land, and the person against whom such action is taken challenges the validity of that law, matters of considerable weight have to be put into the balance to outweigh the desirability of enforcing, in the public interest, what is on its face the law, and so to justify the refusal of an interim injunction in favour of the authority, or to render it just or convenient to restrain the authority for the time being from enforcing the law.

The public interest factor means that it will only be in exceptional cases that an interim injunction will be granted to disapply national law. As Lord Goff stated:[42]

> In the end, the matter is one for the discretion of the court, taking into account all the circumstances of the case. Even so, the court should not restrain a public authority by interim injunction from enforcing an apparently authentic law unless it is satisfied, having regard to all the circumstances, that the challenge to the validity of the law is, *prima facie*, so firmly based as to justify so exceptional a course being taken.

Consequently, a chance of eventual success, which is no more than even, is unlikely to meet Lord Goff's test.[43] Nevertheless, it should always be noted that, even in law enforcement cases, the court's discretion to grant interim relief is not fettered by any rule which requires the individual to show, in all cases, a strong *prima facie* case that the law is invalid.[44] Lord Goff stated:[45]

> It is impossible to foresee what cases may yet come before the courts; I cannot dismiss from my mind the possibility (no doubt remote) that such a party may suffer such serious and irreparable harm in the event of the law being enforced against him that it may be just or convenient to restrain its enforcement by an interim injunction even though so heavy a burden has not been discharged by him.

Effect of *Zuckerfabrik* Subsequently, in Joined Cases 143/88, C–92/89 *Zuckerfabrik Süderdithmarschen AG v Hauptzollamt Itzehoe and Zuckerfabrik*

---

[40] Per Lord Goff in *R v Secretary of State for Transport ex p Factortame (No 2)* [1991] 1 AC 603 at 673, applying *Smith v Inner London Education Authority* [1978] 1 All ER 411 at 422 per Browne LJ and *Sierbein v Westminster City Council* (1987) 86 LGR 431. In *R v Secretary of State For The National Heritage ex p Continental Television BV (Red Hot Dutch)* [1993] 2 CMLR 333 at 348, Leggatt LJ, in refusing an interim injunction, stated 'when the moral welfare of minors is weighed against the applicants' profits there can only be one side upon which the scales can come down'.

[41] [1991] 1 AC 603 at 673C.

[42] Ibid at 674C–D.

[43] See per Glidewell LJ in *R v Secretary of State for National Heritage ex p Continental Television B v (Red Hot Dutch)* [1993] 3 CMLR 357 para 20.

[44] *Cf* Lord Diplock in *F Hoffmann La Roche & Co AG v Secretary of State for Trade and Industry* [1975] AC 295 at 367.

[45] *R v Secretary of State for Transport ex p Factortame (No 2)* [1991] 1 AC 603 at 674C.

Soest GmbH v Hauptzollamt Paderborn[46] the Court of Justice ruled that national courts are not precluded by Community law from suspending a national measure *based* on a Community regulation, even though this has the effect of indirectly suspending the regulation. Referring to *Factortame*, the Court stated that:[47]

> The interim legal protection which Community law ensures for individuals before national courts must remain the same, irrespective of whether they contest the compatibility of national legal provisions with Community law or the validity of secondary Community law, in view of the fact that the dispute in both cases is based on Community law itself.

The Court of Justice also set out the principles to be applied when national courts grant interim relief disapplying national legislation based on Community law. These are, *inter alia*, that there are serious doubts as to the validity of the Community measure, threats of serious and irreparable damage to the applicant and due account taken of the Community's interest.[48] These are difficult conditions to satisfy and are stricter than the conditions laid down for interim relief by Lord Diplock in *American Cyanamid Co v Ethicon Ltd*.[49] Although it has been suggested that these conditions apply equally to the grant of an injunction to disapply national law which is allegedly contrary to Community law, as well as one to disapply national law which is based on Community law,[50] it is unlikely that the Court intended to lay down uniform conditions to be applied in all cases where a national court grants interim relief in a case concerning Community law. Firstly, the passage cited above appears in the part of the judgment which specifically deals with the jurisdiction of national courts to suspend the implementation of Community legislation, whereas the conditions on which such injunctions are granted fall under a completely separate heading. Secondly, the conditions correspond with the principles followed by the Court of Justice in applying article 185 of the EEC Treaty, when the Court is itself suspending Community legislation. There is no logical reason why the strict conditions should apply in a *Factortame*-type situation, where there is no challenge to the validity or uniform application of Community law.

Criminal cases In *Kirklees Metropolitan Borough Council v Wickes Building Supplies*[51] Lord Goff considered the basis upon which an interim injunction should be granted in order to ensure compliance with the criminal law. He emphasised that the right to invoke the assistance of the civil courts in aid of the criminal law is an exceptional power, which must be exercised with great caution. Generally, it is confined to cases where the offence is frequently repeated

---

[46] [1991] ECR I–415. Discussed at pp 99–100.
[47] Ibid para 20.
[48] Ibid para 33.
[49] [1975] AC 396. See pp 87–90.
[50] Advocate-General Mischo in Joined Cases C–6/90, C–9/90 *Francovich and Bonifaci v Italy* [1991] ECR I–5357 para 55 of the Opinion. See also Lord Goff in *Kirklees Metropolitan Borough Council v Wickes Building Supplies* [1993] AC 227 at 280G–281A.
[51] Ibid at 269A–271C.

in disregard of a (usually inadequate) penalty or to cases of emergency. While accepting that, in most cases, it will be necessary to show that the defendant plainly has no defence to a criminal prosecution, this will not apply in all cases. As an example Lord Goff stated that where a defendant invoked a Community law defence, with sufficient substance (but no more) to merit a preliminary reference to the Court of Justice under article 177 of the EEC Treaty, this should not, in itself, prevent the grant of an interim injunction. To hold otherwise would provide encouragement to those seeking to profit from law-breaking activities to adopt this method of prolonging what might prove to be a source of illicit profit. Thus, the existence of an alleged defence is merely a matter to be taken into account in the exercise of the court's discretion, when deciding whether it is just and convenient that interlocutory relief should be granted.[52]

(c) Interim injunction disapplying national law and thereby disapplying Community Law

(i) Jurisdiction to grant interim relief

Zuckerfabrik National courts must have jurisdiction to grant interim injunctions against the State to suspend national legislation adopted on the basis of Community law. This principle was established in Joined Cases C–143/88, C–92/89 *Zuckerfabrik Süderdithmarschen AG v Hauptzollamt Itzehoe and Zuckerfabrik Soest GmbH v Hauptzollamt Paderborn*.[53] In these cases, Zuckerfabrik sought the suspension of a levy which had been imposed by the German authorities pursuant to a Community regulation. It argued that the regulation was invalid and that this vitiated the national decision to impose the levy.[54] The Court of Justice held that, even though regulations are directly applicable in the national legal orders pursuant to article 189 of the EEC Treaty, this does not preclude national courts from suspending an administrative decision which has been adopted on the basis of a Community regulation, even if this has the effect of suspending the application of the regulation. Referring to its judgment in *Factortame*,[55] the Court stated:[56]

> In cases where national authorities are responsible for the administrative implementation of Community regulations, the legal protection guaranteed by Community law includes the right of individuals to challenge, as a preliminary issue, the legality of such regulations before national courts and to induce those courts to refer questions to the Court of Justice for a preliminary ruling. That right would be compromised if, pending delivery of a judgment of the Court, which alone has jurisdiction to declare that a Community regulation is invalid (see judgment in Case 314/85

---

[52] See also *Portsmouth City Council v Brian James Richards and Quietlynn Limited* [1989] 1 CMLR 673.

[53] [1991] ECR I–415.

[54] In *R v Minister of Agriculture Fisheries and Food ex p FEDESA* [1988] 3 CMLR 661 Henry J held that where an instrument of Community secondary legislation is held to be invalid the United Kingdom subordinate legislation adopted to give effect to the Community instrument is also invalid.

[55] Case C–213/89 *R v Secretary of State for Transport ex p Factortame Limited and others* [1990] ECR I–2433.

[56] *Zuckerfabrik Süderdithmarschen AG v Hauptzollamt Itzehoe and Zuckerfabrik Soest GmbH v Hauptzollamt Paderborn* [1991] ECR I–415, paras 16–17, 20.

Foto-Frost v Hauptzollamt Lübeck-Ost [1987] ECR 4199, at paragraph 20), individuals were not in a position, where certain conditions are satisfied, to obtain a decision granting suspension of enforcement which would make it possible for the effects of the disputed regulation to be rendered for the time being inoperative as regards them... The interim legal protection which Community law ensures for individuals before national courts must remain the same, irrespective of whether they contest the compatibility of national legal provisions with Community law or the validity of secondary Community law, in view of the fact that the dispute in both cases is based on Community law itself.

(ii) Conditions for the grant of interim relief

Community law principles are applicable   The principles laid down by Lord Diplock in *American Cyanamid*, which normally guide the English courts in respect of the grant of interim relief, do not apply to the grant of interim injunctions which disapply national law and which thereby disapply Community Law. This power to suspend the operation of Community Law corresponds to the power granted to the EC courts under article 185 of the EEC Treaty to suspend Community measures. Consequently, the Court of Justice in *Zuckerfabrik* considered that, in order to ensure the uniform application of Community law, a national court could only grant an interlocutory injunction in those circumstances where at least the conditions for the grant of interim relief under article 185 were satisfied. On this basis, a national court should only suspend the enforcement of a national measure in such cases where at least the following conditions are satisfied:[57]

(1) there are serious doubts about the validity of the Community measure; and

(2) there is urgency and a threat of serious and irreparable damage to the applicant; and

(3) account is taken of the Community's interest: and

(4) the national court makes a preliminary reference to the Court of Justice concerning the validity of the Community measure (unless the same issue is already pending before the Court of Justice).

Urgency and irreparable damage   There is urgency where the damage is liable to materialise before the ruling of the Court of Justice on the validity of the contested Community measure. Although purely financial damage is not usually regarded as irreparable, interim relief can be granted where the immediate enforcement of the national measure will lead to irreversible damage to the applicant, which could not be made good by compensation if the Community measure were subsequently to be declared invalid.[58]

Community interest   The national court should consider whether the Community measure challenged would be deprived of all effectiveness if it were not immediately enforced. Furthermore, if suspending enforcement would be likely to involve a financial risk for the Community, the applicant should be required to provide adequate guarantees, such as the deposit of money or other security.[59]

---

[57] See Joined Cases C–143/88, C–92/89 *Zuckerfabrik Süderdithmarschen AG v Hauptzollamt Itzehoe and Zuckerfabrik Soest GmbH v Hauptzollamt Paderborn* [1991] ECR I–415, paras 22–33.

[58] *Zuckerfabrik* (above) paras 28–29. See pp 24 5–246.

[59] *Zuckerfabrik* (above) paras 30–32.

Chapter 8

Restitution

1. RESTITUTION CLAIMS INVOLVING THE STATE

(a) Principles of restitution

Right to restitution The EC courts have recognised the right to restitution in a number of situations:

(1) where a Member State has collected taxes, duties or levies which are contrary to Community law (for example, because they are contrary to article 12 or article 95 of the EEC Treaty);

(2) where a Member State has collected monies on behalf of the Community under a Community measure which has subsequently been held to be invalid by the EC courts; and

(3) where a Member State has paid out monies which it mistakenly believed were due to third parties under a Community measure.

Where a Member State has collected monies in contravention of a directly effective provision of Community law, the right to restitution arises from the duty imposed on the national courts by article 5 of the EEC Treaty to ensure the effective protection of directly effective Community rights.[1] Where a Member State has mistakenly paid out monies, which it believed to be due to a person under Community law, a similar right to restitution arises on behalf of the State. The Court of Justice has held that:[2]

> ... it is for the courts of the Member States to provide, in pursuance of the requirement of co-operation embodied in Article 5 of the Treaty, the legal protection made available as a result of the direct effect of the Community provisions both when such provisions create obligations for the subject and when they confer rights on him.

General principles Apart from the recovery of import and export duties, for which specific Community rules have been adopted,[3] no Community legislation has been adopted for the recovery of monies in the other situations outlined

---

[1] Case 33/76 *Rewe-Zentralfinanz eG v Landwirtschaftskammer für das Saarland* [1976] ECR 1989 para 5; Case 45/76 *Comet BV v Produktschap voor Siergewassen* [1976] ECR 2043 paras 11–19.

[2] Case 265/78 *H Ferwerda BV v Produktschap voor Vee en Vlees* [1980] ECR 617 para 10.

[3] Council Regulation 2913/92. See pp 105–106.

above. However, the case law has established the following general principles.[4]

(1) In the absence of harmonising Community rules on the refunding of money,[5] it is for the national courts to apply their own substantive, procedural and evidential rules to determine how the right to restitution may be exercised.

(2) These national rules are subject to two limitations:

    (*a*) such rules cannot be discriminatory and less favourable than those relating to similar actions of a domestic nature, eg a limitation period of six years for national claims and three years for Community claims;

    (*b*) such rules cannot make it impossible in practice to exercise the right to restitution.

Defences Although national rules cannot render the right to restitution impossible to exercise in all cases, the rules can prevent recovery in particular cases. For example, the Court of Justice has held that a Member State may impose a reasonable limitation period on the bringing of restitutionary claims.[6] The Court of Justice has also held that it is permissible for a national legal system to refuse restitution where this would result in the unjust enrichment of the claimant, for example, where he has already passed on the cost of the charges unduly levied in the prices charged to customers.[7] In addition, it is for the national courts to determine whether any interest should be paid in respect of such a claim[8] or whether there may be any set-off against the right to reimbursement.[9]

However, national rules may not have the effect of rendering the *general* right to restitution impossible or excessively difficult to exercise. In Case

---

[4] For cases where Member States have collected monies in contravention of Community Law see: Case 33/76 *Rewe-Zentralfinanz eG v Landwirtschaftskammer für das Saarland* [1976] ECR 1989 para 5; Case 45/76 *Comet BV v Produktschap voor Siergewassen* [1976] ECR 2043 paras 11–19; Case 61/79 *Amministrazione delle Finanze dello Stato v Denkavit Italiana Srl* [1980] ECR 1205 para 25. For a case where a Member State has collected monies under a Community measure subsequently declared to be invalid see Case 130/79 *Express Dairy Foods Ltd v Intervention Board for Agricultural Produce* [1980] ECR 1887. For a case where the Member State has paid money which it mistakenly believed was due under Community Law see Case 265/78 *H Ferwerda BV v Produktschap voor Vee en Vlees* [1980] ECR 617 para 10.

[5] For example, see Case 199/86 *Raiffeisen Hauptgenossenschaft eG v Bundesanstalt für landwirtschaftliche Marktordnung (BALM)* [1988] ECR 1169 paras 12–19.

[6] Case 33/76 *Rewe-Zentralfinanz eG v Landwirtschafskammer für das Saarland* [1976] ECR 1989 para 5; Case 45/76 *Comet BV v Produktschap voor Siergewassen* [1976] ECR 2043 paras 11–19; Joined Cases 119/79, 126/79 *Lippische Hauptgenossenschaft eG v Bundesantalt für landwirtschaftliche Marktordnung* [1980] ECR 1863 paras 7–10; Case 386/87 *Bessin and Salson v Administration des douanes et droits indirects* [1989] ECR 3551 paras 15–18.

[7] Case 68/79 *Hans Just I/S v Danish Ministry for Fiscal Affairs* [1980] ECR 501 paras 25, 26; Case 811/79 *Amministrazione delle Finanze dello Stato v Ariete SpA* [1980] ECR 2545 paras 12–14; Case 826/79 *Amministrazione delle Finanze dello Stato v Sas MIRECO* [1980] ECR 2559 paras 13, 14.

[8] Case 26/74 *Société Roquette Frères v Commission* [1976] ECR 677 paras 9–14; Case 130/79 *Express Dairy Foods v Intervention Board for Agricultural Produce* [1980] ECR 1887 para 15–17; Case 54/81 *Firma Wilhelm Fromme v Bundesanstalt für landwirtschaftliche Marktordnung* [1982] ECR 1449 paras 4–10.

[9] Case 177/78 *Pigs and Bacon Commission v McCarren* [1979] ECR 2161 paras 24–26. See also Case 222/82 *Apple and Pear Development Council v KJ Lewis Ltd* [1983] ECR 4083 paras 36–42.

199/82 *Amministrazione delle Finanze dello Stato v SpA San Giorgio*[10] an Italian trader had paid charges to the Italian authorities which had been levied in breach of Community law. Italian law recognised a right to restitution where charges had been levied contrary to national law and Community law. However, the law presumed that the person who had paid the charges would pass them on to the consumer. In order to recover the charges from the Italian authorities, the trader had to prove, by documentary evidence alone, that they had not been passed on. The Court of Justice considered that such a law was unlawful, as it required the trader to prove a negative by documentary evidence. Although it was not discriminatory, it made it impossible or excessively difficult in practice to exercise the right to restitution granted by Community law.

The Court of Justice has also disapproved of national laws passed to limit reimbursement solely to claimants who had commenced proceedings prior to a judgment by the Court of Justice declaring a national tax to be unlawful.[11]

Temporal limitations Where the State has levied charges on the basis of a Community provision, which is subsequently declared to be invalid, this may give rise to a large number of claims for restitution which might have serious financial consequences for the public purse (the 'floodgates argument'). Consequently, the Court of Justice has on certain occasions limited the temporal effects of judgments made by it concerning the invalidity of a provision of Community law. For example, the Court may exclude any claims for restitution arising prior to the judgment of the Court. It has also limited the right of recovery to the party who brought the proceedings which led to the annulment of the relevant Community measure or to those who had already commenced legal proceedings or made an equivalent claim prior to the judgment of the Court of Justice.[12] The power to impose temporal limitations on the effect of a judgment can only be exercised by the EC Courts in the course of the judgment itself. National courts have no power to impose temporal limitations on the effect of a judgment of the EC courts.[13]

English law: substantive rules It is for the English courts to apply national laws in order to give effect to Community law rights to restitution. However, these laws must not treat Community rights less favourably than comparable national rights nor render the Community rights impossible to exercise in practice. The English law of restitution, although somewhat under-developed, contains some special rules in relation to claims against public bodies.

---

[10] [1983] ECR 3595 paras 11–18. See also Joined Cases 331/85, 376/85, 378/85 *Les Fils de Jules Bianco SA and J Girard Fils SA v Directeur général des douanes et droits indirects* [1988] ECR 1099 paras 8–13; Case 104/86 *Commission v Italy* [1988] ECR 1799 paras 6–13.

[11] Case 309/85 *Barra v Belgium* [1988] ECR 355. See also Case 240/87 *Deville v Administration des Imports* [1988] ECR 3513. Only EC courts may impose temporal limitations on effect of judgments. See pp 201–202.

[12] For example, see Case 145/79 *SA Roquette Frères v France* [1980] ECR 2917 paras 50–53; Case 112/83 *Société des produits de maïs SA v Administration des douanes et droits indirects* [1985] ECR 719 paras 17, 18. See also pp 133–4 and pp 201–202.

[13] Case 309/85 *Bruno Barra v Belgium* [1988] ECR 355 paras 9–15.

Prior to the decision of the House of Lords in *Woolwich Equitable Building Society v Inland Revenue Commissioners*,[14] it was very difficult to succeed in a restitutionary claim against a public body. The normal principles of restitution applied so that a plaintiff would need to establish that payment was made under a mistake of fact or under duress. In most cases, monies were paid under a mistake of law and were, therefore, irrecoverable.[15] However, in *Woolwich*, a majority of the House of Lords established a principle that money paid by a citizen to a public authority in the form of taxes or other levies pursuant to an *ultra vires* demand by the authority is *prima facie* recoverable by the citizen as of right.[16] Lord Goff and Lord Slynn both indicated, *obiter*, that they considered that a *prima facie* right to restitution would also arise where the demand was made because the authority had misconstrued the relevant provision, that is, where there had been a mistake of law.[17] Lord Goff based his reasoning partly on the fact that, under Community law, a person who pays charges levied by a Member State in breach of Community law is entitled to repayment of these charges.[18]

Where a Member State has paid out monies, which it mistakenly believed were due to third parties under a Community measure, it may be able to rely on the principle that, if the Crown pays money out of the consolidated fund without authority, such money is *ipso facto* recoverable if it can be traced.[19] Alternatively, the Member State could rely on the general grounds of restitution (for example, payment under a mistake of fact) to found a claim.[20] However, where the State has paid out monies under a mistake of law, and these monies were not paid out of the consolidated fund or can no longer be traced, it is doubtful whether English law would give a right to recovery, as there is no right to restitution in respect of monies paid under a mistake of law.[21] In such a case, it could be argued that the English courts would be obliged to set aside the rule preventing recovery for a mistake of law because its application renders the Community law right of restitution impossible to exercise in practice.

English law: procedure As RSC Ord 53 does not provide for restitutionary remedies in the context of the judicial review procedure, it appears that restitutionary claims against public bodies must be brought under private law proced-

---

[14] [1993] AC 70. See the comments of Burrows, *The Law of Restitution* 1st edn (Butterworths, 1993), 345–361.

[15] As a result of the principle established in *Bilbie v Lumley* (1802) 2 East 469.

[16] See the speeches of Lord Goff, Lord Browne-Wilkinson, and Lord Slynn (Lord Keith and Lord Jauncey dissented.)

[17] At 177F–178B, per Lord Goff; at 204F–205B, per Lord Slynn.

[18] At 177C–E.

[19] *Auckland Harbour Board v R* [1924] AC 318; *Woolwich Equitable Building Society v Inland Revenue Commissioners* [1993] AC 70 at 177B–C, per Lord Goff. See the comments of Burrows in *The Law of Restitution*, 1st edn (Butterworths, 1993), 330–332.

[20] For example, see *Holt v Markham* [1923] 1 KB 504; *Avon County Council v Howlett* [1983] 1 WLR 605.

[21] *Bilbie v Lumley* (1802) 2 East 469. See also *Holt v Markham* [1923] 1 KB 504; *Avon County Council v Howlett* [1983] 1 WLR 605.

ures, for example, by writ. This is supported by the speech of Lord Slynn in *Woolwich*, where he said:[22]

> If a claim lies for money had and received, judicial review adds nothing. If the money falls in law to be repaid, a direct order for its repayment is more appropriate than a declaration that it should [be repaid] or an order setting aside a refusal to repay it.

(b) Repayment and remission of import and export duties

Council Regulation 2913/92 The Community has adopted specific legislation in relation to the restitution of import and export duties. Council Regulation 2913/92, which establishes the Community Customs Code,[23] sets out the framework rules for the repayment and remission of import and export duties. The duties covered include customs duties and charges having equivalent effect to customs duties, as well as agricultural duties.[24] Repayment means the total or partial refund of import or export duties which have been paid.[25] Remission means the waiver of all or part of a customs debt not yet paid.[26] The Regulation sets out three circumstances where repayment or remission will be granted:

(1) where the duties demanded are not legally due;
(2) where the customs declaration is invalidated; and
(3) where the goods are rejected by the importer on the basis that they are defective or do not correspond with the terms of the contract on the basis of which they were imported.

In addition, the Regulation provides the basis for the adoption of further Community legislation concerning situations in which repayment or remission may be granted.[27]

Duties not legally due[28] Duties which are not legally due may be repaid or remitted where the debtor makes an application to the appropriate customs office within three years of the date on which the amount of those duties was communicated to the debtor, subject to excusable delay caused by unforeseeable circumstances or *force majeure*. In addition, where the customs' authorities discover within this period that duties are not legally due, they are required to repay or remit them on their own initiative. No repayment or remission will be granted where the facts which led to the demand of the relevant duty were the result of deliberate action by the person concerned.

---

[22] *Woolwich Equitable Building Society v Inland Revenue Commissioners* [1993] AC 70 at 200F–G.

[23] Council Regulation 2913/92 of 12 October 1992 establishing the Community Customs Code, OJ No L 302, 19 October 1992, p 1. This regulation repealed Council Regulation 1430/79, OJ No L 175, 12 July 1979, p 1, on the repayment or remission of import or export duties.

[24] Regulation 2913/92, article 4(10), (11). Council Regulation 2913/92 is further supplemented by Commmission Regulation 2454/93 of 2 July 1993 laying down provisions for the implementation of Council Regulation 2913/92 establishing the Community Customs Code, OJ No L 253, 11 October 1993, p 1 (articles 877–912).

[25] Regulation 2913/92, article 235(1).

[26] Ibid article 235(2).

[27] Ibid article 239.

[28] Ibid article 236.

Customs declaration invalidated[29] Where a customs declaration has been invalidated, for example, because goods were placed under a particular type of customs procedure as a result of an error,[30] duties paid may be recovered. The application for repayment must be made within the periods laid down for submission of the application for invalidation of the customs declaration.[31]

Goods rejected by importer[32] Subject to certain conditions, duties may be repaid or remitted where goods are rejected by the importer on the basis that they are defective or do not correspond with the terms of the contract on the basis of which they were imported. An application must be made to the appropriate customs office within 12 months from the date on which the amount of the debt was communicated to the debtor. However, the customs authorities may permit this period to be exceeded in exceptional cases.

Minimum amount[33] Generally, repayment or remission will only be granted if the relevant amount exceeds a minimum sum to be fixed by the Customs Code Committee.[34] However, national customs authorities have discretion to grant repayment or remission in respect of lower amounts.

Interest[35] Interest need not be paid in respect of repayment of duties, unless either a decision to grant a repayment is not implemented within three months of the date of adoption of the decision or national provisions so stipulate.

Appeals Regulation 2913/92 sets down specific rules for appeals from decisions of national customs authorities.[36]

2. RESTITUTION CLAIMS BETWEEN PRIVATE PARTIES

General principles In *Lipkin Gorman v Karpnale Ltd*,[37] the House of Lords expressly recognised that the principle of unjust enrichment formed a part of English law. Where a party has been unjustly enriched as a result of a breach of directly effective Community rights, the person at whose expense the enrichment has been gained should, in principle, be entitled to bring a restitutionary claim in order to protect his Community rights.

Article 85 of the EEC Treaty Restitutionary remedies may prove to be of particular importance in relation to agreements which restrict competition and which are found to contravene article 85(1) of the EEC Treaty. Article 85(2)

---

[29] Ibid article 237.
[30] Ibid article 66.
[31] Ibid article 66(2).
[32] Ibid article 238.
[33] Ibid article 240.
[34] This Committee is to be established under the terms of Regulation 2913/93. See articles 247–249.
[35] Regulation 2913/92, article 241.
[36] Ibid article 243–246.
[37] [1991] 2 AC 548. See generally, Goff and Jones, *The Law of Restitution*, 3rd edn (Sweet & Maxwell, 1986); Birks, *An Introduction to the Law of Restitution*, 1st edn revised (Oxford University Press, 1989); Burrows, *The Law of Restitution*, 1st edn (Butterworths, 1993).

provides that such agreements 'shall be automatically void'. Therefore, no claim for damages can be brought which is based on the agreement itself. Furthermore, difficulties may arise in seeking to bring a tortious claim based on breach of statutory duty.[38] However, where a party has transferred money or property under an illegal contract, he may be entitled to recover it by means of a restitutionary claim (action for money had and received). Generally, a restitutionary claim arising out of an illegal contract will be barred by the principle *ex turpi causa non oritur actio* ('the court will not lend its aid to a man who founds his action upon an immoral or an illegal act'). However, the courts may permit a restitutionary claim where the parties are not *in pari delicto*. In *Browning v Morris*,[39] Lord Mansfield held that:

> ...where contracts or transactions are prohibited by positive statutes, for the sake of protecting one set of men from another set of men; the one, from their situation and condition, being liable to be oppressed or imposed upon by the other; there, the parties are not in pari delicto; and in furtherance of these statutes, the person injured, after the transaction is finished and completed, may bring his action and defeat the contract.

It could be argued that article 85 of the EEC Treaty is intended not only to protect the efficient functioning of the Common Market as a whole, but also to protect certain individuals from anti-competitive behaviour. For example, it could be said to protect individuals who run petrol stations from the greater bargaining power of the oil company which supplies them and which seeks to impose anti-competitive restrictions on them.

3. REPAYMENT OF STATE AIDS

General principle A principle related to the notion of restitution is the power of the Commission to order Member States to recover illegal state aids. Article 92 of the EEC Treaty provides that state aids which distort competition within the EC are unlawful, unless they fall within the categories of aid expressly permitted under article 92. Where a Member State intends to grant new aid or alter existing aid it must inform the Commission of its intentions.[40] The Member State may not put its proposed measures into effect until a definitive decision has been reached under the procedure provided for in article 93(2). If the Member State fails to notify the Commission of the grant of aid or grants aid without awaiting the final decision of the Commission, the Commission has the power, after giving the Member State in question an opportunity to submit its comments on the matter, to issue an interim decision. This interim decision may require the Member State to suspend immediately the payment of aid pending the outcome of the examination of the aid and to provide the Commission, within

---

[38] See pp 68–69.

[39] [1778] 2 Cowp 790, 98 English Reports 1364. Applied in *Kiriri Cotton Co Ltd v Dewani* [1960] AC 192 at 204 by Lord Denning (PC); *Re Cavalier Insurance Co Ltd* [1989] 2 Lloyd's Rep 430 at 449, 450.

[40] EEC Treaty, article 93(3).

such period as specified in the decision, with all such documentation, information and data as are necessary to enable the Commission to examine the compatibility of the aid with the Common Market. Where the Member State complies in full with the interim decision, the Commission is obliged to examine the compatibility of the aid with the Common Market, in accordance with the procedure laid down in articles 93(2), (3). Where the Member State fails to provide the information requested, the Commission is empowered to terminate the procedure and to decide, on the basis of the information available to it, whether or not the aid is compatible with the Common Market. This decision may call for recovery of the amount of aid which has already been paid.[41]

Challenging the Commission's decision   A Commission decision ordering the recovery of aid may be challenged by a Member State or beneficiary of the aid under article 173 of the EEC Treaty. For example, in Case 223/85 *Rijn-Schelde-Verolme (RSV) Maschinefabrieken en Scheepswerven NV v Commission*[42] the Court of Justice annulled a decision of the Commission requiring the Netherlands to recover monies paid to RSV as state aid, on the ground that the Commission had delayed twenty-six months before adopting the decision. This delay had established a legitimate expectation on the part of RSV that it would be entitled to retain the aid.

Recovery takes place under national law   In principle, the recovery of aid unlawfully paid must take place in accordance with the relevant procedural provisions of national law, subject, however, to the proviso that those provisions are to be applied in such a way that the recovery required by Community law is not rendered practically impossible.[43] In Case C–5/89 *Commission v Germany*[44] the Court of Justice held that national legislation which provides that the principles of the protection of legitimate expectations and the assurance of legal certainty should be observed in relation to the recovery of unlawful state aids cannot be considered contrary to Community law, which itself recognises these principles. However, except in exceptional circumstances, beneficiaries of state aid cannot entertain legitimate expectations that the aid is lawful where it has not been granted in compliance with the procedures laid down in article 93 of the

---

[41] Case 301/87 *France v Commission* [1990] ECR I–307 paras 19–22; Case 142/87R *Belgium v Commission* [1990] ECR I–959 paras 14–18, 66; Case C–305/89 *Italy v Commission* [1991] ECR I–1603 paras 38–42. See also Case 310/85 *Deufil GmbH & Co KG v Commission* [1987] ECR 901 para 24.

[42] [1987] ECR 4617 paras 12–19. *Cf* Case 301/87 *France v Commission* [1990] ECR I–307 paras 25–28 where delay by the Commission in reaching a decision was justified due to the time required to obtain all the necessary information. See also Case C–294/90 *British Aerospace plc and Rover Group Holdings plc v Commission* [1992] ECR I–493.

[43] Case C–142/87R *Belgium v Commission* [1990] ECR I–959 para 61. See also Case 94/87 *Commission v Germany* [1989] ECR 175 para 12. For an English case concerning the recovery of state aids, see *Department of Trade and Industry v British Aerospace plc and Rover Group Holdings plc* [1991] 1 CMLR 165. In relation to English law, insofar as monies paid under a mistake of law cannot be recovered, this is unlikely to be acceptable as a bar to recovery of state aids. It would have the effect of making recovery impossible in practice.

[44] [1990] ECR I–3437 paras 12–16. See also Opinion of Advocate-General Darmon in Case 94/87 *Commission v Germany* [1989] ECR 175 at 187, 188.

EEC Treaty.[45] The Commission has published a communication in the *Official Journal*[46] informing potential recipients of state aid of the risk that they might be required to refund aid granted to them illegally. A diligent business man should normally be able to determine whether the necessary procedures have been followed. In addition, time limits imposed by national law must not render the recovery of state aids required by Community law impossible in practice.[47]

Failure to recover Where the Commission adopts a decision requiring recovery of state aids, this imposes an obligation on the Member State to which it is addressed to take the necessary steps. If a Member State does not challenge the validity of the Commission's decision under article 173 of the EEC Treaty, and fails to recover the sums paid as aid, the Commission may commence infraction proceedings against the Member State under article 93(2) of the EEC Treaty.[48] A Member State may not challenge the validity of the original Commission decision in such proceedings, nor may it rely on internal administrative, legal, political, financial or practical difficulties as a defence. However, a Member State will not be found to be in breach of its Community obligations where it can prove that it was absolutely impossible for it to recover the state aid.[49] If a Member State encounters unforeseen difficulties in implementing the order for recovery, it is under an obligation[50] to communicate these difficulties to the Commission in order to seek a solution.[51] In Case 63/87 *Commission v Greece*,[52] Advocate-General Slynn indicated that a further defence available to a Member State is to argue that the Commission decision is unclear or ambiguous. In these circumstances, it may be that it is absolutely impossible for the Member State to comply with the Commission decision because it is not possible to ascertain the nature of the obligation which the decision seeks to impose.[53]

---

[45] For example, see Case C–183/91 *Commission of Greece*, judgment of 10 June 1993, para 19.
[46] Commission Communication, OJ C No 318, 24 November 1983, p 3.
[47] Case C–5/89 *Commission v Germany* [1990] ECR I–3437 para 19.
[48] Article 93(2) of the EEC Treaty establishes a special procedure for infraction proceedings against a Member State in the context of state aids, whereby the Commission is not obliged to follow the procedure under article 169 of the EEC treaty. See generally Ch 11.
[49] Case 52/84 *Commission v Belgium* [1986] ECR 89 paras 13–16; Case 213/85 *Commission v Netherlands* [1988] ECR 281 paras 22–24; Case 63/87 *Commission v Greece* [1988] ECR 2875 paras 8, 14; Case C–5/89 *Commission v Germany* [1990] ECR I–3437 para 18.
[50] Under article 5 of the EEC Treaty.
[51] Case 52/84 *Commission v Belgium* [1986] ECR 89 para 16; Case C–303/88 *Italy v Commission* [1991] ECR I–1433 paras 56–58; Case C–183/91 *Commission v Greece*, judgment of 10 June 1993.
[52] [1988] ECR 2875, Opinion of Advocate-General Slynn at 2884. The Advocate-General referred to Case 70/72 *Commission v Germany* [1973] ECR 813 in support of this argument.
[53] For further discussion of defences in infraction proceedings, see pp 164–168.

Chapter 9

Judicial Review

1. WHEN DOES JUDICIAL REVIEW LIE?

(a) Appropriate procedure

Public and private law rights Where a person seeks to establish that a decision infringes rights which are entitled to protection under public law, he must proceed by way of judicial review, pursuant to RSC Ord 53 and not by way of ordinary action. If the person proceeds by action rather than judicial review the action will be struck out. As Lord Diplock stated in *O'Reilly v Mackman*;[1]

> ... it would in my view as a general rule be contrary to public policy, and as such an abuse of the process of the court, to permit a person seeking to establish that a decision of a public authority infringed rights to which he was entitled to protection under public law to proceed by way of an ordinary action and by this means to evade the provisions of Order 53 for the protection of such authorities.

The distinction between public and private law rights is a difficult, but vital one. It is still uncertain on what basis the English courts will classify rights derived from Community law. Directly effective Community law rights, by definition, create rights for individuals which the national courts are bound to protect.[2] However, in *Bourgoin SA v Ministry of Agriculture, Fisheries and Food*[3] the majority of the Court of Appeal held that a breach *simpliciter* of article 30 of the EEC Treaty, which obliges Member States not to adopt legislative and administrative measures which restrict inter-State trade, would only give rise to public law remedies by way of judicial review. In contrast, the court considered that an abusive breach of article 30 would give rise to private law remedies under the tort of misfeasance in public office.[4] In effect, the nature of the breach determined the nature of the right.

---

[1] [1983] 2 AC 237 at 285D–G.
[2] See Ch 3.
[3] [1986] 1 QB 716.
[4] Ibid at 787E–G, per Parker LJ. Oliver LJ dissented and approached the question by examining the nature of the right. See pp 78–81. See also *An Bord Baine v Milk Marketing Board* (Irish Dairy Board No 2) [1988] 1 CMLR 605. The difficult dichotomy between public and private is also highlighted in *Cato v Ministry of Agriculture, Fisheries and Food* [1989] 3 CMLR 513, especially at 537.

The decision in *Bourgoin* will need to be re-assessed following the decision in Joined Cases C–6/90, C–9/90 *Francovich and Bonifaci v Italy.*[5] It now appears that the English courts will be obliged to grant damages where an individual has suffered loss due to a breach of Community law by the United Kingdom, even where the breach cannot be classified as 'abusive' (for example, where the State has failed to implement a directive).

Collateral public law issues   Where the challenge to a public law act is a collateral issue in a claim for infringement of a private law right, the private law procedure will usually be appropriate.[6] In *Roy v Kensington and Chelsea and Westminster Family Practitioner Committee* Lord Bridge held:[7]

> It is appropriate that an issue which depends exclusively on the existence of a purely public law right should be determined in judicial review proceedings and not otherwise. But where a litigant asserts his entitlement to a subsisting right in private law, whether by way of claim or defence, the circumstance that the existence and extent of the private right asserted may incidentally involve the examination of a public law issue cannot prevent the litigant from seeking to establish his right by action commenced by writ or originating summons, any more than it can prevent him from setting up his private law right in proceedings brought against him.

Homogenised issues of public and private law   Where there are mixed issues of public and private law it will not usually be an abuse of process to proceed by ordinary action. In *An Bord Bainne Co-operative Ltd v Milk Marketing Board*[8] the Irish Dairy Board brought a writ action against the Milk Marketing Board claiming damages and an injunction. The grounds were:

(*a*)   breach of EEC Regulations 1422/78 and 1565/79 and of the (UK) Milk Marketing Scheme (Amendment) Regulations 1981; and

(*b*)   abuse of a dominant position under article 86 of the EEC Treaty.

The Milk Marketing Board applied to strike out the grounds under (a) on the basis that such a claim should have been brought under the judicial review procedure and, therefore, amounted to an abuse of the process of the court. The application was refused by the Court of Appeal which held that, although the Irish Dairy Board's claim involved public law issues, the claim for damages clearly was based upon alleged private law rights. The public and private law issues were inextricably mixed.

It seems likely, therefore, that an action for damages against the State, arising from a breach of EC law for which the State is responsible, could usually be commenced by writ, rather than by judicial review proceedings under RSC Ord 53, r 7.

---

[5]   [1991] ECR I–5357. Discussed at pp 72–74, 80, 82–86.

[6]   *O'Reilly v Mackman* [1983] 2 AC 237 at 285F, per Lord Diplock. See also *Cocks v Thanet District Council* [1983] 2 AC 286; *Davy v Spelthorne Borough Council* [1984] AC 262; *Wandsworth London Borough Council v Winder* [1985] AC 461.

[7]   [1992] 1 AC 624 at 628H–629A, per Lord Bridge; at 654A–B, per Lord Lowry.

[8]   [1984] 2 CMLR 584.

Issues of fact Discovery, interrogatories and cross-examination are available in judicial review proceedings.[9] However, a claim which involves disputed issues of fact should generally proceed by way of private law procedure.[10]

Alternative avenues Judicial review will not normally be granted where there is an alternative avenue for challenging the decision which is sought to be reviewed.[11] In *R v Secretary of State for Employment, ex p Equal Opportunities Commission*[12] a co-applicant, Mrs Day, sought judicial review of the Secretary of State's refusal to amend the Employment Protection (Consolidation) Act 1978 to conform to article 119 of the EEC Treaty, the Equal Pay Directive (75/117),[13] or the Equal Treatment Directive, (76/207).[14] The Employment Protection (Consolidation) Act 1978 provided that part-time workers had to be employed for five years before they were entitled to statutory redundancy pay, whereas full-time employees only had to be employed for two years before they became entitled. Mrs Day was employed part-time by the Hertfordshire Area Health Authority and was made redundant shortly before the expiry of the five-year period. This, she alleged, was contrary to EC law because the time periods laid down by the Act discriminated against women on the basis that more women worked part-time than men. Her application for judicial review of the 1978 Act was dismissed, the appropriate forum being the industrial tribunal, not the divisional court.

(b) Locus Standi

Sufficient interest Pursuant to RSC Ord 53, r 3, an applicant must first apply *ex parte* for leave to bring judicial review proceedings. Pursuant to RSC Ord 53, r 3(7) no leave will be granted unless the applicant has a sufficient interest in the matter to which the application relates. The question of sufficient interest may be examined at two stages.[15] First, the *ex parte* stage acts as a filter, weeding out the hopeless or vexatious applications. If leave is granted, the question of sufficient interest can then be examined afresh at the substantive hearing.

A 'sufficient ' interest is a question of degree, which is examined in light of the legal and factual context of the application. The interest itself usually con-

---

[9] RSC Ord 53, r 8.

[10] *Inland Revenue Commissioners v Rossminster Ltd* [1980] AC 952 at 1025H–1026A, per Lord Scarman; *R v Derbyshire County Council, ex p Noble* [1990] ICR 808 at 813C–D, per Woolf LJ; *Roy v Kensington and Chelsea and Westminster Family Practitioner Committee* [1992] 1 AC 624 at 646F–647C, per Lord Lowry.

[11] *R v Epping and Harlow General Commissioners ex p Goldstraw* [1983] 3 All ER 257 at 262, per Sir John Donaldson MR; *R v Chief Constable of Merseyside ex p Calveley* [1986] QB 424.

[12] [1993] 1 WLR 872. See also *National Union of Public Employees v Lord Advocate, The Times*, 5 May 1993.

[13] Council Directive 117/75 on the approximation of the laws of the Member States relating to the application of the principle of equal pay for men and women, OJ No L 45, 19 February 1975, p 19.

[14] Council Directive 76/207 on the implementation of the principle of equal treatment for men and women as regards access to employment, vocational training and promotion and working conditions, OJ No L 39, 14 February 1976, p 40.

[15] *R v Inland Revenue Commissioners, ex p National Federation of Self-Employed and Small Businesses Ltd* [1982] AC 617.

notes some personal interest in the relief sought. In *R v Attorney General ex p ICI*[16] the Court of Appeal, upholding Woolf J, held that ICI had sufficient interest to challenge, by way of judicial review, the grant of a state aid to one of its competitors, Shell, which was alleged to be in breach of article 92 of the EEC Treaty. However, it is not necessary for the applicant to benefit financially from the application.[17] 'Sufficient interest' is not limited to direct personal interest and has been given a liberal interpretation by the courts. Regard is had, in particular, to whether there has been a failure to carry out public duties. As Lord Diplock stated in *R v Inland Revenue Commissioners ex p National Federation of Self-Employed and Small Businesses Ltd*:[18]

> It would, in my view, be a grave lacuna in our system of public law if a pressure group, like the federation, or even a single public-spirited taxpayer, were prevented by outdated technical rules of locus standi from bringing the matter to the attention of the court to vindicate the rule of law and get the unlawful conduct stopped.

In *R v HM Treasury ex p Smedley*[19] Woolf J and the Court of Appeal both indicated that Mr Smedley would have *locus standi* to challenge the legality of payments, made by the United Kingdom out of the Consolidated Fund to the European Community, to finance the Community's supplementary budget. Similarly, in *R v Secretary of State for Foreign and Commonwealth Affairs ex p Rees-Mogg*[20] the applicant had sufficient interest to challenge the ratification by the United Kingdom of the Maastricht Treaty. It should be noted, however, that the ability of a pressure group to bring judicial review proceedings in respect of an administrative act which has not infringed a personal right of the group is curtailed by the definition of reviewable act.

Reviewable acts Closely linked to the question of sufficient standing is the question of reviewable acts. Administrative action or inaction may be susceptible to judicial review where:
(a) it alters a person's rights or obligations which are enforceable by or against him in private law; or
(b) it deprives him of some benefit or advantage;[21] or
(c) it promulgates advice comparable to a ministerial circular.[22]
The fact that the authority for the act does not derive from the exercise of the prerogative is not fatal, provided that the body in question is performing a public function. Thus, acts of self-regulatory bodies such as The Stock Exchange

---

[16] [1987] 1 CMLR 72.
[17] *R v Legal Aid Board ex p Bateman* [1992] 1 WLR 711 at 718. *R v Inland Revenue Commissioners ex p National Federation of Self-Employed and Small Businesses Ltd* [1982] AC 617 at 646, per Lord Fraser.
[18] Ibid at 644E.
[19] [1985] 1 QB 657; referred to by Lord Woolf in *M v Home Office* [1993] 3 WLR 433 at 454H.
[20] [1993] 3 CMLR 101.
[21] *Council of Civil Service Unions v Minister For Civil Service* [1985] AC 374 at 408 E, per Lord Diplock.
[22] *Gillick v West Norfolk and Wisbech Area Health Authority* [1986] 1 AC 112 at 193G–194B per Lord Bridge.

and the Panel on Take-overs and Mergers may be the subject of judicial review proceedings.[23]

A refusal to amend legislation will not necessarily constitute a reviewable act. In *R v Secretary of State for Employment ex p Equal Opportunities Commission*[24] the majority of the Court of Appeal (Kennedy and Hirst LLJ) held that a refusal by the Minister at the request of the Equal Opportunities Commission (EOC) to amend allegedly discriminatory legislation so as to conform to Community law was not a reviewable act. No directly enforceable right belonging to the EOC had been infringed and no benefit had been withdrawn from it. The argument that the refusal to amend amounted to a reviewable act was rejected. Dillon LJ dissented on this issue, stating:[25]

> I have no doubt that, given that the EOC is a statutory body and that its statutory duties include the elimination of discrimination, and given the clarity of the Secretary of State's statement of the governments' position, the EOC was on receipt of that letter fully entitled to apply for judicial review to challenge the government's position, thus clearly stated, as erroneous in law.

This judgment has a substantial impact on those employed in the private sector. Since directives do not have horizontal directive effect, private individuals cannot rely on the provisions of a directive directly against another private individual. The inability of the EOC, the statutory body charged with eliminating discrimination, to protect these persons, leaves them, as Kennedy LJ acknowledged, with a claim (as yet undefined) for damages against the State in accordance with the principles laid down by the Court of Justice in Joined Cases C–6/90, C–9/90 *Francovich and Bonifaci v Italy*.[26] The liberal approach adopted by Dillon LJ is probably more in keeping with the Court's obligation, under article 5 of the EEC Treaty, to afford legal protection to individuals who derive rights under Community law.[27] The principle of effective protection is not necessarily limited to directly effective or personally enforceable rights, as the decision in *Francovich* makes clear.

Draft legislation In certain circumstances, draft legislation is susceptible to judicial review. In *R v HM Treasury ex p Smedley*[28] the Member States agreed to make certain loans to the Community to finance the Community's supplementary budget. The United Kingdom proposed to make its loan out of the Consolidated Fund using the Order in Council process, permitted by s 1 of the European Communities Act 1972. This process could only be used if the agreement between the Member States could be described as a 'treaty ancillary to any of the

---

[23] *R v Panel on Take-overs and Mergers ex p Datafin* [1987] QB 815; *R v International Stock Exchange ex p Else (1982) Ltd* [1993] QB 534.

[24] [1993] 1 WLR 872. The EOC was successful on appeal to the House of Lords [1994] 2 WLR 409.

[25] Ibid at 883G–H.

[26] [1991] ECR I–5357.

[27] See Ch 5 on effective protection of Community law rights.

[28] [1985] 1 QB 657; referred to by Lord Woolf in *M v Home Office* [1993] 3 WLR 433 at 454H. See also *R v Legal Aid Board ex p Bateman* [1992] 1 WLR 711 at 718; *R v Inland Revenue Commissioners, ex p National Federation of Self-Employed and Small Businesses Ltd* [1982] AC 617 at 646, per Lord Fraser.

[Community] Treaties'. Although the Order was still in draft and had not been approved by both Houses of Parliament, it seems that Mr Smedley would still have had sufficient standing to challenge the legality of certain payments. The Court of Appeal, upholding Woolf J, considered that it was clear that the agreement could be regarded as a treaty ancillary to the Community Treaties and that no disadvantage was involved in clarifying the position at the earliest opportunity. It will only be in exceptional cases that the court will review draft Parliamentary legislation, especially where the draft is to be subject to further debate by Parliament. The better course is to await the adoption of the relevant act.

Time limits Pursuant to RSC Ord 53, r 4, an application for judicial review must be made promptly and, in any event, within three months from the date when grounds for the application first arose. The three-month time period is the limit and not every application which is brought within three months is necessarily made promptly. The Court of Justice has held that Member States may lay down reasonable time limits which, if not observed, will be a bar to claims brought under Community law.[29] The three-month time limit established by RSC Ord 53 appears to be reasonable and in Case C–208/90 *Theresa Emmott v Minister For Social Welfare*[30] the Court of Justice referred, without adverse comment, to Ord 84, r 21, para 1 of the Irish Rules of the Superior Courts 1986, which also imposed a three-month limitation period for judicial review proceedings. However, in that case the Court of Justice held that special considerations apply where a Member State has failed to implement a directive and that, until such time as a directive has been properly implemented, a defaulting Member State may not rely on an individual's delay to bar proceedings, brought against the State, to protect rights conferred on the individual by the directive. Therefore, the three-month time limit for judicial review proceedings does not begin to run until the directive has been properly implemented.

Pursuant to RSC Ord 53, r 9(5), where an individual is seeking a declaration, an injunction or damages and proceeds by judicial review the court may order that the proceedings should continue as if they had begun by writ. However, where an action has begun by writ there is no power of the court to convert it into an application for judicial review, since this would bypass the requirement that leave of the court must first be obtained. The court has power, under RSC Ord 53, r 4(1), to extend the time limit for bringing judicial review proceedings where there is good reason to do so. However, choosing the wrong procedure is not normally considered to be a good reason to extend the time limit, particularly where the extension would cause substantial prejudice to the rights of any person or would be detrimental to good administration.[31] A judgment of the Court of Justice, which clarifies an individual's rights under EC law, will not constitute a good reason for extending the time limit.[32]

---

[29] Case 33/76 *Rewe-Zentralfinanz v Landwirtschaftskammer* [1976] ECR 1989.
[30] [1991] ECR I–4269.
[31] Supreme Court Act 1981, s 31(6).
[32] *R v Ministry of Agriculture, Fisheries and Food ex p Bostock* [1991] 1 CMLR 681.

2. GROUNDS OF REVIEW

(a) General Principles[33]

Grounds of review in English administrative law The grounds on which administrative action or inaction is subject to control by judicial review can be conveniently categorised under three main headings:

(1) illegality;

(2) procedural impropriety; and

(3) irrationality.[34]

Illegality occurs where the decision-maker has misunderstood the law which regulates his decision and includes want or excess of jurisdiction.[35] Procedural impropriety occurs where there has been a failure to comply with the rules of natural justice.[36] Irrationality is often called 'Wednesbury unreasonableness',[37] and means that a decision is liable to be quashed if it is one which no reasonable authority, properly directed, could have made, ie where it is a perverse decision.

(b) Proportionality

Principle of proportionality in Community law It is a general principle of Community law that an administrative or a legislative act can be reviewed on the ground of proportionality.[38] In order for a measure to comply with the principle of proportionality:

(1) the means employed to achieve the measure's objectives must be capable of doing so; and

(2) the means employed must not go beyond what is necessary to achieve those objectives.[39]

In other words, as Lord Diplock stated in *R v Goldstein*:[40] 'You must not use a steam hammer to crack a nut...'

The principle of proportionality is a separate ground of review and has been consistently applied by the Court of Justice in determining the compatibility of national law with Community law. In Case 261/81 *Rau v De Smedt*[41] the Court held that a Belgian law, which prohibited the sale of margarine unless it was

---

[33] See, generally, Wade, *Administrative Law*, 6th edn (Oxford University Press, 1988).

[34] *Council of Civil Service Unions v Minister For Civil Service* [1985] AC 374 at 410D–411B, per Lord Diplock.

[35] In a Community law context, see *Bourgoin v Ministry of Agriculture, Fisheries and Food* [1986] 1 QB 716. *R v Ministry of Agriculture, Fisheries and Food ex p FEDESA* [1988] 3 CMLR 661 (implementing legislation void if directive illegal).

[36] In a Community law context, see *R v Home Secretary ex p Santillo* [1981] QB 778, per Lord Denning.

[37] *Associated Provincial Picture Houses Limited v Wednesbury Corporation* [1948] 1 KB 223.

[38] See pp 12–14.

[39] Case 66/82 *Fromançais SA v Fonds d'Orientation et de Régularisation des Marchés Agricoles (FORMA)* [1983] ECR 395 para 8; Case 15/83 *Denkavit Nederland BV v Hoofdproduktschap voor Akkerbouwprodukten* [1984] ECR 2171 para 25; Joined Cases 279/84, 280/84, 285/84, and 286/84 *Walter Rau Lebensmittelwerke v Commission* [1987] ECR 1069 para 34.

[40] [1983] 1 WLR 151 at 155B.

[41] [1987] ECR 3961 para 17.

sold in cubes, was contrary to the principle of proportionality. The Belgian Government argued that the law was necessary to protect the consumer by preventing any confusion between butter and margarine; the sale of margarine in cubes was 'rooted' in the habits of Belgian consumers. The Court held that although protection of the consumer was a legitimate objective, the law was not necessary to achieve that aim. 'Consumers may in fact be protected just as effectively by other measures, for example, by labelling, which hinder the free movement of goods less'. The principle of proportionality as applied in this way may be described as the 'wide principle of proportionality'.

However, when the Court of Justice reviews the legality of Community legislation, the application of the principle is modified where the act complained of arises from the exercise of a discretionary power involving economic or political responsibilities. In such cases the Court of Justice considers that:[42]

> The legality of a measure adopted in that sphere can be affected only if the measure is manifestly inappropriate having regard to the objective which the competent institution is seeking to pursue.

The Court does not seek to determine whether the measure could have achieved its objective by other, less onerous, means, but rather whether the decision-maker has 'committed a manifest error of assessment in considering that it did not have any other possible way of achieving the desired objectives by more efficient and less onerous means'. The principle of proportionality as applied to this category of acts may be described as the 'narrow principle of proportionality.'

English law: purely domestic cases In English domestic law the principle of proportionality is not a separate ground for seeking judicial review; it is merely a facet of irrationality or *Wednesbury* unreasonableness. This was confirmed, by the House of Lords, in *R v Secretary of State for the Home Department ex p Brind*.[43] The reasons given by Lord Lowry were as follows:

(1) To interfere with the discretion of an administrative body at a level lower than unreasonableness would be an abuse of the judge's supervisory jurisdiction.

(2) Judges are not equipped with the requisite knowledge and advice to decide the answer to an administrative problem where the scales are evenly balanced, but they have a much better chance of reaching the right answer where the question is put in a *Wednesbury* form.

(3) Stability and relative certainty would be jeopardised if the principle of proportionality were introduced.

(4) There would be an unjustifiable increase in applications for judicial review.

In many cases, the application of either the principle of proportionality or the *Wednesbury* unreasonableness test would result in the same answer. However, not every decision to adopt measures which are stricter than necessary can be

---

[42] For example, see Case C–331/88 *R v MAFF, ex p FEDESA* [1990] ECR I–4023 paras 12–18.
[43] [1991] 1 AC 696 at 766C–767G.

classed as perverse. The difference was recognised by Watkins LJ in the Divisional Court in *R v Home Secretary ex p Brind*:[44]

> ... in our view, the law of the United Kingdom has not developed so that a decision, which is neither perverse nor absurd and which is one which a reasonable minister properly taking into account the relevant law could take, becomes unlawful simply because it can be shown that it was not in proportion to the benefit to be obtained or the mischief to be avoided by the taking of the decision. In our opinion the application of such a concept of proportionality would result in the courts substituting their own decisions for that of the minister, and that is something which the courts of this country have consistently declined to do.

English law: cases involving Community rights There can be little doubt that English courts are bound to apply the principle of proportionality, as defined by the Court of Justice, when complying with their duty under article 5 of the EEC Treaty to protect directly effective rights derived from Community law. Section 3(1) of the European Communities Act 1972 provides that:

> For the purposes of all legal proceedings any question as to the meaning or effect of any of the Treaties, or as to the validity, meaning or effect of any Community instrument, shall be treated as a question of law and, if not referred to the European Court, be for determination as such in accordance with the principles laid down by and any relevant decision of the European Court or any court attached thereto.

Section 3(1), therefore, establishes that the Community definition of proportionality should be applied where Community rights are in issue. However, the extent to which English courts are prepared to apply the principle of proportionality, as defined by the Court of Justice, remains unclear.

In *Thomas v Chief Adjudication Officer*[45] the Court of Appeal held that national implementing legislation, which derogated from an individual right laid down in a directive, should be subject to the principle of proportionality. In *R v Minister of Agriculture Fisheries and Food ex p Bell Lines Ltd and An Bord Bainne Co-operative Ltd*[46] Forbes J considered that the principle constituted a separate ground for reviewing whether a national measure was compatible with Community law. In this case the Ministry of Agriculture, Fisheries and Food had banned all imports of milk into the United Kingdom unless they came through seventeen designated ports. Previously, the only milk imported into the United Kingdom was from Ireland and was imported through the ports of Fleetwood in Lancashire and Newport in South Wales. Neither Fleetwood nor Newport was amongst the seventeen designated ports. The plaintiffs, a shipping concern and the Irish Dairy Board, sought a declaration that Fleetwood or Newport should be included as designated ports of entry on the ground that their exclusion constituted a restriction on inter-state trade contrary to article 30 of the EEC Treaty and could not be justified on health grounds under article 36 of the EEC Treaty. There was evidence that the Minister had considered the two ports

---

[44] [1990] 2 WLR 787 at 801, cited by Lord Donaldson MR, [1991] 1 AC 696 at 721H–722B.

[45] [1991] 2 QB 164; applying the Court of Justice's ruling in Case 222/84 *Johnston v Chief Constable of the Royal Ulster Constabulary* [1986] ECR 1651.

[46] [1984] 2 CMLR 502.

but had felt it necessary to confine the importation of milk to the seventeen ports which were 'meat ports'. These ports had previously been designated as ports for the importation of meat and had experience in dealing with health problems arising from the importation of foodstuffs. Forbes J granted the declaration sought. He reached the conclusion that the exclusion of the two ports was not necessary on public health grounds. He stated:

> In my view, there would be other ways in which the desirable object of the Minister could be accomplished than by failing to designate the ports of Fleetwood and Newport for the importation of Irish UHT milk.

By contrast, in *Stoke-on-Trent City Council v B&Q plc*[47] Hoffmann J rejected the principle of proportionality as a ground for reviewing the compatibility of the Shops Act 1950 (the 'Sunday trading' legislation) with article 30 of the EEC Treaty, preferring instead to apply the principle of *Wednesbury* unreasonableness. In proceedings brought by the Council under s 222 of the Local Government Act 1972, Hoffmann J held that the ban on Sunday trading under s 47 of the Shops Act 1950 did not infringe article 30. Relying on Canadian, American and Australian case law, he stated:[48]

> In my judgment it is not my function to carry out the balancing exercise or to form my own view on whether the legislative objective could be achieved by other means. These questions involve compromises between competing interests which in a democratic society must be resolved by the legislature. The duty of the court is only to inquire whether the compromise adopted by the United Kingdom Parliament, so far as it affects community trade, is one which a reasonable legislature could have reached. The function of the court is to review the acts of the legislature but not to substitute its own policies or values.

The Court of Justice, on a preliminary reference by the House of Lords, subsequently ruled that the English Sunday trading rules were not disproportionate.[49] In applying the ruling, the House of Lords was asked by counsel to criticise the approach adopted by Hoffmann J with regard to the question of proportionality. The House declined.[50] Although the approach of Hoffmann J was criticised by Advocate-General Van Gerven,[51] it can be argued that his concerns about the division of powers between the courts and the legislature are legitimate public policy considerations. Indeed, they reflect the concerns of the Court of Justice itself when applying the narrow principle of proportionality in reviewing Community legislation adopted as a result of the exercise of a discretionary power involving economic or political responsibilities. In practical terms, Hoffmann J was doing no more than applying the narrow principle of proportionality to national legislation which balanced important social, political and economic considerations. It remains to be seen, however, whether the

---

[47] [1991] Ch 48. *Cf WH Smith v Peterborough City Council* [1991] 1 QB 304 at 342G–343G, per Schiemann J.

[48] [1991] Ch 48 at 69D–E.

[49] Case C–169/91 *Stoke-on-Trent City Council v B&Q plc*, [1993] AC 900; [1993] 1 CMLR 426.

[50] *Stoke-on-Trent City Council v B&Q plc* [1993] AC 900; [1993] 2 CMLR 509.

[51] [1993] 2 WLR 730 at 764C–H, [1993] 1 CMLR 426 at 457, para 27 of the Opinion.

application, by the English courts, of the narrow principle of proportionality when reviewing the compatibility of national law with Community law will be considered to be acceptable by the EC courts.[52]

(c) Irrationality

English law: purely domestic cases In purely domestic cases, legislative acts or acts involving political judgment cannot be reviewed on the grounds of irrationality. For example, the formulation and implementation of national economic policy are matters which depend on political judgment and any act adopted in this sphere would only be open to challenge on the grounds of bad faith or illegality. As Lord Scarman has stated:[53]

> Judicial review is a great weapon in the hands of the judges: but the judges must observe the constitutional limits set by our parliamentary system upon their exercise of this beneficent power.

English law: cases involving Community rights As a result of the judgment in *Stoke-on-Trent City Council v B&Q plc*,[54] it appears that the English courts may be prepared to review national legislation on the grounds of irrationality in cases involving Community rights. In order to decide whether the national Sunday trading legislation was compatible with Community law, Hoffmann J essentially applied the *Wednesbury* unreasonableness test in seeking to establish whether the United Kingdom Parliament was manifestly unreasonable in applying the legislation.

3. AVAILABLE REMEDIES

Prerogative remedies[55] Under RSC Ord 53, r 1(1) an individual seeking an order of mandamus, prohibition or certiorari must proceed by way of judicial review. 'Certiorari' is an order which quashes an administrative decision, 'prohibition' is an order preventing a public body acting outside its jurisdiction and 'mandamus' is an order requiring a public body to comply with its public duty. In *Bourgoin SA v Ministry of Agriculture, Fisheries and Food*[56] Parker LJ held that a national provision, which prohibited the import of turkeys from France, in breach of article 30 of the EEC Treaty, would give rise to a right to judicial review for anyone with a sufficient interest, a declaration as to the

---

[52] The Court of Justice did not refer to its own application of the narrow principle in *Stoke on Trent*. See also the observations of Dillon LJ in *R v Secretary of State for Employment ex p Equal Opportunities Commission* [1993] 1 WLR 872 at 887C–E. See also the issue of public policy limitations (discussed at p 59).

[53] *R v Secretary of State For the Environment ex p Nottinghamshire County Council* [1986] AC 240 at 250–251. See also *R v Environment Secretary ex p Hammersmith London Borough Council* [1990] 1 AC 521 at 594, per Lord Bridge.

[54] [1991] Ch 48.

[55] See, generally, Wade, *Administrative Law*, 6th edn (Oxford University Press, 1988), 616–664.

[56] [1985] 3 WLR 1027 at 1084E–F.

invalidity of the measure constituting the breach and, *possibly*, a mandamus to the relevant officials to permit the landing of the goods concerned. Mandamus, it seems, will not lie to force the Government to introduce new legislation in Parliament.[57]

Common law remedies[58] RSC Ord 53, r 1(2) provides that a declaration or an injunction may be granted on an application for judicial review where the court considers it just and convenient, having regard to all the circumstances of the case. The power to grant injunctions includes interim injunctions ordering a Minister to disapply an Act of Parliament to protect putative rights derived from Community law.[59]

In *R v Secretary of State for Employment, ex p Equal Opportunities Commission*[60] the majority of the Court of Appeal (Kennedy and Hirst LJJ) held that the Equal Opportunities Commission (EOC) could not seek a declaration that the United Kingdom was in breach of Community law by imposing a five-year threshold for part-time workers and a two-year threshold for full-time workers in respect of their entitlement to statutory redundancy pay. Kennedy LJ stated[61] '... it is not the function of judicial review simply to pronounce upon the law in order to clarify it'. Referring, later, to the possibility of the EC Commission bringing proceedings against the United Kingdom under article 169 of the EEC Treaty, he stated:[62]

> I do not accept that it is possible to use the procedure of judicial review as a form of fast track to give Community Directives full and immediate effect in English law.

In respect of the allegedly discriminatory time period, Dillon LJ would have been prepared to give a declaration.[63] He held that:

> The making of the declarations in these proceedings would further the statutory duties of the EOC by providing an authoritative ruling by a competent national court which can form the basis for claims by persons otherwise discriminated against by the five-year threshold in industrial tribunals or by actions for damages on the basis of *Francovich v Italian Republic* (Case C–6/90) ...

Dillon LJ's view is more 'communautaire' and is to be preferred. The English courts should not be prepared to sit back and wait for the Commission to bring proceedings under article 169 of the EEC Treaty in order to force the Government to change what might be a blatantly discriminatory law. National courts are, in effect, Community courts. They are charged, pursuant to article 5 of the

---

[57] *R v Employment Secretary ex p Equal Opportunities Commission* [1993] 1 WLR 872.

[58] See, generally, Wade, *Administrative Law*, 6th edn (Oxford University Press, 1988), 583–615.

[59] RSC Ord 53, r 3(10)(b). *R v Secretary of State for Transport, ex p Factortame Ltd (No 2)* [1991] 1 AC 603. See also pp 90–100.

[60] [1993] 1 WLR 872, reversed on appeal to the House of Lords, [1994] 2 WLR 409.

[61] Ibid at 894H.

[62] Ibid at 896H–897A.

[63] Ibid at 882H. Curiously, he was not prepared to declare that the method of calculating redundancy pay was discriminatory and, therefore, illegal as he did not believe that the declaration would have any practical effect. It could be argued that the practical effect would have been to produce an authoritative ruling of illegality which would force the Government to change the law.

EEC Treaty, with the duty of 'sincere co-operation' with the Community.[64] This means that they must do everything possible to ensure the full effectiveness of Community law. A declaration by the national court that the United Kingdom is in breach of its EEC Treaty obligations constitutes, as Dillon LJ stated, an authoritative ruling by a competent national court which can form the basis for claims by affected persons. It also acts as a catalyst for the unlawful law to be amended by the State.

A court may award damages on an application for judicial review under RSC Ord 53, r 7.[65]

---

[64] See p 53.

[65] In order to claim damages the statement in support of the application for judicial review must contain a fully particularised claim for damages.

Part III

Preliminary References

Chapter 10

References to the Court of Justice for a Preliminary Ruling

1. INTRODUCTION

(a) The preliminary ruling procedure under Article 177

Article 177 Article 177 of the EEC Treaty provides:

> The Court of Justice shall have jurisdiction to give preliminary rulings concerning: (a) the interpretation of this Treaty; (b) the validity and interpretation of Acts of the institutions of the Community; (c) the interpretation of the statutes of bodies established by an Act of the Council, where those statutes so provide.
>
> Where such a question is raised before any court or tribunal of a Member State, that court or tribunal may, if it considers that a decision on the question is necessary to enable it to give judgment, request the Court of Justice to give a ruling thereon.
>
> Where any such question is raised in a case pending before a court or tribunal of a Member State, against whose decisions there is no judicial remedy under national law, that court or tribunal shall bring the matter before the Court of Justice.

This is the preliminary ruling procedure under which a national court can ask the Court of Justice to give a ruling on certain questions of Community law. The ruling is preliminary because it is made before the national court gives final judgment. References are only made to the Court of Justice and not to the Court of First Instance.[1]

Discretionary and mandatory references Article 177 makes a distinction between discretionary and mandatory references. The second paragraph uses the permissive word 'may' in contrast to the obligatory word 'shall' in the third paragraph. In practice, courts of first instance and the Court of Appeal have a discretion whether or not to refer a question of interpretation to the Court of Justice. Therefore, except for the House of Lords, no other English court is bound to refer such a question to the Court of Justice.[2]

Purpose of the procedure The purpose of the preliminary ruling procedure is to ensure that Community law is applied uniformly by national courts. Divergent national judgments on the validity and interpretation of Community acts or on the exercise of Community rights are liable to jeopardise the unity of the

---

[1] EEC Treaty, article 168a(1).
[2] Discretionary references are dealt with at pp 134–140 and mandatory references at pp 141–146.

Community legal order and to detract from the fundamental requirement of legal certainty.[3] The Court of Justice is best placed to ensure this uniformity. As Bingham J stated:[4]

> It has a panoramic view of the Community and its institutions, a detailed knowledge of the treaties and of much subordinate legislation made under them, and an intimate familiarity with the functioning of the Community market which no national judge denied the collective experience of the Court of Justice could hope to achieve.

The procedure provided for in article 177 is, therefore, an instrument for co-operation between the Court of Justice and the national courts. The Court of Justice provides the national courts with the criteria to interpret Community law or, as the case may be, to settle issues of validity of Community acts.[5]

Role of the parties The parties have no right to demand a reference to the Court of Justice. The right to make a reference is that of the national courts. As the Court of Justice stated in Case 5/72 *Fratelli Grassi fu Davide v Italian Finance Administration:*[6]

> According to Article 177 of the Treaty it is for the national court and not the parties to the main action to bring the matter before the Court of Justice. Since the power to formulate the questions to be referred is vested in the national court alone the parties cannot alter the wording of those questions.

Consequently, any attempt by the parties to bring a matter directly before the Court of Justice will be held to be inadmissible by the Court of Justice.[7] As Lord Denning MR stated in *Bulmer v Bollinger:*[8]

> None of the parties can go off to the European Court and complain. The European court would not listen to any party who went moaning to them. The European court take the view that the trial judge has a complete discretion to refer or not to refer ... with which they cannot interfere. ... If a party wishes to challenge the decision of the trial judge in England—to refer or not to refer—he must appeal to the Court of Appeal in England.

(b) Definition of court or tribunal

'Of a Member State' The court or tribunal must be 'of a Member State'. This includes European territories for whose external relations a Member State is responsible and those overseas countries and territories listed in Annex IV to the EEC Treaty.[9]

---

[3] See Case 66/80 *International Chemical v Amministrazione* [1981] ECR 1191 at 1215; Case 314/85 *Foto-Frost v Haupzollamt* [1987] ECR 4199 at 4231; Case 166/73 *Rheinmühlen v EVST* [1974] ECR 33 at 38.

[4] *Customs & Excise Commissioners v ApS Samex* [1983] 1 All ER 1042 at 1055h.

[5] Joined Cases 297/88, C–197/89 *Massam Dzodzi v Belgium* [1990] ECR I–3763 para 33.

[6] [1972] ECR 443 para 4. See also Joined Cases 31/62 and 33/62 *Wohrman and Lutticke v Commission* [1962] ECR 501; Case 44/65 *Hessische v Singer* [1965] ECR 965; Case 247/86 *ALSATEL v NOVASAM SA* [1988] ECR 5987 para 7, where the Court of Justice refused to hear arguments on article 85 when the reference only mentioned article 86.

[7] Which is what happened in Case 29/68 *Milch v Haupzollamt* [1969] ECR 165; see particularly the Opinion of Advocate-General Gand at 186.

[8] [1974] Ch 401 at 420H.

[9] The territorial ambit of the EEC Treaty is set out in article 227. See Joined Cases C–100/89 and C–101/89 *Kaefer and Procacci v France* [1990] ECR I–4647 and Case C–260/90 *Leplat v French*

Community law concept Whether a body constitutes a 'court or tribunal' is to be decided by reference to Community law, not national law. Thus, in Case 246/80 *Broekmeulen v Huisarts Registratie Commissie*[10] the Court of Justice held that a Medical Appeals Committee could make a reference under article 177, although the Committee did not constitute a court or tribunal under Dutch law. The Court of Justice has given a wide interpretation to the phrase 'court or tribunal' (*juridiction* in the French text) to ensure that it can assist most bodies which determine the exercise of Community rights. In general, the Court of Justice considers that a court or tribunal is one which:

(1) is a permanent body;
(2) is charged with the settlement of disputes;
(3) acts judicially or *quasi*-judicially;
(4) gives the parties the right to be heard and to be legally represented;
(5) has no connection with the person who made the decision which is the subject of the proceedings; and
(6) whose composition entails some degree of State involvement.[11]

Courts and administrative tribunals In England, references may be made by the magistrates' court, the Crown Court, the High Court, the Court of Appeal, the House of Lords and other specialised courts, such as the Patents Court. Many administrative tribunals have the power to make a reference and the Social Security Commissioner,[12] income tax commissioners,[13] industrial tribunals,[14] the Employment Appeal Tribunal[15] and the VAT Tribunal[16] have all done so. However, purely advisory administrative tribunals are not entitled to seek preliminary rulings from the Court of Justice.[17]

Disciplinary tribunals Disciplinary tribunals may make references to the Court of Justice provided that they possess the characteristics listed above.[18] On this basis, the Professional Conduct Committee of the General Medical Council in England, for example, might constitute a tribunal within the meaning of article 177, since its duties and powers are regulated by the Medical Act 1983 and some of its members are nominated by the Privy Council. By contrast, the professional conduct committees of the Bar Council and the Law Society, and the disciplinary committee of bodies such as the Jockey Club, would probably not fall within the definition of tribunal since they are of a private nature.

Polynesia [1992] 2 CMLR 512, where references were made by a court in French Polynesia.
[10] [1981] ECR 2311.
[11] Case 61/65 *Vaassen-Göbbels v Beambtenfonds* [1966] ECR 261; Case 246/80 *Broekmeulen v Huisarts Registratie Commissie* [1981] ECR 2311; *Re Borker* [1980] ECR 1975; Case C–24/92 *Corbiau v Administration de Contributions* judgment of 30 March 1993 (reference by head of Luxembourg tax authorities inadmissible).
[12] Case 150/85 *Drake v Chief Adjudication Officer* [1986] ECR 1995.
[13] Case 44/84 *Hurd v Jones* [1986] ECR 29.
[14] Case 222/84 *Marguerite Johnston v Chief Constable of the Royal Ulster Constabulary* [1986] ECR 1651.
[15] Case 19/81 *Burton v British Railways Board* [1982] ECR 555.
[16] Case 5/84 *Direct Cosmetics Ltd v Customs & Excise Commissioners* [1985] ECR 617.
[17] Case 318/85 *Greis Unterweiger* [1986] ECR 955. Compare Case 61/65 *Vaassen-Göbbels v Beambtenfonds* [1966] ECR 261 and Case 36/73 *Nederlandse Spoorwegen v Minister van Verkeer en Water staat* [1973] ECR 1299, particularly the Opinion of Advocate-General Mayras.
[18] Case 246/80 *Broekmeulen v Huisarts Registratie Commissie* [1981] ECR 2311.

Arbitration Arbitrators appointed voluntarily by contract, by parties to a dispute, cannot make references to the Court of Justice.[19] This fact must be borne in mind by an English judge when he is considering whether to grant leave to appeal against an arbitrator's decision. Usually, leave on general points of law will only be given when the judge considers that a strong *prima facie* case has been made out that the arbitrator was wrong.[20] However, where a point of Community law has been raised before the arbitrator, leave to appeal should normally be granted where the point is 'capable of serious argument'.[21]

(c) Questions which may be referred

Interpretation of the Treaty The Court of Justice has jurisdiction to interpret the EEC Treaty pursuant to article 177(1)(a).[22] Preliminary rulings may also be given concerning the accession treaties[23] and the protocol on the privileges and immunities of the Community, annexed to the EEC Treaty.[24] Interpretation of the Treaty includes interpretation of Community law generally. Thus, in *R v Secretary of State for Transport ex p Factortame*[25] the Court of Justice, on a reference from the House of Lords, ruled that Community law should be interpreted as meaning that a national court must have jurisdiction to grant an interim injunction against the Crown where putative rights of Community law are involved.

Validity and interpretation of acts of Community institutions[26] The Parliament, Council, Commission and the Court of Justice are the only Community institutions.[27] Unlike article 173, which excludes review by the Court of Justice of recommendations or opinions, article 177(1)(b) of the EEC treaty confers on the Court jurisdiction to give a preliminary ruling on the validity and interpreta-

---

[19] Case 102/81 *Nordsee v Reederei* [1982] ECR 1095. Compare Case 61/65 *Vaassen-Göbbels v Beambtenfonds* (arbitration sufficiently connected to the State).

[20] *Pioneer Shipping and BTP Tioxide (the Nema)* [1982] AC 724 at 743, per Lord Diplock. Stricter criteria are applied when dealing with questions of law involved in the construction of a one-off clause in a contract.

[21] *Bulk Oil (Zug) AG v Sun International Limited* [1984] 1 WLR 147 at 154H–155F, per Ackner LJ, confirming the decision of Bingham J to grant leave [1983] 1 Lloyd's Rep 655.

[22] The Court of Justice also has jurisdiction to give preliminary rulings concerning the interpretation of Euratom pursuant to article 150(1)(c) of that Treaty and article 41 of the ECSC Treaty, as interpreted by the Court in Case 221/88 *ECSC v Busseni* [1990] ECR I–495 (ECSC).

[23] See, for example, article 1(3) of the Treaty of Accession 1972, which brings that treaty and the Act of Accession annexed to it within the scope of article 177 of the EEC Treaty. See also Case 44/84 *Hurd v Jones (Inspector of Taxes)* [1986] ECR 29.

[24] Case 32/67 *Van Leeuwen v Rotterdam* [1968] ECR 43.

[25] [1990] ECR I–2433. The ruling was: 'Community law must be interpreted as meaning that a national court which, in a case before it concerning Community law, considers that the sole obstacle which precludes it from granting interim relief is a rule of national law must set aside that rule'.

[26] Although article 41 of the ECSC Treaty gives the Court of Justice sole jurisdiction to give preliminary rulings on the validity of acts of the High Authority and of the Council, the Court of Justice held that it also had jurisdiction to give preliminary rulings concerning the interpretation of such acts: Case C–221/88 *ECSC v Busseni* [1990] ECR I–495 (ECSC).

[27] Part V of the EEC Treaty, articles 137–192. Under the Maastricht Treaty article 177 will also apply to the validity and interpretation of acts of the European Central Bank.

tion of all acts of the institutions of the Community without exception, including (but not limited to) regulations, directives, decisions, recommendations and opinions.[28] Furthermore, the jurisdiction to rule on validity, under article 177, is not subject to the restrictive *locus standi* requirements or the two-month time limit period prescribed under article 173. Different considerations may apply where a party had *locus standi* to challenge the Community measure under article 173, but failed to do so.[28a] Although article 177 does not specify the grounds on which the validity of a Community act may be declared invalid, in practice the grounds are substantially the same under both articles 173 and 177.

Interpretation of international treaties International treaties which the Council has concluded pursuant to articles 228 and 238 of the EEC Treaty constitute acts of the Council within the meaning of article 177(1)(b).[29] The Court of Justice also has jurisdiction to interpret international agreements in relation to which the Community has assumed the Member States' commitments.[30] However, international treaties concluded by Member States outside the framework of Community law do not constitute acts of the institutions, even though they may relate to the Community in some way.[31] Similarly, an agreement concluded by private undertakings does not constitute an act of the institutions, even though the act may be required or envisaged by Community law.[32]

Brussels and Rome Conventions The Convention on Jurisdiction and Enforcement of Judgments in Civil and Commercial Matters (the Brussels Convention 1968) does not constitute an act of the institutions within the meaning of article 177(1)(b) of the EEC Treaty. However, the Court of Justice has jurisdiction to give preliminary rulings on the Brussels Convention by virtue of the 1971 Protocol to the Convention, which is set out in Schedule 2 to the Civil Jurisdiction and Judgments Act 1982. Similarly, the Court will, pursuant to the Brussels Protocol 1988, be able to give rulings on the Rome Convention on the Law applicable to Contractual Relations.[33] The Brussels Protocol is set out in Schedule 3 to the Contracts (Applicable Law) Act 1990. The main difference

---

[28] Case 322/88 *Grimaldi v Fonds des Maladies* [1989] ECR 4416 (recommendations). See also Case 294/83 *Les Verts v European Parliament* [1986] ECR 1339 at 1365.

[28a] Case C–188/92 *TWD Textilwerke Deggendorf GmbH v Germany*, judgment of 9 March 1994.

[29] Case 181/73 *Haegeman v Belgium* [1974] ECR 449 (Greek Association Agreement); Case 87/75 *Bresciani* [1976] ECR 129 (Yaoundé Convention); Case 270/80 *Polydor v Harlequin Record Shops* [1982] ECR 329 (Portuguese Association Agreement); Case 17/81 *Pabst v Richarz* [1982] ECR 1331 (Greek Association Agreement); Case 174/84 *Bulk Oil v Sun International* [1986] ECR 559 (EEC-Israel Agreement); Case C-192/89 *SZ Sevince v Staatssecretaris Van Justitie* [1992] 2 CMLR 57 (Turkish Association Agreement).

[30] Joined Cases 267–269/81 *Amministrazione della Finanze dello Stato v SPI and SAMI* [1983] ECR 801 (GATT); Joined Cases 290/81 and 291/81 *Singer v Geigy* [1983] ECR 847. It is doubtful whether the Court of Justice could rule on the validity of such treaties.

[31] Case 44/84 *Hurd v Jones* [1986] ECR 29 (treaties concluded by the Member State setting up the European schools); see also Case 130/73 *Vandeweghe v Berufsgenossenenschaft* [1973] ECR 1329 (1957 bilateral agreement between Belgium and Germany).

[32] Case 152/83 *Demouche v Fonds de garantie automobile* [1987] ECR 3833 (the agreement between the National Insurance Bureaux relating to the Green Card scheme, which constituted a pre-condition for the entry into force of Council Directive 72/166 on the approximation of laws of the Member States relating to insurance against civil liability in respect of the use of motor vehicles, OJ (English special edition) 1972(ii) p 360).

[33] The Protocol is not yet in force as it has not been ratified by a sufficient number of contracting States.

between the two Protocols and article 177 is that, in principle, only courts sitting in an appellate capacity may request a preliminary ruling under the Protocols.

European Economic Area Article 107 of the Treaty on a European Economic Area (EEA) provides for courts and tribunals in EFTA Treaty States to request the Court of Justice to rule on the interpretation of EEA law. The Court of Justice, in Opinion 1/92, has stated that such rulings will be binding on the EFTA Treaty courts and tribunals.[34]

Interpretation of the statutes of bodies Article 177(1)(c) of the EEC Treaty governs the interpretation of the statutes of bodies established by an act of the Council. This is necessary as the statute of the relevant body may not constitute an act within the meaning of article 177(1)(b). However, the power to interpret statutes of bodies established by an act of the Council has little practical significance. Moreover, the power only exists where the statute so provides.[35]

(d) Limits on the jurisdiction of the Court of Justice to give preliminary rulings

National law Article 177 of the EEC Treaty does not give the Court of Justice jurisdiction, either to interpret national law[36] or to decide upon the compatibility of national law with Community law (as it is possible for it to do under article 169 of the EEC Treaty).[37] Questions concerning whether national law is compatible with Community law will often be reformulated by the Court of Justice.[38]

Finding of fact There is a separation of function between national courts and the Court of Justice and, in this respect, it is not for the Court of Justice to ascertain the facts which have given rise to the dispute before the national court or to apply Community law to the facts of the case.[39] However, although it is for the national court to make the factual assessments in applying Community law, the Court of Justice may inform the national court of the relevance or pertinence of a particular fact when making the assessment. For example, in Case C–298/89 *Rigsadvokaten v Ryborg*[40] a Danish national, Ryborg, who worked in Germany but frequently returned to Denmark to visit his girlfriend, had his car confiscated in Denmark because no car tax had been paid there. He argued that the confiscation was unlawful as it was contrary to Directive 83/182, which exempts from tax the temporary importation of means of transport by persons who are normally resident in another Member State. The Danish court referred a

---

[34] [1992] 2 CMLR 217.
[35] For example article 14 of the rules of the Administration Commission on Social Security for Migrant workers, OJ No C 68, 21 August 1973, p 15.
[36] Joined Cases C–297/88, C–197/89 *Massam Dzodzi v Belgium* [1990] ECR I–3763 para 42.
[37] Case 6/64 *Costa Flaminio v ENEL* [1964] ECR 585 at 593.
[38] Case 148/85 *Direction Générale des Impôts v Forest* [1986] ECR 3449 at 3472; Case 14/86 *Pretore Di Sâlo v Persons Unknown* [1987] ECR 2545 at 2569. See p 148.
[39] Case 17/81 *Pabst & Richarz KG v Hauptzollamt Oldenburg* [1982] ECR 1331; Case 247/86 *ALSATEL v NOVASAM SA* [1988] ECR 5987 para 22.
[40] [1993] 1 CMLR 218.

question to the Court of Justice on the criteria to be adopted to determine normal residence in circumstances such as Ryborg's. The Court ruled that the test for determining normal residence was where a person had established his permanent centre of interests and that, in the circumstances of the case, that test was not satisfied by the mere fact that a person spent nights and weekends with a girl-friend. In effect, the national court was told by the Court that a particular fact was not sufficient to satisfy a particular test laid down by Court of Justice.

The Court of Justice can admit evidence or find additional facts which are necessary to determine a proper interpretation or the validity of a Community provision. This is plain from article 103(1) of the Rules of Procedure, which allows the Court of Justice to conduct preparatory enquiries in article 177 proceedings. As Advocate-General Warner explained in Case 51/75 *EMI v CBS*,[41] the ultimate objective of admitting evidence in article 177 proceedings is to enable the court to frame its answers in a manner likely to be most helpful to the national court. Thus, the Court has accepted evidence in addition to that supplied by the national court in order to determine whether a regulation should be declared invalid[42] or interpreted in a certain way.[43] It is essential that the Court of Justice is able to find additional facts to answer questions of law raised since the facts may not be within the capacity of the referring court to find or the parties to prove.

Occasionally, the Court of Justice may make a finding of fact where it is essential to enable national courts to assess the compatibility of national rules with Community law in a uniform manner. Thus, in Case C–169/91 *Stoke-on-Trent v B&Q plc*[44] the Court considered that the effect on trade of the United Kingdom's Sunday trading laws (such as those contained in the Shops Act 1950) was not excessive to the legitimate aim pursued. The Court held that such rules were not disproportionate, even though previously in Case 145/88 *Torfaen Borough Council v B&Q plc*[45] this was considered by the Court to be a question of fact for the national courts.

(e) Inadmissible references

Exceptional cases It is primarily a matter for the national court whether, having regard to the facts of the case, a preliminary ruling is necessary to enable it to give judgment.[46] In order to provide a satisfactory answer to the national court, the Court of Justice may reformulate the question referred or consider provisions of Community law other than those to which the national court has referred in its question.[47] Nevertheless, the Court of Justice may decline to give a ruling in exceptional cases where the question referred is irrelevant, vague,

[41] [1976] ECR 811 at 854.
[42] Case 131/77 *Milac v Hauptzollamt* [1978] ECR 1041.
[43] Case 47/82 *Gebroeders Vismans BV v Inspecteur de Invoerrechtenen* [1982] ECR 3983.
[44] Judgment of 16 December 1992. See also Case C–312/89 *Union departmentale v SIDEF Conforama* [1991] ECR 997; Case C–332/89 *Marchandise* [1991] ECR 1027.
[45] [1989] ECR 3851.
[46] Joined Cases 98/85, 162/85 and 258/85 *Bertini v Region e Lazio* [1986] ECR 1885.
[47] Case C–315/88 *Italy v Angelo Pennacchiotti* [1992] 3 CMLR 561 para 10.

amounts to an abuse of the Court's procedure or where there is no longer any dispute before the national court.

Obvious irrelevancy A request from a national court may be rejected if it is obvious that the interpretation of Community law or the examination of the validity of Community law bears no relation to the actual nature of the case or to the subject-matter of the main action.[48]

Vagueness of the question referred A request will be held inadmissible if the question asked by the national court is so vague that it is impossible to identify the doubts entertained by the national court. If the Court of Justice is to give a useful reply to the questions referred it is necessary for national courts to describe the factual and legislative background to the questions. Failure to comply with this requirement is likely to lead the Court of Justice to decline jurisdiction by order, pursuant to article 92 of the Rules of Procedure.[49]

Abuse of procedure The Court of Justice will not entertain a reference where it is apparent from the file on the case or the facts stated by the national court that there is no genuine dispute between any parties in the national proceedings. Thus, in Case 104/79 *Foglia v Novello*[50] the Court emphasised that the purpose of article 177 is not to deliver advisory opinions on general or hypothetical questions but to assist in the administration of justice in the Member States.

No dispute The Court of Justice has no jurisdiction to hear a reference for a preliminary ruling when, at the time it is made, the procedure before the referring court has already been terminated. Moreover, it is only the court called upon to resolve the dispute which may make the reference. As the Court of Justice has stated, the right to make a reference is, 'limited to a court or tribunal which considers that a case pending before it raises questions of Community law requiring a decision on *its* part'.[51] The question arises whether a judge hearing an application for an interlocutory injunction may make a reference to the Court of Justice which is not necessary to determine whether the injunction should be granted, but in order to give a final decision on the merits. Although this matter is not entirely clear, an English judge probably does have such power on the basis that it is the same court, albeit a different judge, which will hear both the interlocutory and the substantive proceedings.[52]

---

[48] Case 126/80 *Salonia v Poidamani* [1981] ECR 1563. Case 105/79 *Acting Judge at Hayange* [1979] ECR 2257; Case C–343/90 *Dias v Director Da Alfande do Porto* judgment of 16 July 1992.

[49] Case 14/86 *Pretore di Sâlo v Persons Unknown* [1987] ECR 2545 at 2569; Joined Cases C–320–C322/90 *Telemarsicabruzzo SpA* judgment of 26 January 1993; *Pretore Di Genova v Banchero* Order of 19 March 1993.

[50] Case 104/79 *Foglia v Novello* 1 [1980] ECR 745, criticised by Barav (1980) 5 EL Rev 443; Case 244/80 *Foglia v Novello* 2 [1981] ECR 3045; Case 150/88 *Eau de Cologne v Provide SRL* [1989] ECR 3891; Joined Cases 98/85, 162/85, 258/85 *Bertini v Regione Lazio* [1986] ECR 1885; Case C–83/91 *Wienand Meilicke v ADV/ORGA FA Mayer AG* judgment of 16 July 1992.

[51] Case 338/85 *Pardini v Ministero Del Commcercio Con l'Estro* [1988] ECR 2041 para 10; Case C–159/90 *SPUC v Grogan* [1991] 3 CMLR 849 para 12.

[52] See p 137.

(f) Effect of preliminary rulings

Binding nature A preliminary ruling is binding on the national court which referred the question.[53] Since the main purpose of article 177 of the EEC Treaty is to ensure that Community law is applied uniformly by national courts, a ruling by the Court of Justice under article 177 also binds national courts other than the particular referring court. Thus, a ruling that a Community act is invalid precludes other national courts from giving effect to that act, although they still remain competent to refer a question which has already been settled by the Court.[54] This position is reflected in the United Kingdom by s 3(1) of the European Communities Act 1972, which provides that questions of Community law shall, if not referred to the Court of Justice, be decided 'in accordance with the principles laid down by and any relevant decision of' that Court. Thus, preliminary rulings by the Court of Justice are binding upon all courts in England, including the House of Lords.[55]

Temporal limitations A preliminary ruling on the interpretation of a Community provision clarifies and defines, where necessary, the meaning and scope of that provision as it must be, or ought to have been, understood and applied from the time of its coming into force. Similarly, a ruling that a Community act is invalid takes effect as from the entry into force of that act.[56] The fact that the invalidity of a Community act dates back to its adoption may explain why the Court sometimes uses the words 'invalid' and 'void' interchangeably in article 177 proceedings.[57]

The effect of a judgment *ex tunc* (ie from the date of the adoption of the act), rather than *ex nunc* (ie from the date of the judgment), can often give rise to serious economic repercussions. Consequently, the Court may, by analogy with the second paragraph to article 174 of the EEC Treaty, limit the temporal effect of its rulings for reasons of legal certainty. Temporal limitations may be imposed on rulings concerning the invalidity of Community provisions,[58] as well as on rulings concerning their interpretation.[59] It is for the Court of Justice alone

---

[53] Case 29/68 *Milchkontor v Hauptzollamt Saarbrücken* [1969] ECR 165 at 180; Case 52/76 *Benedetti v Munari* [1977] ECR 163 at 183.

[54] Case 66/80 *International Chemical Corporation* [1981] ECR 1191 at 1215. Occasionally the Court departs from a previous ruling, eg Case C–10/89 *SA CNL-Sucal NV v Hag* [1990] ECR I 3711, effectively overruled Case 192/73 *Van Zuylen Frères v Hag AG* [1974] ECR 731.

[55] See, in particular, the judgment of Lord Diplock in *Garland v British Rail* [1983] 2 AC 751 at 771G; and the Opinion of Advocate-General Warner in Case 112/76 *Manzoni v Finrom* [1977] ECR 1647.

[56] Joined Cases 66/79, 127/79, 128/79 *Amministrazione delle Finanze v Salumi* [1980] ECR 1237 at 1261; Case 61/79 *Amministrazione delle Finanze v Denkavit* [1980] ECR 1205.

[57] See Case 66/80 *International Chemical Corporation v Amministrazione* [1981] ECR 1191 at 1215.

[58] Case 4/79 *Providence Agricole de la Champagne v BNIC* [1980] ECR 2823 at 2852 (invalidity of regulations concerning monetary compensatory amounts); Case 112/83 *Produit de Maïs v Administration des Douanes* [1985] ECR 719 at 748; Case 41/84 *Pinna v Caisse* [1986] ECR 1 at 26 (invalidity of regulation concerning family benefits); Case C–38/90 *R v Lomas* [1992] 2 CMLR 653 at 673 (sheep-meat regulation).

[59] Case 43/75 *Defrenne v Sabena* [1976] ECR 455 at 480 (article 119 of the EEC Treaty); Case 24/86 *Blaizot v University of Liege* [1988] ECR 379 (article 7 of the EEC Treaty and vocational

to decide whether any temporal limitation should be placed on its ruling which, moreover, can only be made in its original judgment.[60] The Court may decide that an exception to a temporal limitation should be made in favour of the party who brought the action before the national court or in favour of any other person who took similar steps before the date of the Court's ruling. It is not certain what steps must be taken and although a letter before action which raises an equivalent claim may sometimes suffice, it is safer for third parties to have initiated legal proceedings themselves (eg by issuing a writ) before the date of the Court's ruling.

The Court also has jurisdiction to declare that a Community provision is invalid, but that it should remain temporarily in force until it is replaced by a new provision. This may happen where the provision has not been adopted on the appropriate legal basis, so that the element vitiating the legality is technical rather than substantive. The Court may make such a ruling where the invalidity of the Community provision would be likely to interfere with the exercise of rights flowing from the EEC Treaty.[61]

2. DISCRETIONARY REFERENCES

Nature of the discretion Courts and tribunals from whose decisions there is a possibility of appeal or of review have the 'widest discretion in referring matters to the Court of Justice'.[62] Consequently, the fact that the High Court is bound by a previous decision of the House of Lords on a particular point of Community law cannot preclude the High Court from referring the question to the Court of Justice, nor can the High Court's discretion be fettered by any rule of practice laid down by higher courts. Article 177 makes it clear that a national court or tribunal should consider two matters in deciding whether to make a reference to the Court of Justice. These are:

(1) whether a decision on the question of Community law is necessary to enable it to give judgment; and

(2) if so, whether the court should, in the exercise of its discretion, order that a reference be made.

(a) A decision on the question of Community law is necessary

The Community point is substantially determinative The word 'necessary' should not be construed too narrowly. The view of Lord Denning MR in *Bulmer v Bollinger*[63] that the point must be 'conclusive' is unduly restrictive and has not

---

training); Case C–262/88 *Barber v Guardian Royal Exchange Assurance Group* [1990] ECR I–1889 at 1956 (article 119 of the EEC Treaty and contracted-out pension schemes).

[60] Case 309/85 *Barra v Belgium* [1988] ECR 355.

[61] By analogy with Case C–295/90 *Re Students' Rights European Parliament v Council* [1992] 3 CMLR 281 (which concerned the right of residence for students for the purposes of vocational training under Council Directive 90/366).

[62] Case 166/73 *Rheinmülen v EVST* [1974] ECR 33 at 38.

[63] [1974] Ch 401 at 420E–421C.

generally been followed. In *Polydor v Harlequin Record Shops*[64] Ormrod LJ said:

> I would not, for my part, be inhibited by any nice questions of necessity, and would regard the word 'necessary' as meaning 'reasonably necessary' in ordinary English and not unavoidable.

On the other hand, the word 'necessary' is stronger than 'desirable' or 'convenient'[65] and is generally understood to mean that the Community law point should be substantially determinative of the case.[66]

Previous ruling of the Court of Justice Where the Court of Justice has made a ruling on the same point or substantially the same point, it may not be necessary for the English court or tribunal to make a reference. The court or tribunal is bound to follow any previous ruling by virtue of s 3 of the European Communities Act 1972.[67] However, if it is considered that the previous ruling of the Court of Justice may have been wrong or there are new factors which ought to be brought to the notice of the Court of Justice, a further reference may be deemed necessary.

The answer is obvious In *R v International Stock Exchange ex p Else Ltd*[68] Sir Thomas Bingham MR stated that if 'the national court has any real doubt, it should ordinarily refer'. Thus, a reference may be unnecessary where the point is reasonably clear and free from doubt. This is known as the doctrine of *acte clair*. However, English courts should not be too ready to hold that, because the meaning of a Community provision seems plain to them, no question of interpretation is involved. As Kerr LJ stated in *R v The Pharmaceutical Society of Great Britain ex p The Association of Pharmaceutical Importers*[69] 'the English authorities show that our courts should exercise great caution in relying on the doctrine of *acte clair* as a ground for declining to make a reference'. Thus, in *Polydor v Harlequin Record Shops*[70] the Court of Appeal considered that the plaintiffs could not prevent records being imported from Portugal (which was not, at that time, part of the Community) into the United Kingdom. This conclusion was based on a particular interpretation of article 14 of the EEC-Portugal Free Trade Agreement. Although the Court of Appeal considered that the plaintiff's action was 'dead', it nevertheless referred the case to the Court of Justice which interpreted article 14 in the plaintiff's favour.[71] In *Henn and Darby v DPP* one of the issues of Community law was whether a total ban on the import of pornographic material could constitute a quantitative restriction

---

[64] [1980] 2 CMLR 413 at 428. See also *R v Plymouth Justices ex p Rogers* [1982] QB 863 at 869, [1982] 3 CMLR 221 at 227.

[65] Neil J in *An Bord Bainne Co-operative Limited v Milk Marketing Board* [1985] 1 CMLR 6 at 10.

[66] See Bingham J in *Customs & Excise Commissioners v APS Samex* [1983] 1 All ER 1042; and Macpherson J in *R v Her Majesty's Treasury ex p Daily Mail* [1987] 2 CMLR 1.

[67] See *R v Secretary of State for Social Services ex p Bomore Medical Supplies Limited* [1986] 1 CMLR 228.

[68] [1993] QB 534 at 545C–G.

[69] [1987] 3 CMLR 951 at 971.

[70] [1980] 2 CMLR 413.

[71] Case 270/80 *Polydor v Harlequin Record Shops* [1982] ECR 329.

under article 30 of the EEC Treaty. The Court of Appeal had little doubt that the answer was in the negative. The House of Lords referred the question to the Court of Justice which answered the question in the affirmative.[72]

Decide the facts first As a general rule, the facts of the case should be decided first, since once the facts have been investigated a decision on the point of Community law may be unnecessary.[73] The case may be decided on another ground altogether. Consequently, a reference should not generally be made before the pleadings have closed.[74] A reference is more likely where the essential facts are agreed or can be settled in a form which will enable the relevant question to be answered. This is consistent with guidelines laid down by the Court of Justice.[75]

This, however, is no more than a general rule to which exceptions may be made.[76] Thus, in *R v Pharmaceutical Society of Great Britain ex p Association of Pharmaceutical Importers*[77] the Court of Appeal referred the question of whether a restriction on a chemist substituting a differently named, but therapeutically identical, imported drug for that prescribed by a doctor was contrary to article 30 of the EEC Treaty on the free movement of goods. The Court of Appeal made the reference even though there were unresolved conflicts on factual matters, such as the effects on health and the importance of the so-called anxiety factor which might be caused by generic drugs.

In criminal trials on indictment it can seldom be a proper exercise of the judge's discretion to seek a preliminary ruling before the facts of the alleged offence have been ascertained.[78] This applies with added force to trials before magistrates.[79] However, where the prosecution's case is based on provisions of Community law, which the defence argues are invalid, an early reference may be desirable. As His Honour Judge Balston stated in *R v Lomas*:[80]

> To subject the defendant to a trial and the possibility of conviction on the basis of EEC law which may well turn out to be defective and of no effect is not only a waste of time and money and unfair to the defendant but to some might appear so farcical as to bring the law into disrepute.

Furthermore, where the issues of fact are not substantially in dispute, the Crown Courts or magistrates' courts are fully entitled to refer questions of

---

[72] [1978] 1 WLR 1031 (CA); [1981] AC 904 (HL); Case 34/79 [1979] ECR 3795.

[73] See Lord Denning MR in *Bulmer v Bollinger* [1974] Ch 401; Bingham J in *Customs & Excise Commissioners v APS Samex* [1983] 1 All ER 1042; Neil J in *An Bord Bainne Co-Operative Limited v Milk Marketing Board* [1985] 1 CMLR 6.

[74] *Lord Bethell v Sabena* [1983] CMLR 1; *Church of Scientology of California v Commissioners of Customs & Excise* [1980] 3 CMLR 114; *Geraldine Patricia Prince v Rt Honourable George Younger* (Court of Session) [1984] 1 CMLR 723.

[75] Case 244/78 *Union Laitière Normande v French Dairy Farmers Ltd* [1979] ECR 2663; Joined cases 36/80, 71/80 *Irish Creamery Milk Suppliers Association v Ireland* [1981] ECR 735 at 748.

[76] *R v Minister of Agriculture Fisheries & Food and the Secretary of State for Health ex p FEDESA* [1988] 3 CMLR 661, per Henry J.

[77] [1987] 3 CMLR 951 .

[78] Lord Diplock in *Henn and Darby v DPP* [1981] AC 904.

[79] Per Lord Lane CJ in *R v Plymouth Justices ex p Rogers* [1982] QB 863 at 871B–C.

[80] [1990] 1 CMLR 513 at 517.

Community law to the Court of Justice if they consider that an answer to those questions is necessary.[81] The unfortunate consequences of not making a reference in cases of this kind can be seen from *R v Tymen*, where the defendant was prosecuted for using fishing nets with meshes which were too small to comply with the requirements of regulations in the Fishing Nets (North East Atlantic) Order 1977, as amended. The facts were undisputed, but the defendant argued that the regulations were contrary to Community law. The Crown Court refused a reference to the Court of Justice, imposed a fine on the defendant and forfeited the offending nets. On appeal, the Court of Appeal referred questions to the Court of Justice to ascertain whether the regulations were contrary to Community law. The ruling by the Court of Justice was to the effect that the regulations were invalid and the conviction contrary to Community law.[82] An early reference by the Crown Court would have avoided the need for an appeal to the Court of Appeal and the defendant would not have been fined and had his nets forfeited.

It is important to note that the desirability of finding the facts first cannot restrict the national court from deciding at what stage of the proceedings it requires a preliminary ruling. The national court is fully entitled to weigh up any 'considerations of procedural organization and efficiency' in determining the appropriate time for making a reference.[83] Thus, procedural efficiency may best be served by an early reference where, for example, the question aims at ascertaining whether a provision of Community law has direct effect and is capable of giving rise to a cause of action.

Interlocutory stage It is permissible for a national court to make a reference to the Court of Justice before granting an interlocutory injunction.[84] However, the circumstances where this is likely to happen will be rare.[85] The national courts will usually either grant or refuse the interlocutory injunction and at the same time make a reference to the Court of Justice in order to give a final judgment. This may happen where the national court does not have to make any further, relevant, factual findings and the only issue to be determined is one of Community law.[86] This is consistent with RSC Ord 114, r 2 which states that a reference may be made at any stage of the proceedings.

---

[81] See *R v Plymouth Justices ex p Rogers* [1982] QB 863; *Portsmouth City Council v Richards and Quietlynn Limited* [1989] 1 CMLR 673 at 704.

[82] *R v Tymen* [1980] 3 CMLR 101, [1981] 2 CMLR 544 (CA), Case 269/80 [1981] ECR 3079, [1982] 2 CMLR 111 (ECJ).

[83] Case 72/83 *Campus Oil Ltd and Others v Minister for Energy* [1984] ECR 2727 para 10, applied in Case 14/86 *Pretore Di Salo v Persons Unknown* [1986] ECR 2545 para 11, and see in particular the comments on *Bulmer v Bollinger* made by Advocate-General Mancini at p 2557.

[84] Case 107/76 *Hoffmann-La-Roche v Centrafarm* [1977] ECR 957 at 973.

[85] Per Kerr LJ in *Portsmouth City Council v Richards and Quietlynn* [1989] 1 CMLR 673 at 704.

[86] Graham J in *EMI Records v CBS* [1975] 1 CMLR 285; see also *Polydor v Harlequin Record Shops* [1980] 2 CMLR 413 (where an interlocutory injunction was refused, but a reference was made). As to whether such references are, in any event, admissible see pp 131–132.

(b) Guidelines as to the exercise of discretion

Delay The average length of time which may elapse before a ruling can be obtained from the Court of Justice is 18.8 months.[87] Since the whole action in the English court is stayed until the ruling is obtained, one of the parties (or both) may be prejudiced, especially where one party seeks an injunction or there are other reasons for expedition. A reference is more likely to be made where the party who will suffer from any delay is the party asking for the reference.[88] Nevertheless, where a reference to the Court of Justice is inevitable at some stage, an early reference may actually save time and costs. As Bingham J stated in *Customs & Excise Commissioners v APS Samex*:[89]

> the reference to the Court of Justice would be unlikely to take longer than appeals have normally taken to reach the Court of Appeal, at least until recently, and unlikely to cost much more. If, at the Court of Appeal stage, a reference were held to be necessary, the delay and expense would be roughly doubled.

Parties' wishes If both parties want the point to be referred to the Court of Justice, the national court should have regard to their wishes. It will be rare for the national court to disagree with the parties. However, in *Portsmouth City Council v Richards and Quietlynn*[90] Kerr LJ stated that:

> It is very important that the concept of so-called references by consent should not creep into our practice. All references are by the court. The court must itself be satisfied of the need for the reference; that the factual material accompanying the reference is sufficient to provide a proper foundation for it, and that it is of sufficient assistance to the European Court to enable it to reach a decision . . . .

Observations by other parties Pursuant to article 20 of the Protocol of the Statute of the Court of Justice (EEC), all Member States, the Commission and, where the validity or interpretation of an act of the Council is in issue, the Council, are entitled to make written and oral observations to the Court of Justice. Consequently, it is a material consideration, in referring a question to the Court of Justice, that where the interests of other Member States and the Community institutions are affected they may make their views known to the Court.[91]

---

[87] This figure is taken from the *Weekly Summaries* of the Court of Justice, Number 35 of 1992.

[88] Per Lloyd LJ in *Generics UK Limited v Smith-Kline and French Laboratories Limited* [1990] 1 CMLR 416 at 435.

[89] [1983] 1 All ER 1042 at 1056. See also *R v The Pharmaceutical Society of Great Britain ex p the Association of Pharmaceutical Importers* [1987] 3 CMLR 951 at 972, per Kerr LJ who stated:
On the view which I take I would respectfully expect the House of Lords to feel bound to make a reference under the last paragraph of Article 177 in any event. On that basis an immediate reference by this court will obviously save considerable time and costs.
See also MacPherson J in *R v Her Majesty's Treasury ex p Daily Mail* [1987] 2 CMLR 1 at 4. For delays in the prosecution of a criminal trial, see *R v Manchester Crown Court ex p Acting DPP* [1992] 3 CMLR 329 at 345, per Leggatt LJ.

[90] [1989] 1 CMLR 673 at 708.

[91] See, generally, Bingham J in *Customs & Excise Commissioners v APS Samex* [1983] 1 All ER 1042 at 1055. See also Kerr LJ in *R v The Pharmaceutical Society of Great Britain ex p the Association of Pharmaceutical Importers* [1987] 3 CMLR 951 at 971.

Experience of the Court of Justice The answer to the question may turn not purely on legal considerations, but on a broader view of what the orderly development of the Community requires. As Kerr LJ stated, in *R v The Pharmaceutical Society of Great Britain ex p Association of Pharmaceutical Importers*:[92]

> There can equally be no doubt that the case is one of great general importance, not only for this country but for the Community in general, and that the Court of Justice in Luxembourg is in a far better position to reach a decision which is *communautaire* than this Court.

The experience of the Court of Justice is also relevant where there is a need to examine the Community text in different languages. As Bingham J stated in *Customs & Excise Commissioners v APS Samex*:[93]

> Where comparison falls to be made between Community texts in different languages, all texts being equally authentic, the multinational Court of Justice is equipped to carry out the task in a way which no national judge, whatever his linguistic skills, could rival.

Point is raised in good faith A reference to the Court of Justice is unlikely where the question is being raised mischievously in order to obstruct or delay an almost inevitable adverse judgment, thus denying the other party his remedy.[94] The reference should be made in a *bona fide* hope of success.

Nature of the court or tribunal Although magistrates' courts or inferior tribunals have the same discretion to refer a case to the Court of Justice as the High Court or the Crown Court, they should exercise considerable caution before referring, even after they have heard all the evidence. As Lord Lane CJ stated in *R v Plymouth Justices ex p Rogers*:[95]

> If they come to a wrong decision on Community law, a higher court can make the reference and frequently the higher court would be the more suitable forum to do so. The higher court is as a rule in a better position to assess whether any reference is desirable. On references the form of the question referred is of importance and the higher court will normally be in a better position to assess the appropriateness of the question and to assist in formulating it clearly.

Temporal limitations Where a particular interpretation of a Community provision would have severe economic consequences for third parties or for Member States, overriding considerations of legal certainty may dictate that the interpretation should have an effect *ex nunc* (from the date of the judgment) rather than *ex tunc* (the date of the adoption of the Community provision). Consequently, it is a material consideration, in deciding whether to refer, that the

---

[92] Ibid at 972. See also Nolan LJ in *R v IRC ex p Commerzbank* [1991] 3 CMLR 633 at 646 and Bingham J in *Customs & Excise Commissioners v APS Samex* [1983] 1 All ER 1042 at 1056.

[93] Ibid at 1055j.

[94] See, generally, MacPherson J in *R v Her Majesty's Treasury ex p Daily Mail* [1987] 2 CMLR 1 at 4; also Bingham J in *Customs & Excise Commissioners v APS Samex* [1983] 1 All ER 1042 at 1056d.

[95] [1982] 3 CMLR 221 at 228.

Court of Justice alone can impose limitations on the time from which an interpretation of Community law is to take effect.[96]

Parallel proceedings If there are parallel actions in other Member States there is a risk that different decisions will be made, thus compromising the uniform interpretation of Community law. In such circumstances it may be best to refer the matter to the Court of Justice. As Graham J stated in *EMI Records v CBS*:[97]

> Different decisions by the three countries concerned in the present case would lead to chaotic results and this shows the logical necessity for such a court.

Similarly, where proceedings under article 169 of the EEC Treaty have been brought by the Commission concerning a point similar, or identical to one before the English court, a reference under article 177 may be appropriate so that the direct action and the indirect action can be heard on the same or successive days.[98]

3. APPEAL AGAINST THE DECISION TO REFER OR NOT TO REFER

Existence of an appeal The Court of Justice has stated that, although the national court has the widest discretion whether or not to make a reference, article 177 of the EEC Treaty does not preclude the exercise of the discretion being subject to an appeal.[99] The Court of Appeal has jurisdiction to hear an appeal from a decision of a judge to make, or refuse, a reference to the Court of Justice (see Precedent E).

Time limit An order to refer is deemed to be a final decision and an appeal against the order lies to the Court of Appeal without leave. However, the period within which a Notice of Appeal must be served under RSC Ord 59, r 4(1) is 14 days and not the usual 28 days.[100] If the judge refuses to refer, his decision is interlocutory and leave to appeal is necessary from the judge or from the Court of Appeal.[101]

Test for appeal On appeal from an order or refusal to refer, the appellate court, whether it be the Court of Appeal or the House of Lords, must not exercise an independent discretion of its own. It must defer to the lower court's exercise of discretion and must not interfere with it merely upon the ground that the members of the appellate court would have exercised the discretion differently. It is

---

[96] See pp 133–134 in relation to temporal limitations of the Court's judgments.
[97] [1975] 1 CMLR 285 at 297.
[98] See Neill J in *An Bord Bainne Co-operative Limited v Milk Marketing Board* [1985] 1 CMLR 6 (but here no reference was made since all the relevant issues of fact had not been resolved and the judge considered that he could not formulate precisely all the questions on which a ruling was sought).
[99] Case 166/73 *Rheinmühlen v EVST* [1974] ECR 139 at 147.
[100] RSC Ord 114, r 6.
[101] Supreme Court Act 1981, s 18(1)(*h*).

only after the appellate court has reached the conclusion that the lower court's exercise of discretion must be set aside that it becomes entitled to exercise an original discretion of its own.[102] As Stevenson LJ stated in *Bulmer v Bollinger* the Court of Appeal will interfere with the exercise of judicial discretion to refer or not to refer 'when and only when the judge's decision "exceeds the generous ambit within which reasonable disagreement is possible and is, in fact, plainly wrong"'.[103] Similarly, Lord Lane CJ stated in *R v Plymouth Justices ex p Rogers* that the Divisional Court would only interfere with the decision of a magistrates' court to refer 'as long as they have not misdirected themselves in law or acted unreasonably'.[104] The Court of Appeal will, it seems, interfere with a judge's discretion where it considers that the answer to the question is obvious and it is, therefore, unnecessary to seek a ruling from the Court of Justice to enable the judge to give judgment.[105]

4. MANDATORY REFERENCES

(a) Questions of invalidity

Suspending a Community measure Although national courts have the power to declare that acts of the Community institutions are valid, they do not have the power to declare such acts invalid. Consequently, where a substantial doubt is raised in the national court on the validity of a Community measure and where it is clear that a decision on the validity of the measure is necessary for the resolution of the dispute, the national court is bound to refer the question to the Court of Justice for a preliminary ruling as to the validity of the Community measure. As the Court of Justice stated in Case 314/85 *Foto-Frost v Hauptzollamt Lübeck-Ost*:[106]

> Since Article 173 gives the Court exclusive jurisdiction to declare void an act of a Community institution, the coherence of the system requires that where the validity of a Community act is challenged before a national court the power to declare the act invalid must also be reserved to the Court of Justice.

This obligation to refer applies to all national courts, despite the fact that the second paragraph of article 177 of the EEC Treaty appears to confer the same discretion, regardless of whether the question of Community law raised is one of interpretation or one of validity.

---

[102] *Hadmor Productions v Hamilton* [1983] 1 AC, per Lord Diplock at 220. See the High Court of Justiciary on appeal from the Sheriff Court in *Procurator Fiscal Elgin v James Cowie* [1990] 3 CMLR 445 para 20:
    ... although this court might not have thought it appropriate at this stage to seek a preliminary ruling from the European Court of Justice if we had been sitting as a court of first instance, we are clearly of opinion that it cannot be held that the sheriff was not entitled to conclude that a preliminary ruling should be sought.
[103] [1974] Ch 401 at 431B.
[104] [1982] 3 CMLR 221 at 227.
[105] See *R v International Stock Exchange of the United Kingdom and the Republic of Ireland ex p Else (1982) Ltd* [1993] QB 534; [1993] 2 CMLR 677.
[106] [1987] ECR 4199 at 4231.

Suspending a national measure based on a Community measure The obligation to refer also arises where a national court suspends the operation of a national measure adopted to implement a Community measure. In Joined Cases C–143/88 and C–92/89 *Zuckerfabrik v Itzehoe*[107] the Court of Justice ruled that a national court may make such an order only if the following conditions are satisfied:

(1) the national court has serious doubts as to the validity of the Community measure;

(2) it refers the question of the validity of the Community measure to the Court of Justice, if this has not already been done;

(3) the matter is urgent;

(4) there is a risk to the applicant of serious and irreparable harm; and

(5) the national court takes due account of the Community's interests.

(b) Courts against whose decisions there is no judicial remedy

(i) Which courts are covered?

Test for final court The third paragraph of article 177 of the EEC Treaty states that where a question is raised in a case pending before a court or tribunal 'against whose decision there is no judicial remedy under national law', that court or tribunal must bring the matter before the Court of Justice. The generally accepted view is that the final court or tribunal means the highest court or tribunal in the case, rather than the highest court or tribunal in the country. Consequently, a final court is one from whose judgment there is no possibility of appeal or review. In Case 6/64 *Costa v ENEL*[108] the Italian National Electricity Board (ENEL) brought proceedings against Mr Costa in the Milan magistrates' court in respect of his failure to pay an electricity bill. Due to the sum of money involved (approximately £2) there was no possibility of appeal against the decision of the court. On a reference by the magistrates' court, the Court of Justice stated, *obiter*, that the magistrates' court was the final court for the purposes of article 177.

House of Lords is final court For most practical purposes, the House of Lords is the only court in England which is bound to refer questions of Community law within the meaning of article 177, since in most cases an appeal lies, albeit with leave, to the House of Lords from any order or judgment made by the Court of Appeal.[109] The Court of Appeal has consistently held that it is not the court of last resort even though, in order to appeal from a decision of the Court of Appeal, leave is required either from the Court of Appeal itself or from the Appel-

---

[107] [1991] ECR I–415; discussed further at pp 99–100.

[108] [1964] ECR 585. See also Case 107/76 *Hoffmann-La-Roche v Centrafarm* [1977] ECR 957 paras 3, 6 and the judgment of Advocate-General Capotorti at 979, 980.

[109] Administration of Justice (Appeals) Act 1934, s 1(1)). See *Halsbury's Statutes* 4th edn (Butterworths, 1989), vol 11. In certain limited cases the Privy Council may constitute the final court, for example on appeal from a decision of the General Medical Council.

late Committee of the House of Lords.[110] Similarly, where the Queen's Bench Divisional Court is the final appellate court for certain criminal matters, subject only to appeal to the House of Lords if the Divisional Court (and it alone) gives leave, the House of Lords is the final court and not the Queen's Bench Divisional Court.[111] Where decisions of a tribunal may only be set aside by an application to the High Court for an order of *certiorari*, there is a judicial remedy against the decision of the tribunal under English law, even though the application can only be made with leave of the High Court.[112]

If the Court of Appeal has given its decision and has then refused leave to the House of Lords, it is strange to then describe the Court of Appeal as the final court: first, because a decision on the question is *ex hypothesi* not necessary since the Court of Appeal has already given a final judgment; and second, since the Court of Appeal is *functus officio*, no such question will be 'pending' before the Court of Appeal within the meaning of article 177.[113] Although there is a passage to the contrary in *Supreme Court Practice*,[114] it is submitted that this is based on an erroneous interpretation of *dicta* by Buckley LJ in *Hagen v Fratelli*[115] where he stated that the Court of Appeal may be the final court within the meaning of article 177 where leave to appeal to the House of Lords is not 'obtainable'. The judge did not say that the Court of Appeal was the final court where leave to appeal was not obtained or not granted. Furthermore, it is most unlikely that, leave to appeal having been refused by the Court of Appeal, the House of Lords must itself then grant leave to appeal so that a reference can be made to the Court of Justice. Until leave is given, no question of Community law is pending before the House of Lords. In any event, the Appellate Committee will consider whether there is a serious question of Community law in deciding whether to grant leave.

Interlocutory proceedings A court or tribunal is not required to make a reference when the question of Community law is raised in interlocutory proceedings, even where there is no judicial remedy against the interlocutory order,

---

[110] *Bulmer (HP) v Bollinger (J) SA* [1974] Ch 401 at 420E–421C, per Lord Denning MR; *R v The Pharmaceutical Society of Great Britain ex p the Association of Pharmaceutical Importers* [1987] 3 CMLR 951 at 969, per Kerr LJ:
    There is a judicial remedy against a decision of this Court by applying for leave to appeal to the House of Lords, first to this Court and then to the House of Lords itself if necessary. A court or tribunal below the House of Lords can only fall within the last paragraph where there is no possibility of any further appeal from it.
Generics UK Ltd v Smith-Kline & French Laboratories [1991] CMLR 416 at 435, per Lloyd LJ:
    We are not, of course, the final appellate court for the purposes of Article 177 of the Treaty, even though an appeal to the House of Lords lies only with leave.
R v Southwark Crown Court ex p Watts [1992] 1 CMLR 446 at 456, per Russell LJ.

[111] *SA Magnavision v General Optical Council (No 2)* [1987] 2 CMLR 262.

[112] *Re A Holiday in Italy* (Decision of the National Insurance Commissioner) [1975] 1 CMLR 184 at 188.

[113] Case 338/85 *Pardini v Ministero Del Commcercio Con l'Estro* [1988] ECR 2041 para 10; Case C–159/90 *SPUC v Grogan* [1991] 3 CMLR 849 para 12.

[114] Sweet & Maxwell, 1993, p 1614.

[115] [1980] 3 CMLR 253 at 255.

provided that the parties are entitled to raise the question again in the substantive proceedings.[116]

(ii) Scope of the obligation to refer
CILFIT Once the House of Lords considers that a decision on a question of
Community law is necessary to give judgment, it has no discretion to decide
whether or not to refer the question to the Court of Justice. The guidelines relevant to the exercise of lower courts' discretion to refer have no application. However, the House of Lords has the same discretion as the lower courts in
ascertaining whether a decision on a question of Community law is necessary to
enable it to give judgment. Consequently, it is not every question of Community
law which must be referred to the Court of Justice. In Case 283/81 *CILFIT v
Ministry of Health*[117] the Court of Justice referred to three exceptions to the obligation on final courts to refer questions to the Court of Justice. These are:
  (1) where the question is irrelevant;
  (2) where there has been a previous judgment of the Court of Justice on the
       question; and
  (3) where the answer is obvious.

Question is irrelevant Final courts or tribunals are not obliged to refer to the
Court of Justice a question concerning the interpretation of Community law
raised before them if that question is not relevant, that is to say, if the answer to
that question, regardless of what it may be, can in no way affect the outcome of
the case. Thus, in *R v Licensing Authority ex p Smith-Kline*[118] the question before the House of Lords was whether licensing authorities under the Medicines
Act 1968 were entitled to make use of information supplied to them by pharmaceutical companies when they were considering whether to grant licences to
market generic versions of the pharmaceutical company's drug. Lord Templeman stated that the only relevant law was English law, which did not protect the
pharmaceutical companies against the use, by the licensing authority, of their
confidential information. His Lordship refused a request for a ruling under article 177 of the EEC Treaty, stating that, in his opinion, 'no question of Community law arises in connection with confidentiality or otherwise'.

Previous judgment of the Court of Justice A previous decision by the Court
of Justice which deals with identical or materially identical issues, may deprive
the obligation to refer of its purpose, although the final court is free to ask the
same question of the Court of Justice. In *Re Sandhu*[119] the question of Community law before the House of Lords was whether a non-EEC spouse of an EEC
worker was dependent for his rights of entry and residence in a Member State
upon the EEC worker exercising EEC Treaty rights or whether the non-EEC

---

[116] Case 107/76 *Hoffmann-La-Roche v Centrafarm* [1977] ECR 957 at 972; Joined Cases 35/82, 36/
       182 *Morson and Jhanjan v Netherlands* [1982] ECR 3723.
[117] [1982] ECR 3415.
[118] [1990] 1 AC 64. See also *Wellcome Foundation v Secretary of State for Social Services* [1988] 1
       WLR 635.
[119] Decision of the House of Lords, 9 May 1985 (unreported).

spouse had an independent claim under Community law. The Appellate Committee of the House of Lords granted leave to appeal on the basis that a reference was necessary, since the answer to the question was not so obvious as to leave no room for reasonable doubt. However, after the hearing by the Appellate Committee, the Court of Justice delivered a judgment in Case 267/83 *Diatta v Land Berlin*[120] which interpreted Community law in such a way that the non-EEC spouse did not have an independent claim under Community law to remain in a Member State. The House of Lords, therefore, dismissed Mr Sandhu's appeal and declined to make a reference on the basis that the second exception in *CILFIT v Ministry of Health* applied.

Answer is obvious (*acte clair*) Where the correct application of Community law is so obvious as to leave no scope for any reasonable doubt, no reference is required. This is known as the doctrine of *acte clair*. However, before the national court reaches that conclusion, it must be convinced that the matter would be equally obvious to the courts of the other Member States and to the Court of Justice. In this respect it must have regard to the following factors.[121]

(1) The characteristic features of Community law and the particular difficulties to which its interpretation gives rise, including the fact that Community legislation is drafted in several languages and that the different language versions are all equally authentic. An interpretation of a provision of Community law, therefore, involves a comparison of the different language versions.

(2) Even when the different language versions are entirely in accord with one another, Community law uses terminology which is peculiar to it. Legal concepts do not necessarily have the same meaning in Community law and in the law of the various Member States.

(3) Every provision of Community law must be placed in its context and interpreted in the light of the provisions of Community law as a whole, having regard to the objectives of the Community and to its state of evolution at the date on which the provision in question is to be applied.

Approach of the House of Lords The House of Lords has, in general, been mindful of its duty to refer under article 177 of the EEC Treaty[122] although it has, on occasions, refused a reference despite a question of Community law being clearly arguable. For example, in *R v London Boroughs Transport Committee ex p Freight Transport Association Limited*[123] and *Kirklees Borough Council v Wickes Building Supplies Ltd*[124] the House of Lords considered that a decision by the Court of Justice on a question of Community law was not necessary to enable it to give judgment, despite reversing the Court of Appeal on the

---

[120] [1985] ECR 567.

[121] Case 283/81 *Srl CILFIT v Ministry of Health* [1982] ECR 3415 paras 16–20.

[122] See, in particular, Lord Diplock in *R v Henn and Derby* [1981] AC 850 at 906 warning English judges 'not to be too ready to hold that because the meaning of the English text . . . seems plain to them no question of interpretation can be involved'.

[123] [1992] 1 CMLR 5.

[124] [1992] 3 WLR 170.

Community law point. In *Re Sandhu*[125] Lord Bridge and Lord Templeman would have refused a reference on the basis of *acte clair*, despite the fact that they differed from the judge at first instance and from one member of the Court of Appeal on the correct answer to the question of Community law and despite the fact that three members of the House of Lords had concluded that the answer was not obvious.

5. PROCEDURE BEFORE ENGLISH COURTS AND TRIBUNALS

(a) Application for a reference

(i) High Court and Court of Appeal

Rules of the Supreme Court, Ord 114   Order 114 of the Rules of the Supreme Court governs the procedure by which the High Court and the Court of Appeal seek preliminary rulings from the Court of Justice under article 177 of the EEC Treaty. An order referring a question to the Court of Justice for a preliminary ruling under article 177 may be made by the High Court or by the Court of Appeal of its own motion at any stage in a cause or matter, or on the application by a party before or at the trial or hearing thereof.[126] Where the application is made before the trial or hearing it is made by motion.[127] In the High Court no order can be made except by a judge in person. Consequently, Masters cannot order references to the Court of Justice.[128] The order to refer must set out, in a schedule, the request for the preliminary ruling of the Court of Justice.[129] The notice of motion issued by the party applying for a reference should usually be accompanied by a draft order and schedule. If the parties agree that a reference should be made, they will usually agree on the form and content of the draft order and schedule, and submit it to the judge for approval.

If a reference is ordered, the Senior Master will send the file of the case (eg the order, together with the schedule and any relevant pleadings) to the Registrar of the Court of Justice. However, the Senior Master does not transmit the file, unless the court otherwise orders, until the time for appealing against the order has expired or, if an appeal is entered within that time, until the appeal has been determined or otherwise disposed of.[130] Where both parties consent to a reference being made, they may waive their rights of appeal and ask the court to order the reference without waiting for the time to appeal to expire. This has the advantage of speeding up the process.

The proceedings in which an order is made are, unless the court otherwise orders, stayed until the Court of Justice has given a preliminary ruling on the ques-

---

[125] Decision of the House of Lords, 9 May 1985 (unreported).

[126] RSC Ord 114, r 2(1).

[127] Ibid, r 2(2). See Precedent C, p 281–282.

[128] Ibid, r 2(3).

[129] Ibid Ord 114, r 3. See Precedent D, pp 283–284.

[130] RSC Ord 114, r 5: The address is: The Registrar, Court of Justice of the European Communities, L–2925 Luxembourg; telephone 010 352 43031; fax 010 352 433766.

tion referred to it,[131] although proceedings may continue in respect of interlocutory matters.[132] In the case of the Court of Appeal (Criminal Division), no appeal or application for leave to appeal will, unless the Court otherwise orders, be determined until the Court of Justice has given a preliminary ruling on the question referred to it.[133]

(ii) County courts

County Court Rules, Ord 19, r 11 The procedure for a reference for a preliminary ruling in the county court is substantially the same as in the High Court. Order 19, r 11 of the County Court Rules provides that an order may be made by the judge before or at the trial or hearing of any action or matter and either of his own motion or on the application of any party. The order must set out, in a schedule, the request for the preliminary ruling. The proceedings in which an order is made shall, unless the judge otherwise orders, be stayed until the Court of Justice has given a preliminary ruling on the question referred to it. Where an order has been made by the county court judge, a copy thereof is sent to the Senior Master of the High Court for transmission to the Registrar of the Court of Justice. However, unless the judge orders otherwise, the copy will not be sent to the Senior Master until the time for appealing to the Court of Appeal against the order has expired or, if an appeal is entered within that time, until the appeal has been determined or otherwise disposed of.

(iii) Crown Court

Crown Court Rules Proceedings in which an order is made by the Crown Court must, unless the court otherwise determines, be adjourned until the Court of Justice has given its preliminary ruling on the questions referred to it. The Crown Court may, however, decide any preliminary or incidental question which may arise in the proceedings after an order is made and before a preliminary ruling is given.[134] The content and form of the order are broadly similar to those required by RSC Ord 114.

(iv) Magistrates' courts and tribunals

Absence of formal rules No formal rules have been made for references from magistrates' courts and tribunals in England and Wales. Nevertheless, they have a wide discretion to refer questions to the Court of Justice for a preliminary ruling. References from these courts or tribunals are transmitted directly to the Registrar of the Court of Justice.

(b) Drafting the order to refer

The schedule Under RSC Ord 114, r 3, an order must set out, in a schedule, the request for the preliminary ruling of the Court of Justice.[135] The schedule should

---

[131] RSC Ord 114, r 4.

[132] *Portsmouth City Council v Richards and Quietlynn* [1989] 1 CMLR 673.

[133] Criminal Appeal (References to the European Court) Rules, 1972 (SI No 1786), r 5.

[134] Crown Court Rules 1982 (SI No 1109), r 29.

[135] *Supreme Court Practice* (Sweet & Maxwell, 1993), vol 2, Appendix A Prescribed form No. 109.

set out a clear and succinct statement of the case to enable the Court of Justice to understand the issues of Community law raised and to enable other Member States and the Community institutions to submit observations. A vague reference will be declared inadmissible by the Court of Justice.[136] Accordingly, a schedule should set out the following:

(a) the description of the parties;

(b) the facts of the case;

(c) any judgment of a lower court;

(d) the relevant provisions of English law;

(e) the relevant provisions of Community law;

(g) the arguments of the parties on the issues of Community law;

(h) the reasons why the answers to the questions are considered necessary; and

(i) the relevant questions.

The questions　The questions referred must be drafted in abstract terms, asking general questions of law rather than enquiring as to the proper application of Community law to the specific facts in issue, or the compatibility of national law with Community law.

6. PROCEDURE IN THE COURT OF JUSTICE

(a) Generally

Procedural rules　The procedure before the Court of Justice is governed by the Protocol on the Statute of the Court of Justice[137] which is annexed to the EEC Treaty, and by the Rules of Procedure of the Court of Justice.[138] The procedure before the Court of Justice for preliminary references is the same as under direct actions, subject to adaptations necessitated by the nature of the reference for a preliminary ruling.[139]

Jurisdiction　The Court of Justice has exclusive jurisdiction over requests for preliminary rulings under article 177 of the EEC Treaty.[140]

Procedure in brief　After the order of the referring court is transmitted to the Court of Justice, the case is registered and given a number; for example, Case C–275/92 means the 275th case of 1992. When a case is registered it is assigned by the President of the Court to one of the judges to act as judge-rapporteur ('reporting judge'). Throughout the proceedings, the judge-rapporteur must ensure that the correct procedure has been followed and he must also prepare, in draft,

---

[136] For inadmissible references see pp 131–132.

[137] Protocol on the Statute of the Court of Justice of the European Economic Community, signed at Brussels on 17 April 1957, as amended by Council Decision 88/591 of 24 October 1988, OJ 1989 No C 215, 21 August 1989, p 1. Reproduced at Appendix B, pp 297–306. See, in particular, article 20 of the Protocol.

[138] Rules of Procedure of the Court of Justice of the European Communities of 19 June 1991, OJ 1991 No L 176, 4 July 1991, p 7. Reproduced at Appendix C, pp 307–357. See, in particular, ECJ Rules of Procedure, articles 103–104.

[139] ECJ Rules of Procedure, article 103. The Rules of Procedure are discussed in detail in Ch 17.

[140] Article 168a(1) of the EEC Treaty.

the judgment of the whole court. Once the order has been registered in the Court of Justice, the order is translated into the official languages of the Community and published in all the official languages in the Official Journal of the European Communities 'C' Series.

The order is notified to the parties in the main action, to all the Member States, to the Commission and, where the order concerns an act of the Council, to the Council. All these parties may submit written observations within a period of two months from the notification of the order. After the two-month period has expired, the judge-rapporteur will report to the Court of Justice whether further enquiries are necessary. The judge-rapporteur will also prepare a report for the hearing which summarises the facts of the case and the arguments in the written observations. The case will be set down in the Court's cause list and, thereafter, all the parties will be given an advance warning of the date for the oral hearing. Some time after the hearing, the Advocate-General will deliver his Opinion and the Court will subsequently give its ruling on the questions referred to it.

Language On a reference from an English court, the language of the case is English and it is the English text which is authentic.[141] Member States who intervene in the proceedings may submit observations in their own official language.[142]

Persons entitled to make observations Only the parties in the main proceedings, the Commission and the Member States are entitled to take part in the proceedings before the Court of Justice on a preliminary ruling.[143] The Council may take part where the interpretation or validity of a Council measure is in issue. No one else may intervene in the proceedings before the Court of Justice.

Representation Member States and institutions of the Community are represented by an agent appointed for each case. The parties in the national proceedings may appear in person, without being represented by a lawyer, if they have rights of audience before the referring court. It is usual, however, for all parties to be represented.[144]

(b) The written procedure

Time limits After the order of the referring court has been registered at the Court of Justice, the Registrar of the Court of Justice must notify the parties, the Member States, the Commission (and the Council where a Council measure is in issue) of the order by registered letter. Within two months of this notification, the parties, the Member States, the Commission and, where appropriate, the Council are entitled to submit written observations to the Court of Justice.[145]

---

[141] ECJ Rules of Procedure, article 29(2). See p 315.
[142] Ibid, article 29(3).
[143] EEC Statute, article 20.
[144] ECJ Rules of Procedure, article 104(2). See p 338.
[145] EEC Statute, article 20.

The written procedure in proceedings under article 177 of the EEC Treaty is, therefore, different from the procedure in direct actions, as there is no sequence of application, defence, reply and rejoinder. A slip is enclosed with the notification which should be returned to the Court of Justice, setting out the date on which the notification was received. The two-month time limit is mandatory and cannot be extended by the Court of Justice, although it is automatically extended by ten days in the case of the United Kingdom, on account of the distance from Luxembourg.[146] Time continues to run during vacations. Where the limitation period would otherwise end on a Saturday, Sunday or official holiday it will be extended until the end of the first following working day.[147] Regardless of the time of day when the parties receive the notification, time does not begin to run until the end of the day of notification. The period expires at the end of the day which, in the second month indicated by the time limit (plus the ten-day extension on account of distance for the United Kingdom), bears the same number as the day from which time was set running. So, for example, where the parties are notified of the order on 5 May, the period for submitting observations expires at midnight on 15 July.[148]

Drafting the written observations There is no obligation on any of the parties to submit written observations. If they choose not to do so, there will be no judgment in default of written observations. The parties may submit written observations and not attend the oral hearing or, alternatively, they may only attend the oral hearing. Since the written observations are to be translated, they should be made clear and concise. The observations are usually divided into two parts, dealing first with any additional facts (if the facts are not sufficiently set out in the reference) and, secondly, setting out the legal submissions. References to additional facts should be kept to a minimum, since the Court of Justice is concerned merely with the interpretation or the validity of Community law. The legal submissions should, in general, follow the questions raised by the referring court and the parties should set out their suggested answers. Since there is only one opportunity to make written submissions, the parties should draft answers to all questions referred and should refrain from stating that a question is irrelevant. The observations should be dated and signed by the legal representative who has drafted them. The original, accompanied by all annexes, should be lodged with five copies at the Court of Justice.[149]

The parties are not required to provide an address for service in Luxembourg, unlike in direct actions. In proceedings under article 177 of the EEC Treaty, service on the parties by the Registrar is usually made at the address of the party's legal representative.[150]

---

[146] ECJ Rules of Procedure, Annex II. See p 350.
[147] ECJ Rules of Procedure, article 80. See p 329.
[148] Case 152/85 *Misset v Council* [1987] ECR 223; Case T–125/89 *Filtrona v Commission* [1990] ECR II–393.
[149] ECJ Rules of Procedure, article 37. See p 318. A model form of written observations is set out as Precedent F, pp 287–288.
[150] Rules on the Internal Organisation of the Court, article 37(4).

Requests for further evidence After the expiry of the two-month time limit and the submission of the written observations, the judge-rapporteur presents a preliminary report to the Court of Justice on the question of whether measures of enquiry are necessary.[151] The following measures may be prescribed: the personal appearance of the parties; a request for information and production of documents; oral testimony; the commissioning of experts' reports; and an inspection of the place or thing in question. In article 177 proceedings such enquiries are rare and are usually limited to requests, by the Court, for the Commission to produce certain information.

(c) The oral procedure

Purpose of the oral hearing The oral hearing is of particular importance in proceedings under article 177 of the EEC Treaty, as it is the only means by which the parties can comment on each others' written observations. However, there is no obligation to appear at the oral hearing. Indeed, the Court of Justice may decide to dispense with the oral hearing, provided that none of the parties or interveners has asked to present an oral argument.[152]

Procedure The judge-rapporteur prepares a report for the hearing summarising the facts of the case and the arguments contained in the written observations. This is circulated to the judges, the parties, the Member States and the other relevant Community institutions, before the hearing. If the report does not adequately set out the facts or the arguments, the parties should first make this point in writing to the Registrar, setting out the proposed amendments. Thereafter, this point can be made at the oral hearing itself.

The procedure at the oral hearing is broadly the same as the procedure in direct actions. The parties are normally given three weeks' advance warning of the date of the oral hearing. Lawyers wear their national robes and the judges are addressed as 'My Lords'. Before the oral hearing begins the legal representatives are invited to a room, behind the Court of Justice, to meet members of the Court and to determine the order of speeches. The order of speeches is, generally, plaintiff and interveners in support, defendant and interveners in support, Member States, the Council (where appropriate) and the Commission. The Commission usually sits on the left of the Court. At the end of the speeches, each speaker has an opportunity to reply. The time for the speeches is usually a maximum of 30 minutes. Simultaneous translation is provided and legal representatives usually provide the interpreters with an *aide-mémoire*, thus facilitating the translation.

Question identical to previous ruling Where a preliminary reference is identical to a question on which the Court of Justice has already ruled, the Court may, after hearing the parties and the interveners, give its decision in the form of a

---

[151] ECJ Rules of Procedure, articles 45, 103. See pp 320, 337
[152] Ibid, article 104(4). See p 338.

reasoned order, referring to its previous judgment.[153] This procedure obviates the need to follow the full procedure to judgment.

Advocate-General Some time after the oral hearing, the Advocate-General will deliver his Opinion. This brings the oral procedure to an end.

(d) Judgment

Judgment The Court of Justice, after the Opinion of the Advocate-General has been given, will then proceed to deliberate its judgment. The judgment is delivered in open court, although it is not necessary for those who made written or oral submissions to attend. Where the meaning of a judgment is unclear, neither the parties nor the national court which made the reference can bring an application for interpretation of the judgment under article 102 of the ECJ Rules of Procedure. In this situation, the court which made the original reference must make a new reference, with the attendant delay which that involves.[154]

Delay In 1992, the average length of proceedings (from lodging of the preliminary reference with the Court of Justice to judgment) was 18.8 months.[155]

(e) Costs and legal aid

Costs It is for the national court which made the reference to decide on the costs of the reference.[156] In *R v Intervention Board for Agricultural Produce, ex p Fish Producers' Organisation Ltd*[157] the Court of Appeal indicated that the cost of making a reference to the Court of Justice falls within the normal English rule that costs follow the event. Member States and Community institutions which intervene before the Court of Justice must bear their own costs.[158]

Legal aid A reference for a preliminary ruling is a step in the proceedings before the national court and, in principle, a party who is legally aided is entitled to have the national legal aid order extended to cover the proceedings before the Court of Justice.[159] Where the national authorities refuse legal aid, the Court of Justice may, itself, grant legal aid to facilitate the legal representation or attendance of a party.[160]

---

[153] Ibid, article 104(3). See p 338.

[154] Case 40/70 *Sirena Srl v Eda Srl* [1979] ECR 3169. See pp 266–267 for the rules concerning the interpretation of judgments delivered in direct actions.

[155] This figure is taken from the *Weekly Summaries* of the Court of Justice, Number 35 of 1992.

[156] ECJ Rules of Procedure, article 104(5). See p 338.

[157] [1993] 1 CMLR 707.

[158] ECJ Rules of Procedure, article 69(4). See p 326.

[159] *R v Marlborough Street Stipendiary Magistrates, ex p Bouchereau* [1977] 1 WLR 414.

[160] ECJ Rules of Procedure, article 104(5). See p 338.

Part IV

Remedies in EC Courts for Breach of EC Law

Chapter 11

Proceedings Against Member States for Breach of EC law—Articles 169 and 170 of the EEC Treaty

1. ARTICLE 169—INFRACTION PROCEEDINGS BY THE COMMISSION

(a) Introduction

Article 169 Article 169 of the EEC Treaty provides:

> If the Commission considers that a Member State has failed to fulfil an obligation under this Treaty, it shall deliver a reasoned opinion on the matter after giving the State concerned the opportunity to submit its observations.
>
> If the State concerned does not comply with the opinion within the period laid down by the Commission, the latter may bring the matter before the Court of Justice.

Purpose of article 169 proceedings One of the roles of the Commission, as defined by article 155 of the EEC Treaty, is to 'ensure that the provisions of this Treaty and the measures taken by the institutions pursuant thereto are applied'. One of the main instruments by which the Commission fulfils this role as 'guardian' of the Treaty is in taking infraction proceedings under article 169 against Member States which it considers to be in breach of EEC Treaty obligations. As the Commission is acting in the general interest of the Community, it does not need to show that it has a specific legal interest in the matter before commencing proceedings under article 169.[1]

Importance to private parties Although the remedy established in article 169 is only available to the Commission, it is also of importance to private parties in that the Commission may be alerted to the possibility that a Member State is in breach of its obligations following a complaint by a private party. The Commission has published a standard form for private parties to make complaints to it.[2]

The advantage to the private party is clear in terms of legal costs, as it is the Commission which brings the case. One disadvantage is that the private party

---

[1] Case 167/73 *Commission v France* [1974] ECR 359 paras 13–16.
[2] OJ 1989 No C 26, 1 February 1989, p 6; [1989] 1 CMLR 617. Reproduced in Precedent G, pp 289–290.

has no say in the running of the case. If the Commission decides to take up the complaint and to bring infraction proceedings under article 169, the private party does not participate in the legal process. Furthermore, the choice whether to bring infraction proceedings or not lies solely within the discretion of the Commission. An individual who has made a complaint cannot challenge a decision of the Commission not to bring infraction proceedings on the basis of that complaint, either under article 173 or article 175 of the EEC Treaty.[3]

(b) Procedural conditions of admissibility

Outline In outline, the procedure followed in infraction proceedings under article 169 is as follows:
  (1) the Commission considers that a Member State is in breach of its EEC Treaty obligations;
  (2) the Commission writes a letter to the Member State concerned inviting its observations;
  (3) the Commission delivers a reasoned opinion; and
  (4) the case is brought before the European Court of Justice.

Stage 1: Existence of breach

(i) Categories of breach

Categories of breach It is impossible to give an exhaustive list of the ways in which a Member State may be found to have infringed Community law. However, it is possible to identify certain main categories of breach.[4]

Adoption of legislation The adoption by a Member State of a national measure which is contrary to Community law will constitute a breach of the EEC Treaty. For example, in Case C–246/89 *Commission v United Kingdom*[5] the United Kingdom was found to be in breach of its Treaty obligations by enacting the Merchant Shipping Act 1988 which contravened, *inter alia*, article 52 of the EEC Treaty.

Failure to abolish legislation The mere continued existence of conflicting national legislation will be a breach of the EEC Treaty, even if the national courts would not apply it due to the existence of overriding directly applicable or directly effective Community provisions. For example, in Case 167/73 *Commission v France*[6] the Court of Justice found that the French *Code du Travail Maritime* conflicted with article 48 of the EEC Treaty and EEC Regulation 1612/68. The Court of Justice held that:

---

[3] Case 48/65 *Alfons Lütticke GmbH v Commission* [1966] ECR 19; Case 247/87 *Star Fruit SA v Commission* [1989] ECR 291 paras 10–14.

[4] See also pp 3–10 for a discussion of the obligations imposed on Member States by the different kinds of Community legislation.

[5] [1991] ECR I–4585 part of the *Factortame* litigation.

[6] [1974] ECR 359 para 41.

... although the objective legal position is clear, namely, that Article 48 and Regulation No 1612/68 are directly applicable in the territory of the French Republic, nevertheless the maintenance in these circumstances of the wording of the Code du Travail Maritime gives rise to an ambiguous state of affairs by maintaining, as regards those subject to the law who are concerned, a state of uncertainty as to the possibilities available to them of relying on Community law.

Failure to implement Failure by a Member State to implement a directive within the implementation period will constitute a breach. In Case 31/69 *Commission v Italy*[7], the Italian Government argued that a failure to implement directly applicable Community legislation constituted a pure omission, the sanction for which did not come within article 169. The Court of Justice rejected this argument and held that:

> A failure to act, like a positive act, may constitute a failure on the part of a Member State to fulfil an obligation.

Failure to implement properly A breach of the EEC Treaty will occur where a Member State introduces national legislation which fails to fully implement a directive.[8] In addition, Member States are under an obligation to implement Community rules in accordance with the general principles of Community law[9] and, as far as possible, in accordance with fundamental human rights.[10]

Failure to co-operate If a Member State fails to co-operate with the Commission in the course of investigations into a possible breach of Community law, that will in itself constitute a breach of the Member State's duty of co-operation which arises under article 5 of the EEC Treaty.[11]

(ii) Breach must be by a Member State
Wide definition of 'the State' Article 169 deals with breaches of Community law by a Member State. In Case 77/69 *Commission v Belgium*, the Court of Justice held that:[12]

> ... the liability of a Member State under Article 169 arises whatever the agency of the State whose action or inaction is the cause of the failure to fulfil its obligations, even in the case of a constitutionally independent institution.

---

[7] [1970] ECR 25 paras 7–10.
[8] For example, see Case C–337/89 *Commission v United Kingdom* judgment of 25 November 1992 ('drinking water case').
[9] Case 230/78 *SpA Eridania v Ministry for Agriculture and Forestry* [1979] ECR 2749 paras 29–32; Joined Cases C–31–44/91 *SpA Alois Lageder and others v Amministrazione delle finanze dello Stato* judgment of 1 April 1993, para 33.
[10] Case 5/88 *Hubert Wachauf v Germany* [1989] ECR 2609 paras 17–19.
[11] Case C–35/88 *Commission v Greece* [1990] ECR I–3125 paras 38–42; Case C–61/90 *Commission v Greece* [1992] ECR I–2407 paras 29–31; Case C–137/91 *Commission v Greece* [1992] ECR I–4023. See also Case 96/81 *Commission v Netherlands* [1982] ECR 1791 paras 7–8 where a directive imposed a specific obligation on Member States to provide certain information to the Commission.
[12] Case 77/69 *Commission v Belgium* [1970] ECR 237 para 15. See also Case 8/70 *Commission v Italy* [1970] ECR 961 paras 8, 9; Case 52/75 *Commission v Italy* [1976] ECR 277 para 14.

National Parliament A Member State is liable for the failure of its national Parliament to adopt legislation required by Community law. In Case 77/69 *Commission v Belgium*,[13] the Belgian Government had placed a draft law before the national Parliament to rectify the situation complained of by the Commission. However, practical difficulties, notably the dissolution of the Belgian Parliament, had prevented the draft law being adopted. The Belgian Government argued that the delay in enacting the law amounted to a case of *force majeure*. This argument was rejected by the Court of Justice in the terms quoted above.

Local or regional entities A Member State is responsible for breaches of Community law caused by local or regional authorities. For example, in Case C–211/91 *Commission v Belgium*,[14] the Belgian Government was held liable for a decree passed by the Flemish regional government which was contrary to the EEC Treaty rules on the freedom to provide services.

National courts Advocate-General Warner, in Case 9/75 *Meyer-Burckhardt v Commission*,[15] stated:

> It is trite law in this Court that compliance with the provisions of Community law is required of all the organs of a Member State, be they executive, legislative or judicial.

However, he recognised that proceedings against a Member State for failure by one of its courts to comply with Community law should not be undertaken lightly by the Commission. In that case, the Advocate-General considered the obligation imposed by article 177 of the EEC Treaty on national courts of last resort to make preliminary references to the Court of Justice. He stated:

> The third paragraph of Article 177 imposes an obligation that is as binding on Member States as any other obligation undertaken by them under the Treaty, for aught that compliance with it is a matter for their judicial organs.

In Case 30/77 *Regina v Bouchereau*,[16] Advocate-General Warner reiterated that Member States could be held liable for breaches of Community law by their national courts. However, he refined the notion of breach occasioned by a national court as follows:

> It is obvious on the other hand that a Member State cannot be held to have failed to fulfil an obligation under the Treaty simply because one of its Courts has reached a wrong decision. Judicial error, whether due to the misapprehension of facts or to misapprehension of the law, is not a breach of the Treaty. In the judicial sphere, Article 169 could only come into play in the event of a court of a Member State deliberately ignoring or disregarding Community law.

---

[13] [1970] ECR 237 para 15. See also, for example, Case 8/70 *Commission v Italy* [1970] ECR 961; Case 52/75 *Commission v Italy* [1976] ECR 277.
[14] Judgment of 16 December 1992. See also Case C–42/89 *Commission v Belgium* [1990] ECR I–2821; Case C–362/90 *Commission v Italy* [1992] ECR I–2353; Case C–33/90 *Commission v Italy* [1991] ECR I–5987 paras 22–27. *Cf* Case C–8/88 *Germany v Commission* [1990] ECR I–2321 paras 12, 13.
[15] [1975] ECR 1171 at 1187.
[16] [1977] ECR 1999, Opinion of Advocate-General Warner at 2020.

In practice, given the importance of the independence of the judiciary within the national constitutions of each Member State, the Commission is very reluctant to commence proceedings against Member States for the actions of their courts.

Commercial undertakings The Court of Justice has considered the question of what constitutes 'the State' in the context of vertical direct effect of directives.[17] In Case 188/89 *Foster v British Gas*[18] the Court of Justice indicated that, 'organizations or bodies which were subject to the authority or control of the State or had special powers beyond those which result from the normal rules applicable to relations between individuals' should be considered as forming part of the State. If this analysis is considered in the context of State liability under article 169 of the EEC Treaty, the potential responsibility of the Member States under that article is very wide. For example, it appears that the United Kingdom could be held responsible under article 169 for breaches of Community law committed by British Gas.[19]

In Case 249/81 *Commission v Ireland*,[20] the Irish Government was held to be responsible for the acts of a private company, the Irish Goods Council, as the Government had appointed the members of the company's management committee, granted the company public subsidies and defined the general scope and nature of the company's activities.

Stage 2: Observations of Member States

Purpose of Commission's initial letter The Commission begins infraction proceedings by sending the Member State a letter inviting it to make observations. The purpose of this pre-litigation procedure under article 169 is twofold; firstly, it gives the Member State concerned an opportunity to comply with its obligations under Community law and, secondly, it allows the State to avail itself of its right of defence against the complaints made by the Commission.[21]

Form of initial letter The form of the initial letter is of great importance as it must clearly define the subject-matter of the dispute and indicate the factors necessary for the Member State to prepare its defence.[22] However, the initial letter need not be as detailed as the reasoned opinion which constitutes the next stage of infraction proceedings. Indeed, the Court of Justice has recognised that the initial letter, 'of necessity will contain only an initial brief summary of the complaints'.[23]

---

[17] See pp 37–39.

[18] [1990] ECR I–3313 para 18.

[19] See *Foster v British Gas* [1991] 2 WLR 1075, in which the House of Lords held that British Gas was part of the State for the purposes of vertical direct effect of a directive.

[20] [1982] ECR 4005.

[21] Case 293/85 *Commission v Belgium* [1988] ECR 305 para 13.

[22] Case 211/81 *Commission v Denmark* [1982] ECR 4547 para 8; Case 51/83 *Commission v Italy* [1984] ECR 2793 para 4; Case 274/83 *Commission v Italian Republic* [1985] ECR 1077 para 19.

[23] Case 274/83 *Commission v Italy* [1985] ECR 1077 para 21.

The Court of Justice has held that the opportunity for the Member State to submit its observations constitutes an essential guarantee required by the EEC Treaty; observance of that guarantee is an essential, formal requirement of the procedure under article 169, even if the Member State does not consider it necessary to avail itself of that opportunity.[24]

If the Commission's initial letter fails to identify in sufficient detail the nature and scope of the complaint, the matter will be held to be inadmissible when it comes before the Court of Justice. Furthermore, the Commission cannot introduce new matters into the proceedings following its initial letter inviting the Member State to submit its observations. Any attempt to do so will render consideration of the new matters inadmissible before the Court of Justice, even if the Member State has submitted observations on the basis of the 'extended' reasoned opinion.[25]

Reasonable time to respond In Case 293/85 *Commission v Belgium*[26] the Court of Justice stated:[27]

> ... the Commission must allow Member States a reasonable period to reply to the letter of formal notice and to comply with a reasoned opinion, or, where appropriate, to prepare their defence. In order to determine whether the period allowed is reasonable, account must be taken of all the circumstances of the case. Thus, very short periods may be justified in particular circumstances, especially where there is an urgent need to remedy a breach or where the Member State concerned is fully aware of the Commission's views long before the procedure starts.

The Commission argued that the time limits laid down in the initial letter (eight days) and the reasoned opinion (15 days) were not absolute and that it would have considered replies submitted by the Belgian Government after those time limits. The Court of Justice rejected this argument as irrelevant as a Member State cannot know in advance whether, and to what extent, the Commission will grant an extension of the time limits it has set down.[28] Having considered all the circumstances, the Court of Justice held that the time limits imposed were too short. In particular, the Court held that the Commission could not rely on urgency which it had itself created by failing to take action earlier.[29] The Court, therefore, declared the action inadmissible as the article 169 prelitigation procedure had not been properly carried out.

Discussions In practice, once the Commission has issued its initial letter, discussions will take place with the Member State in an attempt to resolve the dispute.

---

[24] Case 31/69 *Commission v Italy* [1970] ECR 25 para 13; Case 211/81 *Commission v Denmark* [1982] ECR 4547 para 9; Case 51/83 *Commission v Italy* [1984] ECR 2793 para 5; Case 274/83 *Commission v Italian Republic* [1985] ECR 1077 para 20.

[25] Case 193/80 *Commission v Italy* [1981] ECR 3019 para 12; Case 51/83 *Commission v Italy* [1984] ECR 2793 paras 6–9.

[26] [1988] ECR 305.

[27] Ibid para 14.

[28] Ibid para 17.

[29] Ibid para 16.

Termination of breach before reasoned opinion issued If a Member State puts an end to the breach before the Commission issues its reasoned opinion, the Commission is not entitled to bring infraction proceedings before the Court of Justice in respect of that breach. The Court will declare any such action inadmissible.[30]

Stage 3: Commission's reasoned opinion

Delivery of a reasoned opinion If, after the Commission has sent its initial letter and after the Member State concerned has had the opportunity to submit its observations, the matter has not been satisfactorily resolved, the Commission may continue the infraction process by delivering a reasoned opinion.

Scope of reasoned opinion The reasoned opinion must contain a coherent statement of the reasons why the Commission believes that the Member State is in breach of its obligations under the EEC Treaty, so that the Member State is made fully aware of the complaint being made against it.[31] However, the reasoned opinion is not required to indicate the steps which the Commission considers are necessary to eliminate the breach[32], nor is it required to address all the counter-arguments raised by the Member State in its observations.[33]

As the opportunity for the Member State to submit its observations is an essential guarantee provided for by article 169, the reasoned opinion and the initial letter must be founded on the same grounds and submissions.[34] However, the Commission is entitled to set out in detail in the reasoned opinion the complaints which it has already made more generally in its initial letter. Furthermore, in its reasoned opinion the Commission may reply to defences or arguments raised by the Member State in the State's response to the initial letter.[35]

Reasonable time limit for compliance The Commission must allow the Member State a reasonable time to comply with the reasoned opinion. If it fails to do so, the application to the Court of Justice will be declared inadmissible. In Case 74/82 *Commission v Ireland*,[36] the Court of Justice held that it was unreasonable for the Commission to allow Ireland only five days to amend legislation which had been applied for more than 40 years. However, in the circumstances of the case, this defect did not render the Commission's application to the Court

---

[30] Case 240/86 *Commission v Greece* [1988] ECR 1835.

[31] Case 325/82 *Commission v Germany* [1984] ECR 777 para 8.

[32] Case C–247/89 *Commission v Portugal* [1991] ECR I–3659 para 22.

[33] Case 7/61 *Commission v Italy* [1961] ECR 317 at 326, 327.

[34] *Cf* Case C–152/89 *Commission v Luxembourg* [1991] ECR I–3141 paras 8–11, where the Court of Justice held that the application was admissible even though it was not in exactly the same terms as the reasoned Opinion. This was because the conduct of the whole pre-trial procedure was such that the Luxembourgeois government had not been deprived of the opportunity to reply to the point raised in the application.

[35] Case 74/82 *Commission v Ireland* [1984] ECR 317 para 20. See also the Opinion of Advocate-General Lenz in Case C–337/89 *Commission v United Kingdom*, judgment of 25 November 1992 paras 13–23.

[36] [1984] ECR 317 paras 8–14.

of Justice inadmissible, as the Commission had waited several months until the Irish government replied to the reasoned opinion before bringing the case before the Court of Justice.[37]

The question of whether the time limit set down in the reasoned opinion is reasonable or not must be decided taking into account all relevant circumstances. The Commission may be entitled to impose a short time limit where the Member State concerned has been aware of the Commission's point of view for some time.[38]

Effect of compliance with the reasoned opinion If the Member State complies with the reasoned opinion within the time limit laid down, or if the breach of Community law ceases to exist, for whatever reason, the Commission cannot bring the matter before the Court of Justice.[39] However, where the breach ceases to exist after the time limit set down in the reasoned opinion, the Commission may still bring the question before the Court, as the proceedings still have a purpose, for example, clarification of the legal position by a ruling of the Court or in establishing the basis of civil liability that a Member State can incur as a result of its default as regards other Member States, the Community or private parties.[40]

The Court of Justice will examine the question of whether there has been a breach of Community law as at the date of the expiry of the period laid down in the reasoned opinion and will not take account of any subsequent changes.[41] Thus, the fact that a Member State indicates its willingness to remedy a breach of Community law and has taken steps to do so does not provide a defence.[42] Similarly, the fact that a proposal for a Community legislative measure has already been submitted to the Council which, if adopted, would terminate the Member State's breach, does not provide a defence.[43] In Case C–280/89 *Commission v Spain*,[44] the Court of Justice held that the fact that the regulations in question had been revoked before the hearing did not prevent the Court from adjudging whether Spain had been in breach of those regulations which were in force when the period laid down in the reasoned opinion expired.

In practice, the Commission may be prepared to abandon proceedings where the breach is remedied before the hearing.

---

[37] See also Case 293/85 *Commission v Belgium* [1988] ECR 305 paras 10–20.

[38] Case 85/85 *Commission v Belgium* [1986] ECR 1149 paras 8–13; Case C–247/89 *Commission v Portugal* [1991] ECR I–3659 para 25.

[39] Case C–362/90 *Commission v Italy* [1992] ECR I–2353 paras 9–13.

[40] For example, see Case 7/61 *Commission v Italy* [1961] ECR 317 at 326; Case 39/72 *Commission v Italy* [1973] ECR 101 at paras 9–11; Case 154/85 *Commission v Italy* [1987] ECR 2717 para 6.

[41] Case 200/88 *Commission v Greece* [1990] ECR I–4299 para 13.

[42] Ibid paras 12, 13.

[43] Case 220/83 *Commission v France* [1986] ECR 3663 paras 6, 7; Case C–236/88 *Commission v France* [1990] ECR I–3163 para 19; Case C–310/89 *Commission v Netherlands* [1991] ECR I–1381.

[44] Judgment of 2 December 1992, para 7.

Stage 4: Hearing before the Court of Justice

(i) Application to the Court of Justice

Jurisdiction Proceedings under article 169 must be brought before the Court of Justice.[45]

Commission's discretion The Commission has an absolute discretion whether or not to bring proceedings under article 169.[46] The Court of Justice will not question whether that discretion has been exercised wisely,[47] nor will it consider the motives behind the decision of the Commission to bring proceedings.[48] Furthermore, the Commission has a discretion as to when it will bring an action under article 169 and it is not precluded from commencing proceedings by virtue of the fact that a 'lengthy period' has passed since it first became aware of a Member State's breach.[49] However, in Case C–96/89 *Commission v Netherlands*, the Court of Justice indicated that excessive delay by the Commission may infringe the Member State's rights of defence where this makes it more difficult for the Member State to refute the Commission's arguments.[50]

Grounds of application The Commission's initial, formal letter, inviting the Member State to make observations, delimits the subject-matter of the Commission's complaint. Therefore, the reasoned opinion and the terms of the application to the Court of Justice must be founded on the same grounds as those specified in the initial letter. Matters raised by the Commission which were not put forward in the course of the pre-trial procedure will be declared inadmissible by the Court of Justice.[51] However, the grounds put forward in the application to the Court need not be identical with those contained in the reasoned opinion. The Commission may deal in the application with arguments and defences raised by the Member State in its response to the reasoned opinion.[52] Further, where the Member State replaces the law challenged in the Commission's reasoned opinion with a new law which substantially reproduces the original law, the Commission will be entitled to challenge the new law without commencing new proceedings. Thus, in Case C–105/91 *Commission v Greece*,[53] the

---

[45] EEC Treaty, article 168a.
[46] Case 329/88 *Commission v Greece* [1989] ECR 4159.
[47] Case 200/88 *Commission v Greece* [1990] ECR I–4299 paras 8, 9; Case C–209/88 *Commission v Italy* [1990] ECR I–4313 paras 15, 16.
[48] Case 415/85 *Commission v Ireland* [1988] ECR 3097 paras 8, 9; Case 416/85 *Commission v United Kingdom* [1988] ECR 3127 paras 8, 9.
[49] Case 7/68 *Commission v Italy* [1968] ECR 423 at 428; Case 7/71 *Commission v France* [1971] ECR 1003 paras 2–6; Case C–146/89 *Commission v United Kingdom* [1991] ECR I–3533 para 49.
[50] [1991] ECR I–2461 paras 14–18.
[51] Case 211/81 *Commission v Denmark* [1982] ECR 4547 paras 5–17; Case 298/86 *Commission v Belgium* [1988] ECR 4343 paras 9–11; Case C–52/90 *Commission v Denmark* [1992] ECR I–2187 paras 23–24; Case C–198/90 *Commission v Netherlands* [1991] ECR I–5799 paras 13–16; Case C–279/89 *Commission v United Kingdom*, judgment of 17 November 1992, paras 12–17; Case C–210/91 *Commission v Greece*, judgment of 16 December 1992, paras 8–12.
[52] Case 211/81 *Commission v Denmark* [1982] ECR 4547 paras 5–17; Case C–243/89 *Commission v Denmark*, judgment on 22 June 1993 paras 9–22.
[53] Judgment of 17 November 1992, paras 11–15. See also Case 45/64 *Commission v Italy* [1965]

Greek government argued that the action was inadmissible as the application to the Court of Justice challenged a national law which was not attacked in the Commission's reasoned opinion. The Court of Justice rejected this argument on the basis that the new law mentioned in the application had been adopted after the delivery of the reasoned opinion and had maintained in place the whole system of taxation on cars which had originally been challenged in the reasoned opinion.

Contents of application The application must set out, in sufficient detail, the grounds of fact and law relied upon.[54] It is not permissible simply to refer to the grounds of complaint set out in the initial letter and reasoned opinion.[55]

Interim relief The Commission may make an application to the Court of Justice under article 186 of the EEC Treaty for an order prescribing interim measures. If the conditions for the grant of interim relief are fulfilled, the Court may order the Member State to suspend enforcement of a contested measure.[56]

Burden of proof It is for the Commission to prove that a Member State is in breach of its Community obligations. Failure to provide sufficient evidence will cause the application to be dismissed.[57]

(ii) Defences

(a) Strict approach

Objective nature of breach If the Commission brings an action before the Court, the Court will consider, as an objective fact, whether the Member State is in breach of its Community obligations.[58] The Court adopts a very strict, literal approach to the enforcement of Member States' Community obligations and has considered (and rejected) a wide number of defences mounted by Member States.

(b) Defences rejected by the Court of Justice

Member States may not take the law into their own hands The Member States cannot seek to justify a breach of Community law on the basis that a

---

ECR 857 at 864–865; Case C–42/89 *Commission v Belgium* [1990] ECR I–2821 paras 8–11.

[54] Statute of the Court of Justice, article 19; ECJ Rules of Procedure, article 38(1)(c). See pp 300, 318. Case C–52/90 *Commission v Denmark* [1992] ECR I–2187.

[55] Case C–347/88 *Commission v Greece* [1990] ECR I–4747 paras 26–30; Case C–43/90 *Commission v Germany* [1992] ECR I–1909 paras 5–9. See p 256.

[56] For example, see Case 154/85R *Commission v Italy* [1985] ECR 1753; Case 293/85R *Commission v Belgium* [1985] 3521; Case 45/87R *Commission v Ireland* [1987] ECR 1411. For the law concerning interim measures, see Ch 16.

[57] Case 31/69 *Commission v Italy* [1970] ECR 25 para 22; Case 298/86 *Commission v Belgium* [1988] ECR 4343 paras 15–17; Case C–64/88 *Commission v France* [1991] ECR I–2727 paras 7–11 (where the Commission withheld confidential information); Case C–210/91 *Commission v Greece*, judgment of 16 December 1992, paras 22, 23. *Cf* Opinion of Advocate-General Warner in Case 12/74 *Commission v Germany* [1975] ECR 181 at 213, 214, where he states that, under certain circumstances, the burden of proof may shift onto the Member State.

[58] Case C–209/89 *Commission v Italy* [1991] ECR I–1591 para 6.

Community institution has failed to carry out its obligations.[59] Thus, in Case 232/78 *Commission v France*, the Court of Justice held that:[60]

> A Member State cannot under any circumstances unilaterally adopt, on its own authority, corrective measures or measures to protect trade designed to prevent any failure on the part of another Member State to comply with the rules laid down by the Treaty.

Similar breach by other Member States A Member State cannot seek to justify its own breach by relying on the fact that other Member States have committed a similar breach of Community law.[61]

National interest cannot justify breaches of Community law A Member State cannot justify the failure to give effect to Community legislation on the basis that it had opposed certain aspects of the legislation during its adoption, nor on the basis that it considers the legislation to be contrary to its own national interests.[62]

Breach of directly applicable/directly effective acts Where a Member State is in breach of a directly applicable or directly effective Community measure, the Member State cannot rely on the fact that private parties are entitled to invoke the Community legislation in the national courts as a defence in infraction proceedings.[63]

Internal political or legal difficulties It is settled law that a Member State may not plead 'provisions, practices or circumstances in its internal legal system', in order to justify a failure to comply with Community directives. Thus, the fact that national implementing legislation could not be adopted because of the premature dissolution of Parliament did not provide a defence in Case 94/81 *Commission v Italy*.[64]

Administrative, practical or financial difficulties A Member State cannot plead internal administrative or practical difficulties in order to justify a breach of Community law. For example, in Case 39/72 *Commission v Italy*[65] the Italian Government sought to justify its failure to introduce a system of premiums for slaughtering on the basis of the special characteristics of Italian agriculture and

---

[59] Joined Cases 90/63, 91/63 *Commission v Luxembourg and Belgium* [1964] ECR 625 at 631.

[60] [1979] ECR 2729 para 9. See also Case C–74/91 *Commission v Germany*, judgment of 27 October 1992, paras 23–25.

[61] Case 52/75 *Commission v Italy* [1976] ECR 277 para 11; Case C–146/89 *Commission v United Kingdom* [1991] ECR I–3533 para 47.

[62] Case 39/72 *Commission v Italy* [1971] ECR 101 para 20. This decision was followed in Case 128/78 *Commission v United Kingdom* [1979] ECR 419 para 9.

[63] Case 31/69 *Commission v Italy* [1970] ECR 25 para 9; Case 102/79 *Commission v Belgium* [1980] 1473 para 12; Case 168/85 *Commission v Italy* [1986] ECR 2945 para 11; Case 104/86 *Commission v Italy* [1988] ECR 1799 para 12.

[64] [1982] ECR 739. See also Case 77/69 *Commission v Belgium* [1970] ECR 237; Case 8/70 *Commission v Italy* [1970] ECR 961 paras 8, 9; Case 39/72 *Commission v Italy* [1973] ECR 161 para 11; Case 254/83 *Commission v Italy* [1984] ECR 3395.

[65] [1973] ECR 101 paras 19–23. See also Case 58/83 *Commission v Greece* [1984] ECR 2027 at para 11; Case C–337/89 *Commission v United Kingdom*, judgment of 25 November 1992, paras 14–25.

the lack of adequate lower level administration. These arguments were rejected by the Court of Justice. Equally, financial difficulties do not provide a defence.[66]

Equivalent national legislation A Member State cannot rely on the fact that national legislation already fulfils the aims of a directive by different means where the directive itself sets out particular measures to be adopted.[67]

No adverse effect on the Common Market An argument that a breach of Community obligations produces no adverse effects on the functioning of the Common Market does not provide a defence.[68]

De minimis Member States cannot argue that a breach of Community law should be excused because it is *de minimis*. In Case C–209/89 *Commission v Italy*,[69] the Court held that:

> ... a Member State is guilty of a failure to fulfil its obligations under the Treaty regardless of the frequency or the scale of the circumstances complained of.

Implementation periods of directives too short It is not a defence for a Member State to argue that the implementation period set down in a directive is too short given the complexity of its subject-matter.[70]

Approval by the Commission In Case 288/83 *Commission v Ireland*,[71] the Court of Justice held that:

> ... the Commission cannot, even by approving expressly or by implication a measure adopted unilaterally by a Member State, confer on that State the right to maintain provisions which are objectively contrary to Community law.

Legal uncertainty Where a Member State has acted in breach of Community law, the fact that the legal position was uncertain at the time when it acted does not provide a defence.[72]

(c) Possible defences

Procedural defects The procedure followed by the Commission, prior to bringing an action before the Court of Justice, is a purely administrative stage

---

[66] Case C–42/89 *Commission v Belgium* [1990] ECR I–2835 para 24.

[67] Case 128/78 *Commission v United Kingdom* [1979] ECR 419; Case 215/83 *Commission v Belgium* [1985] ECR 1039 para 25; Case C–313/89 *Commission v Spain* [1991] ECR I–5231 paras 11, 12. See also Case C–28/89 *Germany v Commission* [1991] ECR I–581 para 17, concerning regulations.

[68] Case 95/77 *Commission v Netherlands* [1978] ECR 863 para 13; Case 209/88 *Commission v Italy* [1990] ECR I–4313 paras 12–14; Case C–209/89 *Commission v Italy* [1991] ECR I–1575 para 6.

[69] [1991] ECR I–1575 paras 18, 19. See also Case C–209/88 *Commission v Italy* [1990] ECR I–4313 para 13; Case C–105/91 *Commission v Greece*, judgment of 17 November 1992, paras 19, 20.

[70] Case 52/75 *Commission v Italy* [1976] ECR 277.

[71] [1985] ECR 1761 para 22. See also Joined Cases 142/80, 143/80 *Amministrazione delle Finanze dello Stato v Essevi SpA and Carlo Salengo* [1981] ECR 1413 paras 13–18.

[72] Case 7/71 *Commission v France* [1971] ECR 1003 para 47 (EURATOM).

which is not reviewable under article 173 or 175 of the EEC Treaty.[73] The validity of an initial letter or reasoned opinion cannot be challenged in separate proceedings.[74] Any defects in these documents can, however, be relied on in the main action and may render the Commission's application inadmissible. The Court of Justice may examine, of its own motion, the question of whether the procedural preconditions required by article 169 have been complied with.[75]

Invalidity of Community measure In Case C–258/89 *Commission v Spain*[76] Advocate-General Darmon considered that Member States should be entitled to invoke article 184 of the EEC Treaty in respect of a regulation in the context of proceedings under article 169. In Case 226/87 *Commission v Greece*,[77] the Court of Justice held that Greece could not allege that a Commission decision was invalid in the context of an action under article 169, where Greece had not previously challenged the decision under article 173. However, article 184 was not expressly pleaded, presumably because the measure in issue was a decision and article 184 is expressed to apply only where regulations are in issue.[78]

'Non-existent' Community measure In Case 226/87 *Commission v Greece*[79] the Court of Justice indicated that it would be a defence to proceedings under article 169 if the measure at issue contained such particularly serious and manifest defects that it could be deemed non-existent.

Absolute impossibility The Court of Justice has indicated that where a Member State can show that it was 'absolutely impossible' to comply with its EEC Treaty obligations this will provide a defence to proceedings under article 169.[80] However, where it appears that it is impossible for a Member State to fulfil its EEC Treaty obligations, it is under an obligation to submit these problems to the Commission and to propose appropriate solutions. If the Member State fails to communicate with the Commission, it will be in breach of its duty of co-operation under article 5 of the EEC Treaty.[81]

---

[73] Case 48/65 *Alfons Lütticke GmbH v Commission* [1966] ECR 19.
[74] Joined Cases 6/69, 11/69 *Commission v France* [1969] ECR 523 at 35–37.
[75] Case C–362/90 *Commission v Italy* [1992] ECR I–2353 para 8.
[76] [1991] ECR I–3977 para 23 of the Opinion. See also Case 226/87 *Commission v Greece* [1988] ECR 3611, Opinion of Advocate-General Mancini at 3617.
[77] [1988] ECR 3611.
[78] See also Case 156/77 *Commission v Belgium* [1978] ECR 1881 paras 21, 22, where article 184 was expressly pleaded; Case C–74/91 *Commission v Germany* [1992] ECR I–5437 para 10; Case C–313/89 *Commission v Spain* [1991] ECR I–5231 paras 9, 10, where the Court held that obligations imposed by a Treaty of Accession are not open to challenge; Case C–183/91 *Commission v Greece*, judgment of 10 June 1993. This issue is discussed further at pp 205–206.
[79] [1988] ECR 3611 para 16; Joined Cases 6/69, 11/69 *Commission v France* [1969] ECR 523 paras 10–13; Case C–74/91 *Commission v Germany* [1992] ECR I–5437 para 11. 'Non-existent' acts are discussed at pp 197–198.
[80] Case 52/84 *Commission v Belgium* [1986] ECR 89 paras 14–16; Case 213/85 *Commission v Netherlands* [1988] ECR 281 paras 22–24; Case C–183/91 *Commission v Greece*, judgment of 10 June 1993 paras 10–21. These cases concerned infraction proceedings under the special infraction procedure for state aids. Case C–74/91 *Commission v Germany* [1992] ECR I–5437 para 12, recognises the availability of this defence in the context of proceedings under article 169.
[81] Case C–217/88 *Commission v Germany* [1990] ECR I–2879 para 33.

(iii) Costs

Costs The normal rule on costs is that the unsuccessful party must bear all the costs of the action.[82] However, where a Member State voluntarily suspends the application of the contested measures pending judgment, the Court of Justice may decide that each party should bear its own costs.[83]

2. ARTICLE 170—INFRACTION PROCEEDINGS BY A MEMBER STATE

Article 170 Article 170 of the EEC Treaty provides that:

> A Member State which considers that another Member State has failed to fulfil an obligation under this Treaty may bring the matter before the Court of Justice.
>
> Before a Member State brings an action against another Member State for an alleged infringement of an obligation under this Treaty, it shall bring the matter before the Commission.
>
> The Commission shall deliver a reasoned opinion after each of the States concerned has been given the opportunity to submit its own case and its observations on the other party's case both orally and in writing.
>
> If the Commission has not delivered an opinion within three months of the date on which the matter was brought before it, the absence of such opinion shall not prevent the matter from being brought before the Court of Justice.

Article 170 provides the means for a Member State to bring infraction proceedings against another Member State which it considers is in breach of its EEC Treaty obligations. However, the complaint must first be brought before the Commission. If the Commission issues a reasoned opinion, the procedure which follows is the same as that under article 169. If the Commission does not adopt a reasoned opinion within three months of the complaint made to it, the Member State can take the matter directly before the Court of Justice. Perhaps because of the political implications of proceeding against a fellow Member State, there is only one example of a Member State pursuing an action under article 170 to judgment.[84]

3. SPECIAL INFRACTION PROCEDURES

Special Procedures Some EEC Treaty articles permit the Commission or a Member State to bring infraction proceedings directly before the Court of Justice, without satisfying the procedural preconditions of article 169 or 170.[85]

---

[82] ECJ Rules of Procedure, article 69(2). See p 326.

[83] Case C–146/89 *Commission v United Kingdom* [1991] ECR I–3533 para 60; ECJ Rules of Procedure, article 69(3). See p 326.

[84] Case 141/78 *France v United Kingdom* [1979] ECR 2923.

[85] Article 93(2) (state aids); article 110a(4) (derogations from harmonisation measures); article 225 (derogations on the grounds of national security). See also article 180(a), which sets down a special procedure for the enforcement of Member States' obligations under the Statute of the European Investment Bank. See Cases 156/77 *Commission v Belgium* [1978] ECR 1881 paras

4. EFFECT OF JUDGMENT OF COURT OF JUSTICE

Article 171 Article 171 of the EEC Treaty provides that:

> If the Court of Justice finds that a Member State has failed to fulfil an obligation under this Treaty, the State shall be required to take the necessary measures to comply with the judgment of the Court of Justice.

Effect of judgment A judgment by the Court of Justice under article 169 is declaratory in form and does not, in itself, cure any breach on the part of the Member State. However, it does impose an obligation on the Member State concerned to take all necessary measures to remedy its default. In particular the judgment:[86]

   (1) prohibits competent national authorities from applying a national law adjudged to be incompatible with the Treaty;

   (2) imposes an obligation on the national authorities to introduce, repeal or amend legislative acts so as to ensure compliance with Community law; and

   (3) imposes an obligation on the courts of the Member State concerned to ensure, when performing their duties, that the Court's judgment is complied with.

Where the Commission brings proceedings on the basis that a Member State has failed to take specific measures, the judgment of the Court of Justice will, in practical terms, impose an obligation on the Member State to adopt the relevant measures.[87]

Time for compliance Although article 171 does not specify the period within which a judgment must be complied with, the Court of Justice has held that the process of complying with a judgment must be initiated at once and must be completed as soon as possible.[88]

Failure to comply with judgment If a Member State fails to comply with a judgment of the Court of Justice under article 169, it is in breach of its obligations under article 171 and the Commission may bring new infraction proceedings in respect of the breach of article 171. It is not necessary to bring proceedings based on the original breach.[89] The Court of Justice adopts the same strict approach to breaches of article 171 as it does in proceedings under

---

5–13, C–35/88 *Commission v Greece* [1990] ECR I–3125 paras 8, 13; C–294/90 *British Aerospace plc and Rover Group Holdings plc v Commission* [1992] ECR I–493; C–61/90 *Commission v Greece* [1992] ECR I–2407 paras 25–28, for discussion of the relationship between article 169 and article 93(2). Discussed further at p 109.

[86] Case 48/71 *Commission v Italy* [1972] ECR 527 para 7; Joined Cases 24/80R, 97/80R *Commission v France* [1980] ECR 1319 para 16; Joined Cases 314–316/81, 83/82 *Procureur de la République v Waterkeyn* [1982] ECR 4337 paras 14, 15.

[87] Case 70/72 *Commission v Germany* [1973] ECR 813 paras 10–13.

[88] Case 169/87 *Commission v France* [1988] ECR 4093 paras 13, 14; Case C–375/89 *Commission v Belgium* [1991] ECR I–383; Case C–328/90 *Commission v Greece* [1992] ECR I–425; Case C–75/91 *Commission v Netherlands* [1992] ECR I–549.

[89] For example, see Case 48/71 *Commission v Italy* [1972] ECR 527; Case C–266/89 *Commission v Italy* [1991] ECR I–2411.

article 169. For example, a Member State will not be permitted, under article 171, to rely on political difficulties as a defence.[90] Where the Court has already made a judgment against a Member State under article 169 and the Commission brings fresh proceedings for failure to comply with article 171, the Court of Justice will not grant interim measures where this would simply have the same effect as the original judgment.[91]

Basis of civil liability In Case 39/72 *Commission v Italy*, the Court of Justice held that:[92]

> ... a judgment by the Court under Articles 169 and 171 of the Treaty may be of substantive interest as establishing the basis of a responsibility that a Member State can incur as a result of its default, as regards other Member States, the Community or private parties.

This demonstrates the practical importance of infraction proceedings to private parties. A judgment under article 169, which binds the English courts by virtue of the European Communities Act 1972,[93] can provide the basis for an action by private parties in their own national courts for restitution of monies paid[94] or for damages in respect of any loss which they have suffered as a result of the relevant breach.[95]

In Joined Cases 314–316/81, 83/82 *Procureur de la République v Waterkeyn*,[96] the Court of Justice emphasised that where a judgment under article 169 establishes that a Member State is in breach of directly effective Community provisions, the judgment does not itself create rights on the part of individuals. However, the national courts must take account of the relevant elements of law established by a judgment under article 169 in an action brought in the national courts. Thus, in Joined Cases C–6/90, C–9/90 *Francovich and Bonifaci v Italy*,[97] the Court of Justice relied on an earlier decision taken in the context of proceedings under article 169,[98] as establishing that Italy was in breach of Community law by failing to implement a directive. This breach provided the basis for the Court's decision that a Member State can be liable in damages to individuals who have suffered loss as a result of the State's failure to properly implement a directive.

Maastricht proposals If a Member State fails to respect a judgment of the Court of Justice under article 169, there are no sanctions available to the Court to censure such behaviour. The other Member States may bring political pres-

---

[90] Case 48/71 *Commission v Italy* [1972] ECR 527.
[91] Joined Cased 24/80R, 97/80R *Commission v France* [1980] ECR 1319.
[92] [1973] ECR 101 para 11. See also Case 309/84 *Commission v Italy* [1986] ECR 599 para 18; Case 240/86 *Commission v Greece* [1988] ECR 1835 para 14.
[93] See pp 10–11.
[94] See Ch 8.
[95] See pp 72–86.
[96] [1982] ECR 4337 paras 13–16.
[97] [1991] ECR I–5357. See further at pp 82–85.
[98] Case 22/87 *Commission v Italy* [1989] ECR 143.

sure to bear and the Commission may bring further infraction proceedings for breach of article 171. However, the Maastricht Treaty, if ratified, will amend article 171, to permit the Court of Justice to impose a 'lump sum or penalty payment' on any Member State which fails to comply with a judgment under article 169.

Chapter 12

Judicial Review of EC Acts—Article 173 of the EEC Treaty

1. INTRODUCTION

Article 173 Article 173 of the EEC Treaty provides:

> The Court of Justice shall review the legality of acts of the Council and the Commission other than recommendations or opinions. It shall for this purpose have jurisdiction in actions brought by a Member State, the Council or the Commission on grounds of lack of competence, infringement of an essential procedural requirement, infringement of this Treaty or of any rule of law relating to its application, or misuse of powers.
>
> Any natural or legal person may, under the same conditions, institute proceedings against a decision addressed to that person or against a decision which, although in the form of a regulation or a decision addressed to another person, is of direct and individual concern to the former.
>
> The proceedings provided for in this Article shall be instituted within two months of the publication of the measure or of its notification to the plaintiff, or, in the absence thereof, of the day on which it came to the knowledge of the latter, as the case may be.

Purpose of Article 173 Article 173 provides the basis for judicial review by the EC Courts of acts of the Community institutions. Actions brought under article 173 are often referred to as 'actions for annulment'.

Distinction between privileged and non-privileged applicants Article 173 establishes different rules for judicial review depending on the nature of the applicant. It is necessary to distinguish between the position of the Member States and the Community institutions ('privileged applicants') and the position of private parties ('non-privileged applicants'). In order to establish that it has *locus standi*, a privileged applicant must show that the measure which it wishes to challenge is a 'reviewable act'. A non-privileged applicant must show that the relevant measure is a reviewable act *and* it must show that it has sufficient standing.

Definition of privileged applicants The first limb of article 173 provides that the Council, Commission or any Member State may seek judicial review of the legality of the acts of the Council and the Commission, other than recommendations or opinions. In contrast, the European Parliament is not expressly named as a privileged applicant by article 173. Furthermore, in Case 302/87 *European*

Parliament v Council,[1] the Court of Justice, in refusing to recognise any right for the Parliament to seek review, held that the Parliament could not rely on the second limb of article 173 as it was not a 'natural or legal person'. However, in Case C–70/88 *European Parliament v Council,*[2] the Court of Justice departed from its previous decision in Case 302/87 by recognising, for the first time, the right of the European Parliament to seek review under article 173. The Court held that the Parliament could seek review of acts of the Council or the Commission provided that the action was brought solely to safeguard the Parliament's own prerogatives and that the action was founded only on submissions alleging infringement of those prerogatives. Provided these conditions were met, the Parliament could seek review on the same basis as the other institutions. The Court of Justice considered that it was necessary to recognise the right of the Parliament to seek review in order to maintain the 'institutional balance' created by the Treaties. On the facts of the case, the Parliament sought review of a Council regulation on the grounds that it had been adopted on the wrong legal basis. The regulation had been adopted on the basis of article 31 of the Euratom Treaty, which requires the Council simply to consult the Parliament. The Parliament argued that the regulation should have been based on article 100a of the EEC Treaty, which would have required the Council to co-operate with the Parliament in relation to its adoption, and that the Council's choice of legal basis had, therefore, prevented the Parliament from playing its proper role in the adoption process. In view of these arguments, the Parliament's application was declared to be admissible.[3]

Jurisdiction Actions by privileged applicants under article 173 must be made to the Court of Justice. Actions by non-privileged applicants under article 173 must be made to the Court of First Instance.[4]

Burden of proof The burden of proving the invalidity of a Community act rests on the applicant.[5]

Admissibility Where the defendant Community institution considers that an applicant does not have *locus standi* to challenge the act in question, it may ask the Court to decide the question of admissibility as a preliminary issue.[6] The EC Courts may consider the question of admissibility of their own motion, even where it has not been raised by the parties.[7]

---

[1] [1988] ECR 5615 (the *Comitology* case).

[2] [1990] ECR I–2041 paras 26–27 (the *Chernobyl* case); followed in Case C–65/90 *European Parliament v Council* [1992] ECR I–4593 paras 10–15.

[3] The Treaty on European Union (the 'Maastricht Treaty') provides that both the European Parliament and the European Central Bank will have *locus standi* to bring actions, for the purpose of protecting their prerogatives.

[4] Article 3 of Council Decision 88/591 of 24 October 1988, OJ No L 319, 25 November 1988, p 1 (corrected text at OJ No C 215, 21 August 1989 p 1) as substituted by Council Decision 93/350 of 8 June 1993, OJ No L 144, 16 June 1993, p 21 as amended by Council Decision 94/149 of 7 March 1994, OJ No L 66, 10 March 1994, p 29.

[5] Case T–11/89 *Shell International Chemical Company Ltd v Commission* [1992] ECR II–757 para 374.

[6] ECJ Rules of Procedure, article 91; CFI Rules of Procedure, article 114. See pp 332, 393.

[7] ECJ Rules of Procedure, article 92(2); CFI Rules of Procedure, article 113. See pp 333, 393. Case

2. LOCUS STANDI

(a) Reviewable acts

Test It is not possible to give an exhaustive list of the types of acts which are reviewable under article 173 of the EEC Treaty. However, the Court of Justice has developed a number of principles which serve as guidelines[8]:

(1) It is the substance of the measure under consideration which is decisive, not its form.
(2) In order to be reviewable, a measure must produce binding effects which affect the legal position of the parties concerned.
(3) Measures of a purely preparatory character are not reviewable.
(4) Confirmatory measures are not reviewable.

Substance not form Article 173 provides that acts 'other than recommendations or opinions' are reviewable. Article 189 of the EEC Treaty sets out certain types of act which may be adopted by the Community institutions namely, regulations, directives, decisions, recommendations and opinions. The EC Courts will look at the content and legal effects of an act, rather than at its form, in order to decide whether it is reviewable.[9] It is not necessary for an act to be categorised as a 'regulation', 'directive' or 'decision' for it to be reviewable. This follows from the judgment of the Court of Justice in Case 22/70 *Commission v Council*[10] (the *ERTA* case), in which the Court held that the categories of reviewable acts were not limited to the categories of measures referred to in article 189. The action for annulment is available in respect of all acts of the institutions which satisfy the 'legal effects' test. In the *ERTA* case, it was held that 'conclusions' adopted by the Council, which established the course of action to be taken by the individual Member States in negotiating a European transport agreement with non-member States, amounted to reviewable acts.

In Case C–325/91 *France v Commission*[11] the Court of Justice examined a document which was entitled 'Communication from the Commission to the Member States' and which dealt with the application of the Community rules on state aids and, in particular, with article 5 of Directive 80/723.[12] The directive

---

92/78 *Simmenthal SpA v Commission* [1979] ECR 777 para 22; Case 294/83 *Parti écologiste 'Les Verts' v European Parliament* [1986] ECR 1339 para 19; Joined Cases C–305/86, C–160/87 *Neotype Techmashexport GmbH v Commission and Council* [1990] ECR I–2945 para 18; Case C–313/90 *Comité international de la rayonne et des fibres synthétiques (CIRFS) v Commission* judgment of 24 March 1993 para 23; Case C–225/91 *Matra SA v Commission* judgment of 15 June 1993 para 13.

[8] See the Opinion of Advocate-General Sir Gordon Slynn in Case 60/81 *IBM v Commission* [1981] ECR 2639 at 2662.

[9] Joined Cases 8–11/66 *Cimenteries v Commission* [1967] ECR 75, Opinion of Advocate-General Roemer at 100, 101; Case 60/81 *IBM v Commission* [1981] ECR 2639 para 9; Case C–50/90 *Sunzest (Europe) BV v Commission* [1991] ECR I–2917 para 12; Joined Cases C–213/88, C–39/89 *Luxembourg v European Parliament* [1991] ECR I–5643 para 15.

[10] [1971] ECR 263 paras 34–55. See also Case C–303/90 *France v Commission* [1991] I–5315 paras 7–25.

[11] Judgment of 16 June 1993 paras 1–23.

[12] Commission Directive 80/723 on the transparency of financial relations between Member States

required the Member States to keep certain records which the Commission could demand to inspect. The communication, while purporting simply to clarify the application of the directive, set out a detailed list of information which was to be provided to the Commission on an annual basis. The Court held that this constituted an attempt to impose obligations on the Member States which went beyond those provided for by the original directive. Therefore, the 'Communication' was an act intended to produce legal effects and constituted a reviewable act subject to article 173 of the EEC Treaty. The Court went on to annul the act because it did not state the legal basis on which it was purported to be based.

Legal effects In order to be reviewable, an act must produce legal effects which:

(1) are binding on the party concerned; and
(2) affect the interests of the party concerned by bringing about a distinct change in its legal position.[13]

An example of the application of the 'legal effects' test is the judgment in Joined Cases 8–11/66 *Cimenteries v Commission*.[14] The issue in that case concerned Council Regulation 17/62[15] which sets out the main procedural rules for competition matters. Article 15(5) of Regulation 17/62 provides that undertakings which notify their agreements to the Commission are exempt from the system of fines imposed for anti-competitive behaviour until the Commission reaches a final decision. However, article 15(6) provides that, after a preliminary examination, the Commission may withdraw this exemption, so that undertakings are at risk if they continue with their agreement and it is subsequently found to be contrary to article 85 of the EEC Treaty. The act challenged in *Cimenteries v Commission* was a letter from the Commission withdrawing the exemption from fines under article 15(6). The Court of Justice held that, as the effect of the Commission's letter was that the undertakings ceased to benefit from the exemption from fines, this brought about a distinct change in their legal position and produced binding legal effects affecting the interests of the undertakings. The letter was therefore reviewable under article 173.

---

and public undertakings, OJ No L 195, 28 July 1980, p 35.

[13] Joined Cases 8–11/66 *Cimenteries v Commission* [1967] ECR 75 at 91; Case 133/79 *Sucrimex SA & Westzucker GmbH v Commission* [1980] ECR 1299 paras 16–18; Case 60/81 *IBM v Commission* [1981] ECR 2639 para 9; Case 182/80 *HP Gauff Ingenieure GmbH & Co KG v Commission* [1982] ECR 799 paras 15–18; Case 53/85 *AKZO Chemie v Commission* [1986] ECR 1965 para 16–18; Joined Cases C–66/91, C–66/91R *Emerald Meats Limited v Commission* [1991] ECR I–1143 paras 26–29; Case C–50/90 *Sunzest (Europe) BV v Commission* [1991] ECR I–2917 paras 12–14; Case C–117/91 *Jean-Marc Bosman v Commission* [1991] ECR I–4837 paras 13–15; Case C–170/89 *Bureau Européen des Unions de Consommateurs (BEUC) v Commission* [1991] ECR I–5709 paras 9–12.

[14] [1967] ECR 75.

[15] Regulation 17/62 of 6 February 1962, First Regulation implementing articles 85, 86 of the EEC Treaty (as amended), OJ No 13, 21 February 1962, p 204 (English Special Edition, 1959–1962, p 87).

For a measure to be reviewable it is not enough that it produces legal effects. The legal effects must be capable of affecting the interests of the party concerned by bringing about a distinct change in the party's legal position. For example, in Case 60/81 *IBM v Commission*,[16] a competition case, the measure challenged was a letter from the Commission to IBM, which stated that the Commission had initiated procedures under Regulation 17/62. The Commission also enclosed a 'statement of objections', in which it indicated its views as to why IBM's behaviour was *prima facie* anti-competitive, and invited IBM to submit a written reply. The Court of Justice held that this letter produced legal effects because it put an end to the jurisdiction of the competition authorities in the Member States and crystallised the Commission's case. However, the Court held that these effects did not 'adversely affect the interests of the undertaking concerned' and the Commission's acts were, therefore, not reviewable under article 173.[17]

Preparatory measures Measures which are merely part of the process by which a final decision is reached are not reviewable. However, it is not necessary that the measure is the final step in the whole administrative process; it is enough that the measure puts an end to a certain part of the overall procedure.[18] This distinction is exemplified by a comparison of the judgments in Joined Cases 8–11/66 *Cimenteries v Commission*[19] and Case 60/81 *IBM v Commission*.[20] In *Cimenteries*, the Court of Justice found that a decision to withdraw the exemption from fines under article 15(6) of Regulation 17/62 constitutes the 'culmination of a special procedure' distinct from the procedure under which a decision on the substance of the matter as a whole is taken.[21] In contrast, in *IBM*, the Court of Justice held that both the initiation of the investigative procedure and the statement of objections were merely 'procedural measures adopted preparatory to the decision which represents their culmination'.[22]

A further example is provided by the judgment in Case 48/64 *Alfons Lütticke GmbH v Commission*.[23] Under article 169 of the EEC Treaty, the Commission may bring an action before the Court of Justice if it believes that a Member State is in breach of its EEC Treaty obligations. Prior to doing so, the Commission must give the Member State concerned an opportunity to submit its observations and the Commission must adopt a reasoned opinion on the matter. The Court of Justice held that this part of the procedure is a purely administrative

---

[16] [1981] ECR 2639. See also Case 53/85 *AKZO Chemie v Commission* [1986] ECR 1965.

[17] In Joined Cases 8–11/66 *Cimenteries v Commission* [1967] ECR 75 Advocate-General Roemer stated, at p 103 of his Opinion, that: '... not every kind of legal effect is sufficient ... one must take a narrower view and see whether the legal effects are capable of *adversely affecting substantial interests*'.

[18] Ibid at 92; Case 60/81 *IBM v Commission* [1981] ECR 2639 paras 10, 11; Case 53/85 *AKZO Chemie v Commission* [1986] ECR 1965 paras 19, 20.

[19] [1967] ECR 75.

[20] [1981] ECR 2639.

[21] [1967] ECR 75 at 92.

[22] [1981] ECR 2639 para 21. See also Joined Cases T–10–12/92R and T–14/92, 15/92R *Cimenteries CBR SA v Commission* [1992] ECR II–1571 para 45.

[23] [1966] ECR 19 at 27.

stage which does not have any binding force and, therefore, is not reviewable under article 173.

Whilst measures of a purely preparatory character are not themselves reviewable under article 173, any legal defects in those preparatory acts may be relied on in challenging the definitive act to which they lead.[24]

Confirmatory measures A measure which merely confirms a previous measure is not reviewable.[25] This is important because of the strict, two-month limitation period for actions under article 173.[26] A party who has failed to challenge an original measure within the two-month time limit cannot circumvent that limitation rule by seeking to challenge a later measure which is purely confirmatory of the first measure or by seeking to challenge a subsequent letter refusing to reconsider the original measure.[27] This rule does not apply where there has been a substantial change of circumstances since the adoption of the first measure.[28]

The definition of a 'confirmatory measure' was examined in Case 44/81 *Germany v Commission*.[29] In this case, the Commission had sent letters to the German Federal Ministry of Labour in July 1980 refusing to make certain payments allocated to Germany from the Social Fund. Further letters and dialogue ensued, which came to an end when the Commission wrote another letter in December 1980, again refusing to make the payments. The act challenged under article 173 was the letter of December 1980. The Commission argued that this letter did not constitute a reviewable act as it was purely confirmatory of the July letters. However, the Court of Justice held that it was clear from the context that the Commission only reached a final, unequivocal and definitive decision in December. The July letters were not expressed to be merely provisional but, because the Commission was subsequently prepared to discuss the matter, the July letters could not constitute definitive decisions.[30]

Acts of the European Parliament Although article 173 only provides expressly for review of acts of the Council and Commission, the Court of Justice has held that acts of the European Parliament which are intended to have legal effects *vis-à-vis* third parties are reviewable. In Case 294/83 *Parti écologiste*

---

[24] Case 60/81 *IBM v Commission* [1981] ECR 2639 para 12; Case C–156/87 *Gestetner Holdings plc v Council and Commission* [1990] ECR I–781 paras 7–10.

[25] Joined Cases 42/59, 49/59 *SNUPAT v High Authority* [1961] ECR 53 at 74 (ECSC); Case 22/70 *Commission v Council (ERTA)* [1971] ECR 263 paras 65, 66; Case 26/76 *Metro SB-Großmärkte GmbH & Co KG v Commission* [1977] ECR 1875 paras 3, 4; Case 44/81 *Germany v Commission* [1982] ECR 1855 paras 8–12; Case C–12/90 *Infortec—Projectos e consultadoria Ld^a v Commission* [1990] ECR I–4265 para 10.

[26] See pp 198–200.

[27] Case 2/71 *Germany v Commission* [1971] ECR 669 para 7.

[28] Joined Cases 42/59, 49/59 *SNUPAT v High Authority* [1961] ECR 53 at 76 (ECSC).

[29] [1982] ECR 1855 paras 8–12.

[30] See also the judgment in Case 22/70 *Commission v Council (ERTA)* [1971] ECR 263 paras 65, 66, where the Court of Justice looked at the factual background in deciding that a measure was not purely confirmatory.

'Les Verts' v European Parliament,[31-32] the Court of Justice observed that at the time of its drafting the EEC Treaty merely granted powers of consultation and political control to the Parliament. It was only later that the Parliament acquired power to adopt measures intended to have legal effects *vis-à-vis* third parties and, therefore, it had become essential to interpret article 173 so as to permit the legality of such acts to be reviewable in order to uphold the rule of law in the Community.[33]

Delegated acts In Joined Cases 32/58, 33/58 *SNUPAT v High Authority*[34] the High Authority, which was at that time the equivalent of the Commission under the ECSC Treaty, had set up two subordinate bodies to administer a subsidy system for steel scrap. A steel-making firm sought to challenge a decision of one of the subordinate bodies under article 33 of the ECSC Treaty (which is equivalent to article 173 of the EEC Treaty). Although article 33 only provides for review of acts of the High Authority, the Court of Justice held that the decisions adopted by the subordinate body were *prima facie* reviewable as they were equivalent to decisions of the High Authority. The Court reached this conclusion on the basis that the subordinate body derived its powers from the High Authority and its decisions in fact constituted the final administrative decision under the subsidy system.

(b) Sufficient standing

(i) Introduction

Definition of sufficient standing The right of private parties to seek judicial review is limited by the second limb of article 173, which provides that a private party will have sufficient standing in three situations only:

(1) where a decision has been addressed to the person bringing the proceedings;

(2) where a decision addressed to another person is of direct and individual concern to the person bringing the proceedings; and

(3) where a decision in the form of a regulation is of direct and individual concern to the person bringing the proceedings.

It follows that any private party who wishes to seek review of an act under article 173 must first demonstrate that the act which he wishes to challenge can be classified as a 'decision'. Where a decision is addressed to a particular person, that person can seek review of the decision under article 173 without hav-

---

[31-32] [1986] ECR 1339 paras 20–25. See also Case 78/85 *Group of the European Right v European Parliament* [1986] ECR 1753; Case 34/86 *Council v European Parliament* [1986] ECR 2155; Case 190/84 *Parti écologiste 'Les Verts' v European Parliament* [1988] ECR 1017; Joined Cases C–213/88, C–39/89 *Luxembourg v European Parliament* [1991] ECR I–5643 para 15; Case C–314/91 *Beate Weber v European Parliament*, judgment of 23 March 1993 paras 7–12. See also Case 108/83 *Luxembourg v European Parliament* [1984] ECR 1945.

[33] The Treaty on European Union (the 'Maastricht Treaty') expressly provides for judicial review of acts adopted jointly by the European Parliament and the Council and of acts of the European Parliament intended to produce legal effects *vis-à-vis* third parties. It will also permit review of acts of the European Central Bank.

[34] [1959] ECR 127 at 137, 138 (ECSC).

ing to satisfy any further requirements. However, where a decision is addressed to another person, the person who wishes to seek review of that decision must show that it concerns him 'directly' and 'individually'.

(ii) Definition of decisions

Substance, not form, is determinative Community measures which are, in substance, if not in form, within the definition of decisions under article 189 of the EEC Treaty, are recognised as decisions.[35] For example, letters sent by Community institutions may amount to decisions and, therefore, be subject to review under article 173.[36]

Decision addressed to another person The phrase 'decisions addressed to another person' includes decisions addressed to Member States.[37]

Decisions in the form of regulations The second limb of article 173 provides that a private party may seek review of a decision which, although it is in the form of a regulation, is of direct and individual concern to the applicant. The Court of Justice has held that this provision is intended to prevent Community institutions barring proceedings for review being taken by an individual by adopting an act in the form of a regulation which is, in substance, a decision.[38] The Court of Justice is concerned with the nature of the measure and not the form in which it is adopted.

The Court of Justice has established that the test of what constitutes a regulation and what constitutes a decision is set out in article 189 of the EEC Treaty. Article 189 states that regulations are of general application, whereas decisions are binding only on those to whom they are addressed.[39] Thus, in order to determine whether or not a measure constitutes a decision, one must enquire whether that measure concerns specific persons.[40] In each case, it is necessary to consider the nature of the contested measure and, in particular, the legal effects which it is intended to have, or does in fact have, taking account of all the circumstances of the case.[41] The crucial difference lies in the general

---

[35] Joined Cases 16/62, 17/62 *Confédération nationale des producteurs de fruits et légumes and Others and Fédération nationale des producteurs de raisins de table v Council (Producteurs de fruits)* [1962] ECR 471 para 1.

[36] For example, Joined Cases 8–11/66 *Cimenteries v Commission* [1967] ECR 75 at 90–93. Discussed at pp 174–176.

[37] Case 25/62 *Plaumann & Co v Commission* [1963] ECR 95 and the Opinion of Advocate-General Roemer at 112, 113.

[38] Case 101/76 *Koninklijke Scholten Honig NV v Council and Commission* [1977] ECR 797 para 6; Case 162/78 *Wagner v Commission* [1979] ECR 3467 para 16; Joined Cases 789/79, 790/79 *Calpak SpA v Commission* [1980] ECR 1949 para 7.

[39] See at pp 5–7, 9.

[40] Case 25/62 *Plaumann & Co v Commission* [1963] ECR 95 at 107.

[41] See, for example, Joined Cases 16/62, 17/62 *Confédération nationale des producteurs de fruits et légumes and Others and Fédération nationale des producteurs de raisins de table v Council (Producteurs de fruits)* [1962] ECR 471 paras 2, 3; Case 101/76 *Koninklijke Scholten Honig NV v Council and Commission* [1977] ECR 797 para 6; Case 162/78 *Wagner v Commission* [1979] ECR 3467 para 17; Joined Cases 789/79, 790/79 *Calpak SpA v Commission* [1980] ECR 1949 para 8; Case 242/81 *SA Roquette Frères v Council* [1982] ECR 3213 paras 5, 6; Case 307/81 *Alusuisse Italia SpA v Council and Commission* [1982] ECR 3463 para 8; Case 40/84 *Casteels*

legislative nature of regulations, in contrast to decisions, which affect specific and identifiable legal persons.[42]

A measure does not lose its character as a regulation simply because it may be factually possible to ascertain the number, or even the identity, of the persons to which it applies at any given time.[43] Furthermore, the fact that a legal provision may have different practical effects for the different persons to whom it applies does not prevent it from being a regulation.[44] In Case 6/68 *Zuckerfabrik Watenstedt GmbH v Council*[45] the regulation challenged affected the common organisation of the market in sugar. The fact that it would have been possible to ascertain the buyers and sellers of sugar beet or sugar cane affected by the regulation did not mean that it was, by its nature, a decision and, therefore, reviewable. The applicant was affected solely because it fell within the objective class of sellers of raw beet sugar and not by reason of any more narrowly defined characteristic. The measure was of general application and constituted a regulation.

A more extreme example is provided by the decision in Case 242/81 *SA Roquette Frères v Council*.[46] The regulation challenged again concerned the common organisation of the market in sugar, in particular the production of isoglucose. The applicant, one of the main producers of isoglucose in the Community, argued that, as there were only nine isoglucose producers in the whole of the Community, which were known to the Council and, therefore, perfectly identifiable, and since the quotas allotted to the various regions in fact equated to the production of the producers in those regions, the measure challenged was, in reality, a decision in the form of a regulation. The Court of Justice rejected this argument, applying the principle that:[47]

> ... a measure does not cease to be a regulation because it is possible to determine more or less exactly the number or even the identity of the persons to whom it applies at any given time as long as it is established that such application takes effect by virtue of an objective legal or factual situation defined by the measure in question in relation to its purpose.

    PVBA v Commission [1985] ECR 667 paras 9–12.
[42]   Joined Cases 103–109/78 *Société des Usines de Beauport v Council* [1979] ECR 17 paras 13–19.
[43]   Case 6/68 *Zuckerfabrik Watenstedt GmbH v Council* [1968] ECR 409; Case 101/76 *Koninklijke Scholten Honig NV v Council and Commission* [1977] ECR 797; Joined Cases 789/79, 790/79 *Calpak SpA v Commission* [1980] ECR 1949 para 9; Case 64/80 *F Giuffrida and G Campogrande v Council* [1981] ECR 693; Case 307/81 *Alusuisse Italia SpA v Council and Commission* [1982] ECR 3463 para 11; Case 147/83 *Münchener Import-Weinkellerei Herold Binderer GmbH v Commission* [1985] ECR 257 para 13; Case 26/86 *Deutz und Geldermann, Sektkellerei Breisach/Baden GmbH v Council* [1987] ECR 941.
[44]   [1968] ECR 409; Case 63/69 *La Compagnie Française Commerciale et Financière SA v Commission* [1970] ECR 205 paras 6–10; Case 65/69 *La Compagnie d'Approvisionnement, de Transport et de Crédit, SA v Commission* [1970] ECR 229 paras 6–10; Case 101/76 *Koninklijke Scholten Honig NV v Council and Commission* [1977] ECR 79.
[45]   [1968] ECR 409.
[46]   [1982] ECR 3213.
[47]   Ibid para 7.

Advocate-General Reischl stated in his Opinion that:[48]

The determinant factor is whether it may be assumed that the number of parties concerned will remain unchanged. However, nobody can predict that with certainty. It is in fact impossible to rule out certain changes, either through the disappearance of an undertaking or by the founding of new undertakings, even if that does perhaps appear improbable.

A measure does not cease to have general application by virtue of the fact that it contains temporal or geographical limitations or derogations.[49] In Case 30/67 *Industria Molitaria Imolese v Council,*[50] certain provisions in a regulation fixed intervention prices for common wheat at the Bologna and Ancona marketing centres. The Court of Justice held that an application for review by milling undertakings situated in Bologna and Ancona was inadmissible as the provisions challenged simply affected the interests of users and traders in the abstract, albeit within the ambit of each marketing centre.

Relationship with direct and individual concern   When seeking to challenge a regulation, a private party must satisfy the three stages of the test established by the second limb of article 173. These are:

(1) the contested measure must constitute a decision in substance;

(2) it must be of direct concern to the applicant; and

(3) it must be of individual concern to him.

In some judgments, the Court of Justice has not explicitly followed this approach, but rather has applied only the second and third stages of the test.[51] In practice, it appears that the same issues often arise under the first and third stages of the test.[52] However, an applicant should not assume that it is sufficient to prove that it is directly and individually concerned by a regulation in order to show that it has *locus standi* to challenge that regulation. This suggestion has been expressly rejected in Opinions of Advocates-General and impliedly rejected by several judgments of the Court of Justice.[53] Thus, an applicant should always deal with all three stages in its application to the Court.

---

[48] Ibid at 3233.

[49] Case 6/68 *Zuckerfabrik Watenstedt GmbH v Council* [1968] ECR 409 at 415; Joined Cases 103–109/78 *Société des Usines de Beauport v Council* [1979] ECR 17 paras 12–17; C–298/89 *Government of Gibraltar v Council* judgment of 29 June 1993 para 18.

[50] [1968] ECR 115 at 121.

[51] See, for example Joined Cases 41–44/70 *NV International Fruit Company v Commission* [1971] ECR 411 paras 2–29; Case 100/74 *Société CAM SA v Commission* [1979] ECR 1393 paras 3–20; Case 138–79 *SA Roquette Frères v Council* [1980] ECR 3333 paras 13–16. For further discussion of this point, see Rosa Greaves 'Locus Standi under Article 173 EEC when Seeking Annulment of a Regulation' [1986] 11 EL Rev 119.

[52] The test for individual concern is discussed at pp 183–186.

[53] Case 40/64 *Marcello Sgarlata v Commission* [1965] ECR 215 at 226 and the Opinion of Advocate-General Roemer at 230–235; Case 63/69 *La Compagnie Française Commerciale et Financière SA v Commission* [1970] ECR 205, Opinion of Advocate-General Roemer at 215; Case 65/69 *La Compagnie d'Approvisionnement, de Transport et de Crédit SA v Commission* [1970] ECR 229; Joined Cases 41–44/71 *NV International Fruit Company v Commission* [1971] ECR 411, Opinion of Advocate-General Roemer at 432–435; Case 123/77 *UNICME v Council* [1978] ECR 845 para 7; Joined Cases 103–109/78 *Société des Usines de Beauport v Council* [1979] ECR 17 paras 10–23; Case 113/77 *NTN Toyo Bearing Company Ltd v Council* [1979]

Applicant's participation in adoption of regulation   The fact that an applicant has participated in the procedure leading to the adoption of a regulation does not give the applicant *locus standi* to seek review of that measure. The distinction between a regulation and a decision is based on the nature of the measure and not on the procedures followed for its adoption. For example, in Case 147/83 *Münchener Import-Weinkellerei Herold Binderer GmbH v Commission*[54], the applicant, Binderer, imported wines into Germany. Following the adoption of a regulation laying down detailed rules for the description and presentation of wines, Binderer made a proposal to the Commission concerning the proper translation of certain Hungarian terms. The Commission approved the proposal in a letter, but, subsequently, in an amending regulation, the use of the translations proposed by Binderer was expressly prohibited on the labels of imported wines. Binderer sought to challenge this amendment claiming, *inter alia*, that the way in which the contested provision was adopted proved that it was directed solely at the applicant. This was rejected by the Court of Justice on the basis that the distinction between a regulation and a decision is based solely on the nature of the measure itself and not on the procedures for its adoption.

(iii) Definition of 'direct concern'

Discretion of the Member State   A measure adopted by a Community institution which simply creates a power in favour of the Member States concerned or which leaves a margin of discretion as to the manner of its implementation *prima facie* cannot be of direct concern within the meaning of article 173 of the EEC Treaty.[55] However, the Court of Justice has held that purely facultative Community measures may be of direct concern to an applicant where, in all the circumstances of the case, there is no doubt that the Member State will make use of the power. For example, in Case 62/70 *Werner A Bock v Commission*[56] and Case 11/82 *AE Piraiki-Patraiki v Commission*[57] the Member States concerned had specifically requested that the Commission grant them the relevant facultative powers.

ECR 1185, Opinion of Advocate-General Warner at 1242, 1243; Case 100/74 *Société CAM SA v Commission* [1979] ECR 1393 at 1411–1414, Opinion of Advocate-General Warner; Case 307/81 *Alusuisse Italia SpA v Council and Commission* [1982] ECR 3463, Opinion of Advocate-General Rozès at para 2(a).

[54] [1985] ECR 257 paras 1–15. See also Case 72/74 *Union syndicale-Service public européen v Council* [1975] 401 para 19; Case 307/81 *Alusuisse Italia SpA v Council and Commission* [1982] ECR 3463 paras 12, 13.

[55] Joined Cases 10/68, 18/68 *Società 'Eridania' Zuccherifici Nazionali v Commission* [1969] ECR 459 paras 8–14; Case 69/69 *SA Alcan Aluminium Raeren v Commission* [1970] ECR 385 paras 8, 9; Joined Cases 41–44/70 *NV International Fruit Company v Commission* [1971] ECR 411 paras 23–28; Case 123/77 *UNICME v Council* [1978] ECR 845; Joined Cases 103–109/78 *Société des Usines de Beauport v Council* [1979] ECR 17 paras 20–22; Case 222/83 *Municipality of Differdange v Commission* [1984] ECR 2889 para 12; Joined Cases 87/77, 130/77, 22/83, 9/84, 10/84 *Vittorio Salerno and others v Commission and Council* [1985] ECR 2523 para 31 (a staff case). Case 294/83 *Parti écologiste 'Les Verts' v European Parliament* [1986] ECR 1339 para 31.

[56] [1971] ECR 897 paras 6–8.

[57] [1985] ECR 207 paras 8–10. See also Joined Cases 106/63, 107/63 *Alfred Toepfer and Getreide-Import Gesellschaft v Commission* [1965] ECR 405.

(iv) Definition of 'individual concern'

Test The Court of Justice has consistently held that:[58]

> Persons other than those to whom a decision is addressed may only claim to be individually concerned if that decision affects them by reason of certain attributes which are peculiar to them or by reason of circumstances in which they are differentiated from all other persons and by virtue of these factors distinguishes them individually just as in the case of the person addressed.

In Case 25/62 *Plaumann & Co v Commission*,[59] the applicant, an importer of clementines into Germany, sought to challenge a decision of the Commission which refused an authorisation sought by the German Government to vary the customs duty levied on clementines imported from third countries. Applying the above test, the Court of Justice held that the applicant, who was affected by the disputed decision simply by reason of a commercial activity which might be carried out at any time by any person, was not individually concerned by the decision.[60]

The fact that it is possible to determine, more or less precisely, the number, or even the identity, of the persons to whom a measure applies at any given time does not mean that the measure must be regarded as being of individual concern to them.[61] For example, in Case 307/81 *Alusuisse Italia SpA v Council and Commission*,[62] a regulation which imposed an anti-dumping duty on importers of orthoxylene from Puerto Rico and the United States was held not to be of individual concern to the applicant, even though it might have been possible to identify the limited numbers of traders affected by the regulation at the time of its adoption. The regulation imposed the anti-dumping duty on persons solely by reference to the objective criterion that they were importers of that product. It did not expressly name the persons on whom the duties were to be imposed.

Closed or fixed class Where a measure affects a class of parties which is absolutely fixed and incapable of alteration at the time of adoption of a measure, the members of that class are 'individually concerned' by the measure. One way in which a class may be absolutely fixed is where the only parties affected by the measure are retrospectively defined.[63] In Joined Cases 106/63, 107/63 *Alfred*

---

[58] Case 25/62 *Plaumann & Co v Commission* [1963] ECR 95 at 107; Case 1/64 *Glucoseries Réunies v Commission* [1964] ECR 413 at 417; Case 40/64 *Marcello Sgarlata v Commission* [1965] ECR 215 at 226, 227; Case 169/84 *Cofaz SA v Commission* [1986] ECR 391 para 22.

[59] [1963] ECR 95.

[60] See also Joined Cases 10/68, 18/68 *Società 'Eridania' Zuccherifici Nazionali v Commission* [1969] ECR 459 paras 5–7.

[61] This is the same principle applied in considering whether a measure is, in substance, a regulation or a decision. See pp 179–182.

[62] [1982] ECR 3463 paras 9–12. See also Case 123/77 *UNICME v Council* [1978] ECR 845; Case 231/82 *Spijker Kwasten BV v Commission* [1983] ECR 2559 paras 8–11; Case C–213/91 *Abertal SAT Limitada v Commission* judgment of 15 June 1993 paras 16–24.

[63] See Case 62/70 *Werner A Bock v Commission* [1971] ECR 897 paras 9, 10; Case 88/76 *Société pour l'exportation des sucres SA v Commission* [1977] ECR 709 paras 9–11; Case 232/81 *Agricola Commerciale Olio Srl v Commission* [1984] ECR 3881 paras 10, 11; Joined Cases 87/77, 130/77, 22/83, 9/84, 10/84 *Vittorio Salerno and others v Commission and Council* [1985] ECR 2523 para 30 (a staff case).

Toepfer and Getreide-Import Gesellschaft v Commission,[64] the Court of Justice looked at all the factual circumstances of the case and decided that, when the contested measures were adopted, the only persons who could be affected by them were importers who had applied for an import licence during the course of the day of 1 October 1963. They were, therefore, 'distinguished individually' and were individually concerned. Similarly, in Joined Cases 41–44/70 *NV International Fruit Company v Commission*,[65] the measure challenged affected parties who had made applications for import licences prior to the adoption of the measure. Therefore, when the measure was adopted, the number of applications which could be affected by it was fixed; no new applications could be added. It followed that the measure challenged, which was in the form of a regulation, was to be treated as a 'conglomeration of individual decisions' and the persons within the fixed class were individually concerned by those decisions.

In Case 100/74 *Société CAM SA v Commission*[66] the regulation challenged concerned the import levies and export refunds for cereals and rice. Under Community legislation concerning the common organisation of the market in cereals, the exporters of certain cereals were authorised to request advance fixing of export refunds. The regulation challenged affected a class of traders but, because it affected only those traders who had requested advance fixing, it applied only to a finite and known number of cereal exporters. The Court, therefore, held that an application under article 173 by an exporter thus affected was admissible.

When applying the fixed-class test to a provision which produces both retroactive and prospective effects, the EC Courts will not treat the provision as severed so that it constitutes a decision in respect of the fixed class which can be identified retroactively and a regulation in respect of the open class which it affects prospectively. This follows from Case 45/81 *Alexander Moksel Import-Export GmbH & Co Handels KG v Commission*,[67] where the Court of Justice held that, 'A single provision cannot at one and the same time have the character of a measure of general application and of an individual measure'. Subsequently, in Case 162/87 *Hans-Otto Wagner GmbH Agrarhandel KG v Commission*,[68] Advocate-General Warner suggested in his Opinion that the Court could sever the retroactive effect of a given provision from its prospective effect, so that the retroactive effects of the provision could be said to constitute a decision. This was not followed by the Court of Justice.

Differentiation from other parties Very rarely, the Court of Justice will adopt a more liberal attitude and hold that parties are individually concerned by a measure which causes them to suffer particular detriment over and above that

---

[64] [1965] ECR 405 at 411, 412, see also the Opinion of Advocate-General Roemer at 437–439.
[65] [1971] ECR 411 paras 14–22.
[66] [1975] ECR 1393 paras 3–20.
[67] [1982] ECR 1129 paras 11–19.
[68] [1979] ECR 3467, Opinion of Advocate-General Warner at 3494.

suffered by the objective class affected by the regulation as a whole. For example, in Case C–358/89 *Extramet Industrie SA v Council*,[69] an anti-dumping case, the applicant was the largest importer of the product affected by the anti-dumping duties and was also an end-user of the product. In addition, its business depended heavily on imports, particularly as the sole Community producer was also its main competitor for the processed product. The Court of Justice held that this specific set of circumstances differentiated the applicant from all other importers potentially affected by the regulation, so that the applicant was individually concerned by the measure.

In Case 11/82 *AE Piraiki-Patraiki v Commission*,[70] Greek cotton producers successfully challenged the validity of a Commission decision adopted in October 1981, which authorised France to impose a quota system on imports of cotton yarn from Greece during November 1981 to January 1982. Prior to the adoption of the decision, certain cotton producers had already entered into contracts to export cotton into France during the relevant period. The Court of Justice held that these producers were individually concerned by the decision, as the execution of their contracts was wholly or partly prevented by the adoption of the decision. In contrast, producers who had not entered into export contracts prior to the adoption of the decision were not particularly affected by it and, therefore, were not individually concerned by it.[71]

Applicant named in the measure Where a person is specifically named in a measure that person will generally be individually concerned by it. In Case 138/79 *SA Roquette Frères v Council*,[72] the measure challenged was a regulation which fixed the production quota for isoglucose within the Community. An Annex to the regulation set out the basic quotas for the year in question in relation to six specifically named undertakings. The Court of Justice held that these undertakings were directly and individually concerned by the measure. In his opinion, Advocate-General Reischl stated that:[73]

> The application of the arrangements is thus confined to a closed and unvarying group of precisely-known undertakings, namely those set out in Annex II.

Severability Where a particular provision within a regulation can be characterised as a decision of direct and individual concern to a private party, it can be separately challenged under article 173.[74]

---

[69] [1991] ECR I–2501 paras 13–18.
[70] [1985] ECR 207 paras 11–19.
[71] Contrast the approach of the Court of Justice when applying the 'fixed class' test. In particular see Case 45/81 *Alexander Moksel Import-EXport GmbH & Co Handels KG v Commission* [1982] ECR 1129 paras 11–19. See pp 183–184.
[72] [1980] ECR 3333 paras 13–16.
[73] Ibid, Opinion of Advocate-General Reischl at 3368.
[74] Joined Cases 16/62, 17/62 *Confédération nationale des producteurs de fruits et légumes v Council* [1962] ECR 471 para 2; Case 30/67 *Industria Molitoria Imolese v Council* [1968] ECR 115 at 121; *Société CAM SA v Commission* [1975] ECR 1393 para 19.

Representative organisations Generally, a representative organisation, such as a trade association or trade union, cannot be considered as being individually concerned by a regulation which affects the general interests of its members.[75] However, a representative organisation may have sufficient standing in cases concerning anti-dumping, competition law, or state aids.[76]

(v) Anti-dumping, state aids and competition
Special characteristics Measures adopted in the areas of anti-dumping, state aids and competition have special characteristics as they often involve responses to particular problems involving particular parties. In relation to anti-dumping and competition law, the relevant Treaty articles are supplemented by detailed regulations.[77] The Court of Justice has tended to adopt a more liberal approach to the question of *locus standi* in these areas. In Joined Cases C–15/91, C–108/91 *Josef Buckl & Söhne OHG v Commission*,[78] the Court of Justice recognised that this more liberal approach results largely from the special legislative frameworks in these areas (for example, in relation to complainants) and, therefore, cannot be applied generally.

Complainants Where a measure has been adopted following a procedure initiated by the complaint of a private party, the complainant will have *locus standi* to challenge that measure. In relation to anti-dumping and competition law, the relevant framework regulations contain specific provisions which permit the Commission to act following complaints by natural or legal persons who claim a legitimate interest.[79] The Court of Justice has repeatedly held that undertakings which are entitled to bring complaints before the Commission should be able to institute review proceedings to protect their legitimate interests where their complaints are dismissed in whole or in part.[80]

---

[75] Joined Cases 16/62, 17/62 *Confédération nationale des producteurs de fruits et légumes v Council* [1962] ECR 471 at 479, 480; Case 72/74 *Union syndicale-Service public européen v Council* [1975] ECR 401 paras 16, 17; Case 60/79 *Fédération Nationale des Producteurs de Vins de Table et Vins de Pays v Commission* [1979] ECR 2429; Case 282/85 *Comité de développement et de promotion du textile et de l'habillement (DEFI) v Commission* [1986] ECR 2469; Case 117/86 *Union de Federaciones Agrarias de España (UFADE) v Council and Commission* [1986] ECR 3255 para 12. Contrast Case 135/81 *Groupement des Agences de Voyages asbl v Commission* [1982] ECR 3799 paras 8–13; Case 297/86 *Confederazione Italiana dirigenti di azienda (CIDA) v Council* [1988] ECR 3531, Opinion of Advocate-General Lenz paras 10–17 (not followed by Court of Justice); position in anti-dumping cases (discussed at p 188).

[76] See p 188.

[77] In particular: in relation to competition law, Regulation 17/62 of 6 February 1962, First Regulation implementing articles 85, 86 of the EEC Treaty (as amended), OJ No 13, 21 February 1962, p 204 (English Special Edition, 1959–1962, p 87); and in relation to anti-dumping, Regulation 2423/88 of 11 July 1988 on the protection against dumped or subsidised imports from countries not members of the EEC, OJ No L 209, 2 August 1988, p 1.

[78] Judgment of 24 November 1992, paras 28–30.

[79] Regulation 17/62, article 3; Regulation 2423/88, article 5.

[80] Case 26/76 *Metro SB-Großmärkte GmbH & Co KG v Commission* [1977] ECR 2913 paras 5–13; Case 191/82 *FEDIOL v Commission* [1983] ECR 2913 paras 27–31; Case 210/81 *Demo-Studio Schmidt v Commission* [1983] ECR 3045 paras 10–16; Case 169/84 *Cofaz SA v Commission* [1986] ECR 391 para 23.

In Case 264/82 *Timex Corporation v Council and Commission*,[81] Timex was permitted to challenge a regulation imposing an anti-dumping duty on mechanical wristwatches originating in the Soviet Union. Timex was the leading manufacturer of mechanical watches and watch movements in the Community. The Court of Justice based its decision on the particular facts of the case, namely that:

(1) the complaint which led to the opening of the investigation procedure, lodged by the British Clock and Watch Manufacturers' Association Limited, owed its origin to a complaint previously lodged by Timex, which had been rejected by the Commission;

(2) the conduct of the investigation procedure was largely determined by Timex's observations; and

(3) the preamble to the regulation expressly indicated that the anti-dumping duty imposed took account of '. . .the extent of the injury caused to Timex by the dumped imports'.

This is a particularly liberal decision of the Court of Justice as it was argued by the Council and the Commission that Timex merely formed part of an open class which consisted of all manufacturers of mechanical wristwatches in the Community. This case should be regarded as a borderline decision, but it can be justified on the basis of the finding that Timex was the original source of the complaint which led to the anti-dumping regulation being adopted and on the fact that Timex was expressly named in the regulation itself, albeit in the preamble.

In Case 75/84 *Metro SB-Großmärkte GmbH & Co KG v Commission*,[82] a competition case, the decision which was adopted by the Commission did not stem from a complaint made by the applicant, Metro. The Commission had published a notice in the *Official Journal* indicating its intention to grant an individual exemption in relation to the distribution system operated by SABA. Metro had submitted its observations, as it was entitled to do by virtue of article 19(3) of Regulation 17/62.[83] The Commission recognised that Metro had a legitimate interest in submitting its observations by virtue of article 19(3). The Court of Justice held, therefore, that Metro was individually concerned by the subsequent decision of the Commission, which did not accord with the observations submitted.

In relation to state aids there is no express provision which gives people with a legitimate interest the right to make a complaint. However, in practice, the Commission does act on complaints made by private parties. The Court of Justice has recognised, by analogy, the right of a party who has lodged a complaint with the Commission to seek review of the decision subsequently adopted, pro-

---

[81] [1985] ECR 849 paras 8–17.

[82] [1986] ECR 3021 paras 18–23.

[83] Regulation 17/62 of 6 February 1962, First Regulation implementing articles 85, 86 of the EEC Treaty (as amended), OJ No 13, 21 February 1962, p 204 (English Special Edition, 1959–1962, p 87).

vided that the party in question can show that its position in the market is significantly affected by the state aid which is the subject of the contested decision.[84]

Representative organisations The regulation governing anti-dumping matters specifically provides that an association acting on behalf of a Community industry, which does not have legal personality, may lodge a complaint with the Commission.[85] In Case 191/82 *Fediol v Commission*,[86] the Court of Justice expressly relied on this provision in holding that Fediol, the EEC Seed Crushers' and Oil Processors' Federation, had *locus standi* to challenge a decision adopted by the Commission following a complaint by that organisation. The Court of Justice has also recognised the right of representative organisations to challenge decisions of the Commission in the context of state aids.[87]

Exporters/importers: anti-dumping cases Anti-dumping duties are generally imposed on the basis of investigations concerning the production prices and export prices of undertakings which have been individually identified. The producers and exporters who are identified in the measures adopted have *locus standi* to challenge the specific provisions which affect them.[88] In contrast, importers generally will not be named in regulations imposing anti-dumping duties, and will form simply part of the open class of actual or potential importers of the products concerned. They will not have *locus standi* to bring applications for review under article 173 of the EEC Treaty.[89] However, importers may be held to be directly and individually concerned by anti-dumping regulations where they are associated with exporters and their resale prices have been taken into account in calculating export prices.[90] Furthermore, a particular importer may be individually concerned by an anti-dumping regulation which affects him in a specific way not applicable to all other importers. For example, in Case C–358/89 *Extramet Industrie SA v Council*[91] the applicant was the largest importer of the product concerned and an end-user of the product. In addition,

---

[84] Case 169/84 *Cofaz SA v Commission* [1986] ECR 391 paras 22–25.

[85] Regulation 2423/88 of 11 July 1988, article 5(1), OJ No L 209, 2 August 1988, p 1.

[86] [1983] ECR 2913.

[87] Joined Cases 67/85, 68/85, 70/85 *Kwekerij Gebroeders Van der Kooy BV v Commission* [1988] ECR 219 paras 17–25; Case C–313/90 *Comité international de la rayonne et des fibres synthétiques (CIRFS) v Commission* judgment of 24 March 1993 paras 29, 30.

[88] Joined Cases 239/82, 275/82 *Allied Corporation v Commission* [1984] ECR 1005 paras 10–12. Where a regulation imposes different anti-dumping duties on different undertakings, each undertaking may challenge only the provisions imposing the particular duty on it. See Case 258/84 *Nippon Seiko KK v Council* [1987] ECR 1923 paras 5–7; Case C–156/87 *Gestetner Holdings plc v Council and Commission* [1990] ECR I–781 para 12.

[89] Joined Cases 239/82, 275/82 *Allied Corporation v Commission* [1984] ECR 1005 paras 15, 16.

[90] Case 113/77 *NTN Toyo Bearing Company Ltd v Council* [1979] ECR 1185 paras 7–12; Case 118/77 *Import Standard Office (ISO) v Council* [1979] ECR 1277 paras 8–16; Joined Cases 239/82, 275/82 *Allied Corporation v Commission* [1984] ECR 1005 paras 10–15; Case 279/86 *SA Sermes v Commission* [1987] ECR 3109 paras 14–17; Joined Cases C–305/86, C–160/87 *Neotype Techmashexport GmbH v Commission and Council* [1990] ECR I–2945 paras 17–22; Case C–358/89 *Extramet Industrie SA v Council* [1991] ECR I–2501 para 15.

[91] [1991] ECR I–2501 paras 15–17. Discussed further at p 185.

its business depended heavily on imports, particularly as the sole Community producer was also its main competitor for the processed product.

Intended beneficiaries of state aid Intended beneficiaries of state aid have *locus standi* to challenge Commission decisions concerning such aid. This principle was conceded by the Commission in Case 730/79 *Philip Morris Holland BV v Commission*,[92] where the Dutch Government had sought the Commission's approval for aid to be granted specifically to the applicant.

Competitors: state aid Competitors of beneficiaries of state aid have standing to challenge a Commission decision approving the grant of aid.[93]

3. GROUNDS OF REVIEW

(a) Introduction

Article 173 Article 173 of the EEC Treaty sets out four grounds of review. These are:
  (1) lack of competence;
  (2) infringement of an essential procedural requirement;
  (3) infringement of the EEC Treaty or of any rule of law relating to its application; and
  (4) misuse of powers.
  In addition, the Court of Justice has recognised that certain acts may be so defective as to be 'non-existent'.[94]

Pleadings The grounds of review under article 173 are the same for all applicants, whether privileged or non-privileged. The Court of Justice does not adhere strictly to the four grounds of review and it is not uncommon for the Court to annul an act without expressly referring to the specific grounds set out in article 173. However, as a matter of pleading, an applicant should state the grounds in article 173 on which it relies as the judgment in Case 42/84 *Remia BV v Commission* establishes that submissions must be set out in the application with sufficient precision for it to be possible to ascertain whether they come within the grounds of action enumerated in article 173.[95]

---

[92] [1980] ECR 2671 para 5.

[93] Case C–198/91 *William Cook plc v Commission* judgment of 19 May 1993 paras 13–26; Case C–225/91 *Matra SA v Commission*, judgment of 15 June 1993 paras 10–20. See also Case 323/82 *SA Intermills v Commission* [1984] ECR 3809 para 16; Case C–313/90 *Comité international de la rayonne et des fibres synthétiques (CIRFS) v Commission* judgment of 24 March 1993 para 20.

[94] For a thorough analysis of the principles of administrative procedure, both in Community law and in the laws of the Member States, see Jürgen Schwarze *European Administrative Law*, 1st edn. (Sweet & Maxwell, 1992), Ch 7.

[95] [1985] ECR 2545 para 16. See also Joined Cases 19/60, 21/60, 2/61, 3/61 *Société Fives Lille Cail v High Authority* [1961] ECR 281 at 294, 295 (ECSC).

(b) Lack of competence

Definition Lack of competence arises where a Community institution acts outside its powers in adopting a particular measure. Community institutions can only act on the basis of powers granted by the EEC Treaty (or on the basis of powers granted by secondary legislation which, in turn, is based on a specific EEC Treaty provision). The Community institutions do not have any inherent powers.

Examples The ground of lack of competence is rarely relied on as a reason for annulment of an act. It is more usual for such questions to be raised under the rubric of the third head (infringement of the EEC Treaty or a rule of law relating to its application). However, this should not prevent arguments based on lack of competence being raised in appropriate cases.[96] In Joined Cases 228/82, 229/82 *Ford of Europe Incorporated and Ford-Werke Aktiengesellschaft v Commission*[97] a Commission decision imposing interim measures was declared void by the Court of Justice. The Commission had exceeded the limits of its powers as the terms of the interim order went beyond what the Commission could adopt in a final order. In Case 108/83 *Luxembourg v European Parliament*[98] the European Parliament was held to have exceeded the limits of its powers by adopting a resolution which would have reduced the services carried out and the number of staff in Luxembourg. In Case 9/56 *Meroni Co, Industrie Metallurgiche, SpA v High Authority*[99] (a case under the European Coal and Steel Treaty) a decision taken by an agency to which the High Authority (the Commission) had delegated power was annulled, because the act by which power was delegated to the agency was, itself, illegal. The delegating act was held to be illegal because the High Authority had acted outside the scope of its competence.

(c) Infringement of an essential procedural requirement

Definition Where there have been procedural irregularities, a measure will only be annulled if, in the absence of those irregularities, there would have been a different substantive result.[100] Furthermore, where the breach relates only to

---

[96] For example, see Joined Cases 281/85, 283–285/85, 287/85 *Germany v Commission* [1987] ECR 3203 paras 9–36; Case 264/86 *France v Commission* [1988] ECR 973; Case C–303/90 *France v Commission* [1991] ECR I–5315 paras 27–35.

[97] [1984] ECR 1129 paras 17–24.

[98] [1984] ECR 1945 paras 25–32.

[99] [1957–58] ECR 133.

[100] Joined Cases 40–48/73, 50/73, 54–56/73, 111/73, 113/73, 114/73 *Coöperatieve vereniging 'Suiker Unie' UA v Commission* [1975] ECR 1663 paras 89–92 (where premature public statements were held to be a breach of the right to a fair trial); Case 30/78 *Distillers Company Limited v Commission* [1980] ECR 2229 para 26 (right to be heard), see also the Opinion of Advocate-General Warner at 2290, 2291 and the cases cited therein; Joined Cases 209–215/78, 218/78 *Heintz van Landewyck Sàrl v Commission* [1980] ECR 3125 paras 45–47 (wrongful disclosure of trade secrets); Joined Cases 100–103/80 *Musique Diffusion Française v Commission* [1983] ECR 1825, Opinion of Advocate-General Sir Gordon Slynn at 1927 (right to be heard).

matters of secondary importance, the validity of the whole measure will not be affected.[101]

Examples There is no exhaustive list of what constitutes an essential procedural requirement. However, the following examples will be considered:[102]

(1) requirement to give reasons;
(2) consultation/co-operation;
(3) right to be heard;
(4) internal rules of procedure.

(i) Requirement to give reasons
Article 190 Article 190 of the EEC Treaty provides:

> Regulations, directives and decisions of the Council and of the Commission shall state the reasons on which they are based and shall refer to any proposals or opinions which were required to be obtained pursuant to this Treaty.

The Court of Justice has held that the requirements of article 190 cannot be extended to measures other than regulations, directives or decisions.[103]

Sufficient reasons The reasons given by the Council or the Commission for a particular measure must be *sufficient*. To be sufficient the reasons given must fulfil the following objectives:

(1) they must allow parties to defend their rights; and
(2) they must allow the Court of Justice to exercise its supervisory functions; and
(3) they must allow Member States and all interested private parties to recognise the reasons for the adoption of the measure in question.[104]

Whether the reasons given are sufficient or not will depend on the nature of the measure in question.[105] Regulations, which are measures of general application, will not require as detailed reasoning as decisions, which are addressed to particular parties.[106] In Case 5/67 *W Beus GmbH & Co v Hauptzollamt*

---

[101] Joined Cases 40–48/73, 50/73, 54–56/73, 111/73, 113/73, 114/73 *Coöperatieve vereniging 'Suiker Unie' UA v Commission* [1975] ECR 1663 paras 94–99 (unduly short time limits for submission of observations); Joined Cases 100–103/80 *SA Musique Diffusion Française v Commission* [1983] ECR 1825 paras 24–30 (right to be heard/failure to disclose documents); Case 107/82 *AEG v Commission* [1983] ECR 3151 paras 21–30 (right to be heard/failure to disclose documents).

[102] The principles relating to essential procedural requirements are of particular importance in competition law. The relevant issues are dealt with fully in specialist works such as Bellamy and Child, *Common Market Law of Competition*, 4th edn (Sweet & Maxwell, 1993), Ch 12 and Kerse, *EEC Antitrust Procedure*, 2nd edn (European Law Centre, 1988), Ch 8.

[103] Case 22/70 *Commission v Council, (ERTA)* [1971] ECR 263 paras 97–100.

[104] Case 24/62 *Germany v Commission* [1963] ECR 63 at 69; Case 108/81 *GR Amylum v Council* [1982] ECR 3107 para 19; Case 42/84 *Remia BV v Commission* [1985] ECR 2545 para 26; Case C–69/89 *Nakajima All Precision Co Ltd v Council* [1991] ECR I–2069 para 14.

[105] Case C–181/90 *Consorgan v Commission* [1992] ECR I–3557 paras 13–18.

[106] Case 18/62 *Emilia Barge v High Authority* [1963] ECR 259 at 280 (ECSC); Case 5/67 *W Beus GmbH & Co v Hauptzollamt München* [1968] ECR 83 at 95; Case 108/81 *GR Amylum v Council*

München,[107] the Court of Justice held that the reasoning behind a regulation may be confined to indicating the general situation which led to its adoption and the general objectives which it is intended to achieve. Furthermore, where a regulation forms part of a wider set of provisions, the reasoning must be judged in the context of the whole of the rules of which it forms a part.[108] In contrast, a decision must set out in a concise, clear and relevant manner the principal issues of law and fact upon which it is based. There is no requirement to discuss all the matters of fact and law which may have been discussed or raised prior to the adoption of the decision.[109] This is of particular importance in competition cases. A decision which fits into a well-established line of decisions may be reasoned in a summary manner, for example, by reference to the other decisions. However, if it goes appreciably further than the previous decisions, the Commission must give an account of its reasoning.[110]

Legal basis The legal basis for a particular act must be readily identifiable. However, the measure need not expressly identify the legal basis if this is discernible from the other parts of the measure.[111] For example, in Case 203/86 *Spain v Council*,[112] the Court of Justice held that an implementing regulation adopted under the terms of a basic regulation need only identify the provision of the basic regulation on which it is based. It is not necessary for the implementing regulation to expressly state the Treaty article on which the basic regulation is itself based. In Case T–92/91 *Helmut Henrichs v Commission*,[113] the Court of First Instance held that a decision which did not expressly state the legal basis on which it was adopted was not invalid because there could have been no doubt that the addressee of the decision, who held a doctorate in law, was aware of the correct legal basis. This approach, which bases the question of legality on the personal knowledge of the addressee of an act, is open to criti-

---

[1982] ECR 3107 para 19; Case C–27/90 *Société Industrielle de Transformation de Produits Agricoles (SITPA) v Office National Interprofessionnel des Fruits, des Légumes et de L'horticulture (ONIFLHOR)* [1991] ECR I–133 paras 10, 15, 16 (excusable factual error in reasoning).

[107] [1968] ECR 83 at 95.
[108] Case 78/74 *Deuka v Einfuhr-und Vorratsstelle für Getreide und Futtermittel* [1975] ECR 421 para 6; Case 92/77 *An Bord Bainne Co-operative Limited v Minister for Agriculture* [1978] ECR 497 para 36; Case 125/77 *Koninklijke Scholten-Honig NV v Hoofdproduktschap voor Akkerbouwprodukten* [1978] ECR 1991 paras 17–22; Case 230/78 *SpA Eridania-Zuccherifici nazionali v Minister of Agriculture and Forestry* [1979] ECR 2749 paras 14–16.
[109] Case 24/62 *Germany v Commission* [1963] ECR 63 at 69; Joined Cases 43/82, 63/82 *VBVB and VBBB v Commission* [1984] ECR 19 paras 21, 22; Case 42/84 *Remia BV v Commission* [1985] ECR 2545 para 26; Case T–76/89 *Independent Television Publications Limited v Commission* [1991] ECR II–575 paras 62–66; Case T–3/89 *Atochem SA v Commission* [1991] ECR II–1177 para 222; Case T–44/90 *La Cinq SA v Commission* [1992] ECR II–1 para 41.
[110] Case 73/74 *Groupement des fabricants de papiers peints de Belgique v Commission* [1975] ECR 1491 para 31.
[111] Case 45/86 *Commission v Council* [1987] ECR 1493 paras 5–9.
[112] [1988] ECR 4563 paras 36–38.
[113] Judgment of 24 June 1993 para 15.

cism, as it fails to account for the interests of third parties who may be unable to discern the legal basis of an act from its terms.

Practical limitations The adequacy of reasoning will depend very much on the circumstances of a particular case. In Case 16/65 *Firma C Schwarze v Einfuhr- Und Vorratsstelle Getreide und Futtermittel*[114] the Commission published weekly decisions setting certain agricultural prices. The Court of Justice held that the degree of precision of the statement of reasons for such decisions must be weighed against the practical realities of making such regular, technical decisions. It would be impractical to require the Commission to provide detailed reasoning for such decisions and, therefore, the Court held that it was sufficient for the Commission to confine itself to setting out, in a general form, the essential factors and the procedure followed in taking each decision. Interested parties' rights to judicial review could be adequately protected by the Commission providing the technical data to any party who challenged such a decision before a court.

Applicant's involvement in adoption Where the applicant for review was closely involved in the process of adoption of the contested measure, the EC Courts may require less detailed reasoning than might otherwise be the case.[115] This approach can be criticised on the grounds that it fails to recognise that the rights of third parties who are directly and individually concerned by a measure, but who played no part in its adoption, may be compromised if full and proper reasoning is not adopted for every measure.[116]

Severance Where a measure is composed of several elements, it may be necessary for each element to be properly reasoned.[117] However, where the justification for a particular clause is inherently obvious from the nature of the measure as a whole it does not require special reasoning.[118]

(ii) Consultation/co-operation

Consultation Where the Treaty provides that the European Parliament should be consulted before a measure is adopted,[119] this constitutes an essential element in the democratic and institutional balance of the European Community. Failure by the Council or Commission to seek such consultation will constitute breach of an essential procedural requirement and will render the measure void.[120] It is not sufficient for the Council or Commission simply to request the Parliament's opinion; the Parliament must actually have expressed an opinion

---

[114] [1965] ECR 877 at 887–889.

[115] Case 13/72 *Netherlands v Commission* [1973] ECR 27 paras 11–13; Case 819/79 *Germany v Commission* [1981] ECR 21 paras 19–21; Case 1251/79 *Italy v Commission* [1981] ECR 205 paras 20, 21.

[116] Case 294/81 *Control Data Belgium NV SA v Commission* [1983] ECR 911 paras 12–15.

[117] Joined Cases 4/78, 19/78, 28/78 *Enrico M Salerno v Commission* [1978] ECR 2403.

[118] Case 57/72 *Westzucker GmbH v Einfuhr- und Vorratsstelle für Zucker* [1973] ECR 321 para 19.

[119] For example, articles 43(2) and 100 of the EEC Treaty.

[120] Case 138/79 *SA Roquette Frères v Council* [1980] ECR 3333 para 32; Case 139/79 *Maizena GmbH v Council* [1980] ECR 3393 paras 33, 34; Case 1253/79 *Dino Battaglia v Commission* [1982] ECR 297 para 17.

before an act can be adopted.[121] Where the Parliament has expressed an opinion, the legality of the consultation will not be affected by the fact that the Council or Commission adopts the measure the very next day.[122] Where the proposed measure is altered after the Parliament has given its opinion, the Parliament need be re-consulted only where the alteration is substantial.[123]

Co-operation The Single European Act introduced a strengthened basis for participation by the European Parliament in the legislative process in respect of certain measures, namely the co-operation procedure.[124] Failure by the Council to follow this procedure where it has a duty to do so will be an infringement of an essential procedural requirement.[125]

(iii) Right to be heard

Definition Community law recognises the general rule of natural justice that a person whose interests are perceptibly affected by a decision taken by a public authority must be given the opportunity to make his point of view known (*audi alteram partem*). The right to be heard consists of two closely related concepts:

(1) a decision cannot be based on facts of which the parties concerned are unaware; and

(2) the parties concerned must have the opportunity to give their views on the points which affect their interests.[126]

Substantive effect Where there has been a breach of the right to be heard, the relevant measure will only be annulled where it can be shown that a different substantive result was reached because of that breach.[127] Furthermore, where the breach relates only to matters of secondary importance the validity of the whole decision will not be affected.[128] Where procedural irregularities relating

---

[121] Case 138/79 *SA Roquette Frères v Council* [1980] ECR 3333 paras 34–37; Case 139/79 *Maizena GmbH v Council* [1980] ECR 3393 paras 35–38. Note, however, that in both these cases the Court of Justice seems to indicate that it would be sufficient for the Council or Commission to have exhausted all the possibilities available to them for obtaining the opinion of the Parliament.

[122] Case 114/81 *Tunnel Refineries Limited v Council* [1982] ECR 3189 para 18.

[123] Case 41/69 *ACF Chemiefarma NV v Commission* [1970] ECR 661 paras 68–70; Case 1253/79 *Dino Battaglia v Commission* [1982] ECR 297 para 24, Case C–65/90 *European Parliament v Council* [1992] ECR I–4593 paras 16–21.

[124] EEC Treaty, article 149. See article 100A of the EEC Treaty for an example of a provision where co-operation with the Parliament is required.

[125] This will also be the case for the strengthened role of the Parliament set out in article 189b to be introduced by the Treaty on European Union (Maastricht Treaty).

[126] Case 17/74 *Transocean Marine Paint Association v Commission* [1974] ECR 1063 para 15 and the Opinion of Advocate-General Warner in which he stated (at 1089) that:
> ... the right to be heard forms part of those rights which 'the law' referred to in Article 164 of the Treaty upholds, and of which, accordingly, it is the duty of this Court to ensure observance.

Case 85/76 *Hoffmann-La Roche & Co AG v Commission* [1979] ECR 461 paras 8–11. See also Case 141/80 *Henri de Compte v European Parliament* [1985] ECR 1951 paras 10–21 for an example of the application of the *audi alteram partem* principle in the context of a staff case.

[127] Case 30/78 *Distillers Company Limited v Commission* [1980] ECR 2229 para 26 and the Opinion of Advocate-General Warner at 2290, 2291 and the cases cited therein. Joined Cases 100–103/80 *Musique Diffusion Française v Commission* [1983] ECR 1825, Opinion of Advocate-General Sir Gordon Slynn at 1927.

[128] Ibid paras 24–30; Case 107/82 *AEG v Commission* [1983] ECR 3151 paras 21–30.

to the right to be heard have arisen, they may be rectified during the proceedings before the Court. This occurred in Case 85/76 *Hoffmann-La Roche & Co AG v Commission*,[129] where the Commission produced further information at the request of the Court during the written procedure.

The scope of the right to be heard will depend on the nature of the provision in question.[130] Thus, the procedure followed by an institution in respect of a provisional decision need not be as rigorous as that followed for a final decision.[131] Preparatory steps which are merely part of the process by which the final decision will be reached are not subject to the right to be heard.[132]

Competition cases The right to be heard is of particular importance in competition cases before the Commission, which may lead to the undertakings involved being subject to fines. The specific regulations which set out the procedure to be followed by the Commission in exercising its competition law powers contain express provisions giving effect to the right to be heard.[133]

(iv) Internal rules of procedure
Effect of breach In Case C–69/89 *Nakajima All Precision Co Ltd v Council*[134] the Court of Justice held that the purpose of the rules of procedure of a Community institution is to organise the internal functioning of its services in the interests of good administration. Therefore, private parties may not rely on an alleged breach of those rules because the rules are not intended to ensure protection for individuals. However, in Joined Cases T–79/89, T–84/89 and others *BASF AG v Commission*[135] the Court of First Instance found that irregularities in the process of adoption and subsequent amendment of a Commission decision were so serious that the decision was 'non-existent'.[136]

(d) Infringement of the EEC Treaty or of any rule of law relating to its application

Infringement of the EEC Treaty This is the most important ground of review, as it is very broad in scope. As the EEC Treaty is, in effect, the constitution of

---

[129] [1979] ECR 461 paras 12–19. This aspect of the decision was criticised by Advocate-General Warner in his Opinion in Case 30/78 *Distillers Company Limited v Commission* [1980] ECR 2229 at 2296–2298.
[130] Case C–342/89 *Germany v Commission* [1991] I–5031 para 17; Case C–346/89 *Italy v Commission* [1991] ECR I–5057 para 17.
[131] Case C–342/89 *Germany v Commission* [1991] I–5031 paras 17–21.
[132] Case 136/79 *National Panasonic (UK) Ltd v Commission* [1980] ECR 2033 para 21.
[133] See, in particular, article 19 of Council Regulation 17/62 of 6 February 1962, First Regulation implementing articles 85, 86 of the EEC Treaty, OJ No 13, 21 February 1962, p 204 (Special Edition 1959–1962, p 87) (as amended); and Commission Regulation 99/63 on the hearings provided for in article 19(1), (2) of Council Regulation 17/62, OJ No 127, 20 August 1962, p 2263 (Special Edition 1963–1964, p 47).
[134] [1991] ECR I–2069 paras 48–51.
[135] [1992] ECR II–315 paras 84–100.
[136] *Cf* the Opinion of Advocate-General Van Gerven in Case C–137/92P *Commission v BASF AG*, delivered on 29 June 1993 paras 71–82. Discussed further at pp 197–198.

the Community, any breach of Community law can be said to be a breach of the EEC Treaty.

Review of exercise of discretion The EC Courts will not simply substitute their decision on the facts for the act of the institution which is challenged.[137] In particular, where a Community institution has been required to exercise its discretion in a complex economic situation, the Court will only intervene if the institution has failed to comply with procedural requirements, has failed to provide proper reasoning for the act adopted, has committed a manifest error in its assessment of the facts, has omitted to take any essential matters into consideration or has been guilty of a misuse of powers.[138]

Correct legal basis All measures of Community secondary legislation must be based, directly or indirectly, on specific provisions of the EEC Treaty. Failure to adopt a measure on the correct legal basis is a ground for annulment. The institutions are not free to adopt whatever legal basis they wish. The choice of legal basis depends on objective factors amenable to judicial review, including, in particular, the aim and content of the measure.[139] The practical importance of the choice of legal basis is that it may affect the procedure to be followed for adoption of a measure, for example, whether the measure is to be adopted unanimously or by majority voting and whether the role of the European Parliament is to be one of consultation or co-operation.

Where appropriate, a measure may be based on two provisions of the EEC Treaty.[140] However, reliance on more than one legal basis will not be permitted where this will interfere with the proper role of the Parliament in the legislative process.[141] A measure may only be based on article 235 of the EEC Treaty where no other provision of the EEC Treaty gives the Community institutions the necessary power to adopt the measure.[142]

General principles/human rights A Community measure may be annulled on the ground that it infringes a general principle of Community law or a fundamental human right.[143] For example, in Case 223/85 *Rijn-Schelde-Verolme*

---

[137] Case C–225/91 *Matra SA v Commission* judgment of 15 June 1993 paras 23–25.

[138] Case 29/77 *SA Roquette Frères v France* [1977] ECR 1835 paras 19, 20; Case 98/78 *Firma A Racke v Hauptzollamt Mainz* [1979] ECR 69 para 5; Case 191/82 *EEC Seed Crushers' and Oil Processors' Federation (FEDIOL) v Commission* [1983] ECR 2913 para 30; Case 42/84 *Remia BV v Commission* [1985] ECR 2545 para 34 (competition case); Joined Cases 142/84, 156/84 *British American Tobacco Company Ltd v Commission* [1987] ECR 4487 paras 60–62 (competition case); Case T–7/92 *SA Asia Motor France v Commission* judgment of 29 June 1993 para 33 (competition case).

[139] Case 45/86 *Commission v Council* [1987] ECR 1493 para 11; Case 68/86 *United Kingdom v Council* [1988] ECR 855 paras 4–25; Case 131/86 *United Kingdom v Council* [1988] ECR 905 paras 8–30; Case C–300/89 *Commission v Council* [1991] ECR I–2867 para 10 ('Titanium dioxide'); Case C–70/88 *European Parliament v Council* [1991] ECR I–4529 ('Chernobyl'). See also, Catherine Barnard, 'Where politicians fear to tread?' (1992) 17 EL Rev 127.

[140] Case 165/87 *Commission v Council* [1988] ECR 5545.

[141] Case C–300/89 *Commission v Council* [1991] ECR I–2867.

[142] Case 45/86 *Commission v Council* [1987] ECR 1493; Case 165/87 *Commission v Council* [1988] ECR 5545.

[143] General principles and fundamental rights are discussed at pp 12–20.

(RSV) Maschinefabrieken en Scheepswerven NV v Commission,[144] the Court of Justice annulled a Commission decision which violated the principle of legitimate expectations.

(e) Misuse of powers

Definition Misuse of powers will be established only where it appears, on the basis of objective, relevant and consistent factors, that a measure has been adopted with the exclusive purpose, or at any rate the main purpose, of achieving an end other than that stated, or of evading a procedure specifically prescribed by the EEC Treaty for dealing with the circumstances of the case.[145] This ground of review is rarely successful because of the difficulties in proving that the purpose behind a measure is different from that stated in it. Where more than one aim is pursued by a measure, including an improper aim, this will not render the measure invalid for misuse of powers as long as the improper aim does not prevent the proper aim being achieved.[146]

(f) Non-existent acts

Definition In the interests of legal certainty, a Community measure is presumed to be valid until it has been repealed by a court, or withdrawn by the institution which adopted it, even though it may contain irregularities.[147] However, in exceptional circumstances, a measure may be deemed to be non-existent if it exhibits serious and manifest defects. These defects must be so gross and so obvious that they go far beyond a 'normal' irregularity resulting from an erroneous assessment of the facts or from a breach of the law.[148] Where an act is non-existent, neither the addressee of the measure nor the enacting institution is bound to comply with it. There is no need for the prior intervention of the courts.

---

[144] [1987] ECR 4617. See also Case 112/77 *August Töpfer & Co GmbH v Commission* [1978] ECR 1019 paras 18, 19; Case 234/82 *Ferriere di Roè Volcanio SpA* [1983] ECR 3921.

[145] Case C–331/88 *R v Minister for Agriculture, Fisheries and Food ex p FEDESA* [1990] ECR I–4023 para 24. See also Case 2/57 *Compagnie des Hauts Fourneaux de Chasse v High Authority* [1958] ECR 199 at 207 (ECSC); Case 15/57 *Compagnie des Hauts Fourneaux de Chasse v High Authority* [1958] ECR 211 at 230 (ECSC); Joined Cases 18/65, 35/65 *Max Gutmann v Commission* [1966] ECR 103 at 116–118 (EURATOM); Case 105/75 *Franco Giuffrida v Council* [1976] ECR 1395; Joined Cases 59/80, 129/80 *Mariette Turner v Commission* [1981] ECR 1883 paras 66–71; Case 69/83 *Charles Lux v Court of Auditors* [1984] ECR 2447 paras 28–31; Case C–323/88 *SA Sermes v Directeur des services des douanes de Strasbourg* [1990] ECR I–3027 para 33.

[146] Case 1/54 *France v High Authority* [1954–1956] ECR 1 at 16 (ECSC).

[147] Joined Cases 7/56, 3–7/57 *Dineke Algera v Common Assembly* [1957] ECR 39 at 60, 61 (ECSC); Case 101/78 *Granaria BV v Hoofdproduktschap voor Akkerbouwprodukten* [1979] ECR 623 paras 4, 5; Joined Cases 46/87, 227/88 *Hoechst AG v Commission* [1989] ECR 2859 para 64.

[148] Case 15/85 *Consorzio Cooperative d' Abruzzo v Commission* [1987] ECR 1005 para 10; Case T–156/89 *Iñigo Valverde Mordt v Court of Justice* [1991] ECR II–407 para 84. *Cf* Joined Cases 15–33 and others *Roswitha Schots v Council and Commission* [1974] ECR 177, where an illegal act was held not to be non-existent.

In Joined Cases T–79/89, T–84/89 and others *BASF AG v Commission*,[149] a decision of the Commission, adopted pursuant to an investigation under article 85 of the EEC Treaty, was held to be non-existent by the Court of First Instance due to irregularities in the process of adoption and subsequent amendment of the decision.

No time limit Where an act is alleged to be non-existent, it may be challenged under the article 173 procedure, even where the two-month time limit has expired.[150] Indeed, the Court is obliged to raise the question of non-existence of its own motion if necessary.[151]

Judgment/costs Technically, actions against a non-existent measure will be declared inadmissible, as there is no justiciable act to form the subject-matter of the action.[152] In practical terms, a judgment to this effect will serve as a declaration that the contested act is non-existent. Because such an action is declared inadmissible, the applicant will *prima facie* have to bear his own costs. However, the Rules of Procedure permit the Court to order that the costs be shared or that the parties bear their own costs where the circumstances are exceptional, or that the successful party pays the costs which it has unreasonably or vexatiously caused the other party to incur.[153] In Joined Cases T–79/89, T–84/89 and others *BASF AG v Commission*,[154] the Court of First Instance relied on these provisions and ordered the Commission to pay the applicants' costs.

4. TIME LIMIT FOR APPLICATIONS

Time limits The third limb of article 173 of the EEC Treaty provides that an application must be commenced within two months of the publication of the measure or of its notification to the applicant or, failing that, within two months of the day on which it came to the knowledge of the applicant.[155] The rules for reckoning periods of time are set out in the Rules of Procedure.[156] The two-month time limit begins to run the day after notification or from the fifteenth day after publication in the *Official Journal of the European Communities*.[157] A gen-

---

[149] [1992] ECR II–315 paras 84–100. *Cf* the Opinion of Advocate-General Van Gerven in Case C–137/92P *Commmission v BASF, AG*, delivered on 29 June 1993 paras 71–82.

[150] Joined Cases 6/69, 11/69 *Commission v France* [1969] ECR 523 paras 10–13; Case 15/85 *Consorzio Cooperative d'Abruzzo v Commission* [1987] ECR 1005 para 10; Joined Cases T–79/89, T–84/89 and others *BASF AG v Commission* [1992] ECR II–315 para 101.

[151] Joined Cases T–79/89, T–84/89 and others *BASF AG v Commission* [1992] ECR II–315 para 101.

[152] Ibid para 101. See also Joined Cases 1/57, 14/57 *Société des Usines à Tubes de la Sarre v High Authority* [1957] ECR 105 at 112, 113 (ECSC).

[153] ECJ Rules of Procedure, art 69(3); CFI Rules of Procedure, art 87(3). See pp 326, 386.

[154] [1992] ECR II–315 para 103.

[155] Case 152/85 *Misset v Council* [1987] ECR 223 para 8; Joined Cases 281/85, 283–285/85, 287/85 *Germany v Commission* [1987] ECR 3245 para 5; Case C–59/91 *France v Commission* [1992] I–525 paras 3–7 (meaning of 'calendar month').

[156] ECJ Rules of Procedure, articles 80–82; CFI Rules of Procedure, articles 101–103. See pp 384–385 and 390–391. Case T–125/89 *Filtrona Española Sa v Commission* [1990] ECR II–393.

[157] ECJ Rules of Procedure, article 81(1); CFI Rules of Procedure, article 102(1). See pp 329–330 and 390.

eral extension of ten days exists for the United Kingdom to take account of distance.[158] The EC Courts apply the relevant time limits very strictly, in order to preserve legal certainty.[159] They do not have a general discretion to extend the mandatory time limits set down by article 173.[160] Time limits before the EC Courts are governed exclusively by Community law. A party is not entitled to rely on provisions concerning time under national law in cases before these courts.[161] It is the responsibility of the party alleging that an application is out of time to prove the date on which the measure was notified.[162]

Publication A measure is presumed to be published on the date on the cover of the *Official Journal of the European Communities* in which it appears, unless there is evidence that the issue was not, in fact, available until a later date.[163]

Notification A measure is duly notified once it has been communicated to the person to whom it is addressed and that person is in a position to take cognisance of it. Actual knowledge is not necessary. Notification will usually take place by a registered letter, accompanied by a form headed 'Acknowledgment of Receipt', to be completed by the recipient or delivered by hand against receipt.[164] Regardless of the time of day when the measure in question is notified, time does not begin to run until the end of the day of notification.[165] The fact that there has been an irregularity in the notification procedure will not prevent the time limit from commencing, where the applicant has, in fact, had full knowledge of the text of the measure.[166] An applicant will not be deemed to have been notified of a Community measure until it has been communicated to him with sufficient detail to enable him to identify the measure adopted and to ascertain its precise content in such a way as to enable him to exercise his right to institute

---

[158] ECJ Rules of Procedure, article 81(2) and Annex II, article 1; CFI Rules of Procedure, article 102 (2). See pp 330, 349, 390. The application of the extension of time depends on where the applicant is habitually resident. The place of residence of the applicant's lawyer is irrelevant; see Case 28/65 *Fulvio Fonzi v Commission* [1966] ECR 477.

[159] Case 152/85 *Rudolf Misset v Council* [1987] ECR 223 para 11; Case 257/85 *Dufay v European Parliament* [1987] ECR 1561 paras 9, 10 (Court rejected an argument based on article 6 of the European Convention on Human Rights).

[160] Case 4/67 *Anne Muller v Commission* [1967] ECR 365 (ECSC).

[161] Case 209/83 *Ferriera Valsabbia SpA v Commission* [1984] ECR 3089; Case C–12/90 *Infortec— Projectos e consultadoria Lda v Commission* [1990] ECR I–4265 para 10.

[162] Joined Cases 32/58, 33/58 *SNUPAT v High Authority* [1959] ECR 127 at 136 (ECSC); Case 42/58 *SAFE v High Authority* [1959] ECR 183 at 190 (ECSC); Joined Cases 193/87, 194/87 *Henri Maurissen and European Public Service Union v Court of Auditors* [1989] ECR 1045; Case T–1/90 *Gloria Pérez-Mínguez Casariego v Commission* [1991] ECR II–143 para 37.

[163] Case 99/78 *Weingut Gustav Decker KG v Hauptzollamt Landau* [1979] ECR 101 paras 2–5; Case 337/88 *Società agricola fattoria alimentare SpA (SAFA) v Amministrazione delle finanze dello Stato* [1990] ECR 1 paras 8–12.

[164] Case 48/69 *Imperial Chemical Industries Ltd v Commission* [1972] ECR 619 paras 34–44 (service on subsidiary company unacceptable); Case 6/72 *Europemballage and Continental Can v Commission* [1973] ECR 215 paras 9, 10; Case 42/85 *Cockerill-Sambre SA v Commission* [1985] ECR 3749 para 10 (ECSC); Case T–12/90 *Bayer AG v Commission* [1991] ECR II–219 paras 17–21.

[165] Case 152/85 *Rudolf Misset v Council* [1987] ECR 223.

[166] Case 48/69 *Imperial Chemical Industries Ltd v Commission* [1972] ECR 619 paras 39–44.

proceedings.[167] Once a party is aware of the existence of a decision affecting him, there is an obligation on him to request the whole text thereof, within a reasonable period, should he wish to challenge it.[168]

Exceptions A party's failure to comply with time limits may be excused if he proves the existence of an excusable error, unforeseeable circumstances[169] or *force majeure*.[170] The Court of Justice has held that the concept of *force majeure* covers unusual circumstances which make it impossible for the relevant act to be carried out. Even though it does not require absolute impossibility, it does require abnormal difficulties, which are independent of the will of the person concerned and which are apparently inevitable, even if all due care is taken.[171]

No time limit applies in respect of non-existent acts.[172] The two-month time limit does not apply where the validity of acts is questioned in proceedings under article 177[173] or 184[174] of the EEC Treaty.

5. ARTICLE 174—EFFECT OF JUDGMENT

Article 174 Article 174 of the EEC Treaty provides:

> If the action is well founded, the Court of Justice shall declare the act concerned to be void.
> In the case of a regulation, however, the Court of Justice shall, if it considers this necessary, state which of the effects of the regulation which it has declared void shall be considered as definitive.

---

[167] Case 76/79 *Karl Könecke Fleischwarenfabrik GmbH & Co KG v Commission* [1980] ECR 665 para 7; Case 59/84 *Tezi Textiel BV v Commission* [1986] ECR 887 paras 9–12; Case C–12/90 *Infortec—Projectos e consultadoria Lda v Commission* [1990] ECR I–4265 paras 8, 9.

[168] Case 236/86 *Dillinger Hüttenwerke AG v Commission* [1988] ECR 3761 para 14 (ECSC); Case C–80/88 *Wirtschaftsvereinigung Eisen- und Stahlindustrie v Commission* [1990] ECR I–4413 para 22; Case C–102/92 *Ferriere Acciaierie Sarde SpA v Commission* order of 5 March 1993, para 18 (ECSC).

[169] See Joined Cases 25/65, 26/65 *Simet and Feram v High Authority* [1967] ECR 33 (ECSC), where a postal delay was held to constitute an 'unforeseeable circumstance'. *Cf* Case C–59/91 *France v Commission* [1992] I–525 paras 8–12 where the applicants were not permitted to rely on a postal delay.

[170] Statute of the Court of Justice, article 42. See pp 319–320.

[171] Case 284/82 *Busseni SpA v Commission* [1984] ECR 557 para 11 (ECSC). See also Case 25/68 *André Schertzer v European Parliament* [1977] ECR 1729 paras 10–21 (excusable error); Case 117/78 *Willy Orlandi v Commission* [1979] ECR 1613 paras 6–12 (excusable error); Case 209/83 *Ferriera Valsabbia SpA v Commission* [1984] ECR 3089 (*force majeure*); Case 224/83 *Ferriera Vittoria Srl v Commission* [1984] ECR 2349 (*force majeure*); Case 42/85 *Cockerill-Sambre SA v Commission* [1985] ECR 3749 (ECSC) (unforeseeable circumstances and *force majeure*); Case T–12/90 *Bayer AG v Commission* [1991] ECR II–219 (excusable error and *force majeure*).

[172] See p 198. Joined Cases 6/69, 11/69 *Commission v France* [1969] ECR 523 paras 10–13; Case 15/85 *Consorzio Cooperative d'Abruzzo v Commission* [1987] ECR 1005 para 10; Joined Cases T–79/89, T–84/89 and others *BASF AG v Commission* [1992] ECR II–315 para 101.

[173] See further at p 129.

[174] See p 203.

Effect of judgment   Under the first limb of article 174, the EC Courts may only declare that the act challenged is void; they are not entitled to order an institution to adopt the measures necessary for the enforcement of the judgment.[175] However, article 176 of the EEC Treaty imposes an obligation on the institution concerned to take all necessary measures to comply with the judgment.[176]

A finding that an act is void is of general application; it does not bind only the particular parties. Therefore, it may be relied on in proceedings in both national and EC Courts. In addition, a judgment under article 173 may provide the basis for a claim for damages against the institution under article 215 of the EEC Treaty.[177]

Temporal limitation   The second limb of article 174 allows the EC Courts to declare that only certain provisions of a Community measure are to be treated as void. This power is granted in the interests of legal certainty and the preservation of rights acquired prior to the Court's judgment.[178] Although article 174 refers expressly to regulations only, the Court of Justice has applied this principle to other types of Community acts. For example, in Case 17/74 *Transocean Marine Paint Association v Commission*[179] the Court of Justice annulled a particular provision of a Commission decision, leaving the remainder intact.

The Court will not exercise the power of partial annulment where the invalid parts of the measure are inseparable from the measure as a whole, so that without them the measure would no longer be capable of producing legal effects.[180] An application to the Court may expressly seek the annulment of a particular provision of a measure.[181] However, if the Court decides that it is not possible to sever that provision from the measure as a whole, it may declare the action inadmissible, unless the application seeks the annulment of the whole measure in the alternative.[182]

An act annulled under article 173 of the EEC Treaty is treated as if it had never existed. However, the Court of Justice has relied on the second limb of article 174 to declare that certain provisions found to be void should continue to have effect until new legislation could be adopted.[183] Furthermore, in Case

---

[175] Case 225/82 *Rudy Verzyck v Commission* [1983] ECR 1991 para 19; Case 53/85 *AKZO Chemie BV v Commission* [1986] ECR 1965 para 23; Case 15/85 *Consorzio Cooperative d'Abruzzo v Commission* [1987] ECR 1005 para 18; Case T–156/89 *Iñigo Valverde Mordt v Court of Justice* [1991] ECR II–407 para 157; C–199/91 *Foyer culturel du Sart-Tilman v Commission* judgment of 25 May 1993 paras 15–18.

[176] See Joined Cases 97/86, 99/86, 193/86, 215/86 *Asteris AE and Greece v Commission* [1988] ECR 2181 paras 19–33, for an analysis of the obligations imposed by article 176.

[177] See p 232–233.

[178] For example, see Case 92/78 *Simmenthal SpA v Commission* [1979] ECR 777 paras 106, 107; and Case 34/86 *Council v European Parliament* [1986] ECR 2155 para 48.

[179] [1974] ECR 1063 paras 20, 21. See also Joined Cases 56/64, 58/64 *Consten and Grundig v Commission* [1966] ECR 299 at 344; Case 62/70 *Werner A Bock v Commission* [1971] ECR 897.

[180] Case 37/71 *Michel Jamet v Commission* [1972] ECR 483 para 11.

[181] For example, see Case 17/74 *Transocean Marine Paint Association v Commission* [1974] ECR 1063 paras 20, 21. See also Case 62/70 *Werner A Bock v Commission* [1971] ECR 897.

[182] Case 37/71 *Michel Jamet v Commission* [1972] ECR 483 paras 1–14.

[183] Case 81/72 *Commission v Council* [1973] ECR 575 para 15; Case 59/81 *Commission v Council* [1982] ECR 3329 para 39; Case C–65/90 *European Parliament v Council* [1992] I–4593 paras 22–24.

34/86 *Council v European Parliament*,[184] where the Court of Justice found that the 1986 Community budget was illegal after a substantial part of the financial year had already elapsed, the Court held that the annulment should only have effect from the date of the judgment, so that the validity of payments made and commitments entered into under the illegal budget could not be called into question.

---

[184] [1986] ECR 2155 para 48.

Chapter 13

Plea of Illegality—Article 184 of the EEC Treaty

1. NATURE OF ARTICLE 184

Article 184 Article 184 of the EEC Treaty provides that:

> Notwithstanding the expiry of the period laid down in the third paragraph of Article 173, any party may, in proceedings in which a regulation of the Council or of the Commission is in issue, plead the grounds specified in the first paragraph of Article 173, in order to invoke before the Court of Justice the inapplicability of that regulation.[1]

Purpose Under article 184 a Community regulation may be declared inapplicable in a particular case. Under article 173 the validity of Community measures can only be challenged directly within a time limit of two months. This short limitation period may give rise to injustice where the validity of a regulation is relevant in separate proceedings which challenge another Community measure. Thus, in Joined Cases 87/77, 130/77, 22/83, 9/84, 10/84 *Vittorio Salerno v Commission and Council*,[2] the Court of Justice held:

> ... the sole purpose of Article 184 is to protect parties against the application of an unlawful regulation where the regulation itself can no longer be challenged owing to the expiry of the period laid down in Article 173.

No independent right of action Parties cannot bring a direct action before the Court of Justice based solely on article 184.[3] The plea of illegality will normally arise where a specific implementing measure is being attacked under article 173 or 177 and the validity of the regulation on which the implementing measure is based is called into question. In Case 92/78 *Simmenthal SpA v*

---

[1] The Treaty on European Union ('the Maastricht Treaty') will add regulations adopted jointly by the European Parliament and Council, and regulations adopted by the European Central Bank, to the measures open to challenge under article 184.

[2] [1985] ECR 2523 para 36. See also Joined Cases 31/62, 33/62 *Milchwerke Heinz Wöhrmann & Sohn KG and Alfons Lütticke GmbH v Commission* [1962] ECR 501 at 507.

[3] Joined Cases 31/62, 33/62 *Milchwerke v Commission* [1962] ECR 501 at 506, 507; Case 44/65 *Hessische Knappschaft v Maison Singer et Fils* [1965] ECR 965 at 970; Case 33/80 *Renato Albini v Council and Commission* [1981] ECR 2141 para 17; Joined Cases 87/77, 130/77, 22/83, 9/84, 10/84 *Vittorio Salerno v Commission and Council* [1985] ECR 2523 para 36.

Commission,[4] the applicant had brought an action under article 173 against a decision of the Commission which was of direct and individual concern to it. The Court of Justice held that a plea of illegality aimed at the regulations on which that decision was based was also admissible under article 184.

Article 184 may only be invoked in the context of a separate, independently admissible cause of action. Thus, where the main action is itself inadmissible, an applicant will not be entitled to rely on article 184. In Joined Cases 89/86, 91/86 *L'Etoile commerciale and CNTA v Commission*,[5] the applicant's challenge to a regulation under article 184 was declared to be inadmissible, as the primary claim under article 173, in respect of an implementing measure, was itself inadmissible, the implementing measure not being of direct and individual concern to the applicant.

Particular importance for private parties   Article 184 is of particular importance in relation to private parties. Where a Community institution adopts a regulation, its legality cannot be challenged by private parties under article 173, unless it is of direct and individual concern to them.[6] However, specific measures adopted on the basis of a regulation may be of direct and individual concern to them or may, indeed, be addressed to them. Article 184 permits private parties to challenge not only the implementing measures but also, indirectly, the regulation upon which they are based.[7]

2. POTENTIAL LIMITATIONS ON ARTICLE 184

Narrow approach   The case law of the Court of Justice suggests two possible approaches to the application of article 184 of the EEC Treaty. In Case 92/78 *Simmenthal SpA v Commission*[8], the Court of Justice adopted a narrow approach. It held that:

> Article 184 of the EEC Treaty gives expression to a general principle conferring upon any party to proceedings the right to challenge, for the purpose of obtaining the annulment of a decision of direct and individual concern to that party, the validity of previous acts of the institutions which form the legal basis of the decision which is being attacked, if that party was not entitled under Article 173 of the Treaty to bring a direct action challenging those acts by which it was thus affected without having been in a position to ask that they be declared void.

This approach suggests that the plea of illegality should only be admissible where the applicant would not have had standing to challenge the regulation under article 173 when it was originally adopted. All privileged applicants (that is, the Community institutions and Member States) would be precluded from relying on article 184. In addition, it would prevent private parties from relying on

---

[4] [1979] ECR 777 paras 34–43.

[5] [1987] ECR 3005 para 22.

[6] See pp 178–179.

[7] Case 262/80 *Kirsten Andersen v European Parliament* [1984] ECR 195 paras 5–7.

[8] [1979] ECR 777 para 39; see also para 41.

article 184 where they had standing to challenge a measure under article 173, but had failed to do so.

Broad approach It is possible to argue for a broader approach to article 184 on the basis that, when a regulation is adopted, a private party, or even a Member State, may not appreciate, at the time of its adoption, the practical effects which it will have. The fact that they did not appreciate the effects that the regulation might have on them, and did not bring an action under article 173 at that time, should not preclude them from challenging the validity of the regulation when the practical effects do become apparent.[9]

Member States The difference between the narrow and broad interpretations of article 184 is of particular importance for Member States. If the narrow approach adopted in *Simmenthal* were to be applied to Member States, they would never be able to rely on article 184. In Case 32/65 *Italy v Commission*[10] the Court of Justice indicated that the wording of article 184 refers to 'any party'. This approach was reflected in the opinion of Advocate-General Sir Gordon Slynn in Case 181/85 *France v Commission*,[11] where he considered the argument that a Member State could not rely on article 184 because it was a privileged applicant under article 173. This argument was based on the fact that a Member State, unlike private parties, is entitled to challenge the validity of regulations under article 173. As such, if it chooses not to do so within the two-month time limit imposed by article 173, it should not be given a 'second bite of the cherry' by relying on article 184. Distinguishing *Simmenthal*, the Advocate-General rejected this approach on the basis that the words 'any party' are used in article 184. Furthermore, he rejected the Commission's submission that the rights of the Member States under article 184 should be limited because of their privileged status under article 173 so that a Member State should only be entitled to invoke article 184 where it had been 'taken by surprise' by the way in which a regulation had been implemented. This issue was not addressed by the Court of Justice.

Importance in article 169 proceedings Article 184 provides a potential defence to article 169 proceedings brought by the Commission against Member States for failure to comply with regulations. In Case 156/77 *Commission v Belgium*,[12] the Court of Justice held that a Member State could not rely on article 184 in the context of article 169 proceedings in order to challenge a Commission decision addressed specifically to that Member State. However, it is

---

[9] See the Opinion of Advocate-General Roemer in Case 32/65 *Italy v Commission* [1966] ECR 389 at 414.

[10] [1966] ECR 389 at 409; see also the Opinion of Advocate-General Roemer at 414.

[11] [1987] ECR 689, Opinion of Advocate-General Sir Gordon Slynn at 702, 703. See also the Opinion of Advocate-General Mancini in Case 204/86 *Greece v Council* [1988] ECR 5323 at 5343–5345; and the Opinion of Advocate-General Darmon in Case C–258/89 *Commission v Spain* [1991] ECR I–3977 paras 12–32 of the Opinion.

[12] [1978] ECR 1881 paras 21, 22; see also the Opinion of Advocate-General Mayras paras 1908, 1909.

important to note that the Court relied on the general principle that article 184 may only be invoked in relation to regulations, rather than simply holding that Member States may not rely on article 184 under any circumstances. In Case C–258/89 *Commission v Spain*[13] Advocate-General Darmon considered that Member States should be entitled to invoke article 184 in respect of a regulation in the context of proceedings under article 169.

Community institutions If the approach of Advocate-General Sir Gordon Slynn in Case 181/85 *France v Commission*[14] is adopted by the Court of Justice, it should follow that Community institutions will also be permitted to rely on article 184 on the basis that it refers to 'any party'.

Private parties The difference between the narrow and broad approaches to article 184 is also important in relation to private parties. Under the broad approach, an applicant would be entitled to challenge a measure under article 184 even if he could have challenged that measure under article 173 within the two-month time limit but did not do so. In Case 216/82 *Universität Hamburg v Hauptzollamt Hamburg-Kehrwieder*[15] the Court of Justice appeared to favour the broad approach, when it emphasised that the applicant had not been aware of the general measure which it wished to challenge until a specific decision addressed to the applicant itself was adopted. However, given the judgment in Case 92/78 *Simmenthal SpA v Commission*,[16] the issue of whether the broad or narrow approach applies to private parties remains unclear. On one hand, if the broad approach is to be applied to cases involving Member States then, logically, there is no reason why it should not apply equally to private parties. Even where a regulation which is adopted is of direct and individual concern to a private party, he may not appreciate the practical effects which it will produce within the two-month time limit set down by article 173. On the other hand, the Court of Justice may be reluctant to adopt a broad definition of article 184 as this may undermine the legal certainty maintained by the two-month time limit provided for in article 173.[17]

3. ACTS WHICH MAY BE CHALLENGED

Necessary connection The Court of Justice has consistently held that article 184 of the EEC Treaty may be pleaded to challenge the legality of a regulation which provides the legal basis of a measure which is at issue in the action.[18] It is

---

[13] [1991] ECR I–3977, Opinion of Advocate-General Darmon para 23. See also Case 226/87 *Commission v Greece* [1988] ECR 3611, Opinion of Advocate-General Mancini at 3617.

[14] [1987] ECR 689, Opinion of Advocate-General Sir Gordon Slynn at 702, 703.

[15] [1983] ECR 2771 paras 5–12. This case did not strictly concern Article 184: see at p 208.

[16] [1979] ECR 777. See pp 203–205.

[17] See Case C–188/92 *TWD Textilwerke Deggendorf GmbH v Germany*, judgment of 9 March 1994.

[18] Case 92/78 *Simmenthal SpA v EC Commission* [1979] ECR 777 para 39; Joined Cases 87/77, 130/77, 22/83, 9/84, 10/84 *Vittorio Salerno v Commission and Council* [1985] ECR 2523 para 36.

not clear whether this is the only basis on which article 184 may be invoked. In Case 32/65 *Italy v Council and Commission*,[19] the Court of Justice adopted a more general approach when it indicated that an applicant can challenge the validity of a regulation which is applicable 'directly or indirectly' to the issue with which the main application is concerned. The Court of Justice held, in that case, that the regulation in question could not be attacked under article 184 as there was no 'necessary connection' between it and the measures which formed the primary subject-matter of the action, rather than simply relying on the argument that the regulation did not provide the legal basis for those measures.

Acts other than regulations The wording of article 184 appears to indicate that the plea of illegality can only be raised in respect of regulations. However, in Case 92/78 *Simmenthal SpA v Commission*[20] the Court of Justice held that:

> The field of application of [Article 184] must therefore include acts of the institutions which, although they are not in the form of a regulation, nevertheless produce similar effects and on those grounds may not be challenged under Article 173 by natural or legal persons other than Community institutions and Member States.

In that case, the applicant was contesting a decision taken on the basis of an invitation to tender. The specific decision was of direct and individual concern to the applicant; however, the notice to tender was a measure of general application and, therefore, could not have been challenged by a private party under article 173 of the EEC Treaty. The Court of Justice held that these constituted good grounds for permitting the applicant to challenge the validity of the notice to tender under article 184.[21]

4. GROUNDS OF INAPPLICABILITY

Same grounds as under article 173 The grounds upon which a Community measure may be declared inapplicable under article 184 of the EEC Treaty are the same as those under article 173,[22] namely:
(1) lack of competence;
(2) infringement of an essential procedural requirement;
(3) infringement of the EEC Treaty or of any rule of law relating to its application; and
(4) misuse of powers.

---

[19] [1966] ECR 389 at 409, 410. See also the Opinion of Advocate-General Sir Gordon Slynn in Case 181/85 *France v Commission* [1987] ECR 689 at 703; and the Opinion of Advocate-General Mischo in Joined Cases 181/86, 184/86 *Sergio Del Plato and others v Commission* [1987] ECR 4991 at 5004.
[20] [1979] ECR 777 paras 39–43.
[21] This is in line with the Court's general approach in considering the substance, not form, of Community measures. See also Case 216/82 *Universität Hamburg v Hauptzollamt Hamburg-Kehrwieder* [1983] ECR 2771 paras 5–12.
[22] See pp 189–198.

5. EFFECT OF JUDGMENT

Inapplicable, not void In Joined Cases 31/62, 33/62 *Milchwerke Heinz Wöhrmann & Sohn KG and Alfons Lütticke GmbH v Commission*[23] the Court of Justice emphasised that the purpose of article 184 of the EEC Treaty is limited to rendering a regulation inapplicable in a particular case 'without thereby in any way calling in issue the regulation itself'.

This limitation stems from the fact that a judgment based on article 184 has the effect of circumventing the two-month limitation period set down in article 173, which is imposed in the interests of legal certainty. However, as all other measures based on the same regulation will also be at risk of being held inapplicable under article 184, the Commission or Council will usually take steps to replace the illegal regulation with a legal one.

6. PROCEEDINGS IN NATIONAL COURTS

Comparable principle Although the plea of illegality under article 184 of the EEC Treaty is restricted to proceedings before the EC Courts, the Court of Justice has held that a party may rely on a comparable principle in proceedings brought in the national courts where the validity of a Community regulation is in issue in those proceedings. In Case 216/82 *Universität Hamburg v Hauptzollamt Hamburg-Kehrwieder*[24] the applicant brought proceedings in the German courts to challenge a decision taken by the German customs authorities. The Court of Justice held that the applicant was entitled to challenge the validity of the Commission decision on which the national decision was based because article 184 reflected a general principle of law applicable in all proceedings. Where the validity of a Community measure is challenged in the course of national proceedings, the national court must refer the question of validity to the Court of Justice under article 177 of the EEC Treaty.[25]

---

[23] [1962] ECR 501 at 507.
[24] [1983] ECR 2771 paras 5–12.
[25] Case 314/85 *Foto-Frost v Hauptzollamt Lübeck-Ost* [1987] ECR 4199 paras 11–20. See p 141.

Chapter 14

Judicial Review of Failure to Act—Article 175 of the EEC Treaty

1. INTRODUCTION

Article 175 Article 175 of the EEC Treaty provides that:

> Should the Council or the Commission, in infringement of this Treaty, fail to act, the Member States and the other institutions of the Community may bring an action before the Court of Justice to have the infringement established.
>
> The action shall be admissible only if the institution concerned has first been called upon to act. If, within two months of being so called upon, the institution concerned has not defined its position, the action may be brought within a further period of two months.
>
> Any natural or legal person may, under the conditions laid down in the preceding paragraphs, complain to the Court of Justice that an institution of the Community has failed to address to that person any act other than a recommendation or an opinion.

Nature of Article 175 Article 175 of the EEC Treaty provides the legal basis for review by the EC Courts of failure to act by the Council or Commission. It is intended:[1]

> to prevent an institution, which has wrongly failed to adopt an act or take a given measure, from evading permanently its responsibilities and escaping any judicial sanction by resorting to silence or by giving a procrastinating, evasive or insufficiently binding reply when called upon to act.

If an institution is found to have contravened article 175, the Court of Justice will make a declaration indicating that the institution is in breach of its EEC Treaty obligations. Article 176 then requires the institution to take the necessary measures to comply with the judgment of the Court of Justice.[2]

Proceedings under article 175 are intended to establish an illegal omission. In Joined Cases 10/68, 18/68 *Società 'Eridania' Zuccherifici Nazionali v Commission*,[3] the applicants had called upon the Commission to revoke certain acts.

---

[1] Case 377/87 *Parliament v Council* [1988] ECR 4017, Opinion of Advocate-General Mischo paras 12, 13.
[2] See p 222.
[3] [1969] ECR 459 paras 15–18.

When the Commission failed to respond, the applicants began proceedings under article 175. The Court of Justice held that these proceedings were inadmissible. Their true purpose was the revocation of certain acts, rather than a declaration of failure to act, by the Commission and, therefore, the appropriate means of recourse was under article 173 of the EEC Treaty.

Jurisdiction Actions by privileged applicants under article 175 must be made to the Court of Justice. Actions by non-privileged applicants under article 175 must be made to the Court of First Instance.[4]

2. PARTIES

Defendants On its face, article 175 of the EEC Treaty provides that failure to act by the Council or Commission may be subject to review by the EC Courts. However, it is arguable that proceedings can also be brought against the European Parliament under article 175.[5]

Privileged applicants The Member States and all the institutions of the Community are privileged applicants.[6] Although article 175 refers to 'other institutions' being entitled to seek review of the Commission's and Council's failure to act, the Commission and Council themselves are entitled to bring proceedings under article 175.[7] In Case 13/83 *European Parliament v Council*,[8] the Court of Justice rejected an argument that the Parliament was not entitled to bring an action against the Council under article 175. In the same case, Advocate-General Lenz considered that the Court of Justice would not be entitled to bring an action under article 175 'because it is responsible for legal protection and does not itself seek it'.[9]

---

[4] Article 3 of Council Decision 8/591 of 24 October 1988, OJ No C 215, 21 August 1989, p 1 as substituted by Council Directive 93/350 of 8 June 1993, OJ No L 144, 16 June 1993, p 21 as amended by Council Decision 94/149 of 7 March 1994, OJ No L66, 10 March 1994, p 29.

[5] See the Opinion of Advocate-General Darmon in Case C–41/92 *Liberal Democrats v European Parliament*, Opinion delivered on 24 March 1993, paras 7–24, where he argues that the wording of article 175 already permits actions for failure to act to be brought against the Parliament. The Treaty on European Union ('Maastricht Treaty') will amend article 175 so that failure to act by the European Parliament and the European Central Bank will be subject to review.

[6] The Treaty on European Union ('Maastricht Treaty') will amend article 175 to permit the European Central Bank to bring actions for failure to act in the areas falling within its field of competence.

[7] For example, see Case 383/87 *Commission v Council* [1988] ECR 4051 where the right of the Commission to bring proceedings under article 175 was not challenged.

[8] [1985] ECR 1513 paras 13–19. The Court of Justice held that article 175 gives the same right of action to all the Community institutions and Advocate-General Lenz (at para 2.2 of his Opinion) made it clear that the right of action of the Parliament does not require proof of a special interest requiring protection (compare the position under Article 173, discussed at pp 172–173. In Case 377/87 *European Parliament v Council* [1988] ECR 4017 the right of the Parliament to bring an action under article 175 was not questioned.

[9] Case 13/83 *European Parliament v Council* [1985] ECR 1513, Opinion of Advocate-General Lenz at 1519.

Non-privileged applicants As under article 173 of the EEC Treaty, article 175 distinguishes between 'privileged' and 'non-privileged' applicants. All natural or legal persons are non-privileged applicants. Article 175 establishes two main differences between the position of privileged and non-privileged applicants.

(1) Non-privileged applicants can only challenge the failure to adopt a measure which would have been addressed to them. Privileged applicants can challenge the failure to adopt all measures, including measures of general application.

(2) The category of acts of which non-privileged applicants can challenge the failure to adopt is limited in that it does not include recommendations or opinions.

3. CONDITIONS OF LIABILITY

(a) Relevant acts

(i) Obligation to act

Obligation to act An institution cannot be challenged for failure to adopt a measure which it has no obligation to adopt. This applies whether the applicant is privileged or non-privileged. This principle has been stated explicitly by several Advocates-General.[10] The Court of Justice has been less explicit in enunciating this proposition, but it has played a part in a number of important judgments. In particular, where the Council or Commission has a discretion whether to act or not, it will not be possible to challenge a failure to act by proceedings under article 175. Thus, where the Commission has decided, pursuant to its discretion, not to pursue an article 169 action against a Member State for infringement of the EEC Treaty, its failure to do so cannot be challenged.[11]

Proceedings under article 175 may be declared inadmissible, not only where the Council or Commission have a discretion whether to act or not, but also where they have a discretion as to *how* to act. In Case 13/83 *European Parliament v Council*[12] the Parliament brought proceedings under article 175 alleging that the Council had failed to implement a common transport policy as required by the EEC Treaty. The Court held that, although the EEC Treaty established specific time limits for the adoption of a common transport policy, the Council had a discretion to determine the content and means for implementing such a policy. The Council's obligations in this regard were, therefore, not sufficiently

---

[10] Opinion of Advocate-General Gand in Case 48/65 *Alfons Lütticke GmbH v Commission* [1966] ECR 19 at 32; Opinion of Advocate-General Roemer in Joined Cases 10/68, 18/68 *Società 'Fridania' Zuccherifici Nazionali v Commission* [1969] ECR 459 at 494, Opinion of Advocate-General Gand in Case 6/70 *Giberto Borromeo Arese v Commission* [1970] ECR 815 at 822; Opinion of Advocate-General Sir Gordon Slynn in *Lord Bethell v Commission* [1982] ECR 2277 at 2296; Opinion of Advocate-General Darmon in Joined Cases 166/86, 220/86 *Irish Cement Limited v Commission* [1988] ECR 6473 para 22 of the Opinion.

[11] Case 247/87 *Star Fruit SA v Commission* [1989] ECR 291 paras 10–14.

[12] [1985] ECR 1513.

specific to be the subject of proceedings under article 175.[13] In contrast, the Court held that the obligation to introduce a common transport policy included the obligation to ensure the freedom to provide transport services. This obligation was sufficiently well-defined to be the subject of proceedings under article 175.[14]

Competition matters Private parties are entitled to lodge complaints concerning competition matters with the Commission.[15] If the Commission decides not to act on the complaint, it is under an obligation to inform the complainant of its reasons for not doing so and to invite the complainant to submit any further comments in writing, within a given time limit.[16] If the Commission fails to comply with this obligation, the complainant is entitled to bring proceedings under article 175.[17]

(ii) Legal effects

Legal effects Some authorities suggest that the concept of a measure capable of giving rise to an action is identical under articles 173 and 175.[18] This would mean that only a failure to adopt acts which produce legal effects would be open to challenge under article 175.[19] Thus, in Case 377/87 *European Parliament v Council*,[20] Advocate-General Mischo, equating proceedings under article 175 with proceedings under article 173, considered that a failure to act within article 175 arises wherever the Council or Commission fails to adopt a measure, of whatever nature, form or description, which is capable of producing legal effects *vis-à-vis* third parties.[21]

However, the Court of Justice, in Case 302/87 *European Parliament v Council*,[22] appeared to suggest that, in certain circumstances, failure to adopt an act

---

[13] Ibid paras 47–53 of the judgment.

[14] Ibid paras 64–68.

[15] Article 3(2)(b) of Council Regulation 17/62 of 6 February 1962, First Regulation implementing Articles 85 and 86 of the Treaty (as amended), OJ No 13, 21 February 1962, p 204 (English Special Edition 1959–1962, p 87).

[16] Article 6 of Commission Regulation 99/63 of 25 July 1963, on the hearings provided for in articles 19(1) and (2) of Council Regulation No 17, OJ No 127, 20 August 1962, p 2263 (English Special Edition 1963–1964, p 47).

[17] Case T–28/90 *Asia Motor France SA v Commission* [1992] ECR II–2285 para 29. See also Case 125/78 *GEMA v Commission* [1979] ECR 3173 paras 14–23; Case T–24/90 *Automec Srl v Commission* [1992] ECR II–2223 paras 71–80 (where the Court of First Instance held that the Commission was under an obligation to give proper consideration to the issues of fact and law raised by a complainant before deciding whether or not to act on the complaint).

[18] Case 15/70 *Chevalley v Commission* [1970] ECR 975 para 6. This was cited with approval by Advocate-General Darmon in Joined Cases 166/86, 220/86 *Irish Cement Limited v Commission* [1988] ECR 6473 para 42 of his Opinion.

[19] See pp 175–176 in relation to the notion of binding legal effects in the context of article 173.

[20] [1988] ECR 4017, Opinion of Advocate-General Mischo paras 28–30. Note that this view was not expressly adopted by the Court of Justice in its judgment.

[21] See also Case 8/71 *Kompanistenverband v Commission* [1971] ECR 705, in which Advocate-General Roemer at 715 considered that the concept of an 'act' for the purposes of article 175 includes 'any measure producing certain legal effects binding the institution in a certain way', including some procedural matters.

[22] [1988] ECR 5615 para 16.

which would not produce legal effects might be reviewable under article 175. The Court based this observation on the decision in Case 377/87 *European Parliament v Council*,[23] which it interpreted as establishing that the Parliament would be entitled to obtain a judgment under article 175 where the Council had failed to adopt a draft budget, even though the draft budget itself, once adopted, could not be challenged under article 173 as it is a preparatory measure. Although the draft budget did not produce legal effects, the Council was under a legal obligation to adopt it. It was, therefore, necessary to permit the Parliament to bring proceedings under article 175 in order to ensure that the Council's failure to fulfil its EEC Treaty obligations would not go unchecked.[24] In Case C–41/92 *Liberal Democrats v European Parliament*[25] Advocate-General Darmon suggested that, where an institution fails to adopt a preparatory measure which is a necessary precondition for the adoption by another institution of a definitive measure producing legal effects, that failure to act may itself be reviewable under article 175.

(iii) Recommendations and opinions
Recommendations and opinions The third limb of article 175 of the EEC Treaty expressly excludes the rights of private parties to complain of the failure to adopt recommendations or opinions. In order to determine the nature of the complaint, the Court of Justice will look at the substance of an applicant's complaint, rather than its form. In both Case 6/70 *Giberto Borromeo Arese v Commission*[26] and Case 15/70 *Amedeo Chevalley v Commission*[27] the applicants complained of a failure by the Commission to adopt decisions which they had called upon it to make. However, the Court of Justice held that, in substance, the applicants were not seeking decisions from the Commission, but rather advice as to their own particular situations, which was equivalent to seeking an opinion and, therefore, not subject to review under article 175.[28]

(iv) Party to whom the act is addressed
Distinction between privileged and non-privileged applicants Member States and Community institutions are entitled to challenge the failure to adopt an act which would have been addressed to third parties. In contrast, the wording of article 175 provides that private parties may only challenge the failure to adopt an act which would have been addressed to them.

---

[23] [1988] ECR 4017.
[24] It should be noted that on the actual facts of Case 377/87 *European Parliament v Council* the Court of Justice dismissed the action under article 175 as the Council had adopted a draft budget before judgment was given. See pp 218–219.
[25] Opinion delivered on 24 March 1993 paras 25–83. The Advocate-General considered that the Parliament's failure to act produced legal effects *vis-à-vis* the Council in as much as it made it impossible for the Council to fulfil the task assigned to it.
[26] [1970] ECR 815.
[27] [1970] ECR 975.
[28] See also Case C–257/90 *Italsolar SpA v Commission*, judgment of 14 January 1993, paras 28–31.

Act addressed to complainant Where a private party complains of a failure to adopt a decision which would have been specifically addressed to him, an action under article 175 is admissible.[29] In Case 15/71 *C Mackprang Jr v Commission*,[30] the applicant complained of an alleged failure by the Commission to adopt a decision addressed to the Member States. The Court of Justice held that such a general provision could not be described as an act which could be addressed to the applicant. In Case 246/81 *Lord Bethell v Commission*,[31] Lord Bethell brought an action under, *inter alia*, article 175, for a declaration that the Commission had failed to adopt measures to combat the alleged anti-competitive behaviour of European airlines. The Court of Justice held that this application was inadmissible as, in substance, Lord Bethell was not asking the Commission to adopt a decision in respect of him, but to open an inquiry with regard to third parties and to take decisions in respect of them.

Where the applicant complains of an institution's alleged failure to adopt a decision which would have been addressed to him, the Court of Justice will consider the substance, rather than the form of the complaint, in order to establish whether the institution would have been capable of adopting such a decision.[32] Thus, in Case C–247/90 *Maria-Theresia Emrich v Commission*[33] the applicant complained of the Commission's failure to address a decision to her which would have the effect of allowing her to practise as a *Rechtsanwalt* (lawyer) before the German courts. The Court of Justice held that this action was inadmissible as, within the system of the EEC Treaty, the only measure which the Commission could have taken would have been to initiate proceedings under article 169 against the Federal Republic of Germany. Indeed, the same applicant had previously brought an action complaining of the Commission's failure to initiate article 169 proceedings against Germany, which had, likewise, been held to be inadmissible.[34]

Acts addressed to third parties but of direct and individual concern to applicant It is not clear whether a private party can complain of failure to adopt a measure which, although it would not have been specifically addressed to him, would have been of direct and individual concern to him. This question arises from the possible parallelism between articles 175 and 173 of the EEC Treaty. Under article 173, private parties may challenge the validity, not only of decisions addressed to them, but also of decisions which, although in the form of

---

[29] Case C–371/89R *Maria-Theresia Emrich v Commission* [1990] I–1555; Case C–72/90 *Asia Motor France v Commission* [1990] ECR I–2182 para 10–12; Case T–3/90 *Vereniging Prodifarma v Commission* [1991] ECR II–1 para 35.

[30] [1971] ECR 797 para 4.

[31] [1982] ECR 2277 paras 15–17.

[32] See Case 90/78 *Granaria v Council and Commission* [1979] ECR 1081 paras 12–15, where the Court of Justice held that the only legal instrument which could have satisfied the applicant's complaint would have been a regulation; therefore, the application was rejected. See also Case 60/79 *Fédération Nationale des Producteurs de Vins de Table et Vins de Pays v Commission* [1979] ECR 2429.

[33] [1990] ECR I–3913 paras 5–7.

[34] Case C–371/89 *Maria-Theresia Emrich v Commission* [1990] ECR I–1555.

regulations or addressed to third parties, are of direct and individual concern to the applicant.[35]

The first point to note is that while article 173 expressly provides for review of measures other than decisions addressed to the applicant, article 175 only provides for review where there has been a failure to address to the applicant any act other than a recommendation or opinion. Thus, in Case 125/78 *GEMA v Commission*,[36] Advocate-General Capotorti stated that the difference in wording between articles 173 and 175 indicated that the right to institute proceedings for failure to act does not lie in respect of acts which, while they would be of direct and individual concern to the applicant, would not be addressed to him.

The Court of First Instance considered this issue in Case T–3/90 *Vereniging Prodifarma v Commission*[37] without reaching a definitive decision. The Court held:[38]

... in order for an action for failure to act to be admissible a natural or legal person must establish that he is in the exact legal position of a potential addressee of a legal act that the Commission is obliged to take in his regard.

On the facts of the particular case, the Court held that the applicant was not a potential addressee of the decision sought and that this finding was sufficient to establish that the application was inadmissible.[39] However, having made that finding, the Court then considered whether the decision sought would have been of direct and individual concern to the applicant. The Court held that the decision would not have had that effect and it was, therefore, unnecessary to consider whether there was a parallelism between applications under articles 173 and 175.[40]

In contrast, in Case C–107/91 *ENU v Commission*,[41] the Court of Justice considered article 148 of the EAEC Treaty, which is in identical terms to article 175 of the EEC Treaty, and held that a private party could challenge a decision addressed to a third party which was of direct and individual concern to it. Furthermore, in Case 247/87 *Star Fruit SA v Commission*,[42] Advocate-General Lenz stated:

---

[35] See pp 178–189.

[36] [1979] ECR 3173, Opinion of Advocate-General Capotorti at 3199. See also the comments on this statement by Advocate-General Slynn in Case 246/81 *Lord Bethell v Commission* [1982] ECR 2277 at 2295–2296. In Case 8/71 *Deutscher Komponistenverband eV v Commission* [1971] ECR 705, Advocate-General Roemer (at p 715 of his Opinion), considering the wording of article 175, stated that it could not apply to regulations and directives. See also Case 103/63 *Rhenania v Commission* [1964] ECR 425, Opinion of Advocate-General Roemer at 433; Case 48/65 *Alfons Lütticke GmbH v Commission* [1966] ECR 19, Opinion of Advocate-General Gand at 30.

[37] [1991] ECR II–1.

[38] Ibid para 35.

[39] Ibid paras 36, 37.

[40] Ibid paras 38–45.

[41] Judgment of 16 February 1993, paras 14–19 (EAEC).

[42] [1989] ECR 291, Opinion of Advocate-General Lenz at para 15.

Under the system of judicial protection instituted by the Treaty private individuals clearly have no general right of action but only a limited right depending on their individual interests. As regards actions for annulment, Article 173 expresses this principle by the requirement of direct and individual concern. The criterion 'address to that person any act' in Article 175 should be understood in that sense, that is to say it may only involve acts in which the applicant has a particular interest but in no case acts with a general scope.[43]

A number of Advocates-General have sought to justify different approaches to articles 173 and 175 on the basis that the aims of those articles differ. While the purpose of article 173 is to obtain a declaration that a measure is void, the purpose of article 175 is to prevent 'the clogging of the machinery of justice'.[44] This attempted justification is not attractive as the legal position of a private party may be affected just as much by the failure of an institution to adopt an act which is of direct and individual concern to him and which the institution has a duty to adopt, as by the actual adoption of a measure which is of direct and individual concern to the party.

In addition, if private parties cannot challenge the failure to adopt acts which would have been of direct and individual concern to them under article 175, a curious situation is created whereby a private party is in a stronger position if an institution expressly refuses to act, rather than simply ignoring a call to act. This arises because an express refusal to act can be challenged by private parties under article 173 where the act, if adopted, would itself have been reviewable under article 173. This includes circumstances where the relevant act would have been of direct and individual concern to the private party.[45]

(b) Institution must be called upon to act

Called upon to act An action under article 175 of the EEC Treaty is only admissible if the institution concerned has first been 'called upon to act'.[46] The purpose of this condition of admissibility is to make the institution aware that its failure to act is regarded by the potential applicant as a breach of the EEC Treaty

---

[43] See also Opinion of Advocate-General Dutheillet de Lamothe in Case 15/71 *C Mackprang Jr v Commission* [1971] ECR 797 at 807–809; Case 134/73 *Holtz & Willemsem GmbH v Council* [1974] ECR 1 para 5; Joined Cases C–15/91, C–108/91 *Josef Buckl & Söhne OHG and others v Commission*, judgment of 24 November 1992, Opinion of Advocate-General Gulmann at paras 17–19; Opinion of Advocate-General Darmon in Case C–41/92 *Liberal Democrats v European Parliament*, Opinion delivered on 24 March 1993, paras 84–94.

[44] Case 125/78 *GEMA v Commission* [1979] ECR 3173, Opinion of Advocate-General Capotorti at 3199–3120; Case 13/83 *European Parliament v Council* [1985] ECR 1513, Opinion of Advocate-General Lenz at 1520; Joined Cases 166/86, 220/86 *Irish Cement Ltd v Commission* [1988] ECR 6473, Opinion of Advocate-General Darmon para 14.

[45] See the Opinion of Advocate-General Dutheillet de Lamothe in Case 15/71 *C Mackprang Jr Commission* [1971] ECR 797 at 807, 808; Opinion of Advocate-General Gulmann in Joined Cases C–15/91, C–108/91 *Josef Buckl & Söhne OHG and others v Commission*, judgment of 24 November 1992, para 19. The review of express refusals to act under article 173 is discussed at pp 219–221.

[46] Where an action is brought under article 175, the application commencing the action must be accompanied by documentary evidence of the date on which the institution was called upon to act. See article 19 of the Statute of the Court of Justice, p 300.

and to give the institution the opportunity of avoiding legal proceedings under article 175 of the EEC Treaty by adopting the act requested or suitably defining its position.[47]

In order to satisfy this precondition, the institution should be clearly informed of the nature of the measures called for and it must be made plain that, if the institution fails to act, legal proceedings will be initiated.[48] The document calling upon the institution to act determines the scope of the subject-matter of the action. Thus, if legal proceedings are subsequently commenced under article 175, they must be confined to the scope of the original call to act.[49]

No express limitation period Article 175 of the EEC Treaty does not impose an express time limit on the period which may elapse between an institution's failure to act and its being called upon to act. However, in Joined Cases 166/86, 220/86 *Irish Cement Limited v Commission*[50] Advocate-General Darmon indicated that there should not be an unreasonable period between the time when an applicant becomes aware of the institution's failure to act and the time when the applicant calls upon the institution to rectify that failure. Given the complexity of the issues in that case (state aids), Advocate-General Darmon considered that a delay of eleven months before calling upon the Commission to act was not unreasonable. In Case C–107/91 *ENU v Commission*[51] the Court of Justice held that a period of 16 months did not bar an action for failure to act as there had been frequent contact between the parties concerning the problem.[52] In contrast, in Case 59/70 *Netherlands v Commission*,[53] a case under article 35 of the ECSC Treaty, the Court of Justice held that a delay of eighteen months before calling upon the High Authority (the Commission) to act was unreasonable and rendered the action inadmissible.

---

[47] In Case 302/87 *European Parliament v Council* [1988] ECR 5615, Advocate-General Darmon at 5613, fn 20, noted that article 175 does not expressly require that the applicant before the Court should necessarily be the one which initially called upon the institution to act.

[48] Opinion of Advocate-General Roemer in Case 8/71 *Deutscher Kompanistenverband eV v Commission* [1971] ECR 705 at 716; Case 13/83 *European Parliament v Council* [1985] ECR 1513 paras 35, 36, Opinion of Advocate-General Lenz at 1526–1527; Case 25/85 *Nuovo Campsider v Commission* [1986] ECR 1531 (ECSC); Joined Cases 81/85, 119/85 *Usinor v Commission* [1986] ECR 1777 paras 15, 16; Case T–28/90 *Asia Motor France SA v Commission* [1992] ECR II–2285 paras 25–28. See also the Opinion of Advocate-General Gulmann in Joined Cases C–15/91, C–108/91 *Josef Buckl & Söhne OHG and others v Commission*, judgment of 8 July 1992, para 12 of the Opinion, where the Advocate-General suggested that the Court of Justice should not, of its own motion, declare an action inadmissible where the call to act was deficient, if the defendant institution did not itself raise the point.

[49] Opinion of Advocate-General Lenz in Case 13/83 *European Parliament v Council* [1985] ECR 1513 at 1526, 1527.

[50] [1988] ECR 6473, Opinion of Advocate-General Darmon paras 15–21.

[51] Judgment of 16 February 1993, paras 23–25 (EAEC).

[52] See also Case 13/83 *European Parliament v Council* [1985] ECR 1513 where proceedings under article 175 were partially successful even though the Council had been called upon to act 13 years after its initial failure. Note, however, that the Court did not expressly consider the effect of this delay.

[53] [1971] ECR 639 (ECSC).

(c) No definition of position

Definition of position Having been called upon to act, an institution has two months within which to define its position. If the institution does not respond within that period, judicial proceedings may be commenced within a further period of two months.

An institution will only be held to have defined its position where it has positively and unequivocally given notice of its intention to act or not to act as required.[54] In considering whether the relevant institution has defined its position, the Court of Justice will look at the nature and substance of any reply. In Case 13/83 *European Parliament v Council*,[55] the Parliament had included in its letter to the Council calling upon it to act, a list of actions which, in its opinion, ought to be taken by the Council to remedy its failure to establish a common transport policy. In assessing the Council's reply, the Court of Justice held:[56]

> The Council's reply, on the other hand, was confined to setting out what action it had already taken in relation to transport without commenting 'on the legal aspects' of the correspondence initiated by the Parliament. The reply neither denied nor confirmed the alleged failure to act nor gave any indication of the Council's views as to the measures which, according to the Parliament, remained to be taken. Such a reply cannot be regarded as a definition of position within the meaning of the second paragraph of Article 175.

Failure to respond Obviously, if the institution fails to give any response, having been called upon to act, it will not have defined its position.

Act adopted before judgment Where the relevant institution adopts the act called for after proceedings have been commenced under article 175, but before judgment, the Court of Justice has held that the proceedings become devoid of purpose and must be dismissed.[57] It has been questioned whether it is correct to say that proceedings under article 175 are truly devoid of purpose once the institution has acted, as the applicant may wish to bring an action for damages against the institution under article 215, based on its failure to act.[58] However, an applicant is not required to obtain a judgment under article 175 prior to com-

---

[54] Case 13/83 *European Parliament v Council* [1985] ECR 1513, Opinion of Advocate-General Lenz at para 3.2.2.1.

[55] Ibid paras 20–27 of the judgment. See also Case 6/70 *Giberto Borromeo Arese v Commission* [1970] ECR 815, Opinion of Advocate-General Gand at 821, 822, which rejects the Commission's argument that an 'implied refusal' constitutes a definition of position for the purposes of article 175. However, contrast the approach of Advocate-General Capotorti in Case 125/78 *GEMA v Commission* [1979] ECR 3173 at 3198, 3199, where he indicated that a letter which could be considered as 'information pure and simple' and which did not amount to a decision could be described as a definition of position.

[56] Case 13/83 *European Parliament v Council* [1985] ECR 1513 para 26.

[57] Case 103/63 *Rhenania v Commission* [1964] ECR 425; Case 377/87 *European Parliament v Council* [1988] ECR 4017 paras 8–10; Case 383/87 *Commission v Council* [1988] ECR 4051 paras 8–10. In Case T–28/90 *Asia Motor France SA v Commission* [1992] ECR II–2285 paras 30, 34–38, the Court of Justice indicated that adoption of the act before judgment does not render proceedings under article 175 inadmissible, but it does render them devoid of purpose, so that the Court will not make a decision on that issue.

[58] For example, see Wyatt and Dashwood, *Substantive Law of the EEC*, 3rd edn (Sweet & Maxwell, 1993), 140, 141.

mencing proceedings under article 215. The failure to act can itself be established in proceedings under article 215.[59]

Different act adopted before judgment Proceedings under article 175 will be declared inadmissible where the institution called upon to act has adopted a measure different from that desired by the applicant, as this does not constitute a failure to act.[60] The act adopted may, of course, be open to challenge under the terms of article 173.

Express refusal: private parties In cases involving private parties, an express refusal to act constitutes a definition of position,[61] even if no reasons are given for the refusal.[62] This means that in this situation no proceedings can be brought under article 175. However, the refusal itself can be challenged under article 173 if the positive act which the institution refuses to take could itself have been challenged under article 173.[63] For example, in Case 42/71 *Nordgetreide GmbH & Co KG v Commission*[64] the Court declared as inadmissible an action under article 173 seeking review of a refusal by the Commission to amend a regulation by an act which would itself have taken the form of a regulation and which would not have been of direct and individual concern to the applicant (a private party).

Equally, where the individual calls upon an institution to adopt a measure which does not produce legal effects, a refusal to act will not be reviewable under article 173 because the measure itself would not have been reviewable under article 173 if it had been adopted.[65]

---

[59] Case 4/69 *Alfons Lütticke v Commission* [1971] ECR 325 at 336. See pp 232–233. Compare the position under article 169 (see p 162) where the Court of Justice has held that the proceedings still have an object even where the breach of Community law is remedied after the time limit set down in the reasoned opinion. Advocate-General Mischo discusses this difference between articles 169 and 175 in Case 377/87 *European Parliament v Council* [1988] ECR 4017, paras 114–135 of the Opinion.

[60] Case 8/71 *Deutscher Kompanistenverband eV v Commission* [1971] ECR 705 para 2; Joined Cases 166/86, 220/86 *Irish Cement Limited v Commission* [1988] ECR 6473 para 17. This applies equally where the institution expressly refuses to act prior to the judgment; see Joined Cases C–15/91, C–108/91 *Josef Buckl & Söhne OHG and others v Commission*, judgment of 24 November 1992, paras 1–18; *cf* the Opinion of Advocate-General Gulmann, in the same case, at para 16 of the Opinion.

[61] Case 48/65 *Alfons Lütticke GmbH v Commission* [1966] ECR 19; Case 42/71 *Nordgetreide GmbH & Co KG v Commission* [1972] ECR 105; Case 125/78 *GEMA v Commission* [1979] ECR 3173 paras 14–23; Joined Cases C–15/91, C–108/91 *Josef Buckl & Söhne OHG and others v Commission*, judgment of 24 November 1992, paras 1–18; Case C–250/90 *Control Union Gesellschaft für Warenkontrolle GmbH v Commission* [1991] ECR I–3585.

[62] Case 15/70 *Chevalley v Commission* [1970] ECR 975, Opinion of Advocate-General Dutheillet de Lamothe at 983.

[63] Case 48/65 *Alfons Lütticke GmbH v Commission* [1966] ECR 19 and Opinion of Advocate-General Gand at 31; Case 302/87 *European Parliament v Council* [1988] ECR 5615, Opinion of Advocate-General Darmon at 5630; Joined Cases 166/86, 220/86 *Irish Cement Ltd v Commission* [1988] ECR 6473, Opinion of Advocate-General Darmon paras 37–41; Case C–87/89 *SONITO v Commission* [1990] ECR I–1981 paras 5–9; Joined Cases C–15/91, C–108/91 *Josef Buckl & Söhne OHG and others v Commission*, judgment of 24 November 1992, paras 21–22.

[64] [1972] ECR 105.

[65] For example, see Case 48/65 *Alfons Lütticke GmbH v Commission* [1966] ECR 19.

It has been suggested that the case law of the Court of Justice causes a gap in the judicial protection of private parties.[66] Where a private party calls upon an institution to act, the institution may prevent proceedings being commenced under article 175 by defining its position. However, even if the act which defines the institution's position can be construed as a decision, it cannot be challenged if the positive act called for could not have been challenged by a private party under article 173.[67] This situation does not really constitute a gap in the legal position of private parties, but rather reflects the limited role which the EEC Treaty grants to private parties in the context of judicial review. Just as in English administrative law, a private party only has *locus standi* to challenge public measures which particularly concern him. There is no reason why a private party should be permitted to seek review under article 175 of a refusal to adopt a general act which would not have concerned him individually or which would not have produced legal effects. If it is necessary to take an act in the general interest, it is more appropriate for the other institutions or the Member States to call upon the relevant institution to adopt such an act.

Express refusal: privileged applicants It appears that, in relation to privileged applicants, an express refusal to act does not always constitute a definition of position. In *Case 302/87 European Parliament v Council*,[68] the Court of Justice held that:

> A refusal to act, however explicit it may be, can be brought before the Court under Article 175 since it does not put an end to failure to act.

This distinction between privileged and non-privileged applicants arises due to the special role played by privileged applicants in ensuring that the Community institutions fulfil their general EEC Treaty obligations. In Case 302/87 *European Parliament v Council*, the Court of Justice based its observations on Case 377/87 *European Parliament v Council*,[69] which concerned the Council's failure to adopt a draft budget, despite its legal obligation to do so. The Court of Justice recognised that if the Council's refusal to act in that case was considered to be a definition of position, that would have rendered article 175 proceedings inadmissible. Furthermore, the refusal to act would not have been reviewable under article 173 as the draft budget, being a preparatory measure, would not, in itself, have been open to review under article 173 if it had been adopted. This would have created a gap in the system of judicial review established by the EEC Treaty, as the Council's failure to fulfil its Community obligations would

---

[66] See the comments of Advocate-General Darmon in Joined Cases 166/86, 220/86 *Irish Cement Limited v Commission* [1988] ECR 6473 paras 37–41 of the Opinion, and the academic commentaries referred to therein. See also AG Toth 'The Law as it stands on the Appeal for Failure to Act' (1975) *Legal Issues of European Integration* 65.

[67] Case 48/65 *Alfons Lütticke GmbH v Commission* [1966] ECR 19, Opinion of Advocate-General Gand at 31; Joined Cases 166/86, 220/86 *Irish Cement Limited v Commission* [1988] ECR 6473, Opinion of Advocate-General Darmon at para 38.

[68] [1988] ECR 5615 paras 14–17.

[69] [1988] ECR 4017.

not have been open to challenge by any applicant, under article 173 or 175.[70] The Court of Justice ensured that the Council's failure to act was subject to judicial review by holding that a refusal to act does not constitute a definition of position in relation to privileged applicants and, therefore, can be challenged under article 175.

Pleadings Where an applicant is uncertain whether the institution's response constitutes a definition of its position or not, it may be appropriate to bring proceedings under both articles 175 and 173 in the alternative.[71] An applicant will not be permitted to convert an action originally brought under article 175 to an action under article 173 during the course of proceedings.[72]

4. POSSIBLE DEFENCES

Objective difficulties The existence of objective difficulties for the institution required to act does not provide a defence. Under article 175 of the EEC Treaty, the Court of Justice must hold that there has been an infringement of the EEC Treaty if it finds that the Council or Commission has failed to act when under an obligation to do so. Article 175 takes no account of how difficult it may be for the institution to comply with the obligation.[73]

Direct applicability Where an institution is under an obligation to adopt detailed implementing rules, the fact that the measure which imposes that obligation is itself directly applicable, does not excuse the institution's failure to act.[74]

Absolute impossibility In Case 377/87 *European Parliament v Council*[75] Advocate-General Mischo considered that, where it was absolutely impossible for an institution to comply with its obligation to act, its failure to do so should not be regarded as an infringement of article 175.

---

[70] See the Opinion of Advocate-General Gulmann in Joined Cases C–15/91, C–108/91 *Josef Buckl & Söhne OHG and others v Commission*, judgment of 24 November 1992, paras 9, 14, 15 of the Opinion.

[71] For examples of this approach, see Case 48/65 *Alfons Lütticke GmbH v Commission* [1966] ECR 19; Case 15/70 *Chevalley v Commission* [1970] ECR 975. See also Joined Cases C–15/91, C–108/91 *Josef Buckl & Söhne OHG and others v Commission*, judgment of 24 November 1992, paras 32–34, which discusses the cost implications of such an approach.

[72] Case 125/78 *GEMA v Commission* [1979] ECR 3173 paras 24–26; Case T–28/90 *Asia Motor France SA v Commission* [1992] ECR II–2283, paras 43, 44.

[73] Case 13/83 *European Parliament v Council* [1985] ECR 1513 para 48. See also the detailed discussion of this issue by Advocate-General Lenz in this case at 1546–1549.

[74] Case 13/83 *European Parliament v Council* [1985] ECR 1513 paras 59–63. Articles 59 and 60 of the EEC Treaty (which are themselves directly applicable) required the Council to adopt detailed rules ensuring freedom to provide services in the transport sector.

[75] [1988] ECR 4017, Opinion of Advocate-General Mischo, paras 100–111.

5. ARTICLE 176: EFFECT OF JUDGMENT

Article 176   Article 176 of the EEC Treaty provides:

> The institution whose act has been declared void or whose failure to act has been de-clared contrary to this Treaty shall be required to take the necessary measures to comply with the judgment of the Court of Justice.
> This obligation shall not affect any obligation which may result from the applica-tion of the second paragraph of Article 215.

Therefore, although an order of the EC Courts under article 175 is in the form of a declaration, this gives rise to an obligation on the part of the institution concerned to take the necessary measures to comply with the judgment of the Court.[76] In Case 13/83 *European Parliament v Council*,[77] the Court of Justice held that, since article 176 does not prescribe a time limit for compliance, it must be inferred that the institution has a 'reasonable period' for that purpose. In addition, a judgment under article 176 can provide the basis for an action for damages against the relevant institution under article 215.[78] If the relevant insti-tution fails to fulfil its obligations under article 176, a further application may be made under article 175.[79]

---

[76] Case 377/87 *European Parliament v Council* [1988] ECR 4017 para 9; Case 383/87 *Commission v Council* [1988] ECR 4051 para 9. In Case 8/71 *Deutscher Kompanistenverband eV v Commission* [1971] ECR 705, Advocate-General Roemer (at 715) stated that, in practice, the result attained under article 176 could be equivalent to 'a direct order to the Commission to perform a specific action'.

[77] [1985] ECR 1513 para 69.

[78] Case 377/87 *European Parliament v Council* [1988] ECR 4017 para 9; Case 383/87 *Commission v Council* [1988] ECR 4061 para 9. See Ch 15.

[79] Joined Cases 97/86, 193/86, 99/86, 215/86 *Asteris AE and Greece v Commission* [1988] ECR 2181 paras 32, 33. It is interesting to note that, in this case, the Commission had expressly refused to act in compliance with the Greek Government's call to act, yet the Court of Justice held that this refusal should be declared void, to permit the Commission's failure to comply with a judgment to be enforced under article 175.

Chapter 15

Suing the Community in Damages

1. INTRODUCTION

(a) Contractual liability

Basis of liability Articles 181, 183 and 215, paragraph 1 of the EEC Treaty provide the basis of the contractual liability of the Community.

Article 181 provides:

> The Court of Justice shall have jurisdiction to give judgment pursuant to any arbitration clause contained in a contract concluded by or on behalf of the Community, whether that contract be governed by public or private law.

Article 183 provides:

> Save where jurisdiction is conferred on the Court of Justice by this Treaty, disputes to which the Community is a party shall not on that ground be excluded from the jurisdiction of the courts or tribunals of the Member States.

The first paragraph of article 215 provides:

> The contractual liability of the Community shall be governed by the law applicable to the contract in question.

Relevant court The Community may be sued for breach of contract (eg failing to pay a contractor for repairs done to a building occupied by the Commission) or sue for breach of contract (eg defective repairs on the part of the contractor) in the same way as any party to a contract. Article 183 provides that any action for breach of contract to which the Community is a party may be brought in the national courts of the Member States. Alternatively, article 181 allows the EC Courts to hear any contractual dispute provided that the contract gives the court jurisdiction. The reference to 'arbitration clause' in article 181 should be understood as a reference to 'jurisdiction clause'. Thus, in Case 23/76 *Luigi Pellegrini & C Sas v Commission*[1] a construction contract provided that 'the Court of Justice of the European Communities shall have jurisdiction to give judgment in disputes between the Commission and the contractor concerning this

---

[1] [1976] ECR 1807. See also Case 109/81 *Pace v Commission* [1982] ECR 2469; Case 23/81 *Commission v Sa Royale Belge* [1983] ECR 2685.

223

agreement.' Acting pursuant to article 168a of the EEC Treaty, the Council has transferred, to the Court of First Instance, the jurisdiction of the Court of Justice in contractual disputes (subject to a right of appeal on points of law to the Court of Justice) where the action is brought by a natural or legal person. Where the action is brought by the Community, it seems that the Court of Justice alone has jurisdiction under article 181.[2]

Applicable law Where the Court of Justice is called on to determine a contractual dispute, the Court applies the national law applicable to the contract (article 215, paragraph 1 of the EEC Treaty), there being no Community law of contract. The applicable law is often determined in a choice of law clause in the contract.[3]

(b) Staff cases

Basis for liability Articles 179 and 215, paragraph 3 of the EEC Treaty provide the basis of the Community's liability in staff disputes.

Article 179 provides:

> The Court of Justice shall have jurisdiction in any dispute between the Community and its servants within the limits and under the conditions laid down in the Staff Regulations or the Conditions of Employment.

Article 215, paragraph 3 provides:

> The personal liability of its servants towards the Community shall be governed by the provisions laid down in their Staff Regulations or in the Conditions of Employment applicable to them.

Staff Regulations Disputes between the Community and its servants are governed by Regulation 31,[4] which contains the Staff Regulations of Community officials and the conditions of employment of other servants. Under article 91 of the Staff Regulations, the Court of Justice has jurisdiction to award damages in disputes of a financial nature. In general, a Community employee should make a complaint to the Community institution and bring a claim for compensation within three months following rejection of the complaint. Disputes which originate in the relationship of employment between a Community institution and an employee should be brought under the Staff Regulations and not under article 215, paragraph 1 or 2 of the EEC Treaty.[5]

---

[2] Council Decision 88/591, OJ No L 319, 25 November 1988, p 1 (corrected text at OJ No C 215, 21 August 1989, p 1), as amended by Council Decision 93/350, OJ No L 144, 16 June 1993, p 21. The Court of First Instance only has jurisdiction in relation to actions brought under article 181 where the contract was concluded after 1 August 1993 (article 3 of Council Decision 93/350).

[3] For example, Case 318/81 *Commission v CODEMI* [1985] ECR 3693 (Belgian law applicable in a construction contract); *Luigi Pellegrini & C Sas v Commission* [1976] ECR 1807 (Italian law in a cleaning contract).

[4] Regulation 31 of 18 December 1961, as amended by Regulation 259/68, OJ No L 56, 3 March 1968, p 1 (Special Edition 1968, p 30). For the conditions of employment of Community officials and other servants, see *Halsbury's Laws*, 4th edn (Butterworths), vol 52, paras 1.105–1.117; for a commentary on staff disputes, see *Halsbury's Laws*, 4th edn (Butterworths), vol 52, paras 2.101–2.115.

[5] Case 9/75 *Martin Meyer-Burckhardt v Commission* [1975] ECR 1171; Case 48/76 *Reinarz v Commission* [1977] ECR 291.

Relevant court Acting pursuant to article 168a of the EEC Treaty, the Council transferred, to the Court of First Instance, the jurisdiction of the Court of Justice in staff cases (subject to a right of appeal on points of law to the Court of Justice).[6]

(c) Non-contractual liability

Basis for liability Articles 178 and 215, paragraph 2, of the EEC Treaty provide the basis of the Community's non-contractual liability, which may loosely be described as tortious liability.

Article 178 provides:

> The Court of Justice shall have jurisdiction in disputes relating to compensation for damage provided for in the second paragraph of Article 215.

Article 215, paragraph 2 provides:

> In the case of non-contractual liability, the Community shall, in accordance with the general principles common to the laws of the Member States, make good any damage caused by its institutions or by its servants in the performance of their duties.

Relevant court Acting pursuant to article 168a of the EEC Treaty, the Council has transferred, to the Court of First Instance, the jurisdiction of the Court of Justice in non-contractual disputes (subject to a right of appeal on points of law to the Court of Justice) where the action is brought by a natural or legal person.[7] Non-contractual liability of the Community is determined exclusively by the Court of First Instance and by the Court of Justice. Therefore, any action which is not of a contractual nature and which seeks to establish the liability of the Community in damages should not be brought in the national courts.[8]

Applicable law The applicable law is Community law, but, in applying Community law, the Court of Justice will have regard to the general principles common to the laws of the Member States. For example, the Court has drawn on principles common to certain Member States when reaching conclusions on interest,[9] mitigation,[10] liability for legislative acts,[11] remoteness,[12] assessment of damage,[13] assignment of the cause of action[14] and time bars.[15]

---

[6] Decision 88/591, OJ No L 319, 25 November 1988, p 1 (corrected text at OJ C 215, 21 August 1989, p 1), as amended by Council Decision 93/350, OJ No L 144, 16 June 1993, p 21.

[7] Decision 88/591 OJ No L 319, 25 November 1988, p 1 (corrected text at OJ No C 215, 21 August 1989, p 1), as amended by Council Decision 93/350 OJ No L 144, 16 June 1993, p 21 as amended by Council Decision 94/149 of 7 March 1994, OJ No L66, 10 March 1994, p 29.

[8] Case 101/78 *Granaria BV v Hoofdproduktschap voor Akkerbouwprodukten* [1979] ECR 623.

[9] Case 152/88 *Sofrimport v Commission* [1990] ECR I–2477; Joined Cases 256/80 and others *Birra Wührer v Council and Commission* [1984] ECR 3693.

[10] Joined Cases C–104/89, C–37/90, *Mulder v Council and Commission* judgment of 19 May 1992.

[11] Joined Cases 83/76, 94/76 and others *HNL v Council and Commission* [1978] ECR 1209.

[12] Joined Cases 64/76, 113/76 and others *Dumortier Frères v Council* [1979] ECR 3091 para 21.

[13] Case 261/78 *Interquell Stärke-Chemie v EEC* [1982] ECR 3271.

[14] Case 250/78 *DEKA v EC Community* [1983] ECR 421; Joined Cases 256/80 and others *Birra Wührer v Council and Commission* [1984] ECR 3693.

[15] Case 20/88 *Roquette Frères v Commission* [1989] ECR 1553.

The nature of the non-contractual liability of the Community is described below.

2. ADMISSIBILITY OF ACTIONS IN NON-CONTRACTUAL MATTERS

(a) Parties

Applicant Any natural or legal person, including a Member State, who has suffered damage may bring an action under article 215 of the EEC Treaty. The damage suffered must be personal to the applicant.[16] Where damage has been suffered by members of a trade union or trade association, only the members (and not the trade union or association) may bring the action for damages before the Court of Justice. Consequently, a co-operative cannot seek to enforce a collective right to compensation for damage to the financial interests of its members.[17]

Assignee A claim for damages may be assigned and enforced, by the assignee, against the Community.[18] However, the assignment must be made in good faith. In Case 250/78 *Deka v EC Community*[19] the Court of Justice held that an assignment of a claim for damages by an insolvent assignor was abusive and invalid on the basis that it was intended to prevent the Community from setting off, against the damages claim, a claim for a refund of sums wrongly paid to the assignor. When an applicant assigns his rights he ceases to be entitled to compensation and any claim for damages subsequently brought by him will be dismissed.[20]

Intervener Article 37, paragraph 2, of the Statute of the Court of Justice provides that the right to intervene is open to any person 'establishing an interest in the result of any case submitted to the Court'. The existence of such an interest must be assessed in the light of the purpose of the action which, in non-contractual disputes, is the payment of compensation. In Joined Cases 197/80 and others *Ludwigshafener Walzmühle v Council and Commission*[21] the Court rejected an application by a German trade union to intervene in an action for damages, since the purpose of the intervention was to ensure the economic well-being of the applicants and the continued employment of the employees. This did not constitute a specific interest in any payment of compensation.

---

[16] Case 353/88 *Briantex SAS v Commission* [1989] ECR 3623 para 6.
[17] Case 72/74 *Union Syndicale v Council* [1975] ECR 401 at 411; Case 114/83 *Société d'Initiatives et de Cooperation Agricoles v Commission* [1984] ECR 2589.
[18] Case 238/78 *Ireks Arkady v Council* [1979] ECR 2955 para 5; Case 133/79 *Sucrimex v Commission* [1980] ECR 1299.
[19] [1983] ECR 421.
[20] Joined Cases 256/80 and others *Birra Wührer v Council and Commission* [1984] ECR 3693.
[21] [1981] ECR 1041.

Defendant Although the liability is that of the Community, the proper defendant is the Community institution which is alleged to have caused the damage.[22] If an action arises from a regulation adopted by the Council of Ministers on a proposal from the Commission, an action may be brought against both institutions.[23] The reference to 'institutions' in article 215 should be understood as including not only the institutions of the Community listed in article 4 of the EEC Treaty (eg the Parliament, Council and Commission) but also Community institutions, such as the European Investment Bank.[24]

(b) Time limit for bringing an action

Five-year limitation period Article 43 of the Statute of the Court of Justice provides:

> Proceedings against the Community in matters arising from non-contractual liability shall be barred after a period of five years from the occurrence of the event giving rise thereto. The period of limitation shall be interrupted if proceedings are instituted before the Court or if prior to such proceedings an application is made by the aggrieved party to the relevant institution of the Community. In the latter event the proceedings must be instituted within the period of two months provided for in Article 173; the provisions of the second paragraph of Article 175 shall apply where appropriate.

Commencement of the limitation period The limitation period does not begin until all three conditions for liability are satisfied (ie unlawfulness, damage and causation).[25] Consequently, where the liability of the Community arises from a legislative measure, the limitation period only begins when the harmful effects are produced, not when the regulation is published.[26] Furthermore, time does not start to run where the applicant is unaware of the wrongful act and, thus, does not have a reasonable time to submit an application to the Court or to the relevant institution before the expiry of the limitation period.[27] The five-year period starts at the end of the day on which the conditions for liability are satisfied.

Expiry of the limitation period The limitation period expires at the end of the day which, in the month of the fifth year, bears the same number as the day on which time was set running. If the end of the period falls on a Sunday or on an official holiday, the time is extended until the end of the first following working day.[28] The time limit is extended by ten days in the case of the United Kingdom on account of distance.[29]

---

[22] Case 353/88 *Briantex SAS v Commission* [1989] ECR 3623.

[23] Joined Cases 63–69/72 *Werhahn v Council* [1973] ECR 1229 at 1247.

[24] Case C–370/91 *SGEM v EIB*, judgment of 2 December 1992.

[25] See p 231–237.

[26] Case 256/80, 5/81 *Birra Wührer v Council and Commission* [1982] ECR 85; Case 51/81 *De Franceschi SpA v Council and Commission* [1982] ECR 117.

[27] Case 145/83 *Stanley Adams v Commission* [1985] ECR 3539 para 50.

[28] ECJ Rules of Procedure, article 80 (see p 329), as interpreted in Case 152/85 *Misset v Council* [1987] ECR 223 and Case T–125/89 *Filtrona v Commission* [1990] ECR II 393.

[29] ECJ Rules of Procedure, article 81(2) and Annex II, article 1; CFI Rules of Procedure, article 102 (2). See pp 330, 390.

Suspension of the limitation period The limitation period is suspended if the aggrieved party first submits a claim to the defendant institution; in other words, time does not run while the Community decides whether or not to compensate the applicant. Therefore, if an applicant, for example, submits a claim for compensation to the Commission on 23 June 1982, the applicant can claim compensation for damage incurred after 23 June 1977, even though court proceedings are brought after 23 June 1982.[30] Importantly, article 43, paragraphs 2 and 3 of the Statute of the Court of Justice do not operate to shorten the five-year period so that it is not mandatory to bring an action for damages within two months after the rejection by the Community institution of the applicant's claim. The consequence of not bringing proceedings within the two-month time limit is that the limitation period continues to run throughout the settlement process with the Community institution.[31]

(c) Lack of jurisdiction

Declining jurisdiction The Court of Justice may decline jurisdiction in three situations:
  (1) where the true author of the decision alleged to have caused the decision is a Member State or a national authority;
  (2) where the applicant has not exhausted the national remedies to obtain compensation;
  (3) where the applicant is claiming the repayment of sums paid to a national authority.

Community not the author of the decision The EC Courts only have jurisdiction to award compensation for damage caused by the Community institutions or by their servants in the performance of their duties. Damage caused by Member States or by national authorities cannot give rise to liability on the part of the Community and national courts retain sole jurisdiction to order compensation for such damage. In Case C–72/90 *Asia Motor France v Commission*[32] the Court of Justice held that it had no jurisdiction to hear a claim brought under articles 178 and 215 of the EEC Treaty in respect of attempts by France to prevent the importation into France of Japanese motor cars.

Where the decision adversely affecting the applicant was adopted by a national body acting to implement Community rules, the EC Courts have jurisdiction under article 215 if the unlawful conduct can be attributed to a Community institution. This is so where the Commission dictates what action the national authority should take, so that the Commission is the true author of the national act. In contrast, where the national authority has a discretion to take action the Community will not incur liability for the unlawfulness of the national act. Two

---

[30] Joined Cases 256/80 and others *Birra Wührer v Council and Commission* [1984] ECR 3693 paras 20–23.
[31] Case 11/72 *Giordano v Commission* [1973] ECR 417 paras 5–7; Joined Cases 5/66, 7/66 and others *Kampffmeyer v Commission* [1967] ECR 245.
[32] [1990] ECR I–2181. See also Joined Cases 31/86, 35/86 *Levantina Agricole Industrial SA (LAISA) v Council* [1988] ECR 2285; Case 169/73 *Compagnie Continentale v Council* [1975] ECR 117 (effects of the Act of Accession not an act of the Council).

judgments of the Court of Justice illustrate this distinction: Case 133/79 *Sucrimex v Commission*[33] and Case 175/84 *Krohn v Commission.*[34]

In the first case, Sucrimex sold a quantity of sugar pursuant to export licences which fixed the rate of export refund. The licences were lost. The relevant authorities issued replacement licences and the sugar was exported under those licences. Sucrimex sought export refunds at the rate fixed in the original licences. However, the French authorities paid only the refund applicable on the day when the customs formalities were completed, which was lower than the refund which would have been payable at the fixed rate. The French authorities relied on an opinion given in a telex by the Commission that replacement licences could not be used to obtain refunds at a rate fixed in advance. Sucrimex's claim for compensation against the Commission was dismissed by the Court of Justice as inadmissible, on the basis that Sucrimex should have proceeded against the French authorities for their refusal to grant the disputed refunds. The Commission's opinion was not binding on the French authorities; therefore, it was not the Commission but the national authorities who were the authors of the decision to refuse the refunds.

In the second case, Krohn requested import licences from the German authorities to import a quantity of manioc from Thailand. Under the provisions of Regulation 2029/82 it was the task of the national authorities to issue the licences, except where they were informed by the Commission that the conditions for importation were not fulfilled. The Commission informed the German authorities by telex that the conditions were not fulfilled and the German authorities duly refused the import licences. The Court of Justice held the application for compensation under article 215 admissible on the basis that the regulation did:

> not merely confer upon the Commission the right to give an opinion on the decision to be adopted in the context of the cooperation between itself and the national bodies responsible for applying the Community rules, but actually empower it to insist that such national bodies refuse requests for import licences . . ..

It followed, therefore, that the unlawful conduct alleged by the applicant in order to establish its claim for compensation was to be attributed not to the German authorities, who were bound to comply with the Commission's instructions, but to the Commission itself.

Exhaustion of national remedies The action for damages under article 215 must be examined in the light of the whole system of legal protection for the individual, and the admissibility of such an action is dependent on the exhaustion of national remedies. This principle is particularly important within the framework of the Common Agricultural Policy, where national intervention agencies

---

[33] [1980] ECR 1299. See also Case 217/81 *Compagnie Interagra v Commission* [1982] ECR 2233; Joined Cases 89/86, 91/86 *L'étoile Commerciale and CNTA v Commission* [1987] ECR 3005 (national body ordering the applicant to repay subsidies as a result of the Commission refusing to recognise the subsidies as chargeable to the EAGGF).

[34] [1986] ECR 753 paras 21, 23. See also Case 59/83 *Biovilac v EEC* [1984] ECR 4057.

have an important role to play. In Case 12/79 *Wagner v Commission*,[35] where a national authority refused a request for the cancellation of an export licence pursuant to a Commission regulation, the action for damages against the Commission was inadmissible on the basis that the applicant should first have challenged the national authority's refusal in the domestic courts.

The national proceedings must, nevertheless, provide an effective means of protection for the individual concerned so that, where the national action does not afford the possibility of obtaining compensation for the loss suffered, an action against the Community will be admissible.[36] In Case 281/82 *Unifrex v Commission*[37] Unifrex, an exporter of cereals to Italy, claimed compensation from the Community on the basis that the French authorities had not paid to it the correct level of monetary compensatory amounts (MCAs) due under the applicable Community regulations. The Commission argued that the claim was inadmissible because the applicant had not challenged the amount of the MCAs in the national courts. The Court of Justice rejected this argument on the ground that such a challenge would not have effectively protected the applicant. It stated that:

> Even if the disputed Community rules were declared invalid by a preliminary ruling of the Court given in the context of such proceedings and the national decision were annulled, that annulment could not have required the national authorities to pay higher monetary compensatory amounts to the applicant, without the prior intervention of the Community legislature.

Consequently, an applicant need not incur expense in bringing fruitless proceedings in the national courts to prove that there is no effective remedy. Instead, the applicant may explain the national legal position in its application under article 215.

The requirement that an applicant must first exhaust national remedies has been relaxed by the Court of Justice in Joined Cases 106–120/87 *Asteris v Greece*,[38] where it was held that a national authority which had merely implemented a Community measure could not be responsible for its unlawfulness. Therefore, unless the applicant can obtain an effective remedy in the national courts on some other ground, an article 215 action is admissible.

Repayment of sums paid to a national authority A claim for the reimbursement of sums collected by national authorities for the Community must be brought in the national courts, even though the amount paid was fixed by the

---

[35] [1979] ECR 3657.
[36] Case 175/84 *Krohn v Commission* [1986] ECR 753 paras 27, 28.
[37] [1984] ECR 1969 para 12. Similarly, Case 126/76 *Dietz v Commission* [1977] ECR 2431. See also Case 81/86 *De Boer Buizen v Council and Commission* [1987] ECR 3677 para 10 (where the annulment, by a national court, of a refusal to grant a licence would not have had the effect of either giving the applicant the right to a licence or to compensation); Joined Cases 197–200/80 and others *Ludwigshafener Walzmühle v Council and Commission* [1981] ECR 3211 para 8 (recourse to national courts not open to applicants as manufacturers, only to importers who paid the levy alleged to be unlawful).
[38] [1988] ECR 5515 para 18.

Community. As the Court stated, in Case 99/74 *Grand Moulins v Commission*:[39]

> The refusal by a Community institution to pay a debt which may be owed by a Member State under Community law is not a matter involving the non-contractual liability of the Community.

The extent of reimbursement is, therefore, a matter for national law, insofar as no provisions of Community law are relevant.[40] By contrast, a claim for compensation for the abolition, by the Community, of production refunds which should have been paid by national authorities may be brought under article 215, since this is not a claim for repayment, but for payment.[41]

3. SUBSTANTIVE CONDITIONS OF NON-CONTRACTUAL LIABILITY

General conditions of liability In order to succeed in an action for damages the applicant must prove:[42]
(1) unlawful conduct on the part of the Community;
(2) damage; and
(3) causation.

Liability for legislative acts There are additional conditions which must be proved where the applicant is suing the Community for legislative acts involving choices of economic policy. These are:[43]
(1) there must be unlawfulness AND a sufficiently serious breach of a superior rule of law for the protection of the individual;
(2) the damage must go beyond the bounds of the economic risks inherent in the applicant's business;
(3) there must be overriding considerations of public interest which absolve the Community from liability.

---

[39] [1975] ECR 1531 para 16. See also Case 26/74 *Roquette Frères v Commission* [1976] ECR 677 para 11; Case 46/75 *IBC v Commission* [1976] ECR 65; Case 30/66 *Becher v Commission* [1967] ECR 285 at 298; Case 175/84 *Krohn v Commission* [1986] ECR 753 para 33.

[40] Limited rules have been laid down by the Community relating to the repayment of import and export duties. See pp 105–106.

[41] Joined Cases 64/76, 113/76 and others *Dumortier Frères v Council* [1979] ECR 3091 para 6; Joined Cases 261/78, 262/78 *Interquell Stärke-Chemie v EEC* [1979] ECR 3045 para 6. See also Case 281/84 *Zuckerfabrik v Council and Commission*[1987] ECR 49 para 12; Case 281/82 *Unifrex v Commission* [1984] ECR 1969.

[42] Case 4/69 *Lütticke v Commission* [1971] ECR 325 para 10; Case 59/84 *Tezi v Commission* [1986] ECR 887 para 70; Joined cases 326/86, 66/88 *Francesconi v Commission* [1989] ECR 2087 para 8; Case C–55/90 *Cato v Commission*, judgment of 8 April 1992, para 18.

[43] See p 237–241.

(a) General conditions of liability

(i) Unlawful conduct by the Community

Unlawful conduct The conduct must be unlawful or, as is sometimes stated, illegal or wrongful. Whether unlawful, illegal or wrongful, the conduct must be contrary to law, not merely unfair.[44] The most obvious way of proving unlawfulness is by challenging the Community provision under one of the heads of review listed in article 173 of the EEC Treaty, namely lack of competence, infringement of an essential procedural requirement, infringement of the EEC Treaty or of any rule of law relating to its application or misuse of powers.[45] However, liability for wrongful acts is not limited to these grounds of review. Liability may also arise in respect of the Commission's negligence. In Case C–330/88 *Grifoni v EAEC*[46] Mr Grifoni was contracted to carry out certain work on a meteorological station at the ISPRA research centre, run by the Commission. The Commission did not provide him with a safety harness, nor had it fitted a safety rail along the roof's edge, which was contrary to Italian law on industrial safety. Mr Grifoni fell and suffered serious injury. The Court of Justice held that the Commission was liable to him for the damage suffered, since the Commission had failed to show due diligence with regard to the requisite safety measures.

Independent cause of action Claims for damages often arise after the Court of Justice has annulled a Community provision under article 173 of the EEC Treaty, or has ruled that the provision is invalid under article 177. It is important to note, however, that the action for damages under article 215 is an independent remedy, that is to say, it is not necessary first to bring an action under article 173 to determine the unlawfulness of the Community act[47] or an action under article 175 to determine the unlawfulness of the Community's failure to act.[48] The action for damages differs, in particular, from an action for annulment, in that its purpose is not to set aside a specific measure, but to repair the damage caused by an institution. The autonomous nature of an article 215 action enables a plaintiff to challenge the lawfulness of a Community directive or regulation,

---

[44] For example Case 4/69 *Alfons Lütticke v Commission* [1971] ECR 325 (illegal); Case 56/75Rev *Elz v Commission* [1976] ECR 1097 (wrongful); Case 59/84 *Tezi v Commission* [1986] ECR 887 (unlawful).

[45] See pp 189–198.

[46] [1991] ECR I–1045 (the claim was brought under the EURATOM Treaty, article 188, which is equivalent to article 215 of the EEC Treaty). See also Joined Cases 169/83, 136/84 *Leussink v Commission* [1986] ECR 2801 (failure to exercise due diligence with regard to the maintenance of an official car).

[47] Case C–87/89 *SONITO v Commission* [1990] ECR I–1981; Case 175/84 *Krohn v Commission* [1986] ECR 753; Case 5/71 *Schöppenstedt v Council* [1971] ECR 975, overruling Case 25/62 *Plaumann v Commission* [1963] ECR 95, insofar as the Court there stated that it could: 'not by way of an action for compensation takes steps which would nullify the legal effects of a decision which . . . has not been annulled'. Note that in staff cases the Court does not entertain an action for damages which is, in effect, a dressed-up action for annulment brought out of time. See, for example, Case 106/80 *Fournier v Commission* [1981] ECR 2759 para 17 and, in particular, Advocate-General Sir Gordon Slynn at pp 2777–2780.

[48] Case 4/69 *Alfons Lutticke v Commission* [1971] ECR 325 at 336.

even though the directive or the regulation would not be of direct and individual concern to the plaintiff and could not, therefore, be challenged under article 173.

No fault liability No fault liability exists in some Member States and an application for compensation may be brought with respect to a lawful act of the administration provided that the applicant can show that he has suffered abnormal and severe loss as a result of the act—this is sometimes known under the German legal concept of *Sonderopfer* (special sacrifice) or under the French concept of *rupture de l'égalité devant les charges publiques* (unequal discharge of public burdens). The Court of Justice has not yet accepted the concept of the Community being liable without fault. On the other hand, the Court has not expressly rejected the concept, preferring to base its judgments on other grounds. [49]

Conduct by the Community Liability may arise by virtue of the adoption of any measure, whether by regulation,[50] directive,[51] decision[52] or resolution.[53] The Community cannot be liable for acts which have not been adopted by its institutions. Consequently, the publication of a pamphlet by a political group of the European Parliament on its own initiative was not regarded as an act of the Parliament capable of giving rise to a cause of action in damages.[54]

A failure to comply with an obligation may result in liability in damages. In Case 145/83 *Stanley Adams v Commission*[55] Mr Adams provided the Commission with information concerning a breach of the competition rules by his employer, Hoffman-La-Roche in Switzerland. The Court held that the Commission was under a duty to warn him that he was under investigation by the Swiss authorities and that a failure to fulfil that duty rendered the Community liable in damages. By contrast, it is unlikely that liability will arise for failure to act, unless the Community is under a duty to act. A failure to act on a complaint that an undertaking is in breach of the competition rules would not render the Commission liable in damages because it has a broad discretion whether or not to initiate an investigation.[56]

---

[49] Case 59/83 *Biovilac v EEC* [1984] ECR 4057 paras 27–29 (damage did not exceed limits of the economic risks inherent in the sector concerned); Case 26/81 *Oleifici Mediterranei v EEC* [1982] ECR 3057 para 26 (no causation) (see Advocate-General Verloren Van Themaat at 3089–3090); Joined Cases 9/71, 11/71 *Cie d'Approvisionnement v Commission* [1972] ECR 391 para 45 (measure of general economic interest).

[50] Joined Cases 64/76, 113/76 and others *Dumortier Frères v Council* [1979] ECR 3091.

[51] For example Case C–63/89 *Les Assurances du Crédit v Council and Commission* [1991] ECR I–1799.

[52] Case 30/66 *Becher v Commission* [1967] ECR 285.

[53] Case 169/73 *Compagnie Continentale v Council* [1975] ECR 117 (misleading information contained in a resolution).

[54] Case C–201/89 *Le Penn v Puhl* [1990] ECR 1183.

[55] [1985] ECR 3539. See also Case 289/83 *GAARM v Commission* [1984] ECR 4295 (alleged failure to adopt protective measures); Case 56/75Rev *Elz v Commission* [1976] ECR 1097 (failure to take necessary steps to notify addressee of decision).

[56] Case T–24/90 *Automec v Commission* [1992] 5 CMLR 431; Case 40/75 *Produits Bertrand v Commission* [1976] ECR 1 (failing to initiate a state aid investigation under article 93(2) of the EEC Treaty—the application was dismissed for lack of proof of causation).

Acts of servants Article 215, paragraph 2 of the EEC Treaty provides that the Community is liable to make good any damage caused by its servants in the performance of their duties. The Community is only liable for the acts of its servants which 'by virtue of an internal and direct relationship, are the necessary extension of the tasks entrusted to the institution.' In this respect the Court of Justice has held that a traffic accident caused by a Community civil servant in a private car in the course of his employment could not render the Community liable in damages.[57] The civil servant should be sued in the local national court.

(ii) Damage
Claim for damages The applicant must set out clearly, in the application, the nature of the damage suffered. A claim for damages at large, that is to say, an unspecified form of damages, will be regarded as inadmissible.[58] The fact that the amount of damages cannot be precisely quantified in the application will not render the claim inadmissible. A claim will be admitted where it sets out 'imminent damage foreseeable with sufficient certainty even if the damage cannot yet be precisely assessed'. In Joined Cases 56–60/74 *Kampffmeyer v Commission*[59] German meal producers claimed that a system of aid to durum wheat growers wrongfully put them at a disadvantage *vis-à-vis* their French competitors, the production of durum wheat being localised in France (durum wheat is ground into meal used to make pasta). They claimed damages for loss of profit which they would suffer in the future. The Court held that such a claim was admissible, stating that such loss was imminent and that the applicants could reserve the right to quantify the amount at a later stage, restricting themselves in the application to asking for a finding of the Community's liability. This possibility is important because it may be necessary to bring the matter before the Court as soon as the cause of damage is certain, in order to prevent even greater damage.

Proof of damage The Court of Justice has an unfettered discretion in assessing all the evidence submitted to it.[60] Thus, experts' reports, statistics, accounts and invoices have all been relied on to prove loss. The burden of proving the existence of damage rests with the applicant. 'Conclusive' proof must be adduced and the loss suffered must be particularised.[61]

Heads of damage The non-contractual liability of the Community is a broader concept than tortious liability applied in the English courts. As a result, the type of damage which may be claimed is wider and includes pure economic loss. Damages may be claimed for loss of earnings,[62] for penalties paid for repudi-

---

[57] Case 9/69 *Sayag v Leduc* [1969] ECR 329.
[58] Case 5/71 *Schöppenstedt v Council* [1971] ECR 984 para 9.
[59] [1976] ECR 711 para 8; Case 44/76 *Eier Kontor v Council and Commission* [1977] ECR 393 para 8; Case 281/84 *Zuckerfabrik v Council and Commission* [1987] ECR 49 para 14.
[60] Case 261/78 *Interquell Stärke-Chemie v EEC* [1982] ECR 3271 para 11.
[61] Case 74/74 *CNTA v Commission* [1976] ECR 797 paras 15, 16; Case 49/79 *Pool v Council* [1980] ECR 569 para 12; Case 253/84 *Groupement Agricole (GAEC) v Council and Commission* [1987] ECR 123 para 12.
[62] Joined Cases C–104/89, C–37/90 *Mulder v Council and Commission*, judgment of 19 May 1992.

ation of contracts,[63] for lost profit on concluded or foreseeable contracts[64] and for the wrongful abolition of production refunds.[65] Damages have also been awarded for personal injuries and for pain and suffering.[66]

Award of damages Where a claim is successful, the Court of Justice will make an interlocutory judgment, ordering the parties to agree on the damage suffered, with liberty to apply to the Court failing agreement. Where damages are expressed in ECU (the European Currency Unit), the relevant date for converting the ECU to national currencies is the date of the interlocutory judgment.[67]

(iii) Causation
Direct link Article 215 of the EEC Treaty does not impose an obligation on the Community to make good every harmful consequence of its unlawful conduct. The Court has held that the damage suffered must be a sufficiently direct consequence of the unlawful conduct. In Joined Cases 64/76, 113/76 and others *Dumortier Frères v Council*[68] some applicants claimed that the unlawful abolition of production refunds had forced them to close their factories. The Council argued that the factories had closed because of the obsolescence of the plant and managerial and other financial problems. The Court rejected the claim for compensation for the closures, stating:

> The data supplied by the parties on that question in the course of the proceedings are not such as to establish the true causes of the further damage alleged. However, it is sufficient to state that even if it were assumed that the abolition of the refunds exacerbated the difficulties encountered by those applicants, those difficulties would not be a sufficiently direct consequence of the unlawful conduct of the Council to render the Community liable to make good the damage.

A defective statement of reasons under article 190 of the EEC Treaty, which may result in the annulment of a Community provision, will not normally give rise to liability in damages under article 215 since there will be no direct causal link between the alleged damage and the statement of reasons.[69] Further, the Court will not award damages where this will unjustly enrich the applicant, ie where the applicant has passed on the loss to his customers or has raised his prices when production refunds have been abolished.[70] The insistence on a

---

[63] Joined Cases 5/66, 7/66 and others *Kampffmeyer v Commission* [1967] ECR 245 at 265.
[64] Ibid at pp 266, 267; Case 74/74 *CNTA v Commission* [1975] ECR 533; Case 152/88 *Sofrimport v Commission* [1990] ECR I–2477.
[65] Case 238/78 *Ireks Arkady v Council* [1979] ECR 2955 (interlocutory order); Joined Cases 241/78 and others *DGV v Council* [1979] ECR 3017 (interlocutory order); Joined Cases 261/78, 262/78 *Interquell Stärke-Chemie v Council and Commission* [1979] ECR 3045 (interlocutory order), [1982] ECR 3271 (award); Joined Cases 64/76, 113/76 and others *Dumortier Frères v Council* [1979] ECR 3091 (interlocutory order) [1982] ECR 1733 (award).
[66] Joined Cases 169/83, 136/84 *Leussink v Commission* [1986] ECR 2801; Case 145/83 *Stanley Adams v Commission* [1985] ECR 3539.
[67] Joined Cases 64/76, 113/76 and others *Dumortier Frères v Council* [1982] ECR 1733; Joined Cases 256/80 and others *Birra Wührer v Council and Commission* [1984] ECR 3693 para 34.
[68] [1979] ECR 3091 para 21. See also Case 153/73 *Holtz and Willemsen v Council* [1974] ECR 675 para 7; Joined Cases 71/84, 72/84 *Surcouf v Commission* [1985] ECR 2925 para 9.
[69] Case C–358/90R *Compagnia Italiana Alcool v Commission* [1992] 2 CMLR 876 para 47.
[70] Joined Cases 64/76, 113/76 *Dumortier Frères v Council*; Joined cases 256/80 and others *Birra*

close, causal link is one way of excluding from compensation damage which is considered too remote. Thus, the Court has awarded damages for loss of profit, but has reduced the amount by 90 per cent due to the speculative nature of the transactions.[71]

Contributory negligence The amount of damages may be reduced where the plaintiff has been contributorily negligent[72] or where the damage has been caused by the applicant's own conduct. In Joined Cases 241/78 and others *DGV v Council*[73] DGV and several other manufacturers of gritz successfully claimed compensation for the abolition of production refunds for gritz intended for the brewing of beer. However, the claim by one applicant was rejected on the basis that it had commenced production of maize gritz only after the Council's decision to abolish the refunds for gritz. The Court held that the loss suffered by the applicant was not caused by the Community, but by the applicant's own decision to enter that particular market.

In determining whether the applicant has been partially or exclusively responsible for the damages suffered, the Court applies a 'prudent person' test.[74] This introduces an element of foreseeability of loss, not on the part of the defendant institution, but on the part of the applicant. In Case 74/74 *CNTA v Commission*[75] the Court ordered that the applicant be compensated for loss suffered due to the immediate withdrawal of monetary compensatory amounts, since it was not foreseeable that the Community would re-expose a trader to an exchange risk as regards transactions irrevocably undertaken by it. The Court considered that 'a trader even a prudent one' might legitimately omit to cover himself against such a risk. By contrast, in Case 169/73 *Compagnie Continentale v Council*[76] the applicant claimed compensation for loss suffered due to the Council abandoning a system of fixed compensatory amounts in favour of a flexible system. The Court held that the chain of causation had been broken since a 'prudent exporter fully informed of the conditions of the market' would not have concluded that the monetary compensatory amounts would remain fixed.

Mitigation The injured party must act to mitigate any loss caused by the Community by showing reasonable diligence in limiting the extent of his loss. In Joined Cases C–104/89, C–37/90 *Mulder v Council and Commission*[77] the applicants had taken advantage of the Council's system of paying premiums for

---

Wührer v Council and Commission [1984] ECR 3693 paras 26 et seq (the burden of proving unjust enrichment lies on the defendant institution raising the issue).

[71] Joined cases 5/66, 7/66 and others *Kampffmeyer v Commission* [1967] ECR 245 at 266; Case 30/66 *Becher v Commission* [1967] ECR 285 at 300.

[72] Case 145/83 *Adams v Commission* [1985] ECR 3539; Case 308/87 *Grifoni v EAEC No 1* [1990] ECR I–1203.

[73] [1979] ECR 3017 para 19.

[74] Case 30/66 *Becher v Commission* [1967] ECR 285 at 299; Case 74/74 *CNTA v Commission* [1975] ECR 533 para 41; Case 169/73 *Compagnie Continentale v Council* [1975] ECR 117 para 23; Case 97/76 *Merkur v Commission* [1977] ECR 1063 para 9; Case 26/81 *Oleifici Mediterranei v EEC* [1982] ECR 3057 paras 22–24.

[75] [1976] ECR 797. The applicant could not eventually prove that it had suffered loss.

[76] [1975] ECR 117.

[77] Judgment of 19 May 1992.

the non-marketing of milk and had, accordingly, suspended production for a period of five years. After this period, the applicants were informed that they could not resume production as they had no reference year on which to base the quantity of milk they would be entitled to produce. The Court held that the Community had acted unlawfully and was liable to compensate the applicants for the loss suffered. The quantum of damages was based on the loss of earnings less any income from replacement activities. The Court stated that the replacement income included actual income and income which 'they could have obtained had they reasonably engaged in such activities'. Rather perversely, however, the Court further held that any losses incurred by the applicants in attempting to mitigate their loss would not be recoverable on the basis that there was no direct link betwen that loss and the unlawful Community rules.

(b) Liability in respect of legislative measures

Conditions for liability It is only exceptionally that the Community incurs liability for the adoption of legislative measures. As the Court stated in Joined Cases 83/76, 94/76 and others *HNL v Council and Commission*:[78]

> This restrictive view is explained by the consideration that the legislative authority, even where the validity of its measures is subject to judicial review, cannot always be hindered in making its decisions by the prospect of applications for damages whenever it has occasion to adopt legislative measures in the public interest which may adversely affect the interests of individuals.

Consequently, there are additional conditions which must be proved when the applicant is suing the Community for damage suffered as a result of the adoption of legislative acts involving choices of economic policy. The applicant must prove:

(1) unlawful conduct AND a sufficiently serious breach of a superior rule of law for the protection of the individual;
(2) that the unlawful conduct has caused damage AND that the damage goes beyond the bounds of the economic risks inherent in the applicant's business;
(3) that there is no overriding consideration of public interest which absolves the Community from liability.

(i) Sufficiently serious breach of a superior rule of law for the protection of the individual
Schöppenstedt principle The Community does not incur liability on account of a legislative measure which involves choices of economic policy unless a sufficiently serious breach of a superior rule of law for the protection of the individual has occurred. Consequently, mere unlawfulness is not sufficient to give rise to liability. The Court first laid down this principle in Case 5/71 *Schöppenstedt v Council*[79] and has consistently applied it in later cases.

---

[78] [1978] ECR 1209 para 5.
[79] [1971] ECR 975. See also Case 153/73 *Holtz and Willemsen v Council* [1974] ECR 675; Joined

238 REMEDIES IN EC COURTS FOR BREACH OF EC LAW

Choices of economic policy Legislation adopted within the framework of the Common Agricultural Policy will involve choices of economic policy, since the Community possesses a wide discretion to attain the objectives of the Common Agricultural Policy, particularly those listed in article 39 of the EEC Treaty.[80] Regulations imposing anti-dumping duties[81] and harmonising legislation in the insurance sector have also been held to involve choices of economic policy.[82]

Superior rule of law for the protection of the individual The expression 'rule of law' means that the rule is mandatory for the institutions to observe. However, it is not every breach of a mandatory rule of law which gives rise to liability; the rule of law must serve to protect individuals. The principles of discrimination,[83] legitimate expectation,[84] proportionality,[85] non-retroactivity[86] and free trade between Member States[87] are all examples of rules of law for the protection of the individual.

Sufficiently serious breach In order to show that there is a sufficiently serious breach, the applicant must prove that the Community has manifestly and gravely disregarded the limits on the exercise of its power. 'Grave disregard' implies conduct verging on the arbitrary. This requirement has proved extremely difficult to satisfy. In Case 143/77 *Koninklijke Scholten-Honig v Council and Commission*[88] the Court had found that a production levy on isoglucose was 'manifestly unequal' compared to the lower levy imposed on sugar. However, the claim for damages was dismissed on the basis that a higher production levy on isoglucose was justified in principle, as the Community was faced with an emergency situation characterised by a surplus of sugar due to the production of isoglucose. It was concluded that the error in the amount of the levy was not of such gravity that it could be said that the conduct of the Community had verged on the arbitrary.

Whether the Community has committed a sufficiently serious breach is a question of fact to be determined in each case. The following are material considerations:

(1) the nature of the breach;

(2) the category of persons affected;

Cases 261/78, 262/78 *Interquell Stärke-Chemie v Council and Commission* [1979] ECR 3045; Case 50/86 *Grands Moulins de Paris v Council and Commission* [1987] ECR 4833.

[80] Joined Cases 54–60/76 *Compagnie Industrielle du Comité de Loheac v Council and Commission* [1977] ECR 645 para 15.

[81] Case 122/86 *Epicheiriseon Metalleftikon v Council and Commmission (No 2)* [1989] ECR 3959.

[82] Case C–63/89 *Les Assurances du Crèdit v Council and Commission* [1991] ECR I–1799 (Directive 73/239 on non-life insurance).

[83] Joined Cases 64/76, 113/76 and others *Dumortier Frères v Council* [1979] ECR 3091 para 11.

[84] Joined Cases C–104/89, C–37/90 *Mulder v Council and Commission*; Case 152/88 *Sofrimport v Commission* [1990] ECR I–2477; Case 74/74 *CNTA v Commission* [1975] ECR 533.

[85] Case 281/84 *Zuckerfabrik v Council and Commission* [1987] ECR 49 para 35.

[86] Case 74/74 *CNTA v Commission* [1975] ECR 533 paras 28–32 (dismissed on the facts).

[87] Case 30/66 *Becher v Commission* [1967] ECR 285 at 297.

[88] [1979] ECR 3583; Joined Cases 116/77, 124/77 *Amylum & Tunnel Refineries v Council and Commission* [1979] ECR 3497; Joined Cases C–104/89, C–37/90 *Mulder v Council and Commission*, judgment of 19 May 1992 particularly concerning the 60 per cent rule.

(3) the extent of the damage;

(4) knowledge of the effects.

It is not every breach of a superior rule of law which incurs non-contractual liability of the Community. For example, a lack of reasoning may be sufficient to vitiate a Community measure but does not constitute a sufficiently serious breach of a superior rule of law for the protection of the individual.[89] Mere technical errors, which lead to *de facto* discrimination between producers of similar products, are unlikely to constitute a manifest breach verging on the arbitrary.[90]

A serious breach may occur where there has been a complete failure to have regard to the interests of certain traders. This is illustrated by Joined Cases C–104/89, C–37/90 *Mulder v Council and Commission*[91] where the applicants had taken advantage of the Council's system of paying premiums for the non-marketing of milk and had, accordingly, suspended production for a period of five years. After this period, the applicants were informed that they could not resume production since they had no reference year on which to base the quantity of milk they would be entitled to produce. In a preliminary ruling under article 177 of the EEC Treaty, the Court of Justice held that the Community system was unlawful on the ground that it was in breach of the principle of legitimate expectation, insofar as the system did not provide for the allocation of a reference quantity. Following that judgment, the Council adopted a regulation which provided for a special reference quantity for those dairy farmers who had been paid the premium for not producing milk. The special reference quantity was equal to 60 per cent of the quantity of milk delivered in the year prior to the start of the five-year period. This 60 per cent rule was also declared invalid by the Court in a subsequent preliminary ruling; the rule also infringed the principle of legitimate expectation, since the returning farmers were not treated similarly to existing farmers. In the damages action, the Court held that the complete failure to set any reference quantity constituted a manifest and grave disregard of the limits of the Community's discretionary powers. However, the Community was not held liable in damages for the 60 per cent rule. Although that rule had infringed a superior rule of law, the breach was not regarded as sufficiently serious since there had been some attempt to take account of the returning farmers' interests.

The category of persons affected constitutes a material factor in determining whether the breach is sufficiently serious. A failure to take account of a limited and clearly defined group makes the breach all the more obvious. Thus the Community was held liable in the following cases: in Joined Cases 64/76, 113/76 and others *Dumortier Frères v Council*[92] where the Council was found to have discriminated against the applicants who comprised the entire maize gritz industry of the Community; in Case C–152/88 *Sofrimport v Commission*[93]

---

[89] Case 106/81 *Julius Kind v EEC* [1982] ECR 2885 para 14; Case C–119/88 *AERPO v Commission* [1990] ECR I–2189.

[90] Case 20/88 *Roquette Frères v Commission* [1989] ECR 1553 para 26; Joined Cases 194–206/83 *Asteris v Commission* [1985] ECR 2815 para 23.

[91] Judgment of 19 May 92.

[92] [1979] ECR 3091.

[93] [1990] ECR I–2477.

where the limited and clearly defined group were importers who had goods in transit; in Joined Cases C–104/89, C–37/90 *Mulder v Council and Commission*[94] where the group were dairy producers who had been paid a premium to produce no milk; in Case 74/74 *CNTA v Commission*[95] where the category was traders who had irrevocably undertaken export transactions. However, damages were not awarded in Joined Cases 83/76, 94/76 and others *HNL v Council and Commission*[96] where the unlawful measure affected a very wide category of traders, namely all buyers of compound feeding-stuffs containing protein.

The greater the damage to the applicants, the more likely it is that a manifest breach will have occurred. In *Mulder v Council* the effect of the Community provision was to prevent the dairy producers who had been paid a premium to produce no milk from resuming the marketing of milk. Where the category of persons affected is wide, the effects on the individual undertakings are likely to be lessened. In *HNL v Council* the effect of the Community provision on the price of feeding stuffs as a factor in the production costs of the buyers was limited, since those costs only rose by about 2 per cent.

Where the defendant institution has been put on notice that a limited and clearly defined category of persons has been affected, but has not acted to rectify the situation, the Court is more likely to find that the institution has manifestly disregarded the limits upon its discretionary power. In Joined Cases 64/76, 113/76 and others *Dumortier Frères v Council*[97] the Council abolished, in March 1975, production refunds for gritz intended for the brewing of beer. A factor which persuaded the Court to award damages to the applicants, who were gritz producers, was that the Council had not acted upon a proposal made by the Commission in June 1975 to re-introduce the refunds.[98]

(ii) Damage beyond the bounds of inherent economic risks

Assumption of normal risks Commercial undertakings must accept that a loss of competitiveness or a loss of profit may result from the adoption of Community legislation. These risks form part of the economic risks inherent in the activities of a commercial undertaking, as does, for example, an increase in energy costs. In *HNL v Council* the Court stated that:[99]

> individuals may be required, in the sectors coming within the economic policy of the Community, to accept within reasonable limits certain harmful effects on their economic interests as a result of a legislative measure without being able to obtain compensation from public funds even if that measure has been declared null and void.

In this case the Court held that although a regulation had discriminated against the applicants and was unlawful, no compensation was payable *inter*

---

[94] Judgment of 19 May 1992.
[95] [1975] ECR 533.
[96] [1978] ECR 1209.
[97] [1979] ECR 3091.
[98] See also the Opinion of Advocate-General Tesauro in Case C–63/89 *Les Assurances du Crédit v Council and Commission* [1991] I–1799 at 1839.
[99] [1978] ECR 1209 paras 6, 7. See also Case 50/86 *Grands Moulins de Paris v Council and Commission* [1987] ECR 4833 para 21.

alia because the regulation resulted in a 2 per cent rise in production costs so that the effect on the profit-making capacity of the undertakings did not ultimately exceed the bounds of the economic risks inherent in the activities of the agricultural sector concerned.

Abnormal or unforeseeable damage An abnormal or unforeseeable degree of loss is likely to fall beyond the bounds of economic risks inherent in the sector concerned. In Case C–104/89 *Mulder v Council*[100] the Court held that preventing dairy producers, who had been paid a premium not to produce milk, from resuming the marketing of milk could not be regarded as foreseeable or as falling within the bounds of the normal economic risks inherent in producing milk. Likewise, in Case 152/88 *Sofrimport v Commission*[101] the Commission prevented the applicant from importing Chilean apples into the Community, even though the goods were in transit and a Council regulation required the Commission, when adopting protective measures, to take account of the special position of products in transit. The Court held that the damage suffered by the importer went beyond the limits of the economic risks inherent in the applicants' business, in that the very purpose of the Council regulation was precisely to limit damage to importers with goods in transit.

(iii) No overriding consideration of public interest
Overriding the interests of individuals The Court of Justice has stated that the Community will not be liable to pay compensation where there is an overriding consideration of public interest.[102] For example, where there are serious disturbances in the market or where the market is operating artificially, the Community may have to act in the interest of the Community as a whole, rather than in the individual interests of a specific group of traders. In Case 281/84 *Zuckerfabrik v Council and Commission*[103] the Court rejected a claim by German sugar manufacturers for compensation for loss suffered as a result of a change in monetary compensatory amounts. The change was considered necessary to instill some economic reality into the market which was characterised by artificial prices. It was not, therefore, in the general interest of the market as a whole to postpone the change 'in order to minimize the unfavourable consequences for certain traders'.

---

[100] [1992] ECR I–3061.
[101] [1990] ECR I–2477. See also Case 74/74 *CNTA v Commission* [1975] ECR 533; Joined Cases 64/76, 113/76 and others *Dumortier Frères v Council* [1979] ECR 3091.
[102] Case 74/74 *CNTA v Commission* [1975] ECR 533 para 43; Case 97/76 *Merkur v Commission* [1977] ECR 1063 para 5.
[103] [1987] ECR 49 para 38. See also Joined Cases 9/71, 11/71 *Cie d'Approvisionnement v Commission* [1972] ECR 391 para 46.

Chapter 16

Interim Relief—Articles 185 and 186 of the EEC Treaty

1. NATURE OF INTERIM RELIEF

Purpose The purpose of interim relief is:[1]

> to safeguard the interests of one of the parties to the proceedings in order to prevent the judgment in the main proceedings from being rendered illusory by being deprived of any practical effect.

Any interim relief granted must be provisional and cannot affect or prejudge the final decision of the Court in any way.[2]

(a) Suspending the operation of Community acts

Article 185 Article 185 of the EEC Treaty provides that:

> Actions brought before the Court of Justice shall not have suspensory effect. The Court of Justice may, however, if it considers that circumstances so require, order that application of the contested act be suspended.

Acts which may be suspended Article 185 may only be invoked to suspend the operation of a measure adopted by a Community institution. Only measures which are being specifically challenged in proceedings before the Court may be suspended under article 185.[3] An applicant may seek the suspension of only part of a measure, even if the validity of the whole measure is being challenged in the main action.[4]

---

[1] Case C–313/90R *Comité International de la Rayone et des Fibres Synthétiques v Commission* [1991] ECR I–2557 para 24. Applications for interim relief are identified by the case number of the main action with the suffix 'R'.

[2] Article 36 of the Statute of the Court of Justice; ECJ Rules of Procedure, article 86(4); CFI Rules of Procedure article 107(4). See pp 302, 332, 392. Joined Cases 60/81, 190/81R *International Business Machines Corporation v Commission* [1981] ECR 1857 para 4; Case 231/86R *Breda-Geomineraria v Commission* [1986] ECR 2639 para 18; Case 176/88R *Jack Hanning v European Parliament* [1988] ECR 3915 para 8; Case 321/88R *Jürgen Sparr v Commission* [1988] ECR 6405 para 9; Case 352/88R *Commission v Italy* [1989] ECR 267 para 22; Case 229/88R *Cargill BV v Commission* [1988] ECR 5183 para 14.

[3] ECJ Rules of Procedure, article 83(1); CFI Rules of Procedure, article 104(1). See pp 331, 391.

[4] For example, see Case 20/74R *Kali-Chemie AG v Commission* [1974] ECR 337; Case 27/76R *United Brands Company v Commission* [1976] ECR 425.

Parties who may apply Article 185 may only be invoked by an applicant who is challenging the particular Community measure in proceedings before the Court.[5] The right to seek suspension of a contested measure is granted to applicants for the purpose of protecting their own interests and they cannot rely on disadvantages to third parties in support of their applications.[6] Furthermore, the validity of the measure must be open to challenge by the particular applicant. Thus, where a private party seeks the suspension of a measure of general application which is clearly not of direct and individual concern to him, the Court will reject the application for interim measures.[7]

(b) Other interim relief

Article 186 Article 186 of the EEC Treaty provides that:

> The Court of Justice may in any cases before it prescribe any necessary interim measures.

Parties who may apply An application for interim measures under article 186 may be made by any party to a case before the Court. The measure sought must relate to the case before the Court.[8]

Suspending measures adopted by Member States In the context of proceedings against a Member State for breach of Community law under article 169 of the EEC Treaty, the Commission may make an application under article 186 seeking an interim order that the relevant national measures should be suspended, pending the final judgment of the Court.[9] Where the Court has already made a judgment against a Member State under article 169 and the Commission brings fresh proceedings for failure to comply with article 171, the Court will not grant interim measures where this would simply have the same effect as the original judgment.[10]

Nature of interim orders The Court has a wide discretion as to the nature of the interim measures which it may order under article 186. In some cases, it may simply order a party to take 'the measures necessary' to achieve a particular result.[11] In Case 293/85R *Commission v Belgium*,[12] the Commission sought the suspension of a Belgian law which required students, who were nationals of

---

[5] ECJ Rules of Procedure, article 83(1); CFI Rules of Procedure, article 104(1). See pp 331, 391.

[6] Case 269/84R *Corrado Fabbro v Commission* [1984] ECR 4333 paras 9, 10; Case 292/84R *Hartmut Scharf v Commission* [1984] ECR 4349 para 12.

[7] Case 82/87R *Autexpo SpA v Commission* [1987] ECR 2131 paras 13–16; Case 160/88R *Fédération européenne de la santé animale v Council* [1988] ECR 4121.

[8] ECJ Rules of Procedure, article 83(1); CFI Rules of Procedure, article 104(1). See pp 331, 391. Case 133/87R *Nashua Corporation v Commission* [1987] ECR 2883 para 7.

[9] For example, see Case 61/77R *Commission v Ireland* [1977] ECR 1411; Case 293/85R *Commission v Belgium* [1985] ECR 3521 para 24.

[10] Joined Cases 24/80, 97/80R *Commission v France* [1980] ECR 1319.

[11] Case 154/85R *Commission v Italy* [1985] ECR 1753 para 21.

[12] [1985] ECR 3521. In Case 318/81R *Commission v CODEMI SpA* [1982] ECR 1325 (EAEC) the Court ordered that a technical expert should be appointed to carry out certain tasks and that the Commission should pay the expert's costs.

other Member States to pay a supplementary enrolment fee (the *minerval*) to universities, which Belgian students were not required to pay. The Court of Justice ordered that students of other Member States should be entitled to enrol in Belgian universities without paying the *minerval*, but on condition that they gave a personal undertaking, in writing, to pay the *minerval* if the Belgian Government successfully defended the main action brought against it under article 169.

The Court also has power to order a party to take positive action. In Case 65/87R *Pfizer International Inc v Commission*,[13] the Court of Justice ordered the Commission to take certain steps to ensure that the additive Carbadox could be legally marketed in the Community.

An application for interim measures may be made against an institution which is not the defendant in the main action. For example, in Case 23/86R *United Kingdom v European Parliament*,[14] the United Kingdom brought proceedings under, *inter alia*, article 173 of the EEC Treaty, challenging the Parliament's final approval of the Community's 1986 budget. In the context of those proceedings, the United Kingdom successfully sought interim measures against the Commission in respect of its implementation of the budget.

2. CONDITIONS FOR GRANT OF INTERIM RELIEF

Conditions In order for the Court to grant interim relief, the applicant must show[15]:

(1) a *prima facie* case; and

(2) that such measures are necessary, as a matter of urgency, in order to prevent the occurrence of a situation likely to cause serious and irreparable damage to the party applying for their adoption.

Burden of proof It is for the applicant to provide adequate evidence that the conditions for the grant of interim relief are satisfied.[16]

***Prima facie* case** The applicant must show that he has a *prima facie* case in the main action, not simply in relation to the application for interim relief itself.[17] Thus, for example, where the main action is inadmissible, the application for interim relief may be dismissed.[18] The Court will, generally, refuse to examine the admissibility of the main application in the context of an application for interim

---

[13] [1987] ECR 1691.

[14] [1986] ECR 1085 paras 22–24.

[15] Joined Cases 60/81, 190/81R *International Business Machines Corporation v Commission* [1981] ECR 1857 para 4; Case 120/83R *VIO Raznoimport v Commission* [1983] ECR 2573 para 2; Case 97/85R *Union Deutsche Lebensmittelwerke GmbH v Commission* [1985] ECR 1331 para 17; Case 231/86R *Breda-Geomineraria v Commission* [1986] ECR 2639 para 16.

[16] Case 250/85R *Brother Industries Ltd v Council* [1985] ECR 3459 paras 15–18; Case C–356/90R *Belgium v Commission* [1991] ECR I–2423 para 23.

[17] Case 148/88R *Alessandro Albani v Commission* [1988] ECR 3361; Case 108/88R *Juan Jaenicke Cendoya v Commission* [1988] ECR 2585 para 21.

[18] Case 376/87R *Distrivet SA v Council* [1988] ECR 209; Case 160/88R *Fédération européenne de la santé animale v Council* [1988] ECR 4121.

relief.[19] However, if a party contends that the main action is manifestly inadmissible, the Court will consider whether the main application reveals *prima facie* grounds for concluding that there is a certain probability that it is admissible.[20]

Urgency The party seeking interim relief must furnish proof that he cannot wait until the conclusion of the main action without personally suffering damage which would have serious and irreparable effects for him.[21] Where the applicant has delayed before bringing the main action and the application for interim relief, the Court may be reluctant to find that the condition of urgency is satisfied.[22] However, in Case 23/87R *Mareile Aldinger v European Parliament*[23] the Court of Justice held that:

> ... urgency is not determined by the speed with which a measure is to be applied for and taken but by the extent to which a person may need to obtain the adoption of a measure which is necessary at the present time to avoid certain damage.

Serious and irreparable harm Except in exceptional circumstances, purely financial loss will not be regarded as irreparable where it could be remedied by financial compensation at a later date.[24] Financial loss may be considered serious and irreparable if it would threaten the very existence of the applicant;[25] where the damage, if it occurs, could not be quantified;[26] or where compensation could not restore the applicant to the position he was in prior to the occurrence of the damage.[27] Interim relief will not be granted where financial loss could be recouped by the applicant by bringing subsequent legal proceedings for compensation.[28]

The Court will not grant interim relief where the final judgment of the Court in relation to the main application is likely to be given before any serious harm

---

[19] Case 75/72R *Leitizia Perinciolo v Council* [1972] ECR 1201 para 7; Case 23/86R *United Kingdom v European Parliament* [1986] ECR 1085 para 21; Case 65/87R *Pfizer International Inc v Commission* [1987] ECR 1691 para 15.

[20] Case 118/83R *CMC Cooperativa Muratori e Cementisti v Commission* [1983] ECR 2583 para 37; Case 221/86R *Group of the European Right v European Parliament* [1986] ECR 2969 para 19; Case 82/87R *Autexpo SpA v Commission* [1987] ECR 2131 para 15; Case 160/88R *Fédération européenne de la santé animale v Council* [1988] ECR 4121 paras 22, 23; Case C–117/91R *Jean-Marc Bosman v Commission* [1991] ECR I–3353 para 7.

[21] Case 142/87R *Belgium v Commission* [1987] ECR 2589 para 23; Case C–356/90R *Belgium v Commission* [1991] ECR I–2423 para 23.

[22] Case C–57/89R *Commission v Germany* [1989] ECR 2849 paras 16–18.

[23] [1987] ECR 2841 paras 10–13.

[24] Case T–51/91R *Paul Edwin Hoyer v Commission* [1991] ECR II–679 para 19; Case C–213/91R *Abertal SAT Ltda v Commission* [1991] ECR I–5109 para 24.

[25] Case 310/85R *Deufil GmbH & Co KG v Commission* [1986] ECR 537 paras 23–25; Case 152/88R *Sofrimport Sàrl v Commission* [1988] ECR 2931 paras 31, 32; Cases C–51/90R, C–59/90R *Cosmos-Tank BV, Matex Nederland BV and Mobil Oil BV v Commission* [1990] ECR I–2167 para 24.

[26] Cases C–51/90R, C–59/90R *Cosmos-Tank BV, Matex Nederland BV and Mobil Oil BV v Commission* [1990] ECR I–2167 para 24.

[27] Case C–195/90R *Commission v Germany* [1990] ECR I–3351 para 38.

[28] Case 229/88R *Cargill BV v Commission* [1988] ECR 5183 paras 17, 18.

could occur.[29] Furthermore, the Court is reluctant to conclude that an applicant will suffer serious and irreparable harm where it is within the applicant's own power to ensure that no such harm occurs. In Case T–19/91R *Société d'Hygiène Dermatologique de Vichy v Commission*[30] the Court of First Instance refused to suspend a decision of the Commission to withdraw Vichy's immunity from fines pending the Commission's investigation of its revised distribution system under the Community competition rules. The Court held that the Commission's decision did not cause serious and irreparable harm because Vichy could put an end to the risk of being fined at any time by not pursuing its revised distribution system.

A Member State may rely on national interests, especially economic and social interests, in seeking interim relief, for example where there is a threat to employment levels or the cost of living.[31] However, a Member State may not rely on financial harm to national undertakings unless it can show that this would cause damage to the national economy as a whole.[32]

The Commission, as guardian of the EEC Treaty, may seek interim relief in order to prevent a flagrant breach of Community law.[33] In Case C–246/89R *Commission v United Kingdom*[34] the Commission obtained interim relief requiring the United Kingdom to suspend the application of certain provisions of the Merchant Shipping Act 1988, on the grounds that the provisions discriminated against EC nationals on the basis of their nationality. The Commission was concerned that certain Spanish fishermen would become insolvent as a result of the adoption of the Act, which prevented them from registering their ships in the United Kingdom.

The Court of Justice has indicated that it would be prepared to suspend Community acts where the immediate loss to the applicant (albeit of a provisional nature because it could be remedied after judgment) would be disproportionate to the interests of the institution in having its acts applied, even when they were being challenged before the Court.[35]

Balance of interests In certain cases, particularly where the grant or refusal of interim relief would have the practical effect of substantively deciding the action, the Court will balance the prejudice which one party will suffer if the relief is granted, against the prejudice which the other party will suffer if the relief is

---

[29] Case C–225/91R *Matra SA v Commission* [1991] ECR I–5823 paras 22–25.

[30] [1991] ECR II–265 paras 15–20.

[31] Case C–280/93R *Germany v Council* order of 29 June 1993 paras 22–28.

[32] Case 142/87R *Belgium v Commission* [1987] ECR 2589 para 24; Case 111/88R *Greece v Commission* [1988] ECR 2591 paras 13–19; Case 303/88R *Italy v Commission* [1989] ECR 801; Case C–32/89R *Greece v Commission* [1989] ECR 985 paras 16–18.

[33] Case C–272/91R *Commission v Italy* [1992] ECR I–457 paras 25–29.

[34] [1989] ECR 3125 paras 34–38, part of the '*Factortame*' litigation.

[35] Case 174/80R *Frans Reichardt v Commission* [1980] ECR 2665 para 1; Case 141/84R *Henri de Compte v European Parliament* [1984] ECR 2575 para 4; Case 44/88R *Henri de Compte v European Parliament* [1988] ECR 1669 para 31; Case 176/88R *Jack Hanning v European Parliament* [1988] ECR 3915 para 9.

denied.[36] For example, in Case C–272/91R *Commission v Italy*[37] (an application for interim relief by the Commission), the Court balanced the Commission's interest in preventing an infraction of Community law against the Italian State's interest in achieving a rapid automisation of the national lottery system. The Italian State argued that, if it was prevented from introducing the new system, illegal gambling would flourish and the State would suffer a substantial loss in revenue. The Court emphasised that, if it refused interim relief and the Commission was successful in the main action, the final judgment would be deprived of effect because it would not be possible to reverse the steps taken by the Italian State. Therefore, the Court found in favour of the Commission and ordered the Italian state to take 'all the necessary measures' to suspend the introduction of the new system.

In Case 45/87R *Commission v Ireland*,[38] the Court of Justice refused to grant the interim relief sought by the Commission, even though it had established a *prima facie* case that Ireland was in breach of EC public procurement legislation. The Court held that the risk of aggravating existing health and safety hazards if the award of the contract at issue was delayed outweighed the Commission's interest in ensuring the observance of Community law.

In Joined Cases 76/89, 77/89, 91/89R *Radio Telefis Eireann v Commission*,[39] the Court took into account whether the grant or refusal of interim relief would have the practical effect of substantively deciding the action because the resultant position could not be reversed.

Voluntary undertaking The Court will not grant interim relief where a party voluntarily undertakes to take the measures necessary to preserve the *status quo* pending the final resolution of the action.[40]

Anti-dumping cases Where an applicant is seeking to suspend the application of a definitive anti-dumping duty, it must adduce evidence showing that, firstly, the damage suffered by it as a result of the imposition of the duty is particular to it and, secondly, that the balance of interests is in its favour, in the sense that the

---

[36] Case 278/84R *Germany v Commission* [1984] ECR 4341 para 20; Case 293/85R *Commission v Belgium* [1985] ECR 3521 para 24; Case 194/88R *Commission v Italy* [1988] ECR 4547 para 16; Case C–358/90R *Compagnia italiana alcool Sas di Mario Mariano & Co v Commission* [1990] ECR I–4887 para 29; Case T–45/90R *Alicia Speybrouck v European Parliament* [1990] ECR II–705 para 36; Case T–24/92R, Case T–28/92R *Langnese-Iglo GmbH and Shöller Lebensmittel GmbH & Co KG v Commission* [1992] ECR II–1839 paras 26–30; Case T–29/92R *Vereniging van Samenwerkende Prijsregelende Organisaties in de Bouwnijverheid (SPO) v Commission* [1992] ECR II–2161 paras 37–39.

[37] [1992] ECR I–457 paras 25–29.

[38] [1987] ECR 1369 paras 32, 33.

[39] [1989] ECR 1141 para 15. See also Case C–246/89R *Commission v United Kingdom* [1989] ECR 3125 paras 39–42.

[40] Case 45/84R *European Independent Steelworks Association (EISA) v Commission* [1984] ECR 1759 paras 11–14; Case 64/86R *Giovanni Sergio v Commission* [1986] ECR 1081 para 9; Case 322/87R *Johann Frank v Court of Auditors* [1987] ECR 4375 para 19; Case C–40/92R *Commission v United Kingdom* [1992] ECR I–3389. See also Case C–385/89R *Greece v Commission* [1990] ECR I–561.

grant of the interim measures requested would not cause appreciable harm to the Community industry.[41]

3. PROCEDURE

Application An application for interim measures is made by lodging a separate document with the Registrar of the Court of Justice or the Court of First Instance, as appropriate, in accordance with the general rules for written applications.[42] The application must state:[43]

(a) the name and permanent address of the applicant;

(b) an address for service in Luxembourg and the name of the person authorised to accept service;[44]

(c) the identity of the defendant;

(d) the subject-matter of the proceedings, the circumstances giving rise to urgency and the pleas of fact and law establishing a *prima facie* case for the interim measures applied for;[45]

(e) the form of order sought by the applicant;

(f) where appropriate, the nature of any evidence offered in support;

(g) a claim for costs.

The following documents should be annexed to the application:[46]

(a) a file containing the documents relied on as evidence, together with a schedule listing them;

(b) a certificate establishing that the lawyer acting for the applicant is entitled to act before a court of a Member State;

(c) where the applicant is 'a legal person governed by private law', for example, a company:

  (i) proof of its existence in law (for an English company, copies of the memorandum and articles of association); and

  (ii) proof that the applicant's lawyer is properly authorised to act (for example, a resolution of the board of directors or a declaration sworn before a notary);[47]

(d) in applications under article 173, a copy of the act challenged;

(e) in applications under article 175, documentary evidence of the date on which the relevant institution was called upon to act;

(f) in applications under article 181 or 182, a copy of the relevant arbitration clause or special agreement.

---

[41] Case 77/87R *Technointorg v Council* [1987] ECR 1793 para 17.

[42] ECJ Rules of Procedure, article 83(3); CFI Rules of Procedure, art 104(3). See pp 331, 391.

[43] ECJ Rules of Procedure, article 38; CFI Rules of Procedure, article 44. See pp 318–319, 373–374.

[44] It is usual to instruct a lawyer in Luxembourg for this purpose.

[45] ECJ Rules of Procedure, article 83(2); CFI Rules of Procedure, article 104(2). See pp 331, 391.

[46] ECJ Rules of Procedure, articles 37, 38; CFI Rules of Procedure, articles 43, 44. Statute of the European Court of Justice, article 19. See pp 318–319, 372–374 and 300 respectively.

[47] A lawyer representing a natural person is not required to provide proof of his authority to act when lodging the application, but must be able to provide such proof if his authority to act is challenged. See Case 14/64 *Emilia Gualco v High Authority* [1965] ECR 51 at 57 (ECSC).

The original of every pleading must be signed by the party's agent or lawyer[48] and should be dated. The original, including annexes, should be lodged with the appropriate Registrar, together with five certified copies for the Court and a copy for every other party to the proceedings.[49]

It is possible to seek relief under both articles 185 and 186 in the same application. Applications for interim relief are allotted the case number of the main application with the suffix 'R'. The application is served on the other party, and the President then prescribes a short period within which that party may submit written or oral observations.[50] Although the President has power to order a preparatory inquiry, this is rarely done.[51]

Decision The President may decide the application himself or refer it to the Court.[52] In appropriate cases, for example, where there is extreme urgency, the President may grant the application even before the observations of the opposite party have been submitted. Such a decision may be varied or cancelled without any application being made by any party.[53] Unless the decision specifies a date on which the order is to lapse, the order will lapse only when final judgment is delivered.[54] A party may apply, at any time, for an order to be varied or cancelled on account of a change in circumstances.[55] Where an application for interim measures is rejected, the party who made it is not precluded from making a further application on the basis of new facts.[56]

Costs The question of costs will normally be reserved until the final judgment. Any interlocutory application or response should contain a separate claim for costs in the written pleadings. Failure to do so will mean that the Court will be obliged to award all of the costs to the successful party in the final judgment, without taking separate account of the outcome of any interlocutory applications.[57]

Security The granting of interim measures may be made conditional on the lodging of security by the applicant.[58] Generally, an applicant will only be ordered to provide security where it would be liable for the sums which the security is intended to cover and there is a risk of that party being insolvent.[59]

---

[48] The application should also give a description of the signatory (Statute of the Court of Justice, article 19), for example, 'barrister'.

[49] ECJ Rules of Procedure, article 37; CFI Rules of Procedure, article 43. See pp 318, 372–373.

[50] ECJ Rules of Procedure, article 84(1); CFI Rules of Procedure, article 105(1). See pp 331, 391.

[51] ECJ Rules of Procedure, article 84(2); CFI Rules of Procedure, article 105(2). See pp 331, 391.

[52] ECJ Rules of Procedure, article 85; CFI Rules of Procedure, article 106. See pp 331, 391.

[53] ECJ Rules of Procedure, article 84(2); CFI Rules of Procedure, article 105(2). See pp 331, 391. Case 45/87R *Commission v Ireland* [1987] ECR 783; Case C–195/90R *Commission v Germany* [1990] ECR I–2715.

[54] ECJ Rules of Procedure, article 86(3); CFI Rules of Procedure, article 107(3). See pp 331, 392.

[55] ECJ Rules of Procedure, article 87; CFI Rules of Procedure, article 108. See pp 332, 392. Case C–272/91R *Commission v Italy* [1992] ECR I–3929.

[56] ECJ Rules of Procedure, article 88; CFI Rules of Procedure, article 109. See pp 332, 392.

[57] Case T–50/89 *Jürgen Sparr v Commission* [1990] ECR II–539 para 9.

[58] ECJ Rules of Procedure, article 86(2); CFI Rules of Procedure, article 107(2). See pp 331, 392.

[59] Case C–195/90R *Commission v Germany* [1990] ECR I–3351 paras 48–50. See also Case 160/84R *Oryzomyli Kavallas OEE v Commission* [1984] ECR 3217, including para 14 of the

However, where the measure being challenged is a decision imposing a fine, the Court will require the applicant to provide a bank guarantee in the amount of the fine as security pending resolution of the main action, unless the applicant can demonstrate that exceptional circumstances exist.[60] Exceptional circumstances will exist where the requirement to provide a bank guarantee would, in itself, cause the applicant serious and irreparable damage.[61]

Appeals No appeal lies from a decision of the Court of Justice. However, parties may appeal to the Court of Justice against any judgment of the Court of First Instance concerning interim measures, within two months of the notification of the judgment to them.[62] Appeals in respect of applications for interim relief do not follow the normal appeal procedure but, instead, follow the procedure adopted by the Court of Justice when applications for interim relief are made to it directly in cases pending before it.[63]

4. POWERS OF THE COMMISSION

Powers of the Commission The Commission has the power to adopt interim measures in relation to competition matters.[64] Interim measures may be adopted where there is a *prima facie* breach of the competition rules and where interim measures are required, as a matter of urgency, in order to avoid a situation likely to cause serious and irreparable damage to the party seeking their adoption, or which is intolerable in the public interest. The measures adopted must be of a temporary nature, designed to preserve the *status quo*, and restricted to what is necessary to ensure that the Commission's final decision is not deprived of any practical effect. Therefore, interim measures must not go beyond what can be ordered in the final decision. When adopting interim measures the Commission must respect the essential safeguards accorded to parties under Regulation 17/62,[65] in particular, the right to be heard. Finally, the decisions granting or refusing interim measures must be made in such a form as to be amenable to review by the EC Courts.[66] The EC Courts will not entertain applications for

---

report for the hearing.

[60] Case 107/82R *Allgemeine Elektricitäts-gesellschaft AEG-Telefunken AG v Commission* [1982] ECR 1549 (competition case); Case 86/82R *Hasselblad (GB) Limited v Commission* [1982] ECR 1555 (competition case); Case 263/82R *Klöckner-Werke AG v Commission* [1982] ECR 3995 (ECSC); Case 392/85R *Finisider v Commission* [1986] ECR 959 paras 12–19 (ECSC); Case 213/86R *Montedipe SpA v Commission* [1986] ECR 2623 (competition case).

[61] Case 234/82R *Ferriere di Roè Volciano SpA v Commission* [1983] ECR 725 (ECSC). *Cf* Case 392/85R *Finisider v Commission* [1986] ECR 959 paras 14–19 (ECSC).

[62] Statute of the Court of Justice, article 50. See p 305.

[63] Statute of the Court of Justice, article 50 (see p 305). As described at pp 248–250.

[64] See Bellamy and Child, *The Common Market Law of Competition*, 4th edn (Sweet & Maxwell, 1993), 740–743; Kerse, *EEC Antitrust Procedure*, 2nd edn (European Law Centre, 1988), 155–162.

[65] Council Regulation 17/62 of 6 February 1962, First Regulation implementing articles 85, 86 of the EEC Treaty, OJ No 13, 21 February 1962, p 204 (English Special Edition 1959–1962, p 87) (as amended).

[66] Case 792/79R *Camera Care Limited v Commission* [1980] ECR 119 paras 18–20; Joined Cases 228/82, 229/82 *Ford of Europe Incorporated v Commission* [1984] ECR 1129; Case T–23/90

interim relief which the Commission has primary jurisdiction to deal with. In such cases, the Courts will restrict themselves to judicial review of any decisions adopted by the Commission.[67]

Automobiles Peugeot SA v Commission [1991] ECR II–653; Case T–44/90 *La Cinq SA v Commission* [1992] ECR II–1.

[67] Case 792/79R *Camera Care Limited v Commission* [1980] ECR 119 paras 20, 21; Case T–23/90 *Automobiles Peugeot SA v Commission* [1990] ECR II–195. See also Case 109/75R *National Carbonising Company Limited v Commission* [1975] ECR 1193.

Chapter 17

Procedure Before the EC Courts

1. THE COURT OF JUSTICE AND THE COURT OF FIRST INSTANCE

Role of the Court Article 164 of the EEC Treaty provides that:

> The Court of Justice shall ensure that in the interpretation and application of this Treaty the law is observed.

Procedural rules The composition, organisation and procedure of the EC Courts are governed by the Statute of the Court of Justice[1] and by the Rules of Procedure of the Court of Justice[2] and of the Court of First Instance.[3] The Rules of Procedure are substantially the same for both Courts.

Court of Justice The Court of Justice consists of thirteen Judges and six Advocates-General. The Court of Justice may sit in plenary session or in chambers of three or five judges.[4] Only one Advocate-General will act in each case.[5] The function of the Advocate-General is to present reasoned submissions to the Court in the form of an Opinion, in order to assist the Court in reaching its judgment.[6] The Opinion is not binding in any way on the Court. However, the Court will often follow the approach of the Advocate-General.

Court of First Instance In view of the increasing workload of the Court of Justice, the Single European Act empowered the Council to create a Court of

---

[1] Protocol on the Statute of the Court of Justice of the European Economic Community, signed at Brussels on 17 April 1957, as amended by Council Decision 88/591 of 24 October 1988, OJ No C 215, 21 August 1989, p 1 and Council Decision 93/350 of 8 June 1993, OJ No L 144, 16 June 1993, p 21. The Statute of the Court of Justice is reproduced in Appendix B at pp 297–306.

[2] Rules of Procedure of the Court of Justice of the European Communities of 19 June 1991, OJ No L 176, 4 July 1991, p 7. Reproduced in Appendix C, pp 307–357.

[3] Rules of Procedure of the Court of First Instance of the European Communities of 2 May 1991, OJ No L 136, 30 May 1991, p 1. Reproduced in Appendix D, pp 359–399.

[4] Article 165 of the EEC Treaty. The rules established by article 165 as to when the Court must sit in plenary session will be replaced under the terms of the Treaty on European Union ('the Maastricht Treaty').

[5] Where the Court of Justice is requested to give an Opinion under article 228 of the EEC Treaty, all six Advocates-General will deliver Opinions. See ECJ Rules of Procedure, art 108(2), p 339.

[6] Article 166 of the EEC Treaty.

First Instance attached to the Court of Justice.[7] The Court of First Instance has twelve judges. There are no permanent Advocates-General, although one of the judges may be called upon to perform the task of Advocate-General in a particular case. The Court of First Instance usually sits in chambers of three or five judges, although it may sit in plenary session.[8] Decisions of the Court of First Instance are subject to appeals to the Court of Justice.[9]

President of the Court The judges of each Court elect a President from their number, who is responsible for the overall administration of that Court.[10]

Jurisdiction The Court of First Instance is not competent to hear actions brought by Member States or Community institutions or questions referred for a preliminary ruling under article 177.[11] The Court of First Instance has jurisdiction to hear the following cases under the EEC Treaty:[12]
  (1) staff cases under article 179;
  (2) actions by natural or legal persons under articles 173, 175, 178, 181.[13]

Where the Court of First Instance is seised of a matter in which it has no jurisdiction, it must transfer the matter to the Court of Justice if that Court does have jurisdiction.[14] Where an action which is within the jurisdiction of the Court of First Instance is brought before the Court of Justice, the Court of Justice must refer that action to the Court of First Instance.[15]

Where the Court of Justice and the Court of First Instance are seised of cases in which the same relief is sought, or the same issue of interpretation is raised, or the validity of the same act is challenged, the Court of First Instance may, after hearing the parties, stay the proceedings before it until the Court of Justice has delivered judgment. Equally, the Court of Justice is entitled to stay the proceedings before it to allow the proceedings before the Court of First Instance to con-

---

[7] Article 168a of the EEC Treaty, added by article 11 of the Single European Act. The Court of First Instance was established by Council Decision 88/591 of 24 October 1988, OJ No C 215, 21 August 1989, p 1. The President of the Court of Justice issued a decision dated 11 October 1989, declaring that the Court of First Instance had been duly established, OJ No L 317, 31 October 1989, p 48.

[8] Article 2 of Council Decision 88/591 of 24 October 1988, OJ No C 215, 21 August 1989, p 1; CFI Rules of Procedure, articles 10–19. See pp 311–313.

[9] See pp 269–273.

[10] ECJ Rules of Procedure, articles 7, 8; CFI Rules of Procedure, articles 7, 8. See pp 310–311, 363.

[11] Article 168a of the EEC Treaty. Article 168a is to be replaced under the terms of the Treaty on European Union (the 'Maastricht Treaty'), so that the Council will have power to give the Court of First Instance jurisdiction over actions brought by Member States and Community institutions.

[12] Article 3 of Council Decision 88/591 of 24 October 1988, OJ No C 215, 21 August 1989, p 1; as substituted by Council Decision 93/350 of 8 June 1993, OJ No L 144, 16 June 1993, p 21 as amended by Council Decision 94/149 of 7 March 1994, OJ No L66, 10 March 1994, p 29.

[13] The Court of First Instance only has jurisdiction in relation to actions brought under article 181 where the contract was concluded after 1 August 1993. See article 3 of Council Decision 93/350 of 8 June 1993, OJ No L 144, 16 June 1993, p 21.

[14] Statute of the Court of Justice, article 47. CFI Rules of Procedure, article 112. See pp 304, 393. See Case C–72/90 *Asia Motor France v Commission* [1990] ECR I–2181 paras 16–21.

[15] Statute of the Court of Justice, article 47 (p 304). See Case C–66/90 *Koninklijke PTT Nederland NV and PTT Post BV v Commission* [1991] ECR I–2723.

tinue. Where the validity of the same act is challenged before both Courts, the Court of First Instance may also choose to decline jurisdiction to allow the Court of Justice to rule on the matter.[16]

Lis pendens/res judicata   Where the parties, subject-matter and submissions in two actions are the same, the second action will be declared inadmissible.[17] The Court may raise the issue of *lis pendens* of its own motion.[18] The Court of Justice has also recognised and relied on the principle of *res judicata*.[19]

2. PROCEDURE IN DIRECT ACTIONS[20]

(a) General rules

Direct actions   Direct actions are actions which may be brought directly before the EC Courts, for example, actions against Member States under article 169, actions for annulment under article 173, actions for failure to act under article 175 and actions for damages under article 215. Indirect actions are references for preliminary rulings, mainly under article 177, so-called because they stem from proceedings already before the national courts.

Rights of audience   Private parties must be represented by a lawyer entitled to practise before a court of a Member State. The Member States and the Community institutions are represented by agents appointed for each case.[21]

Language   The pleadings must be in the language of the case, as defined by the Rules of Procedure. Generally, the applicant may choose the language of the case. However, in the Court of Justice, where the defendant is a Member State or a national of a Member State, the language of the case is *prima facie* the official language of that State. A Member State which intervenes in a case is entitled to use its own official language, in both the written and oral procedure. Any supporting documents expressed in another language must be accompanied by a translation into the language of the case. In the case of lengthy documents, translations may be limited to extracts.[22]

---

[16]   Statute of the Court of Justice, article 47. ECJ Rules of Procedure, article 82a; CFI Rules of Procedure, articles 77–80. See pp 304, 330, 383–384. Case T–42/91 *Koninklijke PTT Nederland NV and PTT Post BV v Commission* [1991] ECR II–273.

[17]   For example, see Joined Cases 358/85, 51/86 *France v European Parliament* [1988] ECR 4821 paras 6–12.

[18]   Joined Cases 58/72, 75/72 *Letizia Perinciolo v Council* [1973] ECR 511 para 5.

[19]   Joined Cases 79/63, 82/63 *Jean Reynier and Piero Erba v Commission* [1964] ECR 259 at 266; Case 57/70 *August Josef van Eick v Commission* [1971] ECR 613; Joined Cases 159/84, 267/84, 12/85, 264/85 *Alan Ainsworth v Commission* [1987] ECR 1579; C–281/89 *Italy v Commission* [1991] ECR I–347 paras 12–16.

[20]   For a comprehensive review of procedure before the Court of Justice, see KPE Lasok, *The European Court of Justice, Practice and Procedure*, 2nd edn (Butterworths, 1993).

[21]   Statute of the Court of Justice, article 17. See pp 299–300.

Lodging with the Court The original of all applications, of whatever nature, should be signed by the party's agent or lawyer[23] and should be dated. The original, including annexes, should be lodged with the appropriate Registrar, together with five certified copies for the Court and a copy for every other party to the proceedings.[24] Applications, of whatever nature, should be addressed to the Registrar of the Court of Justice or the Court of First Instance, as appropriate.[25]

Costs All applications, of whatever nature, should include a claim for costs. Failure to claim costs will mean that a party will have to bear his own costs, even if his application is successful.[26]

Four stage procedure The procedure before the Courts in divided into four main parts:
  (1) the written procedure;
  (2) preparatory inquiries;
  (3) the oral procedure; and
  (4) judgment.

(b) Written procedure

Bringing an action[27] An action is commenced by lodging a written application with the Registrar of the Court of Justice or the Court of First Instance, as appropriate.[28]

Notice of the application is published in the *Official Journal*.[29]

Contents of application The application must state:[30]
  (1) the name and permanent address of the applicant;
  (2) an address for service in Luxembourg and the name of the person authorised to accept service;[31]
  (3) the identity of the defendant;
  (4) the subject-matter of the proceedings and a summary of the pleas in law on which the application is based;
  (5) the form of order sought by the applicant;
  (6) where appropriate, the nature of any evidence offered in support.

---

[22] ECJ Rules of Procedure, articles 29–31; CFI Rules of Procedures, articles 35–37. See pp 315–316, 370–371.

[23] The application should also give a description of the signatory (Statute of the Court of Justice, article 19—see p 300), for example 'barrister'.

[24] ECJ Rules of Procedure, article 37; CFI Rules of Procedure, article 43. See pp 318, 372–373.

[25] Addresses: Registrar, Court of Justice of the European Communities, L–2925 Luxembourg; Registrar, Court of First Instance of the European Communities, L–2925 Luxembourg.

[26] ECJ Rules of Procedure, article 69(2); CFI Rules of Procedure, article 87(2). See pp 326, 386. Case T–50/89 *Jürgen Sparr v Commission* [1990] ECR II–539 para 9 (interlocutory applications).

[27] See *Lodging with the Court*, above.

[28] Statute of the Court of Justice, article 19. See p 300. For addresses, see fn 25 above.

[29] ECJ Rules of Procedure, article 16(6); CFI Rules of Procedure, article 24(6). See pp 312–313, 367.

[30] ECJ Rules of Procedure, article 38; CFI Rules of Procedure, article 44. See pp 318–319, 373–374.

[31] It is usual to instruct a lawyer in Luxembourg for this purpose.

Co-defendants   An application may be made against co-defendants.[32] However, a new defendant cannot be joined to the original application once proceedings have commenced. In Case 90/77 *Hellmut Stimming KG v Commission*,[33]
the applicant brought an action for damages against the Commission and, in its
reply, sought to join the Council as a co-defendant. This attempt was rejected by
the Court of Justice, which emphasised that the Rules of Procedure do not allow
such an alteration in the person of the defendant.

Pleas of fact and law   The applicant should ensure that he sets out his case fully
in the application. The Court will not allow later amendments, even in the reply,
which seek to extend the subject-matter of the proceedings as defined in the application.[34] In order to be admissible, the pleading must not be, 'such as to prevent the [defendant] from effectively defending its interests or to hinder the
Court in the exercise of its judicial review'.[35] The applicant must set out the
facts and law relied on in support of his claim and must present his conclusions
in an unequivocal manner.[36] It is not sufficient to refer to the submissions made
in another, related, case.[37] Nor is it sufficient, in proceedings under article 169
of the EEC Treaty, simply to refer to the grounds of complaint set out in the initial letter and reasoned opinion.[38]

Costs/interest   The application should also include a claim for costs. Failure to
claim costs will mean that the applicant will have to bear his own costs, even if
his application is successful.[39] In the context of monetary claims, the application should include a claim for interest which specifies the rate of interest
claimed. The Court may reduce the interest claimed, but not award interest
at a rate higher than that claimed. In past cases, the Court has awarded interest at
between six and eight per cent.[40]

---

[32] For example, see Case 264/82 *Timex Corporation v Council and Commission* [1985] ECR 849.
[33] [1977] ECR 2113. Compare Case 294/83 *Parti écologiste 'Les Verts' v European Parliament*
[1986] ECR 1339 paras 1–18, where the applicant merged with other associations to form a new
body, which was allowed to continue the original action.
[34] Case 191/84 *Jean-Pierre Barcella v Commission* [1986] ECR 1541 paras 5, 6; Case T 41/89
Georg Schwedler v European Parliament [1990] ECR II–79 para 34.
[35] Case 74/74 *CNTA v Commission* [1975] ECR 533 paras 2–6; Case T–18/90 *Egidius Jongen v
Commission* [1991] ECR II–187 para 13.
[36] Joined Cases 46/59, 47/59 *Meroni v High Authority* [1962] ECR 411 at 419 (ECSC); Case
C–52/90 *Commission v Denmark* [1992] ECR I–2187. *Cf* Case T–21/90 *Günter Generlich v
Commission* [1991] ECR II–1323 paras 32, 33 where the Court of First Instance adopted a less
strict approach. Also Case T–18/90 *Egidius Jongen v Commission* [1991] ECR II–187 para 13
where the failure to explicitly refer to the relevant legal act in the application did not render the
application inadmissible.
[37] Joined Cases 19/63, 65/63 *Satya Prakash v Commission* [1965] ECR 533 at 546 (EAEC).
[38] Case C–347/88 *Commission v Greece* [1990] ECR I–4747 paras 26–30; Case C–43/90
Commission v Germany [1992] ECR I–1909 paras 5–9.
[39] ECJ Rules of Procedure, article 69(2); CFI Rules of Procedure, article 87(2). See pp 326, 386.
[40] For example, see Case 261/78 *Interquell Stärke-Chemie GmbH & Co KG v European Economic
Community* [1982] ECR 3271; Joined Cases 64/76, 113/76, 167/78, 239/78, 27/79, 28/79, 45/79
P Dumortier Frères SA v Council [1982] ECR 1733; Joined Cases C–104/89, C–37/90 *JM
Mulder v Council and Commission* [1992] ECR I–3061.

Form of application There is no set form for the application, but it usually falls into three parts: the title; the submissions; and the form of order.[41]

Annexes The following documents should be annexed to the application.[42]

(1) A file containing the documents relied on as evidence, together with a schedule listing them.

(2) A certificate establishing that the lawyer acting for the applicant is entitled to act before a court of a Member State.

(3) Where the applicant is 'a legal person governed by private law', for example, a company:

  (*a*) proof of its existence in law (for an English company, copies of the memorandum and articles of association should be produced); and

  (*b*) proof that the applicant's lawyer is properly authorised to act (for example, a resolution of the board of directors or a declaration sworn before a notary);[43]

(4) In applications under article 173 of the EEC Treaty, a copy of the act challenged.

(5) In applications under article 175 of the EEC Treaty, documentary evidence of the date on which the relevant institution was called upon to act.

(6) In applications under article 181 or 182 of the EEC Treaty, a copy of the relevant arbitration clause or special agreement.

Confidential documents A party may request that confidential documents forming part of the pleadings should be placed in a special file, to be disclosed only to the principal parties and the officers of the Court.[44]

Case numbers Cases are assigned a docket number when they are first lodged with the Courts' Registries. Since the foundation of the Court of First Instance in 1989, cases before the Court of Justice have borne the prefix 'C–'. Cases before the Court of First Instance are denoted by the prefix 'T–'.[45] Each case is given a case number, which includes the year of registration, for example Case C–275/92.

Judge-rapporteur As soon as an application is lodged, the President of the Court designates a 'judge-rapporteur' (reporting judge) for that case. His

---

[41] See Precedent H, p 291.

[42] ECJ Rules of Procedure, articles 37, 38; CFI Rules of Procedure, articles 43, 44. Statute of the Court of Justice, article 19. See pp 318–319, 372–373 and 300 respectively.

[43] A lawyer representing a natural person is not required to provide proof of his authority to act when lodging the application, but must be able to provide such proof if his authority to act is challenged. See Case 14/64 *Emilia Gualco v High Authority* [1965] ECR 51 at 57 (ECSC).

[44] Case 236/81 *Celanese Chemical Company Inc v Council and Commission* [1982] ECR 1183.

[45] This reflects the Court of First Instance's French title 'Tribunal de première instance'.

function is to ensure that the proper procedure is complied with and to oversee the general conduct of the case.[46]

Service Once the Registrar is satisified that the application is in order he serves it on the defendant.[47] In addition, copies of the application (and defence) are sent to the Council and the Commission, even where they are not named as parties in the application.[48]

Defence The defendant must lodge a defence within one month after service of the application. The time limit may be extended by the President of the Court following an application by the defendant.[49] The defence must contain the following information:[50]

(1) the name and permanent address of the defendant;
(2) an address for service in Luxembourg and the name of the person authorised to accept service;
(3) the arguments of fact and law relied on;[51]
(4) the form of order sought by the applicant;[52]
(5) the nature of any evidence offered.

There is no set form for the defence, but it usually falls into three parts: the title; the submissions; and the form of order. The defence should also include a claim for costs. Failure to claim costs will mean that the defendant will have to bear his own costs, even if his defence is successful.[53]

Annexes The following documents should be annexed to the defence.[54]

(1) A file containing the documents relied on as evidence, together with a schedule listing them;

(2) A certificate establishing that the lawyer acting for the defendant is entitled to act before a court of a Member State;

(3) Where the defendant is 'a legal person governed by private law', for example a company:

(*a*) proof of its existence in law (for an English company, copies of the memorandum and articles of association should be produced); and

(*b*) proof that the applicant's lawyer is properly authorised to act (for example, a resolution of the board of directors or a declaration sworn before a notary);

---

[46] ECJ Rules of Procedure, article 9(2); CFI Rules of Procedure, article 13(2). See pp 311, 365.
[47] ECJ Rules of Procedure, articles 39, 79; CFI Rules of Procedure, articles 45, 100. See pp 319, 329, 374, 389.
[48] ECJ Rules of Procedure, article 16(7); CFI Rules of Procedure, article 24(7). See pp 313, 367.
[49] ECJ Rules of Procedure, article 40(2); CFI Rules of Procedure, article 46(3). See pp 319, 374.
[50] ECJ Rules of Procedure, article 40(1); CFI Rules of Procedure, article 46(1). See pp 319, 374.
[51] The defendant should ensure that he sets out his case fully in the defence. The Court will not allow later amendments, even in the rejoinder, which seek to extend the subject-matter of the proceedings as defined in the application and defence. See p 259–260.
[52] This will usually ask for the rejection of the application and costs.
[53] ECJ Rules of Procedure, article 69(2); CFI Rules of Procedure, article 87(2). See pp 326, 386.
[54] ECJ Rules of Procedure, articles 37(4), 40(1); CFI Rules of Procedure, articles 43(4), 46(1). Statute of the European Court of Justice, article 19. See pp 318, 319, 373, 374 and 300 respectively.

(4) In applications under article 173 of the EEC Treaty, a copy of the act challenged;

(5) In applications under article 175 of the EEC Treaty, documentary evidence of the date on which the relevant institution was called upon to act.

Default judgment The Rules of Procedure provide for judgment in default where a defendant fails to lodge a defence in the proper form within the time prescribed.[55]

Reply and rejoinder The application and the defence may be supplemented by a reply from the applicant and by a rejoinder from the defendant. The President of the Court fixes the time limits within which these pleadings are to be lodged.[56] The applicant is entitled to expand in his reply upon points clearly made in his application.[57] Further evidence may be put forward in the reply or rejoinder, provided that reasons are given for the delay in offering it. Thereafter, no fresh issue may be raised unless it is based on matters of law or of fact already raised in the written procedure.[58]

Amendment The Rules of Procedure provide that no new plea in law may be introduced in the course of proceedings, unless it is based on matters of law or fact which come to light in the course of the procedure.[59] For a new fact to justify the raising of a fresh issue during the proceedings, it must not have existed or must not have been known to the applicant when the action was commenced.[60] The Court of Justice has taken a strict approach to amendments and has consistently held that an amendment may not seek to extend the subject-matter of the proceedings as established in the application and defence.[61] An amendment may be permitted, for example, where the decision originally challenged in the application has been replaced by another decision with the same subject matter,[62] or where the scope of the original decision is extended without affecting the general principle to which it gives effect.[63] Equally, a later submission which amplifies a submission, express or implied, previously

---

[55] ECJ Rules of Procedure, article 94; CFI Rules of Procedure, article 122. See pp 334, 396–397.
[56] ECJ Rules of Procedure, article 41; CFI Rules of Procedure, article 47. See pp 319, 374.
[57] Case T–21/90 *Günter Generlich v Commission* [1991] ECR II–1323 para 32.
[58] ECJ Rules of Procedure, article 42; CFI Rules of Procedure, article 48. See pp 319–320, 375.
[59] ECJ Rules of Procedure, article 42(2); CFI Rules of Procedure, article 48(2). See pp 319–320, 375.
[60] Case 11/81 *Firma Anton Dürbreck v Commission* [1982] ECR 1251 para 17.
[61] Case 232/78 *Commission v France* [1979] ECR 2729 paras 2, 3; Case 125/78 *GEMA v Commission* [1979] ECR 3173 para 26; Case 124/81 *Commission v United Kingdom* [1983] ECR 203 para 6; Case T–64/89 *Automec Srl v Commission* [1990] ECR II–367 paras 66–70. *Cf* Cases 82, 83/85R *Eurasian Corporation Ltd v Commission* [1985] ECR 1191, where amendments to an application for interim measures were permitted as, on the facts of the case, the Commission's opportunity to defend itself was not affected thereby.
[62] Case 14/81 *Alpha Steel Ltd v Commission* [1982] ECR 749 paras 7, 8; Case 103/85 *Stahlwerke Peine-Salzgitter AG v Commission* [1988] ECR 4131 paras 10–13.
[63] Joined Cases 351/85, 360/85 *Fabrique de fer de Charleroi SA v Commission* [1987] ECR 3639 paras 8–11 (ECSC).

made in the original application, will also be permitted.[64] These amendments may be made in the reply or rejoinder, or even at the oral hearing.[65]

Joinder of cases The Court may, at any time, order that cases concerning the same subject-matter should be joined for the written or oral procedure or for final judgment.[66] Joint applications may be permitted where the applicants' conclusions refer only to identical measures or to measures which concern them all equally.[67]

Intervention[68] Member States and Community institutions may apply to intervene in cases before the Court.[69] The same right is open to any other person establishing an interest in the result of any case submitted to the Court, except in cases between Member States, between institutions of the Community or between Member States and institutions of the Community.[70] Submissions made by an intervener are limited to supporting or opposing the remedies claimed by the parties. This does not prevent an intervener from presenting arguments different from those put forward by the party which it is supporting.[71]

An application to intervene must be made within three months of the publication of the notice in the *Official Journal* that the case has been registered. The application must satisfy the formal requirements for the main pleadings referred to above, but must also set out:[72]

(1) the description of the case and the parties; and

(2) the reasons why the intervener has an interest in the result of the case.

The Registrar serves the application to intervene on the other parties and, after they have been given an opportunity to make submissions, the President or the Court gives its decision in the form of an order. If the Court allows the inter-

---

[64] Case 306/81 *Constantin Verros v European Parliament* [1983] ECR 1755 para 9.

[65] Case 33/59 *Compagnie des hauts fourneaux de Chasse v High Authority* [1962] ECR 381 at 388 (ECSC).

[66] ECJ Rules of Procedure, article 43; CFI Rules of Procedure, article 50. See pp 320, 375.

[67] Joined Cases 18/64, 19/64 *Alvino and Benoit v Commission* [1965] ECR 789 at 796.

[68] Statute of the Court of Justice, article 37. ECJ Rules of Procedure, article 93; CFI Rules of Procedure, articles 115, 116. See pp 302, 333–334, 393–394. Intervention is only permissible on the basis of these procedural rules; see Case T 1/90 *Gloria Pérez-Mínguez Casariego v Commission* [1991] ECR II–143 paras 41–44.

[69] Member States and Community institutions are not required to demonstrate that they have an interest in the result of the case in order to be permitted to intervene. See Case 138/79 *SA Roquette Frères v Council* [1980] ECR 3333 paras 17–21.

[70] In Joined Cases 41/73, 43–48/73 and others *Société anonyme Générale Sucrière v Commission* [1973] ECR 1465 the Court of Justice held that a body without legal personality (the National Union of Italian Consumers) was entitled to intervene in an action. In Joined Cases 91/82, 200/82 *Chris International Foods Ltd v Commission* [1983] ECR 417 a non-Member State (Dominica) was permitted to intervene in an action. In Case T–84/91 *Mirielle Meskens v European Parliament* [1992] II–1565 a trade union was permitted to intervene in a staff case. See Case T–35/91 *Eurosport Consortium v Commission* [1991] ECR II–1359 for a discussion of the right to intervene in competition cases.

[71] Case 30/59 *De Gezamenlijke Steenkolenmijnen in Limburg v High Authority* [1961] ECR 1 at 17, 18 (ECSC).

[72] See Joined Cases 197–200/80, 243/80, 245/80, 247/80 *Ludwigshafener Walzmühle Erling KG v EEC* [1981] ECR 1041 in which the degree of interest which a person must demonstrate in order to intervene is considered.

vention, the intervener receives a copy of all the documents served on the parties, unless they contain confidential information.[73]

Time limits The rules for reckoning periods of time are set out in the Rules of Procedure.[74] An extension of ten days exists for the United Kingdom to take account of distance.[75] The Court applies the time limits very strictly in order to preserve legal certainty[76] and, if necessary, it will consider, of its own motion, whether the time limits prescribed for bringing actions have been complied with.[77] The Court does not have a general discretion to extend the mandatory time limits set down by the EEC Treaty or Rules of Procedure.[78] Time limits before the EC Courts are governed exclusively by Community law and a party is not entitled to rely on provisions as to time under national law in cases before these Courts.[79] It is the responsibility of the party alleging that an application is out of time to prove the date on which the measure was notified.[80]

A party's failure to comply with time limits may be excused if he proves the existence of an excusable error, unforeseeable circumstances[81] or *force majeure*.[82] The Court of Justice has held that the concept of *force majeure* essentially covers unusual circumstances which make it impossible for the act to be

---

[73] See Joined Cases T–24/92R, T–28/92R *Langnese-Iglo GmbH and Schöller Lebensmittel GmbH & Co KG v Commission* [1992] ECR II–1713 paras 5–10; Case T–24/93R *Compagnie Maritime Belge Transport NV v Commission* judgment of 13 May 1993.

[74] ECJ Rules of Procedure, articles 80–82; CFI Rules of Procedure, articles 101–103. See pp 329–330, 390–391. Case T–125/89 *Filtrona Española Sa v Commission* [1990] ECR II–393; Case C–59/91 *France v Commission* [1992] I–525 paras 3–7 (meaning of 'calendar month').

[75] ECJ Rules of Procedure, article 81(2) and Annex II, article 1; CFI Rules of Procedure, article 102 (2). See pp 330, 349, 390. The application of the extension of time depends on where the applicant is habitually resident. The place of residence of the applicant's lawyer is irrelevant; see Case 28/65 *Fulvio Fonzi v Commission* [1966] ECR 477.

[76] Case 152/85 *Rudolf Misset v Council* [1987] ECR 223 para 11; Case 257/85 *Dufay v European Parliament* [1987] ECR 1561 paras 9, 10 (Court rejected an argument based on article 6 of the European Convention on Human Rights).

[77] Case 108/79 *Salvatore Belfiore v Commission* [1980] ECR 1769 para 3.

[78] Case 4/67 *Anne Muller v Commission* [1967] ECR 365 (ECSC).

[79] Case 209/83 *Ferriera Valsabbia SpA v Commission* [1984] ECR 3089; Case C–12/90 *Infortec—Projectos e consultadoria, Lda v Commission* [1990] ECR I–4265 para 10.

[80] Joined Cases 32/58, 33/58 *SNUPAT v High Authority* [1959] ECR 127 at 136; Case 42/58 *SAFE v High Authority* [1959] ECR 183 at 190 (ECSC); Joined Cases 193/87, 194/87 *Henri Maurissen and European Public Service Union v Court of Auditors* [1989] ECR 1045; Case T–1/90 *Gloria Pérez-Mínguez Casariego v Commission* [1991] ECR II–143 para 37. See also Case 6/72 *Europemballage and Continental Can v Commission* [1973] ECR 215 paras 9, 10 (definition of 'notification'); Case 76/79 *Karl Könecke Fleischwarenfabrik GmbH & Co KG v Commission* [1980] ECR 665 (definition of 'notification'); Case 42/85 *Cockerill-Sambre SA v Commission* [1985] ECR 3749 (definition of 'notification'); Case 152/85 *Rudolf Misset v Council* [1987] ECR 223 (regardless of time of day when measure notified, time does not begin to run until the end of the day of notification); Case T–12/90 *Bayer AG v Commission* [1991] ECR II–219 (definition of 'notification' and 'date of notification').

[81] See Joined Cases 25/65, 26/65 *Simet and Feram v High Authority* [1967] ECR 33 (ECSC), where a postal delay was held to constitute an 'unforeseeable circumstance'. *Cf* Case C–59/91 *France v Commission* [1992] I–525 paras 8–12 where the applicants were not entitled to rely on a postal delay.

[82] Statute of the Court of Justice, article 42. See p 303.

carried out. Even though *force majeure* does not require absolute impossibility, it does require abnormal difficulties, which are independent of the will of the person concerned and which are apparently inevitable even if all due care is taken.[83]

Judge-rapporteur's preliminary report[84] After the rejoinder (if any), the President fixes the date on which the judge-rapporteur is to present his preliminary report to the Court at its weekly case administrative meeting. The report should contain recommendations as to whether further evidence is required and whether the case should be referred to a particular chamber.

(c) *Preparatory inquiries*

Obtaining further evidence The Court of Justice and the Court of First Instance have wide powers for obtaining further evidence, usually exercisable both of their own motion or on an application by one of the parties.[85] Either Court may adopt the following measures of inquiry.

(1) The Court may require the parties to produce documents and information which they consider desirable.[86] They may require Member States and institutions which are not parties to the case to supply all information necessary for the proceedings.[87]

(2) The Court may summon and orally examine witnesses, whether parties or non-parties.[88]

(3) The Court may order that an expert's report be obtained.[89]

(4) The Court may issue letters rogatory for the examination of witnesses or experts.[90]

---

[83] Case 284/82 *Busseni SpA v Commission* [1984] ECR 557 para 11 (ECSC). See also Case 25/68 *André Schertzer v European Parliament* [1977] ECR 1729 paras 10–21 (excusable error); Case 117/78 *Willy Orlandi v Commission* [1979] ECR 1613 paras 6–12 (excusable error); Case 209/83 *Ferriera Valsabbia SpA v Commission* [1984] ECR 3089 *(force majeure)*; Case 224/83 *Ferriera Vittoria Srl v Commission* [1984] ECR 2349 (ECSC) *(force majeure)*; Case 42/85 *Cockerill-Sambre SA v Commission* [1985] ECR 3749 (ECSC) (unforeseeable circumstances and *force majeure)*; Case T–12/90 *Bayer AG v Commission* [1991] ECR II–219 (excusable error and *force majeure)*.

[84] ECJ Rules of Procedure, article 44; CFI Rules of Procedure, article 52. See pp 320, 375–376.

[85] See, generally, Statute of the Court of Justice, articles 21–27; ECJ Rules of Procedure, articles 45–54, 124; CFI Rules of Procedure, articles 64–76. See pp 301, 320–324, 342, 377–383. Preparatory measures can only be ordered by the Court and cannot be ordered by the President in the context of an interlocutory application, see Case C–358/89R *Extramet Industrie SA v Council* [1990] ECR I–431.

[86] See Joined Cases 121/86, 122/86R *Epicheiriseon v Council and Commission* [1987] ECR 833 on the appropriate procedure to be followed by a party to obtain discovery of documents.

[87] Statute of the Court of Justice, article 21. See p 301.

[88] Statute of the Court of Justice, article 23; ECJ Rules of Procedure, articles 47, 48; CFI Rules of Procedure, articles 68, 69. See pp 301, 321–322, 379–381.

[89] Statute of the Court of Justice, article 22; ECJ Rules of Procedure, article 49; CFI Rules of Procedure, article 70. See pp 301, 322–323, 381.

[90] Statute of the Court of Justice, article 26. See p 301. ECJ Rules of Procedure, article 52, Supplementary Rules, articles 1–3 (OJ No L 350, 28 December 1974, p 29, as amended by OJ 1987 No L 165, 24 June 1987, p 4). CFI Rules of Procedure, article 75. See p 383. For example, see Case 160/84 *Oryzomyli Kavalla v Commission* [1985] ECR 675.

(5) The Court may inspect the place or thing in question.[91]

In addition, the Court of First Instance may invite the parties to make written or oral submissions on certain aspects of the proceedings and may summon the parties or their agents to meetings.[92]

Where a party makes an application for the adoption of measures of inquiry he must provide evidence of why such measures are necessary.[93]

After the preparatory inquiry has been completed, the President will usually fix the date for the opening of the oral procedure.[94]

(d) Interlocutory matters

Admissibility A challenge to the admissibility of an application may be raised in the defence, in which case it will normally be considered by the Court in its final judgment. Alternatively, a party may raise the question of admissibility as a preliminary issue by making an application to the Court setting out the pleas of fact and law relied on and the form of order sought by the applicant.[95] Any supporting documents must be annexed to the application. Having given the other party the opportunity to make submissions on the matter, there will usually be an oral hearing and the Court will then decide the question of admissibility as an interlocutory matter, or reserve its decision until the final substantive judgment.

The Court may declare an action inadmissible of its own motion where the Court has no jurisdiction on the matter or where the action is manifestly inadmissible.[96]

The admissibility of an action is judged as of the date when the application was lodged. If, at that time, the conditions for an action to be brought are not fulfilled, the action is inadmissible, unless the defect is rectified within the period prescribed for proceedings to be instituted. In Case 50/84 *SRL Bensider v Commission*,[97] an application made on the last day of the prescribed period was declared to be inadmissible, as the applicant, a company, had not acquired legal personality under its national law at that date and was not, therefore, entitled to bring legal proceedings.

---

[91] ECJ Rules of Procedure, article 45(2)(e); CFI Rules of Procedure, article 65(e). See pp 321, 378.
[92] CFI Rules of Procedure, article 64(3). See p 378.
[93] Case 51/65 *ILFO v High Authority* [1966] ECR 87 (ECSC).
[94] ECJ Rules of Procedure, article 54. See pp 323–324. See Case 77/70 *Maurice Prelle v Commission* [1971] ECR 561 paras 6, 7, where the Court of Justice indicated that a party could make an application for a measure of inquiry after the oral procedure had closed, but only if it related to facts which were capable of having a decisive influence and which the party concerned was not able to put forward before the closure of the oral procedure.
[95] ECJ Rules of Procedure, article 91; CFI Rules of Procedure, article 114. See pp 332, 393.
[96] ECJ Rules of Procedure, article 92; CFI Rules of Procedure, articles 111, 113. See pp 333, 393, 394. See Case C–72/90 *Asia Motor France v Commission* [1990] ECR I–2181 paras 9–15.
[97] [1984] ECR 3991 (ECSC).

Interim measures The substantive and procedural law relating to interim measures is considered separately in Chapter 16.

Expedition There are no explicit general rules providing for expedition. The President may, in special circumstances, order that a case be given priority over others in respect of the oral hearing, once any necessary preparatory inquiries have been completed.[98]

Stay of proceedings The Court of Justice has a general power to stay proceedings subject to the conditions established in the Rules of Procedure.[99] In contrast, the Rules of Procedure permit the Court of First Instance to stay proceedings in specific instances, for example at the joint request of the parties.[100]

Costs in interlocutory applications Any interlocutory application or response should contain a separate claim for costs. Failure to do so will mean that the Court is obliged to award all of the costs in the action to the successful party in the final judgment, without taking separate account of the outcome of any interlocutory applications.[101]

Discontinuance A case may be withdrawn from the register if the parties agree a settlement (except in applications under article 173 or 175 of the EEC Treaty) or if the applicant informs the Court, in writing, that he wishes to discontinue the proceedings.[102] In these circumstances, the President will give a decision on costs in accordance with the specific provisions set down in the Rules of Procedure. The general rule is that the party who discontinues or withdraws from the proceedings must pay the other party's costs, subject to any agreement between the parties themselves as to costs.[103]

(e) Oral procedure

Report for the hearing The judge-rapporteur prepares a report for the hearing, which summarises the facts of the case and the arguments contained in the written observations. This is circulated to the judges, the parties and any interveners prior to the hearing. If a party considers that the report for the hearing does not adequately set out the facts or the arguments, he should endeavour to inform the Registrar of this before the hearing and suggest appropriate amendments.

Public hearing The oral hearing will be a public hearing, unless the Court, of its own motion, or on application by the parties, decides otherwise.[104]

---

[98] ECJ Rules of Procedure, article 55; CFI Rules of Procedure, article 55. See pp 324, 376.
[99] ECJ Rules of Procedure, article 82a; Statute of the Court of Justice, article 47. See pp 330, 374.
[100] CFI Rules of Procedure, articles 77–79, 123(4), 128, 129(4); Statute of the Court of Justice, article 47. See pp 383–384, 397, 398, 399 and 304 respectively.
[101] Case T–50/89 *Jürgen Sparr v Commission* [1990] ECR II–539 para 9.
[102] ECJ Rules of Procedure, articles 77, 78; CFI Rules of Procedure, articles 98, 99. See pp 328–329, 389.
[103] ECJ Rules of Procedure, article 69(5); CFI Rules of Procedure, article 87(5). See pp 326–327, 386–387.
[104] Statute of the Court of Justice, article 28. See p 301.

Conduct of the oral hearing A written *aide-mémoire* may be prepared, setting out the contents of the advocate's speech, and given to the translators prior to the hearing. This facilitates the simultaneous translation of the advocate's speech.[105] Before the oral hearing begins, the legal representatives are usually invited to a room behind the Court to meet members of the Court and, in particular, the judge-rapporteur.

Lawyers and agents wear their national robes. Barristers usually address the Court as 'My Lords'. A party may address the Court only through his agent, adviser or lawyer.[106] The order of speeches, is generally, applicant, interveners in support, defendant, interveners opposed to the application and, finally, the Commission. The time allowed for the speeches is usually a maximum of 30 minutes each,[107] which is rigorously enforced by the President.[108] The main purpose of the oral hearing is not to repeat the written observations already made, but to emphasise points of particular importance and to comment on the written observations of the other parties. The Judges and Advocate-General may ask questions.[109] At the end of the speeches, each speaker is given an opportunity to reply.

Advocate-General's Opinion In the Court of Justice, the Advocate-General delivers his Opinion orally, some time following the oral hearing.[110] Once the Opinion has been delivered the oral procedure is declared closed.[111] In the Court of First Instance, the oral procedure is generally declared closed at the end of the oral hearing.[112]

(f) Judgment

Secret deliberation The Court reaches its judgment by deliberation in closed session. Only the Judges who were present at the oral hearing take part in the deliberations. If necessary, decisions are reached by majority following a vote. Only one judgment is delivered; there are no dissenting judgments. The conduct of the deliberations is confidential.[113]

---

[105] The interpreters read all the case papers and any relevant authorities cited in the written submissions prior to the hearing.

[106] Statute of the Court of Justice, article 29; ECJ Rules of Procedure, article 58; CFI Rules of Procedure, article 59. See pp 301, 324, 377.

[107] In cases before Chambers of three judges, the time permitted is limited to 15 minutes.

[108] A party may apply for a longer period by sending a request to the Registrar at least 14 days before the hearing (15 days in the Court of First Instance). The request must detail the reasons on which it is based and must stipulate the amount of time considered necessary.

[109] ECJ Rules of Procedure, article 57; CFI Rules of Procedure, article 58. See pp 324, 376. The time limit of 30 minutes does not include the time used to reply to questions asked by the Court.

[110] The Advocate-General will usually indicate the date on which he intends to deliver his Opinion at the end of the oral hearing.

[111] ECJ Rules of Procedure, article 59. See p 324.

[112] CFI Rules of Procedure, articles 60–62. See p 377.

[113] Statute of the Court of Justice, articles 32–34. ECJ Rules of Procedure, articles 27, 63–65; CFI Rules of Procedure, articles 33, 81–83. See pp 302, 314–315, 325, 369, 384–385.

Delivery of judgment Judgment is delivered in open court. The parties need not attend. All parties to the action are served with certified copies of the judgment,[114] which is binding as from its date of delivery.[115]

Delay In 1992, the average length of proceedings for direct actions (from lodging of the application to judgment) was 25.8 months. The average delay for special proceedings, such as applications for interim measures and challenges concerning admissibility, was 2.7 months.[116]

Slip rule The Court may rectify clerical mistakes, errors in calculation or obvious slips in any judgment, either of its own motion or on application by a party within two weeks of the delivery of the judgment.[117]

Omissions Equally, if the Court omits to make a decision on any head of the claim or on costs, a party can apply to the Court to supplement its judgment within a month after service of the judgment.[118]

Interpretation of judgments Any party or any Community institution with an interest can make an application to the Court to clarify the meaning or scope of a judgment.[119] A person who was not a party to the case cannot make an application for interpretation.[120] Where several actions are brought against the same measure and where, as a result of one of those actions, the measure is annulled, the applicants in the other actions may be entitled to make an application for interpretation of the judgment, provided that those applicants had put forward the same reasons for annulment in their own application as the Court relied on in its judgment.[121] Interveners may also submit an application for interpretation, even if the party whose conclusions they supported does not do so.[122]

An application for interpretation must be based on the obscurity or ambiguity of the judgment in question, and may not raise questions on the effect of the judgment.[123] An interpreting judgment is binding not only on the applicants, but

---

[114] ECJ Rules of Procedure, article 64; CFI Rules of Procedure, article 82. See pp 325, 385.

[115] ECJ Rules of Procedure, article 65; CFI Rules of Procedure, article 82. See pp 325, 385. See the exception in relation to decisions of the Court of First Instance declaring regulations to be void in the Statute of the Court of Justice, article 53 (p 305).

[116] These figures are taken from the Weekly Summaries of the Court of Justice, Number 35 of 1992.

[117] ECJ Rules of Procedure, article 66; CFI Rules of Procedure, article 84. See pp 325–326, 385.

[118] ECJ Rules of Procedure, article 67; CFI Rules of Procedure, article 85 (limited to a failure to give a decision on costs). See pp 326, 386.

[119] Statute of the Court of Justice, article 40; ECJ Rules of Procedure, article 102; CFI Rules of Procedure, article 129. See pp 303, 337, 399.

[120] Case 24/66 bis *Gesellshaft für Getreidehandel mbH v Commission* [1973] ECR 1599.

[121] Case 5/55 *ASSIDER v High Authority* [1955] ECR 135 at 141 (ECSC).

[122] Joined Cases 146/85, 431/85 *Claude Maindiaux v Economic and Social Committee and others* [1988] ECR 2003 para 4.

[123] Case 5/55 *ASSIDER v High Authority* [1955] ECR 135 at 142 (ECSC); Case 70/63A *High Authority v Collotti and Court of Justice* [1965] ECR 275 (ECSC); Case 110/63 *Alfred Williame v Commission* [1966] ECR 287; Case 9/81 *Court of Auditors v Williams* [1983] ECR 2859 para 12; Case 206/81 A *José Alvarez v European Parliament* [1983] ECR 2865.

also on any other party, insofar as that party is affected by the passage in the judgment which the Court is asked to interpret or by a passage which is exactly similar thereto.[124]

Revision of judgments An application for revision of a judgment may be made to the Court within three months of the discovery of a fact, 'which is of such a nature as to be a decisive factor,[125] and which, when the judgment was given, was unknown to the Court and to the party claiming the revision'.[126] The fact must have existed before the delivery of the judgment.[127] The conditions of review are construed strictly by the Court, as an application for revision is not a means of appeal but an exceptional review procedure which may render the principle of *res judicata* inapplicable.[128] No application for revision can be made later than ten years from the date of the judgment. The Court will not permit revision of a judgment which was based on purely legal considerations (for example, a judgment whereby the Court of Justice, on an appeal from a decision of the Court of First Instance, referred the matter back to the Court of First Instance on the basis that it had breached Community law).[129]

Review at the request of third parties Member States, Community institutions and any private party may, subject to the conditions set out in the Rules of Procedure, institute third party proceedings to contest a judgment which was rendered without their being heard, where the judgment is prejudicial to their rights.[130] This is an exceptional procedure and is subject to strict control by the Court in order to protect legal certainty in respect of judgments.

Enforcement Enforcement of judgments is governed by the rules of civil procedure in force in the State in which enforcement is carried out.[131] Enforcement

---

[124] Joined Cases 41/73, 43/73, 44/73 *Société anonyme générale Sucrière v Commission* [1977] ECR 445 paras 27–30.

[125] For example, see Case 285/81Rev *Jean-Jacques Geist v Commission* [1984] ECR 1789 paras 8, 9.

[126] Statute of the Court of Justice, article 41; ECJ Rules of Procedure, articles 99, 100; CFI Rules of Procedure, articles 125–128. See pp 303, 336, 398. Case 56/70 *Fondeire Acciaierie Giovanni Mandelli v Commission* [1971] ECR 1; Case 235/82 Rev *Ferriere San Carlo SpA v Commission* [1986] ECR 1799; Case T–4/89Rev *BASF AG v Commission* [1992] ECR II–1591.

[127] Case 267/80Rev *Riseria Modenese Srl v Council and Commission and Birra Peroni SpA* [1985] ECR 3499 para 10; Case C–185/90 *Walter Gill v Commission* [1992] ECR I–993 para 12. *Cf* Case 56/75Rev *Raymond Elz v Commission* [1977] ECR 1617 paras 6, 7.

[128] Case 116/78Rev *Arturo Bellintani v Commission* [1980] ECR 23; Case 267/80R *Riseria Srl v Council and Commission and Birra Peroni SpA* [1985] ECR 3499 para 10.

[129] Case C–185/90 *Walter Gill v Commission* [1992] ECR I–993 paras 11–16.

[130] Statute of the Court of Justice, article 39; ECJ Rules of Procedure, article 97; CFI Rules of Procedure, articles 123, 124. See pp 302–303, 335, 397. See Case T–35/89 *Inigo Ascasibar Zubizarreta v Alessandro Albani* [1992] ECR II–1599. See also Joined Cases 9/60, 12/60 *Belgium v Vloeberghs and High Authority* [1962] ECR 171 (ECSC); Joined Cases 42/59, 49/59 *Breedband NV v Société des Aciéries du Temple* [1962] ECR 145 (ECSC); Case 267/80 TO *Birra Dreher SpA v Risria Modenese Srl, Council and Commission* [1986] ECR 3901; Case 292/84 TP *F Bolognese v H Scharf and Commission* [1987] ECR 3563 paras 7–10; Case 147/86 TO 1–3 *POIFXG and others v Greece and Commission* [1989] ECR 4103.

[131] Articles 187, 192 of the EEC Treaty. It is for the appropriate national authority to oversee the enforcement process; see Case 4/73 *J Nold Kohlen- und Baustoffgroßhandlung v Ruhrkohle AG* [1977] ECR 1 (ECSC).

may only be suspended by means of an application to the Court of Justice or the Court of First Instance, as appropriate.[132]

(g) Costs

Order as to costs The final judgment or order which closes the proceedings must contain a decision as to costs. The rules as to costs are set out in the Rules of Procedure.[133] The general rule is that the unsuccessful party must bear all the costs of the action if the costs have been applied for in the successful party's written pleadings. If costs are not claimed in the written pleadings, the parties must bear their own costs.[134] Member States and institutions which intervene in proceedings must bear their own costs.[135] Costs incurred prior to the proceedings before the Court of Justice or the Court of First Instance may not be recovered by an order of either of those Courts.[136]

The Court may order a successful party to pay costs which it considers that party to have 'unreasonably or vexatiously' caused the opposite party to incur.[137] In Case 14/63 *Forges de Calbecq v High Authority*,[138] the Court of Justice held that, where defective drafting of a measure by a Community institution was the decisive factor in the making of an application which was dismissed, it was appropriate to order that the parties should bear their own costs. In Joined Cases 5/60, 7/60, 8/60 *Meroni, FERAM and SIMET v High Authority*,[139] the High Authority revoked the contested decisions during the course of the proceedings. The successful parties were ordered to pay the costs incurred after the revocation, as they had chosen to continue the proceedings, even though they no longer had an interest in doing so.

The party which is awarded costs should send an account of the costs which it claims to the other party within a reasonable period.[140]

---

[132] Article 192 of the EEC Treaty. Statute of the Court of Justice, article 36; ECJ Rules of Procedure, articles 89, 97(2); CFI Rules of Procedure, articles 110, 123(2). See pp 302, 332, 335, 392, 397.

[133] ECJ Rules of Procedure, articles 69–75; CFI Rules of Procedure, articles 87–93. See pp 326–334, 386–388. See also Statute of the Court of Justice, article 35, p 302.

[134] ECJ Rules of Procedure, article 69(2); CFI Rules of Procedure, article 87(2). See pp 326, 386. See also Joined Cases 23/63, 24/63, 52/63 *Société Anonyme Usines Emile Henricot v High Authority* [1963] ECR 217 at 225 (ECSC); Joined Cases 53/63, 54/63 *Lemmerz-Werke GmbH v High Authority* [1963] ECR 239 at 248, 249 (ECSC).

[135] ECJ Rules of Procedure, article 69(4); CFI Rules of Procedure, article 87(4). See pp 326, 386. These rules were introduced in 1991.

[136] Case 75/69 *Ernst Hake & Co v Commission* [1970] ECR 535.

[137] ECJ Rules of Procedure, article 69(3); CFI Rules of Procedure, article 87(3). See pp 326, 386.

[138] [1963] ECR 357 at 374 (ECSC). See also Case 49/64 *Emmanuel Stipperger v High Authority of the ECSC* [1965] ECR 521 at 527.

[139] [1961] ECR 107 (ECSC).

[140] In Case 126/76 *Firma Gebrüder Dietz v Commission* [1977] ECR 2431 para 1 the Court of Justice held that the Commission had not waived its right to recover costs where it had allowed six months to pass before sending a detailed account of the costs claimed to the unsuccessful party.

Interlocutory applications Any interlocutory application should contain a separate claim for costs. Failure to do so will mean that the Court is obliged to award all of the costs in the action to the successful party in the final judgment, without taking separate account of the outcome of any interlocutory applications.[141]

Taxation If there is a dispute concerning the amount of costs, a party can apply for the matter to be settled by the Court.[142] The Court will undertake a general appreciation of the object and nature of the dispute, its importance from the point of view of Community law, the difficulties of the proceedings, the amount of work undertaken by the lawyer and the financial implications of the dispute for the parties.[143]

(h) Legal aid

A party, or prospective party, may apply directly to the Court, at any time, for legal aid. The application must be accompanied by evidence of the applicant's need for assistance, in particular a document from a competent authority certifying his lack of means.[144] Legal aid will not be granted unless the applicant establishes that he has a *prima facie* case.[145]

3. APPEALS AGAINST DECISIONS OF THE COURT OF FIRST INSTANCE

Availability of appeals Judgments and interlocutory orders of the Court of First Instance may be appealed to the Court of Justice.

---

[141] Case T–50/89 *Jürgen Sparr v Commission* [1990] ECR II–539 para 9.

[142] ECJ Rules of Procedure, article 74(1); CFI Rules of Procedure, article 92(1). See pp 327, 387. The Court will tax the costs only if they are disputed; see Case 25/65 *Simet v High Authority* [1967] ECR 113 (ECSC); Joined Cases 9/65, 58/65 *Acciaierie San Michele SpA (in liquidation) v High Authority* [1968] ECR 259 (ECSC).

[143] Case 6/72 *Europemballage Corporation and Continental Can Company Inc v Commission* [1975] ECR 495; Case 238/78 *Ireks-Arkady GmbH v EEC* [1981] ECR 1723; Joined Cases 241/78, 242/78, 246/78 *DGV GmbH v EEC* [1981] ECR 1731; Case 24/79 *Dominique Noëlle Oberthür v Commission* [1981] ECR 2229; Case 318/82 *Leeuwarder Papierwarenfabriek BV v Commission* [1985] ECR 809; Case 43/83 *De Naeyer v Commission* [1987] ECR 3569 para 14. See Case 126/76 *Firma Gebrüder Dietz v Commission* [1974] ECR 2431 for the costs recoverable by the Community institutions in respect of legal representation.

[144] ECJ Rules of Procedure, article 76 (p 328); Supplementary Rules, articles 4, 5 (OJ No L 350, 28 December 1974, p 29, as amended by OJ No L 165, 24 June 1987, p 4); CFI Rules of Procedure, articles 94–97 (see pp 388–389). Presumably, a 'competent authority' would be the authority responsible for legal aid in the Member State concerned; see Case T–13/91R *Michael Harrison v Commission* [1991] ECR II–179 para 27.

[145] Case T–13/91R *Michael Harrison v Commission* [1991] ECR II–179 para 27. ECJ Rules of Procedure, article 76(3); CFI Rules of Procedure, article 94(2). See pp 328, 388.

(a) Appeal from final decisions

(i) Nature of appeal

Notification Final judgments of the Court of First Instance, decisions disposing of substantive issues in part only and decisions disposing of procedural issues concerning lack of competence or inadmissibility are notified by the Registrar of the Court of First Instance to all parties, as well as to all the Member States and Community institutions, even if they did not intervene in the case.[146]

Parties entitled to appeal An appeal on any of the above matters may be brought before the Court of Justice by any party which has been wholly, or partly, unsuccessful. Interveners, other than Member States or Community institutions, may only appeal against decisions which directly affect them. An appeal may be brought by a Member State or Community institution which did not intervene at first instance (except in staff cases).

Time limits for appeal Any appeal must be brought within two months of notification.[147]

Grounds of appeal Appeals to the Court of Justice are limited to points of law,[148] that is:

(1) lack of competence of the Court of First Instance;
(2) a breach of procedure which adversely affects the interests of the appellant; and
(3) infringement of Community law by the Court of First Instance.

There is no right to appeal as to the amount of costs awarded or as to the party ordered to pay them.

(ii) Procedure

Application for appeal An appeal is brought by lodging an application with the Registry of the Court of Justice or the Registry of the Court of First Instance.[149] The appeal must state:[150]

(1) the name and permanent address of the appellant;
(2) an address for service in Luxembourg and the name of the person authorised to accept service;
(3) the names of the other parties to the proceedings before the Court of First Instance;
(4) the date on which the decision appealed against was notified to the appellant;
(5) the pleas in law and legal arguments relied on;
(6) the form of order sought by the appellant, either:[151]

---

[146] Statute of the Court of Justice, article 48. See p 304.
[147] Statute of the Court of Justice, article 49. See pp 304–305.
[148] Statute of the Court of Justice, article 51. See p 305. Case C–283/90 *Vidrányi v Commission* [1991] ECR I–4339 paras 12, 13; Case C–346/90P *MF v Commission* [1992] ECR I–2691.
[149] ECJ Rules of Procedure, article 111. See pp 339–340.
[150] Ibid, article 112. See p 340.
[151] Ibid, article 113. See p 340. The subject-matter of the proceedings before the Court of First Instance may not be changed in the appeal.

(*a*) to set aside, in whole or in part, the decision of the Court of First Instance; or

(*b*) the same form of order, in whole or in part, as that sought at first instance. The appeal may not seek a different form of order.

Annexes The following documents should be annexed to the appeal:[152]

(1) the decision of the Court of First Instance appealed against;

(2) a certificate establishing that the lawyer acting for the appellant is entitled to act before a court of a Member State;

(3) a file containing documents relied on as evidence, together with a schedule listing them.

Lodging with the Court The original of the appeal must be signed by the appellant's agent or lawyer and should be dated. The original, including annexes, should be lodged with the Registrar, together with five certified copies for the Court and a copy for every other party to the proceedings.[153] Upon registration, appeals from the Court of First Instance are assigned a case number in the form, for example 'C–345/90P'.[154]

Further pleadings The pattern of pleadings follows the procedure at first instance. Any party to the first instance proceedings may lodge a response within two months after service on him of the notice of appeal.[155] This may be followed by a reply and rejoinder or any other pleading, within time limits prescribed by the President of the Court of Justice.[156]

Further procedure Following the written pleadings the procedure followed by the Court of Justice on an appeal is similar to the procedure in other cases. In particular, the same rules apply in relation to:[157]

(1) stay of proceedings;

(2) discontinuance;

(3) the slip rule;

(4) rectification of omissions;

(5) interpretation of judgments;

(6) revision of judgments;

(7) review at the request of third parties;

(8) legal aid.

Intervention The general rules as to intervention apply also to appeals.[158] An application to intervene in appeal proceedings must be lodged within three months of the date on which the appeal was lodged.[159]

---

[152] Ibid, article 112. See p 340.
[153] Ibid, article 112. See p 340.
[154] The 'P' derives from the French term, 'pourvoi'.
[155] ECJ Rules of Procedure, articles 115, 116. See pp 340–341.
[156] Ibid, article 117. See p 341.
[157] Ibid, article 118. Note that the powers to order preparatory inquiries do not apply to appeals.
[158] Ibid, article 118. See p 341.
[159] Ibid, article 123. See p 342.

Interim measures An appeal does not have suspensory effect. However, articles 185 and 186 of the EEC Treaty and the general rules of procedure for their application apply to appeals and a party may apply to the Court of Justice to suspend the application of a judgment of the Court of First Instance, pending an appeal to the Court of Justice.[160]

Inadmissibility The Court of Justice may, of its own motion, dismiss an appeal in whole or in part where it is clearly inadmissible or clearly unfounded.[161]

Oral hearing The Court of Justice may decide to dispense with the oral part of the procedure, unless one of the parties objects on the ground that the written procedure did not enable him fully to defend his point of view.[162] If an oral hearing is held, it will follow the same procedure as in other actions.[163]

(iii) Judgment

Nature of judgment Where an appeal is well founded, the Court of Justice will quash the decision of the Court of First Instance. It may give final judgment in the matter or refer the case back to the Court of First Instance for judgment. If the matter is referred back to the Court of First Instance, that Court is bound by any decisions of the Court of Justice on points of law.[164]

Where the Court of First Instance has adopted reasoning which is incorrect, but the decision can be justified on other, valid, grounds, an appeal against that decision will be rejected.[165]

Delay In 1992, the average length of proceedings for an appeal (from lodging of the appeal to judgment) was 17.5 months.[166]

(iv) Costs

The general rules as to costs apply.[167] Where the appeal fails, or where the appeal succeeds and the Court of Justice gives final judgment, the Court of Justice will make an order as to costs.[168] Where the case is referred back to the Court of First Instance, that Court makes an order covering the costs of the proceedings instituted before it, as well as the costs of the appeal proceedings before the Court of Justice.[169]

---

[160] Statute of the Court of Justice, article 53; ECJ Rules of Procedure, article 118. See pp 305, 341. Case C–345/90PR *European Parliament v Jack Hanning* [1991] ECR I–231; Case T–77/91R *Hochbaum v Commission* [1991] ECR II–1285 paras 19–22.

[161] ECJ Rules of Procedure, article 119. See p 341.

[162] Statute of the Court of Justice, article 52; ECJ Rules of Procedure, articles 120, 121. See pp 305, 341.

[163] ECJ Rules of Procedure, article 118. See p 341.

[164] Statute of the Court of Justice, article 54. See pp 305–306. The procedure to be followed where a case is referred back to the Court of First Instance is contained in CFI Rules of Procedure, articles 117–121. See p 341.

[165] Case C–30/91 *Jean Lestelle v Commission* [1992] ECR I–3755 para 28.

[166] These figures are taken from the Weekly Summaries of the Court of Justice, Number 35 of 1992.

[167] ECJ Rules of Procedure, article 118. See p 341.

[168] Ibid, article 122. See p 341–342.

[169] CFI Rules of Procedure, article 121. See p 341.

(b) Appeal from interlocutory decisions

Interim measures/suspension of enforcement Parties may appeal to the Court of Justice against any decision of the Court of First Instance concerning interim measures (under article 185 or 186 of the EEC Treaty) or the suspension of enforcement (article 192 of the EEC Treaty) within two months of the notification of the decision to the parties.[170]

Interveners Any person whose application to intervene has been dismissed by the Court of First Instance may appeal to the Court of Justice within two weeks of the notification of the decision dismissing the application.[171]

Procedure Appeals on interlocutory decisions do not follow the normal appeal procedure; instead, they follow the procedure adopted by the Court of Justice when called upon to consider such matters in cases brought directly before it.[172]

---

[170] Statute of the Court of Justice, article 50. See p 305.
[171] Ibid.
[172] Ibid.

Part V

Precedents

A: Damages Against a Private Party—Statement of Claim

IN THE HIGH COURT OF JUSTICE   199[ ] A No [ ]
QUEEN'S BENCH DIVISION

BETWEEN:

AB LIMITED

Plaintiff

and

CD LIMITED

Defendant

STATEMENT OF CLAIM

1 The Plaintiff carries on business in the United Kingdom and Italy as an exporter/importer and retailer of computer games and has a registered office at [ ].

2 The Defendant is a manufacturer of computer games and has a registered office at [ ].

3 In or about June 1993 the Plaintiff sought to export computer games manufactured by the Defendant ('Computer Games') from the United Kingdom to Italy. The Plaintiff intended to re-sell Computer Games in Italy.

4 The Plaintiff was prevented from exporting Computer Games to Italy as the Defendant instructed all of its authorised distributors in the United Kingdom not to sell Computer Games to the Plaintiff.

5 At all material times the Defendant was in a dominant position in a substantial part of the Common Market within the meaning of Article 86 of the EEC Treaty. In support of this contention the Plaintiff relies on the following facts and matters.

    (a) [   ]

    (b) [   ], etc

277

6 The Defendant has abused its dominant position contrary to Article 86. In support of this contention the Plaintiff relies on the following facts and matters.

   (a) [   ]

   (b) [   ], etc

7 The above abuses of a dominant position have had an appreciable effect on trade between Member States. In support of this contention, the Plaintiff relies on the following facts and matters.

   (a) [   ]

   (b) [   ], etc

8 The Defendant owes to the Plaintiff a statutory duty under the European Communities Act 1972 or other duty to comply with the provisions of the EEC Treaty and in particular Article 86 thereof.

9 For the reasons set out above the Defendant has acted in breach of the said duty.

10 Further or alternatively, the Defendant has acted unlawfully with the intention of harming the business of the Plaintiff alternatively the Defendant should reasonably have foreseen that its conduct as set out above would harm the business of the Plaintiff.

11 In the premises the conduct of the Defendant constitutes unlawful interference by the Defendant with the business of the Plaintiff.

12 The Plaintiff has suffered loss and damage as a result of the said breach of duty and/or unlawful interference.

PARTICULARS

[*Give particulars of loss*]

13 The Plaintiff is entitled to interest pursuant to section 35A of the Supreme Court Act 1981 on such sums and at such rate and for such period as the Court deems fit.

AND the Plaintiff claims:

(1) damages;

(2) interest pursuant to section 35A of the Supreme Court Act 1981.

[*Name of Counsel*]

Served this [   ] day of [   ] 199[   ] by [*firm name*] of [*address*], Solicitors for the Plaintiff.

B: Damages Against the State— Statement of Claim

IN THE HIGH COURT OF JUSTICE   199[   ] A No [   ]
QUEEN'S BENCH DIVISION

BETWEEN:

AB LIMITED

Plaintiff

and

DEPARTMENT OF
TRADE AND INDUSTRY

Defendant

STATEMENT OF CLAIM

1 The plaintiff carries on business in the United Kingdom as an importer and retailer of contact lenses and associated care products.

2 In or about June 1992 the Plaintiff commenced the importation of Cleareye contact lenses and associated care products from Belgium ('the Goods') for resale to opticians throughout the United Kingdom.

3 By The Importation of Contact Lenses Regulations 1993, Statutory Instrument 1993 No 000, ('the Regulations') the Defendant prohibited the importation into the United Kingdom of the Goods with effect from 1 February 1993.

4 The Regulations constitute a measure having equivalent effect to a quantitative restriction and are contrary to Article 30 of the EEC Treaty.

5 The Regulations were adopted following a complaint made to the Defendant by Clearsight (UK) Limited, who distribute the Goods in the United Kingdom under the terms of an exclusive distribution agreement with Fineview GmbH, a company incorporated under the laws of Germany and the manufacturer of the Goods.

6 The Defendant knew or should have known that the Regulations are contrary to Article 30 of the EEC Treaty. The Defendant adopted the Regulations in order to protect the economic interest of Clearsight (UK) Limited and Fineview GmbH by preventing the Goods being imported into the United Kingdom from elsewhere within the European Community and sold at prices inferior to those charged by Clearsight (UK) Limited. It was reasonably foreseeable that the adoption of the Regulations would cause loss to the Plaintiff.

7 The Defendant owes the Plaintiff a statutory duty under the European Communities Act 1972 or other duty to comply with the provisions of the EEC Treaty and in particular Article 30 thereof.

8 For the reasons set out above the Defendant has acted in breach of the said duty.

9 Further or alternatively for the reasons set out above the Defendant misconducted itself in the discharge of its public duties and in its public offices in that it exercised its powers to prevent the import of the Goods for a purpose that was contrary to Article 30 of the EEC Treaty and/or was calculated to and did unlawful damage to the Plaintiff in its business and/or was not the purpose for which the said powers had been conferred upon the Defendant.

10 The Plaintiff has suffered loss and damage as a result of the said breach of duty and/or misfeasance.

PARTICULARS

[*Give particulars of loss*]

11 The Plaintiff is entitled to interest pursuant to section 35A of the Supreme Court Act 1981 on such sums and at such rate and for such period as the Court deems fit.

AND the Plaintiff claims:

(1) damages;

(2) interest pursuant to section 35A of the Supreme Court Act 1981.

[*Name of Counsel*]

Served this [   ] day of [   ] 199[   ] by [*firm name*] of [*address*], Solicitors for the Plaintiff.

C: Preliminary Reference—Notice of Motion

IN THE HIGH COURT OF JUSTICE   199[   ] A No [   ]
[QUEEN'S BENCH/CHANCERY DIVISION]

BETWEEN:

AB LIMITED

Plaintiff

and

CD LIMITED

Defendant

NOTICE OF MOTION

TAKE NOTICE that this Honourable Court will be moved before Mr Justice [   ] at the Royal Court of Justice, Strand, London WC2 2LL, on the [   ] day of [   ] 199[   ] at [   ] o'clock in the [fore/after]noon or so soon thereafter as Counsel can be heard for an order that:

(1) the questions set out in the draft Schedule hereto concerning the [interpretation/validity] of Commission Directive 000/93 of 24 June 1993 on the approximation of the laws of the Member States relating to the labelling of foodstuffs be referred to the Court of Justice of the European Communities for a preliminary ruling in accordance with Article 177 of the EEC Treaty;

(2) all further proceedings in this action be stayed until after the Court of Justice shall have given its ruling on the said question or until further Order in the meantime;

(3) the costs of this Motion be costs reserved.

[Signature]
Solicitors for the Plaintiff

Dated this [   ] day of [   ] 199[   ].

To the Defendant
and to [*name*] of [*address*], Solicitors for the Defendant.

281

SCHEDULE

REQUEST FOR A PRELIMINARY RULING OF THE COURT OF JUSTICE
OF THE EUROPEAN COMMUNITIES

[The Schedule should contain the following:

    (a) description of the parties;

    (b) facts of the case;

    (c) details of any judgment of a lower court;

    (d) description of relevant provisions of English law;

    (e) description of relevant provisions of Community law;

    (f) reasons why preliminary reference is necessary;

    (g) arguments of the parties on issues of Community law.]

The preliminary ruling of the Court of Justice is accordingly requested on the following questions:

(1)

(2)

(3)

D: Preliminary Reference—Order

IN THE HIGH COURT OF JUSTICE   199[   ] A No [   ]
[QUEEN'S BENCH/CHANCERY DIVISION]
THE HONOURABLE MR JUSTICE [   ]

BETWEEN:

AB LIMITED

Plaintiff

and

CD LIMITED

Defendant

ORDER

UPON READING the Notice of Motion herein dated the [   ] day of [   ] 199[   ] filed on behalf of the Plaintiff.

AND UPON READING the affidavit[s] of [   ] sworn on [   ] together with the exhibits referred to therein filed on behalf of the Plaintiff and the Statement of Facts set out in the Schedule thereto.

AND UPON READING the affidavit[s] of [   ] sworn on [   ] together with the exhibits referred to therein filed on behalf of the Defendant.

AND UPON HEARING counsel for the Plaintiff and for the Defendant.

IT IS ORDERED that:

(1) the questions set out in the Schedule hereto concerning the [interpretation/ validity] of Commission Directive 000/93 of 24 June 1993 on the approx- imation of the laws of the Member States relating to the labelling of food- stuffs be referred to the Court of Justice of the European Communities for a preliminary ruling in accordance with Article 177 of the EEC Treaty;

(2) all further proceedings in this action be stayed until after the Court of Justice shall have given its ruling on the said question or until further Order in the meantime;

[(3)the Senior Master of the Queen's Bench Division do send a copy of this Order to the Registrar of the Court of Justice without waiting for the expiry of the time to appeal against this Order pursuant to Order 114 Rule 5 of the Rules of the Supreme Court];[1]

(4) the costs of this Motion be Costs reserved.

SCHEDULE

REQUEST FOR A PRELIMINARY RULING OF THE COURT OF JUSTICE OF THE EUROPEAN COMMUNITIES

[*The Schedule should contain the following:*

> *(a) description of the parties;*
> *(b) facts of the case;*
> *(c) details of any judgment of a lower court;*
> *(d) description of relevant provisions of English law;*
> *(e) description of relevant provisions of Community law;*
> *(f) reasons why preliminary reference is necessary;*
> *(g) arguments of the parties on issues of Community law.*]

The preliminary ruling of the Court of Justice is accordingly requested on the following questions:

(1)

(2)

(3)

Dated this [   ] day of [   ] 199[   ].

---

[1] All parties may agree to waive their rights to appeal. See further at p 146.

E: Preliminary Reference—Notice of Appeal

IN THE COURT OF APPEAL   199[   ] A No [   ]
ON APPEAL FROM THE HIGH COURT OF JUSTICE
[QUEEN'S BENCH/CHANCERY DIVISION]

BETWEEN:

AB LIMITED

Plaintiff

and

CD LIMITED

Defendant

NOTICE OF APPEAL

TAKE NOTICE that the Court of Appeal will be moved as soon as Counsel can be heard on behalf of the above-named [Defendant] on appeal from the judgment and order of Mr Justice [   ] given at the hearing of the [Plaintiff's] Motion on the [   ] day of [   ] 199[   ] whereby on the [Plaintiff's] application under Order 114 of the Rules of the Supreme Court the Court ordered that there be referred to the Court of Justice of the European Communities for a preliminary ruling under Article 177 of the EEC Treaty the following questions:

(1) [*reproduce question*];

(2) [*reproduce question*];

(3) [*reproduce question*].

FOR AN ORDER that the said judgment be set aside AND for an Order that the [Plaintiff] pay to the [Defendant] the costs of this appeal.

AND FURTHER TAKE NOTICE that the grounds of the appeal are:

(1)

(2) , etc.

[Signature of Counsel]

Dated this [   ] day of [   ] 199[   ].

[Name of solicitors]
Solicitors to the Defendant.
To the Plaintiff and *[name of solicitors]*, Solicitors to the Plaintiff.

F: Preliminary Reference— Observations to the Court of Justice

IN THE COURT OF JUSTICE OF THE EUROPEAN COMMUNITIES

CASE C-000/94

ON A REFERENCE FOR A PRELIMINARY RULING UNDER ARTICLE 177 OF THE EEC TREATY MADE BY THE [QUEEN'S BENCH DIVISION OF THE HIGH COURT OF JUSTICE OF ENGLAND AND WALES], IN THE CASE PENDING BEFORE IT BETWEEN:

AB Limited

and

CD Limited

WRITTEN OBSERVATIONS
OF CD LIMITED

Facts

[Set out additional facts not sufficiently dealt with in reference or indicate agreement with facts as set out in reference.]

Legal Submissions

First Question
[Set out text of question.]
[Submissions.]

Consequently, CD Limited submits that the Court of Justice should answer the first question as follows:
[For example 'Article 5 of Commission Directive 000/93 of 24 June 1993 on the approximation of the laws of the Member States relating to the labelling of foodstuffs precludes a national law from requiring the exclusive use of a specific language for the labelling of foodstuffs'.]

Second Question

Third Question

Dated this [   ] day of [   ] 199[   ].

Signed [*Counsel*], instructed by [   ], Solicitors of [*address*].

G: Article 169—Complaint to the Commission (OJ No C26/6, 1 February 1989)

The Commission is issuing this standard complaint form to assist complainants in cases of failure to comply with Community law.

COMPLAINT TO THE COMMISSION OF THE EUROPEAN COMMUN-
ITIES FOR FAILURE TO COMPLY WITH COMMUNITY LAW

(89/C 26/07)

Name of complainant([1]):

Nationality:

Address or registered office:

Sphere of activity:

Member State, body or undertaking which has failed to comply with Community law:

Subject-matter of complaint and damage suffered, if any:

Steps taken before national or Community authorities:

— Administrative steps:

— Proceedings, if any, before courts or tribunals:

---

[1] The Commission undertakes to observe the customary rules of confidentiality when investigating the complaint.

Documentary or other evidence available in support of the complaint:

(Note to appear on the back of the form)

The Commission of the European Communities is responsible under the Treaties for ensuring the correct application of their provisions and of measures taken by the Community institutions.

Any individual may lodge a complaint with the Commission concerning a practice or a measure which, in his opinion, infringes a Community provision.

The complaint may be made on this form. It may either be sent direct to Brussels (Commission of the European Communities, 200 rue de la Loi, B-1049 Brussels) or be handed in at one of the Commission's information offices.

The following administrative safeguards exist for the complainant's benefit:

— an acknowledgement of receipt will be sent to the complainant as soon as the complaint is registered,

— the complainant will be informed of the action taken in response to his complaint, including representations made to the national authorities, Community bodies or undertakings concerned;

— the complainant will be informed of any infringement proceedings that the Commission intends to institute against a Member State as a result of the complaint and of any legal action it intends to take against an undertaking. Where appropriate, the complainant will be informed of proceedings that have already been instituted in relation to the subject-matter of the complaint.

H: Article 173—Application to the Court of First Instance

IN THE COURT OF FIRST INSTANCE OF THE EUROPEAN
COMMUNITIES

X Limited, a company incorporated in England, of [registered office], represented by [   ] barrister of Gray's Inn, instructed by [name], solicitor, with an
address for service at [name of Luxembourg agent and Luxembourg address for
service].

Applicant

and

The Commission of the European Communities

Defendant

APPLICATION under Article 173 of the EEC Treaty
for a declaration that Commission Decision 000/93
of 23 October 1993 relating to a proceeding under
Article 85 of the EEC Treaty is void

Facts

Legal arguments

Order sought

AB Limited respectfully asks the Court:

(1) to declare that Commission Decision 000/93 of 23 October 1993 is void;
(2) to order the Commission to pay costs.

Signed: [*signature of legal representative*]

Dated the [   ] day of [   ] 199[   ].

[*plus necessary annexes*]

Appendices

Appendix A

List of Directly Effective Treaty Articles
(OJ No C177/13, 4 July 1983)

1. Treaty Articles which have direct effect

Article 7 — Case 22/80 *Boussac Saint-Frères SA v Gerstenmeier* [1980] ECR 3427

Article 9 — Cases 2 and 3/69 *Sociaal Fonds voor de Diamantarbeiders v SA Ch Brachfeld & Sons* [1969] ECR 211

Article 12 — Case 26/62 *SACE SpA v Italian Ministry for Finance* [1963] ECR 1

Article 13 (2) — Case 33/70 *NV Algemene Transport-en Expeditie Onderneming van Genden Loos v Nederlandse Tarief Commissie* [1970] ECR 1213

Article 16 — Case 18/71 *Eunomia di Porro e C v Italian Ministry for Education* [1971] ECR 811

Article 30 — Case 74/76 *Iannelli and Volpi SpA v Meroni* [1977] ECR 557

Article 31 and first paragraph of Article 32 — Case 13/68 *Salgoil SpA v Italian Ministry for Foreign Trade* [1968] ECR 453

Article 34 — Case 83/78 *Pigs Marketing Board v Redmond* [1978] ECR 2347

Article 37 (1) — Case 59/75 *Pubblico Ministero v Manghera* [1976] ECR 91

Article 37 (2) — Case 6/64 *Costa v ENEL* [1964] ECR 585

Article 48 (2) — Case 167/73 *EC Commission v France* [1974] ECR 359

Article 52 — Case 2/74 *Reyners v Belgium* [1974] ECR 631

Article 53 — Case 6/64 *Costa v ENEL* [1964] ECR 585

First paragraph of Article 59 and third paragraph of Article 60 — Case 33/74 *Van Binsbergen v Bestuur van de Bedrijfsvereniging voor de Metaalnijverheid* [1974] ECR 1299

Article 85 — Case 13/61 *Kledingverkoopbedrijf de Geus un Uitdenbogerd v Robert Bosch GmbH* [1962] ECR 45

Article 86 (in conjunction with Article 90) — Case 155/73 *Sacchi* [1974] ECR 409

Final sentence of Article 93 (3) — Case 6/64 *Costa v ENEL* [1964] ECR 585

First paragraph of Article 95 — Case 57/65 *Lütticke GmbH v Hauptzollamt Saarlouis* [1966] ECR 205

Second paragraph of Article 95 — Case 27/67 *Fink-Frucht GmbH v Hauptzollamt München-Landsbergerstraße* [1968] ECR 223

Article 119 — Case 43/75 *Defrenne v SA Belge de Navigation Aérienne* [1976] ECR 455

Except for Article 119, which is an exception from the general rule for specific reasons, the date on which a provision of the Treaty becomes directly applicable does not depend on the date of the Court judgment.

2. Treaty Articles which do not have direct effect

Second paragraph of Article 32 — Case 13/68 *Salgoil SpA v Italian Ministry for Foreign Trade* [1968] ECR 453

Article 33 — Ibid.

Article 67 — Case 203/80 *Casati* [1981] ECR 2595

First paragraph of Article 71 — Case 203/80 *Casati* [1981] ECR 2595

Article 90 (2) — Case 10/71 *Ministère Public of Luxembourg v Muller* [1971] ECR 723

Article 97 — Case 57/65 *Lütticke GmbH v Hauptzollamt München-Landsbergerstraße* [1966] ECR 205

Article 102 — Case 6/64 *Costa v ENEL* [1964] ECR 585

Articles 5 and 107 — Case 9/73 *Schlüter v Hauptzollamt Kehl* [1973] ECR 1135

Appendix B

Statute of the Court of Justice (EEC Statute)[1]

Article 1

The Court established by Article 4 of this Treaty shall be constituted and shall function in accordance with the provisions of this Treaty and of this Statute.

TITLE I

Judges and Advocates-General

Article 2

Before taking up his duties each Judge shall, in open court, take an oath to perform his duties impartially and conscientiously and to preserve the secrecy of the deliberations of the Court.

Article 3

The Judges shall be immune from legal proceedings. After they have ceased to hold office, they shall continue to enjoy immunity in respect of acts performed by them in their official capacity, including words spoken or written.

The Court, sitting in plenary session, may waive the immunity.

Where immunity has been waived and criminal proceedings are instituted against a Judge, he shall be tried, in any of the Member States, only by the Court competent to judge the members of the highest national judiciary.

Article 4

The Judges may not hold any political or administrative office.

They may not engage in any occupation, whether gainful or not, unless exemption is exceptionally granted by the Council.

When taking up their duties, they shall give a solemn undertaking that, both during and after their term of office, they will respect the obligations arising therefrom, in particular the duty to behave with integrity and discretion as regards the acceptance, after they have ceased to hold office, of certain appointments or benefits.

Any doubt on this point shall be settled by decision of the Court.

---

[1] Protocol of the Statute of the Court of Justice, signed at Brussels on 17 April 1957.

Article 5

Apart from normal replacement, or death, the duties of a Judge shall end when he resigns.

Where a Judge resigns, his letter of resignation shall be addressed to the President of the Court for transmission to the President of the Council. Upon this notification a vacancy shall arise on the bench.

Save where Article 6 applies, a Judge shall continue to hold office until his successor takes up his duties.

Article 6

A Judge may be deprived of his office or of his right to a pension or other benefits in its stead only if, in the unanimous opinion of the Judges and Advocates-General of the Court, he no longer fulfils the requisite conditions or meets the obligations arising from his office. The Judge concerned shall not take part in any such deliberations.

The Registrar of the Court shall communicate the decision of the Court to the President of the European Parliament and to the President of the Commission and shall notify it to the President of the Council.

In the case of a decision depriving a Judge of his office, a vacancy shall arise on the bench upon this latter notification.

Article 7

A Judge who is to replace a member of the Court whose term of office has not expired shall be appointed for the remainder of his predecessor's term.

Article 8

The provisions of Articles 2 to 7 shall apply to the Advocates-General.

TITLE II

Organization

Article 9

The Registrar shall take an oath before the Court to perform his duties impartially and conscientiously and to preserve the secrecy of the deliberations of the Court.

Article 10

The Court shall arrange for replacement of the Registrar on occasions when he is prevented from attending the Court.

Article 11

Officials and other servants shall be attached to the Court to enable it to function. They shall be responsible to the Registrar under the authority of the President.

Article 12

On a proposal from the Court, the Council may, acting unanimously, provide for the appointment of Assistant Rapporteurs and lay down the rules governing their service. The Assistant Rapporteurs may be required, under conditions laid down in the rules of procedure, to participate in preparatory inquiries in cases pending before the Court and to cooperate with the Judge who acts as Rapporteur.

The Assistant Rapporteurs shall be chosen from persons whose independence is beyond doubt and who possess the necessary legal qualifications; they shall be appointed by the Council. They shall take an oath before the Court to perform their duties impartially and conscientiously and to preserve the secrecy of the deliberations of the Court.

Article 13

The Judges, the Advocates-General and the Registrar shall be required to reside at the place where the Court has its seat.

Article 14

The Court shall remain permanently in session. The duration of the judicial vacations shall be determined by the Court with due regard to the needs of its business.

Article 15

Decisions of the Court shall be valid only when an uneven number of its members is sitting in the deliberations. Decisions of the full Court shall be valid if seven members are sitting. Decisions of the Chambers shall be valid only if three Judges are sitting; in the event of one of the Judges of a Chamber being prevented from attending, a Judge of another Chamber may be called upon to sit in accordance with conditions laid down in the rules of procedure.

Article 16

No Judge or Advocate-General may take part in the disposal of any case in which he has previously taken part as agent or adviser or has acted for one of the parties, or in which he has been called upon to pronounce as a Member of a court or tribunal, of a commission of inquiry or in any other capacity.

If, for some special reason, any Judge or Advocate-General considers that he should not take part in the judgment or examination of a particular case, he shall so inform the President. If, for some special reason, the President considers that any Judge or Advocate-General should not sit or make submissions in a particular case, he shall notify him accordingly.

Any difficulty arising as to the application of this Article shall be settled by decision of the Court.

A party may not apply for a change in the composition of the Court or of one of its Chambers on the grounds of either the nationality of a Judge or the absence from the Court or from the Chamber of a Judge of the nationality of that party.

TITLE III

Procedure

Article 17

The States and the institutions of the Community shall be represented before the Court by an agent appointed for each case: the agent may be assisted by an adviser or by a lawyer entitled to practise before a court of a Member State.

Other parties must be represented by a lawyer entitled to practise before a court of a Member State.

Such agents, advisers and lawyers shall, when they appear before the Court, enjoy the rights and immunities necessary to the independent exercise of their duties, under conditions laid down in the rules of procedure.

As regards such advisers and lawyers who appear before it, the Court shall have the powers normally accorded to courts of law, under conditions laid down in the rules of procedure.

University teachers being nationals of a Member State whose law accords them a right of audience shall have the same rights before the Court as are accorded by this Article to lawyers entitled to practise before a court of a Member State.

Article 18

The procedure before the Court shall consist of two parts: written and oral.

The written procedure shall consist of the communication to the parties and to the institutions of the Community whose decisions are in dispute, or applications, statements of case, defences and observations, and of replies, if any, as well as of all papers and documents in support or of certified copies of them.

Communications shall be made by the Registrar in the order and within the time laid down in the rules of procedure.

The oral procedure shall consist of the reading of the report presented by a Judge acting as Rapporteur, the hearing by the Court of agents, advisers and lawyers entitled to practise before a court of a Member State and of the submissions of the Advocate-General, as well as the hearing, if any, of witnesses and experts.

Article 19

A case shall be brought before the Court by a written application addressed to the Registrar. The application shall contain the applicant's name and permanent address and the description of the signatory, the name of the party against whom the application is made, the subject matter of the dispute, the submissions and a brief statement of the grounds on which the application is based.

The application shall be accompanied, where appropriate, by the measure the annulment of which is sought or, in the circumstances referred to in Article 175 of this Treaty by documentary evidence of the date on which an institution was, in accordance with that Article, requested to act. If the documents are not submitted with the application, the Registrar shall ask the party concerned to produce them within a reasonable period, but in that event the rights of the party shall not lapse even if such documents are produced after the time-limit for bringing proceedings.

Article 20

In the cases governed by Article 177 of this Treaty the decision of the Court or tribunal of a Member State which suspends its proceedings and refers a case to the Court shall be notified to the Court by the court or tribunal concerned. The decision shall then be notified by the Registrar of the Court to the parties, to the Member States and to the Commission, and also to the Council if the act the validity or interpretation of which is in dispute originates from the Council.

Within two months of this notification, the parties, the Member States, the Commission and, where appropriate, the Council, shall be entitled to submit statements of case or written observations to the Court.

Article 21

The Court may require the parties to produce all documents and to supply all information which the Court considers desirable. Formal note shall be taken of any refusal.

The Court may also require the Member States and institutions not being parties to the case to supply all information which the Court considers necessary for the proceedings.

Article 22

The Court may at any time entrust any individual body, authority, committee or other organization it chooses with the task of giving an expert opinion.

Article 23

Witnesses may be heard under conditions laid down in the rules of procedure.

Article 24

With respect to defaulting witnesses the Court shall have the powers generally granted to courts and tribunals and may impose pecuniary penalties under conditions laid down in the rules of procedure.

Article 25

Witnesses and experts may be heard on oath taken in the form laid down in the rules of procedure or in the manner laid down by the law of the country of the witness or expert.

Article 26

The Court may order that a witness or expert be heard by the judicial authority of his place of permanent residence.

The order shall be sent for implementation to the competent judicial authority under conditions laid down in the rules of procedure. The documents drawn up in compliance with the letters rogatory shall be returned to the Court under the same conditions.

The Court shall defray the expenses, without prejudice to the right to charge them, where appropriate, to the parties.

Article 27

A Member State shall treat any violation of an oath by a witness or expert in the same manner as if the offence had been committed before one of its courts with jurisdiction in civil proceedings. At the instance of the Court, the Member State concerned shall prosecute the offender before its competent court.

Article 28

The hearing in court shall be public, unless the Court, of its own motion or on application by the parties, decides otherwise for serious reasons.

Article 29

During the hearings the Court may examine the experts, the witnesses and the parties themselves. The latter, however, may address the Court only through their representatives.

Article 30

Minutes shall be made of each hearing and signed by the President and the Registrar.

Article 31

The case list shall be established by the President.

Article 32

The deliberations of the Court shall be and shall remain secret.

Article 33

Judgments shall state the reasons on which they are based. They shall contain the names of the Judges who took part in the deliberations.

Article 34

Judgments shall be signed by the President and the Registrar. They shall be read in open court.

Article 35

The Court shall adjudicate upon costs.

Article 36

The President of the Court may, by way of summary procedure, which may, in so far as necessary, differ from some of the rules contained in this Statute and which shall be laid down in the rules of procedure, adjudicate upon applications to suspend execution, as provided for in Article 185 of this Treaty, or to prescribe interim measures in pursuance of Article 186 or to suspend enforcement in accordance with the last paragraph of Article 192.

Should the President be prevented from attending, his place shall be taken by another Judge under conditions laid down in the rules of procedure.

The ruling of the President or of the Judge replacing him shall be provisional and shall in no way prejudice the decision of the Court on the substance of the case.

Article 37

Member States and institutions of the Community may intervene in cases before the Court.

The same right shall be open to any other person establishing an interest in the result of any case submitted to the Court, save in cases between Member States, between institutions of the Community or between Member States and institutions of the Community.

Submissions made in an application to intervene shall be limited to supporting the submissions of one of the parties.

Article 38

Where the defending party, after having been duly summoned, fails to file written submissions in defence, judgment shall be given against that party by default. An objection may be lodged against the judgment within one month of it being notified. The objection shall not have the effect of staying enforcement of the judgment by default unless the Court decides otherwise.

Article 39

Member States, institutions of the Community and any other natural or legal persons may, in cases and under conditions to be determined by the rules of procedure, institute third-party proceedings to contest a judgment rendered without their being heard, where the judgment is prejudicial to their rights.

Article 40

If the meaning or scope of a judgment is in doubt, the Court shall construe it on application by any party or any institution of the Community establishing an interest therein.

Article 41

An application for revision of a judgment may be made to the Court only on discovery of a fact which is of such a nature as to be a decisive factor, and which, when the judgment was given, was unknown to the Court and to the party claiming the revision.

The revision shall be opened by a judgment of the Court expressly, recording the existence of a new fact, recognizing that it is of such a character as to lay the case open to revision and declaring the application admissible on this ground.

No application for revision may be made after the lapse of 10 years from the date of the judgment.

Article 42

Periods of grace based on considerations of distance shall be determined by the rules of procedure.

No right shall be prejudiced in consequence of the expiry of a time-limit if the party concerned proves the existence of unforeseeable circumstances or of *force majeure*.

Article 43

Proceedings against the Community in matters arising from non-contractual liability shall be barred after a period of five years from the occurrence of the event giving rise thereto. The period of limitation shall be interrupted if proceedings are instituted before the Court or if prior to such proceedings an application is made by the aggrieved party to the relevant institution of the Community. In the latter event the proceedings must be instituted within the period of two months provided for in Article 173; the provisions of the second paragraph of Article 175 shall apply where appropriate.

TITLE IV

The Court of First Instance of the European Communities

Article 44

Articles 2 to 8, and 13 to 16 of this Statute shall apply to the Court of First Instance and its members. The oath referred to in Article 2 shall be taken before the Court of Justice and the decisions referred to in Articles 3, 4 and 6 shall be adopted by that Court after hearing the Court of First Instance.

Article 45

The Court of First Instance shall appoint its Registrar and lay down the rules governing his service. Articles 9, 10 and 13 of this Statute shall apply to the Registrar of the Court of First Instance *mutatis mutandis*.

The President of the Court of Justice and the President of the Court of First Instance shall determine, by common accord, the conditions under which officials and other servants attached to the Court of Justice shall render their services to the Court of First Instance to enable it to function. Certain officials or other servants shall be responsible to the Registrar of the Court of First Instance under the authority of the President of the Court of First Instance.

Article 46

The procedure before the Court of First Instance shall be governed by Title III of this Statute, with the exception of Article 20.

Such further and more detailed provisions as may be necessary shall be laid down in the Rules of Procedure established in accordance with Article 168a (4) of this Treaty.

Notwithstanding the fourth paragraph of Article 18 of this Statute, the Advocate-General may make his reasoned submissions in writing.

Article 47

Where an application or other procedural document addressed to the Court of First Instance is lodged by mistake with the Registrar of the Court of Justice it shall be transmitted immediately by that Registrar to the Registrar of the Court of First Instance; likewise, where an application or other procedural document addressed to the Court of Justice is lodged by mistake with the Registrar of the Court of First Instance, it shall be transmitted immediately by that Registrar to the Registrar of the Court of Justice.

Where the Court of First Instance finds that it does not have jurisdiction to hear and determine an action in respect of which the Court of Justice has jurisdiction, it shall refer that action to the Court of Justice; likewise, there the Court of Justice finds that an action falls within the jurisdiction of the Court of First Instance, it shall refer that action to the Court of First Instance, whereupon that Court may not decline jurisdiction.

Where the Court of Justice and the Court of First Instance are seised of cases in which the same relief is sought, the same issue of interpretation is raised or the validity of the same act is called in question, the Court of First Instance may, after hearing the parties, stay the proceedings before it until such time as the Court of Justice shall have delivered judgment. Where applications are made for the same act to be declared void, the Court of First Instance may also decline jurisdiction in order that the Court of Justice may rule on such applications. In the cases referred to in this subparagraph, the Court of Justice may also decide to stay the proceedings before it; in that event, the proceedings before the Court of First Instance shall continue.

Article 48

Final decisions of the Court of First Instance, decisions disposing of the substantive issues in part only or disposing of a procedural issue concerning a plea of lack of competence or inadmissibility, shall be notified by the Registrar of the Court of First Instance to all parties as well as all Member States and the Community institutions even if they did not intervene in the case before the Court of First Instance.

Article 49

An appeal may be brought before the Court of Justice, within two months of the notification of the decision appealed against, against final decisions of the Court of First Instance and decisions of that Court disposing of the substantive issues in part only or disposing of a procedural issue concerning a plea of lack of competence or inadmissibility.

Such an appeal may be brought by any party which has been unsuccessful, in whole or in part, in its submissions. However, interveners other than the Member States and the

Community institutions may bring such an appeal only where the decision of the Court of First Instance directly affects them.

With the exception of cases relating to disputes between the Committee and its servants, an appeal may also be brought by Member States and Community institutions which did not intervene in the proceedings before the Court of First Instance. Such Member States and institutions shall be in the same position as Member States or institutions which intervened at first instance.

Article 50

Any person whose application to intervene has been dismissed by the Court of First Instance may appeal to the Court of Justice within two weeks of the notification of the decision dismissing the application.

The parties to the proceedings may appeal to the Court of Justice against any decision of the Court of First Instance made pursuant to Article 185 or 186 or the fourth paragraph of Article 192 of this Treaty within two months from their notification.

The appeal referred to in the first two paragraphs of this Article shall be heard and determined under the procedure referred to in Article 36 of this Statute.

Article 51

An appeal to the Court of Justice shall be limited to points of law. It shall lie on the grounds of lack of competence of the Court of First Instance, a breach of procedure before it which adversely affects the interests of the appellant as well as the infringement of Community law by the Court of First Instance.

No appeal shall lie regarding only the amount of the costs or the party ordered to pay them.

Article 52

Where an appeal is brought against a decision of the Court of First Instance, the procedure before the Court of Justice shall consist of a written part and an oral part. In accordance with conditions laid down in the Rules of Procedure the Court of Justice, having heard the Advocate-General and the parties, may dispense with the oral procedure.

Article 53

Without prejudice to Articles 185 and 186 of this Treaty, an appeal shall not have suspensory effect.

By way of derogation from Article 187 of this Treaty, decisions of the Court of First Instance declaring a regulation to be void shall take effect only as from the date of expiry of the period referred to in the first paragraph of Article 49 of this Statute or, if an appeal shall have been brought within that period, as from the date of dismissal of the appeal, without prejudice, however, to the right of a party to apply to the Court of Justice, pursuant to Articles 185 and 186 of this Treaty, for the suspension of the effects of the regulation which has been declared void or for the prescription of any other interim measure.

Article 54

If the appeal is well founded, the Court of Justice shall quash the decision of the Court of First Instance. It may itself give final judgment in the matter, where the state of the proceedings so permits, or refer the case back to the Court of First Instance for judgment.

Where a case is referred back to the Court of First Instance, that Court shall be bound by the decision of the Court of Justice on points of law.

When an appeal brought by a Member State or a Community institution, which did not intervene in the proceedings before the Court of First Instance, is well founded the Court of Justice may, if it considers this necessary, state which of the effects of the decision of the Court of First Instance which has been quashed shall be considered as definitive in respect of the parties to the litigation.

Article 55

The rules of procedure of the Court provided for in Article 188 of this Treaty shall contain, apart from the provisions contemplated by this Statute, any other provisions necessary for applying and, where required, supplementing it.

Article 56

The Council may, acting unanimously, make such further adjustments to the provisions of this Statute as may be required by reason of measures taken by the Council in accordance with the last paragraph of Article 165 of this Treaty.

Article 57

(text not reproduced)

Appendix C

Rules of Procedure—Court of Justice

**RULES OF PROCEDURE OF THE COURT OF JUSTICE OF THE EUROPEAN
COMMUNITIES OF 19 JUNE 1991**[1]

CONTENTS

---

[1] OJ No L 176 of 4 July 1991, p 7 and No L 383 (Corrigenda) of 29 December 1992, p 117.

THE COURT OF JUSTICE,

Having regard to the powers conferred on the Court of Justice by the Treaty establishing the European Coal and Steel Community, the Treaty establishing the European Economic Community and the Treaty establishing the European Atomic Energy Community (Euratom),

Having regard to Article 55 of the Protocol on the Statute of the Court of Justice of the European Coal and Steel Community,

Having regard to the third paragraph of Article 188 of the Treaty establishing the European Economic Community,

Having regard to the third paragraph of Article 160 of the Treaty establishing the European Atomic Energy Community (Euratom),

Whereas it is necessary to revise the text of its Rules of Procedure in the various languages in order to ensure coherence and uniformity between those language versions;

With the unanimous approval of that revision, given by the Council on 29 April 1991;

And whereas, after the numerous amendments to its Rules of Procedure, it is necessary, in the interests of clarity and simplicity to establish a coherent authentic text,

With the unanimous approval of the Council, given on 7 June 1991,

REPLACES ITS RULES OF PROCEDURE BY THE FOLLOWING RULES:

Interpretation

Article 1

In these Rules:

'ECSC Treaty' means the Treaty establishing the European Coal and Steel Community;

'ECSC Statute' means the Protocol on the Statute of the Court of Justice of the European Coal and Steel Community;

'EEC Treaty' means the Treaty establishing the European Economic Community;

'EEC Statute' means the Protocol on the Statute of the Court of Justice of the European Economic Community;

'Euratom Treaty' means the Treaty establishing the European Atomic Energy Community (Euratom);

'Euratom Statute' means the Protocol on the Statute of the Court of Justice of the European Atomic Energy Community.

For the purposes of these Rules, 'institutions' means the institutions of the European Communities and the European Investment Bank.

TITLE 1

Organization of the Court

Chapter 1

JUDGES AND ADVOCATES-GENERAL

Article 2

The term of office of a Judge shall begin on the date laid down in his instrument of appointment. In the absence of any provisions regarding the date, the term shall begin on the date of the instrument.

Article 3

1. Before taking up his duties, a Judge shall at the first public sitting of the Court which he attends after his appointment take the following oath:

'I swear that I will perform my duties impartially and conscientiously; I swear that I will preserve the secrecy of the deliberations of the Court'.

2. Immediately after taking the oath, a Judge shall sign a declaration by which he solemnly undertakes that, both during and after his term of office, he will respect the obligations arising therefrom, and in particular the duty to behave with integrity and discretion as regards the acceptance, after he has ceased to hold office, of certain appointments and benefits.

Article 4

When the Court is called upon to decide whether a Judge no longer fulfils the requisite conditions or no longer meets the obligations arising from his office, the President shall invite the Judge concerned to make representations to the Court, in closed session and in the absence of the Registrar.

Article 5

Articles 2, 3 and 4 of these Rules shall apply in a corresponding manner to Advocates-General.

Article 6

Judges and Advocates-General shall rank equally in precedence according to their seniority in office.

Where there is equal seniority in office, precedence shall be determined by age.

Retiring Judges and Advocates-General who are reappointed shall retain their former precedence.

Chapter 2

PRESIDENCY OF THE COURT AND CONSTITUTION OF THE CHAMBERS

Article 7

1. The Judges shall, immediately after the partial replacement provided for in Article 32b of the ECSC Treaty, Article 167 of the EEC Treaty and Article 139 of the Euratom Treaty, elect one of their number as President of the Court for a term of three years.

2. If the office of the President of the Court falls vacant before the normal date of expiry thereof, the Court shall elect a successor for the remainder of the term.

3. The elections provided for in this Article shall be by secret ballot. If a Judge obtains an absolute majority he shall be elected. If no Judge obtains an absolute majority, a second ballot shall be held and the Judge obtaining the most votes shall be elected. Where two or more Judges obtain an equal number of votes the oldest of them shall be deemed elected.

Article 8

The President shall direct the judicial business and the administration of the Court; he shall preside at hearings and deliberations.

Article 9

1. The Court shall set up Chambers in accordance with the provisions of the second paragraph of Article 32 of the ECSC Treaty, the second paragraph of Article 165 of the EEC Treaty and the second paragraph of Article 137 of the Euratom Treaty and shall decide which Judges shall be attached to them.

The composition of the Chambers shall be published in the *Official Journal of the European Communities*.

2. As soon as an application initiating proceedings has been lodged, the President shall assign the case to one of the Chambers for any preparatory inquiries and shall designate a Judge from that Chamber to act as Rapporteur.

3. The Court shall lay down criteria by which, as a rule, cases are to be assigned to Chambers.

4. These Rules shall apply to proceedings before the Chambers.

In cases assigned to a Chamber the powers of the President of the Court shall be exercised by the President of the Chamber.

Article 10

1. The Court shall appoint for a period of one year the Presidents of the Chambers and the First Advocate-General.

The provisions of Article 7 (2) and (3) shall apply.

Appointments made in pursuance of this paragraph shall be published in the *Official Journal of the European Communities*.

2. The First Advocate-General shall assign each case to an Advocate-General as soon as the Judge-Rapporteur has been designated by the President. He shall take the necessary steps if an Advocate-General is absent or prevented from acting.

Article 11

When the President of the Court is absent or prevented from attending or when the office of President is vacant, the functions of President shall be exercised by a President of a Chamber according to the order of precedence laid down in Article 6 of these Rules.

If the President of the Court and the President of the Chambers are all prevented from attending at the same time, or their posts are vacant at the same time, the functions of President shall be exercised by one of the other Judges according to the order of precedence laid down in Article 6 of these Rules.

Chapter 3

REGISTRY

Section 1—The Registrar and Assistant Registrars

Article 12

1. The Court shall appoint the Registrar. Two weeks before the date fixed for making the

appointment, the President shall inform the Members of the Court of the applications which have been made for the post.

2. An application shall be accompanied by full details of the candidate's age, nationality, university degrees, knowledge of any languages, present and past occupations and experience, if any, in judicial and international fields.

3. The appointment shall be made following the procedure laid down in Article 7 (3) of these Rules.

4. The Registrar shall be appointed for a term of six years. He may be reappointed.

5. The Registrar shall take the oath in accordance with Article 3 of these Rules.

6. The Registrar may be deprived of his office only if he no longer fulfils the requisite conditions or no longer meets the obligations arising from his office; the Court shall take its decision after giving the Registrar an opportunity to make representations.

7. If the office of Registrar falls vacant before the normal date of expiry of the term thereof, the Court shall appoint a new Registrar for a term of six years.

Article 13

The Court may, following the procedure laid down in respect of the Registrar, appoint one or more Assistant Registrars to assist the Registrar and to take his place in so far as the Instructions to the Registrar referred in Article 15 of these Rules allow.

Article 14

Where the Registrar and Assistant Registrar are absent or prevented from attending or their posts are vacant, the President shall designate an official to carry out temporarily the duties of Registrar.

Article 15

Instructions to the Registrar shall be adopted by the Court acting on a proposal from the President.

Article 16

1. There shall be kept in the Registry, under the control of the Registrar, a register initialled by the President, in which all pleadings and supporting documents shall be entered in the order in which they are lodged.

2. When a document has been registered, the Registrar shall make a note to that effect on the original and, if a party so requests, on any copy submitted for the purpose.

3. Entries in the register and the notes provided for in the preceding paragraph shall be authentic.

4. Rules for keeping the register shall be prescribed by the Instructions to the Registrar referred to in Article 15 of the Rules.

5. Persons having an interest may consult the register at the Registry and may obtain copies or extracts on payment of a charge on a scale fixed by the Court on a proposal from the Registrar.

The parties to a case may on payment of the appropriate charge also obtain copies of pleadings and authenticated copies of judgments and orders.

6. Notice shall be given in the *Official Journal of the European Communities* of the date of registration of an application initiating proceedings, the names and addresses of the

parties, the subject-matter of the proceedings, the form of order sought by the applicant and a summary of the pleas in law and of the main supporting arguments.

7. Where the Council or the Commission is not a party to a case, the Court shall send to it copies of the application and of the defence, without the annexes thereto, to enable it to assess whether the inapplicability of one of its acts is being invoked under the third paragraph of Article 36 of the ECSC Treaty, Article 184 of the EEC Treaty or Article 156 of the Euratom Treaty.

Article 17

1. The Registrar shall be responsible, under the authority of the President, for the acceptance, transmission and custody of documents and for effecting service as provided for by these Rules.

2. The Registrar shall assist the Court, the Chambers, the President and the Judges in all their official functions.

Article 18

The Registrar shall have custody of the seals. He shall be responsible for the records and be in charge of the publications of the Court.

Article 19

Subject to Articles 4 and 27 of these Rules, the Registrar shall attend the sittings of the Court and of the Chambers.

Section 2—Other departments

Article 20

1. The official and other servants of the Court shall be appointed in accordance with the provisions of the Staff Regulations.

2. Before taking up his duties, an official shall take the following oath before the President, in the presence of the Registrar:

'I swear that I will perform loyally, discreetly and conscientiously the duties assigned to me by the Court of Justice of the European Communities'.

Article 21

The organization of the departments of the Court shall be laid down, and may be modified, by the Court on a proposal from the Registrar.

Article 22

The Court shall set up a translating service staffed by experts with adequate legal training and a thorough knowledge of several official languages of the Court.

Article 23

The Registrar shall be responsible, under the authority of the President, for the administration of the Court, its financial management and its accounts; he shall be assisted in this by an administrator.

Chapter 4

ASSISTANT RAPPORTEURS

Article 24

1. Where the Court is of the opinion that the consideration of and preparatory inquiries in cases before it so require, it shall, pursuant to Article 16 of the ECSC Statute and Article 2 of the EEC and Euratom Statutes, propose the appointment of Assistant Rapporteurs.

2. Assistant Rapporteurs shall in particular assist the President in connection with applications for the adoption of interim measures and assist the Judge-Rapporteurs in their work.

3. In the performance of their duties the Assistant Rapporteurs shall be responsible to the President of the Court, the President of a Chamber or a Judge-Rapporteur, as the case may be.

4. Before taking up his duties, an Assistant Rapporteur shall take before the Court the oath set out in Article 3 of these Rules.

Chapter 5

THE WORKING OF THE COURT

Article 25

1. The dates and times of the sittings of the Court shall be fixed by the President.

2. The dates and times of the sittings of the Chambers shall be fixed by their respective Presidents.

3. The Court and the Chambers may choose to hold one or more sittings in a place other than that in which the Court has its seat.

Article 26

1. Where, by reason of a Judge being absent or prevented from attending, there is an even number of Judges, the most junior Judge within the meaning of Article 6 of these Rules shall abstain from taking part in the deliberations unless he is the Judge-Rapporteur. In that case the Judge immediately senior to him shall abstain from taking part in the deliberations.

2. If after the Court has been convened it is found that the quorum of seven Judges has not been attained, the President shall adjourn the sitting until there is a quorum.

3. If in any Chamber the quorum of three Judges has not been attained, the President of that Chamber shall so inform the President of the Court who shall designate another Judge to complete the Chamber.

Article 27

1. The Court and Chambers shall deliberate in closed session.

2. Only those Judges who were present at the oral proceedings and the Assistant Rapporteur, if any, entrusted with the consideration of the case may take part in the deliberations.

3. Every Judge taking part in the deliberations shall state his opinion and the reasons for it.

4. Any Judge may require that any questions be formulated in the language of his choice and communicated in writing to the Court or Chamber before being put to the vote.

5. The conclusions reached by the majority of the Judges after final discussion shall determine the decision of the Court. Votes shall be cast in reverse order to the order of precedence laid down in Article 6 of these Rules.

6. Differences of view on the substance, wording or order of questions, or on the interpretation of the voting shall be settled by decision of the Court or Chamber.

7. Where the deliberations of the Court concern questions of its own administration, the Advocates-General shall take part and have a vote. The Registrar shall be present, unless the Court decides to the contrary.

8. Where the court sits without the Registrar being present it shall, if necessary, instruct the most junior Judge within the meaning of Article 6 of these rules to draw up minutes. The minutes shall be signed by this Judge and by the President.

Article 28

1. Subject to any special decision of the Court, its vacations shall be as follows:

— from 18 December to 10 January,

— from the Sunday before Easter to the second Sunday after Easter,

— from 15 July to 15 September.

During vacations, the functions of President shall be exercised at the place where the Court has its seat either by the President himself, keeping in touch with the Registrar, or by a President of Chamber or other Judge invited by the President to take his place.

2. In a case of urgency, the President may convene the Judges and the Advocates-General during the vacations.

3. The Court shall observe the official holidays of the place where it has its seat.

4. The Court may, in proper circumstances, grant leave of absence to any Judge or Advocate-General.

Chapter 6

LANGUAGES

Article 29

1. The language of a case shall be Danish, Dutch, English, French, German, Greek, Irish, Italian, Portuguese or Spanish.

2. The language of a case shall be chosen by the applicant, except that:

(a) where the defendant is a Member State or a natural or legal person having the nationality of a Member State, the language of the case shall be the official language of that State; where that State has more than one official language, the applicant may choose between them;

(b) at the joint request of the parties the Court may authorize another of the languages mentioned in paragraph (1) of this Article to be used as the language of the case for all or part of the proceedings;

(c) at the request of one of the parties, and after the opposite party and the Advocate-General have been heard, the Court may, by way of derogation from subparagraphs (a) and (b), authorize another of the languages mentioned in paragraph (1) of this Article to be used as the language of the case for all or part of the proceedings; such a request may not be submitted by an institution of the European Communities.

In cases to which Article 103 of these Rules applies, the language of the case shall be the language of the national court or tribunal which refers the matter to the Court.

3. The language of the case shall be used in the written and oral pleadings of the parties and in supporting documents, and also in the minutes and decisions of the Court.

Any supporting documents expressed in another language must be accompanied by a translation into the language of the case.

In the case of lengthy documents, translations may be confined to extracts. However, the Court or Chamber may, of its own motion or at the request of a party, at any time call for a complete or fuller translation.

Notwithstanding the foregoing provisions, a Member State shall be entitled to use its official language when intervening in a case before the Court or when taking part in any reference of a kind mentioned in Article 103. This provision shall apply both to written statements and to oral addresses. The Registrar shall cause any such statement or address to be translated into the language of the case.

4. Where a witness or expert states that he is unable adequately to express himself in one of the languages referred to in paragraph (1) of this Article, the Court or Chamber may authorize him to give his evidence in another language. The Registrar shall arrange for translation into the language of the case.

5. The President of the Court and the Presidents of Chambers in conducting oral proceedings, the Judge-Rapporteur both in his preliminary report and in his report for the hearing, Judges and Advocates-General in putting questions and Advocates-General in delivering their opinions may use one of the languages referred to in paragraph (1) of this Article other than the language of the case. The Registrar shall arrange for translation into the language of the case.

Article 30

1. The Registrar shall, at the request of any Judge, of the Advocate-General or of a party, arrange for anything said or written in the course of the proceedings before the Court or a Chamber to be translated into the languages he chooses from those referred to in Article 29 (1).

2. Publications of the Court shall be issued in the languages referred to in Article 1 of Council Regulation No. 1.

Article 31

The texts of documents drawn up in the language of the case or in any other language authorized by the Court pursuant to Article 29 of these rules shall be authentic.

Chapter 7

RIGHTS AND OBLIGATIONS OF AGENTS, ADVISERS AND LAWYERS

Article 32

1. Agents representing a State or an institution, as well as advisers and lawyers, ap-

pearing before the Court or before any judicial authority to which the Court has addressed letters rogatory, shall enjoy immunity in respect of words spoken or written by them concerning the case or the parties.

2. Agents, advisers and lawyers shall enjoy the following further privileges and facilities:

(a) papers and documents relating to the proceedings shall be exempt from both search and seizure; in the event of a dispute the customs officials or police may seal those papers and documents; they shall then be immediately forwarded to the Court for inspection in the presence of the Registrar and of the person concerned;

(b) agents, advisers and lawyers shall be entitled to such allocation of foreign currency as may be necessary for the performance of their duties;

(c) agents, advisers and lawyers shall be entitled to travel in the course of duty without hindrance.

Article 33

In order to qualify for the privileges, immunities and facilities specified in Article 32, persons entitled to them shall furnish proof of their status as follows:

(a) agents shall produce an official document issued by the State or institution which they represent; a copy of this document shall be forwarded without delay to the Registrar by the State or institution concerned;

(b) advisers and lawyers shall produce a certificate signed by the Registrar. The validity of this certificate shall be limited to a specified period, which may be extended or curtailed according to the length of the proceedings.

Article 34

The privileges, immunities and facilities specified in Article 32 of these Rules are granted exclusively in the interests of the proper conduct of proceedings.

The Court may waive the immunity where it considers that the proper conduct of proceedings will not be hindered thereby.

Article 35

1. Any adviser or lawyer whose conduct towards the Court, a Chamber, a Judge, an Advocate-General or the Registrar is incompatible with the dignity of the Court, or who uses his rights for purposes other than those for which they were granted, may at any time be excluded from the proceedings by an order of the Court or Chamber, after the Advocate-General has been heard; the person concerned shall be given an opportunity to defend himself.

The order shall have immediate effect.

2. Where an adviser or lawyer is excluded from the proceedings, the proceedings shall be suspended for a period fixed by the President in order to allow the party concerned to appoint another adviser or lawyer.

3. Decisions taken under this Article may be rescinded.

Article 36

The provisions of this Chapter shall apply to university teachers who have a right of audience before the Court in accordance with Article 20 of the ECSC Statute and Article 17 of the EEC and Euratom Statutes.

APPENDIX C

TITLE II

Procedure

Chapter 1

WRITTEN PROCEDURE

Article 37

1. The original of every pleading must be signed by the party's agent or lawyer.

The original, accompanied by all annexes referred to therein, shall be lodged together with five copies for the Court and a copy for every other party to the proceedings. Copies shall be certified by the party lodging them.

2. Institutions shall in addition produce, within time-limits laid down by the Court, translations of all pleadings into the other languages provided for by Article 1 of Council Regulation No. 1. The second subparagraph of paragraph (1) of this Article shall apply.

3. All pleadings shall bear a date. In the reckoning of time-limits for taking steps in proceedings, only the date of lodgment at the Registry shall be taken into account.

4. To every pleading there shall be annexed a file containing the documents relied on in support of it, together with a schedule listing them.

5. Where in view of the length of a document only extracts from it are annexed to the pleading, the whole document or a full copy of it shall be lodged at the Registry.

Article 38

1. An application of the kind referred to in Article 22 of the ECSC Statute and Article 19 of the EEC and Euratom Statutes shall state:

(a) the name and address of the applicant;

(b) the designation of the party against whom the application is made;

(c) the subject-matter of the proceedings and a summary of the pleas in law on which the application is based;

(d) the form of order sought by the applicant;

(e) where appropriate, the nature of any evidence offered in support.

2. For the purpose of the proceedings, the application shall state an address for service in the place where the Court has its seat and the name of the person who is authorized and has expressed willingness to accept service.

If the application does not comply with these requirements, all service on the party concerned for the purpose of the proceedings shall be effected, for so long as the defect has not been cured, by registered letter addressed to the agent or lawyer of that party. By way of derogation from Article 79, service shall then be deemed to be duly effected by the lodging of the registered letter at the post office of the place where the Court has its seat.

3. The lawyer acting for a party must lodge at the Registry a certificate that he is entitled to practise before a Court of a Member State.

4. The application shall be accompanied, where appropriate, by the documents specified in the second paragraph of Article 22 of the ECSC Statute and in the second paragraph of Article 19 of the EEC and Euratom Statutes.

5. An application made by a legal person governed by private law shall be accompanied by:

(a) the instrument or instruments constituting or regulating that legal person or a recent extract from the register of companies, firms or associations or any other proof of its existence in law;

(b) proof that the authority granted to the applicant's lawyer has been properly conferred on him by someone authorized for the purpose.

6. An application submitted under Articles 42 and 89 of the ECSC Treaty, Articles 181 and 182 of the EEC Treaty and Articles 153 and 154 of the Euratom Treaty shall be accompanied by a copy of the arbitration clause contained in the contract governed by private or public law entered into by the Communities or on their behalf, or, as the case may be, by a copy of the special agreement concluded between the Member States concerned.

7. If an application does not comply with the requirements set out in paragraphs (3) to (6) of this Article, the Registrar shall prescribe a reasonable period within which the applicant is to comply with them whether by putting the application itself in order or by producing any of the abovementioned documents. If the applicant fails to put the application in order or to produce the required documents within the time prescribed, the Court shall, after hearing the Advocate-General, decide whether the non-compliance with these conditions renders the application formally inadmissible.

Article 39

The application shall be served on the defendant. In a case where Article 38(7) applies, service shall be effected as soon as the application has been put in order or the Court has declared it admissible notwithstanding the failure to observe the formal requirements set out in that Article.

Article 40

1. Within one month after service on him of the application, the defendant shall lodge a defence, stating:

(a) the name and address of the defendant;

(b) the arguments of fact and law relied on;

(c) the form of order sought by the defendant;

(d) the nature of any evidence offered by him.

The provisions of Article 38 (2) to (5) of these Rules shall apply to the defence.

2. The time-limit laid down in paragraph (1) of this Article may be extended by the President on a reasoned application by the defendant.

Article 41

1. The application initiating the proceedings and the defence may be supplemented by a reply from the applicant and by a rejoinder from the defendant.

2. The President shall fix the time-limits within which these pleadings are to be lodged.

Article 42

1. In reply or rejoinder a party may offer further evidence. The party must, however, give reasons for the delay in offering it.

2. No new plea in law may be introduced in the course of proceedings unless it is based on matters of law or of fact which come to light in the course of the procedure.

If in the course of the procedure one of the parties puts forward a new plea in law which is so based, the President may, even after the expiry of the normal procedural time-limits, acting on a report of the Judge-Rapporteur and after hearing the Advocate-General, allow the other party time to answer on that plea.

The decision on the admissibility of the plea shall be reserved for the final judgment.

Article 43

The Court may, at any time, after hearing the parties and the Advocate-General, if the assignment referred to in Article 10 (2) has taken place, order that two or more cases concerning the same subject-matter shall, on account of the connection between them, be joined for the purposes of the written or oral procedure or of the final judgment. The cases may subsequently be disjoined.

Article 44

1. After the rejoinder provided for in Article 41 (1) of these Rules has been lodged, the President shall fix a date on which the Judge-Rapporteur is to present his preliminary report to the Court. The report shall contain recommendations as to whether a preparatory inquiry or any other preparatory step should be undertaken and whether the case should be referred to the Chamber to which it has been assigned under Article 9 (2).

The Court shall decide, after hearing the Advocate-General, what action to take upon the recommendations of the Judge-Rapporteur.

The same procedure shall apply:

(a) where no reply or no rejoinder has been lodged within the time-limit fixed in accordance with Article 41 (2) of these Rules;

(b) where the party concerned waives his right to lodge a reply or rejoinder.

2. Where the Court orders a preparatory inquiry and does not undertake it itself, it shall assign the inquiry to the Chamber.

Where the Court decides to open the oral procedure without an inquiry, the President shall fix the opening date.

Article 44(a)

Without prejudice to any special provisions laid down in these Rules, and except in the specific cases in which, after the pleading referred to in Article 40 (1) and, as the case may be, in Article 41 (1) have been lodged, the Court, acting on a report from the Judge-Rapporteur, after hearing the Advocate-General and with the express consent of the parties, decides otherwise, the procedure before the Court shall also include an oral part.

Chapter 2

PREPARATORY INQUIRIES

Section 1—Measures of inquiry

Article 45

1. The Court, after hearing the Advocate-General, shall prescribe the measures of inquiry that it considers appropriate by means of an order setting out the facts to be proved. Before the Court decides on the measures of inquiry referred to in paragraph (2) (c), (d) and (e) the parties shall be heard.

The order shall be served on the parties.

2. Without prejudice to Articles 24 and 25 of the ECSC Statute, Articles 21 and 22 of the EEC Statute or Articles 22 and 23 of the Euratom Statute, the following measures of inquiry may be adopted:

(a) the personal appearance of the parties;

(b) a request for information and production of documents;

(c) oral testimony;

(d) the commissioning of an expert's report;

(e) an inspection of the place or thing in question.

3. The measures of inquiry which the Court has ordered may be conducted by the Court itself, or be assigned to the Judge-Rapporteur.

The Advocate-General shall take part in the measures of inquiry

4. Evidence may be submitted in rebuttal and previous evidence may be amplified.

Article 46

1. A Chamber to which a preparatory inquiry has been assigned may exercise the powers vested in the Court by Articles 45 and 47 to 53 of these Rules; the powers vested in the President of the Court may be exercised by the President of the Chamber.

2. Articles 56 and 57 of the Rules shall apply in a corresponding manner to proceedings before the Chamber.

3. The parties shall be entitled to attend the measures of inquiry.

Section 2—The summoning and examination of witnesses and experts

Article 47

1. The Court may, either of its own motion or on application by a party, and after hearing the Advocate-General, order that certain facts be proved by witnesses. The order of the Court shall set out the facts to be established.

The Court may summon a witness of its own motion or on application by a party or at the instance of the Advocate-General.

An application by a party for the examination of a witness shall state precisely about what facts and for what reasons the witness should be examined.

2. The witness shall be summoned by an order of the Court containing the following information:

(a) the surname, forenames, description and address of the witness;

(b) an indication of the facts about which the witness is to be examined;

(c) where appropriate, particulars of the arrangements made by the Court for reimbursement of expenses incurred by the witness, and of the penalties which may be imposed on defaulting witnesses.

The order shall be served on the parties and the witnesses.

3. The Court may make the summoning of a witness for whose examination a party has applied conditional upon the deposit with the cashier of the Court of a sum sufficient to cover the taxed costs thereof; the Court shall fix the amount of the payment.

The cashier shall advance the funds necessary in connection with the examination of any witness summoned by the Court of its own motion.

4. After the identity of the witness has been established, the President shall inform him that he will be required to vouch the truth of his evidence in the manner laid down in these Rules.

The witness shall give his evidence to the Court, the parties having been given notice to attend. After the witness has given his main evidence the President may, at the request of a party or of his own motion, put questions to him.

The other Judges and the Advocate-General may do likewise.

Subject to the control of the President, questions may be put to witnesses by the representatives of the parties.

5. After giving his evidence, the witness shall take the following oath:

'I swear that I have spoken the truth, the whole truth and nothing but the truth.'

The Court may, after hearing the parties, exempt a witness from taking the oath.

6. The Registrar shall draw up minutes in which the evidence of each witness is reproduced.

The minutes shall be signed by the President or by the Judge-Rapporteur responsible for conducting the examination of the witness, and by the Registrar. Before the minutes are thus signed, witnesses must be given an opportunity to check the content of the minutes and to sign them.

The minutes shall constitute an official record.

Article 48

1. Witnesses who have been duly summoned shall obey the summons and attend for examination.

2. If a witness who has been duly summoned fails to appear before the Court, the Court may impose upon him a pecuniary penalty not exceeding ECU 5 000 and may order that a further summons be served on the witness at his own expense.

The same penalty may be imposed upon a witness who, without good reason, refuses to give evidence or to take the oath or where appropriate to make a solemn affirmation equivalent thereto.

3. If the witness proffers a valid excuse to the Court, the pecuniary penalty imposed on him may be cancelled. The pecuniary penalty imposed may be reduced at the request of the witness where he establishes that it is disproportionate to his income.

4. Penalties imposed and other measures ordered under this Article shall be enforced in accordance with Articles 44 and 92 of the ECSC Treaty, Articles 187 and 192 of the EEC Treaty and Articles 159 and 164 of the Euratom Treaty.

Article 49

1. The Court may order that an expert's report be obtained. The order appointing the expert shall define his task and set a time-limit within which he is to make his report.

2. The expert shall receive a copy of the order, together with all the documents necessary for carrying out his task. He shall be under the supervision of the Judge-Rapporteur, who may be present during his investigation and who shall be kept informed of his progress in carrying out his task.

The Court may request the parties or one of them to lodge security for the costs of the expert's report.

3. At the request of the expert, the Court may order the examination of witnesses. Their examination shall be carried out in accordance with Article 47 of these Rules.

4. The expert may give his opinion only on points which have been expressly referred to him.

5. After the expert has made his report, the Court may order that he be examined, the parties having been given notice to attend.

Subject to the control of the President, questions may be put to the expert by the representatives of the parties.

6. After making his report, the expert shall take the following oath before the Court:

'I swear that I have conscientiously and impartially carried out my task.'

The Court may, after hearing the parties, exempt the expert from taking the oath.

Article 50

1. If one of the parties objects to a witness or to an expert on the ground that he is not a competent or proper person to act as witness or expert or for any other reason, or if a witness or expert refuses to give evidence, to take the oath or to make a solemn affirmation equivalent thereto, the matter shall be resolved by the Court.

2. An objection to a witness or to an expert shall be raised within two weeks after service of the order summoning the witness or appointing the expert; the statement of objection must set out the grounds of objection and indicate the nature of any evidence offered.

Article 51

1. Witnesses and experts shall be entitled to reimbursement of their travel and subsistence expenses. The cashier of the Court may make a payment to them towards these expenses in advance.

2. Witnesses shall be entitled to compensation for loss of earnings, and experts to fees for their services. The cashier of the Court shall pay witnesses and experts their compensation or fees after they have carried out their respective duties or tasks.

Article 52

The Court may, on application by a party or of its own motion, issue letters rogatory for the examination of witnesses or experts, as provided for in the supplementary rules mentioned in Article 125 of these Rules.

Article 53

1. The Registrar shall draw up minutes of every hearing. The minutes shall be signed by the President and by the Registrar and shall constitute an official record.

2. The parties may inspect the minutes and any expert's report at the Registry and obtain copies at their own expense.

Section 3—Closure of the preparatory inquiry

Article 54

Unless the Court prescribes a period within which the parties may lodge written observations, the President shall fix the date for the opening of the oral procedure after the preparatory inquiry has been completed.

Where a period had been prescribed for the lodging of written observations, the President shall fix the date for the opening of the oral procedure after that period has expired.

Chapter 3

ORAL PROCEDURE

Article 55

1. Subject to the priority of decisions provided for in Article 85 of these Rules, the Court shall deal with the cases before it in the order in which the preparatory inquiries in them have been completed. Where the preparatory inquiries in several cases are completed simultaneously, the order in which they are to be dealt with shall be determined by the dates of entry in the register of the applications initiating them respectively.

2. The President may in special circumstances order that a case be given priority over others.

The President may in special circumstances, after hearing the parties and the Advocate-General, either on his own initiative or at the request of one of the parties, defer a case to be dealt with at a later date. On a joint application by the parties the President may order that a case be deferred.

Article 56

1. The proceedings shall be opened and directed by the President, who shall be responsible for the proper conduct of the hearing.

2. The oral proceedings in cases heard *in camera* shall not be published.

Article 57

The President may in the course of the hearing put questions to the agents, advisers or lawyers of the parties.

The other Judges and the Advocate-General may do likewise.

Article 58

A party may address the Court only through his agent, adviser or lawyer.

Article 59

1. The Advocate-General shall deliver his opinion orally at the end of the oral procedure.

2. After the Advocate-General has delivered his opinion, the President shall declare the oral procedure closed.

Article 60

The Court may at any time, in accordance with Article 45 (1), after hearing the Advocate-General, order any measure of inquiry to be taken or that a previous inquiry be repeated or expanded. The Court may direct the Chamber or the Judge-Rapporteur to carry out the measures so ordered.

Article 61

The Court may after hearing the Advocate-General order the reopening of the oral procedure.

Article 62

1. The Registrar shall draw up minutes of every hearing. The minutes shall be signed by the President and by the Registrar and shall constitute an official record.

2. The parties may inspect the minutes at the Registry and obtain copies at their own expense.

Chapter 4

JUDGMENTS

Article 63

The judgment shall contain:

— a statement that it is the judgment of the Court,

— the date of its delivery,

— the names of the President and of the Judges taking part in it,

— the name of the Advocate-General,

— the name of the Registrar,

— the description of the parties,

— the names of the agents, advisers and lawyers of the parties,

— a statement of the forms of order sought by the parties,

— a statement that the Advocate-General has been heard,

— a summary of the facts,

— the grounds for the decision,

— the operative part of the judgment, including the decision as to costs.

Article 64

1. The judgment shall be delivered in open court; the parties shall be given notice to attend to hear it.

2. The original of the judgment, signed by the President, by the Judges who took part in the deliberations and by the Registrar, shall be sealed and deposited at the Registry; the parties shall be served with certified copies of the judgment.

3. The Registrar shall record on the original of the judgment the date on which it was delivered.

Article 65

The judgment shall be binding from the date of its delivery.

Article 66

1. Without prejudice to the provisions relating to the interpretation of judgments the

Court may, of its own motion or on application by a party made within two weeks after the delivery of a judgment, rectify clerical mistakes, errors in calculation and obvious slips in it.

2. The parties, whom the Registrar shall duly notify, may lodge written observations within a period prescribed by the President.

3. The Court shall take its decision in closed session after hearing the Advocate-General.

4. The original of the rectification order shall be annexed to the original of the rectified judgment. A note of this order shall be made in the margin of the original of the rectified judgment.

Article 67

If the Court should omit to give a decision on a specific head or claim or on costs, any party may within a month after service of the judgment apply to the Court to supplement its judgment.

The application shall be served on the opposite party and the President shall prescribe a period within which that party may lodge written observations.

After these observations have been lodged, the Court shall, after hearing the Advocate-General, decide both on the admissibility and on the substance of the application.

Article 68

The Registrar shall arrange for the publication of reports of cases before the Court.

Chapter 5

COSTS

Article 69

1. A decision as to costs shall be given in the final judgment or in the order which closes the proceedings.

2. The unsuccessful party shall be ordered to pay the costs if they have been applied for in the successful party's pleadings.

Where there are several unsuccessful parties the Court shall decide how the costs are to be shared.

3. Where each party succeeds on some and fails on other heads, or where the circumstances are exceptional, the Court may order that the costs be shared or that the parties bear their own costs.

The Court may order a party, even if successful, to pay costs which the Court considers that party to have unreasonably or vexatiously caused the opposite party to incur.

4. The Member States and institutions which intervene in the proceedings shall bear their own costs.

The Court may order an intervener other than those mentioned in the preceding subparagraph to bear his own costs.

5. A party who discontinues or withdraws from proceedings shall be ordered to pay the costs if they have been applied for in the other party's pleadings. However, upon applica-

tion by the party who discontinues or withdraws from proceedings, the costs shall be borne by the other party if this appears justified by the conduct of that party.

Where the parties have come to an agreement on costs, the decision as to costs shall be in accordance with that agreement.

If costs are not claimed, the parties shall bear their own costs.

6. Where a case does not proceed to judgment the costs shall be in the discretion of the Court.

Article 70

Without prejudice to the second subparagraph of Article 69 (3) of these Rules, in proceedings between the Communities and their servants the institutions shall bear their own costs.

Article 71

Costs necessarily incurred by a party in enforcing a judgment or order of the Court shall be refunded by the opposite party on the scale in force in the State where the enforcement takes place.

Article 72

Proceedings before the Court shall be free of charge, except that:

(a) where a party has caused the Court to incur avoidable costs the Court may, after hearing the Advocate-General, order that party to refund them;

(b) where copying or translation work is carried out at the request of a party, the cost shall, in so far as the Registrar considers it excessive, be paid for by that party on the scale of charges referred to in Article 16 (5) of these Rules.

Article 73

Without prejudice to the preceding Article, the following shall be regarded as recoverable costs:

(a) sums payable to witnesses and experts under Article 51 of these Rules;

(b) expenses necessarily incurred by the parties for the purpose of the proceedings, in particular the travel and subsistence expenses and the remuneration of agents, advisers or lawyers.

Article 74

1. If there is a dispute concerning the costs to be recovered, the Chamber to which the case has been assigned shall, on application by the party concerned and after hearing the opposite party and the Advocate-General, make an order, from which no appeal shall lie.

2. The parties may, for the purposes of enforcement, apply for an authenticated copy of the order.

Article 75

1. Sums due from the cashier of the Court shall be paid in the currency of the country where the Court has its seat.

At the request of the person entitled to any sum, it shall be paid in the currency of the country where the expenses to be refunded were incurred or where the steps in respect of which payment is due were taken.

2. Other debtors shall make payment in the currency of their country of origin.

3. Conversions of currency shall be made at the official rates of exchange ruling on the day of payment in the country where the Court has its seat.

Chapter 6

LEGAL AID

Article 76

1. A party who is wholly or in part unable to meet the costs of the proceedings may at any time apply for legal aid.

The application shall be accompanied by evidence of the applicant's need of assistance, and in particular by a document from the competent authority certifying his lack of means.

2. If the application is made prior to proceedings which the applicant wishes to commence, it shall briefly state the subject of such proceedings.

The application need not be made through a lawyer.

3. The President shall designate a Judge to act as Rapporteur. The Chamber to which the latter belongs shall, after considering the written observations of the opposite party and after hearing the Advocate-General, decide whether legal aid should be granted in full or in part, or whether it should be refused. The Chamber shall consider whether there is manifestly no cause of action.

The Chamber shall make an order without giving reasons, and no appeal shall lie therefrom.

4. The Chamber may at any time, either of its own motion or on application, withdraw legal aid if the circumstances which led to its being granted alter during the proceedings.

5. Where legal aid is granted, the cashier of the Court shall advance the funds necessary to meet the expenses.

In its decision as to costs the Court may order the payment to the cashier of the Court of the whole or any part of amounts advanced as legal aid.

The Registrar shall take steps to obtain the recovery of these sums from the party ordered to pay them.

Chapter 7

DISCONTINUANCE

Article 77

If, before the Court has given its decision, the parties reach a settlement of their dispute and intimate to the Court the abandonment of their claims, the President shall order the case to be removed from the register and shall give a decision as to costs in accordance with Article 69 (5), having regard to any proposals made by the parties on the matter.

This provision shall not apply to proceedings under Articles 33 and 35 of the ECSC Treaty, Articles 173 and 175 of the EEC Treaty and Articles 146 and 148 of the Euratom Treaty.

Article 78

If the applicant informs the Court in writing that he wishes to discontinue the proceedings, the President shall order the case to be removed from the register and shall give a decision as to costs in accordance with Article 69 (5).

Chapter 8

SERVICE

Article 79

Where these Rules require that a document be served on a person, the Registrar shall ensure that service is effected at that person's address for service either by the dispatch of a copy of the document by registered post with a form for acknowledgement of receipt or by personal delivery of the copy against a receipt.

The Registrar shall prepare and certify the copies of documents to be served, save where the parties themselves supply the copies in accordance with Article 37 (1) of these Rules.

Chapter 9

TIME LIMITS

Article 80

1. Any period of time prescribed by the ECSC, EEC or Euratom Treaties, the Statutes of the Court or these Rules for the taking of any procedural step shall be reckoned as follows:

(a) where a period expressed in days, weeks, months or years is to be calculated from the moment at which an event occurs or an action takes place, the day during which that event occurs or that action takes place shall not be counted as falling within the period in question;

(b) a period expressed in weeks, months or in years shall end with the expiry of whichever day in the last week, month or year is the same day of the week, or falls on the same date, as the day during which the event or action from which the period is to be calculated occurred or took place. If, in a period expressed in months or in years, the day on which it should expire does not occur in the last month, the period shall end with the expiry of the last day of that month;

(c) where a period is expressed in months and days, it shall first be reckoned in whole months, then in days;

(d) periods shall include official holidays, Sundays and Saturdays;

(e) periods shall not be suspended during the judicial vacations.

2. If the period would otherwise end on a Saturday, Sunday or an official holiday, it shall be extended until the end of the first following working day.

A list of official holidays drawn up by the Court shall be published in the *Official Journal of the European Communities*.

Article 81

1. The period of time allowed for commencing proceedings against a measure adopted

by an institution shall run from the day following the receipt by the person concerned of notification of the measure or, where the measure is published, from the 15th day after publication thereof in the *Official Journal of the European Communities*.

2. The extensions, on account of distance, of prescribed time limits shall be provided for in a decision of the Court which shall be published in the *Official Journal of the European Communities*.

Article 82

Any time limit prescribed pursuant to these Rules may be extended by whoever prescribed it.

The President and the Presidents of Chambers may delegate to the Registrar power of signature for the purpose of fixing time limits which, pursuant to these Rules, it falls to them to prescribe or of extending such time limits.

Chapter 10

STAY OF PROCEEDINGS

Article 82a

1. The proceedings may be stayed:

(a) in the circumstances specified in the third paragraph of Article 47 of the ECSC Statute, the third paragraph of Article 47 of the EEC Statute and the third paragraph of Article 48 of the Euratom Statute, by order of the Court or of the Chamber to which the case has been assigned, made after hearing the Advocate-General;

(b) in all other cases, by decision of the President adopted after hearing the Advocate-General and, save in the case of references for a preliminary ruling as referred to in Article 103, the parties.

The proceedings may be resumed by order or decision, following the same procedure.

The orders or decisions referred to in this paragraph shall be served on the parties.

2. The stay of proceedings shall take effect on the date indicated in the order or decision of stay or, in the absence of such indication, on the date of that order or decision.

While proceedings are stayed time shall cease to run for the purposes of prescribed time limits for all parties.

3. Where the order or decision of stay does not fix the length of stay, it shall end on the date indicated in the order or decision of resumption or, in the absence of such indication, on the date of the order or decision of resumption.

From the date of resumption time shall begin to run afresh for the purposes of the time limits.

TITLE III

Special Forms of Procedure

Chapter 1

SUSPENSION OF OPERATION OR ENFORCEMENT AND OTHER INTERIM MEASURES

Article 83

1. An application to suspend the operation of any measure adopted by an institution, made pursuant to the second paragraph of Article 39 of the ECSC Treaty, Article 185 of the EEC Treaty and Article 157 of the Euratom Treaty, shall be admissible only if the applicant is challenging that measure in proceedings before the Court.

An application for the adoption of any other interim measure referred to in the third paragraph of Article 39 of the ECSC Treaty, Article 186 of the EEC Treaty and Article 158 of the Euratom Treaty shall be admissible only if it is made by a party to a case before the Court and relates to that case.

2. Any application of a kind referred to in paragraph (1) of this Article shall state the subject-matter of the proceedings, the circumstances giving rise to urgency and the pleas of fact and law establishing a *prima facie* case for the interim measures applied for.

3. The application shall be made by a separate document and in accordance with the provisions of Articles 37 and 38 of these Rules.

Article 84

1. The application shall be served on the opposite party, and the President shall prescribe a short period within which that party may submit written or oral observations.

2. The President may order a preparatory inquiry.

The President may grant the application even before the observations of the opposite party have been submitted. This decision may be varied or cancelled even without any application being made by any party.

Article 85

The President shall either decide on the application himself or refer it to the Court.

If the President is absent or prevented from attending, Article 11 of these Rules shall apply.

Where the application is referred to it, the Court shall postpone all other cases, and shall give a decision after hearing the Advocate-General. Article 84 shall apply.

Article 86

1. The decision on the application shall take the form of a reasoned order, from which no appeal shall lie. The order shall be served on the parties forthwith.

2. The enforcement of the order may be made conditional on the lodging by the applicant of security, of an amount and nature to be fixed in the light of the circumstances.

3. Unless the order fixes the date on which the interim measure is to lapse, the measure shall lapse when final judgment is delivered.

4. The order shall have only an interim effect, and shall be without prejudice to the decision of the Court on the substance of the case.

Article 87

On application by a party, the order may at any time be varied or cancelled on account of a change in circumstances.

Article 88

Rejection of an application for an interim measure shall not bar the party who made it from making a further application on the basis of new facts.

Article 89

The provisions of this Chapter shall apply to applications to suspend the enforcement of a decision of the Court or of any measure adopted by another institution, submitted pursuant to Articles 44 and 92 of the ECSC Treaty, Articles 187 and 192 of the EEC Treaty and Articles 159 and 164 of the Euratom Treaty.

The order granting the application shall fix, where appropriate, a date on which the interim measure is to lapse.

Article 90

1. An application of a kind referred to in the third and fourth paragraphs of Article 81 of the Euratom Treaty shall contain:

(a) the names and addresses of the persons or undertakings to be inspected;

(b) an indication of what is to be inspected and of the purpose of the inspection.

2. The President shall give his decision in the form of an order. Article 86 of these Rules shall apply.

If the President is absent or prevented from attending, Article 11 of these Rules shall apply.

Chapter 2

PRELIMINARY ISSUES

Article 91

1. A party applying to the Court for a decision on a preliminary objection or other preliminary plea not going to the substance of the case shall make the application by a separate document.

The application must state the pleas of fact and law relied on and the form of order sought by the applicant; any supporting documents must be annexed to it.

2. As soon as the application has been lodged, the President shall prescribe a period within which the opposite party may lodge a document containing a statement of the form of order sought by that party and its pleas in law.

3. Unless the Court decides otherwise, the remainder of the proceedings shall be oral.

4. The Court shall, after hearing the Advocate-General, decide on the application or reserve its decision for the final judgment.

If the Court refuses the application or reserves its decision, the President shall prescribe new time-limits for the further steps in the proceedings.

Article 92

1. Where it is clear that the Court has no jurisdiction to take cognizance of an action or where the action is manifestly inadmissible, the Court may, by reasoned order, after hearing the Advocate-General and without taking further steps in the proceedings, give a decision on the action.

2. The Court may at any time of its own motion consider whether there exists any absolute bar to proceeding with a case, and shall give its decision in accordance with Article 91 (3) and (4) of these Rules.

Chapter 3

INTERVENTION

Article 93

1. An application to intervene must be made within three months of the publication of the notice referred to in Article 16 (6) of these Rules.

The application shall contain:

(a) the description of the case;

(b) the description of the parties;

(c) the name and address of the intervener;

(d) the intervener's address for service at the place where the Court has its seat;

(e) the form of order sought, by one or more of the parties, in support of which the intervener is applying for leave to intervene;

(f) except in the case of applications to intervene made by Member States or institutions, a statement of the reasons establishing the intervener's interest in the result of the case.

The intervener shall be represented in accordance with the first and second paragraphs of Article 20 of the ECSC Statute and with Article 17 of the EEC and Euratom Statutes.

Articles 37 and 38 of these Rules shall apply.

2. The application shall be served on the parties.

The President shall give the parties an opportunity to submit their written or oral observations before deciding on the application.

The President shall decide on the application by order or shall refer the application to the Court.

3. If the President allows the intervention, the intervener shall receive a copy of every document served on the parties. The President may, however, on application by one of the parties, omit secret or confidential documents.

4. The intervener must accept the case as he finds it at the time of his intervention.

5. The President shall prescribe a period within which the intervener may submit a statement in intervention.

The statement in intervention shall contain:

(a) a statement of the form of order sought by the intervener in support of or opposing, in whole or in part, the form of order sought by one of the parties;

(b) the pleas in law and arguments relied on by the intervener;

(c) where appropriate, the nature of any evidence offered.

6. After the statement in intervention has been lodged, the President shall, where necessary, prescribe a time-limit within which the parties may reply to that statement.

Chapter 4

JUDGMENTS BY DEFAULT AND APPLICATIONS TO SET THEM ASIDE

Article 94

1. If a defendant on whom an application initiating proceedings has been duly served fails to lodge a defence to the application in the proper form within the time prescribed, the applicant may apply for judgment by default.

The application shall be served on the defendant. The President shall fix a date for the opening of the oral procedure.

2. Before giving judgment by default the Court shall, after hearing the Advocate-General, consider whether the application initiating proceedings is admissible, whether the appropriate formalities have been complied with, and whether the application appears well founded. The Court may order a preparatory inquiry.

3. A judgment by default shall be enforceable. The Court may, however, grant a stay of execution until the Court has given its decision on any application under paragraph (4) to set aside the judgment, or it may make execution subject to the provision of security of an amount and nature to be fixed in the light of the circumstances; this security shall be released if no such application is made or if the application fails.

4. Application may be made to set aside a judgment by default.

The application to set aside the judgment must be made within one month from the date of service of the judgment and must be lodged in the form prescribed by Articles 37 and 38 of these Rules.

5. After the application has been served, the President shall prescribe a period within which the other party may submit his written observations.

The proceedings shall be conducted in accordance with Articles 44 *et seq.* of these Rules.

6. The Court shall decide by way of a judgment which may not be set aside. The original of this judgment shall be annexed to the original of the judgment by default. A note of the judgment on the application to set aside shall be made in the margin of the original of the judgment by default.

Chapter 5

CASES ASSIGNED TO CHAMBERS

Article 95

1. The Court may assign to a Chamber any appeal brought against a decision of the Court of First Instance pursuant to Article 49 of the ECSC Statute, Article 49 of the EEC Statute and Article 50 of the Euratom Statute, any reference for a preliminary ruling of a kind mentioned in Article 103 of these Rules and any other case, with the exception of those brought by a Member State or an institution, in so far as the difficulty or the import-

ance of the case or particular circumstances are not such as to require that the Court decide it in plenary session.

2. The decision so to assign a case shall be taken by the Court at the end of the written procedure upon consideration of the preliminary report presented by the Judge-Rapporteur and after the Advocate-General has been heard.

However, a case may not be so assigned if a Member State or an institution, being a party to the proceedings, has requested that the case be decided in plenary session. In this subparagraph the expression 'party to the proceedings' means any Member State or any institution which is a party to or an intervener in the proceedings or which has submitted written observations in any reference of a kind mentioned in Article 103 of these Rules.

The request referred to in the preceding subparagraph may not be made in proceedings between the Communities and their servants.

3. A Chamber may at any stage refer a case back to the Court.

Article 96

(repealed)

Chapter 6

EXCEPTIONAL REVIEW PROCEDURES

Section 1—Third-party proceedings

Article 97

1. Articles 37 and 38 of these Rules shall apply to an application initiating third-party proceedings. In addition such an application shall:

(a) specify the judgment contested;

(b) state how that judgment is prejudicial to the rights of the third party;

(c) indicate the reasons for which the third party was unable to take part in the original case.

The application must be made against all the parties to the original case.

Where the judgment has been published in the *Official Journal of the European Communities*, the application must be lodged within two months of the publication.

2. The Court may, on application by the third party, order a stay of execution of the judgment. The provisions of Title III, Chapter I, of these Rules shall apply.

3. The contested judgment shall be varied on the points on which the submissions of the third party are upheld.

The original of the judgment in the third-party proceedings shall be annexed to the original of the contested judgment. A note of the judgment in the third-party proceedings shall be made in the margin of the original of the contested judgment.

Section 2—Revision

Article 98

An application for revision of a judgment shall be made within three months of the date on which the facts on which the application is based came to the applicant's knowledge.

Article 99

1. Articles 37 and 38 of these Rules shall apply to an application for revision. In addition such an application shall:

(a) specify the judgment contested;

(b) indicate the points on which the judgment is contested;

(c) set out the facts on which the application is based;

(d) indicate the nature of the evidence to show that there are facts justifying revision of the judgment, and that the time-limit laid down in Article 98 has been observed.

2. The application must be made against all parties to the case in which the contested judgment was given.

Article 100

1. Without prejudice to its decision on the substance, the Court, in closed session, shall, after hearing the Advocate-General and having regard to the written observations of the parties, give in the form of a judgment its decision on the admissibility of the application.

2. If the Court finds the application admissible, it shall proceed to consider the substance of the application and shall give its decision in the form of a judgment in accordance with these Rules.

3. The original of the revising judgment shall be annexed to the original of the judgment revised. A note of the revising judgment shall be made in the margin of the original of the judgment revised.

Chapter 7

APPEALS AGAINST DECISIONS OF THE ARBITRATION COMMITTEE

Article 101

1. An application initiating an appeal under the second paragraph of Article 18 of the Euratom Treaty shall state:

(a) the name and address of the applicant;

(b) the description of the signatory;

(c) a reference to the arbitration committee's decision against which the appeal is made;

(d) the description of the parties;

(e) a summary of the facts;

(f) the pleas in law or and the form of order sought by the applicant.

2. Articles 37 (3) and (4) and 38 (2), (3) and (5) of these Rules shall apply.

A certified copy of the contested decision shall be annexed to the application.

3. As soon as the application has been lodged, the Registrar of the Court shall request the arbitration committee registry to transmit to the Court the papers in the case.

4. Articles 39, 40, 55 *et seq.* of these Rules shall apply to these proceedings.

5. The Court shall give its decision in the form of a judgment. Where the Court sets aside the decision of the arbitration committee it may refer the case back to the committee.

Chapter 8

INTERPRETATION OF JUDGMENTS

Article 102

1. An application for interpretation of a judgment shall be made in accordance with Articles 37 and 38 of these Rules. In addition it shall specify:

(a) the judgment in question;

(b) the passages of which interpretation is sought.

The application must be made against all the parties to the case in which the judgment was given.

2. The Court shall give its decision in the form of a judgment after having given the parties an opportunity to submit their observations and after hearing the Advocate-General.

The original of the interpreting judgment shall be annexed to the original of the judgment interpreted. A note of the interpreting judgment shall be made in the margin of the original of the judgment interpreted.

Chapter 9

PRELIMINARY RULINGS AND OTHER REFERENCES FOR INTERPRETATION

Article 103

1. In cases governed by Article 20 of the EEC Statute and Article 21 of the Euratom Statute, the procedure shall be governed by the provisions of these Rules, subject to adaptations necessitated by the nature of the reference for a preliminary ruling.

2. The provisions of paragraph (1) shall apply to the references for a preliminary ruling provided for in the Protocol concerning the interpretation by the Court of Justice of the Convention of 29 February 1968 on the mutual recognition of companies and legal persons and the Protocol concerning the interpretation by the Court of Justice of the Convention of 27 September 1968 on jurisdiction and the enforcement of judgments in civil and commercial matters, signed at Luxembourg on 3 June 1971, and to the references provided for by Article 4 of the latter Protocol.

The provisions of paragraph (1) shall apply also to references for interpretation provided for by other existing or future agreements.

3. In cases provided for in Article 41 of the ECSC Treaty, the text of the decision to refer the matter shall be served on the parties in the case, the Member States, the Commission and the Council.

These parties, States and institutions may, within two months from the date of such service, lodge written statements of case or written observations.

The provisions of paragraph (1) shall apply.

Article 104

1. The decisions of national courts or tribunals referred to in Article 103 shall be communicated to the Member States in the original version, accompanied by a translation into the official language of the State to which they are addressed.

2. As regards the representation and attendance of the parties to the main proceedings in the preliminary ruling procedure the Court shall take account of the rules of procedure of the national court or tribunal which made the reference.

3. Where a question referred to the Court for a preliminary ruling is manifestly identical to a question on which the Court has already ruled, the Court may, after informing the court or tribunal which referred the question to it, hearing any observations submitted by the persons referred to in Article 20 of the EEC Statute, Article 21 of the Euratom Statute and Article 103 (3) of these Rules and hearing the Advocate-General, give its decision by reasoned order in which reference is made to its previous judgment.

4. Without prejudice to paragraph (3) of this Article, the procedure before the Court in the case of a reference for a preliminary ruling shall also include an oral part. However, after the statements of case or written observations referred to in Article 20 of the EEC Statute, Article 21 of the Euratom Statute and Article 103 (3) of these Rules have been submitted, the Court, acting on a report from the Judge-Rapporteur, after informing the persons who under the aforementioned provisions are entitled to submit such statements or observations, may, after hearing the Advocate-General, decide otherwise, provided that none of those persons has asked to present oral argument.

5. It shall be for the national court or tribunal to decide as to the costs of the reference.

In special circumstances the Court may grant, by way of legal aid, assistance for the purpose of facilitating the representation or attendance of a party.

Chapter 10

SPECIAL PROCEDURES UNDER ARTICLES 103 TO 105 OF THE EURATOM TREATY

Article 105

1. Four certified copies shall be lodged of an application under the third paragraph of Article 103 of the Euratom Treaty. The Commission shall be served with a copy.

2. The application shall be accompanied by the draft of the agreement or contract in question, by the observations of the Commission addressed to the State concerned and by all other supporting documents.

The Commission shall submit its observations to the Court within a period of 10 days, which may be extended by the President after the State concerned has been heard.

A certified copy of the observations shall be served on that State.

3. As soon as the application has been lodged the President shall designate a Judge to act as Rapporteur. The First Advocate-General shall assign the case to an Advocate-General as soon as the Judge-Rapporteur has been designated.

4. The decision shall be taken in closed session after the Advocate-General has been heard.

The agents and advisers of the State concerned and of the Commission shall be heard if they so request.

Article 106

1. In cases provided for in the last paragraph of Article 104 and the last paragraph of Article 105 of the Euratom Treaty, the provisions of Articles 37 *et seq.* of these Rules shall apply.

2. The application shall be served on the State to which the respondent person or undertaking belongs.

Chapter 11

OPINIONS

Article 107

1. A request by the Council for an Opinion under Article 228 of the EEC Treaty shall be served on the Commission. Such a request by the Commission shall be served on the Council and on the Member States. Such a request by a Member State shall be served on the Council, the Commission and the other Member States.

The President shall prescribe a period within which the institutions and Member States which have been served with a request may submit their written observations.

2. The Opinion may deal not only with the question whether the envisaged agreement is compatible with the provisions of the EEC Treaty but also with the question whether the Community or any Community institution has the power to enter into that agreement.

Article 108

1. As soon as the request for an Opinion has been lodged, the President shall designate a Judge to act as Rapporteur.

2. The Court sitting in closed session shall, after hearing the Advocates-General, deliver a reasoned Opinion.

3. The Opinion, signed by the President, by the Judges who took part in the deliberations and by the Registrar, shall be served on the Council, the Commission and the Member States.

Article 109

Requests for the Opinion of the Court under the fourth paragraph of Article 95 of the ECSC Treaty shall be submitted jointly by the Commission and the Council.

The Opinion shall be delivered in accordance with the provisions of the preceding Article. It shall be communicated to the Commission, the Council and the European Parliament.

TITLE IV

Appeals against decisions of the Court of First Instance

Article 110

Without prejudice to the arrangements laid down in Article 29 (2) (b) and (c) and the fourth subparagraph of Article 29 (3) of these Rules, in appeals against decisions of the Court of First Instance as referred to in Articles 49 and 50 of the ECSC Statute, Articles 49 and 50 of the EEC Statute and Articles 50 and 51 of the Euratom Statute, the language of the case shall be the language of the decision of the Court of First Instance against which the appeal is brought.

Article 111

1. An appeal shall be brought by lodging an application at the Registry of the Court of Justice or of the Court of First Instance.

2. The Registry of the Court of First Instance shall immediately transmit to the Registry of the Court of Justice the papers in the case at first instance and, where necessary, the appeal.

Article 112

1. An appeal shall contain:

(a) the name and address of the appellant;

(b) the names of the other parties to the proceedings before the Court of First Instance;

(c) the pleas in law and legal arguments relied on;

(d) the form or order sought by the appellant.

Article 37 and Article 38 (2) and (3) of these Rules shall apply to appeals.

2. The decision of the Court of First Instance appealed against shall be attached to the appeal. The appeal shall state the date on which the decision appealed against was notified to the appellant.

3. If an appeal does not comply with Article 38 (3) or with paragraph (2) of this Article, Article 38 (7) of these Rules shall apply.

Article 113

1. An appeal may seek:

— to set aside, in whole or in part, the decision of the Court of First Instance;

— the same form of order, in whole or in part, as that sought at first instance and shall not seek a different form of order.

2. The subject-matter of the proceedings before the Court of First Instance may not be changed in the appeal.

Article 114

Notice of the appeal shall be served on all the parties to the proceedings before the Court of First Instance. Article 39 of these Rules shall apply.

Article 115

1. Any party to the proceedings before the Court of First Instance may lodge a response within two months after service on him of notice of the appeal. The time-limit for lodging a response shall not be extended.

2. A response shall contain:

(a) the name and address of the party lodging it;

(b) the date on which notice of the appeal was served on him;

(c) the pleas in law and legal arguments relied on;

(d) the form of order sought by the respondent.

Article 38 (2) and (3) of these Rules shall apply.

Article 116

1. A response may seek:

— to dismiss, in whole or in part, the appeal or to set aside, in whole or in part, the decision of the Court of First Instance;

— the same form of order, in whole or in part, as that sought at first instance and shall not seek a different form of order.

2. The subject-matter of the proceedings before the Court of First Instance may not be changed in the response.

Article 117

1. The appeal and the response may be supplemented by a reply and a rejoinder or any other pleading, where the President expressly, on application made within seven days of service of the response or of the reply, considers such further pleading necessary and expressly allows it in order to enable the party concerned to put forward its point of view or in order to provide a basis for the decision on the appeal.

2. Where the response seeks to set aside, in whole or in part, the decision of the Court of First Instance on a plea in law which was not raised in the appeal, the appellant or any other party may submit a reply on that plea alone within two months of the service of the response in question. Paragraph (1) shall apply to any further pleading following such a reply.

3. Where the President allows the lodging of a reply and a rejoinder, or any other pleading, he shall prescribe the period within which they are to be submitted.

Article 118

Subject to the following provisions, Articles 42 (2), 43, 44, 55 to 90, 93, 95 to 100 and 102 of these Rules shall apply to the procedure before the Court of Justice on appeal from a decision from the Court of First Instance.

Article 119

Where the appeal is, in whole or in part, clearly inadmissible or clearly unfounded, the Court may at any time, acting on a report from the Judge-Rapporteur and after hearing the Advocate-General, by reasoned order dismiss the appeal in whole or in part.

Article 120

After the submission of pleadings as provided for in Articles 115 (1) and, if any, Article 117 (1) and (2) of these Rules, the Court may, acting on a report from the Judge-Rapporteur and after hearing the Advocate-General and the parties, decide to dispense with the oral part of the procedure unless one of the parties objects on the ground that the written procedure did not enable him fully to defend his point of view.

Article 121

The report referred to in Article 44 (1) shall be presented to the Court after the pleadings provided for in Article 115 (1) and Article 117 (1) and (2) of these Rules have been lodged. The report shall contain, in addition to the recommendations provided for in Article 44 (1), a recommendation as to whether Article 120 of these Rules should be applied. Where no such pleadings are lodged, the same procedure shall apply after the expiry of the period prescribed for lodging them.

Article 122

Where the appeal is unfounded or where the appeal is well founded and the Court itself gives final judgment in the case, the Court shall make a decision as to costs.

In proceedings between the Communities and their servants:

— Article 70 of these Rules shall apply only to appeals brought by institutions;

— by way of derogation from Article 69 (2) of these Rules, the Court may, in appeals brought by officials or other servants of an institution, order the parties to share the costs where equity so requires.

If the appeal is withdrawn Article 69 (5) shall apply.

When an appeal brought by a Member State or an institution which did not intervene in the proceedings before the Court of First Instance is well founded, the Court of Justice may order that the parties share the costs or that the successful appellant pay the costs which the appeal has caused an unsuccessful party to incur.

Article 123

An application to intervene made to the Court in appeal proceedings shall be lodged before the expiry of a period of three months running from the date on which the appeal was lodged. The Court shall, after hearing the Advocate-General, give its decision in the form of an order on whether or not the intervention is allowed.

Miscellaneous Provisions

Article 124

1. The President shall instruct any person who is required to take an oath before the Court, as witness or expert, to tell the truth or to carry out his task conscientiously and impartially, as the case may be, and shall warn him of the criminal liability provided for in his national law in the event of any breach of this duty.

2. The witness shall take the oath either in accordance with the first subparagraph of Article 47 (5) of these Rules or in the manner laid down by his national law.

Where his national law provides the opportunity to make, in judicial proceedings, a solemn affirmation equivalent to an oath as well as or instead of taking an oath, the witness may make such an affirmation under the conditions and in the form prescribed in his national law.

Where his national law provides neither for taking an oath nor for making a solemn affirmation, the procedure described in paragraph (1) shall be followed.

3. Paragraph (2) shall apply *mutatis mutandis* to experts, a reference to the first subparagraph of Article 49 (6) replacing in this case the reference to the first subparagraph of Article 47 (5) of these Rules.

Article 125

Subject to the provisions of Article 188 of the EEC Treaty and Article 160 of the Euratom Treaty and after consultation with the Governments concerned, the Court shall adopt supplementary rules concerning its practice in relation to:

(a) letters rogatory

(b) applications for legal aid;

(c) reports of perjury by witnesses or experts, delivered pursuant to Article 28 of the ECSC and Euratom Statutes and Article 27 of the EEC Statute.

Article 126

These Rules replace the Rules of Procedure of the Court of Justice of the European Communities adopted on 4 December 1974 (*Official Journal of the European Communities* No L 350 of 28 December 1974, p. 1), as last amended on 15 May 1991.

Article 127

These Rules, which are authentic in the languages mentioned in Article 29 (1) of these Rules, shall be published in the *Official Journal of the European Communities* and shall enter into force on the first day of the second month following their publication.

Done at Luxembourg, 19 June 1991.

APPENDIX C

Annex I

Decision on Official Holidays

THE COURT OF JUSTICE OF THE EUROPEAN COMMUNITIES,

Having regard to Article 80 (2) of the Rules of Procedure, which requires the Court to draw up a list of official holidays;

DECIDES

Article 1

For the purposes of Article 80 (2) of the Rules of Procedure the following shall be official holidays:

New Year's Day;

Easter Monday;

1 May;

Ascension Day;

Whit Monday;

23 June;

24 June, where 23 June is a Sunday;

15 August;

1 November;

25 December;

26 December.

The official holidays referred to in the first paragraph hereof shall be those observed at the place where the Court of Justice has its seat.

Article 2

Article 80 (2) of the Rules of Procedure shall apply only to the official holidays mentioned in Article 1 of this Decision.

Article 3

This Decision, which shall constitute Annex I to the Rules of Procedure, shall enter into force on the same day as those Rules.

It shall be published in the *Official Journal of the European Communities*.

Done at Luxembourg, 19 June 1991.

ANNEX II

Decision on Extension of Time Limits on account of Distance

THE COURT OF JUSTICE OF THE EUROPEAN COMMUNITIES,

Having regard to Article 81 (2) of the Rules of Procedure relating to the extension, on account of distance, of prescribed time limits;

DECIDES

Article 1

In order to take account of distance, procedural time limits for all parties save those habitually resident in the Grand Duchy of Luxembourg shall be extended as follows:

— for the Kingdom of Belgium: two days,

— for the Federal Republic of Germany, the European territory of the French Republic and the European territory of the Kingdom of the Netherlands: six days,

— for the European territory of the Kingdom of Denmark, for the Hellenic Republic, for Ireland, for the Italian Republic, for the Kingdom of Spain, for the Portuguese Republic (with the exception of the Azores and Madeira) and for the United Kingdom: 10 days,

— for other European countries and territories: two weeks,

— for the autonomous regions of the Azores and Madeira of the Portuguese Republic: three weeks,

— for other countries, departments and territories: one month.

Article 2

This Decision, which shall constitute Annex II to the Rules of Procedure, shall enter into force on the same day as those Rules.

It shall be published in the *Official Journal of the European Communities*.

Done at Luxembourg, 19 June 1991.

APPENDIX C

SUPPLEMENTARY RULES

Chapter I

LETTERS ROGATORY

Article 1

Letters rogatory shall be issued in the form of an order which shall contain the names, forenames, description and address of the witness or expert, set out the facts on which the witness or expert is to be examined, name the parties, their agents, lawyers or advisers, indicate their addresses for service and briefly describe the subject-matter of the proceedings.

Notice of the order shall be served on the parties by the Registrar.

Article 2

The Registrar shall send the order to the competent authority named in Annex I of the Member State in whose territory the witness or expert is to be examined. Where necessary, the order shall be accompanied by a translation into the official languages of the Member State to which it is addressed.

The authority named pursuant to the first paragraph shall pass on the order to the judicial authority which is competent according to its national law.

The competent judicial authority shall give effect to the letters rogatory in accordance with its national law. After implementation the competent judicial authority shall transmit to the authority named pursuant to the first paragraph the order embodying the letters rogatory, any documents arising from the implementation and a detailed statement of costs. These documents shall be sent to the Registrar of the Court.

The Registrar shall be responsible for the translation of the documents into the language of the case.

Article 3

The Court shall defray the expenses occasioned by the letters rogatory without prejudice to the right to charge them, where appropriate, to the parties.

Chapter II

LEGAL AID

Article 4

The Court, by any order by which it decides that a person is entitled to receive legal aid, shall order that a lawyer be appointed to act for him.

If the person does not indicate his choice of lawyer, or if the Court considers that his choice is unacceptable, the Registrar shall send a copy of the order and of the application for legal aid to the authority named in Annex II, being the competent authority of the State concerned.

The Court, in the light of the suggestions made by that authority, shall of its own motion appoint a lawyer to act for the person concerned.

Article 5

The Court shall advance the funds necessary to meet expenses.

It shall adjudicate on the lawyer's disbursements and fees; the President may, on application by the lawyer, order that he receive an advance.

Chapter III

REPORTS OF PERJURY BY A WITNESS OR EXPERT

Article 6

The Court, after hearing the Advocate-General, may decide to report to the competent authority referred to in Annex III of the Member State whose courts have penal jurisdiction in any case of perjury on the part of a witness or expert before the Court, account being taken of the provisions of Article 110 of the Rules of Procedure.

Article 7

The Registrar shall be responsible for communicating the decision of the Court.

The decision shall set out the facts and circumstances on which the report is based.

FINAL PROVISIONS

Article 8

These Supplementary Rules replace the Supplementary Rules of 9 March 1962 (OJ, 1962, p. 1113).

Article 9

These Rules, which shall be authentic in the languages referred to in Article 29 (1) of the Rules of Procedure, shall be published in the *Official Journal of the European Communities*.

These Rules shall enter into force on the date of their publication.

APPENDIX C

LIST REFERRED TO IN THE FIRST PARAGRAPH OF ARTICLE 2

Belgium
The Minister for Justice
Denmark
The Minister for Justice
France
The Minister for Justice
Germany
The Federal Minister for Justice
Greece
The Minister for Justice
Ireland
The Minister for Justice
Italy
The Minister for Justice
Luxembourg
The Minister for Justice
Netherlands
The Minister for Justice
Portugal
The Minister for Justice
Spain
The Minister for Justice
United Kingdom
The Secretary of State

ANNEX II

LIST REFERRED TO IN THE SECOND PARAGRAPH OF ARTICLE 4

Belgium
The Minister for Justice
Denmark
The Minister for Justice
France
The Minister for Justice
Germany
Bundesrechtsanwaltskammer
Greece
The Minister for Justice
Ireland
The Minister for Justice
Italy
The Minister for Justice
Luxembourg
The Minister for Justice
Netherlands
Algemene Raad van de Nederlandse Orde van Advocaten
Portugal
The Minister for Justice
Spain
The Minister for Justice
United Kingdom
The Law Society, London (for applicants resident in England or Wales)
The Law Society of Scotland, Edinburgh (for applicants resident in Scotland)
The Incorporated Law Society of Northern Ireland, Belfast (for applicants resident in Northern Ireland)

Annex II

LIST REFERRED TO IN ARTICLE 6

Belgium
The Minister for Justice
Denmark
The Minister for Justice
France
The Minister for Justice
Germany
The Federal Minister for Justice
Greece
The Minister for Justice
Ireland
The Attorney-General
Italy
The Minister for Justice
Luxembourg
The Minister for Justice
Netherlands
The Minister for Justice
Portugal
The Minister for Justice
Spain
The Minister for Justice
United Kingdom
Her Majesty's Attorney-General, for witnesses or experts resident in England or Wales
Her Majesty's Advocate, for witnesses or experts resident in Scotland
Her Majesty's Attorney-General, for witnesses or experts resident in Northern Ireland

PROTOCOL ON THE INTERPRETATION BY THE COURT OF JUSTICE OF THE CONVENTION OF 27 SEPTEMBER 1968 ON JURISDICTION AND THE ENFORCEMENT OF JUDGMENTS IN CIVIL AND COMMERCIAL MATTERS

Article 1

The Court of Justice of the European Communities shall have jurisdiction to give rulings on the interpretation of the Convention on jurisdiction and the enforcement of judgements in civil and commercial matters and the Protocol annexed to that Convention, signed at Brussels on 27 September 1968, and also on the interpretation of the present Protocol.

The Court of Justice of the European Communities shall also have jurisdiction to give rulings on the interpretation of the Convention on the accession of the Kingdom of Denmark, Ireland and the United Kingdom of Great Britain and Northern Ireland to the Convention of 27 September 1968 and to this Protocol.

The Court of Justice of the European Communities shall also have jurisdiction to give rulings on the interpretation of the Convention on the accession of the Hellenic Republic to the Convention of 27 September 1968 and to this Protocol, as adjusted by the 1978 Convention.

The Court of Justice of the European Communities shall also have jurisdiction to give rulings on the interpretation of the Convention on the accession of the Kingdom of Spain and the Portuguese Republic to the Convention of 27 September 1968 and to this Protocol, as adjusted by the 1978 Convention and the 1982 Convention.

Article 2

The following courts may request the Court of Justice to give preliminary rulings on questions of interpretation:

1— in Belgium: la Cour de Cassation (het Hof van Cassatie) and le Conseil d'Etat (de Raad van State),

— in Denmark: Højesteret,

— in the Federal Republic of Germany: die obersten Gerichtshöfe des Bundes,

— in Greece: the τα ανώτατα Διχαστήρια,

— in Spain: el Tribunal Supremo,

— in France: la Cour de Cassation and le Conseil d'Etat,

— in Ireland: the Supreme Court,

— in Italy: la Corte Suprema di Cassazione,

— in Luxembourg: la Cour Supérieure de Justice, when sitting as Cour de Cassation,

— in the Netherlands: de Hoge Raad,

— in Portugal: o Supremo Tribunal de Justiça and o Supremo Tribunal Administrativo,

— in the United Kingdom: the House of Lords and courts to which application has been made under the second paragraph of Article 37 or under Article 41 of the Convention;

2— the courts of the Contracting States when they are sitting in an appellate capacity;

3— in the cases provided for in Article 37 of the Convention, the courts referred to in that Article.

Article 3

1. Where a question of interpretation of the Convention or of one of the other instruments referred to in Article 1 is raised in a case pending before one of the courts listed in point 1 of Article 2, that court shall, if it considers that a decision on the question is necessary to enable it to give judgment, request the Court of Justice to give a ruling thereon.

2. Where such a question is raised before any court referred to in point 2 or 3 of Article 2, that court may, under the conditions laid down in paragraph 1, request the Court of Justice to give a ruling thereon.

Article 4

1. The competent authority of a Contracting State may request the Court of Justice to give a ruling on a question of interpretation of the Convention or of one of the other instruments referred to in Article 1 if judgments given by courts of that State conflict with the interpretation given either by the Court of Justice or in a judgment of one of the courts of another Contracting State referred to in point 1 or 2 of Article 2. The provisions of this paragraph shall apply only to judgments which have become *res judicata*

2. The interpretation given by the Court of Justice in response to such a request shall not affect the judgments which gave rise to the request for interpretation.

3. The Procurators-General of the Courts of Cassation of the Contracting States, or any other authority designated by a Contracting State, shall be entitled to request the Court of Justice for a ruling on interpretation in accordance with paragraph 1.

4. The Registrar of the Court of Justice shall give notice of the request to the Contracting States, to the Commission and to the Council of the European Communities; they shall then be entitled within two months of the notification to submit statements of case or written observations to the Court.

5. No fees shall be levied or any costs or expenses awarded in respect of the proceedings provided for in this Article.

Article 5

1. Except where this Protocol otherwise provides, the provisions of the Treaty establishing the European Economic Community and those of the Protocol on the Statute of the Court of Justice annexed thereto, which are applicable when the Court is requested to give a preliminary ruling, shall also apply to any proceedings for the interpretation of the Convention and the other instruments referred to in Article 1.

2. The Rules of Procedure of the Court of Justice shall, if necessary, be adjusted and supplemented in accordance with Article 188 of the Treaty establishing the European Economic Community.

Article 11

The Contracting States shall communicate to the Secretary-General of the Council of the European Communities the texts of any provisions of their laws which necessitate an amendment to the list of courts in point 1 of Article 2.

Article 12

This Protocol is concluded for an unlimited period.

Article 14

This Protocol, drawn up in a single original in the Dutch, French, German and Italian languages, all four texts being equally authentic, shall be deposited in the archives of the Secretariat of the Council of the European Communities. The Secretary-General shall transmit a certified copy to the Government of each signatory State.

FIRST PROTOCOL ON THE INTERPRETATION BY THE COURT OF JUSTICE OF THE EUROPEAN COMMUNITIES OF THE CONVENTION ON THE LAW APPLICABLE TO CONTRACTUAL OBLIGATIONS, OPENED FOR SIGNATURE IN ROME ON 19 JUNE 1980

Article 1

The Court of Justice of the European Communities shall have jurisdiction to give rulings on the interpretation of:

(a) the Convention on the law applicable to contractual obligations, opened for signature in Rome on 19 June 1980, hereinafter referred to as 'the Rome Convention';

(b) the Convention on accession to the Rome Convention by the States which have become Members of the European Communities since the date on which it was opened for signature;

(c) this Protocol.

Article 2

Any of the courts referred to below may request the Court of Justice to give a preliminary ruling on a question raised in a case pending before it and concerning interpretation of the provisions contained in the instruments referred to in Article 1 if that court considers that a decision on the question is necessary to enable it to give judgment:

(a)— in Belgium: la Cour de Cassation (het Hof van Cassatie) and le Conseil d'Etat (de Raad van State),

— in Denmark: Højesteret,

— in the Federal Republic of Germany: die obersten Gerichtshöfe des Bundes,

— in Greece: τα ανώτατα Διχαστήρια,

— in Spain: el Tribunal Supremo,

— in France: la Cour de Cassation and le Conseil d'Etat,

— in Ireland: the Supreme Court,

— in Italy: la Corte Suprema di Cassazione and il Consiglio di Stato,

— in Luxembourg: la Cour Supérieure de Justice, when sitting as Cour de Cassion,

— in the Netherlands: de Hoge Raad,

— in Portugal: o Supremo Tribunal de Justiça and o Supremo Tribunal Administrativo

— in the United Kingdom: the House of Lords and other courts from which no further appeal is possible;

(b)— the courts of the Contracting States when acting as appeal courts.

Article 3

1. The competent authority of a Contracting State may request the Court of Justice to give a ruling on a question of interpretation of the provisions contained in the instruments referred to in Article 1 if judgments given by courts of that State conflict with the interpretation given either by the Court of Justice or in a judgment of one of the courts of another Contracting State referred to in Article 2. The provisions of this paragraph shall apply only to judgments which have become *res judicata*.

2. The interpretation given by the Court of Justice in response to such a request shall not affect the judgments which gave rise to the request for interpretation.

3. The Procurators-General of the Supreme Courts of Appeal of the Contracting States, or any other authority designated by a Contracting State, shall be entitled to request the Court of Justice for a ruling on interpretation in accordance with paragraph 1.

4. The Registrar of the Court of Justice shall give notice of the request to the Contracting States, to the Commission and to the Council of the European Communities; they shall then be entitled within two months of the notification to submit statements of case or written observations to the Court.

5. No fees shall be levied or any costs or expenses awarded in respect of the proceedings provided for in this Article.

Article 4

1. Except where this Protocol otherwise provides, the provisions of the Treaty establishing the European Economic Community and those of the Protocol on the Statute of the Court of Justice annexed thereto, which are applicable when the Court is requested to give a preliminary ruling, shall also apply to any proceedings for the interpretation of the instruments referred to in Article 1.

2. The Rules of Procedure of the Court of Justice shall, if necessary, be adjusted and supplemented in accordance with Article 188 of the Treaty establishing the European Economic Community.

Article 5

This Protocol shall be subject to ratification by the Signatory States. The instruments of ratification shall be deposited with the Secretary-General of the Council of the European Communities.

Article 6

1. To enter into force, this Protocol must be ratified by seven States in respect of which the Rome Convention is in force. This Protocol shall enter into force on the first day of the third month following the deposit of the instrument of ratification by the last such State to take this step. If, however, the Second Protocol conferring on the Court of Justice of the European Communities certain powers to interpret the Convention on the law applicable to contractual obligations, opened for signature in Rome on 19 June 1980, concluded in Brussels on 19 December 1988, enters into force on a later date, this Protocol shell enter into force on the date of entry into force of the Second Protocol.

2. Any ratification subsequent to the entry into force of this Protocol shall take effect on the first day of the third month following the deposit of the instrument of ratification, provided that the ratification, acceptance or approval of the Rome Convention by the State in question has become effective.

Article 7

The Secretary-General of the Council of the European Communities shall notify the Signatory States of:

(a) the deposit of each instrument of ratification;

(b) the date of entry into force of this Protocol;

(c) any designation communicated pursuant to Article 3 (3);

(d) any communication made pursuant to Article 8.

Article 8

The Contracting States shall communicate to the Secretary-General of the Council of the European Communities the texts of any provisions of their laws which necessitate an amendment to the list of courts in Article 2 (a).

Article 9

This Protocol shall have effect for as long as the Rome Convention remains in force under the conditions laid down in Article 30 of that Convention.

Article 11

This Protocol, drawn up in a single original in the Danish, Dutch, English, French, German, Greek, Irish, Italian, Portuguese and Spanish languages, all 10 texts being equally authentic, shall be deposited in the archives of the General Secretariat of the Council of the European Communities. The Secretary-General shall transmit a certified copy to the Government of each Signatory State.

Joint Declaration

The Governments of the Kingdom of Belgium, the Kingdom of Denmark, the Federal Republic of Germany, the Hellenic Republic, the Kingdom of Spain, the French Republic, Ireland, the Italian Republic, the Grand Duchy of Luxembourg, the Kingdom of the Netherlands, the Portuguese Republic and the United Kingdom of Great Britain and Northern Ireland,

On signing the First Protocol on the interpretation by the Court of Justice of the European Communities of the Convention on the law applicable to contractual obligations, opened for signature in Rome on 19 June 1980,

Desiring to ensure that the Convention is applied as effectively and as uniformly as possible,

Declare themselves ready to organize, in cooperation with the Court of Justice of the European Communities, an exchange of information on judgments which have become *res judicata* and have been handed down pursuant to the Convention on the law applicable to contractual obligations by the courts referred to in Article 2 of the said Protocol. The exchange of information will comprise:

— the forwarding to the Court of Justice by the competent national authorities of judgments handed down by the courts referred to in Article 2 (a) and significant judgments handed down by the courts referred to in Article 2 (b),

— the classification and the documentary exploitation of these judgments by the Court of Justice including, as far as necessary, the drawing up of abstracts and translations, and the publication of judgments of particular importance,

— the communication by the Court of Justice of the documentary material to the competent national authorities of the States parties to the Protocol and to the Commission and the Council of the European Communities.

SECOND PROTOCOL CONFERRING ON THE COURT OF JUSTICE OF THE EUROPEAN COMMUNITIES CERTAIN POWERS TO INTERPRET THE CONVENTION ON THE LAW APPLICABLE TO CONTRACTUAL OBLIGATIONS, OPENED FOR SIGNATURE IN ROME ON 19 JUNE 1980

Article 1

1. The Court of Justice of the European Communities shall, with respect to the Rome Convention, have the jurisdiction conferred upon it by the First Protocol on the interpretation by the Court of Justice of the European Communities of the Convention on the law applicable to contractual obligations, opened for signature in Rome on 19 June 1980, concluded in Brussels on 19 December 1988. The Protocol on the Statute of the Court of Justice of the European Communities and the Rules of Procedure of the Court of Justice shall apply.

2. The Rules of Procedure of the Court of Justice shall be adapted and supplemented as necessary in accordance with Article 188 of the Treaty establishing the European Economic Community.

Article 2

This Protocol shall be subject to ratification by the Signatory States. The instruments of ratification shall be deposited with the Secretary-General of the Council of the European Communities.

Article 3

This Protocol shall enter into force on the first day of the third month following the deposit of the instrument of ratification of the last Signatory State to complete that formality.

Article 4

This Protocol, drawn up in a single original in the Danish, Dutch, English, French, German, Greek, Irish, Italian, Portuguese and Spanish languages, all 10 texts being equally authentic, shall be deposited in the archives of the General Secretariat of the Council of the European Communities. The Secretary-General shall transmit a certified copy to the Government of each signatory.

Appendix D

Rules of Procedure—Court of First Instance

RULES OF PROCEDURE OF THE COURT OF FIRST INSTANCE OF THE EUROPEAN COMMUNITIES[1]

CONTENTS

[1] OJ No L 136 of 30 May 1991, p 1 and No L 317 (Corrigenda) of 19 November 1991, p 34.

THE COURT OF FIRST INSTANCE OF THE EUROPEAN COMMUNITIES,

Having regard to Article 32d of the Treaty establishing the European Coal and Steel Community,

Having regard to Article 168a of the Treaty establishing the European Economic Community,

Having regard to Article 140a of the Treaty establishing the European Atomic Energy Community,

Having regard to the Protocol on the Statute of the Court of Justice of the European Coal and Steel Community, signed in Paris on 18 April 1951,

Having regard to the Protocol on the Statute of the Court of Justice of the European Community, signed in Brussels on 17 April 1957,

Having regard to the Protocol on the Statute of the Court of Justice of the European Atomic Energy Community, signed in Brussels on 17 April 1957,

Having regard to Council Decision 88/591 ECSC, EEC, Euratom of 24 October 1988 establishing a Court of First Instance of the European Communities (OJ No L 319 of 25 November 1988, with corrigendum in OJ No L 241 of 17 August 1989), and in particular Article 11 thereof,

Having regard to the agreement of the Court of Justice,

Having regard to the unanimous approval of the Council, given on 21 December 1990 and 29 April 1991,

Whereas the Court of First Instance is to establish its rules of procedure in agreement with the Court of Justice and with the unanimous approval of the Council and to adopt them immediately upon its constitution;

Whereas it is necessary to adopt the provisions laid down for the functioning of the Court of First Instance by the Treaties, by the Protocols on the Statutes of the Court of Justice and by the Council Decision of 24 October 1988 establishing a Court of First Instance of the European Communities and to adopt any other provisions necessary for applying and, where required, supplementing those instruments;

Whereas it is necessary to lay down for the Court of First Instance procedures adapted to the duties of such a court and to the task entrusted to the Court of First Instance of ensuring effective judicial protection of individual interests in cases requiring close examination of complex facts;

Whereas it is, moreover, desirable that the rules applicable to the procedure before the Court of First Instance should not differ more than is necessary from the rules applicable to the procedure before the Court of Justice under its Rules of Procedure adopted on 4 December 1974 (OJ No L 350 of 28 December 1974), as subsequently amended,

adopts the following

RULES OF PROCEDURE
INTERPRETATION

Article 1

In these Rules:

'ECSC Treaty'   means the Treaty establishing the European Coal and Steel Community;

'ECSC Statute'	means the Protocol on the Statute of the Court of Justice of the European Coal and Steel Community;
'EEC Treaty'	means the Treaty establishing the European Economic Community;
'EEC Statute'	means the Protocol on the Statute of the Court of Justice of the European Economic Community;
'Euratom Treaty'	means the Treaty establishing the European Atomic Energy Community (Euratom);
'Euratom Statute'	means the Protocol on the Statute of the Court of Justice of the European Atomic Energy Community.

For the purposes of these Rules, 'institutions' means the institutions of the European Communities and the European Investment Bank.

TITLE 1

Organization of the Court of First Instance

Chapter 1

PRESIDENT AND MEMBERS OF THE COURT OF FIRST INSTANCE

Article 2

§ 1

Every Member of the Court of First Instance shall, as a rule, perform the function of Judge.

Members of the Court of First Instance are hereinafter referred to as 'Judges'.

§ 2

Every Judge, with the exception of the President, may, in the circumstances specified in Articles 17 to 19, perform the function of Advocate-General in a particular case.

References to the Advocate-General in these Rules shall apply only where a Judge has been designated as Advocate-General.

Article 3

The term of office of a Judge shall begin on the date laid down in his instrument of appointment. In the absence of any provision regarding the date, the term shall begin on the date of the instrument.

Article 4

§ 1

Before taking up his duties, a Judge shall take the following oath before the Court of Justice of the European Communities:

'I swear that I will perform my duties impartially and conscientiously; I swear that I will preserve the secrecy of the deliberations of the Court.'

§ 2

Immediately after taking the oath, a Judge shall sign a declaration by which he solemnly undertakes that, both during and after his term of office, he will respect the obligations arising therefrom, and in particular the duty to behave with integrity and discretion as regards the acceptance, after he has ceased to hold office, of certain appointments and benefits.

Article 5

When the Court of Justice is called upon to decide, after consulting the Court of First Instance, whether a Judge of the Court of First Instance no longer fulfils the requisite conditions or no longer meets the obligations arising from his office, the President of the Court of First Instance shall invite the Judge concerned to make representations to the Court of First Instance, in closed session and in the absence of the Registrar.

The Court of First Instance shall state the reasons for its opinion.

An opinion to the effect that a Judge of the Court of First Instance no longer fulfils the requisite conditions or no longer meets the obligations arising from his office must receive the votes of at least seven Judges of the Court of First Instance. In that event, particulars of the voting shall be communicated to the Court of Justice.

Voting shall be by secret ballot; the Judge concerned shall not take part in the deliberations.

Article 6

With the exception of the President of the Court of First Instance and of the Presidents of the Chambers, the Judges shall rank equally in precedence according to their seniority in office.

Where there is equal seniority in office, precedence shall be determined by age.

Retiring Judges who are reappointed shall retain their former precedence.

Article 7

§ 1

The Judges shall, immediately after the partial replacement provided for in Article 32 (d) of the ECSC Treaty, Article 168 (a) of the EEC Treaty and Article 140 (a) of the Euratom Treaty, elect one of their number as President of the Court of First Instance for a term of three years.

§ 2

If the office of President of the Court of First Instance falls vacant before the normal date of expiry thereof, the Court of First Instance shall elect a successor for the remainder of the term.

§ 3

The elections provided for in this Article shall be by secret ballot. If a Judge obtains an absolute majority he shall be elected. If no Judge obtains an absolute majority, a second ballot shall be held and the Judge obtaining the most votes shall be elected. Where two or more Judges obtain an equal number of votes the oldest of them shall be deemed elected.

Article 8

The President of the Court of First Instance shall direct the judicial business and the administration of the Court of First Instance. He shall preside at plenary sittings and deliberations.

Article 9

When the President of the Court of First Instance is absent or prevented from attending or when the office of President is vacant, the functions of President shall be exercised by a President of a Chamber according to the order of precedence laid down in Article 6.

If the President of the Court and the Presidents of the Chambers are all prevented from attending at the same time, or their posts are vacant at the same time, the functions of President shall be exercised by one of the other Judges according to the order of precedence laid down in Article 6.

Chapter 2

CONSTITUTION OF THE CHAMBERS AND DESIGNATION OF JUDGE-RAPPORTEURS AND ADVOCATES-GENERAL

Article 10

§ 1

The Court of First Instance shall set up Chambers composed of three or five Judges and shall decide which Judges shall be attached to them.

§ 2

The composition of the Chambers shall be published in the *Official Journal of the European Communities*.

Article 11

§ 1

Cases before the Court of First Instance shall be heard by Chambers composed in accordance with Article 10.

Cases may be heard by the Court of First Instance sitting in plenary session under the conditions laid down in Articles 14, 51, 106, 118, 124, 127 and 129.

§ 2

In cases coming before a Chamber, the term 'Court of First Instance' in these Rules shall designate that Chamber.

Article 12

§ 1

Subject to the provisions of Article 14, disputes between the Communities and their servants shall be assigned to Chambers of three Judges.

Other cases shall, subject to the provisions of Article 14, be assigned to Chambers of five Judges.

§ 2

The Court of First Instance shall lay down criteria by which, as a rule, cases are to be assigned to Chambers composed of the same number of Judges.

Article 13

§ 1

As soon as the application initiating proceedings has been lodged, the President of the

Court of First Instance shall assign the case to one of the Chambers.

§ 2

The President of the Chamber shall propose to the President of the Court of First Instance, in respect of each case assigned to the Chamber, the designation of a Judge to act as Rapporteur; the President of the Court of First Instance shall decide on the proposal.

Article 14

Whenever the legal difficulty or the importance of the case or special circumstances so justify, a case may be referred to the Court of First Instance sitting in plenary session or to a Chamber composed of a different number of Judges.

Any decision to refer a case shall be taken under the conditions laid down in Article 51.

Article 15

The Court of First Instance shall appoint for a period of one year the Presidents of the Chambers.

The provisions of Article 7 (2) and (3) shall apply.

The appointments made in pursuance of this Article shall be published in the *Official Journal of the European Communities*.

Article 16

In cases coming before a Chamber the powers of the President shall be exercised by the President of the Chamber.

Article 17

When the Court of First Instance sits in plenary session, it shall be assisted by an Advocate-General designated by the President of the Court of First Instance.

Article 18

A Chamber of the Court of First Instance may be assisted by an Advocate-General if it is considered that the legal difficulty or the factual complexity of the case so requires.

Article 19

The decision to designate an Advocate-General in a particular case shall be taken by the Court of First Instance sitting in plenary session at the request of the Chamber before which the case comes.

The President of the Court of First Instance shall designate the Judge called upon to perform the function of Advocate-General in that case.

Chapter 3

REGISTRY

Section 1—The Registrar

Article 20

§ 1

The Court of First Instance shall appoint the Registrar.

Two weeks before the date fixed for making the appointment, the President of the Court of First Instance shall inform the Judges of the applications which have been submitted for the post.

§ 2

An application shall be accompanied by full details of the candidate's age, nationality, university degrees, knowledge of any languages, present and past occupations and experience, if any, in judicial and international fields.

§ 3

The appointment shall be made following the procedure laid down in Article 7 (3).

§ 4

The Registrar shall be appointed for a term of six years. He may be reappointed.

§ 5

Before he takes up his duties the Registrar shall take the oath before the Court of First Instance in accordance with Article 4.

§ 6

The Registrar may be deprived of his office only if he no longer fulfils the requisite conditions or no longer meets the obligations arising from his office; the Court of First Instance shall take its decision after giving the Registrar an opportunity to make representations.

§ 7

If the office of Registrar falls vacant before the usual date of expiry of the term thereof, the Court of First Instance shall appoint a new Registrar for a term of six years.

Article 21

The Court of First Instance may, following the procedure laid down in respect of the Registrar, appoint one or more Assistant Registrars to assist the Registrar and to take his place in so far as the Instructions to the Registrar referred in Article 23 allow.

Article 22

Where the Registrar is absent or prevented from attending and, if necessary, where the Assistant Registrar is absent or so prevented, or where their posts are vacant, the President of the Court of First Instance shall designate an official or servant to carry out the duties of Registrar.

Article 23

Instructions to the Registrar shall be adopted by the Court of First Instance acting on a proposal from the President of the Court of First Instance.

Article 24

§ 1

There shall be kept in the Registry, under the control of the Registrar, a register initialled by the President of the Court of First Instance, in which all pleadings and supporting documents shall be entered in the order in which they are lodged.

§ 2

When a document has been registered, the Registrar shall make a note to that effect on the original and, if a party so requests, on any copy submitted for the purpose.

§ 3

Entries in the register and the notes provided for in the preceding paragraph shall be authentic.

§ 4

Rules for keeping the register shall be prescribed by the Instructions to the Registrar referred to in Article 23.

§ 5

Persons having an interest may consult the register at the Registry and may obtain copies or extracts on payment of a charge on a scale fixed by the Court of First Instance on a proposal from the Registrar.

The parties to a case may on payment of the appropriate charge also obtain copies of pleadings and authenticated copies of orders and judgments.

§ 6

Notice shall be given in the *Official Journal of the European Communities* of the date of registration of an application initiating proceedings, the names and addresses of the parties, the subject-matter of the proceedings, the form of order sought by the applicant and a summary of the pleas in law and of the main supporting arguments.

§ 7

Where the Council or the Commission is not a party to a case, the Court of First Instance shall send to it copies of the application and of the defence without the annexes thereto, to enable it to assess whether the inapplicability of one of its acts is being invoked under the third paragraph of Article 36 of the ECSC Treaty, Article 184 of the EEC Treaty or Article 156 of the Euratom Treaty.

Article 25

§ 1

The Registrar shall be responsible, under the authority of the President, for the acceptance, transmission and custody of documents and for effecting service as provided for by these Rules.

§ 2

The Registrar shall assist the Court of First Instance, the Chambers, the President and the Judges in all their official functions.

Article 26

The Registrar shall have custody of the seals. He shall be responsible for the records and be in charge of the publications of the Court of First Instance.

Article 27

Subject to Articles 5 and 33, the Registrar shall attend the sittings of the Court of First Instance and of the Chambers.

Section 2—Other Departments

Article 28

The officials and other servants whose task is to assist directly the President, the Judges and the Registrar shall be appointed in accordance with the Staff Regulations. They shall be responsible to the Registrar, under the authority of the President of the Court of First Instance.

Article 29

The officials and other servants referred to in Article 28 shall take the oath provided for in Article 20 (2) of the Rules of Procedure of the Court of Justice before the President of the Court of First Instance in the presence of the Registrar.

Article 30

The Registrar shall be responsible, under the authority of the President of the Court of First Instance, for the administration of the Court of First Instance, its financial management and its accounts; he shall be assisted in this by the departments of the Court of Justice.

Chapter 4

THE WORKING OF THE COURT OF FIRST INSTANCE

Article 31

§ 1

The dates and times of the sittings of the Court of First Instance shall be fixed by the President.

§ 2

The Court of First Instance may choose to hold one or more sittings in a place other than that in which the Court of First Instance has its seat.

Article 32

§ 1

Where, by reason of a Judge being absent or prevented from attending, there is an even number of Judges, the most junior Judge within the meaning of Article 6 shall abstain from taking part in the deliberations unless he is the Judge-Rapporteur. In this case, the Judge immediately senior to him shall abstain from taking part in the deliberations.

§ 2

If, after the Court of First Instance has been convened in plenary session, it is found that the quorum of seven Judges has not been obtained, the President of the Court of First Instance shall adjourn the sitting until there is a quorum.

§ 3

If in any Chamber the quorum of three Judges has not been attained, the President of that Chamber shall so inform the President of the Court of First Instance who shall designate another Judge to complete the Chamber.

§ 4

If in any chamber of three or five Judges the number of Judges assigned to that Chamber is higher than three or five respectively, the President of the Chamber shall decide which of the Judges will be called upon to take part in the judgment of the case.

Article 33

§ 1

The Court of First Instance shall deliberate in closed session.

§ 2

Only those Judges who were present at the oral proceedings may take part in the deliberations.

§ 3

Every Judge taking part in the deliberations shall state his opinion and the reasons for it.

§ 4

Any Judge may require that any question be formulated in the language of his choice and communicated in writing to the other Judges before being put to the vote.

§ 5

The conclusions reached by the majority of the Judges after final discussion shall determine the decision of the Court of First Instance. Votes shall be cast in reverse order to the order of precedence laid down in Article 6.

§ 6

Differences of view on the substance, wording or order of questions, or on the interpretation of a vote shall be settled by decision of the Court of First Instance.

§ 7

Where the deliberations of the Court of First Instance concern questions of its own administration, the Registrar shall be present, unless the Court of First Instance decides to the contrary.

§ 8

Where the Court of First Instance sits without the Registrar being present it shall, if necessary, instruct the most junior Judge within the meaning of Article 6 to draw up minutes. The minutes shall be signed by this Judge and by the President.

Article 34

§ 1

Subject to any special decision of the Court of First Instance, its vacations shall be as follows:

— from 18 December to 10 January,

— from the Sunday before Easter to the second Sunday after Easter,

— from 15 July to 15 September.

During the vacations, the functions of President shall be exercised at the place where the Court of First Instance has its seat either by the President himself, keeping in touch with the Registrar, or by a President of Chamber or other Judge invited by the President to take his place.

§ 2

In a case of urgency, the President may convene the Judges during the vacations.

§ 3

The Court of First Instance shall observe the official holidays of the place where it has its seat.

§ 4

The Court of First Instance may, in proper circumstances, grant leave of absence to any Judge.

Chapter 5

LANGUAGES

Article 35

§ 1

The language of a case shall be Danish, Dutch, English, French, German, Greek, Irish, Italian, Portuguese or Spanish.

§ 2

The language of the case shall be chosen by the applicant, except that:

(a) at the joint request of the parties the Court of First Instance may authorize another of the languages mentioned in paragraph (1) of this Article to be used as the language of the case for all or part of the proceedings.

(b) at the request of one of the parties, and after the opposite party and the Advocate-General have been heard, the Court of First Instance may, by way of derogation from subparagraph (a), authorize another of the languages mentioned in paragraph (1) of this Article to be used as the language of the case for all or part of the proceedings; such a request may not be submitted by an institution.

§ 3

The language of the case shall be used in the written and oral pleadings of the parties and in supporting documents, and also in the minutes and decisions of the Court of First Instance.

Any supporting documents expressed in another language must be accompanied by a translation into the language of the case.

In the case of lengthy documents. translations may be confined to extracts. However, the Court of First Instance may, of its own motion or at the request of a party, at any time call for a complete or fuller translation.

Notwithstanding the foregoing provisions, a Member State shall be entitled to use its official language when intervening in a case before the Court of First Instance. This provision shall apply both to written statements and to oral addresses. The Registrar shall cause any such statement or address to be translated into the language of the case.

§ 4

Where a witness or expert states that he is unable adequately to express himself in one of the languages referred to in paragraph (1) of this Article, the Court of First Instance may authorize him to give his evidence in another language. The Registrar shall arrange for translation into the language of the case.

§ 5

The President in conducting oral proceedings, the Judge-Rapporteur both in his preliminary report and in his report for the hearing, Judges and the Advocate-General in putting questions and the Advocate-General in delivering his opinion may use one of the languages referred to in paragraph (1) of this Article other than the language of the case. The Registrar shall arrange for translation into the language of the case.

Article 36

§ 1

The Registrar shall, at the request of any Judge, of the Advocate-General or of a party, arrange for anything said or written in the course of the proceedings before the Court of First Instance to be translated into the languages he chooses from those referred to in Article 35 (1).

§ 2

Publications of the Court of First Instance shall be issued in the language referred to in Article 1 of Council Regulation No.1.

Article 37

The texts of documents drawn up in the language of the case or in any other language authorized by the Court of First Instance pursuant to Article 35 shall be authentic.

Chapter 6

RIGHTS AND OBLIGATIONS OF AGENTS, ADVISERS AND LAWYERS

Article 38

§ 1

Agents representing a State or an institution, as well as advisers and lawyers, appearing before the Court of First Instance or before any judicial authority to which it has addressed letters rogatory, shall enjoy immunity in respect of words spoken or written by them concerning the case or the parties.

§ 2

Agents, advisers and lawyers shall enjoy the following further privileges and facilities:

(a) papers and documents relating to the proceedings shall be exempt from both search and seizure; in the event of a dispute the customs officials or police may seal those papers and documents; they shall then be immediately forwarded to the Court of First Instance for inspection in the presence of the Registrar and of the person concerned;

(b) agents, advisers and lawyers shall be entitled to such allocation of foreign currency as may be necessary for the performance of their duties;

(c) agents, advisers and lawyers shall be entitled to travel in the course of duty without hindrance.

Article 39

In order to qualify for the privileges, immunities and facilities specified in Article 38, persons entitled to them shall furnish proof of their status as follows:

(a) agents shall produce an official document issued by the State or institution which they represent; a copy of this document shall be forwarded without delay to the Registrar by the State or institution concerned;

(b) advisers and lawyers shall produce a certificate signed by the Registrar. The validity of this certificate shall be limited to a specified period, which may be extended or curtailed according to the length of the proceedings.

Article 40

The privileges, immunities and facilities specified in Article 38 are granted exclusively in the interests of the proper conduct of proceedings.

The Court of First Instance may waive the immunity where it considers that the proper conduct of proceedings will not be hindered thereby.

Article 41

§ 1

Any adviser or lawyer whose conduct towards the Court of First Instance, the President, a Judge or the Registrar is incompatible with the dignity of the Court of First Instance, or who uses his rights for purposes other than those for which they were granted, may at any time be excluded from the proceedings by an order of the Court of First Instance; the person concerned shall be given an opportunity to defend himself.

The order shall have immediate effect.

§ 2

Where an adviser or lawyer is excluded from the proceedings, the proceedings shall be suspended for a period fixed by the President in order to allow the party concerned to appoint another adviser or lawyer.

§ 3

Decisions taken under this Article may be rescinded.

Article 42

The provisions of this Chapter shall apply to university teachers who have a right of audience before the Court of First Instance in accordance with Article 20 of the ECSC Statute and Article 17 of the EEC and Euratom Statutes.

TITLE 2

Procedure

Chapter 1

WRITTEN PROCEDURE

Article 43

§ 1

The original of every pleading must be signed by the party's agent or lawyer.

The original, accompanied by all annexes referred to therein, shall be lodged together with five copies for the Court of First Instance and a copy for every other party to the proceedings. Copies shall be certified by the party lodging them.

§ 2

Institutions shall in addition produce, within time-limits laid down by the Court of First

Instance, translations of all pleadings into the other languages provided for by Article 1 of Council Regulation No 1. The second subparagraph of paragraph (1) of this Article shall apply.

§ 3

All pleadings shall bear a date. In the reckoning of time-limits for taking steps in proceedings only the date of lodgment at the Registry shall be taken into account.

§ 4

To every pleading there shall be annexed a file containing the documents relied on in support of it, together with a schedule listing them.

§ 5

Where in view of the length of a document only extracts from it are annexed to the pleading, the whole document or a full copy of it shall be lodged at the Registry.

Article 44

§ 1

An application of the kind referred to in Article 22 of the ECSC Statute and Article 19 of the EEC and Euratom Statutes shall state:

(a) the name and address of the applicant;

(b) the designation of the party against whom the application is made;

(c) the subject-matter of the proceedings and a summary of the pleas in law on which the application is based;

(d) the form of order sought by the applicant;

(e) where appropriate, the nature of any evidence offered in support.

§ 2

For the purpose of the proceedings, the application shall state an address for service in the place where the Court of First Instance has its seat and the name of the person who is authorized and has expressed willingness to accept service.

If the application does not comply with these requirements, all service on the party concerned for the purposes of the proceedings shall be effected, for so long as the defect has not been cured, by registered letter addressed to the agent or lawyer of that party. By way of derogation from Article 100, service shall then be deemed to have been duly effected by the lodging of the registered letter at the post office of the place where the Court of First Instance has its seat.

§ 3

The lawyer acting for a party must lodge at the Registry a certificate that he is entitled to practise before a court of a Member State.

§ 4

The application shall be accompanied, where appropriate, by the documents specified in the second paragraph of Article 22 of the ECSC Statute and in the second paragraph of Article 19 of the EEC and Euratom Statutes.

§ 5

An application made by a legal person governed by private law shall be accompanied by:

(a) the instrument or instruments constituting and regulating that legal person or a recent extract from the register of companies, firms or associations or any other proof of its existence in law;

(b) proof that the authority granted to the applicant's lawyer has been properly conferred on him by someone authorized for the purpose.

§ 6

If an application does not comply with the requirements set out in paragraphs (3) to (5) of this Article, the Registrar shall prescribe a reasonable period within which the applicant is to comply with them whether by putting the application itself in order or by producing any of the abovementioned documents. If the applicant fails to put the application in order or to produce the required documents within the time prescribed, the Court of First Instance shall decide whether the non-compliance with these conditions renders the application formally inadmissible.

Article 45

The application shall be served on the defendant. In a case where Article 44 (6) applies, service shall be effected as soon as the application has been put in order or the Court of First Instance has declared it admissible notwithstanding the failure to observe the formal requirements set out in that Article.

Article 46

§ 1

Within one month after service on him of the application, the defendant shall lodge a defence, stating:

(a) the name and address of the defendant;

(b) the arguments of fact and law relied on;

(c) the form of order sought by the defendant;

(d) the nature of any evidence offered by him.

The provisions of Article 44 (2) to (5) shall apply to the defence.

§ 2

In proceedings between the Communities and their servants the defence shall be accompanied by the complaint within the meaning of Article 90 (2) of the Staff Regulations of Officials and by the decision rejecting the complaint together with the dates on which the complaint was submitted and the decision notified.

§ 3

The time-limit laid down in paragraph (1) of this Article may be extended by the President on a reasoned application by the defendant.

Article 47

§ 1

The application initiating the proceedings and the defence may be supplemented by a reply from the applicant and by a rejoinder from the defendant.

§ 2

The President shall fix the time-limits within which these pleadings are to be lodged.

Article 48

§ 1

In reply or rejoinder a party may offer further evidence. The party must, however, give reasons for the delay in offering it.

§ 2

No new plea in law may be introduced in the course of proceedings unless it is based on matters of law or of fact which come to light in the course of the procedure.

If in the course of the procedure one of the parties puts forward a new plea in law which is so based, the President may, even after the expiry of the normal procedural time-limits, acting on a report of the Judge-Rapporteur and after hearing the Advocate-General, allow the other party time to answer on that plea.

Consideration of the admissibility of the plea shall be reserved for the final judgment.

Article 49

At any stage of the proceedings the Court of First Instance may, after hearing the Advocate-General, prescribe any measure of organization of procedure or any measure of inquiry referred to in Articles 64 and 65 or order that a previous inquiry be repeated or expanded.

Article 50

The President may, at any time, after hearing the parties and the Advocate-General, order that two or more cases concerning the same subject-matter shall, on account of the connexion between them, be joined for the purposes of the written or oral procedure or of the final judgment. The cases may subsequently be disjoined.

Article 51

In the cases specified in Article 14, and at any stage in the proceedings, the Chamber hearing the case may, either on its own initiative or at the request of one of the parties, propose to the Court of First Instance sitting in plenary session that the case be referred to the Court of First Instance sitting in plenary session or to a Chamber composed of a different number of Judges. The Court of First Instance sitting in plenary session shall, after hearing the parties and the Advocate-General, decide whether or not to refer a case.

Article 52

§ 1

Without prejudice to the application of Article 49, the President shall, after the rejoinder has been lodged, fix a date on which the Judge-Rapporteur is to present his preliminary report to the Court of First Instance. The report shall contain recommendations as to whether measures of organization of procedure or measures of inquiry should be undertaken and whether the case should be referred to the Court of First Instance sitting in plenary session or to a Chamber composed of a different number of Judges.

§ 2

The Court of First Instance shall decide, after hearing the Advocate-General, what action to take upon the recommendations of the Judge-Rapporteur.

The same procedure shall apply:

(a) where no reply or no rejoinder has been lodged within the time-limit fixed in accordance with Article 47 (2);

(b) where the party concerned waives his right to lodge a reply or rejoinder.

Article 53

Where the Court of First Instance decides to open the oral procedure without undertaking measures of organization of procedure or ordering a preparatory inquiry, the President of the Court of First Instance shall fix the opening date.

Article 54

Without prejudice to any measures of organization of procedure or measures of inquiry which may be arranged at the stage of the oral procedure, where, during the written procedure, measures of organization or procedure or measures of inquiry have been instituted and completed, the President shall fix the date for the opening of the oral procedure.

Chapter 2

ORAL PROCEDURE

Article 55

§ 1

Subject to the priority of decisions provided for in Article 106, the Court of First Instance shall deal with the cases before it in the order in which the preparatory inquiries in them have been completed. Where the preparatory inquiries in several cases are completed simultaneously, the order in which they are to be dealt with shall be determined by the dates of entry in the register of the applications initiating them respectively.

§ 2

The President may in special circumstances order that a case be given priority over others.

The President may in special circumstances, after hearing the parties and the Advocate-General, either on his own initiative or at the request of one of the parties, defer a case to be dealt with at a later date. On a joint application by the parties the President may order that a case be deferred.

Article 56

The proceedings shall be opened and directed by the President, who shall be responsible for the proper conduct of the hearing.

Article 57

The oral proceedings in cases heard *in camera* shall not be published.

Article 58

The President may in the course of the hearing put questions to the agents, advisers or lawyers of the parties.

The other Judges and the Advocate-General may do likewise.

Article 59

A party may address the Court of First Instance only through his agent, adviser or lawyer.

Article 60

Where an Advocate-General has not been designated in a case, the President shall declare the oral procedure closed at the end of the hearing.

Article 61

§ 1

Where the Advocate-General delivers his opinion in writing, he shall lodge it at the Registry, which shall communicate it to the parties.

§ 2

After the delivery, orally or in writing, of the opinion of the Advocate-General the President shall declare the oral procedure closed.

Article 62

The Court of First Instance may, after hearing the Advocate-General, order the re-opening of the oral procedure.

Article 63

§ 1

The Registrar shall draw up minutes of every hearing. The minutes shall be signed by the President and by the Registrar and shall constitute an official record.

§ 2

The parties may inspect the minutes at the Registry and obtain copies at their own expense.

Chapter 3

MEASURES OF ORGANIZATION OF PROCEDURE AND MEASURES OF INQUIRY

Section 1—Measures of organization of procedure

Article 64

§ 1

The purposes of measures of organization of procedure shall be to ensure that cases are prepared for hearing, procedures carried out and disputes resolved under the best possible conditions. They shall be prescribed by the Court of First Instance, after hearing the Advocate-General.

§ 2

Measures of organization of procedure shall, in particular, have as their purpose:

(a) to ensure efficient conduct of the written and oral procedure and to facilitate the taking of evidence;

(b) to determine the points on which the parties must present further argument or which call for measures of inquiry;

(c) to clarify the forms of order sought by the parties, their pleas in law and arguments and the points at issue between them;

(d) to facilitate the amicable settlement of proceedings.

§ 3

Measures of organization of procedure may, in particular, consist of:

(a) putting questions to the parties;

(b) inviting the parties to make written or oral submissions on certain aspects of the proceedings;

(c) asking the parties or third parties for information or particulars;

(d) asking for documents or any papers relating to the case to be produced;

(e) summoning the parties' agents or the parties in person to meetings.

§ 4

Each party may, at any stage of the procedure, propose the adoption or modification of measures of organization of procedure. In that case, the other parties shall be heard before those measures are prescribed.

Where the procedural circumstances so require, the Registrar shall inform the parties of the measures envisaged by the Court of First Instance and shall give them an opportunity to submit comments orally or in writing.

§ 5

If the Court of First Instance sitting in plenary session decides to prescribe measures of organization of procedure and does not undertake such measures itself, it shall entrust the task of so doing to the Chamber to which the case was originally assigned or to the Judge-Rapporteur.

If a Chamber prescribes measures of organization of procedure and does not undertake such measures itself, it shall entrust the task to the Judge-Rapporteur.

The Advocate-General shall take part in measures of organization of procedure.

Section 2—Measures of inquiry

Article 65

Without prejudice to Articles 24 and 25 of the ECSC Statute, Articles 21 and 22 of the EEC Statute or Articles 22 and 23 of the Euratom Statute, the following measures of inquiry may be adopted:

(a) the personal appearance of the parties;

(b) a request for information and production of documents;

(c) oral testimony;

(d) the commissioning of an expert's report;

(e) an inspection of the place or thing in question.

Article 66

§ 1

The Court of First Instance, after hearing the Advocate-General, shall prescribe the measures of inquiry that it considers appropriate by means of an order setting out the facts to be proved. Before the Court of First Instance decides on the measures of inquiry referred to in Article 65 (c), (d) and (e) the parties shall be heard.

The order shall be served on the parties.

§ 2

Evidence maybe submitted in rebuttal and previous evidence may be amplified.

Article 67

§ 1

Where the Court of First Instance sitting in plenary session orders a preparatory inquiry and does not undertake such an inquiry itself, it shall entrust the task of so doing to the Chamber to which the case was originally assigned or to the Judge-Rapporteur.

Where a Chamber orders a preparatory inquiry and does not undertake such an inquiry itself, it shall entrust the task of so doing to the Judge-Rapporteur.

The Advocate-General shall take part in the measures of inquiry.

§ 2

The parties may be present at the measures of inquiry.

Section 3—The summoning and examination of witnesses and experts

Article 68

§ 1

The Court of First Instance may, either of its own motion or on application by a party, and after hearing the Advocate-General and the parties, order that certain facts be proved by witnesses. The order shall set out the facts to be established.

The Court of First Instance may summon a witness of its own motion or on application by a party or at the instance of the Advocate-General.

An application by a party for the examination of a witness shall state precisely about what facts and for what reasons the witness should be examined.

§ 2

The witness shall be summoned by an order containing the following information:

(a) the surname, forenames, description and address of the witness;

(b) an indication of the facts about which the witness is to be examined;

(c) where appropriate, particulars of the arrangements made by the Court of First Instance for reimbursement of expenses incurred by the witness, and of the penalties which may be imposed on defaulting witnesses.

The order shall be served on the parties and the witnesses.

§ 3

The Court of First Instance may make the summoning of a witness for whose examination a party has applied conditional upon the deposit with the cashier of the Court of First Instance of a sum sufficient to cover the taxed costs thereof; the Court of First Instance shall fix the amount of the payment.

The cashier of the Court of First Instance shall advance the funds necessary in connexion with the examination of any witness summoned by the Court of First Instance of its own motion.

§ 4

After the identity of the witness has been established, the President shall inform him that he will be required to vouch the truth of his evidence in the manner laid down in paragraph (5) of this Article and in Article 71.

The witness shall give his evidence to the Court of First Instance, the parties having been given notice to attend. After the witness has given his main evidence the President may, at the request of a party or of his own motion, put questions to him.

The other Judges and the Advocate-General may do likewise.

Subject to the control of the President, questions may be put to witnesses by the representatives of the parties.

§ 5

Subject to the provisions of Article 71, the witness shall, after giving his evidence, take the following oath:

'I swear that I have spoken the truth, the whole truth and nothing but the truth.'

The Court of First Instance may, after hearing the parties, exempt a witness from taking the oath.

§ 6

The Registrar shall draw up minutes in which the evidence of each witness is reproduced.

The minutes shall be signed by the President or by the Judge-Rapporteur responsible for conducting the examination of the witness, and by the Registrar. Before the minutes are thus signed, witnesses must be given an opportunity to check the content of the minutes and to sign them.

The minutes shall constitute an official record.

Article 69

§ 1

Witnesses who have been duly summoned shall obey the summons and attend for examination.

§ 2

If a witness who has been duly summoned fails to appear before the Court of First Instance, the latter may impose upon him a pecuniary penalty not exceeding 5 000 ECU and may order that a further summons be served on the witness at his own expense.

The same penalty may be imposed upon a witness who, without good reason, refuses to give evidence or to take the oath or where appropriate to make a solemn affirmation equivalent thereto.

§ 3

If the witness proffers a valid excuse to the Court of First Instance, the pecuniary penalty imposed on him may be cancelled. The pecuniary penalty imposed may be reduced at the request of the witness where he establishes that it is disproportionate to his income.

§ 4

Penalties imposed and other measures ordered under this Article shall be enforced in accordance with Articles 44 and 92 of the ECSC Treaty, Articles 187 and 192 of the EEC Treaty and Articles 159 and 164 of the Euratom Treaty.

Article 70

§ 1

The Court of First Instance may order that an expert's report be obtained. The order appointing the expert shall define his task and set a time-limit within which he is to make his report.

§ 2

The expert shall receive a copy of the order, together with all the documents necessary for carrying out his task. He shall be under the supervision of the Judge-Rapporteur, who may be present during his investigation and who shall be kept informed of his progress in carrying out his task.

The Court of First Instance may request the parties or one of them to lodge security for the costs of the expert's report.

§ 3

At the request of the expert, the Court of First Instance may order the examination of witnesses. Their examination shall be carried out in accordance with Article 68.

§ 4

The expert may give his opinion only on points which have been expressly referred to him.

§ 5

After the expert has made his report, the Court of First Instance may order that he be examined, the parties having been given notice to attend.

Subject to the control of the President, questions may be put to the expert by the representatives of the parties.

§ 6

Subject to the provisions of Article 71, the expert shall, after making his report, take the following oath before the Court of First Instance:

'I swear that I have conscientiously and impartially carried out my task.'

The Court of First Instance may, after hearing the parties, exempt the expert from taking the oath.

Article 71

§ 1

The President shall instruct any person who is required to take an oath before the Court of First Instance, as witness or expert, to tell the truth or to carry out his task conscientiously and impartially, as the case may be, and shall warn him of the criminal liability provided for in his national law in the event of any breach of this duty.

§ 2

Witnesses and experts shall take the oath either in accordance with the first subparagraph of Article 68 (5) and the first subparagraph of Article 70 (6) or in the manner laid down by their national law.

§ 3

Where the national law provides the opportunity to make, in judicial proceedings, a solemn affirmation equivalent to an oath as well as or instead of taking an oath, the witnesses and experts may make such an affirmation under the conditions and in the form prescribed in their national law.

Where their national law provides neither for taking an oath nor for making a solemn affirmation, the procedure described in the first paragraph of this Article shall be followed.

Article 72

§ 1

The Court of First Instance may, after hearing the Advocate-General, decide to report to the competent authority referred to in Annex III to the Rules supplementing the Rules of Procedure of the Court of Justice of the Member State whose courts have penal jurisdiction in any case of perjury on the part of a witness or expert before the Court of First Instance, account being taken of the provisions of Article 71.

§ 2

The Registrar shall be responsible for communicating the decision of the Court of First Instance. The decision shall set out the facts and circumstances on which the report is based.

Article 73

§ 1

If one of the parties objects to a witness or to an expert on the ground that he is not a competent or proper person to act as witness or expert or for any other reason, or if a witness or expert refuses to give evidence, to take the oath or to make a solemn affirmation equivalent thereto, the matter shall be resolved by the Court of First Instance.

§ 2

An objection to a witness or to an expert shall be raised within two weeks after service of the order summoning the witness or appointing the expert; the statement of objection must set out the grounds of objection and indicate the nature of any evidence offered.

Article 74

§ 1

Witnesses and experts shall be entitled to reimbursement of their travel and subsistence expenses. The cashier of the Court of First Instance may make a payment to them towards these expenses in advance.

§ 2

Witness shall be entitled to compensation for loss of earnings, and experts to fees for their services. The cashier of the Court of First Instance shall pay witnesses and experts their compensation or fees after they have carried out their respective duties or tasks.

Article 75

§ 1

The Court of First Instance may, on application by a party or of its own motion, issue letters rogatory for the examination of witnesses or experts.

§ 2

Letters rogatory shall be issued in the form of an order which shall contain the name, forenames, description and address of the witness or expert, set out the facts on which the witness or expert is to be examined, name the parties, their agents, lawyers or advisers, indicate their addresses for service and briefly describe the subject-matter of the proceedings.

Notice of the order shall be served on the parties by the Registrar.

§ 3

The Registrar shall send the order to the competent authority named in Annex I to the Rules supplementing the Rules of Procedure of the Court of Justice of the Member State in whose territory the witness or expert is to be examined. Where necessary, the order shall be accompanied by a translation into the official language or languages of the Member State to which it is addressed.

The authority named pursuant to the first paragraph shall pass on the order to the judicial authority which is competent according to its national law.

The competent judicial authority shall give effect to the letters rogatory in accordance with its national law. After implementation the competent judicial authority shall transmit to the authority named pursuant to the first paragraph the order embodying the letters rogatory, any documents arising from the implementation and a detailed statement of costs. These documents shall be sent to the Registrar.

The Registrar shall be responsible for the translation of the documents into the language of the case.

§ 4

The Court of First Instance shall defray the expenses occasioned by the letters rogatory without prejudice to the right to charge them, where appropriate, to the parties.

Article 76

§ 1

The Registrar shall draw up minutes of every hearing. The minutes shall be signed by the President and by the Registrar and shall constitute an official record.

§ 2

The parties may inspect the minutes and any expert's report at the Registry and obtain copies at their own expense.

Chapter 4

STAY OF PROCEEDINGS AND DECLINING OF JURISDICTION BY THE COURT OF FIRST INSTANCE

Article 77

Without prejudice to Article 123 (4), Article 128 and Article 129 (4), proceedings may be stayed:

(a) in the circumstances specified in the third paragraph of Article 47 of the ECSC Statute, the third paragraph of Article 47 of the EEC Statute and the third paragraph of Article 48 of the Euratom Statute;

(b) where an appeal is brought before the Court of Justice against a decision of the Court of First Instance disposing of the substantive issues in part only, disposing of a procedural issue concerning a plea of lack of competence or inadmissibility or dismissing an application to intervene;

(c) at the joint request of the parties.

Article 78

The decision to stay the proceedings shall be made by order of the Court of First Instance, after hearing the parties and the Advocate-General. The Court of First Instance may, following the same procedure, order that the proceedings be resumed. The orders referred to in this Article shall be served on the parties.

Article 79

§ 1

The stay of proceedings shall take effect on the date indicated in the order of stay or, in the absence of such an indication, on the date of that order.

While proceedings are stayed time shall, except for the purposes of the time-limit prescribed in Article 115 (1) for an application to intervene, cease to run for the purposes of prescribed time-limits for all parties.

§ 2

Where the order of stay does not fix the length of the stay, it shall end on the date indicated in the order of resumption, or, in the absence of such indication, on the date of the order of resumption.

From the date of resumption time shall begin to run afresh for the purposes of the time-limits.

Article 80

Decisions declining jurisdiction in the circumstances specified in the third paragraph of Article 47 of the ECSC Statute, the third paragraph of Article 47 of the EEC Statute and the third paragraph of Article 48 of the Euratom Statute shall be made by the Court of First Instance by way of an order which shall be served on the parties.

Chapter 5

JUDGMENTS

Article 81

The judgment shall contain:

— a statement that it is the judgment of the Court of First Instance,

— the date of its delivery,

— the names of the President and of the Judges taking part in it,

— the name of the Advocate-General, if designated,

— the name of the Registrar,

— the description of the parties,

— the names of the agents, advisers and lawyers of the parties,

— a statement of the forms of order sought by the parties,

— a statement, where appropriate, that the Advocate-General delivered his opinion,

— a summary of the facts,

— the grounds for the decision,

— the operative part of the judgment, including the decision as to costs.

Article 82

§ 1

The judgment shall be delivered in open court; the parties shall be given notice to attend to hear it.

§ 2

The original of the judgment, signed by the President, by the Judges who took part in the deliberations and by the Registrar, shall be sealed and deposited at the Registry; the parties shall be served with certified copies of the judgment.

§ 3

The Registrar shall record on the original of the judgment the date on which it was delivered.

Article 83

Subject to the provisions of the second paragraph of Article 53 of the ECSC Statute, the second paragraph of Article 53 of the EEC Statute and the second paragraph of Article 54 of the Euratom Statute, the judgment shall be binding from the date of its delivery.

Article 84

§ 1

Without prejudice to the provisions relating to the interpretation of judgments, the Court of First Instance may, of its own motion or on application by a party made within two weeks after the delivery of a judgment, rectify clerical mistakes, errors in calculation and obvious slips in it.

§ 2

The parties, whom the Registrar shall duly notify, may lodge written observations within a period prescribed by the President.

§ 3

The Court of First Instance shall takes its decision in closed session.

§ 4

The original of the rectification order shall be annexed to the original of the rectified judgment. A note of this order shall be made in the margin of the original of the rectified judgment.

Article 85

If the Court of First Instance should omit to give a decision on costs, any party may within a month after service of the judgment apply to the Court of First Instance to supplement its judgment.

The application shall be served on the opposite party and the President shall prescribe a period within which that party may lodge written observations.

After these observations have been lodged, the Court of First Instance shall decide both on the admissibility and on the substance of the application.

Article 86

The Registrar shall arrange for the publication of cases before the Court of First Instance.

Chapter 6

COSTS

Article 87

§ 1

A decision as to costs shall be given in the final judgment or in the order which closes the proceedings.

§ 2

The unsuccessful party shall be ordered to pay the costs if they have been applied for in the successful party's pleadings.

Where there are several unsuccessful parties the Court of First Instance shall decide how the costs are to be shared.

§ 3

Where each party succeeds on some and fails on other heads, or where the circumstances are exceptional, the Court of First Instance may order that the costs be shared or that each party bear its own costs.

The Court of First Instance may order a party, even if successful, to pay costs which it considers that party to have unreasonably or vexatiously caused the opposite party to incur.

§ 4

The Member States and institutions which intervened in the proceedings shall bear their own costs.

The Court of First Instance may order an intervener other than those mentioned in the preceding subparagraph to bear his own costs.

§ 5

A party who discontinues or withdraws from proceedings shall be ordered to pay the costs if they have been applied for in the other party's pleadings. However, upon application by the party who discontinues or withdraws from proceedings, the costs shall be borne by the other party if this appears justified by the conduct of that party.

Where the parties have come to an agreement on costs, the decision as to costs shall be in accordance with that agreement.

If costs are not claimed in the written pleadings, the parties shall bear their own costs.

§ 6

Where a case does not proceed to judgment, the costs shall be in the discretion of the Court of First Instance.

Article 88

Without prejudice to the second subparagraph of Article 87 (3), in proceedings between the Communities and their servants the institutions shall bear their own costs.

Article 89

Costs necessarily incurred by a party in enforcing a judgment or order of the Court of First Instance shall be refunded by the opposite party on the scale in force in the State where the enforcement takes place.

Article 90

Proceedings before the Court of First Instance shall be free of charge, except that:

(a) where a party has caused the Court of First Instance to incur avoidable costs, the Court of First Instance may order that party to refund them;

(b) where copying or translation work is carried out at the request of a party, the cost shall, in so far as the Registrar considers it excessive, be paid for by that party on the scale of charges referred to in Article 24 (5).

Article 91

Without prejudice to the preceding Article, the following shall be regarded as recoverable costs:

(a) sums payable to witnesses and experts under Article 74;

(b) expenses necessarily incurred by the parties for the purpose of the proceedings, in particular the travel and subsistence expenses and the remuneration of agents, advisers or lawyers.

Article 92

§ 1

If there is a dispute concerning the costs to be recovered, the Court of First Instance hearing the case shall, on application by the party concerned and after hearing the opposite party, make an order, from which no appeal shall lie.

§ 2

The parties may, for the purposes of enforcement, apply for an authenticated copy of the order.

Article 93

§ 1

Sums due from the cashier of the Court of First Instance shall be paid in the currency of the country where the Court of First Instance has its seat.

At the request of the person entitled to any sum, it shall be paid in the currency of the country where the expenses to be refunded were incurred or where the steps in respect of which the payment is due were taken.

§ 2

Other debtors shall make payment in the currency of their country of origin.

§ 3

Conversions of currency shall be made at the official rates of exchange ruling on the day of payment in the country where the Court of First Instance has its seat.

Chapter 7

LEGAL AID

Article 94

§ 1

A party who is wholly or in part unable to meet the costs of the proceedings may at any time apply for legal aid.

The application shall be accompanied by evidence of the applicant's need of assistance, and in particular by a document from the competent authority certifying his lack of means.

§ 2

If the application is made prior to proceedings which the applicant wishes to commence, it shall briefly state the subject of such proceedings.

The application need not be made through a lawyer.

The President of the Court of First Instance shall designate a Judge to act as Rapporteur. The Chamber to which the latter belongs shall, after considering the written observations of the opposite party, decide whether legal aid should be granted in full or in part, or whether it should be refused. The Chamber shall consider whether there is manifestly no cause of action.

The Chamber shall make an order without giving reasons, and no appeal shall lie therefrom.

Article 95

§ 1

The Court of First Instance, by any order by which it decides that a person is entitled to receive legal aid, shall order that a lawyer be appointed to act for him.

§ 2

If the person does not indicate his choice of lawyer, or if the Court of First Instance considers that his choice is unacceptable, the Registrar shall send a copy of the order and of the application for legal aid to the authority named in Annex II to the Rules supplementing the Rules of Procedure of the Court of Justice, being the competent authority of the State concerned.

§ 3

The Court of First Instance, in the light of the suggestions made by that authority, shall of its own motion appoint a lawyer to act for the person concerned.

Article 96

The Court of First Instance may at any time, either of its own motion or on application, withdraw legal aid if the circumstances which led to its being granted alter during the proceedings.

Article 97

§ 1

Where legal aid is granted, the cashier of the Court of First Instance shall advance the funds necessary to meet the expenses.

§ 2

The Court of First Instance shall adjudicate on the lawyer's disbursements and fees; the President may, on application by the lawyer, order that he receive an advance.

§ 3

In its decision as to costs the Court of First Instance may order the payment to the cashier of the Court of First Instance of the whole or any part of amounts advanced as legal aid.

The Registrar shall take steps to obtain the recovery of these sums from the party ordered to pay them.

Chapter 8

DISCONTINUANCE

Article 98

If, before the Court of First Instance has given its decision, the parties reach a settlement of their dispute and intimate to the Court of First Instance the abandonment of their claims, the President shall order the case to be removed from the register and shall give a decision as to costs in accordance with Article 87 (5) having regard to any proposals made by the parties on the matter.

This provision shall not apply to proceedings under Articles 33 and 35 of the ECSC Treaty, Articles 173 and 175 of the EEC Treaty and Articles 146 and 148 of the Euratom Treaty.

Article 99

If the applicant informs the Court of First Instance in writing that he wishes to discontinue the proceedings, the President shall order the case to be removed from the register and shall give a decision as to costs in accordance with Article 87 (5).

Chapter 9

SERVICE

Article 100

Where these Rules require that a document be served on a person, the Registrar shall ensure that service is effected at that person's address for service either by the dispatch of a copy of the document by registered post with a form for acknowledgement of receipt or by personal delivery of the copy against a receipt.

The Registrar shall prepare and certify the copies of documents to be served, save where the parties themselves supply the copies in accordance with Article 43 (1).

Chapter 10

TIME-LIMITS

Article 101

§ 1

Any period of time prescribed by the ECSC, EEC or Euratom Treaties, the Statutes of the Court of Justice or these Rules for the taking of any procedural step shall be reckoned as follows:

(a) Where a period expressed in days, weeks, months or years is to be calculated from the moment at which an event occurs or an action takes place, the day during which that event occurs or that action takes place shall not be counted as falling within the period in question;

(b) A period expressed in weeks, months or in years shall end with the expiry of whichever day in the last week, month or year is the same day of the week, or falls on the same date, as the day during which the event or action from which the period is to be calculated occurred or took place. If, in a period expressed in months or in years, the day on which it should expire does not occur in the last month, the period shall end with the expiry of the last day of that month;

(c) Where a period is expressed in months and days, it shall first be reckoned in whole months, then in days;

(d) Periods shall include official holidays, Sundays and Saturdays;

(e) Periods shall not be suspended during the judicial vacations.

§ 2

If the period would otherwise end on a Saturday, Sunday or official holiday, it shall be extended until the end of the first following working day.

The list of official holidays drawn up by the Court of Justice and published in the *Official Journal of the European Communities* shall apply to the Court of First Instance.

Article 102

§ 1

The period of time allowed for commencing proceedings against a measure adopted by an institution shall run from the day following the receipt by the person concerned of notification of the measure or, where the measure is published, from the 15th day after publication thereof in the *Official Journal of the European Communities*.

§ 2

The extensions, on account of distance, of prescribed time-limits provided for in a decision of the Court of Justice and published in the *Official Journal of the European Communities* shall apply to the Court of First Instance.

Article 103

§ 1

Any time-limit prescribed pursuant to these Rules may be extended by whoever prescribed it.

§ 2

The President may delegate power of signature to the Registrar for the purpose of fixing time-limits which, pursuant to these Rules, it falls to the President to prescribe, or of extending such time-limits.

TITLE 3

Special Forms of Procedure

Chapter 1

SUSPENSION OF OPERATION OR ENFORCEMENT AND OTHER INTERIM MEASURES

Article 104

§ 1

An application to suspend the operation of any measure adopted by an institution, made pursuant to the second paragraph of Article 39 of the ECSC Treaty, Article 185 of the EEC Treaty or Article 157 of the Euratom Treaty, shall be admissible only if the applicant is challenging that measure in proceedings before the Court of First Instance.

An application for the adoption of any other interim measure referred to in the third paragraph of Article 39 of the ECSC Treaty, Article 186 of the EEC Treaty or Article 158 of the Euratom Treaty shall be admissible only if it is made by a party to a case before the Court of First Instance and relates to that case.

§ 2

An application of a kind referred to in paragraph (1) of this Article shall state the subject-matter of the proceedings, the circumstances giving rise to urgency and the pleas of fact and law establishing a *prima facie* case for the interim measures applied for.

§ 3

The application shall be made by a separate document and in accordance with the provisions of Articles 43 and 44.

Article 105

§ 1

The application shall be served on the opposite party, and the President of the Court of First Instance shall prescribe a short period within which that party may submit written or oral observations.

§ 2

The President of the Court of First Instance may order a preparatory inquiry.

The President of the Court of First Instance may grant the application even before the observations of the opposite party have been submitted. This decision may be varied or cancelled even without any application being made by any party.

Article 106

The President of the Court of First Instance shall either decide on the application himself or refer it to the Chamber to which the case has been assigned in the main proceedings or to the Court of First Instance sitting in plenary session if the case has been assigned to it.

If the President of the Court of First Instance is absent or prevented from attending, he shall be replaced by the President or the most senior Judge, within the meaning of Article 6, of the bench of the Court of First Instance to which the case has been assigned.

Where the application is referred to a bench of the Court of First Instance, that bench shall postpone all other cases and shall give a decision. Article 105 shall apply.

Article 107

§ 1

The decision on the application shall take the form of a reasoned order. The order shall be served on the parties forthwith.

§ 2

The enforcement of the order may be made conditional on the lodging by the applicant of security, of an amount and nature to be fixed in the light of the circumstances.

§ 3

Unless the order fixes the date on which the interim measure is to lapse, the measure shall lapse when final judgment is delivered.

§ 4

The order shall have only an interim effect, and shall be without prejudice to the decision on the substance of the case by the Court of First Instance.

Article 108

On application by a party, the order may at any time be varied or cancelled on account of a change in circumstances.

Article 109

Rejection of an application for an interim measure shall not bar the party who made it from making a further application on the basis of new facts.

Article 110

The provisions of this Chapter shall apply to applications to suspend the enforcement of a decision of the Court of First Instance or of any measure adopted by another institution, submitted pursuant to Articles 44 and 92 of the ECSC Treaty, Articles 187 and 192 of the EEC Treaty and Articles 159 and 164 of the Euratom Treaty.

The order granting the application shall fix, where appropriate, a date on which the interim measure is to lapse.

Chapter 2

PRELIMINARY ISSUES

Article 111

Where it is clear that the Court of First Instance has no jurisdiction to take cognizance of an action or where the action is manifestly inadmissible, the Court of First Instance may, by reasoned order, after hearing the Advocate-General and without taking further steps in the proceedings, give a decision on the action.

Article 112

The decision to refer an action to the Court of Justice, pursuant to the second paragraph of Article 47 of the ECSC Statute, the second paragraph of Article 47 of the EEC Statute and the second paragraph of Article 48 of the Euratom Statute, shall, in the case of manifest lack of competence, be made by reasoned order and without taking any further steps in the proceedings.

Article 113

The Court of First Instance may at any time of its own motion consider whether there exists any absolute bar to proceeding with it, and shall give its decision in accordance with Article 114 (3) and (4).

Article 114

§ 1

A party applying to the Court of First Instance for a decision on admissibility, on lack of competence or other preliminary plea not going to the substance of the case shall make the application by a separate document.

The application must contain the pleas of fact and law relied on and the form of order sought by the applicant; any supporting documents must be annexed to it.

§ 2

As soon as the application has been lodged, the President shall prescribe a period within which the opposite party may lodge a document containing a statement of the form of order sought by that party and its pleas in law.

§ 3

Unless the Court of First Instance otherwise decides, the remainder of the proceedings shall be oral.

§ 4

The Court of First Instance shall, after hearing the Advocate-General, decide on the application or reserve its decision for the final judgment. It shall refer the case to the Court of Justice if the case falls within the jurisdiction of that Court.

If the Court of First Instance refuses the application or reserves its decision, the President shall prescribe new time-limits for further steps in the proceedings.

Chapter 3

INTERVENTION

Article 115

§ 1

An application to intervene must be made within three months of the publication of the notice referred to in Article 24 (6).

§ 2

The application shall contain:

(a) the description of the case;

(b) the description of the parties;

(c) the name and address of the intervener;

(d) the intervener's address for service at the place where the Court of First Instance has its seat;

(e) the form of order sought, by one or more of the parties, in support of which the intervener is applying for leave to intervene;

(f) except in the case of applications to intervene made by Member States or institutions, a statement of the reasons establishing the intervener's interest in the result of the case.

Articles 43 and 44 shall apply.

§ 3

The intervener shall be represented in accordance with the first and second paragraphs of Article 20 of the ECSC Statute and with Article 17 of the EEC and Euratom Statutes.

Article 116

§ 1

The application shall be served on the parties.

The President shall give the parties an opportunity to submit their written or oral observations before deciding on the application.

The President shall decide on the application by order or shall refer the decision to the Court of First Instance. The order must be reasoned if the application is dismissed.

§ 2

If the President allows the intervention, the intervener shall receive a copy of every document served on the parties. The President may, however, on application by one of the parties, omit secret or confidential documents.

§ 3

The intervener must accept the case as he finds it at the time of his intervention.

§ 4

The President shall prescribe a period within which the intervener may submit a statement in intervention.

The statement in intervention shall contain:

(a) a statement of the form of order sought by the intervener in support of or opposing, in whole or in part, the form of order sought by one of the parties;

(b) the pleas in law and arguments relied on by the intervener;

(c) where appropriate, the nature of any evidence offered.

§ 5

After the statement in intervention has been lodged, the President shall, where necessary, prescribe a time-limit within which the parties may reply to that statement.

Chapter 4

JUDGMENTS OF THE COURT OF FIRST INSTANCE DELIVERED AFTER ITS DECISION HAS BEEN SET ASIDE AND THE CASE REFERRED BACK TO IT

Article 117

Where the Court of Justice sets aside a judgment or an order of the Court of First Instance and refers the case back to that Court, the latter shall be seised of the case by the judgment so referring it.

Article 118

§ 1

Where the Court of Justice sets aside a judgment or an order of a Chamber, the President of the Court of First Instance may assign the case to another Chamber composed of the same number of Judges.

§ 2

Where the Court of Justice sets aside a judgment delivered or an order made by the Court of First Instance sitting in plenary session, the case shall be assigned to that Court as so constituted.

§ 3

In the cases provided for in paragraphs (1) and (2) of this Article, Articles 13 (2), 14 and 51 shall apply.

Article 119

§ 1

Where the written procedure before the Court of First Instance has been completed when the judgment referring the case back to it is delivered, the course of the procedure shall be as follows:

(a) Within two months from the service upon him of the judgment of the Court of Justice the applicant may lodge a statement of written observations.

(b) In the month following the communication to him of that statement, the defendant may lodge a statement of written observations. The time allowed to the defendant for lodging it may in no case be less than two months from the service upon him of the judgment of the Court of Justice.

(c) In the month following the simultaneous communication to the intervener of the observations of the applicant and the defendant, the intervener may lodge a statement of written observations. The time allowed to the intervener for lodging it may in no case be less than two months from the service upon him of the judgment of the Court of Justice.

§ 2

Where the written procedure before the Court of First Instance had not been completed when the judgment referring the case back to the Court of First Instance was delivered, it shall be resumed, at the stage which it had reached, by means of measures of organization of procedure adopted by the Court of First Instance.

§ 3

The Court of First Instance may, if the circumstances so justify, allow supplementary statements of written observations to be lodged.

Article 120

The procedure shall be conducted in accordance with the provisions of Title II of these Rules.

Article 121

The Court of First Instance shall decide on the costs relating to the proceedings instituted before it and to the proceedings on the appeal before the Court of Justice.

Chapter 5

JUDGMENTS BY DEFAULT AND APPLICATIONS TO SET THEM ASIDE

Article 122

§ 1

If a defendant on whom an application initiating proceedings has been duly served fails to lodge a defence to the application in the proper form within the time prescribed, the applicant may apply to the Court of First Instance for judgment by default.

The application shall be served on the defendant. The President shall fix a date for the opening of the oral procedure.

§ 2

Before giving judgment by default the Court of First Instance shall consider whether the application initiating proceedings is admissible, whether the appropriate formalities have been complied with, and whether the application appears well founded. It may order a preparatory inquiry.

§ 3

A judgment by default shall be enforceable. The Court of First Instance may, however, grant a stay of execution until it has given its decision on any application under paragraph (4) of this Article to set aside the judgement, or it may make execution subject to the provision of security of an amount and nature to be fixed in the light of the circumstances; this security shall be released if no such application is made or if the application fails.

§ 4

Application may be made to set aside a judgment by default.

The application to set aside the judgment must be made within one month from the date of service of the judgment and must be lodged in the form prescribed by Articles 43 and 44.

§ 5

After the application has been served, the President shall prescribe a period within which the other party may submit his written observations.

The proceedings shall be conducted in accordance with the provisions of Title II of these Rules.

§ 6

The Court of First Instance shall decide by way of a judgment which may not be set aside. The original of this judgment shall be annexed to the original of the judgment by default. A note of the judgment on the application to set aside shall be made in the margin of the original of the judgment by default.

Chapter 6

EXCEPTIONAL REVIEW PROCEDURES

Section 1—Third-party proceedings

Article 123

§ 1

Articles 43 and 44 shall apply to an application initiating third-party proceedings. In addition such an application shall:

(a) specify the judgment contested;

(b) state how that judgment is prejudicial to the rights of the third party;

(c) indicate the reasons for which the third party was unable to take part in the original case before the Court of First Instance.

The application must be made against all the parties to the original case.

Where the judgment has been published in the *Official Journal of the European Communities*, the application must be lodged within two months of the publication.

§ 2

The Court of First Instance may, on application by the third party, order a stay of execution of the judgment. The provisions of Title III, Chapter 1, shall apply.

§ 3

The contested judgment shall be varied on the points on which the submissions of the third party are upheld.

The original of the judgment in the third-party proceedings shall be annexed to the original of the contested judgment. A note of the judgment in the third-party proceedings shall be made in the margin of the original of the contested judgment.

§ 4

Where an appeal before the Court of Justice and an application initiating third-party proceedings before the Court of First Instance contest the same judgment of the Court of First Instance, the Court of First Instance may, after hearing the parties, stay the proceedings until the Court of Justice has delivered its judgment.

Article 124

The application initiating third-party proceedings shall be assigned to the Chamber which delivered the judgment which is the subject of the application; if the Court of First Instance sitting in plenary session delivered the judgment, the application shall be assigned to it.

Section 2—Revision

Article 125

Without prejudice to the period of ten years prescribed in the third paragraph of Article 38 of the ECSC Statute, the third paragraph of Article 41 of the EEC Statute and the third paragraph of Article 42 of the Euratom Statute, an application for revision of a judgment shall be made within three months of the date on which the facts on which the application is based came to the applicant's knowledge.

Article 126

§ 1

Articles 43 and 44 shall apply to an application for revision. In addition such an application shall:

(a) specify the judgment contested;

(b) indicate the points on which the application is based;

(c) set out the facts on which the application is based;

(d) indicate the nature of the evidence to show that there are facts justifying revision of the judgment, and that the time-limits laid down in Article 125 have been observed.

§ 2

The application must be made against all parties to the case in which the contested judgment was given.

Article 127

§ 1

The application for revision shall be assigned to the Chamber which delivered the judgment which is the subject of the application; if the Court of First Instance sitting in plenary session delivered the judgment, the application shall be assigned to it.

§ 2

Without prejudice to its decision on the substance, the Court of First Instance shall, after hearing the Advocate-General, having regard to the written observations of the parties, give its decision on the admissibility of the application.

§ 3

If the Court of First Instance finds the application admissible, it shall proceed to consider the substance of the application and shall give its decision in the form of a judgment in accordance with these Rules.

§ 4

The original of the revising judgment shall be annexed to the original of the judgment revised. A note of the revising judgment shall be made in the margin of the original of the judgment revised.

Article 128

Where an appeal before the Court of Justice and an application for revision before the Court of First Instance concern the same judgment of the Court of First Instance, the Court of First Instance may, after hearing the parties, stay the proceedings until the Court of Justice has delivered its judgment.

Section 3—Interpretation of judgments

Article 129

§ 1

An application for interpretation of a judgment shall be made in accordance with Articles 43 and 44. In addition it shall specify:

(a) the judgment in question;

(b) the passages of which interpretation is sought.

The application must be made against all the parties to the case in which the judgment was given.

§ 2

The application for interpretation shall be assigned to the Chamber which delivered the judgment which is the subject of the application; if the Court of First Instance sitting in plenary session delivered the judgment, the application shall be assigned to it.

§ 3

The Court of First Instance shall give its decision in the form of a judgment after having given the parties an opportunity to submit their observations and after hearing the Advocate-General.

The original of the interpreting judgment shall be annexed to the original of the judgment interpreted. A note of the interpreting judgment shall be made in the margin of the original of the judgment interpreted.

§ 4

Where an appeal before the Court of Justice and an application for interpretation before the Court of First Instance concern the same judgment of the Court of First Instance, the Court of First Instance may, after hearing the parties, stay the proceedings until the Court of Justice has delivered its judgment.

Miscellaneous Provisions

Article 130

These Rules, which are authentic in the languages mentioned in Article 35 (1), shall be published in the *Official Journal of the European Communities*. They shall enter into force on the first day of the second month from the date of their publication.

Done at Luxembourg on 2 May 1991.

H. JUNG

Registrar

JL CRUZ VILAÇA

President

INDEX

401